Principles of
Sociology

Fourth Edition

Principles of
Sociology

Canadian
Perspectives

EDITED BY

Lorne Tepperman
Patrizia Albanese

OXFORD
UNIVERSITY PRESS

OXFORD
UNIVERSITY PRESS

Oxford University Press is a department of the University of Oxford.
It furthers the University's objective of excellence in research, scholarship,
and education by publishing worldwide. Oxford is a registered trade mark of
Oxford University Press in the UK and in certain other countries.

Published in Canada by
Oxford University Press
8 Sampson Mews, Suite 204,
Don Mills, Ontario M3C 0H5 Canada

www.oupcanada.com

Copyright © Oxford University Press Canada 2018

The moral rights of the author have been asserted

Database right Oxford University Press (maker)

First Edition published in 2006
Second Edition published in 2009
Third Edition published in 2014

Library and Archives Canada Cataloguing in Publication
Principles of sociology (Don Mills, Ont.)
Principles of sociology : Canadian perspectives / edited by Lorne Tepperman
and Patrizia Albanese. – Fourth edition.

Includes bibliographical references and index.
ISBN 978-0-19-902373-8 (softcover)

1. Sociology—Textbooks. 2. Canada—Social conditions–1991—Textbooks.
3. Canada—Social conditions–Statistics. I. Tepperman, Lorne, 1943–, editor
II. Albanese, Patrizia, editor III. Title.

HM586.P75 2017   301   C2017-901830-2

Introduction opener: zaragyemo/BigStock.com; Part 1 opener: robertharding / Alamy Stock Photo;
Chapter 1 opener: Photo by Stanley Chou/Getty Images; Part 2 opener: Photo by Harry How/Getty Images;
Chapter 2 opener: Carlos Osorio/Toronto Star via Getty Images; Chapter 3 opener: Hero Images/Getty Images;
Chapter 4 opener: © Guangliang Huo | Dreamstime.com; Chapter 5 opener: MENAHEM KAHANA/AFP/
Getty Images; Part 3 opener: Cebas/Thinkstock; Chapter 6 opener: Kamyar Adl / Alamy Stock Photo;
Chapter 7 opener: MarijaRadovic/iStockphoto; Chapter 8 opener: robertharding / Alamy Stock Photo;
Part 4 opener: © Wangkun Jia | Dreamstime.com; Chapter 9 opener: monkeybusinessimages/iStockphoto;
Chapter 10 opener: Linda Goodhue Photography/Getty Images; Chapter 11 opener: pcruciatti/iStockphoto;
Chapter 12 opener: Photo by Rick Madonik/Toronto Star via Getty Images; Chapter 13 opener: Steve Russell/
Toronto Star via Getty Images; Part 5 opener: Photo by Martin Seras Lima/ActionPlus/Corbis via Getty Images;
Chapter 14 opener: franckreporter/iStockphoto; Chapter 15 opener: Witold Skrypczak/Getty Images;
Chapter 16 opener: Vertigo3d/Getty Images.

Cover image: Moonlight/Getty Images

Oxford University Press is committed to our environment.
Wherever possible, our books are printed on paper which comes from
responsible sources.

Printed and bound in Canada

4 5 6 - 22 21 20

BRIEF CONTENTS

CONTENTS

PART III | TYPES OF INEQUALITY   131

8 | Ethnic and Race Relations   172
NIKOLAOS I. LIODAKIS

PART IV | SOCIAL INSTITUTIONS   199

9 | Families and Health Issues   200
JUANNE CLARKE AND PATRIZIA ALBANESE

10 | Education   222
TERRY WOTHERSPOON

TABLES

FIGURES

BOXED FEATURES

SOCIOLOGY IN ACTION

Research That Helps Us Understand Our World

HUMAN DIVERSITY

World Views and Ways of Life of Different Cultures and Social Groups

OPEN FOR DISCUSSION

Contemporary Social Issues and Debates

GLOBAL ISSUES

UNDER THE WIRE

RESEARCHERS IN ACTION ▶

PREFACE

FROM THE PUBLISHER

Oxford University Press is delighted to present the fourth edition of *Principles of Sociology: Canadian Perspectives*. While preparing this new edition, the general editors, contributing authors, and publisher kept in mind one paramount goal: to produce the most authoritative, accessible, and interesting introduction to sociology available for Canadian students.

This revision builds on the success of the previous editions and incorporates new content designed to enhance the book's usefulness for students and instructors alike.

HIGHLIGHTS OF THE FOURTH EDITION

New Chapter on Media and Technology

Anabel Quan-Haase joins David Young to craft a brand-new chapter that deals with the sociological implications of both the media and technology. The chapter examines a range of fascinating topics such as gender performativity with respect to social media, the digital divide, and surveillance technology.

Vibrant New Design

The book has been completely redesigned and modernized to enhance readability and engagement with the text. The vibrant four-colour aesthetic has been updated to better reflect the vitality of Canadian sociology as an academic discipline.

Top Canadian Contributors

Sociology is a global discipline, but one to which sociologists working in Canada have made unique contributions. Not merely an adaptation of a book originally written for American undergraduates, this text was conceived and written from the ground up to provide a Canadian perspective on this fascinating field. Experts in their particular sub-disciplines not only examine the key concepts and terminology of sociology as an academic discipline but also use those concepts to shed light on the nature of Canadian society and Canada's place in the world.

Global Perspective

Although this is a book written by and for Canadians, the editors and authors never forget that Canada is but one small part of a vast, diverse, and endlessly fascinating social world. Along with Canadian data, examples, and illustrations, a wealth of information about how humans live and interact around the world is presented across the text.

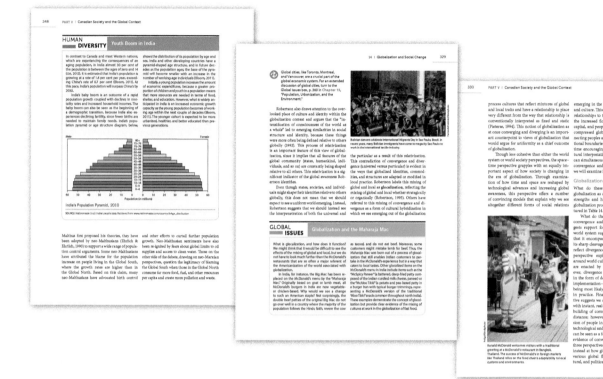

Theoretical Balance

The overriding goal of *Principles of Sociology: Canadian Perspectives* has been not just to make the theories that underpin the discipline comprehensible but to show how they inform an understanding of the data that sociologists gather—and how the choice of which theoretical perspective to use can yield new and surprising insights. Throughout the text, emerging paradigms are also discussed when they shed new light on longstanding questions.

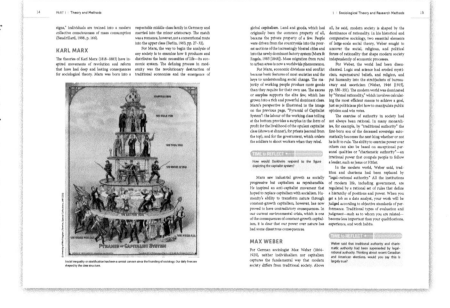

Insightful Theme Boxes

"Why study sociology?" is a question frequently asked by students. There are many reasons, of course: sociology provides a unique insight into the nature of the human world; it shows us things about society and ourselves that we might not otherwise know; and the lessons of sociology can be intriguing, touching, tragic, and even fun. The dozens of theme boxes scattered throughout the text illustrate all of these dimensions of the discipline.

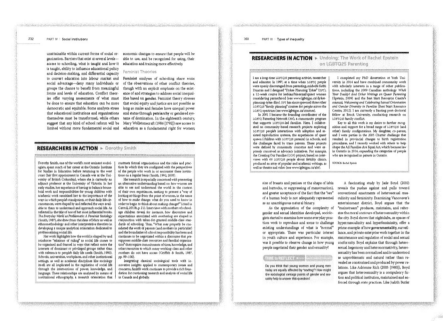

◀ **NEW "Researchers in Action" boxes** profile leading Canadian sociologists, giving students insight into the exciting work that has been undertaken in various sub-disciplines of sociology, right here in Canada.

▶ **"Open for Discussion" boxes** use contemporary social issues and debates to broaden student understanding of core sociological concepts.

◀ **"Sociology in Action" boxes** show how sociological research can help us better understand the everyday world.

◀ **"Global Issues" boxes** draw upon examples from around the world to illustrate the effects of globalization and show what sociologists have to say about, for instance, immigration or fast food.

▶ **"Human Diversity" boxes** seek to introduce students to the ways of life, experiences, and world views of different cultures and social groups.

◀ **"Under the Wire" boxes** analyze the ways in which current media and new technologies influence social patterns and behaviours.

Aids to Student Learning

A textbook must fulfill a double duty: while meeting instructors' expectations for accuracy, currency, and comprehensiveness, it must also speak to today's students, providing them with an accessible introduction to a body of knowledge. To that end, numerous features to promote student learning are incorporated throughout the book.

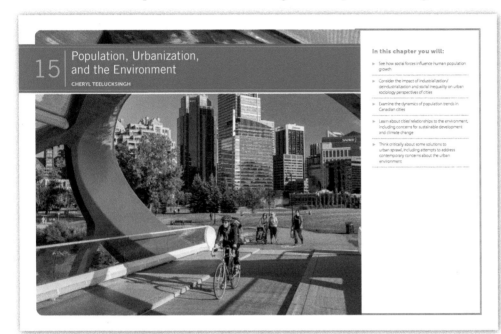

Learning Objectives at the start of each chapter provide a concise overview of the key concepts that will be covered.

Graphs and Tables Colourful and informative graphs and charts are featured throughout the text and allow students to accurately analyze quantitative data.

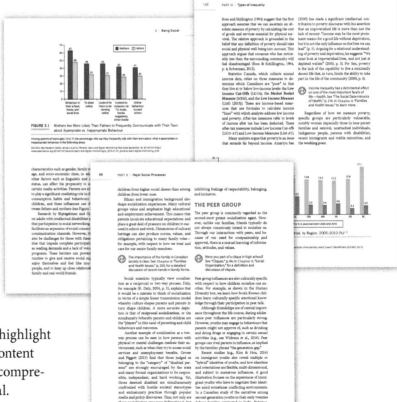

Cross-Chapter References highlight the interconnectedness of content across chapters to ensure a comprehensive study of the material.

◀ **Time to Reflect** questions placed throughout the text prompt students to analyze the material both in and out of the classroom.

▶ NEW **"Sociological Explorations"** found at the end of each chapter provide some ideas for sociological activities students can conduct outside of class.

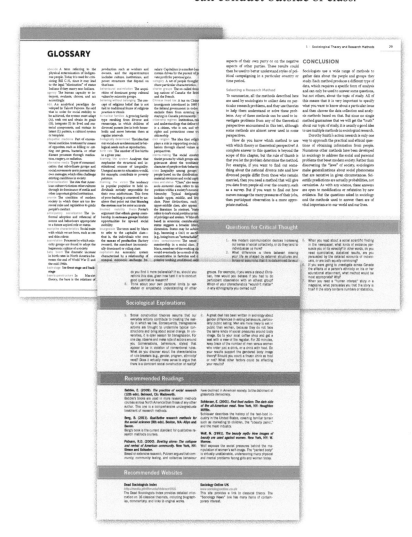

◀ NEW End-of-chapter Glossary, as well as Questions for Critical Thought, Recommended Readings, and Recommended Websites at the end of each chapter encourage readers to think deeply and point students toward useful sources for further research.

Robust Supplements Package

Today's texts are no longer volumes that stand on their own. Rather, they are but the central element in a complete learning and teaching package. *Principles of Sociology: Canadian Perspectives* is no exception and is supported by an outstanding array of ancillary materials for both students and instructors.

For Instructors

Online Instructor's Manual

This updated online resource includes comprehensive outlines of the text's various chapters, suggested class activities and assignments, questions for encouraging classroom discussion, suggestions on how to use media to enhance classes, and extra resource material for use in lectures.

Online Test Generator

A comprehensive test generator allows instructors to sort, edit, import, and distribute hundreds of questions in multiple-choice, short-answer, true/false, and essay formats.

PowerPoint® Slides

Hundreds of slides for classroom presentation incorporate graphics and tables from the text, summarize key points from each chapter, and can be edited to suit individual instructors' needs.

Sociology Streaming Video Collection

An exciting online collection provides instant access to a variety of feature-length videos and shorter clips, with an accompanying video guide that includes learning objectives, discussion questions, and assignment suggestions for each video included.

For Students

Companion Website

A one-stop online study guide provides hundreds of review questions, automatically graded self-assessment quizzes, annotated lists of useful readings and Web resources, and other material designed to enhance student learning.

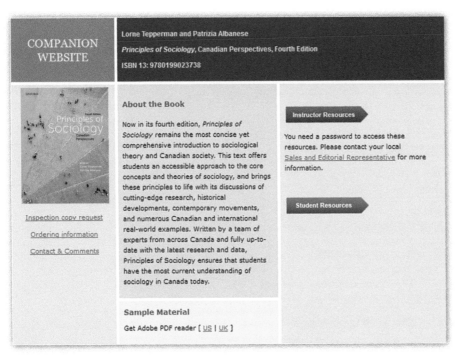

www.oupcanada.com/Principles4e

FROM THE GENERAL EDITORS

So much has changed since the first edition of this book in 2006. In the past 10 years, Canada has been jolted by financial events originating in our neighbour-state, the United States. Canada has been drawn into inconclusive but costly warfare in the Middle East set in motion by a reckless American president. Many young Canadians died in this enterprise.

The Americans eventually elected a less-reckless president—their first African-American president ever—leading to hopes that global power would be exercised in a new, more peaceful, and more collegial way than in the recent past. But the mere change of personnel, even of presidents, did not change the institutional structure and fundamental interests of the world's power-brokers, as you will see through various chapters in this book and in a new chapter on culture by Eric Weissman. A separate but related enduring reality, represented by another chapter in this edition, was that religion continued to exercise a dominant ideological force in the world. For reasons made clear in Lori G. Beaman's chapter in this book, religion continues to shape the thoughts, hopes, and actions of people around the world—especially in the war-torn Middle East. Religion still inspires people to noble deeds, as well as to violent, foolhardy ones.

Here in Canada, we elected a new Liberal government in 2015, one that (at least) seems more willing than the previous government to "commit sociology." Of course, the country is still fractured by regional differences, and with the decline of the oil economy in Alberta and Newfoundland and Labrador, regional conflict has started to heat up again. Canada remains a minor player in the world's political and military dramas, and the Liberal government has so far avoided putting ground troops at risk in the Middle East. Here at home, our everyday lives are still mainly focused on friends and family, school and work, cyberspace and popular culture. As Canadians, we still live in a society widely viewed as moderate, civilized, tolerant, and healthy. Therefore, many people around the world want to immigrate here, and many do, giving us one of the highest rates of immigration in the world. With this comes continuing concern about immigrant assimilation—economically, culturally, and socially.

People in Canada are rightly concerned about the economy and the occupational futures of our younger generations. With unions weakened and many manufacturing jobs lost to low-wage, overseas countries, many people—especially young people, less educated people, minorities, immigrants, and people with disabilities—are forced to earn a living from "precarious work" in the service sector. They have a hard time getting a financial foothold that would allow them to pay off their debts, marry, buy a home, and raise a family. It is unclear how the new Liberal government will solve the multiple economic, educational, and social issues that Canadians face in a society that has become more unequal and less generous over the last 10 years.

In short, Canada continues to be a complicated society: rich and poor, calm and fearful, cooperative and conflictual, stable and tempestuous. This new edition of *Principles of Sociology* tries to capture, describe, and explain Canadian society today, and we think you will like it. We think you will find it even more interesting, provocative, and readable than the last edition. And our mission is no less important than it was the last time: namely, to educate Canadians about the society in which they live. We have a duty to study and understand this country and to make it serve our collective needs.

The publisher, Oxford University Press Canada, has continued to help our contributors provide the clearest possible portrait of Canadian society. Developmental editor Tanuja Weerasooriya has done a masterful job of keeping us on track, smoothing chapters, and otherwise taking care of the backstage, practical matters at Oxford—making sure that all the pieces come together when and where they should. We also want to thank Leslie Saffrey for performing a very thorough read-through of the manuscript. And thanks go to those talented people who selected the photos that appear in this great-looking book.

We would also like to acknowledge the following reviewers, along with the reviewers who chose to remain anonymous, whose insightful comments have helped to shape the new edition of *Principles of Sociology: Canadian Perspectives*:

Sonia Bookman, University of Manitoba

Ricardo Duchesne, University of New Brunswick

Christopher Helland, Dalhousie University

Liam Kilmurray, University of Ottawa

Sarah Knudson, St. Thomas More College, University of Saskatchewan

Timothy MacNeill, University of Ontario Institute of Technology

Sandria Officer, Seneca College

Katarzyna Rukszto, Sheridan College

Holly Thomas, Carleton University

We extend our most profound thanks to the authors of the chapters in the most recent edition of *Sociology: A Canadian Perspective*, whose work formed the basis of this streamlined version. Without their contribution, this book would not exist. They put up with our (seemingly endless) demands, and somehow everything was done on time and as needed. It has been a great privilege working with this distinguished group of Canadian scholars from all over the country. Thank you, authors.

In closing, we dedicate this book to our students, who face many challenging decisions. Never in recent times has the world economy been so troubled or the future so murky. It will take great courage, dedication, and maturity to forge ahead, to make plans, and to keep them alive. We wish you well; you are the next generation of our country and our best chance. We hope sociological analysis will prove a useful guide in your lives.

Lorne Tepperman, University of Toronto

Patrizia Albanese, Ryerson University

CONTRIBUTORS

Patrizia Albanese is a professor of sociology at Ryerson University.

Bruce Arai is the dean of the Faculty of Human and Social Sciences at Wilfrid Laurier University (Brantford).

Lori G. Beaman is a professor of religious studies at the University of Ottawa.

Juanne Clarke is a professor of sociology at Wilfrid Laurier University.

Sara J. Cumming is a professor in the Faculty of Humanities and Social Sciences at Sheridan College.

Ann D. Duffy is a professor of sociology at Brock University.

Andrea Doucet is a professor of sociology at Carleton University.

Randle Hart is an associate professor of sociology at Saint Mary's University.

Alicia D. Horton is a PhD candidate in the Department of Sociology at Queen's University.

Nikolaos I. Liodakis is an associate professor of sociology at Wilfrid Laurier University.

Barbara A. Mitchell is a professor of sociology and gerontology at Simon Fraser University.

Dorothy Pawluch is an associate professor of sociology at McMaster University.

Anabel Quan-Haase is an associate professor in the Department of Sociology, cross-appointed with the Faculty of Information and Media Studies, at Western University.

Howard Ramos is a political sociologist at Dalhousie University.

Vincent F. Sacco is a professor of sociology at Queen's University.

William Shaffir is a professor and associate chair in the Department of Sociology at McMaster University.

Janet Siltanen is a professor of sociology at Carleton University.

Karen Stanbridge is an associate professor of sociology at Memorial University of Newfoundland.

Pamela Sugiman is the dean of Arts and a professor of sociology at Ryerson University.

Liam Swiss is an associate professor of sociology at Memorial University.

Cheryl Teelucksingh is an associate professor of sociology at Ryerson University.

Lorne Tepperman is a professor of sociology at the University of Toronto and past president of the Canadian Sociological Association.

Anthony Thomson is a professor of sociology at Acadia University.

John Veugelers is an associate professor of sociology at the University of Toronto.

Eric Weissman has a PhD from Concordia University and is a principal investigator in a critical ethnography of the Tony Di Pede Residences.

Terry Wotherspoon is a professor and the head of sociology at the University of Saskatchewan.

David Young is a teaching professor in the Department of Sociology at McMaster University.

Principles of
Sociology

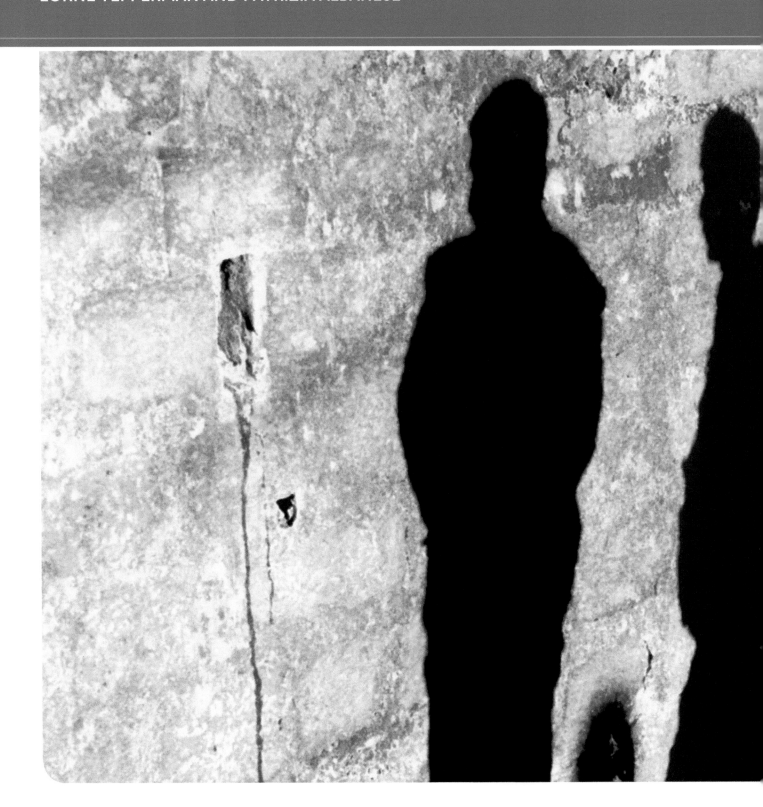

Why Not Become a Sociologist?

LORNE TEPPERMAN AND PATRIZIA ALBANESE

INTRODUCTION

INTRODUCTION

In April 2013, Prime Minister Steven Harper, a Conservative, was asked about the arrest of two men who were accused of conspiring to carry out a terrorist attack on a VIA Rail train. Shortly before this, Conservative MPs had criticized Liberal leader (now prime minister) Justin Trudeau for suggesting it was important to look at the root causes of the Boston Marathon bombings. The Conservatives viewed such thoughts as signs of weakness and dithering—as an attempt to rationalize, justify, or excuse the bombings. Said Harper about the VIA case, "I think . . . this is not a time to commit sociology, if I can use an expression. . . . These things are serious threats, global terrorist attacks, people who have agendas of violence that are deep and abiding threats to all the values our society stands for."

Harper's inclination to view sociological explanation as a means of excusing bad behaviour or avoiding action was demonstrated a second time the following year, when government critics called for an investigation of the large number of murders of Indigenous women. In August 2014, after the death of 15-year-old Tina Fontaine, Prime Minister Harper urged Canadians not to think of the disappearance and murders of Indigenous women as a "sociological phenomenon" but rather to "view it as a crime" that merely required policing and punishment, not analysis.

A great many Canadians disagreed with this Conservative approach to solving social problems and voted Prime Minister Harper out of office in 2015. But this episode of intentional ignorance focused public attention on the questions, What is sociology? When and how should sociology be used for social policy-making? What's more, why don't we all commit sociology more often? In fact, why don't we all become sociologists?

It is likely that everyone—even Stephen Harper—at one point or another has been on the brink of becoming a sociologist. At some point, all people experience idiosyncracies of social life that affect their opportunities, and they try to understand them. It does not take a bomb threat or a murdered Indigenous woman to jump-start sociological thinking. It can be something much more familiar, something that a person has experienced in daily life. This is where sociology begins for most people. What could be more fascinating, more empowering, and more personal than to begin to understand the society that shapes our lives? For these reasons, sociology is an inherently attractive area of study, and many people do study it.

Consider some examples. Maybe as a child you noticed the following:

- Parents sometimes treat their sons differently from their daughters.
- Salespeople treat well-dressed youth better than poorly dressed youth.
- Movies typically portray people with "accents" as strange or suspicious.

If you noticed these things, you may have wondered why they happen. They may even have affected you, as a daughter or son, a poorly dressed or well-dressed person, or a person with or without an "accent." You may have felt ashamed, angry, or pleased, depending on whether you identified with the favourably treated or the unfavourably treated category of people.

If you noticed or experienced these things, you may have wanted to understand them better. These are the kinds of circumstances in which sociological curiosity begins. All sociologists got hooked on trying to better understand their own lives and the lives of people around them. They came to understand that common sense gave them incomplete or inaccurate explanations about people's behaviour and the society in which they live. They were not satisfied with the explanations they received and wanted to know more.

For much of what we do, common-sense understanding is just fine. But for anyone who wants to understand how society works, it is not good enough. You may already realize there are many questions common sense cannot answer adequately, such as the following:

- Why do seemingly similar people lead such different lives?
- Why do we often treat "different" people worse than others?
- What do people do to escape from being treated badly?
- What can citizens do to make Canadian society a more equitable place?
- Can we bring about social change by changing the laws of the country?

Sociologists want to understand how societies change and how people's lives change with them. Social changes, inequalities, and conflicts captivate sociologists because such issues—war and peace, wealth and poverty, environmental destruction and technological innovation, for example—are important for people's lives. Sociologists know that "personal problems" are similar across many individuals. They also know that many of our personal problems are the private side of public issues. American sociologist C. Wright Mills called this knowledge or ability "the sociological imagination." With this ability or approach, we know we need to deal with personal problems collectively and, often, politically—with full awareness that we share these problems and their solutions with others.

And that is why we need to understand the causes of terrorist plots and Indigenous victimization—among other things—before we can take meaningful action to solve the problem. Solving problems requires understanding them, and this, in turn, requires clear thinking and careful research. So social theorists and social science researchers have developed concepts, theories, and research methods that help them to study the social world more effectively. Our goal as sociologists is to be able to explain social life, critique social inequities, and work toward effecting social change. In this book, you will learn how sociologists go about these tasks and some of what sociologists have found out about the social world.

Our starting point is a formal definition of "sociology," comparisons of sociology with other related fields of study, and a discussion of sociology's most basic subject matter.

A DEFINITION OF SOCIOLOGY

Scholars have defined "sociology" in many ways, but most practising sociologists think of their discipline as the systematic study of social behaviour in human societies. Humans are intensely social beings and spend most of their time interacting with others. That is why sociologists study the social units people create when they join with others. As we will see in the following chapters, these units range from small groups—comprising as few as two people—to large corporations and even whole societies (see, for example, Chapter 4, on social organization). Sociologists are interested in learning about how group membership affects individual behaviour. They are also interested in learning how individuals change the groups of which they are members.

However, it is impossible for any sociologist to study all social issues or to become an expert in all the sub-disciplines of sociology. As a result, most sociologists specialize in either macrosociology or microsociology—two related

Women hold images of murdered and missing Indigenous women during a rally on Parliament Hill. Sociologists are particularly interested in social change. What do you think a sociologist would say about the murder of Indigenous women in many parts of rural Canada?

but distinct approaches to studying the social world—and choose problems for study from within these realms.

Macrosociology is the study of large social **organizations** (for example, the Roman Catholic Church, universities, corporations, or government bureaucracies) and large social categories (for example, ethnic minorities, seniors, or university students). Sociologists who specialize in the macrosociological approach to the social world focus on the complex social patterns that people form over long periods.

On the other hand, **microsociology** focuses on the typical processes and patterns of face-to-face interaction in small groups. A microsociologist might study a marriage, a clique, a business meeting, an argument between friends, or a first date. In short, a microsociologist would study the common, everyday interactions and negotiations that together produce lasting, secure patterns. You can see many examples of this in Chapter 3, on being social.

Combining macro and micro approaches improves our understanding of the social world. Consider a common social phenomenon: the domestic division of labour—who does what chores around the home. From the micro perspective, who does what is constantly open to negotiation. It is influenced by personal characteristics, the history of the couple, and many other unique factors. Yet viewed from a macro perspective, different households have similar divisions of labour despite different personal histories. This suggests the answer lies in a society's history, culture, and economy. It is far from accidental that across millions of households, men enjoy the advantage of a better salary and more social power both in a great many workplaces and at home.

While these approaches are different, they are also connected. They have to be: after all, both macro- and microsociologists are studying the same people in the same society. All of us are leading unique lives within a common social context, faced by common problems. The question is, how can sociologists bring these elements together? As noted above, C. Wright Mills (1959) gave the answer when he introduced the notion of the sociological imagination as something that enables us to relate personal biographies—the lives of millions of ordinary people like ourselves—to the broad sweep of human history. The sociological imagination is what we need to use to understand how societies control and change their members and, at the same time, are constantly changed by the actions of their members.

How Sociology Differs from Other Academic Fields

Sociology is just one of several fields of study designed to help describe and explain human behaviour; others include journalism, history, philosophy, and psychology. How does sociology differ from these other endeavours? Canadian sociologist Kenneth Westhues (1982) has compared sociology's approach with those of the other fields. He stresses that journalism and history describe real events, as does sociology. However, journalism and history only sometimes base

Meghann Dionne/Radio-Canada

Sunni and Shia Muslims in Calgary stand together in protesting ISIS. Even though they are both used by sociologists all the time, micro- and macrosociology are two distinct approaches. For example, a macrosociology approach would examine rates of terrorist violence throughout the world, whereas a microsociology approach would focus on the motives and socialization of individual terrorists.

their descriptions on a theory or interpretation, and then it is often an implicit or hidden theory.

Sociologists strive to make their theories clear, to be able to test them. Telling a story is important for sociologists but less so than the explanation on which the story is based. Besides, stories often make the news because they are unusual; sociologists instead are drawn to issues that are common events or form recurring patterns.

Sociology also differs from philosophy. Both are *analytical*—that is, concerned with testing and refining theory. However, sociology is firmly *empirical*, or concerned with gathering evidence and doing studies, while philosophy is not. Philosophy has greater concern with the internal logic of its arguments. Sociological theories must stand up logically, but they must also stand up to evidence in a way philosophical theories need not. Sociologists will not accept a sociological theory, no matter how logical, whose predictions are not supported by evidence gathered in a sound way.

Finally, sociology differs from psychology, which is also analytical, empirical, and interpretive. The difference here lies in the subject matter. Psychologists study the behaviour of individual humans or, sometimes, animals. Generally, they do so under experimental conditions. Sociology's subject matter is **social relationships** or groups viewed in society. As you will see, sociologists study families, schools, workplaces, the media—even the total society. Sociology and psychology come close together in a field called *social psychology*, but this field is defined differently by sociologists and by psychologists. Studies by sociologists are more likely to focus on the effects of group living on people's views and behaviours. By contrast, psychologists are more likely to focus on particular individuals and how they respond under certain experimental conditions.

Another way of characterizing sociology and what makes it unique has been put forward by Earl Babbie (1988). He states that sociologists hold some basic or fundamental ideas that set them apart from those in other fields:

1. Society has an existence of its own.
2. Society can be studied scientifically.
3. Society creates itself.
4. Cultures vary over time and place.
5. Individual identity is a product of society.
6. Social structure must satisfy survival requirements.
7. Institutions are inherently conservative.
8. Societies constrain and transform.
9. Multiple paradigms or fundamental models of reality are needed.

There are multiple ways to approach questions like the causes of violent terrorism and the murder of Indigenous women. Sociologists might approach them in somewhat different ways, but as we will see, there is a basic, shared core to sociological knowledge and research. The goal of this book is to highlight that shared core.

As we will see in the chapters that follow, the most basic ideas or assumptions of sociology are shared by all sociologists. Accordingly, Chapter 1 introduces the theoretical underpinnings and methodologies of sociology. This is followed by chapters on culture (Chapter 2), being social (Chapter 3), social organization (Chapter 4), and deviance (Chapter 5). The next three chapters present different forms of inequality people experience: class and status (Chapter 6), sexuality and gender relations (Chapter 7), and ethnic and race relations (Chapter 8). Reading the next part of the book, you will learn about different social institutions that shape and constrain our lives, including health and families (Chapter 9), education (Chapter 10), work and the economy (Chapter 11), religion (Chapter 12), and politics and social movements (Chapter 13). Increasingly, understanding Canadian society means also understanding global issues (Chapter 14); population, urbanization, and the environment (Chapter 15); and media and technology (Chapter 16).

Sociology is one of the fields of study designed to help describe and explain human behaviour. Unlike psychologists, who focus on the individual, sociologists prefer to study social relationships and groups.

People who major or specialize in sociology gain valuable skills in critical thinking and research methods. This prepares them for a variety of second-entry college and university programs, including law, social work, teaching, industrial relations, human resources, opinion polling, public health, and public administration as well as other fields. People who go on to get an MA or PhD in sociology often end up teaching in colleges or universities or holding positions as researchers, consultants, or policy planners.

CONCLUSION

Sociology is a broad field of study. This is obvious in the broad theoretical perspectives used to guide most sociological research. Sociology highlights both micro- and macro-level analyses and the complex relationships between the two, as noted in Mills's idea of the sociological imagination. Sociology also covers a broad subject matter—consider the subject matter of the following chapters, ranging across deviance, family, education, religion, politics, the economy, health, and beyond.

Sociology allows people to move beyond a purely common-sense approach to a better understanding of social life. In response to social problems like terrorism and hate-based murders of minorities, sociology seeks explanations, proposes solutions, and tests alternative programs of response. Unlike blind blaming and punishment, sociology gives people powerful tools to explore the connections between social institutions and processes. As they do so, they recognize that much common-sense knowledge is faulty.

Yet, for all its importance in public affairs, sociology also has obvious personal relevance, since it addresses everyday life issues. Sociology, in the attempt to understand both personal troubles and public issues, has an important goal overall: to contribute positively to the future of humanity. Our sincere hope is that this text will set you on your way to developing your own sociological imagination.

Key Terms

macrosociology The study of social institutions and large social groups; the study of the processes that depict societies as a whole and of the social-structural aspects of a given society.

microsociology A sociological approach that focuses analysis on small groups, face-to-face interactions, and everyday life activities.

organization A set of people connected by regular relationships that conform to shared norms and values.

social relationships Interactions of people in a society. Because people share culture and a sense of collective existence, these interactions are to some extent recurrent and predictable.

Theory and Methods

As we noted in the introduction of this book, sociology is both similar to and different from other disciplines in the social sciences and humanities. *What* we study in the social sciences—individuals, social groups, social interactions, social relations, and social change—makes us "social." *How* we choose to study what we study—using theories and methods—makes sociology and other social sciences a *science*. While some sociologists criticize or even reject the idea that sociology is an empirically driven, positivist science, especially those who align themselves with more qualitative approaches, few can dispute the fact that combining social theory with clear and precise sociological methods lies at the core of contemporary sociology.

Sociology is the study of social behaviour. It is the job of sociologists to ask critical questions, to dig deeply and challenge common-sense assumptions about how the social world seems to work, and even to challenge inequitable social order and relations. Experience shows that to understand the "how" and "why" of social life, we need both theories and methods.

A *theory* is a set of interrelated concepts that can be used to describe, explain, or predict social phenomena. Sociologists use theories as a lens through which to seek to understand society. As you will see, conflict theory is an example of one such lens. That lens focuses our attention on power differences at the root of social, political, or material inequalities that exist in any given society. Feminist theorists use that critical lens to focus on the impact of gender (sometimes in conjunction with other things like class, race, ethnicity, sexuality, age, ability, etc.) on access to power and privilege.

All of the sociologists presented in this collection have particular theoretical lenses through which they have approached their area of research. Their theoretical lens has in turn shaped the kinds of questions they have asked, the methods that they have chosen to use, and the insights they have shared through their findings. Throughout this collection, you will see cited examples of a wide range of research methods or research tools used to test, measure, uncover, and explore the complex phenomena that make up our social world.

Chapter 1 in this collection, by Bruce Arai and Anthony Thomson, sets the stage for your journey into sociological inquiry. The chapter focuses on sociological theories and research methods commonly used in the discipline. The chapter will help you distinguish between objectivity and subjectivity in social theory, identify the key ideas of the major classical theorists, and understand how they have shaped contemporary sociological theories, including functionalism, conflict theories, interactionism, feminist theories, and post-structuralism. The chapter will also introduce you to the basic notions needed to understand social research methods.

You will learn that quantitative methods typically look for causal explanations (i.e., they identify a series of variables that help explain why things are happening) using mathematical or statistical models, and report their results using numbers. Qualitative methods, on the other hand, often ask individuals to share experiences or insights in richer, more personal and descriptive ways—in their own words and in their own ways. Each methodological approach that you will encounter in this and other sociology books aims to provide insights into the large (macro) and small (micro) things that make up our often taken-for-granted social worlds. That is why you will begin your exploration of the discipline of sociology, and its probing of everyday life, with an introduction to sociological theories and methods.

1 | Sociological Theory and Research Methods

BRUCE ARAI AND ANTHONY THOMSON

In this chapter you will:

▶ Distinguish between objectivity and subjectivity in social theory

▶ Identify the key ideas of the major classical theorists: Durkheim, Marx, and Weber

▶ Relate classical social theory to perspectives in contemporary sociology: functionalist, conflict, interactionist, feminist, and post-structuralist

▶ Identify the distinctive features of surveys, field research, interviewing, and ethnographic research

▶ Determine some of the major uses of different types of existing data and how they are analyzed

INTRODUCTION: WHY THEORY AND METHODS?

In one sense, we are all sociologists because we try to make sense of the world in which we live. Understanding the world and our places within it is almost as important as eating. The majority of Canadians (though certainly far from all) can take eating pretty much for granted. This is a great privilege. In our increasingly connected but greatly unequal globe, a full stomach cannot be assumed. Our privilege is also our responsibility. Not only are we able to use our intellect to understand the world, it is a crucial ingredient for guiding the actions we take. From a sociological perspective, what we do—our day-to-day actions—are part of the making and remaking of the actual world we live in.

If physically we are what we eat, mentally, as novelist Dean Koontz says, we are the ideas we swallow (2007, p. 299). Like eating, much of our understanding of the world, of what we do and think, is simply taken for granted, as if it were natural. But the rules of nature—for example, if you are deprived of food long enough, you will die—are not the same as the rules of society: you will not have enough to eat if you do not have the money to pay for it.

Like food distribution, the ideas we consume are open to question. They may be popular fictions, part of the problems in the world, not the solutions. And they can be violated and changed. Social rules are human constructions; for better or ill, they shape the world we live in. In this chapter, we focus on the theories sociologists have devised to understand social life and the methods they use to collect the data that have informed these theories and produced the many findings you will read about throughout this text.

THE BIRTH OF CLASSICAL SOCIOLOGY IN THE AGE OF REVOLUTION

How do sociologists go about building a theory for understanding social life? Quite a lot depends on how they approach some basic questions about individuals and society. On the one hand, we are born into pre-existing social arrangements or structures, including physical objects such as cities and buildings as well as social codes of behaviour and morality. These pre-existing structures and institutions set the limits and boundaries of our lives.

But real life is complicated. First, people choose one course of action over others. For example, you chose to enter university, but you may toss the whole project aside tomorrow and travel to Bali. People are thinking and acting individuals; in short, they exercise **agency**. Second, sociologists look at more than just the existing facts, such as how food is unevenly dispensed and also ask questions about values, such as how food *should justly* be shared. Sociology considers both the existing **objective** facts and our **subjective** understandings about them.

Sociology was developed in Europe in the chaos of the Industrial and French Revolutions by scholars who were aware that their traditional world was changing rapidly and fundamentally (Thomson, 2010). People who are part of the generation now reaching adulthood are used to rapid change in the ways they communicate, travel, work, and experience diversions and pleasures. But the gap between the older generations and the new microchip one seems to be widening: "I *used to be* with it," Grandpa Simpson says, but now what is "it" seems pretty weird and scary to him.

Sociology thrives in these periods of large-scale social change. European social theorists in the 1800s understood that a more modern world was replacing the older, traditional one. In contrast to the traditional world of magic, mystery, and arbitrary authority, they saw modern Western society as entering a new world of **Enlightenment**. Through the use of reason, it was assumed, the human mind could shine light into the darkest caves and discover "true" knowledge.

Just as Isaac Newton had discovered the law of gravity, the French social theorist who invented the term "sociology," Auguste Comte (1798–1857), intended to create a science of social life. As Comte (1974, pp. 19–27) saw it, the

"Mind controlled video games. In our day we had to use our thumbs!"

We live in a world of rapid change. What do you think sociologists a century from now will be saying about the large-scale social changes happening today?

knowledge developed by his new social science would give humans power over social change. But as sociologists proliferated, the search for absolute laws led to quite different—indeed opposite—conclusions. More than 200 years after Comte, we are no closer to this elusive and improbable universal understanding.

Societies in the world today are not uniformly modern, but they are all subject to the forces of modernity. Western institutions and values intrude everywhere in the Global South, disrupting traditional practices, beliefs, and structures of power. This Westernization is double-edged. Its consequences are both beneficial (women's education, for example) and harmful (global warming). Social change is embraced by some; it is feared and resisted by others, sometimes violently.

Studying sociological theory entails grasping the perspectives of the founding generation of sociologists (classical theorists) who strove to carve out the new discipline. Three of the most important are Émile Durkheim, Karl Marx, and Max Weber. They are cited frequently throughout this text, so at this point it is useful to outline their thinking. Briefly, all three focused on fundamental ways that traditional society had been transformed by modernity.

ÉMILE DURKHEIM

Émile Durkheim (1858–1917) was born in eastern France to a close-knit, strictly orthodox Jewish family, part of a small and cohesive minority community. Durkheim broke with the Jewish faith and with religious belief generally, but he understood the powerful hold that custom and religion have on people in society (Lukes, 1972, pp. 39–46). Durkheim's social theory examined society as a totality of interconnected parts in which all social groups perform necessary functions to support the whole society. He stamped this functionalist approach on the new discipline he helped to create.

In contemporary society, Durkheim's functional theories explain the ways different institutions function to maintain social order and reproduce society over time. A strong sense of social togetherness, Durkheim said, originated in the simplest societies through regular feasts and celebrations. In joyous, often delirious festivals, people experienced a "collective effervescence" that bound them together and generated not only a feeling of spirituality, but belief in a sacred or spiritual power greater than themselves. Think of a religious revival meeting or even the hysteria of a rock concert.

For Durkheim, modern individualism had undermined the traditional, community-based world of shared customs and spiritual beliefs. The secular had overwhelmed the sacred. People had lost the solid and shared code of morality that had acted as the glue holding society together—in Durkheim's terms, people no longer shared a collective conscience. Instead, they lived in a paralyzing uncertainty he termed **anomie** (Durkheim, 1965 [1912], pp. 5–6).

Jean Baudrillard (1929–2007) suggests it may be only the definition of the collective conscience that is changing. Through the ostentatious display of goods for sale in shop windows and big-box malls, "things" take on an almost sacred aura, even when they are merely worshipped through gazing (window-shopping). At every moment in consumer society, "in the streets . . . on advertising hoardings and neon signs," individuals are trained into a modern collective consciousness of mass consumption (Baudrillard, 1998, p. 166).

KARL MARX

The theories of Karl Marx (1818–1883) have inspired movements of revolution and reform that have had deep and lasting consequences for sociological theory. Marx was born into a respectable middle-class family in Germany and married into the minor aristocracy. The match was a romance, however, not a conventional route into the upper class (Berlin, 1963, pp. 27–32).

For Marx, the way to begin the analysis of any society is to examine how it produces and distributes the basic necessities of life—its economic system. The defining process in modernity was the revolutionary destruction of traditional economies and the emergence of

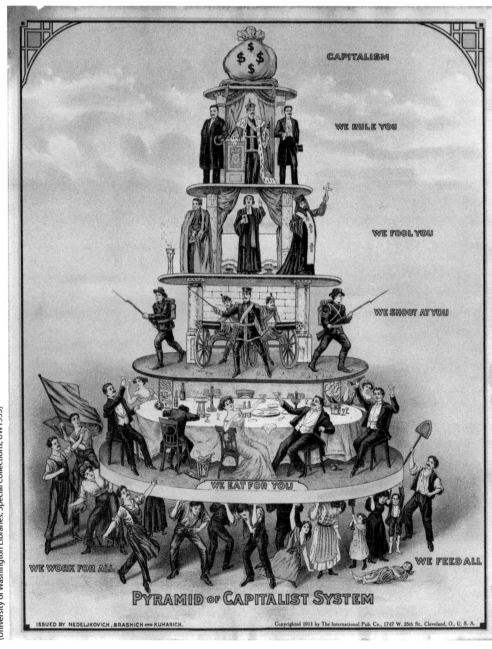

Social inequality or stratification has been a central concern since the founding of sociology. Our daily lives are shaped by the class structure.

global **capitalism**. Land and goods, which had originally been the common property of all, became the private property of a few. People were driven from the countryside into the poorest sections of the increasingly bloated cities and into the newly dominant factory system (Marx & Engels, 1985 [1848]). Mass migration from rural to urban areas is now a worldwide phenomenon.

For Marx, economic divisions and conflict became basic features of most societies and the keys to understanding social change. The majority of working people produce more goods than they require for their own use. The excess or **surplus** supports the elite few, which has grown into a rich and powerful dominant class. Marx's perspective is illustrated in the image on the previous page, "Pyramid of Capitalist System": the labour of the working class toiling at the bottom provides a surplus in the form of profit for the livelihood of the opulent capitalist class (shown at dinner), for priests (second from the top), and for the government, which orders the soldiers to shoot workers when they rebel.

> **TIME to REFLECT**
>
> How would Durkheim respond to the figure depicting the capitalist system?

Marx saw industrial growth as socially progressive but capitalism as reprehensible. He inspired an anti-capitalist movement that hoped to replace capitalism with socialism. Humanity's ability to transform nature through constant-growth capitalism, however, has now proved to have contradictory consequences. In our current environmental crisis, which is one of the consequences of constant-growth capitalism, it is clear that our power over nature has had some disastrous consequences.

MAX WEBER

For German sociologist Max Weber (1864–1920), neither individualism nor capitalism captures the fundamental way that modern society differs from traditional society. Above all, he said, modern society is shaped by the dominance of rationality. In his historical and comparative sociology, two essential elements of large-scale social theory, Weber sought to uncover the social, religious, and political forces of rationality that shape modern society independently of economic processes.

For Weber, the world had been disenchanted. Logic and science had eroded mysticism, supernatural beliefs, and religion, and put humanity into the straitjackets of bureaucracy and asceticism (Weber, 1946 [1915], pp. 350–351). The modern world was dominated by "formal rationality," which involves calculating the most efficient means to achieve a goal, just as politicians plot how to manipulate public opinion and win votes.

The exercise of authority in society had not always been rational. In many monarchies, for example, by "traditional authority" the first-born son of the deceased sovereign automatically becomes the next king whether or not he is fit to rule. The ability to exercise power over others can also be based on exceptional personal qualities or "charismatic authority"—an irrational power that compels people to follow a leader, such as Jesus or Hitler.

In the modern world, Weber said, tradition and charisma had been replaced by "legal–rational authority." All the institutions of modern life, including government, are regulated by a rational set of rules that define a hierarchy of positions and power. When you get a job as a data analyst, your work will be judged according to objective standards of performance. Traditional types of evaluation and judgment—such as to whom you are related—become less important than your qualifications, experience, and work habits.

> **TIME to REFLECT**
>
> Weber said that traditional authority and charismatic authority had been superseded by legal-rational authority. Thinking about recent Canadian and American elections, would you say this is largely true?

In contemporary sociology, French social theorist Pierre Bourdieu (1930–2002) redefined Weber's analysis of modern society to examine the various ways in which people can acquire resources of power and control. For Bourdieu (1984), if you are well-educated and have acquired the necessary knowledge and "taste" to be able to fit seamlessly into higher classes, you have **cultural capital**. If you are well connected and have an "in" with important people, you can benefit by using these connections and have **social capital**, says Bourdieu.

George Ritzer terms the spread of formal rationality in contemporary globalization "McDonaldization," since the fast-food chain's finely calculated techniques of production and marketing are emulated worldwide. McDonaldization is evident in "education, work, health care, travel, leisure, dieting, politics, the family, and virtually every other aspect of society" (Ritzer, 2000a, pp. 1–2).

POST–WORLD WAR II SOCIOLOGY

The European perspectives of Durkheim and Weber were soon exported to new sociology departments in the United States and Canada. As immigrant nations, both were constructing multi-ethnic and pluralistic societies in which the traditionalism of many new arrivals clashed with the values and priorities of modernity. This drama continues to unfold daily as refugees come to Canada by the thousands from conflict zones such as Syria, and as migrants seek to escape the desolation wrought by poverty and climate change. The debate about wearing hijabs and other traditional female coverings reflects

---

GLOBAL ISSUES
Sociology: A Subversive Discipline

When sociology was born in Western Europe in the nineteenth century, it was deeply dyed with the birthmarks of its time and place. Europe had embarked on global conquest and Eurocentric ideas were an integral part of colonialism. Western society adopted the ideology of Orientalism: Europe was the pinnacle of progress; all other societies were culturally backward; Europe had assumed the "burden" of "civilizing" the "natives" (Saïd, 1978). Sociological views, which frequently questioned taken-for-granted institutions and values, did not spread quickly to the east and south. Authoritarian regimes, whether imperialist or traditional, felt threatened by the critical and reformist bent of early sociology.

When sociological analysis did spread globally, it often took an explicitly political character, closely linked to anti-colonialism and the critique of Western capitalism. For Latin American theorists such as Andre Gunder Frank and Fernando Cardoso, global capitalism was an engine designed to siphon wealth from underdeveloped colonies to further enrich the industrialized north. During the right-wing dictatorship of Augusto Pinochet in Chile, sociology became the "forbidden discipline" (Simbürger, 2014). Sociology departments were closed, faculty and graduate students fled for their lives, and sociology was identified as socialist and subversive. Ironically perhaps, in left-wing China under Mao Zedong, sociology was eliminated in universities because it was deemed a Western, bourgeois pseudo-science—and subversive.

Since then, sociology has been established as a legitimate discipline in most countries. At its best, sociology is an "underdog" perspective. "Committing sociology," as Stephen Harper once put it, means being critical of institutions and practices that reproduce the myriad forms of oppression that continue to exist. Sociology is still threatening to repressive regimes. In 2016, Canadian anthropologist Homa Hoodfar was imprisoned in Iran, her home country, where she had been conducting sensitive research on Muslim women. Turkish sociologist Pinar Selek actively supports the rights of women, as well as those of sexual and ethnic minorities. She has been acquitted three times for alleged involvement in an explosion in 1998. In 2013 she was tried again and given a life sentence. Critics say her actual "crime" was researching Kurdish minority rebels in Turkey and then refusing to divulge her sources (Banerjee, 2016). Speaking truth to power and protecting the powerless are always dangerous undertakings.

the dilemmas of assimilation and racism in Canada. All these social conflicts and upheavals are grist for the sociological mill. Sociology is now a global enterprise, but its critical perspective has not always made it a welcome addition to university curricula.

After World War II (1939–1945), the United States and Canada entered an era of unprecedented prosperity—a time of job growth and high spending that now seems a dream. America dominated the globe, and Canada was tied to its soaring kite strings. On both sides of the undefended border it sometimes appeared that all was right with the world. In this age of complacency, sociology was dominated by one perspective: **structural functionalism**.

Sociologists who looked at society through the structural functional lens wanted to know why society seemed to be so orderly, so organized, and so free of conflict. Led by American sociologist Talcott Parsons (1902–1979), they studied the forces that hold societies together, as Durkheim had done half a century before. In this viewpoint, what is most important about society is how a society is reproduced over time; how it remains, day-to-day, basically unchanged—in a word, sameness. Look around your classroom and imagine the things you and your classmates *could* be doing together here and now. But what you *are* doing allows the lecture to go on, in an orderly and routine way. No society can operate without rules, functioning institutions, social roles, belief systems, and commonly accepted values. Many of the complexities of these rules, beliefs, and values are discussed in separate chapters below.

As functionalist theory developed in the age of prosperity and complacency, however, it became one-sided. Do people really think, believe, and act on a single set of values and assumed truths? Canadian-born sociologist Dennis Wrong (1961) complained that functional theory incorrectly viewed people as over-socialized, as more trained into conformity than they actually were.

Sociologists developed two critical responses to functionalism. Microsociologists rejected the view that people were merely puppets of institutional structures and social forces. They focused on the way our daily lives are shaped by our intentions and interactions with others. Conflict sociologists complained that functionalism assumed too much harmony and consensus. They viewed society as fundamentally conflict-ridden and said we could learn more by examining the deep fault lines dividing society, such as race, gender, and class.

MICROSOCIOLOGY

It is not possible to study people the way you study rocks or plants. If you push a rock, you can predict how far and in what direction it will move. But what happens if you push a human being? Rocks do not push back; they do not run away or turn and fight. The thinking and acting side of humanity is known as agency.

If I predicted that you would close this book now in frustration and turn to Snapchat or Tinder instead, you could choose not to, precisely to refute my prediction. Human beings are not simply objects that are analyzed and acted upon; they have intentions they want to carry out; they have interpretations of their own actions and those of others; they have desires and needs they seek to fulfill; and they make choices.

The study of these subjective processes led to **symbolic interactionism**, a theory that is a form of microsociology because it focuses attention on the smallest units of society—individual people and small groups (Blumer, 1969). W.I. Thomas said everyone enters a social occasion with a specific "definition of the situation," which affects how they act and what they hope to achieve from the interaction (Thomas & Znaniecki, 1958, pp. 68–69). People orient their action according to what they think others think—a calculation involving **intersubjectivity**. In his modern novel *Ulysses*, James Joyce (1968, p. 602) asks this question about Leopold Bloom and Stephen Dedalus, two of his characters: "What . . . were Bloom's thoughts about Stephen's thoughts about Bloom, and Bloom's thoughts about Stephen's thoughts about Bloom's thoughts about Stephen?" But not everyone's opinion counts equally. In *The Social Network*, it does not matter to the Mark Zuckerberg character if a neighbour down the hall thinks he is an "asshole," but it is different when his girlfriend comes to the same conclusion.

Similarly, G.H. Mead (1863–1931) argued that we learn to stand in others' shoes and see the world from their point of view; to see what they see, feel what they feel. The better socialized we are, in Mead's terms, the better we are able to "take the role of the other" and learn to think reflexively (1934, pp. 73, 133–134).

 For a more complete discussion of symbolic interactionism and Mead's perspective, see "Symbolic Interactionist Frame of Reference," p. 64, in **Chapter 3**, "Being Social."

Interactionists and the **social constructionist** perspective they engendered (Berger & Luckmann, 1966) generally see society as an ensemble of relationships, communications, and interpretations. Social institutions exist only because people continually, minute by minute, act in ways that reproduce them. Some people, however, particularly those in positions of power, have more opportunity to construct society according to their interests. This insight is crucial to **conflict theory** in sociology.

CONFLICT THEORY

While functionalism still dominated the sociological imagination, what US President Lyndon Johnson called the "Great Society" was being torn apart. The violent repression of the often desperate struggles for basic civil rights among African Americans was vividly broadcast by the new medium of television. Mass protests denounced the Vietnam War and supported the anti-colonial struggles of so-called Third World nations.

A new generation of young and radical activists calling itself the **New Left** found a congenial home in sociology departments. Making sociology relevant for the times meant tackling the big issues of war, poverty, inequality, and injustice. Conflict theorists took on this task. From Dalhousie University in Halifax to Simon Fraser in Vancouver, students protested, occupied

---

SOCIOLOGY IN ACTION   Michel Foucault

Born in France, Michel Foucault (1936–1984) established a career in intellectual history and remains influential in many disciplines, including sociology. Educated at an elite school in France, the solitary Foucault found life unbearable. He became fascinated with authors who dealt with **transgression**, "limit experiences" (such as death), and excess. His book *Discipline and Punish* (1979 [1975]) uses the rise of the penitentiary, with its constant surveillance of prisoners and strict discipline, as a metaphor for the same processes as they spread throughout modern society (schools, hospitals, public spaces).

For Foucault, authority surrounds and acts upon people, seeking to turn them into docile and obedient objects. Scientific knowledge gives authorities the power to control both the body and the mind though "stricter methods of surveillance . . . [and] more effective techniques of . . . obtaining information." Power to normalize and punish operates throughout society, regulating those who depart only slightly "from a rule, an average, a demand, a norm" (Foucault, 1979 [1975], pp. 77, 198–199). The result is a modern biopolitics of power directed at certain populations distinguished by bodily markers (race, gender, ability, etc.). Simultaneously, however, there arises a biopolitics of resistance to power along lines of solidarity established through these same physical markers.

As an "engaged philosopher," Foucault became politically active in the 1970s. He supported prisoners' rights and exposed the intolerable realities of incarceration. By then, he had come to terms with a homosexual identity and followed his new lifestyle with abandon. Foucault died at 47 from complications linked to AIDS (Eribon, 1991).

university buildings, and went on strike, none more aggressively than at Sir George Williams University in Montreal (now part of Concordia).

The concepts of **power** and inequality in society—including top-down domination and resistance from the bottom—are important elements in the modern conflict perspective. Learning the rules of domination begins early in our upbringing. Kindergarten is referred to in sociology as "boot camp" for children because teachers impose rules on the way students eat and drink, cover parts of their bodies, form lines, sit in their places, and obey the rule of silence. In Michel Foucault's terms, people are taught to regulate themselves.

Nevertheless, no one is powerless. Ask any teacher or parent. When people such as teachers, judges, or parole officers exercise power, they simultaneously provoke resistance—the ways people find to subvert power, transgress rules, and achieve their aims. Students have invented many strategies to resist school. They copy homework, skip classes, feign sickness, cheat on tests, plagiarize—in short, they learn the informal anti-rules of schooling (Raby, 2009, p. 127). Children as a group may be the most oppressed of all—Charles Dickens thought so—but **feminism**, which focuses on the inequality between men and women, is one of the most important contemporary perspectives to emerge from conflict theory.

FEMINIST SOCIOLOGY: SECOND AND THIRD WAVES

The New Left proliferated throughout the 1960s and inspired social movements among various disadvantaged groups. Ironically, however, many male activists could not see beyond the masculine privileges of their personal realm. A separate women's movement—second-wave feminism—responded to these entrenched sexist practices.

As more and more women entered sociology and undertook professional studies, it became increasingly clear that sexism also wore

In a show of rejection of contemporary models of international governance and authority, demonstrators damage police cars during the 2010 G20 protests in Toronto.

Photo by Steve Russell/Toronto Star via Getty Images

academic garb. Women were absent from classical, male theory and were subsumed under a male point of view. Liberals in the women's movement sought to equalize conditions for women within the existing social structures (Friedan, 1963). Over time, women in modern society have been more successful in acquiring the *rights* to equality than in achieving *actual* equality in the dominant political and economic spheres.

In contrast to liberal feminists, radical feminists demand more than an equal chance to gain unequal power (Firestone, 1970). They identify male power—**patriarchy**—as the original and most persistent form of social injustice. They demand changes in the everyday relationships between men and women, such as stopping violence against women, the freedom to express sexuality in all its variations, and the equal recognition of alternative forms of families or no families at all.

In Canada, sociologist Dorothy Smith (b. 1926) developed a women's standpoint perspective that is critical of the dominant, top-down model of conventional sociology. Smith argues that feminist research should begin with the everyday experiences of women and with their subjective understanding of these "lived experiences." Smith's activist research method is engaged, explicit in its goals, and not value free.

She integrates her "subjects" into all aspects of the research process. The results address the issues that sparked the research and are shared with the participants (Smith, 1987).

 Dorothy Smith was a pioneer of Canadian feminist sociology. To learn more about her perspective, see "Gender and Sexuality as Critical Vantage Points," p. 156, in **Chapter 7**, "Gender and Sexuality."

The present generation has inherited a degree of gender equality their parents worked hard to achieve. But second-wave feminism proved to have its own blinders. A number of contemporary third-wave feminists realize that the experiences of poor, or minority, or sexually differentiated women are likely to be misunderstood when seen through the eyes of the white, middle-class, professional, heterosexual women who had inspired second-wave feminism (Thomson, 2016). Among these critics is Patricia Hill Collins.

Collins (b. 1948) grew up an only child in a black, working-class family in Philadelphia. At Brandeis University she felt overwhelmed and silenced by the daily assaults that came from being socially denigrated as an African American, working-class woman. Collins asserts in *Black Feminist Thought* (2000) that sociology must integrate issues of race, gender, and social class, give a voice to the voiceless, and privilege the standpoint of black women. Transnationally, women of African descent exist within a multi-dimensional **matrix of domination**. They "encounter recurring social issues such as poverty, violence, reproductive concerns, lack of education, sex work, and susceptibility to disease." All these forms of intersecting oppression have to be targeted simultaneously. Black feminist thought aims to empower its subjects and stimulate resistance (Collins, 2000, pp. 25–32).

Contemporary sociology is a magnet for women, as undergraduates, graduate students, and faculty members. Much of the work of women sociologists is highlighted in this text. They bring to their research an understanding of what it means to see society from different and "othered" vantage points, an understanding that reflects the emergence of **post-structuralism**.

TIME to REFLECT

Why is it that women now make up the majority (over 60 per cent) of university graduates in Canada?

POST-STRUCTURALISM AND POST-MODERNISM

The New Left–inspired sociologists who have dominated sociological theory since the heady, romantic 1960s focused on criticizing and resisting the dominant social structures of power and wealth. And when no new society emerged from all the exuberance, disillusionment replaced optimism. In this vacuum, a host of social theorists rejected any sociological thought with its roots in the Enlightenment. Rather than focusing on the general structures and patterns of society, they concentrated on marginalized and repressed minorities and on acts of transgression beyond the limits of the dominant rules—in a word, difference. The result was not so much a coherent, new theory as a radically oppositional outlook. It became known as post-structuralism.

Much contemporary post-structural theory is rooted in a wider theoretical attitude known as **post-modernism**, which can be traced back to nineteenth-century Romanticism, the anti-theoretical twin of Enlightenment rationalism (Thomson, 2010). Romantics claimed there were deeper, more profound sources of knowledge than rationality and that people were at heart emotional, feeling, wilful, and desiring beings. The Romantic impulse resurfaced among the youthful rebels of the 1950s (the Beats) and 1960s (Hippies), in much of the alternative arts scene (music and film), and among contemporary anarchists.

No Great Wall separated cultural theory from sociology. In the 1980s, the post-modernist attack flowed into sociological theory. Postmodernists argued there is no single "reality" to be understood and transformed. What we think of as "real" consists more and more of images fabricated for our consumption and spread through various forms of media. And there are as many different perceptions about what is real as there are people to think about it.

The binary, either/or ideas of functionalist and conflict theory not only had failed to describe the complexities of life, but had led to false, often authoritarian solutions. New problems had emerged, such as ethnic cleansing, religious intolerance, and individual and state-sponsored terrorism. Ultimately, post-modernism leads to extreme relativism, leaving us defenceless in the post-truth world of false news. Evidence-based probable truths are discredited and overwhelmed by pseudo-science, self-interested beliefs, and hyperbolic "alternative facts." In terms of action, all that anyone could do was respond individually, particularly by transgressing (consciously and publicly violating) social regulations about such things as authority, sexuality, and gender roles (for example, becoming transgender).

As theoretical criticism, post-structuralism highlights new cultural forces in global society that affect the way people experience, understand, and respond to social problems. It denies the existence of an essential and unitary "self"; it emphasizes diversity, identity politics, and the role of media and technology in creating the taken-for-granted images that form the spectacles of modern life (Thomson, 2016). An adequate sociology for the present must face the challenges of post-structuralist thought.

The contemporary generation faces a litany of deeply rooted social problems, such as climate change, widening global inequality, nuclear proliferation, civil wars, and economic crises. We are living in an unprecedented new age that is "weird and scary" in more ways than one. As with any technology, the microchip revolution is a double-edged sword (see the "Under the Wire" box). Sociology can best approach this world by criticizing existing structures and focusing on the human ability to understand, criticize, make choices, and take actions. Dorothy Smith's action research is only one way to approach the practical and ethical questions of obtaining information from people. Numerous other methods have been developed in sociology to address the social and personal problems that beset modern society, as discussed below.

UNDER THE WIRE   What Difference Do the Differences Make?

In contemporary times—at least in the Western world—new technology, international travel, and the Internet have modified the way we experience our world. The implications of our new and different lifestyle for us and future generations are issues of vital public interest.

Sociologists are not just interested in what the differences are—they want to know *what difference the differences make*. Does modern communication technology enable us to be better informed about socially significant events or only about everyday trivia? Do the new media provide platforms for the greater realization of democratic decision-making, or are they tools of Big Brother? Do they create more communities of interest and sharing, or do they more thoroughly individualize us? Do they deepen our actual engagement with the world or merely make even the most horrendous event seem like a spectacle, to be gazed at but not acted upon?

Every new communication technology creates new possibilities for control but also for resistance. Protesters in Egypt and Tunisia in 2011, who (perhaps temporarily) drove their dictatorial leaders from power, frequently communicated via social networking. Blurred Vision, a Toronto-based rock group fronted by two Iranian brothers, covered Pink Floyd's transgressive anthem "Another Brick in the Wall." Posted on YouTube in 2010, the song created an underground sensation among disaffected Iranian youth.

One of the most controversial theorists in contemporary times, Jean Baudrillard, challenges our view of "the real." For Baudrillard (1998), we perceive society through the veil of mass media so that "reality" has been overtaken by simulations, such as Walt Disney World, that impose upon us images of what we take to be real. No wonder the Hollywood "culture industry" speculates about what is real or virtual (*The Matrix*, *Ex Machina*) and what is only a dream (*Inception*).

THEORY AND RESEARCH

For most sociologists, it is important that their research be closely connected with a theory or set of theories. Briefly, *theories* are abstract ideas about the world. Most sociological research is designed to evaluate a theory, either by testing it or by exploring the applicability of a theory to different situations. As can be seen throughout the many chapters in this text, sociologists investigate substantive problems and try to use their theories to help them understand these problems better. For instance, sociologists may be interested in understanding crime, the family, the environment, or education, and they will almost always use their theories to provide a deeper appreciation of these issues.

Sociologists use theories as models of how the world works, and they use research methods to gather data that are relevant to these theories. Thus, theories and methods are always intertwined in the research process. There are hundreds of different theories in sociology, but most of them can be grouped into the four main theoretical perspectives that can be found throughout this text. Theories cannot be tested directly, because they are only abstract ideas. Theories must be translated into observable ideas before they can be tested. This process of translation is called **operationalization**.

It is important to understand the difference between dependent and in- dependent variables. For example, your hypothesis may be that finding a well- paid job is *dependent* on obtaining a higher level of education. Thus, higher education is an independent variable, while a well-paid job is a dependent variable.

Operationalization

Operationalization is the process of translating theories and concepts into hypotheses and variables. Theories are abstract ideas, composed of concepts. **Concepts** are single ideas. Usually, theories explain how two or more concepts are related to each other. For instance, Karl Marx used concepts such as "exploitation" and "class" to construct a theory of capitalism.

Once we have a theory, we need some way to test it. We need an observable equivalent of a theory or at least a set of observable statements that are consistent with our theory. These are called hypotheses. In the same way that theories express relationships between concepts, **hypotheses** express relationships between variables. Unlike the typical definition of a hypothesis as simply an "educated guess," hypotheses must be observable or testable. This means they must express relationships between variables.

A **variable** is the empirical or observable equivalent of a concept. The two key points about a variable are that it must be observable and that it must have a range of different values it can take on. For instance, ethnicity, age, and annual income are variables. We can collect information on all these items (that is, they are observable), and people can have different ages, ethnicities, and so on.

In most cases, our hypotheses contain a minimum of two types of variables: independent variables and dependent variables. Independent variables are roughly equivalent to causes, and dependent variables are roughly equivalent to effects. For instance, if you wanted to investigate differences between the average earnings of men and women, then sex or gender would be the independent variable, and earnings would be the dependent variable. This is because people's earnings may depend on their gender.

RESEARCH TECHNIQUES

A popular image is that the experiment is the primary method scientists use to conduct research. However, even in the natural sciences, experiments often are the exception rather than the rule. A great deal of biology, astronomy, geology, and other science is not done—and in many cases cannot be done—experimentally. Nevertheless, the image persists, and it has traditionally been the standard against which science of all types, natural or social, has been measured.

Despite the fact that sociologists do not use experiments very often, the logic of the experiment still dominates at least one of the major techniques of sociological research. Surveys almost always collect a great deal of extra information from respondents in an attempt to recreate the controlled environment of the experiment after the fact. Surveys are often referred to as *quasi-experimental* designs, because they are only able to construct a controlled environment after the data have been collected. In other words, in true experiments the controlled conditions are set in place, and then the experiment is allowed to run, while in quasi-experiments observations of "naturally occurring" phenomena are made and an attempt is made to remove the effects of confounding variables during the analysis stage.

Surveys

Surveys are the most widely used technique in social scientific research. Sociologists, economists, political scientists, psychologists, and others use them regularly (Gray & Guppy, 2008). They are an excellent way to gather data on large populations that cannot be studied effectively face-to-face. The goals of almost all social scientific surveys are to produce detailed data that will allow researchers to describe the characteristics of the group under study, to test theories about that group, and to generalize results beyond the people who responded to the survey.

At first glance, it might seem that designing good questions for a survey would be easy. The reality is that it is quite difficult— sociologists can spend months trying to figure out what questions they will ask, how they will word them, and the order in which they will

---

OPEN FOR DISCUSSION — Max Weber and *Verstehen*

In many of the chapters in this text, you will come across the ideas of Max Weber. One of his most enduring contributions to research methods in sociology is his elaboration of a concept he called *verstehen* (German for "to understand"). His idea is that in order to properly study the cultures of other peoples, a researcher needs to develop not just knowledge but an "empathetic understanding" of their lives as well in order to see the world as that group sees it.

Verstehen became a cornerstone of qualitative sociology as researchers tried to understand the lives of others "from the inside." In Weber's view, developing *verstehen* was a bit of an art, but in theory anyone who was good at it could understand the world view of any other group. In other words, the views of any group could be understood regardless of the personal characteristics of the researcher.

But this view has been criticized as too simplistic. Some researchers have argued that there are limits to *verstehen*, because the personal characteristics of the researcher will affect how the group reacts to her or him, and this will limit the depth of *verstehen* or understanding that a researcher can achieve. For instance, a person's sex or gender may have a decisive impact not only on how much a person can empathize with another group, but also on how much and what kind of information members of the group will provide. In Killingsworth's (2006) study of mom and tot groups discussed later in this chapter, it might be the case that as a male, he might not have had the same access to the ongoing discussions around motherhood and child care. So, are there factors that would limit the level of *verstehen* that a researcher can achieve? And if so, what are those factors, and how do we identify them? At one extreme, this would mean that a researcher would have to match up with her or his participants on everything from gender, to education level, to hair colour, to fashion sense. So neither extreme position is particularly convincing, but exactly where we draw this line remains "open for discussion."

ask them. One of the reasons it is so difficult is that each question must be unambiguous for both the respondent and the researcher. A question with several different interpretations is not useful, because respondents may answer it from a perspective different from that intended by the researcher. Similarly, questions that are too complicated for respondents to answer will not produce useful data. There are many, many issues to consider in designing good questions and the order they appear on the questionnaire, and unless sufficient attention is paid to these issues before the survey is administered, the results will affect the legitimacy of the whole research project.

Random Sampling, Sample Size, and Response Rates

In virtually all social science research, it is impossible to include each member of the whole population in a study. For instance, sending a survey to everyone in Canada each time a sociologist wants to conduct some research is not practical. Luckily, we can use a small **sample** of a population in any study, as long as we choose that sample randomly. Random sampling is so important because it is the only way that we can be confident that our sample is representative of (that is, it looks like) the population we

are interested in. If our sample is representative, then we can be fairly confident that the patterns we find among our sample also will be present in the larger population. And although randomization does not guarantee that our sample will be representative, by minimizing both intentional and unintentional biases we maximize our chances that the sample will be representative. However, randomization does not solve all problems in sociological research and is not always appropriate or necessary in field research.

There are many procedures for choosing a truly random sample, but all are based on the principle that each person (or element) in a population has an equal (and non-zero) chance of being selected into the sample. The simplest random-sampling procedure is known as *simple random sampling*: each person in a population is put on a list, and then a proportion of them are chosen from this list completely at random. The usual way of ensuring that people are chosen at random is to use a table of random numbers as the basis for selection.

Generating truly random samples is not as easy as the word "simple" suggests. The problem lies not in choosing the actual people or elements but in constructing a complete list of every person or element in the population. For

Table 1.1 ▶ Guidelines for Designing Good Survey Questions

Focus	Each question should have one specific topic. Questions with more than one topic are difficult to answer, and the answers are often ambiguous.
Brevity	Generally, shorter questions are preferable to longer questions. They are easier for respondents to understand. An important exception to this guideline is when asking about threatening topics, when longer questions are often preferable.
Clarity	Use clear, understandable words, and avoid jargon. This is especially important for general audiences, but if you are surveying a distinct group or population (such as lawyers), then specialized language is often preferable.
Bias	Avoid biased words, phrases, statements, and questions. If one answer to a question is more likely or is more socially acceptable than others, then the question is probably biased and should be reworded. For instance, if you are asking people about their religious preferences, do not use words like "ungodly," "heathen," or "fanatic" in your questions or you will bias your answers.
Relevance	Ensure that the questions you ask of your respondents are relevant to them and to your research. Also, in most surveys, some questions will not be relevant to all respondents; filter questions allow people to skip questions that are not pertinent to them. For instance, if you want to know why some people did not complete high school, you should first filter out high school graduates and ask them not to answer the questions about not completing high school.

SOURCE: Adapted from George Gray and Neil Guppy, Successful Surveys: Research Methods and Practices, 4th edn (Toronto: Nelson Thomson, 2008).

this reason, other sampling techniques, such as **stratified** sampling and cluster sampling, are frequently used to choose samples.

So how big a sample do you need in order to be able to generalize your results? Actually, this is the wrong question to ask—it is not the size of the sample but rather how it is chosen that determines how confident you can be that your results are applicable to the population. That is, even a very large sample, if it is not chosen randomly, offers no guarantee about the generalizability of the results. On the other hand, a small sample, properly chosen, can produce very good results. So never assume that because a sample is large it must be representative. Always find out how the sample was chosen before making any judgments about its generalizability.

Another crucial factor in determining the generalizability of survey results is how many people from the original sample actually complete the survey. This percentage is called the *response rate*, and it is an important, although not the only, issue to consider in determining the generalizability of the results of a survey. The reason it is important is that unless a large proportion of the people in the original sample actually complete the survey, it is quite possible that the people who do not respond to it are different from those who do respond.

Field Research

In surveys, the primary aim is to collect quantitative or numerical data that can be generalized to a larger population. In contrast, field researchers are concerned about collecting qualitative or non-numerical data that may or may not be generalized. In field research, the aim is to collect rich, nuanced data by going into the "field" to observe and talk to people directly. Researchers spend time getting to know their subjects in order to be able to capture their world view.

Several separate techniques fall under the rubric of field research. They include participant observation or ethnography, in-depth interviewing, and documentary analysis. In many studies, more than one of these techniques is used.

Many organizations create pools of respondents who are willing to answer polls and surveys online. In many cases, respondents are rewarded for their participation with gifts or cash. Does this make you wonder about bias in polling more generally? Why?

Ethnographic or Participant Observation Research

In *ethnographic* or *participant observation* research, the researcher participates in the daily activities of his or her research subjects, usually for an extended period of time. This may include accompanying them on their daily activities (such as following police officers on patrol), interviews and discussions about their lives, and occasionally even living with them. During these activities, researchers take field notes (or make recordings) during and after an episode in the field.

A good example of participant observation research is Killingsworth's study (2006) of how mothers interact with each other in a "mom and tot" playgroup to construct ideas about what a good mother is and how mothers can reconcile that with the consumption of alcohol. Killingsworth participated in a playgroup of mothers and toddlers, and as is typical of participant observation research, he did not have a rigid research design while in the field. Rather, his main interest was in the women's conversations about alcohol, personal consumption, and how they used these conversations to reconstruct ideas about "good mothers." He did not direct the women's conversations; he simply participated in the playgroup and allowed the conversations to occur naturally. He found that the women were able to reconcile their understandings of good motherhood with the consumption of alcohol by recapturing the importance of alcohol to their previous identities as childless women and using that to build ideals of themselves as women first and good mothers second.

Killingworth's research is interesting for several reasons, but one is particularly relevant to his use of participant observation. By focusing on naturally occurring conversations, he was able to show how cultural ideals about things like motherhood and womanhood are embedded in and recreated by seemingly mundane discussions among mothers. In other words, ideals about good mothers do not just appear out of nowhere and exert pressure on people through "norms" or "society." Instead, ideals about good mothers are defined, interpreted, and reconstructed by actual people in actual interactions.

Another example that highlights the role of gender in the ethnographic research process is a study by John Pruit (2015) on male Montessori preschool teachers. He spent two years as a participant-observer in Montessori classrooms, where he found that male preschool teachers were viewed with high levels of suspicion about their sexuality, their masculinity, and even their potential for violence. And, as a male researcher,

he had to develop a series of strategies to gain trust from parents, school board members, children, and other teachers. In this case, being a male in a largely female environment may have been an advantage and allowed him to see more deeply into the taken-for-granted suspicions around male preschool teachers and the strategies these men use to overcome those fears.

TIME to REFLECT

What role did gender play in the research by Killingsworth and by Pruit? Would either of them have reached different conclusions if they were women?

In-depth Interviews

The in-depth interview is another popular field research technique and may be used in conjunction with participant observation. *In-depth interviews* are extensive interviews that are often recorded and later transcribed into text. In some cases, these interviews are highly structured, and neither the researchers nor the respondents are permitted to deviate from a specific set of questions. At the other extreme, unstructured interviews may seem like ordinary conversations in which researchers and respondents simply explore topics as they arise. Striking the right balance between structured and unstructured questions can pose problems for sociologists, as can asking the right questions.

Documentation

In some field studies, researchers have access not only to people but also to documents. This is more common in the study of formal organizations like police forces or law firms, but it can also be the case with churches, political groups, and even families. These documents (case records, files, diaries, photos) can be analyzed to provide a more complete picture of the group under study.

Conducting Field Research

The elaborate procedures needed to choose a sample for a survey are not necessary for selecting the research site and the sample in field

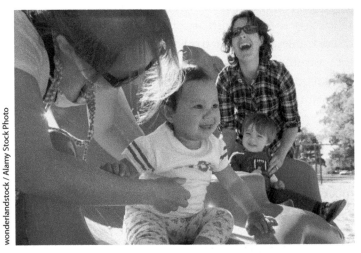

wonderlandstock / Alamy Stock Photo

Ethnographic research is highly context-dependent. How might a study on mothers and motherhood conducted presently in Canada differ from a study conducted a decade ago in Australia?

research. The goal here is to gain greater understanding through the collection of detailed data, not through generalization. Nevertheless, it is important to choose both the research site and the subjects or informants carefully (Bryman, Teevan, & Bell, 2009).

The first consideration in choosing a site for field research is the topic of study. A field study of lawyers or police officers likely will take place at the offices or squad rooms of the respective groups. Choosing which offices and squad rooms to study involves many factors, including which ones will be most useful for the purposes of the research. But a practical element impinges on much field research—the actual choice of research site can come down to which law offices or squad rooms will grant access (Monahan & Fisher, 2015).

Once the site has been chosen, the issues of whom to talk to, what types of data to record, and how long to stay in the field become important. Some things can be planned in advance, but many things are decided during the course of the field research. The selection of key informants—the people who will be most valuable in the course of the study—cannot always be made beforehand. Similarly, figuring out what to write down in field notes, whom to quote, and which observations to record cannot always be determined until after the research has begun.

When to leave the field is almost always determined during the course of the research. Most researchers stay in the field until they get a sense that they are not gaining much new information. This is often taken as a sign that the researcher has reached a deep enough level of understanding to be confident that he or she will not learn much from additional time in the field (Bryman, Teevan, & Bell, 2009).

This flexibility during the course of the study is one of the great advantages of field research over survey research. Mistakes in research design and the pursuit of new and unexpected opportunities are possible in field research but not usually possible in quantitative survey research. Once a survey has been designed, pre-tested, and administered to a sample, it is impractical to recall the survey to make changes. This is one reason that pre-testing is so important in surveys.

Existing Data

Both in surveys and in field research, sociologists are involved in collecting new, original data. However, a great deal of sociological research is done with data already collected. Of the several different types of existing data, most are amenable to different modes of analysis. Some of the major types of existing data are official statistics and surveys done by other researchers; books, magazines, newspapers, and other media; case files and records; and historical documents.

Secondary Data Analysis

The analysis of official statistics and existing surveys—also known as *secondary data analysis*—has grown immensely with the development of computers and statistical software packages. It has become one of the most common forms of research reported in major sociological journals such as the *American Journal of Sociology*.

Quantitative data can be presented in tables like Table 1.2. However, tables can be designed in many different ways, and the type of information being presented will determine the types of comparisons that can be made. In Table 1.2, on marital status in Canada, comparisons can be made within or across the values of marital status (for example, how many people are married versus single), by sex, and across five different years.

We can see that the number of divorced males increased by more than 45,000 between 2011 and 2015 and the number of divorced females rose by more than 64,000, while the numbers of married men and women increased by about 447,000 and 376,000 respectively. However, the table does not tell us anything about why these numbers may have changed, nor can we make any comparisons with the number of married and divorced people in other countries. Also, the numbers are very precise, but

Table 1.2 ▶ Population by Marital Status and Sex, Canada, 2011–2015

Marital Status	Sex	2011	2012	2013	2014	2015
Total	Males	17,015,959	17,225,198	17,430,739	17,626,354	17,776,719
	Females	17,326,821	17,526,278	17,724,760	17,917,304	18,075,055
Single	Males	7,446,612	7,491,032	7,529,598	7,567,087	7,587,028
	Females	6,561,711	6,590,937	6,616,609	6,642,696	6,658,591
Married	Males	6,520,600	6,637,698	6,757,878	6,872,242	6,968,467
	Females	6,479,531	6,577,938	6,678,366	6,774,674	6,855,878
Common-law	Males	1,634,450	1,652,638	1,669,822	1,685,494	1,695,031
	Females	1,559,565	1,574,013	1,587,536	1,599,931	1,607,024
Widowed	Males	312,018	323,993	336,289	348,688	360,632
	Females	1,276,651	1,312,019	1,348,740	1,385,666	1,421,421
Divorced	Males	751,365	764,063	776,491	787,745	797,005
	Females	1,012,609	1,029,760	1,047,061	1,063,287	1,077,424

SOURCE: Statistics Canada. CANSIM, Table 051-0042. Last modified: 2 Nov. 2015.

the fact is that these are estimates of the true numbers. So while it is possible to discern trends in tables like this, be careful about reading too much into the precision of the numbers.

Personal computers, statistical software packages, and the ready availability of many national and international datasets have made secondary data analysis possible for almost every social scientist. The advantages of secondary analysis are that the coverage of the data is broad and that the hard work involved in constructing and administering a survey has already been done, usually by an agency with far more expertise and resources than most individual researchers. The disadvantages are that the data collected are often not precise enough to test the specific ideas that interest researchers and that mastering the techniques to analyze the data properly can be challenging.

Historical Research and Content Analysis

The analysis of historical documents, print and other media, and records and case materials can be done by several methods. The two most common forms of analysis are historical research and content analysis. Historical sociology relies on all kinds of historical documents, from organizational records, old newspapers, and magazines to speeches and sermons, letters and

diaries, and even interviews with people who participated in the events of interest. In *content analysis*, documents such as newspapers, magazines, TV shows, and case records are subjected to careful sampling and analysis procedures to reveal patterns. (See Warren & Karner [2009] for a good discussion of historical research and content analysis.)

One of the major issues facing historical sociologists is that someone or some organization has created the records used in their analyses, but the potential biases and reasons for recording the information in the documents are not always clear. Documents get lost or destroyed with the passing of time. Why have certain documents survived while others have not? Is there any significance to the ordering or cataloguing of the documents? These and other issues must be dealt with continually in historical research.

Content analysis can be done in a number of ways, but it usually involves taking a sample of relevant documents and then rigorously and methodically identifying and classifying particular features, words, or images in these documents. For instance, in studying political posters, content analysis could be used to determine whether the posters from particular parties put more emphasis on the positive aspects of their own party or on the negative aspects of other parties. These results could then be used to better understand styles of political campaigning in a particular country or time period.

Selecting a Research Method

To summarize, all the methods described here are used by sociologists to collect data on particular research problems, and they use theories to help them understand or solve these problems. Any of these methods can be used to investigate problems from any of the theoretical perspectives encountered in this text, although some methods are almost never used in some perspectives.

How do you know which method to use with which theory or theoretical perspective? A complete answer to this question is beyond the scope of this chapter, but the rule of thumb is that you let the problem determine the method. For example, if you want to find out something about the national divorce rate and how divorced people differ from those who remain married, then you need a method that will give you data from people all over the country, such as a survey. But if you want to find out how nurses manage the many pressures of their jobs, then participant observation is a more appropriate method.

CONCLUSION

Sociologists use a wide range of methods to gather data about the people and groups they study. Each method produces a different type of data, which requires a specific form of analysis and can only be used to answer some questions, but not others, about the topic of study. All of this means that it is very important to specify what you want to know about a particular issue and then choose the data collection and analysis methods based on that. But since no single method guarantees that we will get the "truth" about our topic of study, it is usually a good idea to use multiple methods in sociological research.

Dorothy Smith's action research is only one way to approach the practical and ethical questions of obtaining information from people. Numerous other methods have been developed in sociology to address the social and personal problems that beset modern society. Rather than discovering the "laws" of society, sociologists make generalizations about social phenomena that are tentative in given circumstances. Scientific predictions are actually probabilities, not certainties. As with any science, these answers are open to modification or refutation by new evidence. But the questions asked in sociology and the methods used to answer them are of vital importance to our world and our lives.

Questions for Critical Thought

1. Are modern communication devices increasing our sense of social collectivity, or do they tend to individualize us more?
2. What difference is there between viewing your life as shaped by external structures and forces or assuming that it is determined by your agency?
3. Considering her public performances and what the public may know of her private life, does Beyoncé represent a feminist model that young women today should emulate?
4. If contemporary sociological theory leads to relativism, is this socially beneficial or otherwise?
5. When you read about a social scientific finding in the newspaper, what kinds of evidence persuade you of its veracity? In other words, do you need quantitative, statistical results, are you persuaded by the detailed accounts of individuals, or are both equally convincing?
6. If you were going to investigate across Canada the effects of a person's ethnicity on his or her educational attainment, what method would be most appropriate? Why?
7. When you read a "human interest" story in a magazine, what persuades you that the story is true? If the story contains numbers or statistics,

do you find it more believable? If so, should you rethink this idea, given how hard it is to conduct good quantitative research?

8. Think about your own personal limits to *verstehen* or empathetic understanding of other groups. For example, if you were a devout Christian, how would you behave if you had to do participant observation with an atheist group? Which of your characteristics "wouldn't matter" in any ethnography you carried out?

Sociological Explorations

1. Social construction theories assume that our everyday actions contribute to creating the reality in which we live. Consequently, transgressive actions are thought to undermine typical constructions and bring about social change. In universities, it is open season for transgression. For one day, observe and make note of actions around you (conversations, behaviours, styles) that appear to be in violation of conventional rules. What do you discover about the characteristics of rule-breakers (e.g., gender, program, ethnicity/race)? Does it actually make sense to argue that there is a dominant social construction of reality?

2. A great deal has been written in sociology about gender differences in eating behaviours, particularly public eating. Men are more likely to eat in public than women, because they do not face the same kinds of social pressures around body image. Go to your local coffee shop and get a seat with a view of the register. For 30 minutes, keep track of the number of men versus women who order just a drink, or a drink with food. Do your results support the gendered body image theory? Should you count a frozen drink as food or not? What other factors could be affecting your results?

Recommended Readings

Babbie, E. (2009). *The practice of social research* (12th edn). Belmont, CA: Wadsworth.
Babbie's books are used in more research methods courses across North America than those of any other author. This one is a comprehensive undergraduate treatment of research methods.

Berg, B. (2011). *Qualitative research methods for the social sciences* (8th edn). Boston, MA: Allyn and Bacon.
Berg's book is the current standard for qualitative research methods courses.

Putnam, R.D. (2000). *Bowling alone: The collapse and revival of American community*. New York, NY: Simon and Schuster.
Based on extensive research, Putnam argues that community, community feeling, and collective behaviour have declined in American society, to the detriment of grassroots democracy.

Schlosser, E. (2001). *Fast food nation: The dark side of the all-American meal*. New York, NY: Houghton Mifflin.
Schlosser describes the history of the fast-food industry in the United States, covering familiar terrain such as marketing to children, the "obesity panic," and the meat industry.

Wolf, N. (1991). *The beauty myth: How images of beauty are used against women*. New York, NY: W. Morrow.
Wolf exposes the social pressures behind the manipulation of women's self-image. The "perfect body" is virtually unattainable, underscoring many physical and mental problems facing girls and women today.

Recommended Websites

Dead Sociologists Index
http://media.pfeiffer.edu/lridener/DSS
The Dead Sociologists Index provides detailed information on 16 classical theorists, including biographies, commentary, and links to original works.

Sociology Online UK
www.sociologyonline.co.uk
This site provides a link to classical theory. The "Sociology News" link has many items of contemporary interest.

Free Resources for Program Evaluation and Social Research Methods

http://gsociology.icaap.org/methods

This is a free resource page on social science research methods, with an emphasis on quantitative rather than qualitative methods.

Organisation for Economic Co-operation and Development (OECD)

www.oecd.org

The OECD is a major data-generating organization, but the focus is international rather than national and is more directly tied to economic and social development policies around the world.

Statistics Canada

www.statcan.gc.ca

Statistics Canada is one of the world's most respected national statistical organizations. This is a huge site full of quantitative data, survey materials, statistical analyses, and much more on Canada.

Embracing Otherness, Embracing Oneself

www.ted.com/talks/thandie_newton_embracing_otherness_embracing_myself?language=en

A TED Talk by actor Thandie Newton, who explores how her racialized heritage, gender, and acting career affected the development of her sense of self.

Key Terms

agency The human capacity to interpret, evaluate, choose, and act accordingly.

anomie The condition of modern society in which there are too few moral rules and regulations to guide people's conduct.

capitalism An economic system characterized by a relationship of unequal economic exchange between capitalists (employers) and workers. Because they do not own the means of production, workers must sell their labour to employers in exchange for a wage or salary.

concept An abstract idea that cannot be tested directly. Concepts can refer to anything, but in social research they usually refer to characteristics of individuals, groups, or artifacts or to social processes. Some common sociological concepts include religiosity (strength of religious conviction), social class, and alienation.

conflict theory A theoretical paradigm linked to the work of Marx and Weber that emphasizes conflict and change as the regular and permanent features of society, because society is made up of various groups that wield varying amounts of power. Conflict theorists often stress the importance of status, economic inequality, and political power.

cultural capital A term coined by Pierre Bourdieu for cultural and linguistic competence, such as prestigious knowledge, tastes, preferences, and educational expertise and credentials, that individuals possess and that influences the likelihood of their educational and occupational success.

Enlightenment An era in the 1700s when theorists believed that human reason could be the instrument of perfecting social life; emotions had to be controlled, and the roles of religion, custom, and authority were criticized.

feminism A theoretical paradigm, as well as a social movement, that focuses on causes and consequences of inequality between men and women, especially patriarchy and sexism.

hypotheses Testable statements composed of at least two variables and how they are related.

intersubjectivity The notion that we adjust our behaviour according to the back-and-forth interpretation of what we think is on others' minds; for example, what I think *you* think of me.

matrix of domination Complex structures of power within which people live and in which various forms of oppression intersect, such as colour, gender, poverty, ability, and health; these must be resisted simultaneously.

New Left A radical social and political movement with roots in conflict theory that emerged among mostly privileged students in the 1960s seeking liberation from oppressive social conditions and influencing a generation of young, critical academics in the 1970s and beyond.

objective Something completely unaffected by the characteristics of the person or instrument observing it. "Objective" observations were used in the past to establish the truth of scientific theories until it became clear that completely objective observations are impossible.

operationalization The translation of abstract theories and concepts into observable hypotheses and variables. Once abstract ideas are operationalized, they can be tested in a study.

patriarchy A society or family system in which men have more authority than women.

post-modernism An intellectual trend that became current in the arts and social theory in the 1980s and that opposes and deconstructs the dominant ideologies of rationality, progress, science, social democracy, and social regulation.

post-structuralism A social theory that became current in the late twentieth century and that depicts the construction of social life as complex, diverse, interconnected, multi-dimensional, undetermined, interpretive, and ultimately fragile.

power In the classic formulation, refers to the ability to exercise one's will, even in the face of opposition from others. In Marxist sociology, it refers to a social relationship that has a material base. Those who own the means of production have the power to exploit workers through the appropriation of their labour efforts. In Weberian sociology, power is more broadly defined and can reflect the capacity of individuals or groups to exert their will over others. Contemporary analysts point out that power may also involve a wide variety of indirect and subtle manifestations, including the ability to mobilize bias or define a situation in one's own interests.

sample The group of people or objects drawn from the whole population that will be studied. In quantitative research, a great deal of time and effort is devoted to the selection of truly random samples, while in qualitative research, samples are often selected on the basis of the theoretical importance of the people or objects.

social capital The power that is derived from ties to social networks; a concept widely thought to have been developed by American sociologist James Coleman in 1988 but discussed by Pierre Bourdieu in a similar way in the early 1980s.

social constructionism (constructionist) The sociological theory that argues that social problems and issues are less objective conditions than they are collective social definitions based on how they are framed and interpreted.

stratified Hierarchically ordered; in relation to power, stratification occurs when some groups control more material, cultural and social, and institutional resources than others and block others from challenging their control or gaining access to them.

structural functionalism A theoretical paradigm that emphasizes the way each part of a society functions to fulfill the needs of society as a whole.

subjective The opposite of "objective"; refers to the observer's mind, to perceptions, intentions, interpretations, and so on that affect how she or he acts in the world.

surplus That part of the value of goods produced by working people that is taken by the dominant class and used to maintain social inequalities; a measure of the exploitation of the working class.

symbolic interactionism An intellectual tradition in sociology akin to interpretive theory, founded in the early-twentieth-century work of Charles Horton Cooley and George Herbert Mead, although the term itself was not coined until years later by Herbert Blumer. Symbolic interactionism emphasizes the importance of understanding the meanings of social action and uses ethnographic methods to discover these meanings for individuals in an effort to explain human conduct.

transgression The usually deliberate violation of social rules. In post-structuralism, this is the only viable, liberating, and non-oppressive strategy of personal and social change.

variable The operational or observable equivalent of concepts. Many concepts require more than one variable for proper operationalization. The key characteristic of variables is that there must be a range of different values that can be observed.

Major Social Processes

PART
II

The term "culture" has many meanings. However, for most sociologists, culture broadly refers to the knowledge, traditions, values, practices, and beliefs held by members of an organization, community, or society. Defined this way, we are all familiar with culture and cultures. Most of us have likely engaged in conversations about what makes up Canadian culture, or about ethnic cultures, or our personal experiences in and with the various subcultures that affect our lives.

Chapter 2, by Eric Weissman, explores what culture means and why the concept of culture is essential to doing sociology. The chapter maps the interplay of material and immaterial elements of culture and shows how both types of elements help us establish "webs of significance." Weissman compares contemporary views of culture (as manifested in queer theory, for example) to traditional sociological theoretical approaches. He also shows how the Internet and globalization have decentred culture, and provocatively asks what role we, as individuals, can play in consciously changing our culture.

The development of our individual identities is also of great interest to sociologists, and it implicates the learning of culture. Historically, within the discipline of sociology, identity formation has been studied in relation to socialization. Socialization is a lifelong process through which we learn the norms, values, and behaviours that we need to master to successfully participate in social life. Chapter 3, by Barbara Mitchell, explores the idea of being social and what it means to be human. In the chapter you will review how theorists explain processes of socialization and examine different agents of socialization, including the family, school, peer group, and mass media. Mitchell critically evaluates how socialization experiences are socially structured and vary by social

class, gender, sexual orientation, ethnicity, generation, and geographical location.

Chapter 4, by Dorothy Pawluch, William Shaffir, and Lorne Tepperman, explores another important part of sociological analysis, social organization. Their chapter on social organization is about two distinct but interrelated sociological concerns. The first of these, related to the previous chapter, is about how people develop their personal identity. As the authors show, identities grow out of social roles. The second has to do with how individuals build organizations and establish organizational roles; to repeat, it is through those roles that identities develop. The authors begin by defining the key terms involved in this process, including *status*, *role*, *self*, and *identity*. They also show how each of these notions is interrelated. They challenge us to think about how we define ourselves and others, and to understand how groups, networks, communities, and cliques function inside larger organizations. They pose challenging questions, including, How could we organize social groupings to increase the chances that people will achieve their collective goals?

Where there are roles, rules, and social expectations, there are rule-breakers we call deviants. Chapter 5, on deviance, by Alicia Horton and Vincent Sacco, tackles specifically what happens when roles, rules, and social expectations are violated. They begin the chapter by defining the sociological concepts of *deviance* and *social control*. They then identify the major questions that sociological theories of deviance and control attempt to answer. In this context, they also consider the nature of crime and punishment, an ever-interesting topic in the mass media. The chapter examines interesting social and demographic factors that are related to particular forms of deviant conduct and show how behaviours and people come to be labelled as deviant.

2 | Culture and Cultural Change

ERIC WEISSMAN

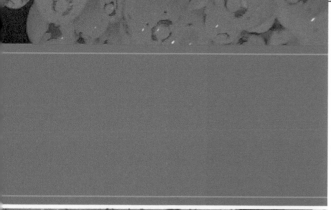

In this chapter you will:

► Learn what culture means and why it is essential to doing sociology

► Understand the interplay of material and immaterial elements of culture in helping us establish "webs of significance"

► Discover the ways that culture can be a conservative and liberating force, mediating a constant tension between stability and conflict

► Compare the symbiotic view of culture and structure inherent to traditional sociological theoretical approaches with current views such as queer theory

► Recognize how the Internet and globalization have decentred culture, and ask what role we can play in consciously shaping culture change

INTRODUCTION

Culture is a difficult concept to comprehend. People often use the words **culture** and **society** interchangeably. In this chapter we discuss society as *a group of people who live in a certain place* and who *share* culture, and culture as *a shared system of values and practices about how to live in that group*, but not the group itself.

Sociobiology is an anti-cultural approach. It argues that universal biological tendencies tell us more about human behaviour than culture. Yet, most things we do with biological purposes, such as kissing or eating, are governed by rules, which are produced by culture. This means that they are **socially constructed**. So to understand culture, we will examine the tension between schools of thought that suggest nature is responsible for how we act and those which argue that culture, by defining the rules of conduct, is really responsible for the social world.

We will also look at the elements of culture. These include **material elements** such as technology and natural resources, and **immaterial** ones such as language and rules about social behaviour. Some elements, such as beliefs and practices about birth, death, or shelter, are necessary to all societies. We call these **cultural universals**. Because there is so much **cultural diversity** in what these elements look like from place to place, we will discuss debates about how culture works.

Hockey fans from diverse genders, backgrounds, and ages celebrate their city's hockey team in the Stanley Cup finals. Hockey is a big part of Canadian culture.

Sergei Bachlakov/Shutterstock

With its implications for finding **consensus** and conflict, culture is a central concern to major theoretical positions such as Marxism, functionalism, symbolic interaction, post-modernism, and queer studies. It is the only concept that can help us understand why Canadian women are paid less than men for the same job or why transgendered individuals hold a sacred place in some social systems while being **stigmatized** in others.

We will also learn that humans have the power to deliberately change culture and thus change the world. This is evidenced by **subcultures**, which are smaller groups of people who do things differently than do most people in the dominant culture in which they live. Hippies and some religious sects are examples of subcultures.

There is a traditional sense that culture is specific to people in a certain place at a certain time in history. However, in our Web-linked and globalized world cultures are no longer restricted to specific geographical locations. Understanding that culture is both a local and a trans-local force is essential to looking at social worlds and problems. A major concern for sociology is bringing about social change. Given that cultural principles tend to reinforce existing social practices, how is it possible that social life can change? The online linking of cultures on a global scale means people from different societies can interact through **defiant publics** in important debates about social justice and the environment; it is, however, uncertain whether this will produce a more just state of affairs.

> **TIME to REFLECT**
>
> How do you define your culture? Can you list five things and five ideas that define who you are?

A DEFINITION OF CULTURE

"Culture" is a commonly used word, yet it is difficult to define in a manner that satisfies everyone. Traditionally, culture has been understood as something that ties people to particular places.

Edward S. Casey (1993) traces the word "culture" to the Latin *colere*, which means "to care for," and to *cultus*, or "cult." He sees culture as a locally interpreted creative force for producing the physical and symbolic conditions by which to build civilizations, unique places of human social life. In 60 BCE, the Roman philosopher Cicero used the expression *cultura anims* to describe a cultivation of the human soul as that part of our nature that distinguishes us from all other living things—a capacity for and measure of our creativity.

The most cited definition comes from E.B. Tylor, the founder of British cultural anthropology. For him, culture is that "complex whole which includes knowledge, belief, art, morals, law, custom, and any other capabilities and habits acquired by man as a member of society" (1920 [1871], p. 1). Such a broad definition tends to conflate social and cultural aspects into an image of a whole society as a collection of observable parts that mistakenly become focal points for understanding that society. So, Clifford Geertz, one of the leading American anthropologists of the twentieth century, wrote that the definition of culture had reached the point "where it obscures more than it reveals" (1973, p. 4). He thought that those who studied culture were too wrapped up in the materials and forms that cultural practices required.

Geertz shared with sociologist Max Weber that "man" was an animal "suspended in **webs of significance** that he himself has spun" (Geertz, 1973, p. 5). Claude Lévi-Strauss, an important structural anthropologist, echoed this view, arguing that the basic elements of culture were "signs," such as words or anything else one could touch, taste, or see, that "made sense" (1966, p. 18, in Atkinson et al., 2007, p. 41). For many scholars, the concept of culture was not about finding universal practical rules and tools for social life but rather a **semiotic** problem that asked how we establish and share meaning with others in our local group.

All these positions have merit. Sociology is interested in the ways culture helps people organize and do practical things. When these ways are common between people, they are members of webs of significance. For sociology, culture is a key concept because it helps us understand how different groups of people might approach the social world in different ways. So the way the social world appears to us is the result of how culture drives people to act in social ways based on what those actions mean to them.

Culture is ironic: on the one hand, it makes getting along in human societies uniquely possible, while on the other, it produces conflict. Much of the conflict we see in the world results from economic and political competition between nations, but some arises from different systems of meaning trying to assert themselves over others. Within Canadian society, we can observe some very peaceful and stable social practices, such as the way we shop at malls or celebrate national holidays. When students violently strike against tuition hikes, or hockey fans hurl obscenities at each other, these are part of our culture too.

Culture Is Human

Most contemporary sociology rejects the notion that our biology determines how we act. Yet there is agreement that only human societies have culture. In animals other than humans, natural drives govern an organism's reactions, whereas humans can place an idea or a rule about conduct above their natural urges.

Sociobiology argues that behaviours like aggression, passion, and competition are the result of biological imperatives that force humans to develop cultural rules governing social practices that manage these needs. E.O. Wilson wrote *Sociobiology: the New Synthesis* in 1975 as a way of linking the ecological and sociological causes of human evolution. A synthesis of various branches of sociobiology reveals the central claim that social behaviour evolving over time reflects the successful adaptation of human groups to their environments and their natural or biological needs. Especially problematic behaviours like murder and violence were rationalized as the result of an individual's inherent drive to protect or reproduce itself at all costs even if there was risk associated with such acts.

This approach is questionable. Bourgois (1995, 2010) and others show that problematic social behaviours like aggression reflect social environmental pressures rather than biological attributes. Sociobiology is a complicated idea with many variations and adaptations too broad to confront here, but in its essence, the claim that behaviour is **biologically determined** and unchangeable is clearly anti-culture.

Very often when scholars write of the conflict between natural or biological drives and culture, they use the example of kissing. In the West we grow up learning that deep kissing is a biological and social part of the courtship and reproduction process. Kissing is interpreted as a way of testing the bio-chemical appropriateness of a potential partner and to stimulate sexual and other hormones in the human body. So it has its biological function. We can argue that this function is the same wherever kissing *is part of the reproductive process.* Yet people kiss for many other reasons. In Canada, it is generally inappropriate for siblings to kiss the same way that lovers might. So kissing is symbolic too. In fact, in the West, kissing on the cheek or mimicking a kiss by brushing one's cheek against another is considered polite and reasonable when greeting a non-romantic loved one, like an aunt or a sibling. So we have romantic kissing that includes the mouth, the lips and tongue in full contact. And yet in other cultures such as the **Tinguian of Austronesia**, kissing does not occur at all, not even as a part of reproduction, because it is considered unclean and undesirable (Ford & Beach, 1951; Cole, 1915).

 Chapter 3, "Being Social," addresses the role of nurturing and important institutions in producing social outcomes.

Sociobiological approaches have given weight to moral positions that use racism and evolutionism to control people on the basis of gender or medical conditions. In Canada the most notable example is the Alberta Sexual Sterilization Act of 1929, which, until its repeal in 1972, gave authorities the power to sterilize patients deemed mentally defective. In even more perverse and extreme cases, biological determinism has justified the murder of groups of people based on racialized biological categorizations. Nazis applied **eugenics** to Jews and other ethnic groups in Europe between 1936 and 1945. American eugenicists, including some black scholars, advocated selective breeding to raise the status of African Americans and poor whites near the beginning of the twenty century (Sherman, 2014).

Defeating such biological discrimination is the moral call of modern **feminism** and **queer theory**. Each of us knows, for example, that women continue to be paid less than men for the same work. Laws and privileges, formulated by men, that discriminated against women on the basis of their sex produced this inequality. The idea that men were more naturally appropriate and better suited to governing is an aspect of **patriarchal** society, in which power and privilege are culturally constructed to favour men. Yet, patriarchy is a value system, not a natural state of affairs. For example, in Canadian Indigenous culture before contact with Europeans, women were in charge of the clan's economic and domestic practices (Native Women's Association of Canada, 2007). It was the Indian Act of 1876 that gave the Canadian government the legal power to place men in charge of Indigenous households and clans, a law that reflected the dominance of European patriarchal culture over that of Indigenous people.

We sociologists avoid purely biological explanations because we are interested in how things change. If it were true that women were naturally suited only for child-rearing and housework, how could we explain their current success as soldiers, professionals, statespersons, and so on? Today sociologists accept that human social worlds are possible because of the way culture helps members of groups learn the socially appropriate manners. It also tells us what the costs for not doing this might be. So culture helps us understand the extent and rules of our webs of significance, which we can now call societies. We have to work at culture to make it happen. It is in some ways, we should remember, like growing a garden.

ELEMENTS OF CULTURE

Material elements include *things* such as tools, natural resources, modes of transportation, weaponry, ritual objects, and even types of textile or other body coverings. Immaterial elements might be the *signs* that Lévi-Strauss spoke of: symbols, languages, beliefs, values, norms, and spiritual practices. These cannot be touched like one can touch a canoe, but they are meaningful. Material elements are manipulable and tangible. Immaterial elements organize people along values and principles or beliefs, such as picking a legal spouse or establishing rules for being a good parent or whom you should kiss. While sociology respects and looks for diversity, it needs to understand what the essential elements of a culture might be to identify how different ways of doing culture might conflict and present problems in high-density, highly diversified cultural spaces like Toronto or other global cities. This is why we might ask, with Garrett-Petts et al. (2014), "Whose culture is it anyway?"

Émile Durkheim (1964 [1893]) famously discussed mechanical and organic solidarity. **Mechanical solidarity** is the prevailing form of social organization in smaller communities where people have strong common values and beliefs. In terms of culture, people in these groups share symbols so well they have a very strong **collective conscience**, which tends to establish who else is included in their webs of significance. **Organic solidarity** occurs in large-scale groups like industrial cities where the sharing of meaning is made more difficult by complex and interdependent divisions of labour.

In each type of solidarity, material needs like food and technology are indispensable, but so too is a sense of belonging and integration.

These needs are satisfied because material and immaterial elements are linked by rules, role descriptions, and symbolic values. So let's look at all these elements to see what their implications are.

Artifacts

Artifacts are things we can actually touch. Tylor (1920) used archaeological evidence to compare "primitive" societies largely on the complexity of their tools, art, homes, and modes of production. For **cultural evolutionists** like Tylor, greater complexity and diversity of artifacts is a measure of cultural superiority. The fallacy of this evolutionary perspective is clear: the most civilized and complicated cultures—ours—have come to dominate the world by being the most violent and by relying on the most unsustainable modes of production. Many people, aware of this, are changing the way we do things like housing.

Symbols

Symbols can have physical forms we can see or touch. A painted stop sign, the logo on a sports team's jersey, and a flag are examples of symbols with physical forms that mean something. Housing is a particularly strong symbol. The stop sign organizes traffic, the logo represents a person's attachment to a team or a brand, a flag identifies members of political groups, and housing types symbolize wealth and social class. These and other symbols help us understand the webs of significance to which we belong.

Other symbols are non-verbal and immaterial, like the wave of a hand, the sound of a police car siren, or even something as simple as a smile. A waving hand can be a call for help or a recognition of friendship, a siren warns us to be alert, and a smile generally signifies that someone is happy or pleased with our actions. Symbols, then, are things that stand in the place of something else and produce reactions in social actors. Symbols are created and found in all cultures, so they belong to an analytical category George Murdoch (1945) called cultural universals. He found that universal elements

SOCIOLOGY IN ACTION

Community-Based Ethnographic Research

Imagine going without housing. Housing is a particularly important artifact. The tiny home movement is an emerging social movement in the US and Canada in which people give up their large homes for very small cottage-like structures. These places resemble the shacks at Dignity Village in Portland, Oregon, the first city-sanctioned homeless camp in US history, where Eric Weissman (2012, 2014) did his PhD fieldwork. Weissman found that to most of Portland's conventionally housed residents, the shacks in the camp symbolized despair and economic failure. Even residents of Dignity Village felt some despair at living in poverty and had a poor image of themselves. Portlanders and villagers felt a disconnect in their webs of significance. So Weissman and photographer Nigel Dickson used photos to help the two groups see each other differently, which meant changing the symbolic value of the village and its villagers.

Weissman (2014) lived in one of 50 crudely manufactured shacks built out of discarded or donated lumber. The village had no electricity or Wi-Fi except in one community building. There was one phone and only two water outlets. Five outhouses served 60 people. Still, the homeless people Weissman met on the streets of Portland referred to Dignity Village as a hotel and envied the villagers for their donated clothes, access to shelter, and clean running water. For most residents of Portland, however, the village was troubling because the community was defined by poverty.

However, by using images to show the villagers and their homes as part of the much broader and more acceptable tiny house movement, Weissman and other researchers helped many critics of the village to see the community as an acceptable part of the city's homelessness policies. The images helped Portlanders see what they had in common with the villagers, thus forging a symbolic connection that made room for villagers in their webs of significance. Now tiny home activists from around the globe visit Dignity Village for ideas and inspiration. Many US cities are currently building similar communities to house the very poor.

Eric Weissman

(Left) Interior of Weissman's shack, six feet by eight feet, constructed out of scrap wood. (Right) Scott and Lisa in front of their "cottage" at Dignity Village. Such positive images make the concept of a homeless camp less foreign to the dominant city culture.

were associated with basic needs: food, shelter, support, and common life experiences like birth and death. All cultures—hunters and gatherers, cultivators, or industrial powers—share the meaning of social life through symbols.

Language

All societies have a symbolic system that serves the function of a language. Language can take the form of basic hand gestures, spoken words,

HUMAN DIVERSITY

Symbols, Signs, and Sharing Ideas

In Canada we sometimes shake hands or wave hello to each other. We can use a thumbs-up symbol to indicate agreement. (We also have other hand signals that are less polite.) The thumbs-up signal in Canada is usually a positive sign, but in other places, such as Australia, it can be offensive.

In the small fishing village of San Agustinillo, Mexico, the boat captains (*lancheros*) can rarely speak to each other over their radios because of the loud wind and the slapping of waves. They developed a complex system of hand gestures that help them silently but effectively communicate among themselves the locations of schools of tuna and approaching storms.

Lancheros can tell other captains and their clients even from far distances where to look for fish or how to avoid obstacles, using a series of very subtle hand gestures. For example, on land, a thumbs-up means everything is okay and well, but at sea, a thumb pointing up and a finger pointing down means "the fish are here all around us." Learning the

(Photograph by Eric Weissman, 2008)

Lidio, a *lanchero*, signals "the tuna are here below the boat."

hand signals was vital to Weissman's participation as a fishing guide in San Agustinillo.

---

uttered sounds, or even organized symbols, such as computer codes. Language is a logic-based and shared symbolic system that structures how people communicate with each other. Languages have rules, such as grammar and spelling, which tend to mirror important cultural values.

The English alphabet has 26 letters combining to make over 500,000 words. The rules for using these words varies within different English-speaking cultures. For example, in some parts of the US, the word for a carbonated drink such as Coca-Cola is "soda" but in Canada we call it "pop." In Canada, "boot" refers to a type of footwear but in England it is also the trunk of a car.

Linguist Edward Sapir (1921) and his student Benjamin Whorf (1956) developed theories about language and cultural identity. Though they never co-authored a specific hypothesis, they are understood to have shared the hypothesis that people experience the social world primarily though language. They argued that language shapes the way we think because it is a

structured element with implicit built-in rules. According to this hypothesis, if we do not have a word to describe a thing or an experience, we lack the underlying conceptual frameworks to make sense of it to ourselves or to others. Though it has been critiqued by scholars like Noam Chomsky (1975), the **Sapir–Whorf hypothesis** still helps us to understand how, for example, gender values permeate the structure of language. In English, the pronouns "he" and "his" have more commonly been used to refer to unspecified individuals than their opposites, "she" and "her." For example, a text might read, "When a student wishes to dispute a failing grade, he must notify the dean of students." While this is intended to apply to all genders, the language makes a masculine student seem to be the norm. Using this hypothesis, feminist critiques of language have shown that words such as "mankind," "chairman," and "journeyman" imply that men properly occupy positions of importance and place the feminine in a subjugated role. Language, then, is something we can look at when studying culture in order to prove that social change does happen. "Humankind," "chairperson," and other now-common words reveal how cultures change over time.

TIME to REFLECT

Can you write a paragraph about one of your friends without using a value-laden, gendered pronoun?

Norms and Values

Values and **norms** are interrelated. Values speak to how a person identifies what is good or bad, or desirable and important. Norms and values are found in all cultures but are not universally the same: what is desirable or considered good in one place is not necessarily the same in other cultures. For example, in the fishing village of San Agustinillo, Mexico, childbirth is highly valued and considered a sacred blessing. Being single past one's late teen years is considered abnormal and undesirable; children pair off as young as 10 or 11, and by 16 many of the girls are pregnant, often before they are married. In Canada, such behaviour would be criticized as irresponsible and children born into such circumstances considered unfortunate.

Underlying this fear of having children at a young age is a value that sociologists like to call the **work ethic**. While advanced capitalist cultures value family and children, they also promote individuality as vital to our economic prosperity. We therefore think having children must be delayed to the years following our departure from our parents' home. Within our cultural work ethic, personal freedom and individualism make it reasonable for people to avoid having babies as teenagers, even if their bodies are ready.

In 1838, Harriet Martineau, considered the first feminist sociologist, revealed the gap between **ideal culture** and **real culture**. Ideal culture refers to the strictly expressed code that tells us how life should be lived. In Canada, for example, we believe strongly in equality and multiculturalism. Ideally, therefore, in our culture all people should have equal access to resources and

education. However, careful sociological examination shows that in Canada, women and ethnic minorities are paid less than men of European descent for work of equal value. Even though we talk about equality and tolerance as basic tenets of ideal Canadian culture, in reality these values are difficult to achieve.

Over time, the repetition of value-based social performances produces a sense of what is normal in a given society, and this contributes to what we understand as norms. Norms are best understood as explicitly and implicitly known standards and expectations for regulating social behaviour. **Mores** are formal norms scripted in laws and codes of conduct. In Canada, these kinds of norms are recognized in laws and regulations we must follow, such as traffic laws, criminal codes, and professional standards.

Implicit or informal norms are sometimes called folkways and customs. These are behaviours or practices that are not enshrined in law, but which are regularly associated with a certain social practice. For example, in Mexico once again, it is illegal, and subject to severe punishment, to kill sea turtles or eat their eggs, but it is customary to eat the eggs (with lime juice and sea salt) at weddings and important birthdays. Not partaking of the eggs is considered very poor manners and an insult.

Formal mores change less frequently and in different ways than do customs. For a more to change, a law must be passed through a formal political process. In Canada, one of the most urgent areas where norms and mores are changing is sexual identity and marriage. For almost 150 years, legal marriage in Canada was between a man and a woman. In this **heteronormative** moral and political frame, other types of love and coupling were stigmatized, a form of discrimination based on a negatively perceived identity (Goffman, 1963). Homosexual and transgendered couples could not be recognized as married under the law. However, since about 2005 in Canada, this has changed. While LGBTQ identities and unions are not statistically normal, meaning most marriages are still heterosexual, it is now legal in Canada for people with these identities to wed someone of their own sex. It is common for stigmatized groups who want social change to join together in order to be heard and, hopefully, to change norms.

Informal and formal norms are linked. In our culture, widespread support for legalization of an activity may bring about change. For example, as of this writing, the recreational use of marijuana is illegal in Canada. But this is likely to change because in our culture we are starting to think differently about marijuana. Canadians elected a federal government in 2015 that promised to legalize recreational marijuana use. Various interests use mass media—newspapers, television ads, and online blogs—to discuss this and other issues important to Canadians.

This **mass media** can impact mores. The mass media include newspapers, films, television, the Internet, social media, and print advertising such as what we see on buses or on billboards. Some argue the Internet is more than just a part of the mass media because it is a conduit for people to directly communicate, and is a way for people to shop, do research, and develop their own ideas. But there are very powerful patterns of usage in the Internet, and it does convey the messages of highly concentrated and powerful media corporations.

The media manipulate symbols and language to produce behaviours in those who consume them. When we see a series of symbols and ideas repeatedly in the media we begin to see the world as a kind of story or narrative. We learn how to anticipate social situations and to navigate our own roles based on a certain **narrative inevitability**, or ongoing assumptions

OPEN FOR DISCUSSION
Classic Literature—Legacy of "The Culture of Poverty"

In "The Culture of Poverty" (1966), Oscar Lewis argues that through childhood socialization, poverty is inscribed in individuals and thus into culture. The culture of poverty suggests that poor people experience the following:

(1) A cash economy, wage labor and production for profit;

(2) A persistently high rate of unemployment and underemployment for unskilled labor;

(3) low wages;

(4) The failure to provide social, political or economic organization, either on a voluntary basis or by government imposition, for the low-income population;

(5) The existence of a bilateral kinship system rather than a unilateral one; and finally,

(6) The existence in the dominant class of a set of values that stresses the accumulation of wealth and property, the possibility of upward mobility, and thrift and that explains low economic status as the result of personal inadequacy or inferiority (Lewis, 1996, pp. 393–403).

Lewis's image of a "poor" personality echoes claims that individuals, not structural conditions, were to blame for poverty. However, Phillip Bourgois, who wrote *In Search of Respect: Selling Crack in El Barrio* (1995) and *Righteous Dopefiend* (Bourgois & Schonberg, 2009), criticizes the notion of the culture of poverty:

In the USA, irrespective of the theoretical orientation of researchers, most discussions on poverty polarize around value judgments concerning individual self worth or around racial/ethnic stereotypes. US attitudes towards poverty are rooted in the country's colonial Calvinist/Puritanical heritage and are exacerbated by the historical importance of racialized hierarchies that have legitimized genocide, slavery, colonization, and immigration generate so much emotional heat while shedding so little conceptual light. (Bourgois, 2001, p. 906)

The "culture of poverty" approach promoted an image of undeserving and pathological poor people, a negative view that resonated well with the "blame the victim" discourse so prevalent in the West under capitalism in the 1960s and 1970s, and under neo-liberal governmentality as it entered the twenty-first century; critique of the poor rewards the capable self-governed citizen.

about how the social world should play out in terms of unavoidable outcomes (Weissman, 2017, forthcoming). So when news media consistently report on the potential for marijuana legalization, for example, it becomes more likely to happen.

While language is necessary to make these stories comprehensible, the image of the social world produced in these stories is shaped by powerful points of view, called **discourses**. A discourse itself is not objective and real; like other systems of meaning, as we suggested earlier, it is socially constructed, yet because it is widely shared, it seems both real and inevitable (Foucault, 1969, 1975; Rose, 1999).

For example, when homelessness is repeatedly characterized as the result of people causing their own problems because they are drug addicts, the general public adopts this discourse. Homelessness is still understood by many in terms of the "blame the victim" discourse. This view steers critical opinions away from the failure of the government or the economy to provide opportunity and affordable living conditions for poor people; rather, it emphasizes the character defects of some homeless people (Caton, 1990, Wright, 1997). One such powerful discourse, which still inflects our view of poverty, is Oscar Lewis's "The Culture of Poverty" which he theorized in the 1960s.

Subcultures and Cultural Change

Commonly in large complex societies like ours we find subcultures. Very simply, subcultures are groups such as hippies, rockers, gamers, the Amish and Mennonites, and, some would argue, LGBTQ groups; even devoted yoga practitioners are subcultural because their most meaningful signs and practices are concentrated on certain smaller webs of significance that happen within larger social systems.

One of the ways that subcultures change society is by offering to conventional members of society different symbols and ways of doing common things. When people see or hear about alternative ways of doing something, there is often resistance, but there is also potential for

change. Veganism (like some other food paradigms) started out as a very uncommon and esoteric practice, but through the popularization of this subcultural mode over the Internet, in the press, and in conversation, even the largest fast-food companies are now experimenting with vegan offerings for their menus.

Very often subcultural practices need an anchor place, spaces where like-minded people can gather and socialize free from mainstream interventions. A number of scholars such as Michel Foucault (1984) and Victor Turner (1969) have written extensively about how people often come together for short periods of time to temporarily explore unconventional practices in places that cultures actually produce for this kind of experimentation. Festivals like Halloween, theatrical spaces, places of worship, dance clubs—all are examples of spaces where people can act differently than they would in their daily lives. And sometimes people meet in these spaces regularly to socialize with others who share these interests.

Turner refers to these subcultural practices as *ludic* experiences: experiences that are short-lived and playful, presenting an alternative vision of dominant cultural practices, like a dance or music festival where words and movement shed dominant ideas. Turner argued that in these ludic subcultural spaces, which he called "communitas," people were more equal to one another than in the outside world.

Foucault (1984) said that all cultures produce places for alternative cultural practices. He called these "heterotopias," of which there are many—theatres and alternative festivals like "Burning Man" are examples of concentrated subcultural practices that occur in such heterotopic places. That people who are wrapped up in large webs of significance might find meaningful ties in smaller webs—subcultures—is important for understanding how the social world changes. When people return to their normal lives after a subcultural experience, they bring with them residual ways of looking at the world, which can then change the values and norms that they practise in the dominant culture, especially values about social justice, equality, and power relations.

While subcultures might, for example, reflect musical tastes such as hip hop, they can also concern themselves with political and environmental issues, and all of them have the potential to permanently change the way the social world works. For example, the current movement at the level of national governments to reduce carbon footprints and create more sustainable communities originated in small local subcultural activist organizations in universities around the globe. Current campaigns against building oil pipelines over Indigenous peoples' lands take the form of occupations of space by people sharing clearly alternative visions of a just world that conflict with mainstream values.

In their book on community engagement, *Whose Culture Is It Anyway?*, Garrett-Petts et al. (2014) argue that social justice–oriented change uses values like dignity and equality in the workplace, but that these needs look different in specific places. This means that social change must reflect the needs of people in specific localities, with unique cultures. Very often new ideas and alternative visions of how to order the social world start in the ludic and temporary practices we just discussed, and over time, by attraction and promotion, enter mainstream value systems.

Rituals and Rites of Passage

A ritual is usually defined as a group activity carried out by people in accordance with "social custom or normal protocol" (Ritual, n.d.). Very often such protocols attach to specific purposes of which the ritual might be a part. This is especially true of religious practices such as Christian communion, a practice in which bread and wine are consecrated and shared as part of a religious service, or a bat mitzvah, a Jewish girl's coming of age ceremony at the age of 13, in which she recites passages from the Torah (part of the Hebrew bible) in a synagogue.

Some people have routines they call rituals. But when someone says they are used to reading

A bride and groom during a typical Western wedding ceremony enjoy their "first dance" symbolizing their new status as a married couple.

redstallion/iStockphoto

the newspaper, eating their breakfast, and listening to the radio before going to work, this is not a ritual. Rituals speak to a series of beliefs and symbols that unite people into discrete groups, such as Jews or Christians, and are not just repetitive routines.

With Canada's renewed commitment to its Indigenous peoples, much attention is drawn to their traditional cultures. In some Native North American cultures, an important ritual is the vision quest. There is great variation in this ritual, which often combines the mentorship of elders with physical stresses endured in a sweat lodge to help a young man see his guiding spirit and achieve his transition into manhood.

TIME to REFLECT

Can you think of important rituals in your life, who leads them, and what they mean to your own personal growth?

Arnold Van Gennep (1908) describes **rites of passage** as ritual events that help us improve our **status** by transitioning us from lesser to better **roles** in society. Looking at African tribes, he focused on the necessity of ritual and key persons like shamans who had the wisdom or skill to oversee rituals. Victor Turner (1969) argued that industrial cultures were equally dependent on rituals and specially trained leaders to guide people through the **liminal** phase of social development, a transitional period where we move from previous statuses to new ones. Parents and teachers, for example, help us move through roles in modern societies.

What happens when rites of passage do not work? Lewis observed that poverty is very much related to the failure of the capitalist social system to provide meaningful economic roles for some people. Very basic institutions, such as family and school, that help young people become adults and to find a place in the social world clearly fail to provide the necessary transitional experiences. According to Lewis, a lack of strong parental leadership and few positive role models trap young people into a dismal future. People stuck in the liminal phase of homelessness are evidence that capitalism creates poverty just as it creates wealth (Snow & Anderson, 1993; Hopper & Baumohl, 2003). In addition, as we have seen, Western culture produces a story, a narrative, that helps people blame themselves for systemic issues.

Governmentality, Neo-liberalism, and Self-help Culture

Based on the work of Michel Foucault (1975, 1991), a number of scholars including Mitchell Dean (1991, 2010) and Robert Fairbanks II (2004) have shown that current Western liberal democracies represent a very deliberately crafted type of governing mentality, or **governmentality**, called **neo-liberalism**. In neo-liberal societies, the **self-help** culture is a natural response to the needs of individuals to look after themselves by being healthy, going to school, saving money, and managing themselves well, because governments do a poor job of it. Furthermore, neo-liberal governmentality and the self-help culture shun those who do not or cannot self-govern well. So our culture produces the basis for conflict because people who succeed can blame those who fail for poor self-governing.

Insomuch as we now see how complicated a concept culture is, we can rest assured that its

relationship to and role in society have always been the subjects of intense theoretical debate.

THEORETICAL PERSPECTIVES ON CULTURE

Marxism

Classical Marxism is derived directly from the work of Karl Marx and Friedrich Engels (1985 [1848]). The key tenet of Marxism is the **base/ superstructure** model of society, where the economy is the base above which sits a superstructure that establishes social relations. Classic Marxists argue that in all societies, from hunting and gathering groups to complex capitalist systems, cultures exist to serve the needs of the economy.

Marxism warns that if the poor stay poor and the rich continue to get richer, *there will be a revolution to overturn the prevailing capitalist relations of production.* For Marxism, sometimes called **conflict theory**, the capitalist **mode of production** presents an antagonism between wealthy owners of the means of production (the bourgeoisie) and poor workers who labour to produce this wealth (the proletariat). In this model, the historical role of culture is to provide beliefs and rules that sustain the economic relations of production. Thus culture is both a force and a tool for sustaining social inequality. Inequality is inevitable because capitalism manufactures a capitalist **ideology**, a powerful set of beliefs in which inequality is acceptable. Engels (1968 [1893]) argued that culture deluded workers into buying into this ideology through a **false consciousness**, a kind of delusion that inequality was inevitable.

Cultural Marxism, associated with Antonio Gramsci, gives culture rather than the economy a central role in producing inequalities. A key part of this perspective is the notion of **cultural hegemony** (1971). For Gramsci, hegemony means the domination of the masses by prevailing ideas and cultural forms important to smaller but more dominant groups in society. He argues that non-economic institutions such as religion and the family have self-serving interests that produce hegemony. His work influenced the Frankfurt School of Critical Theory.

Critical theory based on the works of Theodor Adorno (1985), Max Horkheimer (1985), Herbert Marcuse (1941) and others centred on revealing to the masses how they were duped by capitalistic institutions and media. The expressed goal was mobilizing society toward its **immanent transcendence**: its latent, inherent capacity to progress toward a more just order of civil life. As an empirically based sociology grounded in an image of society as political, critical theory sought to disclose a world of misleading facts disguised by ideology, and to change how the world is envisioned (Delanty, 2011, p. 73).

This is key for cultural Marxism: civil society, including central institutions like the church, education, and media, rather than the economic sphere, is the part of the social world necessary for establishing hegemony and making webs of significance meaningful. So, culture for Marxists is something that serves the interests of the few and is an obstacle to justice.

Functionalism

The functionalist perspective is very different from cultural Marxism. If the enemy of equality and social justice is the falsely produced consensus that Marxists touted, functionalism is equally marked by its fancy for consensus, or finding a general state of agreement and cooperation. Functionalism was called **consensus theory** in the 1960s and criticized for ignoring conflict and social change. This perspective tends to regard society as an organism with parts that work together to make social life possible and mostly stable.

The origin of functionalism is generally located in the work of Émile Durkheim around the beginning of the twentieth century. Durkheim (1964 [1893], 1982 [1895], 2001 [1912]) tells us that when cultural practices fail to unite people, society can become very unstable. Durkheim looked at rituals and religion and argued that cultural practices have the social impact of integrating people into social groups. Culture,

then, is a function of the social structure that helps guarantee the overall economic, religious, demographic, material, and spiritual needs of the group. Culture works by creating powerful values about how to be a good member of society, manifesting in what we earlier described as the collective conscience.

Talcott Parsons (1951) was an American structural functionalist sociologist who developed a model of society called action theory and a model of the social based on the AGIL **paradigm**. In this model, four interdependent systems help us understand how society tends to reproduce itself: the behavioural organism, personality system, social system, and cultural system. Of these, it is the cultural system that is the most encompassing and essential to ensuring that members share the appropriate meanings for their actions and those of others. For Parsons, then, culture is linked to but transcends the other systems. If we could understand a particular culture, we could show how these other systems were encoded by practices and values with a tendency toward stability. So, for Parsons and in other functionalist orientations like Durkheim's, culture is a force that is responsible for the sustenance and growth of the social structure and for the integration of people in the social world. In order to understand the person as a social being we need to look at how culture works through social structures.

 Chapter 5, "Deviance," discusses how social structures and classes produce inequalities that can lead to major conflicts.

Symbolic Interaction

Symbolic interaction is an empirical school of thought that uses many investigative methods, especially fieldwork and ethnographic examination, to test and create theories about how the world works. At the very core of this approach is not modes of production or institutions but the human actor, a person (or more usually a group) whose essential need is to establish meaning in their own identities and in those of others. If we think back to the webs of significance from the beginning of this chapter, then for social interactionists it is the actual processes by which people interact in these webs that is important, not the underlying economic or structural arrangements.

Here, culture is a system of symbols, ideas, and language that facilitates actual interaction. This is how you and I know what our identities mean and what we should do with each other. Many of the ideas associated with this approach originated in the Chicago School of Sociology. Everett C. Hughes (1971) argued that the social interaction was the main unit of analysis for understanding the social world. This was a view shared by other interactionists such as Herbert Blumer (1969) and Erving Goffman (1963). The idea here is that social life cannot be understood if the social actor is stripped of any originality or the capacity to think differently on his or her own. Social order thus is not something that culture guarantees by reinforcing the values of the dominant classes over the poor or by creating the total range of meanings that people get from institutions, but is the conceptual basis for what we can call "negotiated order."

The negotiation concept is most directly associated with Anselm Strauss (1978) but is present in most of this approach. Strauss argued that social order is a constant negotiation of obligations and reciprocations, which are not always

binding and must be "continually worked out." The role of culture, then, is to give people the cognitive tools to understand who they are in these negotiations and how to use symbol to establish shared meanings.

For Goffman, this negotiation is understandable if we think of the world as a stage and that each of us has a role to play and a script to follow. This is called the **dramaturgical approach**; it depends largely on how we learn to act in public and in private. For Goffman, culture teaches people what their appropriate roles are and how to perform them in public or the **front-stage**. What we do in private is called the **back-stage**. Western culture tells us that our politicians should appear clean, organized, sober, and honest. So when Rob Ford, the belligerent mayor of Toronto, appeared on video smoking crack and issuing gender-phobic comments, his back-stage behaviour became front-stage and he lost all credibility. Back-stage acts are not necessarily bad or illegal, but every culture decides which behaviours should be public and which should be private.

These rules are learned through the process of socialization and are reinforced out of the myriad negotiations we make as we grow and life unfolds. None of this is to say that economic inequality is not real, or that institutions do not play an important role in structuring our lives, but regarding culture specifically, symbolic interactionists are interested in how it equips people for their performances within those other structural contexts. And, in this way we can change these structures by altering our scripts and performances.

 Chapter 5, "Deviance"; Chapter 7, "Gender and Sexuality"; and Chapter 8, "Ethnic and Race Relations," speak to the many ways that cultures produce rules about crime, deviance, gender, and ethnic identity.

Production of Culture

Unlike these other perspectives, the production of culture approach rejects the symbiotic nature

How do certain symbols, ideas, or language give meaning to our identities? How are they used in communicating our identities to others?

of culture and social structure or organization. The assertion here is that "culture and social structure are elements in an ever-changing patchwork" (Peterson & Anand, 2004, p. 312). Originally this approach attended to the material aspects of culture, like art and movies, that were intentionally produced by members of a society and explained how symbolic aspects of meaning found their expression:

> The production of culture perspective focuses on how the symbolic elements of culture are shaped by the systems within which they are created, distributed, evaluated, taught, and preserved.... Recently, the perspective has been successfully applied to a range of quite different situations in which the manipulation of symbols is a by-product rather than the purpose of the collective activity. (Peterson & Anand, 2004, p. 313)

As an example of rapid cultural change, Peterson and Anand looked at how the production of the culture of rock music supplanted swing bands. In just four short years, through new mobile recording technologies, financial credit, and a proliferation of sounds and bands, the structure of the entire music industry changed, allowing a new and persuasive genre to take over the popular charts and dominate music culture (Peterson & Anand, 2004, p. 325). The domination of four major record labels was replaced by competition among hundreds of smaller independent labels. In other words, the social structure of that industry changed quickly and massively because the music-making culture—the values and tools—changed.

Consumer Culture Theory and British Cultural Studies

Consumer culture theory asserts that people's choices are governed not by foundational economic or moral beliefs but by the way class and markets of consumption tell us what to want and how to spend in order to live up to cultural expectations. In this view, how we see ourselves and others in our webs of significance depends mostly on how commercially produced products

Some theorists assert that our choices are governed by advertisers and media telling us what to want and what to spend our money on. Think about a purchase you made recently. Do you agree with these theorists? Why or why not?

and activities like social media link us to others caught up in the pursuit of social and material resources. These links are established and confirmed by how consumption symbolically unites us with others who make similar choices.

Much of consumer theory is influenced by the early work of Stuart Hall between 1964 and 1979 and of Paul Willis, who became influential in the 1970s. Hall was a founder and Willis a prominent member of the Birmingham Centre for Contemporary Cultural Studies. Sometimes the centre's approach is called British cultural studies. Hall (1971) argued that people are producers and consumers of culture at the same time and that language plays an important part in this dynamic. For Hall, it is culture that produces the possibility of social action and is the part of the social world where power conflicts play out. Willis's work emphasizes the tendency of social structures to constrain people's choices along class lines because symbolic attachments to others tend to be reinforced by the possibilities that these structures hold. In this sense, people tend to make choices similar to those of people whom they know and interact with. Hall was captivated by people's creativity despite the limiting effects of class inequality. Sometimes choosing not to consume the same ideas or practices is a way for subcultural groups to assert their uniqueness and establish important ties among their members. Because these approaches give individuals a role in creating unstable cultural practices, they relate to post-modernism, the next perspective we will discuss.

Post-modernism, Cultural Construction, and New Takes on Culture

Post-modernism is a term describing a general shift in how social and cultural researchers presented their findings following the **critical turn** of the late 1970s. Prior to that, written texts and sociological studies were assumed to represent truthful accounts of the social world based on objectively knowable facts. The culturally inscribed ideas that a scholar brought to bear on his or her work were largely disregarded.

After critical studies such as James Clifford and George Marcus's *Writing Culture* (1986), social scientists began to regard all texts, including academic work, advertising, laws, rules, and codes of living, as ways of looking at the world that reflected very strong underlying cultural assumptions. There is no truth, not even in social analysis, because everything, every word, is based on learned ideas and evaluations peculiar to specific cultures that exclude other ideas.

We began to question if there were transcendent morals and truths that justified certain political acts: wars and civil codes, limiting free democratic participation or the rights of same-sex unions, for example, were revealed to arise from powerful stories that excluded alternative visions of the world, made believable by even more powerful interest groups such as religious, medical, and political organizations (Foucault, 1975, 1991). The more we looked at cultural practices such as rules about gender choices (Butler, 1990) or the pursuit of freedom (Rose, 1999), the more we came to realize that such ideas were not universal or inherent in human experience, but were the result of

specific mediations of knowledge and powerful interests over time, or discourses produced in specific cultures.

But post-modernism is difficult to entertain as a theory because few scholars identify their work as post-modern. Still, when we discuss approaches that make room for excluded ideas and discourses or that invite new ways to investigate the social world, we speak to a post-modern approach. The destabilization of ideal types of author, subject, gender, and time invoked by post-modernists paved the way for an entire range of **culture-jamming** research and scholarship that dominates the social sciences today. The most critical of these is queer theory.

Queer Theory and Culture

Queer theory includes both studies of queer identities and a mode of looking at all dominant cultural practices in search of excluded possibilities, an intellectual process called **queering**. Through the liberating impact of post-modern thinking, feminist and lesbian movements of the 1980s were empowered to question how culturally inscribed discourse (value-laden stories) about sex and gender had created the myth of fixed sexual identities. In so doing, they completely destabilized the notion of the normal gender binary of male and female. In reaction to the stigma of being homosexual, largely because of the public fear of the AIDS epidemic, gay and lesbian people increasingly joined forces to question the social construction of sexuality. Much of the power of dominant culture arises from its production of stable categories of the *other* and the *normal* in order to protect the interests of powerful groups. The term "queer theory" has come to mean any approach that questions the stable and exclusive categories of identity, time, space, sex, gender, and so on that enable power and discrimination in Western culture.

Not only does queer theory question the normative validity of **compulsory heterosexuality**, it questions all practices that seem normal merely out of repetition, but which are actually clearly constructed to serve particular interest over time. These interests tend to discriminate and exclude other ways of seeing and doing. Edward Soja (1996), for example, in *Third Space*, "queers" city spaces by critiquing the dominant rules governing them.

In queer culture there is a conscious attempt to use inclusionary language such as the singular "them" instead of "him" or "her." There is as well an almost militant sense of protecting the marginalized and excluded. Queers speak of blended and merged identities, multi-spirited and gender-neutral spaces. In the book *Dignity in Exile* (2012) Weissman describes a Dignity Villager who physically transitioned from female to male and replaced the name "Roslyn" with "Ptery" (after *pterodactyl*, the flying dinosaur) in order to be completely queer-friendly and gender-neutral. Whereas "queer" started out as a term that stood outside of heteronormative culture, today we can queer gender, space, medicine—everything—by arguing for the inclusion of excluded and marginalized ways of doing these things—ways that tend to turn dominant culture inside out.

CULTURE CHANGE AND GLOBALIZATION

While it is true that culture makes each society possible, this does not mean that cultures do not influence each other. Alan Lomax (1966), for example, found that sounds and instruments from various cultures combined to produce different kinds of "American" music. In this sense, people bring their cultures with them and impact other people's ways of thinking and doing things, like making music, in subtle but significant ways.

In some places, speaking of a self-contained and unique culture is very difficult. Canada's official policy of **multiculturalism** was introduced in the 1970s. Canadian culture is an inclusive system of many ethnic webs of significance, which maintain their traditional beliefs and customs while being united in larger political, social, and economic practices. Some argue that this system helps new immigrants to adjust to Canadian society, while others argue this ethnic diversity makes it impossible to build a unified Canadian culture. Today, however, both positions are somewhat moot unless we look at how all cultures are influenced by the Internet and globalization.

We know that globalization is the process by which powerful nations and their economies extend their power into other nations by controlling media, the Internet, world economies, and the politics of other countries. In some ways the effects of globalization are easy to understand (Featherstone, 1990). The term **cultural imperialism** is used to describe the success of American-run media in infiltrating the symbolic and value systems of many nations. In Canada, television broadcasters must by law present a regulated percentage of Canadian content, in order to protect Canadian culture from **Americanization**.

Other positions, like that held by Daniel Drache (2008), argue for the unprecedented capacity of the Internet to fight these global powers by providing social actors the tools to form defiant publics. Publics are communities organized around a cause or some basic principle of social change. Drache argues that we have entered an era of digital publics and the **culture of dissent**. Defiant publics are communities often united only online but that share the symbols and language of dissent. He cites studies showing that when connected by the Internet, people from many cultures feel empowered against the traditional strength of imperial states and corporations.

It is likely, then, that culture is no longer simply a way for people to attach to local places. The culture of dissent actually provides the language, symbols, and tools for people to unite in transnational, transcultural webs of significance. Not only are public opinion and popular culture going global, the social changes that occur in one nation, in one culture, are now immediately rendered in the meanings people use to establish webs of significance in other places. None of this is to say that culture is dead.

In fact, culture, freed of its traditional academic tie to specific places, can change and provide social change and freedom like never before.

 Chapter 14, "Globalization and Social Change," provides a comprehensive discussion of globalization and international relations.

CONCLUSION

Culture is a force that affects all human beings by making it possible to establish webs of significance, or societies. At one time, these webs may have been mostly local, or even comprehensible as national cultures, but today, the cultivation of the human mind and the rules that affect our choices for action are increasingly global in origin. Cultural elements in both material and immaterial forms, such as computers or gender values, are increasingly becoming shared and negotiated on a global scale. However, if we look at culture from different schools of thought, even this global emancipation may not promote social justice.

Cultural Marxists will tell us that hidden in the Internet is the false belief that we benefit from our participation in it; what we are really doing is buying bandwidth and technology to feed our addiction to social media and make a few companies wealthy. Functionalists will tell us that the Internet serves to help governments survey us and help the economy find new ways to extract resources while making us feel connected. Symbolic interactionists will explain that we are becoming addicted to ourselves and our images and losing the capacity to organize in actual and effective social movements. There is little potential for positive social change in this self-compulsion. Even production of culture theorists would be wary of the kind of abusive and anti-humane cultural production that occurs on the Internet. We can therefore leave off where we began: culture is responsible for all that is good and all that is harmful in society. But culture is not fixed—it is rarely written in stone—and we have the capacity to change, beginning with new ideas.

According to Tony Bennett (2007), the key to effecting social change through culture is by illuminating the complex connections between government and culture, or to do what Luc Boltanski (2011) has suggested, namely linking dominant institutions and their messages with the individuals who control them. These positions suggest that there is a social and transformative role for cultural information, and the goal for a safe world is to activate this knowledge before global economic or environmental disasters force us to think differently about how we live.

Questions for Critical Thought

1. The Internet holds the promise of great freedoms of expression, but consider whether our need to be online is proof that our culture is becoming dependent on technology. Are we hopeless without these much larger webs of significance?

2. Can you identify fundamental beliefs you have and the symbolic elements attached to them? Are they the same as those of everyone in your classroom? Are you united with people because you share the same symbols or because you each use symbols regardless of what they mean?

3. Are same-sex unions acceptable? Do you think they should be called "marriage"; why or why not?

Sociological Explorations

1. Leave your cell phone or other digital communication device at home for one day. Keep notes of every time you feel the need to borrow someone else's phone. What does this tell you about this culture?
2. Interview your parents or grandparents about their lives when they were your age. What did people do for entertainment? What were their views on same-sex marriage? Did any of your family face stigmas, and if so, why? What does their experience suggest to you? Will future generations be more or less technological?
3. Volunteer with a community organization and keep a journal of your experiences. When the volunteer commitment is over, ask yourself if your webs of significance have changed. Are they larger, smaller, more intense, more satisfying, more confusing, or something else?

Recommended Readings

Berger, P.L., & Luckmann, T. (1966). *The social construction of reality: A treatise in the sociology of knowledge.* **New York, NY: Anchor.**
This book is the foundational work for understanding the role culture plays in the social construction of reality and what this construction means for doing sociology.

Drache, D. (2008). *Defiant publics: The unprecedented reach of the global citizen.* **Cambridge, UK: Polity.**
Though largely a book about digitally supported global political activism, the book confronts the problem of culture as a way of seeing new ways to change the social world on local and global scales.

Featherstone, M. (2007). *Consumer culture and postmodernism* **(2nd edn). London, UK: Sage.**
This book looks at the historic roots of post-modern discourses on consumption and identity and offers a thorough rendition of consumer culture.

Recommended Websites

Village Building Convergence
www.villagebuildingconvergence.com/#about
This website shows how citizens of Portland, Oregon, use art and technology to modify city spaces into alternative visions of community.

Dignity Village
www.dignityvillage.org
The official site of Dignity Village, Oregon. It discusses the history of this US tent camp and its challenges.

LGBTQ Nation
www.lgbtqnation.com/
The "world's most followed LGBTQ news source."

The Webby Awards
http://webbyawards.com
This website examines and rates the top websites on the planet based on content, message, and usage. It is an interesting resource for understanding how the Web is shaping our ideas through language, symbols, and discourses.

Key Terms

AGIL An analytical paradigm developed by Talcott Parsons. He said that in order for social stability to be achieved the system must adapt (A), seek out and obtain its goals (G), integrate (I) its lived and material components, and sustain its latent (L) pattern, a cultural system or template.

Americanization The idea that American culture victimizes other cultures through its dominance of media and other important global institutions.
back-stage See **front-stage and back-stage**.
base/superstructure In Marxist theory, the base is the relations of production such as workers and owners,

and the superstructure includes culture, institutions, and power structures that depend on that base.

biologically determined The idea that our social acts are determined by biological needs such as reproduction.

collective conscience Durkheim's term for the shared system of beliefs that provide our basis for solidarity.

communitas A term popularized in 1969 by Victor Turner to describe a **ludic**, egalitarian social space that is found in places of festival and dance, for example. Because people gather to have fun, there is less direction, less governance, and more equality than in participants' daily lives.

compulsory heterosexuality A term coined by Adrienne Rich (1978) to explain that heterosexuality is a politically reinforced value in patriarchal society.

conflict theory A theoretical paradigm linked to the work of Marx and Weber that emphasizes conflict and change as the regular and permanent features of society, because society is made up of various groups that wield varying amounts of power. Conflict theorists often stress the importance of status, economic inequality, and political power.

consensus General agreement within a population.

consensus theory A term used to describe functionalism in the 1960s.

critical turn The paradigm shift in the social sciences and humanities which began in the early 1980s. The turn is marked by a destabilization of the concept of the "other" and the recognition that objective reality is impossible because the measures we use to see it are socially constructed. Also called the *post-modern turn*.

culture-jamming A term for anti-capitalist, anti-consumerist activists taking over advertising billboards and other symbolic tools used by powerful organizations and replacing those symbols with the activists' own ideas. An example would be an ad on a bus saying "Corporate advertising is bad."

cultural diversity A way to explain how different cultures meet people's material and immaterial needs in different ways.

cultural evolution The idea that cultures evolve to meet the biological requirements of human societies, a notion sometimes linked to social Darwinism.

cultural hegemony A concept developed by Marxist theorist Antonio Gramsci, describing how, in culturally diverse societies, powerful social classes dominate others through their ownership and dominance of culturally powerful institutions, making their vision of the social world seem normal; as a result, class distinctions persist.

cultural imperialism The idea that by controlling popular culture and economies, a powerful culture can dominate others. See also **Americanization**.

cultural universals Those elements shared by all cultures, such as beliefs and practices about birth and death, shelter, and food.

culture The set of beliefs, values, and practices that help people establish their places and carry out their roles in webs of significance, or society.

culture of dissent A term used by Drache (2008) to explain how a global sense of disenfranchisement and political activism is uniting people into transnational, often Web-supported, cultures of activism.

defiant publics Those people united by their political activism into cultures of dissent.

discourses Powerful stories usually supported by dominant institutions and powerful people to force a vision of the world on others.

dramaturgical approach The idea of a stage (Goffman, 1963) to explain how people act, as if it were a performed drama.

eugenics A moral position that advocated sterilization and murder of persons or entire "races" deemed genetically defective.

false consciousness A person's misunderstanding of his or her lot in life and the wider social structure and relationships that shape power and politics. A term coined by Karl Marx as a label for ignorance or delusion about one's objective class position.

feminism A theoretical paradigm, as well as a social movement, that focuses on causes and consequences of inequality between men and women, especially patriarchy and sexism.

front-stage and back-stage The two realms of human behaviour in Goffman's dramaturgical approach. The front-stage is how we present ourselves based on socially acceptable public conventions. The back-stage is the realm of our private selves.

governmentality A term popularized by Foucault (1991) to describe how neo-liberal states cause people to self-govern according to discourses of which they rarely are aware.

heteronormative The assumption that being heterosexual is normal.

heterotopia A term coined by Foucault (1984) to describe spaces where people take part in or act out in ways that are different from their daily activities. These spaces are real and representative. For example, one can go to the theatre or to a cemetery and experience other ways of being without acting or dying oneself.

ideal culture The way a culture presents itself in its mores and norms or prescriptions for social action. It rarely achieves this status.

ideology A powerful system of knowledge supported by dominant institutions that rationalizes different perceptions about social justice and order.

immaterial/material elements The intangible and tangible aspects of culture, such as ideas and technology.

immanent transcendence The misguided belief held by the Frankfurt School that society contained the potential and destiny to transcend capitalist exploitation.

LGBTQ(s) An acronym for lesbian, gay, bi(sexual), trans, queer, and straight alliances that work together to fight gender discrimination.

liminal A term used to described the transitional moments that people go through during rites of passage.

ludic A term describing essentially unmonitored, unrestricted acts of fun. Anthropologist Victor Turner (1969) refers to fun festivities as ludic spaces that make **communitas** possible.

mass media The technologies, practices, and institutions through which information and entertainment are produced and disseminated on a mass scale.

mechanical and organic solidarity Durkheim's terms for understanding how social integration occurs in simple and complex social groups.

mode of production A Marxist term for how the economy works (e.g., agriculture vs. industry).

mores The legalized forms of norms.

multiculturalism Canada's official political and inclusive disposition toward race and ethnicity.

narrative inevitability The idea that discourses impact social action by making people expect certain outcomes from certain situations.

neo-liberalism A form of liberal-democratic politics where the state decreasingly serves its social function and increasingly leans toward economic initiatives.

norms Values that tend to be repeatedly expressed or practised such that they seem normal.

patriarchal A term used to describe cultures where males are granted privilege.

queering A way of looking at traditional ideas, such as rules for using public space or the meaning of marriage, and turning them inside out to allow for other perceptions.

queer theory A number of approaches oriented toward social justice by abandoning traditional theories about normal identities in favour of inclusive and fluid categories of sexual, psychological, social, and other experience.

real culture The way culture actually happens, despite what **ideal culture** would imply.

Rites of passage A term coined by Arnold Van Gennep in his 1908 study of culture and folklore to describe rituals performed when a person enters a more advanced status in a cultural group, such as graduating from college or getting married.

roles The kinds of things we do as social beings such as being a wife, mother, sister, teacher, and so on.

Sapir–Whorf hypothesis A theory that helps us to understand how gender values permeate the structure of language.

self-help A term that refers to the idea that individuals are responsible for their own well-being. The idea of self-help is different from self-conduct or self-governing. The latter two concepts are very old and refer to codes often enshrined in religious and civil codes, and as such refer to moral and ethical behaviour. Self-help is popularized under neo-liberalism such that those who are ill, for example, must pay for medical care on their own, thus releasing the state from financial responsibility for people's well-being.

semiotics A perspective on how language is constructed to establish powerful meanings.

socially constructed The idea that nothing is innate or natural and that all social truths are the result of humans acting toward ideas produced by culture.

society A group of people living in a certain and sharing a culture, or otherwise sharing mechanisms for establishing webs of significance.

sociobiology A contentious paradigm that argues that human behaviour is the result of social and cultural evolution that reflects universal biological tendencies.

status The kind of prestige or relative power attributed to one's possessing an important role or economic power; a way of understanding one's social place relative to another (boss vs. worker, single vs. married).

stigmatized Discriminated against based on a negatively perceived personal attribute (from the word "stigma").

subcultures Groups of people, such as religious sects or fetishists, who establish their own webs of significance and social practices that set them apart from the larger society in which they live.

Tinguian of Austronesia A group of tribal people who do not kiss for any reason.

values Central beliefs that underlie the way people perceive justice or injustice in social situations. For example, freedom and autonomy are key values in North America.

webs of significance A term for a way of looking at culture. These are our social and other ties with people who share a similar understanding of the world and who, therefore, do things similarly enough that together we form a culture.

work ethic A Western value that places the need to work and reach economic solvency above other needs and values.

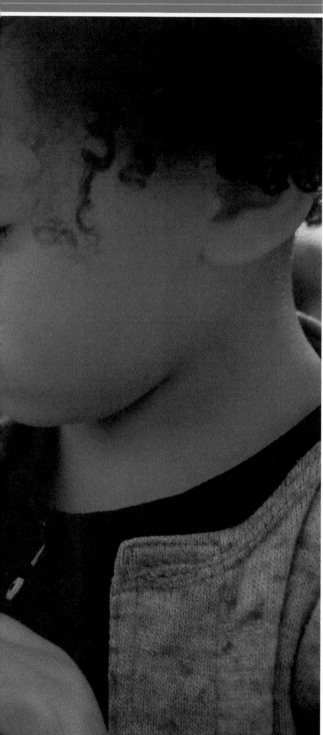

In this chapter you will:

▶ Comprehend basic patterns of socialization and what it means to be human

▶ Situate the social experience within the nature–nurture debate

▶ Learn how different theorists explain processes of socialization

▶ Examine different agents of socialization, such as the family, the school, the peer group, and the mass media

▶ Critically evaluate how socialization experiences are socially structured and vary by social class, gender/sexual orientation, ethnicity, generation, and geographical location

▶ Explore how socialization is a reciprocal, dynamic, and lifelong process that changes over the life course

INTRODUCTION: WHAT IS SOCIALIZATION?

In the 2010 television documentary mini-series *Into the Universe with Stephen Hawking*, the famous British scientist asserts that "aliens are out there, but it could be too dangerous for humans to interact with extraterrestrial life." Hawking further speculates that most extra-terrestrials would be similar to microbes or small animals, but that communicating with them could be "too risky." But imagine, for a moment, a slightly different scenario. Imagine that you arrive home one day to a neighbour-hood that has been newly inhabited by creatures that are biologically identical to adult humans. Intelligent, cooperative, and peaceful (although occasionally combative), they do not recog-nize our language or comprehend our customs, norms, or ways of interacting. Instead, they ex-change thoughts sonically using suction-like pods, and they make intense eye contact with strangers. After setting up camp in the local park, they quickly begin to learn our language and engage in local community affairs. Over time, they internalize and copy many of our behaviours, beliefs, and technologies, and most become accepted and productive citizens of our society.

Although this hypothetical situation reads like a scene out of a science fiction movie, it illustrates the process of **socialization**, which can be defined as the acquisition of knowledge, skills, and motivation to participate in social life. In other words, it is the process whereby individuals learn, through interaction with others, that which they must know in order to survive, function, and become members of our society. Moreover, socialization is not confined to babies and children but consti-tutes a complex, lifelong learning process that enables us to develop our selves, roles, and identities.

Yet socialization is not a uniform phenom-enon whereby we are all churned out by some kind of giant socialization factory. Although humans share many values and norms, differ-ences are found by such aspects as geographic region, ethnic/immigration background, gender/sexual orientation, religion, and social class. Additionally, each generation experiences so-cializing effects particular to their birthplace and historical location. Growing up during the Great Depression (1929–1939) in Canada, for instance, would have been vastly different from what it is today, given the very different social, economic, and technological environ-ments. Further, criminologists point out that socialization does not necessarily mean that what is learned is acceptable to the "main-stream" or is positive for us. Take, for example, youth gang behaviour whereby a young adult self-identifies with a certain group (e.g., the Crips, the Bloods). Through interaction with other gang members, youths learn and display "anti-social" norms and behaviours, such as participating in delinquent acts, crime sprees, drug-trafficking, and slayings.

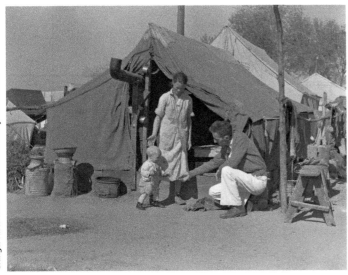

The socialization of each generation is very different due to the social, eco-nomic, and technological environment. For instance, growing up during the Great Depression presented challenges unknown to most youths now.

Granger Historical Picture Archive / Alamy Stock Photo

TIME to REFLECT

How have your opportunities in life been affected by your historical location—the generational time and place in which you were born?

HUMAN BEHAVIOUR— NATURE OR NURTURE?

For more than a century, social scientists have argued over the relative contributions of biology and the environment to human development, popularly called "the nature–nurture debate." By way of example, consider your own musical abilities. Are you an awesome singer, or can you play a musical instrument such as a guitar or piano with ease and finesse? Do you think that your musical talent (or lack thereof) is the result of your biology (nature) or environmental influences (nurture)? If you lean toward a biological explanation, you might attribute your musical talent to the unfolding of "hardwired" genetic factors. You might believe, for example, that you inherited strong music genes from your parents or from your Uncle Albert, who might be a professional musician. However, if you lean toward an environmental explanation, you might focus more on the role of social forces in producing your musical talents. For instance, maybe you had lots of opportunities to take music lessons growing up, and your parents made you diligently practise what you learned.

Alternatively, you might argue that both sides of the debate have some merit. In short, we may be predisposed toward certain abilities, but our environment will determine the extent to which these abilities can be realized.

One of the most exciting advances in this area is the emerging science of epigenetics, or the study of how the environment modifies the way that genes are expressed (Landecker & Panofsky, 2013). The *New York Times* ran a series of articles on this topic, one of which reviewed Shenk's (2010) bestselling book *The Genius in All of Us: Why Everything You've Been Told about Genetics, Talent, and IQ Is Wrong*. In this article, Paul (2010) discusses Shenk's major thesis that our genes are constantly activated by environmental stimuli, nutrition, and so on. Consequently, there can be "no guaranteed genetic windfalls or fixed genetic limits . . . instead, there is a continually unfolding interaction between our heredity and our world, a process that may be in some measure under our control." From this lens, Shenk asserts that epigenetics introduces a "new paradigm" that "reveals how bankrupt the phrase 'nature versus nurture' really is."

In summary, one useful way to conceptualize socialization is that it provides the link between biology and culture. We are born with the capacity to learn (e.g., music), to use language, and to forge social and emotional bonds, all of which are necessary for normal childhood development. However, our environment may limit (or facilitate) the extent to which innate gifts or propensities are realized. But what happens when our biological potential is not actualized? In order to examine this question more closely, let's consider a case study that illustrates this phenomenon—the effects of social deprivation on human development.

TIME to REFLECT

Many children throughout the world do not have the opportunity to grow up in a safe, secure, and loving environment. For example, children may be living in a war-ravaged country or be forced into child-labour camps. How might these early life experiences affect the socialization process and later adult life?

The Case of Genie

Throughout history, reports have surfaced of young children who have been isolated from society and who, in one way or another, have lived in a "wild" state. For example, one study compiled a list of 53 cases of isolated children, beginning with the Hesse Wolf-Child (purportedly raised by wolves) discovered in Germany in 1344 (Newton, 2002). More recent examples include the cases of Isabelle, Anna, and Genie. Genie, for instance, was discovered at the age of 13 in her home in Los Angeles, California, on 4 November 1970 (Rymer, 1993; Curtiss, 1977). Tied to a potty chair during the day, she had been locked in a room alone for more than 10 years.

At first, people were shocked to find out that Genie was 13 years old, since she weighed only 59 pounds and was just 54 inches tall. She could understand only a few words like "stopit" and "nomore," and she had a strange bunny-like gait. She was not toilet trained, and she could not eat solid food. After she was placed in the Children's Hospital in Los Angeles, her mental and physical development started to improve immediately and she was always eager to learn new words. A team of scientists (known as the Genie Team) began to work with her and wondered whether Genie would have a normal learning capacity. Notably, could a nurturing, enriched environment compensate for her horrible past? It appeared that this partially happened, since Genie's vocabulary grew significantly. Unfortunately, scientists were never able to fully answer this question. After five years, Genie's mother forbade the team from having contact with Genie because she claimed that their "tests" constituted cruel treatment.

Although case studies such as this one are obviously extreme, research documents that even milder forms of social isolation can have profound effects for children later in life. Moreover, a lack of these supports at other times in our life as we age can similarly hinder our health and well-being. For example, LGBT elders often experience a higher risk of social isolation later in life, and this may hinder their opportunities for socialization (e.g., in recreational activities) and their feelings of inclusion (Harley, Gassawy, & Dunkley, 2015).

In conclusion, socialization is the essential bridge between the individual and society, and it is the process through which we become human. And although humans are resilient creatures, there is a point at which abuse, neglect, or social isolation (especially in infancy) results in irreparable developmental damage.

THEORIZING SOCIALIZATION

In this section, major theoretical approaches to socialization are reviewed. These approaches include learning/behaviourist theory, Freud's psychoanalytic theory, developmental approaches (Erikson, Piaget, and Kohlberg), the symbolic interactionist view on the development of the self, functionalist and conflict approaches, and feminist theory (especially in relation to critical perspectives on gender-role socialization).

Theories on Childhood Socialization
Learning/Behaviourist Frame of Reference

Learning theory, which has its roots in behaviourism, assumes that the same concepts and principles that apply to animals apply to humans. Although there are many variations of this theory, socialization as applied to the newborn infant involves changes that result from maturations that include classical or instrumental conditioning. Classical conditioning links a response to a known stimulus. A popular example is Pavlov's dog experiment in which a hungry dog is placed in a soundproof room and hears a tuning fork (a conditioned stimulus) before receiving some meat. After this situation is repeated several times, the dog begins to salivate upon hearing the tuning fork. The same principles are assumed to hold true with an infant upon hearing his or her mother's voice or approaching footsteps.

Operant or instrumental conditioning focuses attention on the response, which is not related to any known stimulus. Instead, it functions in an instrumental manner in that one learns to make a certain response on the basis of the outcome that the response produces. According to Skinner (1953), it is the response that correlates with positive reinforcement or a reward. For example, imagine that a baby is picked up after saying "da-da-da" because the father is convinced that the baby is saying "Daddy." Consequently, the baby begins to say "da-da-da" all day long because there may be lots of rewards. As children grow older, different reinforcements (e.g., praise, candy, allowance) are used as deliberate techniques to teach children approved forms of behaviour.

While there is some usefulness in this theory, there may be limited applicability in generalizing animal behaviour to socialized humans. Humans, unlike animals, have the capacity to share symbolic meanings and symbols in ways that animals cannot.

Psychoanalytic Frame of Reference

Developed by Sigmund Freud (1856–1939) and his followers, psychoanalytic theory stresses the importance of childhood experiences, biological drives and unconscious processes, and cultural influences. Beneath the surface of each individual's consciousness are impulsive, pleasure-seeking, and selfish energies that Freud termed the *id*. Individuals also have *egos* and engage in cognitive, conscious thought processes that make each one of us a unique individual. Both the id and the ego are controlled by the individual's gradual internalization of societal restraints (the *superego*). Parents play a key role in *impulse taming* by transmitting cultural values and rules that guide the ego and repress the id.

Accordingly, socialization consists of a number of stages of development that occur and are called the *oral*, *anal*, and *phallic stages*, followed later by a period of *latency* and then a *genital phase*. An individual's passage through all these stages culminates in a healthy, mature personality with a well-developed superego, which channels libidinal forces in appropriate directions. However, Freud theorized that it is also possible for one to remain in one stage for an inordinate length of time (fixation) or return to an earlier stage (regression) and that this can be the source of inappropriate or problematic social behaviour (Freud, 1938).

Child Development Frames of Reference

Similar to Freud, both Erik Erikson (1963, 1982) and Jean Piaget (1932, 1950) emphasized the early stages of childhood development. Unlike Freud, both extended their stages beyond the early years and focused more attention on social structure and reasoning. Erikson, who was one of Freud's students, viewed socialization as a lifelong process. He developed eight stages of human development, which range from *trust versus mistrust* (first year of infancy) to *integrity versus despair* (old age). As individuals create solutions to developmental concerns, those solutions become institutionalized in our culture. Swiss social psychologist Piaget, who wrote during the 1920s, was also interested in maturational stages. However, his interest was more in cognitive development, which he characterized as the ability to think and reason abstractly and logically.

Piaget also developed four major cumulative stages of intellectual development, which include the *sensorimotor period* (birth to two years), *pre-operational period* (two to seven years), *concrete operational period* (seven to 11 years), and *formal operational period* (age 11 through adulthood). Children develop their cognitive abilities through interaction with the world and adaptation to their environment. They adapt by assimilating, which means making new information compatible with their understanding of the world. Children also learn to accommodate by adjusting their cognitive framework to incorporate new experiences as they become socialized into adults.

Lawrence Kohlberg (1969, 1975) expanded on Piaget's ideas with his stages of moral development. His ideas were based on his research in which children were presented with moral dilemmas that asked what they would do and why they would do it. In one such dilemma, a man's wife was dying, and the druggist (who had invented the only medicine that could save her) was charging 10 times what the medicine cost to produce, a cost that was also considerably higher than what the husband could afford. Subjects were then asked whether the husband had the right to steal the drug and why.

Subject responses clustered into three general levels of moral reasoning, each of which could be subdivided into more specific stages. In the earliest stages, children say "it is wrong to steal" and "it is against the law," but they are unable to elaborate any further. By stage 4 (the most prevalent stage, usually reached as children mature), moral decisions are made from the perspective of society as a whole, since we think from a full-fledged member-of-society perspective.

In summary, so far we have reviewed frames of reference that emphasize overt behaviour (i.e., behaviourism, learning theory), the unconscious role of motives and emotions (i.e., the Freudians), and motor skills, thought, and moral reasoning processes (i.e., child developmentalists). Next we will review perspectives that shine the spotlight on societal influences on socialization.

Symbolic Interactionist Frame of Reference

In sociology, the symbolic interactionist (SI) perspective has had one of the greatest influences on theories of socialization. Central importance is placed on interactions with others and the internalized definitions, meanings, and interpretations of our interactions (Charon, 1979; Mitchell, 2012). Basic assumptions include the following:

(1) *Humans must be studied on their own level.* Social life involves sharing meanings and communicating symbolically via language, which enables humans alone to deal with events in terms of past, present, or future.

(2) *An analysis of society is the most valuable method in understanding society.* Individual behaviour needs to be contextualized within the structure of society. When one is born into a given society, one learns the language, customs, and expectations of that culture.

(3) *At birth, the human infant is asocial.* Newborns are born with impulses and needs and with the potential to become a social being. Babies begin to learn to channel their behaviours in specific directions via training and socialization from their parents.

(4) *A socialized being is an actor as well as a reactor.* Humans are minded beings, actively responding to a symbolic environment that involves responses to interpreted and anticipated stimuli. In this way, they assess new ways of responding and can dream of future possibilities.

Another key concept is the idea of the development of a social self, which takes place in interaction with others. For example, a young adult may occupy the status of child, student, sister, athlete, and many others. These statuses have expectations (roles) assigned to them and are organized and integrated into the social self. In this way, the social self is never fixed, static, or in a final state.

Of central importance are the roles of **significant others** and reference groups. Although parents are usually the most significant socializers, other people or groups are important. These individuals can be other family members or even role models presented in the media, such as pop-star sensations like Taylor Swift or Katy Perry. Reference groups, on the other hand, constitute a source of comparison and provide standards for conduct (e.g., Boy Scouts) that operates in a similar fashion.

TIME to REFLECT

Who are your most significant role models? How do they influence what you say and do? How do they contribute to your feelings of self-worth and your self-identity?

Popular SI theorists include George Herbert Mead (1934) and Charles Horton Cooley (1902, 1962). To Mead, social, not biological, forces are the primary source of human behaviour. He maintained that a newborn baby is *tabula rasa*, or a "blank slate," without predisposition to develop any particular type of personality. Mead referred to this spontaneous and unsocialized self as the "I." Through interaction, our personalities develop and the socialized self ("Me") emerges.

Another central concept is his notion of **generalized other**. According to Mead, children usually pass through three stages in developing a full sense of selfhood: the *play stage* (whereby the child models significant others); the *game stage* (whereby children pretend to be other people); and finally, the *generalized other stage* (learning generalized values and cultural rules). This final stage signifies how individuals become consistent and predictable in their behaviour and how people learn to view themselves from the perspective of others. Thus, behaviour results less from drives and needs, unconscious processes, and biological forces and more from social interaction processes and internalized meanings of self and others.

Functionalist and Conflict Perspectives

While many theories of socialization describe and analyze the *process* of socialization, functionalist and conflict theories place emphasis on understanding the *role* and the *importance* of socialization. A functionalist approach addresses the ways in which conformity helps to preserve and meet the needs of society. It does so by providing knowledge that is passed from generation to generation. Thus, the fundamental task of any society is to reproduce itself such that the needs of society become the needs of the individual (Newman, 2006).

Conflict perspectives (which often have roots in Marxist theories) focus more on issues of power and control, and how socialization helps the powerful and wealthy pass on their advantages to the next generation. Socialization does so by supporting ideologies and practices that work to the advantage of dominant groups and by social channelling. In this way, children are prepared for future societal roles, and gender, class, and racial inequities are reproduced. Notably, poor children are channelled toward a life of poverty through the educational and employment system. **Gender-role socialization** also prepares women and men for different and unequal roles in society, a topic to which we now turn.

Feminist Theories, Intersectionality, and Critical Perspectives on Gender-role Socialization

Although one unified feminist theory does not exist, feminists often critique functionalist views and build upon conflict theorizing by emphasizing how gender is a fundamental organizing feature of social life. Focus is often placed on how social interaction, including discourse (i.e., the usage of language and symbols), is socially constructed and on how gender-role socialization mirrors and perpetuates inequities found throughout society.

There is little denying that gendered divisions are found in virtually all societies. For many centuries, it was assumed that "anatomy is destiny" and that these differences were largely innate or inborn. However, many feminists assert that this belief provides a major (functionalistic) ideological justification for a system of stratification that subordinates women and privileges men. Instead, we must also consider the organization and practices of society. Fundamental differences in gender-role socialization and stereotyping continue to exist, and this begins at birth and continues throughout one's life. This is seen in the sexualization of girls and women in society and the media (Gunter, 2014).

Although there has been some positive social change in this regard, many feminists observe that progress has been slow. A study by Auster and Mansbach (2012), for instance, documents that Disney continues to market "traditional" toys for "boys only" or for "girls only" on their US website. "Traditionally" (in the 1950s, for example), little girls were often given dolls, sewing machines, and makeup, while little boys were often presented with toy guns, action figures, cars, and games that contain violent content—practices that remain popular.

Another example of how social institutions are highly gendered is our educational system, which also plays an important role in the formation of gender identities through curriculum and its local culture. Connell (1996) maintains that each school has its own "gender regime," which contributes to the ongoing negotiation and renegotiation of femininity or masculinity. A school's style of dress can act as a powerful signifier of social acceptability and expression of identity, as well as a signifier of fashion that separates "the girls from the boys." For instance, at some schools, "the look for boys" is to appear somehow connected to sports, athleticism, strength, and power, and this becomes the hegemonic norm (Swain, 2004).

Fox (2001, 2014) reveals other structural sources of gender differences and how they can resurface beyond childhood (i.e., in young families). Her research uncovered how the transition to parenthood can produce a more conventional division of labour in the home. Gender inequity arises out of the gendered division of paid and unpaid work, and these conditions further shape and constrain options and behaviours. In today's society, a shortage of outside community supports and the privatization of parenthood also mean that women continue to have the ultimate responsibility for their babies' welfare. This creates women's dependence on men or other family members (e.g., on their own mothers), and this further strengthens gendered divisions.

In short, gender socialization does not end in childhood. It continues (and can even deepen) through certain institutional practices and discourses that produce gendered adults and identities.

Moreover, many feminists have produced work that reveals the complex factors and processes that shape gendered and human lives by drawing upon an intersectionality approach. As discussed by Hankivsky (2014, p. 2), "Intersectionality promotes an understanding of human beings as shaped by the integration of different locations" (e.g., race/ethnicity, Indigeneity, gender, class, sexuality, geography, age, disability/ability, migration status, religion). These interactions happen within a context of intertwined structures of power (e.g., laws, policies, media). Therefore, it is argued that our social lives cannot be explained simply by taking into account single categories such as gender, since people's lives are multi-dimensional.

There is also growing recognition that we need to better understand men's daily lives. It is increasingly acknowledged that "maleness" or being of the male gender does not necessarily confer the same socialization experiences and privileges in the same way across all men. Overall, an intersectionality approach shows promise in helping theorists, researchers, and social activists to better conceptualize the complexity

and consequences of diverse socialization processes in relation to social inequities and social justice.

TIME to REFLECT

In her bestselling book *The Beauty Myth* (first published in 1990), Naomi Wolf argues that media images place a great deal of pressure on women to conform to an impossible standard of physical perfection. Do you agree or disagree? Have times changed at all since she wrote the book?

From the preceding discussion, it is clear that families are a **primary agent of socialization** but that other (secondary) agents, such as the educational system, also contribute to socialization processes.

In the next section, we will examine more closely the role of families in socialization, followed by the **secondary socialization** that takes place in the wider society. We will consider how these secondary agents—school, peer group, and mass media/technology—differentially shape our social experiences.

THE FAMILY

Clearly, during infancy and childhood, the family constitutes the most significant agent of socialization. Families provide the primary source of our early emotional attachments and learning, although other agents (e.g., daycare, the mass media) also shape children's basic beliefs and values. Families also play a critical role in transmitting culture from one generation to the next.

Experiences within contemporary families are very different from those of the past. Although family life has never been homogeneous, changes in family structure (e.g., the rise in step-, common-law, single-father, and childless families), transformations in work and greater gender-role equality (e.g., dual-career households), and continuing high rates of immigration contribute to the diversification and experience of "family." For example, Gazso (2014) notes that newcomers to Canada may experience a social context with cultural norms about child-rearing or discipline that can be very different than those in their country of origin.

Historical state and family policies have also affected today's Canadian families in important ways. Notably, traditional Indigenous child-rearing practices in Canada have been significantly disrupted in the context of colonialism and historical trauma caused by the residential school experience (Muir & Bohr, 2014). Taking Indigenous children away from their families and placing them in church- and government-run boarding schools—a common practice in Canada from 1892 to 1996—meant that many children spent most of their childhood in punitive and harsh institutions and without positive role models. Consequently, these children lost the experience of growing up with their traditional family life and knowing their cultural heritage. Sadly, many of these children reached adulthood without having any sense of parenting, love, or warmth, a situation that has negatively impacted subsequent generations.

Regardless of the disruption or continuation of many family practices, family experiences are variable and occur within unique social/ecological contexts. Extra-familial factors, such as the neighbourhood in which the family lives, social supports, work/employment experiences, social class background, and culture, also play a role in these experiences.

Further, social class and ethnic/cultural background can influence the kinds of life chances and values that are being transmitted to children. For example, a recent study (Irwin & Elley, 2012) found that a substantial proportion of working-class parents, more commonly fathers, saw a skilled trade as a good job for their sons. This finding reinforces the idea that parental expectations and styles of engagement reflect the material contexts in which families are embedded. Parents at a higher socio-economic level are also more likely to provide opportunities and resources for learning, such as through travel and exposure to more "cultured" lifestyles. Thus, it is not surprising that the enrolment rates in university are higher among

Photo by Mario Tama/Getty Images

Extra-familial factors can have a major impact on socialization. People growing up and living in highly policed, high-risk, low-income areas, such as the *favelas* of Rio de Janeiro, will experience very different socialization processes than people growing up and living in, for example, suburban Canada.

children from higher social classes than among children from lower ones.

Ethnic and immigration background also shape socialization experiences. Many cultural groups value and emphasize high educational and employment achievement. This means that parents inculcate educational expectations and place a great deal of pressure on children to succeed in school and work. Dimensions of cultural heritage can also produce norms, values, and obligations pertaining to many family roles—for example, with respect to how we treat and care for our senior family members.

 The importance of the family in Canadian society is clear. See **Chapter 9**, "Families and Health Issues," p. 200, for a detailed discussion of recent trends in family forms.

Social scientists typically view socialization as a reciprocal or two-way process. Daly, for example (K. Daly, 2004, p. 5), explains that it would be a mistake to think of socialization in terms of a simple linear transmission model whereby culture shapes parents and parents in turn shape children. A more accurate depiction is that of **reciprocal socialization**, or the simultaneity (whereby parents and children are the "players" in this case) of parenting and child behaviours and outcomes.

Another example of socialization as a two-way process can be seen in how persons with physical or mental challenges mediate their environment, such as when they try to access social services and unemployment benefits. Grover and Piggott (2013) find that those judged as belonging to the "category" of "disabled persons" are strongly encouraged by the state and many formal organizations to be responsible, independent, and hard working. Yet, those deemed disabled are simultaneously confronted with hostile societal stereotypes and exclusionary practices through popular media and policy discourses. Thus, not only are these socialization processes bidirectional, but they can also be competing and contradictory. Ironically, these practices work to further marginalize and stigmatize disabled persons by inhibiting feelings of respectability, belonging, and inclusion.

THE PEER GROUP

The peer group is commonly regarded as the second-most potent socialization agent. However, unlike our families, friends typically do not always consciously intend to socialize us. Through our interactions with peers, and because of our need for companionship and approval, there is a mutual learning of information, attitudes, and values.

 Were you part of a clique in high school? See "Cliques," p. 94, in **Chapter 4**, "Social Organization," for a definition and discussion of cliques.

Peer group influences are also culturally specific with respect to how children socialize one another. For example, as shown in the Human Diversity box, we learn how South Korean children learn culturally specific emotional knowledge through their participation in peer talk.

Although friendships are of central importance throughout the life course, during adolescence peer influences are particularly strong. However, youths may engage in behaviours that parents might not approve of, such as drinking and doing drugs or engaging in certain sexual activities (e.g., see Widman et al., 2016). Peer groups can rival parents in influence, as implied by the familiar phrase "the generation gap."

Recent studies (e.g., Kim & Hou, 2016) on immigrant youths also reveal multiple or "hybrid" identities of youths, and how identities and orientations are flexible, multi-dimensional, and subject to numerous influences. A good illustration focuses on the experiences of immigrant youths who have to negotiate their identities amid sometimes conflicting environments. In a Canadian study of the narratives among second-generation youths in their early twenties (whose families originated in India, Pakistan, and Bangladesh), most youths had a profound appreciation of their family heritage even as they participated in "dominant" Canadian culture.

HUMAN ▬ DIVERSITY

"Don't Cry, You're Not a Baby!": Emotion, Role, and Hierarchy in Korean Language Socialization Practice

In this excerpt based on an intensive observational study of South Korean children and teacher/peer group interactions, Ahn finds that the socialization of culturally specific emotional stances and habits

. . . occurs not simply through children's exposure to adult-contrived language routines but through children's active participation in peer talk. The Korean cultural model of emotions presented through teachers' everyday emotional discourses emphasises attuning and subduing one's inner feelings to display socially appropriate emotions, that is, role specific and specific hierarchically sensitive emotional displays. Rather than passively adopting these culturally specific theories of emotions,

children actively appropriate and transform them to construct their own emotional worlds. Children observed for this article know how to restrain, control, or express emotions according to rules of affective conduct vested in their roles and in the hierarchical order of human relationships as prescribed by Korean culture. The interactive realisation of these affective structures and habits are possible not simply thorough adults' socializing efforts, but equally through children's active participation in peer talk, wherein they observe and experience the effects emotion talk can play on their societal sphere.

SOURCE: Ahn, J. 2016. Children and Society, Volume 30, 12–24.

These findings challenge the prevailing discourse that children of immigrants are a "problem group" living in "two worlds"—caught between their "old" culture and the mainstream (Tyyskä, 2009).

In addition to age and ethnic background, peer networks are socially structured by other sociological variables such as gender, sexual orientation, and social class.

SCHOOLS

As a key socializing agent, schools provide a social environment that is separate from the family, and teachers and schoolmates widen our early learning and experiences. Consequently, a major socializing dimension of schools encompasses its many informal and social elements, including interactions among students and between teachers and students. Moreover, on a more macro level, the school plays an important role in political socialization, since it inculcates children with the basic beliefs and values of their society.

In modern society, the role of the school in the socialization process has become even more pronounced. It is relatively common for children under the age of five to attend some type of daycare or preschool program. Further, the amount of specialized technical and scientific knowledge required to participate in society has expanded well beyond what parents can teach in the home. Youths in Canada and other industrialized countries are more educated than previous generations, and a post-secondary education is now an expected part of many young people's lives. And while critics note that this trend has delayed the transition to adulthood and created greater dependency on parents for economic and housing support, benefits are also documented. Living at home with parents, for instance, can help young adults while attending school and create more peer-like intergenerational socialization experiences (Mitchell, 2012).

Yet as previously mentioned, not all Canadian children have the opportunity to achieve higher levels of education, since family and cultural background and gender have a significant effect on educational experiences. There is also concern over the sizable inequalities in educational pathways of Indigenous and First Nations youth, which can be traced to a legacy of

Structured learning environments, including classrooms and extracurricular activities, provide unique opportunities for socialization separate from the family. Dance, for example, may teach students to expect certain types of treatment based on their genders.

colonization, marginalization, and discrimination, as previously mentioned. Overall, racialized youths, visible minorities, and immigrants (with the exception of Asian students) are less likely to attend college and university (Thiessen, 2009).

It is argued that the continuation of unequal educational patterns and experiences lies in the institutionalization of classism, racism, and sexism. One aspect of this is the "hidden curriculum," which refers to implicit messages in education that may not be consciously taught or planned. These messages emphasize "dominant" societal values (such as competition and that our society's way of life is morally good) and social hierarchies based on social class, gender/sexual orientations, and race.

Therefore, it is not surprising that young adults who have the privilege and opportunity to attend post-secondary school face many advantages in life relative to their poorer counterparts.

For example, elite universities are credited as "launch points" for the active construction of meanings about career and work trajectories and the funnelling of students into prestigious jobs. Binder, Davis, and Bloom (2016) found that while most of their study participants (students at Harvard and Stanford) experienced confusion about career paths when arriving on campus, student culture and campus structures quickly steered them into high-wealth, high-status occupational disciplines. Through this process, students received important knowledge and planning advice through highly structured campus recruitment pathways into the most lucrative job sectors.

Finally, other pressing issues of interest and concern with respect to student social interactions and how they affect learning and identity include sexual and gender harassment, bullying, and school violence.

TIME to REFLECT

Why do children bully other children? Consider how various socializing agents play a role in this behaviour. What do you think might prevent children from bullying or being bullied? For example, should we specifically target "at risk" children, their families, or the school system?

MASS MEDIA

Television, computers, newspapers, radio, magazines, and entertainment such as movies are readily available and constitute another powerful source of socialization. The media environment experienced by children today is vastly different and expanded from the one their parents or grandparents faced. Children can now participate in a much wider range of media-related activities than ever before, including online social networking and shopping, texting, and watching video on demand.

Although the adoption of social media has been rapid and widespread, rates and types of usage can vary among socio-demographic groups (Stevens et al., 2016). Indeed, social

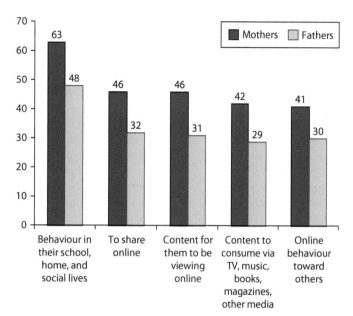

FIGURE 3.1   Mothers Are More Likely Than Fathers to Frequently Communicate with Their Teen about Appropriate vs. Inappropriate Behaviour

Among parents of teens ages 13 to 17, the percentage who say they frequently talk with their teen about what is appropriate or inappropriate behaviour in the following areas.

SOURCE: Pew Research Centre. January 5.,2016. "Parents, Teens, and Digital Monitoring." Retrieved September 24, 2016 from http://www.pewinternet.org/2016/01/07/parents-teens-and-monitoring/pi_2016-01-07_parents-teens-digital-monitoring_2-03

characteristics such as gender, family structure, age, and socio-economic class, in addition to other factors such as linguistic and disability status, can affect the propensity to engage in certain media activities. Parents are also found to play a significant mediating role in the media consumption habits and behaviours of their children, and these influences can differ between fathers and mothers (see Figure 3.1).

Research by Shpiegelman and Gill (2014) on adults with intellectual disabilities also finds that participation in social networking sites can facilitate an expansion of social connections and communication channels. However, there may also be challenges for those with these disabilities that impede complete participation, such as reading demands and a lack of voice-control programs. These barriers can prevent opportunities to give and receive social support, to enjoy themselves and feel like non-disabled people, and to keep up close relationships with family and real-world friends.

Social scientists observe that media and technology influences have always been controversial. However, there is concern that modern-day media technologies exert too much control over our daily lives and that they contribute to unhealthy behaviours. By way of illustration, a popular video-game series called *Grand Theft Auto* encourages the player to take on the role of a criminal in a big city and engage in numerous illegal activities, such as killing police and military personnel. Women are typically depicted as prostitutes and men as violent thugs—stereotypes that appear in other media venues (Dill & Thill, 2007). Video games in general are purported to overtly sexualize female characters at a time when children are beginning to develop attitudes toward body types and ideas about male and female sexuality (Downs & Smith, 2010; Gunter, 2014). Other critics link media exposure to the significant rise in body image disorders (e.g., through "body shaming") and to youth becoming too celebrity obsessed.

UNDER THE ▬▬ WIRE | Parental Perceptions of the Internet and Its Impact on Children

Parents in this study viewed the Internet as having a more positive than negative influence on their children. The key benefit of the Internet was its usefulness as a resource. Parents believed that the Internet made their children more knowledgeable as it provides an unlimited amount of information and enables the children to find information easily and quickly. The informants regarded the Internet as a useful information source, especially helpful when children worked on school assignments requiring information search:

> I find that she has become more knowledgeable, more resourceful. . . . She is more resourceful now because she knows that if she needs to know something, she can go to Google and find out herself. Then she learns the use of certain words sometimes. . . . I think she has become smarter. [Father, age 40, with a 9-year-old daughter]
>
> He relies on the Internet to do a lot of research (for school assignments). A lot of things he doesn't know and he does a Google search. All the answers come out. It is easier, faster, and saves time. [Mother, age 36, with a 9-year-old son]

While the informants' accounts of positive influences of the Internet on children converged on resourcefulness, their accounts of negative influences were rather diverse, with half of the informants not mentioning any negative aspects of it. Some parents thought the resourcefulness of the Internet had made children somewhat lazier ("everything is under fingertips"), but they indicated the benefits of the Internet (i.e. resourcefulness and convenience) outweighed its detriment (i.e. becoming lazier). Some informants indicated it was sometimes difficult to stop the children from using the Internet due to its addictive nature.

However, they did not think their children were seriously addicted to the Internet because they regulated the amount of time the children use the Internet at home.

Overall, the informants presumed more positive than negative influences of the Internet on their children, and they were not greatly concerned about its detrimental impact. Still, some parents expressed concerns. The most common concern was children's exposure to child-inappropriate online content. The Internet's resourcefulness can be "a double-edged sword" as described by an informant. While the tremendous amount of information available on the Internet can keep children better informed and more knowledgeable, not all information found is suitable for them. Parents knew that a simple keyword typed in on a search engine could take young ones to less desirable websites. In the words of an informant: You know these days, when you google, anything will come out. So sometimes certain things that he googles might come with some undesirable outcomes, adult websites and stuff like that, especially since he is almost into the puberty stage. [Father, age 38, with an 11-year-old son]

Other concerns mentioned by the parents, but not as prominent as concerns pertinent to exposure to inappropriate content, include the addictive nature of the Internet, contact risks on social networking sites, and privacy issues. However, most concerns were about "what might happen in the future" rather than "how children currently use the Internet."

SOURCE: Shin, W. and W.K. Wee. 2015. "Parental Socialization of Children's Internet Use: A Qualitative Approach." New Media and Society, 17, pp. 5–6.

Critics are also concerned about the power of music and lyrics, given that numerous studies have documented potential harmful effects in the areas of violence, smoking and drinking behaviour, and risky sexual activity. Other critics point out that overall, we live in a society in which sexual images and content predominate because of these new technologies (Barrie, 2014). Greater access and availability to pornography through the privacy of the Internet is argued to weaken other family socialization practices. For example, Perry (2015) found that pornography consumption (particularly by fathers) threatened the transmission of religious heritage to children because of reduced time spent together.

And, as media industries grow, Strasburger et al. (2009) assert that they become increasingly global and commercial in nature. Notably, media corporations target children and youths as a profitable group of consumers. Websites like Nicktropolis (which also contain a lot of advertising) encourage young children to enter an immersive 3-D virtual world where they can create avatars, interact with cartoon characters (e.g., SpongeBob SquarePants), and chat with other kids in "real time." Consequently, it is deemed that children are increasingly being socialized to become self-indulgent lifelong consumers as well as to form imaginary "para-social" (one-sided) relationships (Chung, DeBuys, & Nam, 2007).

Finally, socialization also takes place in other institutionalized settings, such as in organized sports, in religious contexts, and in other professional and formal organizations, such as in health-care settings. With respect to religious institutions, Statistics Canada documents that attendance at formal religious services has fallen dramatically over the past several decades, particularly among younger age groups, a trend that has many implications for other socialization processes. Religious norms influence many facets of family life, such as gender roles, parent–child relations, attitudes toward moral issues (e.g., abortion), and how families celebrate rituals and holidays. At the same time the number of adherents to religions such as Islam, Hinduism, Sikhism, and Buddhism has increased substantially in Canada as the result of changing sources of immigration (Statistics Canada, 2011c). Taken together, these trends contribute to more diverse profiles of Canadian families and further support the notion that socialization experiences vary across social groups.

The debate continues about the extent to which celebrity-watching socializes young people and whether the resulting socialization (e.g., attitudes toward body image, sex, and violence) is benign or malignant.

Featureflash Photo Agency/Shutterstock

THE LIFE COURSE, AGING, AND SOCIALIZATION

Throughout this chapter, it has been emphasized that socialization occurs throughout the life course, although the basic, formative instruction occurs fairly early in life. Some of the socialization that takes place during this time is called **anticipatory socialization**, a term used to refer to how individuals acquire the values and orientations they will likely take up in the future. In childhood, this might include doing household chores, a childhood job, sports, dance lessons, and dating—experiences that give youngsters an opportunity to rehearse for the kinds of roles that await them in adulthood. During adolescence and the teenage years, young people often adopt norms and behaviours of certain peer or reference groups before transitioning into them. Dukes and Stein's (2014) research on "wannabe" tattooed adolescents found that many of them already considered themselves as "outsiders." Making plans to mimic the behaviours of tattooed persons, therefore, allowed them to prepare for future "deviant" behaviours and roles (e.g., risk-taking and rebelliousness).

As we age, other experiences can also give us the opportunity to rehearse for the kinds of adult roles that we might eventually adopt.

> **TIME to REFLECT**
>
> How have your family and religious/spiritual background influenced your current opinions or attitudes with respect to some controversial social issues (e.g., abortion, same-sex marriage, assisted suicide, the death penalty)?

OPEN FOR
DISCUSSION

Should You Raise a Gender-Neutral Baby?

Blue is for boys and pink is for girls—that's what most of us were raised to believe. But some parents are taking the opposite approach to parenting by choosing to raise their children gender neutral. In fact, Sweden took a big step last year in addressing this trend by adding a gender-neutral personal pronoun, "hen," to the country's vocabulary. A children's clothing company in Sweden has done away with its designated boys' and girls' sections to become a gender-neutral outlet, and a toy catalog in the same country featured a boy in a Spider-Man costume pushing a pink baby carriage. Although the Swedes are embracing this parenting style, it's still a controversial topic here in the United States. Although some think it's a great way to encourage a child to embrace his or her true identity, others believe it will confuse the child and alienate him socially. Here, some common questions and answers about this parenting style.

What exactly is gender-neutral parenting?

There are different degrees of gender-neutral parenting. Some parents take an extreme approach. One couple from Toronto still hasn't revealed the gender of their 3-year-old, Storm. According to the *Toronto Star*, Storm's parents wrote in an e-mail to family and friends, explaining that their decision was "a tribute to freedom and choice in place of limitation, a standup to what the world could become in Storm's lifetime (a more progressive place?)."

Parents who want to practice a lesser form of gender-neutral parenting might simply encourage their children to play with both "boy" and "girl" toys, keep clothing and room décor neutral, and allow their children to pick their own clothes—even if that means their son goes to school in a tutu or their daughter goes out dressed as Spider-Man.

Lisa Cohn of Portland, Oregon, is raising her kids in her family's version of gender-neutral parenting. "We definitely avoid stereotypes about Mom doing the dishes and Dad mowing the lawn. That's not what our kids see at all," Cohn says. "I generally let my youngest son wear pink if he wants to, and he often appears in public wearing a headband. And I'm very careful about how I talk about girls and boys—and don't choose books that stereotype men and women."

Is it healthy for the child?

It depends on whom you ask. "A major pro to raising a gender-neutral baby is that you will be allowing your child to develop without the artificially created limitations that society has placed around gender," says Israel Martinez, a licensed clinical social worker. "As human beings, we crave to make life simpler and new information easier to digest. So we naturally want to establish categories, or boxes, that everything needs to fit into." Unfortunately, Martinez says, these gender norms are too limiting and can make kids feel like they have to be something they're not--and this can keep kids from being as happy and healthy as possible.

For Jane Ward, an associate professor of Women's Studies at the University of California, Riverside, the decision to parent her son this way was an easy one. "Raising a child under these strict gender guidelines is denying them an entire world of colors—they become tracked into the characteristics of their biological sex." Ward's 4-year-old son has grown up wearing both jeans and dresses, plays with all types of toys, and, until recently, had long hair. He told his parents not long ago that although he identifies with being a boy, he doesn't want to give up wearing girls' clothes.

But other experts—like Fran Walfish, a psychotherapist based in Beverly Hills, California—disagree. "Every boy and girl child must make a strong identification as a male or female person. Without it, the child feels lost and confused about [his or her] own identity. Gender and sexuality are only aspects of a person's identification. The goal is for clarity. Without male or female gender clarity, the child is not a full person."

SOURCE: excerpt from: DiProperzio, L. 2013. Retrieved September 23, 2016 from http://www.parents.com/parenting/gender-neutral-parenting/

A Swedish Top-Toy catalogue ad.
SOURCE: T. Gara. (2012). Highlights from the gender-neutral Swedish Toys "R" Us catalog. Retrieved 21 July 2016 from http://blogs.wsj.com/corporate-intelligence/2012/11/29/highlights-from-the-gender-neutral-swedish-toys-r-us-catalogue

Barnes (2015) illustrates this idea in her symbolic interactionist study focused on the anticipatory socialization of pregnant women. These women were in the process of transitioning to parenthood and had learned of their child's sex prior to childbirth. Her findings show that once women find out whether their child is a "girl" or "boy" they begin to engage in gendered interactions with the unborn fetus. Many mothers assigned a formal name to the unborn child and began to interact with the fetus in gender-typical ways. This "doing of motherhood" prepared them not only in their new role as "mother" but also in more specific roles such as "mother-to-son" and "mother-to-daughter."

Socialization to many new roles continues as we age and face new transitions and responsibilities. Older adults, for example, may have to "reverse" and learn new family roles as they care for frail and dependent aging parents. Moreover, adjustment to grandparenthood, retirement, and the death of friends and family members, as well as acceptance of the inevitability of one's own death, are part of socialization for aging adults.

It is also possible that during any time of our lives, we may become resocialized because of changing circumstances—a term that reflects the learning of new ways of life. Notably, events (e.g., migration, wars, recessions), social movements (e.g., the women's movement, gay rights), and technological developments can affect our behaviours, relationships, and self-images.

This **resocialization** can cause stress, because old behaviours must be unlearned and new behaviours acquired, and the tension between the old and new behaviours may be contradictory or confusing.

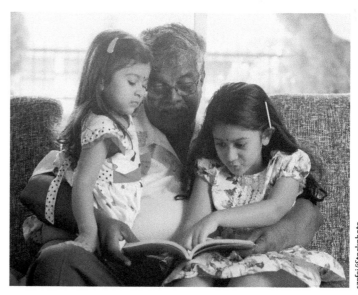

szefei/iStockphoto

Socialization to new roles (such as grandparenthood, retirement, or widowhood) occurs throughout the life course.

SOCIALIZATION PROCESSES: PAWNS, PUPPETS, OR FREE AGENTS?

In summary, we have learned that socialization is lifelong and shapes the individual and society. Societal order and continuity rely on members learning to share norms, values, and language. On an individual level, socialization allows us to realize our potential as human beings. However, because socialization is such a powerful process, you might ask yourself: To what extent are we free, active agents? Or are we just pawns subject to the invisible hands of larger social forces? This latter view has been called the *over-socialized conception of man*, a term coined by American sociologist Dennis Wrong in 1961. It reflects a critique of Parsons's functionalist theory of socialization that assumes we passively accept what is taught to us in order to conform to societal norms.

Fortunately, while socialization processes have a significant impact on our lives, we are not necessarily prisoners of this process or non-thinking clones. As Peter Berger points out, "unlike puppets, we have the possibility of stopping in our movements, looking up and perceiving the machinery by which we have

TIME to REFLECT •——

Think back to your first paid work experience. What kinds of skills and "lessons" did you learn? How did your interactions with others on the job (e.g., bosses, co-workers, customers) specifically influence your experience and what you learned?

been moved" (1963, p. 176). Studies also document that some of us are in a better position (e.g., cognitively, materially, or socially) than others to decide whether we want to accept what we learn.

Moreover, although we are not completely passive in the socialization process, resocialization by **total institutions** can occur. Developed by Goffman (1961), this term refers to any group or organization that has almost total, continuous control over the individual and that attempts to erase the effects of previous socialization. It often denotes a setting in which people are isolated in some way from the rest of society and manipulated by others (e.g., by administrative staff). This might entail brainwashing, religious conversion, military propaganda, physical brutality, and "rehabilitation" programs in prisons and mental hospitals designed to change one's personality.

CONCLUSION

This chapter explored the social experience and what it means to be human. Although there are biological or genetic limits to how socialization shapes us, socialization is an extremely powerful process that makes us functioning, "civilized" members of society. It is a major link between the individual and society, and social relationships are of fundamental importance to our experiences, health, and well-being. Sociologists theorize and study socialization processes at various levels, ranging from day-to-day interactions between individuals to the organization of society. On an individual level, socialization

moulds our tastes and preferences, attitudes and values, and tendencies to act in particular ways in particular situations. Think back to your last family meal or business meeting, for example, and visualize what could have transpired if there were no customs, rules, or rituals governing everyone's behaviour. Similarly, imagine what our society would be like in the absence of such cultural norms and behavioural guidelines.

Another major theme was that beliefs, values, and norms of society are not transmitted through various agents in a uniform, passive, and unidirectional fashion. Diversity is found not only across cultures but also within cultures. Further, in line with popular sociological theory, although socialization performs key functions for the individual and society and can perpetuate inequities in society, individuals are not like the fabled lemmings (small rodents) that blindly or unquestioningly follow others. Instead, individuals have some capacity to reflect upon or even resist certain socializing forces, depending upon factors such as social and economic position.

Finally, it was emphasized that socialization is a dynamic, lifelong process and that our social experiences change as we age, along with other societal transformations. Globalization, rapid population aging, and continuing high rates of immigration in Canadian society may provide the potential to learn and experience an even wider array of roles, identities, and behaviours. Technological advancements in communication and medical fields also mean that our social worlds and social selves are constantly shifting.

Questions for Critical Thought

1. What kinds of challenges and opportunities do immigrant children face in trying to become socialized into Canadian society?
2. While watching television or surfing the net, observe any ads marketing a household domestic product (e.g., a cleaning product, appliance). Do these ads perpetuate rigid and binary gender stereotypes or are they typically gender-neutral?
3. How might your social class membership shape your specific tastes and preferences in food, entertainment, and leisure activities?

4. Make a list of contradictory lessons that different agents of socialization taught you as a child. How have you resolved these contradictions?

5. To what extent, and how, do new communication technologies shape the socialization experiences of older adults in today's society?

Sociological Explorations

1. Toys play an important role in children's lives and socialization experiences. Visit a local toy store and observe the types (e.g., characters, colours) of toys and products that are being sold in the store. To what extent are these toys marketed and sold on the basis of gender? Are any gender neutral?

2. Interview several members of your family who belong to different generations and ask them what they think were the most significant socializing agents during their childhood years. For example, you could interview a grandparent, a parent, and a sibling or niece/nephew. How does each person's answer reflect his or her historical time and place and its state of technological advancement (e.g., in communications)?

Recommended Readings

Berns, R. (2013). *Child, family, school, community: Socialization and support* (9th edn). Florence, KY: Wadsworth Publishing.
Examining how the school, family, and community shape children's socialization, this text focuses on issues of diversity. Topics related to culture, ethnicity, gender, sexual orientation, and special needs are addressed, drawing from a social ecological approach.

Frones, I. (2016). *The autonomous child: Theorizing socialization*. New York, NY: Springer.
This book addresses how different perspectives theorize socialization and the genetic interplay of genetics and environments. It argues that socialization does not constitute a fixed trajectory into static social order and it offers an integrated multi-disciplinary framework for understanding the socialization process. In particular, the child is conceived as a subject, in an interplay with others in micro environments, as well as the macro-conditions of modern knowledge-based economies.

Griswold, W. (2013). *Cultures and societies in a changing world* (4th edn). Thousand Oaks, CA: Sage.
This book focuses on the role that culture plays in shaping our norms, values, beliefs, and practices. Cultural phenomena, including stories, beliefs, media, art, religious practices, fashion, and rituals from a global sociological perspective are critically examined. The effects of political symbols and rituals are also examined to highlight the interplay of culture and power.

Kimmel, M., Aronson, A., & Kaler, A. (2015). *The gendered society* (3rd Canadian edn). Toronto, ON: Oxford University Press.
This book investigates contemporary gender relations and shows how gender differences are often exaggerated in society. The author also illustrates that gender is not just an element of individual identity, but also a socially constructed phenomenon. A wide range of topics are covered that address socialization processes such as gender, race and racialization, the gendered body, family life, the classroom and workplace, and media.

Pursell, C. (2015). *From playgrounds to PlayStation*. New York, NY: Johns Hopkins University Press.
In this book, the author explores how play reflects and drives the evolution of culture and the ways in which technology is shaped by and shapes people. In particular, the objects that children (and adults) play with and play on, along with their games and the hobbies they pursue, can both reinforce and challenge gender roles and cultural norms. Drawing on a wide variety of primary and secondary sources, this text informs readers how capitalist structures focus as much on leisure as they do on work and politics.

Sandstrom, K., Lively, K., Martin, D., & Fine, G. (2014). *Symbols, selves, and social reality: A symbolic interactionist approach to social psychology and sociology* (4th edn). New York, NY: Oxford University Press.
This book provides students with an engaging introduction to symbolic interactionalism by focusing on

how elements of race and gender affect identity. Interesting research topics such as self-development, impression management, identity transformation, gender play, rumour transmissions, and collective action are covered.

Recommended Websites

Life Learning: Canadian Home-Based Learning Resources
www.life.ca/lifelearningca/
Provides information and resources on topics such as unschooling, self-learning, and socialization in addition to a short history of the home-schooling movement in Canada.

Genie: Secret of the Wild Child
www.pbs.org/wgbh/nova/transcripts/
2112gchild.html
www.youtube.com/watch?v=VjZolHCrC8E&list=
PLgd-bynF6dnYxOvd_FniK83ErCxJtJj17
Originally produced as an episode in the *Nova* TV series, this 2003 TLC documentary presents the unique case of Genie, who was abused as a child and raised in complete isolation. This case study raises many questions about the great debate about nature vs nurture. Above find the links to the *Nova* TV series transcripts and a short video from TLC.

The Goffman Page
http://people.brandeis.edu/~teuber/goffmanbio.html
The Goffman Page outlines the contributions of well-known Canadian-born sociologist Erving Goffman in terms of his insightful analyses of human social interaction.

The Lawson Foundation, Healthy Active Children Program
http://lawson.ca/about
The Lawson Foundation provides programs, reports, and resources dedicated to the healthy social, educational, and physical well-being of Canadian children and youth.

Media Awareness Network
http://democraticeducation.org/index.php/library/
resource/media_awareness_network/
This is a Canadian not-for-profit centre for media literacy that helps teach young people the critical thinking skills to engage with media as active and informed digital citizens.

Ontario Federation of Teaching Parents
http://ontariohomeschool.org/socialization.shtml
The Ontario Federation of Teaching Parents provides articles and research on the socialization of home-schooled children, in addition to Web links related to various socialization issues in schools.

Key Terms

anticipatory socialization The informal adoption and rehearsal of norms and behaviours appropriate to a future aspired role or status.
gender-role socialization The process of learning the societal and cultural norms and expectations associated with being a male or a female.
generalized other This developmental stage of the self signifies how individuals become consistent and predictable in their behaviour and how people learn to view themselves from the perspective of others.

primary agent of socialization The most important transmitter of societal and cultural norms, typically the family.
reciprocal socialization The idea that socialization is not unidirectional, but a two-way process that can occur simultaneously, for example, between a parent and a child.
resocialization The unlearning of old behaviours so that new behaviours, roles, and statuses can be acquired and adopted.

secondary socialization The transmission of societal and cultural norms through the second-most important agents of socialization (after the family), such as the school, the mass media, religion, the workplace, and peer groups.

significant others Those persons who are of sufficient importance to influence an individual's sense of self, emotions, and behaviours.

socialization A lifelong process of learning in order to become a capable, functioning member of society that is shaped by institutions such as the family, peer groups, schools, and the mass media.

total institutions Any group or organization that has an almost complete, continuous control over the individual.

4 | Social Organization

DOROTHY PAWLUCH, WILLIAM SHAFFIR, AND LORNE TEPPERMAN

In this chapter you will:

▶ Learn how sociologists define the terms "status," "role," "self," and "identity"

▶ Learn how these concepts are interrelated

▶ Explore themes related to how we define ourselves and others

▶ Learn about the different sociological "sets" of people

▶ Understand how groups and cliques function inside larger organizations

▶ Learn the reasons behind the bureaucratic form of organization

INTRODUCTION

This chapter on social organization is really about two interrelated sociological concerns: how people figure out their personal identity, and how people build organizations that give them roles to play and, through those roles, develop identities.

Consider the question of personal identity. Who am I? Take a moment to think about it. Would you say that you are a woman, man, daughter, son, brother, or sister? Do you identify as a Canadian, atheist, or gay? Would you say you are working-class, Indigenous, or immigrant? Would you say that you are honest, outgoing, shy, messed up? What difference does it make how you define yourself? How do these definitions affect your experience of life? The study of "social organization" touches on two main questions: (1) How do people typically act in social groupings of different size and purpose? (2) How could we organize social groupings to increase the chances that people will achieve their collective goals? We can address these questions to a wide variety of social groupings ranging in size from (two-person) dyads to cliques, small groups, large groups, social networks, communities, and formal organizations. We will start small and build up to bureaucracies, because large and small organizations are more similar than you might think.

A FUNCTIONALIST VIEW OF STATUSES AND ROLES

Functionalists take a macrosociological perspective, which means they take a broad view of society, focusing on how societies organize themselves and persist over time. They are drawn to the part that large-scale structures or institutions, such as the family, religion, and education, play in ensuring that societies endure.

Functionalists underscore the patterned ways in which social institutions are integrated through norms—that is, on sets of socially derived expectations about appropriate behaviour in particular settings. The most important norms are learned in childhood. Later in life, people continue to act in ways that are socially approved. As they enter new social institutions, such as universities, corporations, or organizations, they learn new norms.

Norms in turn are organized around statuses and roles. **Status** refers to particular social positions that individuals hold. All positions occupied by individuals are statuses—hockey player, restaurant server, social worker, or sex trade worker. Attached to every status are one or more roles. **Roles** consist of the responsibilities, behaviours, and privileges connected with the position. In other words, roles are the action element of status. A status is something we occupy, while a role is something we play. A status describes what one is, while a role describes what one does. "Student" is a status, while studying and attending class are part of the role.

Statuses

Statuses can be ascribed or achieved. One can be born into a status or have it imposed by nature or chance; this is an ascribed status. For the most part, we have little control over whether we are young or old, male or female, black or white. By contrast, other statuses are a matter of choice. We can achieve them by seeking them out and through our own effort. In our society, most individuals can decide whether to be an entertainer, a parent, or a vegetarian.

All of us hold many statuses simultaneously. One can be a construction worker, jogger, chess player, and much more at the same time, though not necessarily all in the same situation. The cluster of statuses held by any individual at one time is called a **status set**. People continuously enter into, and exit from, statuses over their lives. Status sets are far from fixed—they are regularly reconfigured.

Roles

The roles connected with any particular status carry both rights and responsibilities. In fact, roles are often organized in such a way that the rights attached to one are linked with the responsibilities of another. Sociologists refer to this as the reciprocity of roles. Members of a sports team have the right to expect training opportunities and support from their coach, and a coach has the responsibility to provide these things; on the other hand, coaches have the right to expect commitment and effort from their players, and players are obliged to display the required level of dedication to the team. Parents and children, professors and students, and salespersons and customers are all similarly linked.

Holding different statuses, each with different roles attached, has the potential to create conflict. What happens when the behavioural expectations attached to one role interfere with those of another role? Sociologists refer to this as **role conflict**. Women trying to juggle motherhood with a career may experience role conflict. Mothering demands devotion to one's children, but work roles come with their own set of demands, including staying late or working on days off if required. To play one role well mothers may feel that they are letting down those who rely on them in their other role.

By contrast, the concept of **role strain** involves competing demands built into a single role, causing tension and stress. Multiple expectations are built into most work roles. Lawyers, for example, are expected to represent their clients but also to mentor junior colleagues, generate clients, and keep their billing hours up. As in most areas of work, lawyers often feel as though there are not enough hours in the day for them to properly fulfill their duties.

A functionalist view of roles emphasizes constraints. Although people have some control over the statuses they hold and whether or not to act out institutional roles, they have little choice in how to play their roles. Each role comes with pre-existing scripts, demands, and expectations. The scripts are more or less agreed upon and do not allow for much flexibility.

SYMBOLIC INTERACTIONISM: ROLES, SELF, IDENTITY

An interactionist view of roles is closely tied to symbolic interactionism, a perspective concerned with how social actors make sense of their worlds. From a symbolic interactionist perspective, individuals are constantly involved in assessing and defining things around them and working out how they are going to act. In contrast to the functionalist approach, which sees individuals as buffeted by outside social forces, symbolic interactionism emphasizes how individuals interact to create, sustain, and transform social relationships (Sandstrom et al., 2013). According to symbolic interactionists, human behaviour does not occur in a vacuum but arises out of how social actors define situations. The phrase "definition of the situation" was coined by W.I. Thomas and D.S. Thomas (1928, p. 572), who maintained that "[i]f men define situations as real, they are real in their consequences." The process of defining is ongoing and allows interaction to flow smoothly. Indeed, when a definition of the situation is lacking or unclear, we focus on establishing one that is satisfactory and can help guide ongoing interaction.

The symbolic interactionist approach focuses less on social structure and more on the interactive process. For symbolic interactionists, the conventional approach to roles offers a misleading portrayal of how people actually behave. Statuses and roles, for the interactionist, do not determine social interaction. Rather, they merely provide a context. While human beings make use of norms to guide their interactions, they do not blindly conform to norms. Instead, they engage in ongoing appraisals of what is going on and then act. Individuals carry around a repertoire of roles, determining which of them to use. While they may act within roles, they do so with considerable latitude and flexibility. Far from being locked into particular role configurations or structures, they have the capacity to use and play around with roles.

TIME to REFLECT

How do structural functionalists and symbolic interactionists view roles differently?

Role-taking

Two concepts that further emphasize the symbolic interactionist view are role-taking and role-making. Role-taking is the process by which we coordinate or align our actions with those of others. When we engage in role-taking, we put ourselves in the shoes of others and try to determine how they are defining the situation. What roles are they projecting, what meanings are they attaching to the situation, what course of action are they likely to follow? Role-taking also entails looking at ourselves from the point of view of others and trying to anticipate the consequences of our own plan of action. This process continues as we initiate a response. We are constantly monitoring how others are reacting and performing their roles and adjusting or fine-tuning our role performance accordingly. Or we might abandon a particular performance altogether if it is not working. These ongoing adjustments are what make joint action possible.

Role-making

In playing our roles, we do not follow rigid, predetermined, or prewritten scripts. The expectations attached to any given role provide us with a rough guideline at best. There is room for innovation and creativity. Not everyone who performs the role of student does so in precisely the same way. Indeed, there is remarkable variability in how the role is played. In this sense, the concept of role-making comes closer than role-playing to describing how we enact our roles.

Role-taking and role-making are linked. There can be no role-making in the absence of role-taking. The construction of a role is impossible without being able to view oneself from the vantage point of another. Behaviour is not simply a matter of repeating pre-set lines of a script, and roles are not merely packages of mandatory behaviour. Roles are perspectives from which people organize lines of behaviour that fit the situation.

TIME to REFLECT

How are role-taking and role-making different? How are they related?

We have stressed that symbolic interactionists see human beings as agents, actively defining the things to which they respond. Among the things we define are our selves. Our capacity to role-take means that we can treat ourselves as an object. As with all objects, the meaning we attach to our selves is not fixed but constantly changing. We acquire our sense of **self** by imagining how others see us. This is what symbolic interactionists mean when they say that individuals and society are in a dialectical relationship. Society cannot exist without individuals, but self-aware individuals cannot exist without others (society). Symbolic interactionist Charles Horton Cooley captures the interdependence between individuals and society in his concept of "the looking glass self." Others (society) are the mirror that reflects back an image of who we are.

Another interactionist, George Herbert Mead, pointed out that the capacity to take the role of others is not present at birth but acquired as we develop a self. The self is made up of an "I" and a "me." The "I" is spontaneous, impulsive, and unsocialized, while the "me" is the socialized part of the self, conscious of social norms, values, and expectations.

 The concept of the self is further explained in "Symbolic Interactionist Frame of Reference," p. 64, in **Chapter 3**, "Being Social."

Identity

If the self is an object to which we assign meaning, **identity** refers to the names we give ourselves or use to announce to others who we are. Sociologist Erving Goffman (1959) has written extensively about identity. He analyzes everyday interaction using a dramaturgical approach. Borrowing from the imagery and language of theatre, Goffman argues that every encounter is an occasion for social actors to present one or more of their social roles, much as in a stage performance. Through a process called **impression management**, actors try to shape how others will define them. University of Manitoba sociologists Daniel Albas and Cheryl Albas offer the example of university students receiving their grades on exams. Those who have done well—the aces—engage in behaviours like "sitting tall" at their desks, grinning broadly, and walking jauntily. Those who have done poorly or failed—the bombers—use these behaviours to figure out who to avoid, since they do not want to come out of the encounter looking (and feeling) lazy, irresponsible, or "dumb" (Albas & Albas, 1988).

Goffman distinguishes between *role* and **role performance**. For Goffman, *role* refers to behaviours expected of those in particular positions. By contrast, *role performance* reflects the actual behaviour of individuals acting out their roles. Goffman also divides the social world into two regions: front-stage and back-stage. In the front-stage, social actors carefully manage the presentations of themselves they project to others in the hope of creating a positive impression. A student who wishes to impress attends class regularly, participates in class discussions, and may seek out the professor during office hours. In the back-stage region, the same student is likely to be more relaxed, venting perhaps about the course content or the professor's teaching style. Back-stage behaviour is generally displayed among those with whom we share close social bonds and trust with often unflattering information about ourselves.

Identity Work

Sociologists have focused considerable attention on how identities are "created, shaped, maintained, communicated, presented, negotiated, challenged, reproduced, reinvented and narrated" (Scott, 2015). These processes are referred to as **identity work**. We project our identities using appearance, behaviours, and props of various kinds. For example, a study about the "punk" scene (Force, 2009) discovered a gendered quality to the identity work of its members. Men wear band shirts or pins and baseball caps, while women wear mainstream clothes with a subversive twist, like re-stitched seams. The messy hair look that most punks work hard to achieve is described as a "scene cut" on men and "JBF" ("just been fucked") hair on women. Talk too is a way to project or distance ourselves from certain identities. How we talk about who our friends are and what social networks we belong to gives others an idea of who we are (Anthony & McCabe, 2015).

Some identity work happens at a collective level, where individuals construct a sense of their "we-ness" on the basis of the distinctiveness of the interests, attitudes, and experiences that bind them and communicate this sense to others through self-presentation, writings, documents, videos, and other media. These collective efforts have been studied in connection with a broad range of groups including the homeless (Snow & Anderson, 1987), atheists (Smith, 2013), and Canadian Indigenous peoples (Ramos, 2006).

TIME to REFLECT

Think of a role that is central to how you define yourself; what identity work do you engage in to communicate to others who you are?

Over the past several decades, the body and identity have attracted increasing attention. Sociologists have looked at how we experience our bodies and use them to communicate who we are. Leanne Joanisse (2005) studied women who had undergone bariatric surgery for obesity. She found that when the surgery was successful, women reported that they were "new" people. Removing the layers of fat, they explained, brought out their "real" selves (2005, p. 257).

cosmetic surgery among men is rising. Atkinson links the increase to the "crisis of masculinity" or uncertainty about what it means to be a man in the face of gender equity movements, ideologies of political correctness, and attitudes of misandry (male-bashing). In an effort to create what Atkinson calls "a mask of masculinity," men are willing to subject themselves to both invasive (e.g., eyelid surgery, liposuction, hair transplantation) and non-invasive (e.g., chemical peels, hair removal, Botox collagen injections) procedures.

Social versus Personal Identities

There can be a gap between the roles we play (social identity) and who we understand ourselves to be (personal identity). Where this gap exists, we may try to distance ourselves from our roles. This role distancing work can be contrasted with role embracement—situations in which there is such congruence between roles and self-definition that we feel that we *are* our roles.

Another key concept is the authentic self. We typically become aware of our authentic self when we view ourselves as at odds with normative guidelines concerning appropriate behaviours attached to our roles. In the airline industry, for example, trainers instruct flight attendants not only in tasks such as serving meals and giving safety instructions; they train them to control their feelings and expressions in order to shape passengers' emotions, keeping them calm and satisfied. Over time, the forced

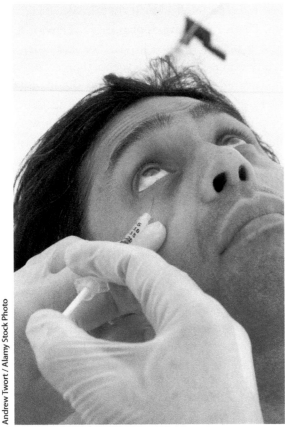

Andrew Twort / Alamy Stock Photo

It is a common misconception that only women choose to have plastic surgery. New research suggests that the way men experience their appearance is pivotal to their self-identity.

Michael Atkinson (2016) looked at men who undergo plastic surgery as a way of dealing with what they consider to be deficient (aged, overweight, unattractive) bodies. It is generally assumed that cosmetic surgery is performed almost exclusively on women. However, Atkinson presents data to show that the rate of elective

UNDER THE WIRE   The Quantified Self

There is a growing trend toward using the steady stream of newly emerging mobile apps and technological gadgets flooding the market to track and analyze one's diet, mood, habits, activities, body sensations, friendship networks, and so on. In fact, new devices and software are being developed precisely for this purpose. "Self-trackers" or "life-loggers" are taking data-gathering practices that are common in government, business, and organizations and applying them to their personal lives. They are using the data as a mirror or self-knowledge tool to gain greater awareness and insight into who they are. Do you think that the increasing digitalization of society will fundamentally change how we define and experience our selves?

For a 5-minute TED Talk on the quantified self, see www.ted.com/talks/gary_wolf_the_quantified_self.

smiles become divorced from their true feelings. The same must happen to any worker in the service sector—salespeople, teachers, or entertainers. All require emotional labour both to present themselves and to control the responses of the people they serve.

Protective Identity Work

How do we shape others' view of us in situations in which our identity or actions may invite negative interpretations? In these situations, we often offer disclaimers, accounts, excuses, and justifications. These verbal devices all fall under the category of vocabularies of motive, a concept first used by C. Wright Mills (1940) to describe the standardized forms people use to explain and excuse their behaviour. According to Mills, certain stated motives for our actions are more acceptable than others, and how we explain our actions will vary depending on whom we are talking to.

Erving Goffman (1963) too considered the consequences of others' negative views. He pointed out that negative evaluations can be based on physical abnormalities or deformities, membership in a discredited group, or behaviour that deviates from a moral standard. The related concept of courtesy stigma describes a situation in which individuals find themselves dealing with a spoiled identity not by virtue of who they are but because of their connection to someone else whose identity is tainted. Children of alcoholics, as much as their alcoholic parent(s), often find themselves dealing with the stigmatizing reactions of others.

Deviant labels are consequential, because they generally become a master status. Master status, as defined by Everett Hughes (1945), is a status that overshadows all others in terms of how others see us. Someone who suffers from mental illness is more than his or her condition. That person may be a father, mother, business owner, marathon runner. However, in most situations the person will be judged primarily on the basis of the mental illness. Hughes suggested that statuses such as gender,

race, class, and age are master statuses. For better or for worse, we generally begin our interactions with assumptions about who people are on the basis of these characteristics. Deviant statuses work in the same way in that they have the power to shape how others see and interact with us.

 See "The Process of Labelling," p. 121, in **Chapter 5**, "Deviance," for more information on deviant labels and the master status.

According to Sykes and Matza (1957), techniques of neutralization are ways of thinking that allow social actors to maintain a more positive, non-deviant identity in the face of social disapproval. Based on their research on youth offenders, Sykes and Matza identified five such techniques (see Table 4.1).

Table 4.1 ▶ Sykes and Matza's Techniques of Neutralization

Denial of responsibility	"I'm not to blame."
Denial of injury	"No one got hurt."
Denial of victim	"They deserved it."
Condemning the condemners	"Who are you to judge me?"
Appealing to a higher loyalty	"I didn't do it for me."

TIME to REFLECT

Think of a transgression you have committed—buying an essay, lying to a friend, shoplifting, drinking underage, and so on. What technique(s) of neutralization did you use?

Identity Change

Sociologists are also interested in how individuals move through statuses, roles, and identities. Anselm Strauss (1959) referred to these movements as *status passages* and to the key junctures along the way as *turning points*. According to Strauss (1959, p. 93), turning points are critical incidents that signal to individuals "I am not the same as I was, as I used to be." How these turning points are experienced depends on whether the changes are voluntary or involuntary, desirable or undesirable, important or insignificant, sudden or gradual, planned or unexpected, reversible or irreversible, and individual or collective.

The interest in understanding how these identity changes occur is reflected in a study (Shaffir, 1991) that compared the experiences of secular Jews who decide to become Orthodox Jews (*baalei tshuvah* in Hebrew) with those of Jews born into ultra-Orthodox communities who choose to pursue a more secular way of life (*haredim*). Though both processes involved a radical transformation in lifestyle, relationships with others, and self-definition, there were differences. The *baalei tshuvah* changed their behaviours before completely redefining themselves. Outwardly, they adopted the appropriate behavioural trappings of Orthodox Judaism, including dress, language, study, and prayer, while inwardly they were still realigning their understanding of themselves. This sequence was reversed for the *haredim*, who took on a more secular lifestyle only after going through a process of questioning their authenticity as part of the *haredi* community.

The process of exiting from a social role and shedding an identity has also been studied. Helen Rose Ebaugh (1988) compared the experiences of various sorts of "exes": those who had exited occupational roles (ex-students, ex-nuns, ex-doctors, retirees), family roles (divorcees, mothers without custody of their children), and deviant roles (ex-convicts, ex-alcoholics, and transsexuals). She developed a model that divides the exiting process into four stages. The process starts with first doubts or individuals questioning the roles and identities that they have taken for granted. These doubts can be precipitated by disappointments, burnout, organizational changes, or changing relationships with others. The second stage, seeking and weighing alternatives, involves considering options, weighing the pros and cons, seeking out new reference groups, and in some cases

rehearsing new roles. In the third stage, turning point, individuals decide that there is no turning back and are ready to "announce to the world" that they have left an old role behind. In the final stage, creating an ex-role, individuals adjust to the new self-definitions, working out how to manage such issues as dealing with one's own and others' expectations attached to the hangover identity.

TIME to REFLECT

Think of a role that you have exited. Do Ebaugh's four steps describe your experience?

Now we turn to the discussion of **social forms**, through which people express their personal identities in social settings.

A founder of sociology, Georg Simmel, defined social interactions and social forms—the essential features of groups and organizations—as the basic subject matter of sociology. Simmel noted that these two elements are only distinguishable analytically. For groups, social interactions are the purpose or motive of interaction. For organizations, social forms are the *forms* through which the interaction communicates its meaning. This is important, as these distinctions mark the differences between groups and organizations—although they work similarly, groups and organizations have differences in size and purpose.

Fashion is a good example because it speaks to both interactions and form at the same time. Fashion is one form through which people display themselves in a way that (they feel) displays their individuality. As such, fashion can be considered a social form. Yet fashion, by nature, is social. The group as a whole decides what is in or out of fashion. Individuals themselves cannot make fashion—they can only select from it and try to personalize it. Indeed, fashion is created through social interactions with one another. Together, people determine what will be fashionable—also, beautiful or ugly, eye-catching or grotesque—and what will be considered passé or tasteless.

SETS OF PEOPLE, DIFFERENTLY ORGANIZED

Imagine five sets of 20 people. Call them categories, networks, communities, groups, and organizations. Sociologists study these five sets differently, because they are organized differently and have different effects on their members.

Categories

First, imagine 20 people who are unconnected with one another—say, a random sample of Canadian 19-year-olds. They are all different, but because they have one thing in common (their age), we can say that they fit into an (age) **category**. If they represent the attitudes and behaviours of 19-year-olds across the country, this category of teenagers would be of interest to sociologists. This is because if we analyze their attitudes and behaviours, we may help predict future behaviour, or explain current behaviour, of 19-year-olds.

Often, categories become sociologically interesting only when people dramatize (or socially construct) meanings for the differences between one category and another. Can you think of any big differences between the categories of 18-, 19-, and 20-year-olds? These groups have no meaningful distinguishing features between them. To be 19 is not much different than to be 20. However, socially constructed differences do exist between the categories named "male" and "female," "young" and "old," and, in some societies, "white" and "black." As a result, these categories assume social importance. Also, these distinctions can carry problematic cultural connotations: males are often seen as more powerful than females, old people are often seen as more rational than young people, and white people can hold more privileges in society than black people. Unfortunately, certain categories can carry sexism, ageism, and racism along with them.

Networks

Generally, sociologists are more interested in what they call social networks. Imagine the same 20 people all connected to one another, whether directly or indirectly. By direct connections, we mean links of kinship, friendship, and acquaintance. Indirect connections also interest sociologists. These are people to whom we are linked only through our direct connections to other people: for example, our best friend's boss or our girlfriend's mother. In fact, some sociologists, such as Mark Granovetter (1974), argue that weakly tied networks, based largely on indirect links, may be even more useful than strongly tied or completely connected networks. This is because, surprisingly, information, social support, and other valuable resources flow more through weakly tied networks than through strongly tied networks.

Nicholas Christakis, an American physician and sociologist, has created a fascinating body of work on network-related imitative behaviour, showing the range and power of this mode of analysis. One of Christakis' most widely cited articles, "The Spread of Obesity in a Large Social Network over 32 Years" (2007), reports that a person is more likely to gain weight if another person in their social network is obese. Christakis found that obese people were generally clustered within a social network—that is, tended to associate with one another—but they did have associations with others who were not originally obese. A non-obese person's likelihood of becoming obese increased by 57 per cent if one's friend was obese, 40 per cent if one's sibling was obese, and 37 per cent if one's spouse was obese.

Moreover, an individual's weight was more likely to be influenced by someone of the same sex, especially among pairs of friends. Similar findings were reported in Christakis's study of smoking prevalence, "The Collective Dynamics of Smoking in a Large Social Network" (2008). Here, Christakis found that although the prevalence of smoking has decreased, clusters of smokers remained the same size across time. This suggests that people quit in groups, if they quit at all. Put another way, quitting smoking is very much influenced by the behaviour of other people in your social network. For example, a

GLOBAL ISSUES   Digital Activism in a Changing World

While youth have always been idealistic and eager to change the world, advances in communication technologies (especially social media) and the ease of travel have created new possibilities. Young people are more likely to be linked to individuals, communities, cultures, and organizations across the world and to think of the entire globe as an arena for self-expression and social action. The role of the digital activism of young people in the series of political revolutions that started in 2011, referred to as the Arab Spring, is well recognized. In writing about that phenomenon, DeLong-Bas (n.d.) has observed that youth are developing a collective identity as change-makers. The "lost generation" is becoming the "miracle generation." "Perhaps the greatest sense of empowerment," DeLong-Bas writes, "has come through the ability to use cyberspace as a location for doing what could not otherwise be done in reality: assemble to discuss ideas, concerns, and complaints, and to share frustrations, while also providing the social networking opportunity to unite, strategize and plan for change" (n.d.). Consider as well the impact of the digital activism of youth on such movements as Black Lives Matter and Idle No More.

person's chances of smoking decrease by 67 per cent if their spouse stops, 25 per cent if their sibling stops, and 25 per cent if their friend stops smoking. To generalize, collective pressures influence individual behaviour. However, some people in networks are also more likely to catch contagious diseases than others. People who are more "central," and have more contacts with a diverse set of friends are more likely to catch diseases—also, more likely to spread them.

In recent years, Internet-based social networking services such as LinkedIn, Instagram, and Facebook have rapidly increased in popularity. These services collect information from an individual's profile and their list of social contacts to create a display of their personal social network. Such networking services claim that by allowing members to "get to know one's friends of friends [they can] expand their own social circle" (Adamic & Adar, 2005, p. 188). Increasingly, people set up virtual networks in cyberspace as well as real ones. For example, people can become friends on Facebook even though they do not know each other in real life. Consider another example—people who post in the *New York Times* comment section. Regular commenters form a virtual network of acquaintances to discuss current events with. As such, they form online friendships with people that they do not know outside of cyberspace (*New York Times*, 2015).

But virtual communities go beyond that. In their 2011 book *The Tender Cut: Inside the Hidden World of Self-Injury*, sociologists Patricia Adler and Peter Adler draw on 150 interviews with self-injurers from all over the world, along with 30,000–40,000 Internet posts in chat rooms to study the 10-year evolution of a virtual community of self-injurers—people who cut, burn, and brand their bodies, and even break their own bones. Self-injury has moved from being a suicidal gesture to being a type of subcultural rebellion, turning unbearable emotional pain into tolerable physical pain. In the past people hid such behaviour; today a subculture has formed via cyberspace that shares similar norms, values, lore, vocabulary, and interests.

Social networks are important and interesting. However, much of social life is not well understood in terms of networks. That is because networks lack several key characteristics. First, people in networks lack a **community's** sense of collective identity. Second, people in networks lack a **group's** awareness of their membership and its characteristics. Third, people in networks lack an **organization's** collective goal. In what follows, we will examine communities, groups, and organizations.

In particular, we will analyze how they work and what distinguishes these social organizations from one another.

Communities

Sets of people with a common sense of identity are typically called communities. Imagine a community of only 20 people—say, a community of like-minded people living together in the country (perhaps a hippie commune in 1960s British Columbia or a utopian farming community in nineteenth-century upstate New York) or in the city (perhaps a community of anarchist or bohemian youths living in a broken-down squat in twenty-first-century Amsterdam).

What do these communities have in common? They likely comprise people who share common sentiments, or they may be people who have grown up together and share common values that differ from societal norms. Moreover, what make a community distinct? Nineteenth-century German sociologist Ferdinand Tönnies (1957 [1887]) distinguished community (rural) life, which he called

Increasingly, we spend time in Internet contact with people we know well, people we know slightly, and people we know only through friends and acquaintances.

aelitta/iStockphoto

Gemeinschaft, from non-community (urban) life, which he called *Gesellschaft*.

Gemeinschaft refers to the typical features of rural and small-town life. They include a stable, homogeneous group of residents with a strong attachment to one particular place. The

---

RESEARCHERS IN ACTION ▶ Robert Charles Prus

Born and raised in rural Manitoba, Robert Charles Prus began his studies in the sciences, but gradually became interested in sociology and social psychology. He earned his PhD in sociology from the University of Iowa in 1973. Prus credits his summer job as an encyclopedia salesman—not a particularly successful one, he says—with fuelling his interest in interactions between people. The encyclopedia industry's loss is certainly sociology's gain. Prus has influenced the sociological scene in Canada, as well as internationally, in ways that few others have. The author of over 10 books and a long list of articles and book chapters, he has become one of the most prolific and influential symbolic interactionists writing today.

Prus's research has focused on studying how people make sense of the situations they find themselves in and develop lines of action through the interactions with each other. This has meant examining people's activities, viewpoints, relationships, identities, emotions, and participation in subcultures and collective events. It is easy to see, in his work, how this creation of identities and subcultures is related to the creation and maintenance of communities.

Prus's studies have taken him into the life worlds of priests and ministers, hustlers and thieves, and magicians; the hotel community and entertainment venues; marketing and consumer behaviour; and economic development. He has also studied accounts of the human lived experience in classical Greek and Latin writing. The common thread through all this work is underlying patterns across time and social worlds of how people experience their lives and organize their behaviour as individuals and as part of a collective. Prus calls these *generic social processes* (GSPs). He has paid particular attention to GSPs such as achieving identities, experiencing relationships, making commitments, and persuading others—this last one a GSP that would well serve anyone in the encyclopedia-selling business.

The Currier and Ives Foundation

American popular artists Currier and Ives captured nineteenth-century North American conceptions of "community," in this case the pleasure of sharing one another's company in a simple holiday pastime—skating on a frozen river.

Gemeinschaft is marked by dense or highly connected networks, centralized and controlling elites, and multiple social ties.

By contrast, *Gesellschaft* refers to city life. This kind of organization brings together a fluid, diverse group of residents with different personal histories and impersonal, brief relationships. They interact around similar interests, not similar characteristics or histories. They share few moral values and few moral guardians to enforce a common moral code. In short, people who live in a *Gesellschaft* are less cohesive and, largely for this reason, less controlled.

Tönnies saw *Gesellschaft* (city life) as an example of non-community living. Do you agree? Sociologists debate whether city life represents a loss of community, or, rather, a *new* kind of community. This is because most sociologists today believe that people are not as isolated and atomized in large cities as once thought. Indeed, most city-dwellers form small communities based on friendship, whether they are residentially close or scattered.

Groups

Groups are another form of social organization, and what makes groups distinct is that all group members are aware of their *membership* in the group. Members are connected with one another (directly or indirectly) and to varying degrees communicate, interact, and conduct exchanges with one another.

Sociologists have long distinguished between primary groups and secondary groups (Cooley, 1962 [1909]). Primary groups are small and marked by regular face-to-face interaction—for example, a family. Secondary groups are larger, and many members may not interact with one another regularly.

All small or primary groups have similar characteristics and patterns, whatever their purpose or goal. For example, they are all based on intense, face-to-face interaction, and the members tend to identify with one another. Indeed, as people identify closely with the group, they may find it hard to leave or betray it.

Teams, bands, and gangs (let's use the abbreviation TBG) are three types of larger groups. Unlike families, they do not always command our primary social loyalty. However, many people consider the teams, bands, and gangs they belong to almost like surrogate families. TBGs are very similar, despite the different goals of their members. Each TBG has a clear set of goals and main activities as well as a leadership structure. One or more leaders have the responsibility to set goals, mobilize resources to achieve these goals, and motivate members to take part, according to group rules. TBGs also have a simple political structure (with leaders and followers), legal system (with procedures to resolve conflicts), economy (with a treasury and assets), and culture (with a shared memory of great events, heroes, and villains).

The influence of group membership is especially evident in the realm of deviant behaviour—for example, binge drinking. People—especially young people—tend to drink as much as they think is normal in their group. If they think it is cool to binge drink, they will emulate the behaviour, even if it hurts them physically or undermines their studies. So, efforts to get students to drink more sensibly and moderately will fail unless they address the group dynamic that makes excessive drinking seem like not just normal behaviour, but ideal.

Secondary groups, though less strongly integrated, are no less important. We spend most of our waking hours as members of secondary groups, where we interact, communicate, and exchange resources with other people. Secondary groups can include our school friends, work colleagues, or members of a team sport. Can you think of any secondary groups you participate in?

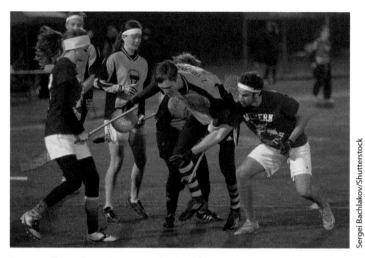

Teams at Simon Fraser University play Quidditch, the game popularized by the Harry Potter books. Are these teams primary groups or secondary groups? Justify your answer.

Like primary groups, secondary groups bind people in fairly stable patterns of social interaction. Formal organizations are subtypes of secondary groups. In turn, bureaucracies are subtypes of formal organizations. So in the end, almost everything in this chapter—except the discussion of cliques—is about secondary groups.

Organizations

Organizations are secondary groups with a collective goal or purpose. Examples of organizations include giant multinational corporations (like General Motors), small convenience stores, political parties, churches, school, or sports clubs. Given the endless variety of organizational forms and the millions of specific examples, what do all organizations have in common?

Every organization comprises a group of people who work together, through communication and leadership, to achieve a common goal or goals. At the same time, organizations have many variations. For example, organizations may come together spontaneously or deliberately. The division of labour within organizations may be crude or complex. The communication and leadership may be informal or formal. Organizations may have a specific goal or various loosely related goals.

TIME to REFLECT ⊸

Organizations vary widely in size and purpose. Why, then, do sociologists want to lump them together and generalize about them, despite these variations? What do they have in common that is worth remembering?

One important distinction to make about organizations is between spontaneous and formal organizations. A spontaneous organization arises quickly to meet a single goal, and then disbands when the goal is achieved. Bucket brigades and search parties are two common examples of spontaneous organizations. They each have a single goal—for example, to keep a barn from burning down, or to find a lost child. Each arises spontaneously, and its leaders emerge informally, without planning. Each has a crude division of labour—for example, to fill buckets, pass them along, and empty them on the fire. Moreover, each disappears when the job is completed. Mobs, such as those formed to riot in Vancouver after the final Stanley Cup game in 2011, also fall into the category of spontaneous organization. Cliques are also spontaneous organizations, but they tend to persist over time and have no obvious reason to exist.

Cliques mainly exist to exclude people from membership, thereby raising the value of being a member. Why is clique membership more critically important to teenagers than to adults?

CLIQUES

Defining the Clique

Organizations with unstated goals and/or little division of labour are considered informal organizations. One familiar example is the clique. Dictionaries define *clique* as "a small exclusive set," a "faction," a "gang," or a "noisy set." In current sociological thinking, a clique is a group of tightly interconnected people—a friendship circle whose members are connected to one another, and to the outside world, in similar ways. Clique members spend more time with one another than with non-clique members, share their knowledge, and think and behave similarly. In short, cliques are built on friendship and the exclusion of "outsiders." They survive largely through what psychologist Irving Janis (1982) called "groupthink."

Though seemingly without goals, cliques have an unstated "mission" or purpose: popularity—to raise the status of clique members at the expense of non-members. Though cliques lack an organizational chart or stated division of labour, school cliques (for example) have a clear hierarchy of influence and popularity, with the leader on top surrounded by his or her favourites. In this sense, then, a clique is clearly an organization: a group of people who work together to achieve a common goal.

Cliques in School Settings

Cliques are not only organizations: they are communities and miniature societies. In cliques, for the first time, children learn the rules and expectations of society outside their family home. Through games and play with clique members, children internalize the beliefs, values, and attitudes of their group. By these means, children also form judgments of themselves. For example, they learn what it means to be "good-looking," "sexy," and "popular," to be chosen or passed over.

Cliques, though often supportive, can also offer excellent examples of structured cruelty. It was perhaps unavoidable that the reach of cliques would extend into cyberspace. Online

SpeedKingz/Shutterstock

bullying by clique members is a new phenomenon and potentially just as damaging as face-to-face bullying. With online or e-bullying, youths can constantly harass their victims through text messages or online posts.

The cohesion of a clique is based both on loyalty to the leader and on loyalty to the group. This loyalty, in turn, is based as much on exclusion as it is on inclusion. Clique members use gossip to reinforce their ignorance of outsiders and keep social distance from them.

BUREAUCRACIES

Formal Organizations

Organizations are formal if they are deliberately planned and organized. Within formal organizations, roles and statuses provide the skeleton for all communication and leadership. Often, formal organizations have multiple goals, and they usually have a long lifespan. The Roman Catholic Church is a formal organization that has lasted nearly 2,000 years.

We can define a formal organization as a deliberately planned social group that coordinates people, capital, and tools through formalized roles, statuses, and relationships, in order to achieve a specific set of goals.

The most successful form of organization in the past century or so has been the bureaucracy. The word calls to mind images of red tape, books of rules and regulations, inefficient and unwieldy groups moving at a tortoise-like pace. To sociologists, however, bureaucracies are merely formal organizations that thrive everywhere in modern societies because they are relatively efficient and effective.

The Emergence of the Bureaucratic Form of Organization

It was obvious to Max Weber—the first sociologist to study bureaucracies—that this form of organization held enormous advantages over earlier organizational forms. Because of its formal characteristics, bureaucratic organization holds the potential for rational planning.

Bureaucracies can state clear goals, plan team strategies, train the most able people, mobilize the needed resources, evaluate effectiveness, and carry out organizational improvements. This makes IBM or the Canadian Forces (see Figure 4.1), both bureaucracies, very different from the Italian mafia or the court of Louis XIV, which are patron–client organizations—that is, organizations founded on favouritism (or kinship) and lacking written rules. And, people in organizations—whether devised for educational, religious, governmental, or military purposes—feel very differently depending on whether they are at the top or the bottom.

The Characteristics of Bureaucracy

Weber (1958c [1922]) identified seven essential characteristics of bureaucracy in his classic work on the topic:

- division of labour
- hierarchy of positions
- formal system of rules
- reliance on written documents
- separation of the person from the office
- hiring and promotion based on technical merit
- protection of careers

Division of Labour

In earlier eras, individual workers handcrafted a commodity from start to finish. Gradually, this production process gave way to specialization (the creation of many different, more specific, tasks) and the technological takeover of division of labour. Specialization became the foundation for modern industry and bureaucratization. An automotive assembly line is perhaps the typical modern example of such a division of labour.

As on an assembly line, every member of a bureaucracy performs a certain duty. The bureaucracy itself provides the facilities and resources to carry out these duties. Workers use equipment they do not own; in other words, as Marx notes, they are separated from the means of production.

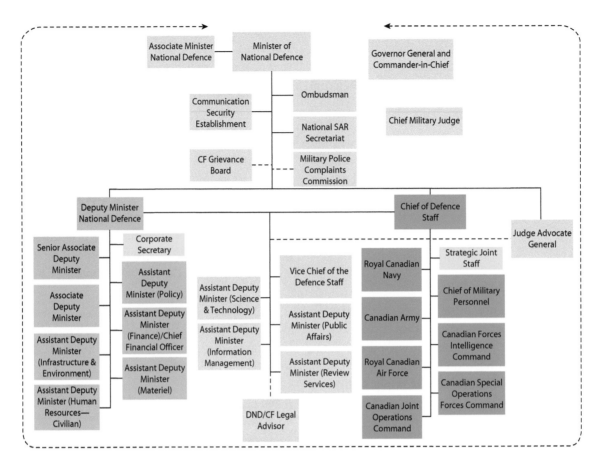

FIGURE 4.1   Organizational Structure of the Canadian Forces, 2015

Bureaucracies are hierarchical organizations—i.e., organizations with many levels or ranks—and many written rules. No wonder people at the bottom of a large bureaucracy may feel very small.

SOURCE: © All rights reserved. Reproduced with the permission of DND/CAF 2017

Hierarchy of Positions

We can imagine the structure of an organization as a pyramid, with authority centralized at the top. Authority filters down toward the base through a well-defined hierarchy of command. Within this hierarchy, each person is responsible to a specific person one level up the pyramid and for a specific group of people one level down.

The organizational chart of any large corporation is shaped roughly like a Christmas tree. The number of workers increases as you move down toward the bottom of the hierarchy. With the other characteristics of bureaucracy, this feature serves to increase efficiency: all communications flow upward to "control central" from large numbers of workers "at ground level."

Formal System of Rules

Bureaucracies also rely on, and work according to, written rules. The rules allow a bureaucracy to classify the countless circumstances it routinely confronts. For each situation, decision-makers can find or develop a rule that provides for an objective and impersonal response. Therefore, rules guarantee impersonal, predictable responses to specific situations. In turn, rules help organizations achieve their objectives.

Separation of the Person from the Office

In a bureaucracy, each person is an office-holder in a hierarchy. The duties, roles, and authority of this office all are clearly defined. For example, an organization spells out the duties of a Level 3 manager in relation to a Level 4 manager (her superior) or a Level 2 manager (her subordinate). Thus, the relations between positions in a bureaucracy are impersonal relations between roles, not personal relations between people. So, personal feelings between colleagues are subordinated to the impersonal demands of the office. This separation of person and office means that people are replaceable functionaries. People come and go, but the organization remains intact.

Hiring and Promotion Based on Technical Merit

An ideal bureaucracy hires employees impartially. Decisions are made based on candidates' technical competence, not on inborn features like gender, race, or ethnicity. Promotion is based on technical competence, or sometimes seniority. People are neither discriminated against nor favoured because of their personalities or connections to the boss.

Protection of Careers

The final characteristic of bureaucracies is that people's careers are protected within them. People can look forward to long careers in a bureaucracy, because they are not subject to arbitrary dismissal for personal reasons. As long as they follow the rules attached to their office or position, they are secure in their job.

Merton's Bureaucratic Personality

Sociologists have found that often bureaucracies do not behave rationally in terms of their long-term interests and survival. This occurs for several reasons.

First, there is the issue of "bureaucratic personalities." As sociologist Robert Merton (1957) pointed out, bureaucracies force their members to conform to rigid bureaucratic rules. This pressure, combined with intensive training, overemphasizes knowledge of and adherence to these rules. In turn, this makes it easy for bureaucrats to act in routine ways. Inevitably, the routines become similar to "blinkers" on a horse—bureaucrats stick to their rules, even when they do not work, or are unfair to others. Moreover, bureaucrats can be loath to change rules. As Merton argued, bureaucrats develop a "trained incapacity" to deal with new situations.

Also, the existence of rules means that bureaucrats have to classify all situations with objective criteria. The result is that bureaucrats often fail to see both employees and clients as people with unique wants and needs, and instead see them only as impersonal categories. This viewpoint causes bureaucrats to fail to meet the unique needs of individual employees and clients.

Informal Organizations in Bureaucracies

A bureaucracy is intended to be an impersonal form of organization; however, bureaucratic roles are filled by actual people. As human beings, workers resist becoming faceless cogs in the bureaucratic machine (replaceable cogs at that). So, within formal organizations, employees develop complex personal and informal networks, informal organizations, and even cliques.

Informal networks among people who interact on the job serve many purposes. First, they humanize the organization. They also provide support and protection to workers at the lower levels of the hierarchy. They serve as active channels of information flow (the grapevine) and mechanisms to exchange favours. Paradoxically, informal networks can serve to free people from the limits of formal organization and, occasionally, allow them to protest and change their working conditions for the better.

HOW BUREAUCRACIES ACTUALLY WORK

Weber's idea of bureaucracy is a useful model for studying this complex form of organization. However, it is an idealization.

Ideally, every member understands his or her role in a bureaucratic network of reporting relationships. In graphic form, a bureaucracy is a Christmas tree–shaped structure that repeatedly branches out as you go down the hierarchy. Thus, at the bottom of the hierarchy there are many people whose job it is to carry out orders from above and report work-related information up the tree to their superiors. At the top of the hierarchy, a few people issue orders, process information received from below, and preserve links with other organizations.

In practice, organizations do not work this way. There is the ideal or formal structure, which prescribes how a bureaucracy ought to work, and there is the actual, informal structure, which is how it really works.

Actual Flows of Information

In theory, a failure to report information up the hierarchy would never occur. In practice, it occurs all the time. Moreover, sometimes people purposely subvert the flow of information as a means to change the power balance between superiors and subordinates. For example, workers may use information to help one another. Sometimes they may even leak information for personal gain or to subvert the boss or the organization as a whole.

Bureaucracies also appear to work differently for men and women. When playing a managerial role, women often adopt a collaborative approach that draws on qualities learned in family relations. Women's managerial styles stress good employer–employee relations and sharing information and power. By contrast, men are more likely to stress purely rational or economic considerations (Occhionero, 1996).

As the French sociologist Michel Crozier (1964) showed, bureaucracies work differently in different societies. This is because people raised in different cultures have different ideas about inequality, deference, openness, and secrecy.

TIME to REFLECT

Can you explain Crozier's findings that people raised in different cultures, with different ideas about inequality and secrecy, behave differently in bureaucratic organizations? How might this fact affect the operation of multinational organizations?

Many organizations function in environments where distrust is routine and justifiable. When information is a matter of organizational survival, secrecy, security, and intelligence strategies become vital.

An increasingly critical problem is the effect of secrecy on science. The scientific community has historically relied on norms of objectivity and open sharing of scientific information. However, national security and corporate interests increasingly infringe on these norms of openness. The public has an interest in an open scientific establishment, so that it can democratically discuss the values and interests that science is serving. While scholars may disagree about the extent of the problem, the need remains to clarify the ownership of intellectual property and the conditions of free intellectual flow.

Governments frequently use secrecy to gain political or economic advantage. Reconciling publicly declared goals of freedom of information, the right to privacy, and national security poses problems for democratic societies. For example, Britain's Official Secrets Act forces civil servants to promise never to reveal anything deemed an official secret; ironically, some employees do not even know what secrets they are supposed to safeguard.

Secrets—in government and business, as in private life—are a currency of exchange. People, organizations, and even nations hoard secrets so that they can trade them. The belief in and quest for secret information creates elaborate structures, procedures, and mechanisms, the most familiar of which are spy organizations like the CIA, MI5, and the KGB.

TIME to REFLECT

What are some the benefits of secrecy in government or business organizations? What are some costs or potentially harmful consequences? Do the benefits usually outweigh the costs?

The Problem of Rationality

Over the long term, through impersonal decisions and rewards for excellence, bureaucracies are able to pursue strategic goals with huge amounts of wealth and power.

However, the sheer size of large bureaucracies and their long-term outlook introduces certain types of irrationality that may also undermine the organization. A concern with the long-term survival of the organization may undermine shorter-term concerns with the quality of decisions, products, and services the organization provides to its customers. Equally, research has shown that large bureaucratic organizations are as likely to imitate other organizations, simply to follow organizational fashion, as they are to innovate for internal reasons. This process is discussed in work on institutional isomorphism, beginning with a classic study by DiMaggio and Powell in 1983.

In the late nineteenth century, a prominent French social scientist, Gabriel de Tarde (1903), proposed that two master processes shape all social life: innovation and imitation. All other processes and their resulting social patterns can be traced to these two. Not surprisingly, then, we see examples of organizational and political imitation in a wide variety of situations. Organizations imitate one another because it is cheaper, easier, and safer to imitate than it is to invent new ideas, technologies, and practices. Imitation also increases legitimacy and the chances of success.

To be sure, imitation can be problematic, given that different institutions have different needs, and adopting an ill-fitting process can lead to inefficiency rather than improvement. However, some organizational research suggests that imitating the practices of current institutions on the whole increases both the survival prospects and the legitimacy of a new institution. Once bureaucracies adopt practices or policies, they are often slow to change them. For instance, Lowry (2008) suggests that public bureaucracies are reluctant to alter long-standing policies even if doing so would enhance efficiency. Instead, bureaucracies want to avoid the backlash that often arises when attempting to alter practices with deep historical roots.

A large body of literature demonstrates the inefficiencies and irrationalities of bureaucratic organization, contrary to Weber's supposition that bureaucracies are (and would inevitably be) more rational than other forms of organization. In fact, it would not be an exaggeration to say that most sociological literature about bureaucracy is concerned with the nature of this paradox: that an organization designed to be rational and predictable is, more often than not, neither of these. In large part, this is because bureaucracies do what they must in order to survive, even at the expense of their original goals.

What's more, the gap between the theoretical, rational ideal and the actual, irrational functioning of bureaucracies has been exacerbated in recent decades. With the advent of globalization and the development of a "post-capitalist society," there has been pressure on bureaucracies to transform themselves in order to cope with some of the dramatic changes in the economic and political environment. Some scholars believe that traditional bureaucracies will become obsolete and unable to cope, and that a new organizational structure will emerge: one that "liberates" employees from hierarchical "constraints" and increases their ability to cope with a rapidly changing world order.

Since the end of World War II, organizational imitation has increasingly gone global, with the globalization of the world's economy. Imitation is generally asymmetrical, meaning that influence flows from the most powerful down to the least powerful people (or organizations) in the network. That is another way of asserting the truth that, in the social world, there are inequalities of influence, just as there are inequalities of power, wealth, authority, and prestige.

During the same period, the global diffusion of organizational practices has taken many forms. Some are purely cultural while others are financial and organizational: for example, currency devaluations with global consequences, free-trade agreements (e.g., NAFTA), free-trade zones (e.g., the European Community), and the widening of military alliances (e.g., NATO's opening its membership to states in Eastern Europe).

The world's financial system has become structurally interlocked due to high-speed, high-stakes international finance, the growing availability of tax havens, and a diversity of free-trade areas. Multinational corporations, international humanitarian organizations, and a global recognition of refugee, drug, debt, environmental, and terrorist problems have all accelerated this process of globalization and global imitation.

Whether we are talking about the world as a whole or particular parts of the world, we have witnessed increasingly organizational complexity. As a bureaucracy grows, and more rules are added, the system becomes increasingly complex. This can lead to a situation in which no one person knows all the rules. Then, different offices act independently of each other and create rules that conflict with one another. As such, the bureaucratic system can become out of control, as a few examples below will show.

Total Institutions

Total institutions are the ultimate bureaucratic organizations, as they control large numbers of people, 24/7. Examples of total institutions include mental hospitals, prisons, residential schools, and military installations. Although these organizations seem very diverse, they have many things in common (Goffman, 1961). True, they have different institutional goals and provide different services to society; they also employ different kinds of experts and oversee different kinds of "customers." However, what they have in common far outweighs these

differences: through the extreme and expert control of human inmates, they are able to bring about *identity change* through degradation. Often, through harmful practices, mental institutions change patients from "sick" to healthy, prisons change inmates from criminals to law-abiding citizens, residential schools change Indigenous children from "wild Natives" to "civilized Christians," and military training camps change soldiers from ordinary citizens to disciplined, hardened combatants. Susie Scott (2011) has recently extended the idea of total institutions to look at the growing phenomenon of individuals who voluntarily commit themselves to places that confine and control them around the clock—like rehab or meditation centres and spiritual communities—in order to pursue a regimen of self-improvement. The circumstances may be different and techniques may be more humane in these settings, but the goal (identity change) is the same.

What Goffman tells us about mental institutions and prisons reminds us of life in totalitarian societies like Nazi Germany and Soviet Russia. Under both Nazism and communism, people were dominated by uncontrollable rulers through government and party bureaucracies. It turns out that totalitarian societies are like Goffman's "total institutions," only larger. So, it is not surprising that totalitarian societies make liberal use of total institutions to punish, brainwash, and resocialize uncooperative citizens.

Often, they do this without adverse publicity, let alone public condemnation. Large organizations often punish whistleblowers—employees who bring forward valid information about wrongdoing or illegal conduct—for criticizing the organization. Even organizations that publicly claim they want employees to "participate" and those that pledge to uphold high ethical standards may move to discredit or dismiss the whistleblower out of fear that information about waste, fraud, or abuses of power will harm the organization or its executives.

As a result, so-called collective decisions, typically taken by the top executives of bureaucracies, are liable to be foolish, harmful, or even

Provincial Archives of Saskatchewan, R-A8223-1, A-8223-2

Like other bureaucracies, and especially like other total institutions, residential schools saw their job as controlling and re-socializing people who did not fit the norm. In this case, they set out to change young Indigenous children who did not dress, talk, and think like young white Canadians. A first step was to change how they dressed.

criminal. In corporate and government bureaucracies, information control, norms, rewards, and the actions of organizational elites may encourage deviant—even criminal—behaviour and lead to socially undesirable outcomes. For one thing, no one in the organization may have enough information to evaluate the decisions taken or understand why people have taken them. Executives actively discourage or even prevent subordinates from gaining this information.

As Weber warned, modern bureaucratic society is an "iron cage": our ambitions for success, efficiency, and progress trap us (1958a [1904], p. 181). Bureaucracy has enormous potential for enslavement, exploitation, and cruelty. It also has enormous potential to promote human progress. For example, it can promote economic development and scientific discovery, high-quality mass education, or the delivery of humane social services to the needy. However, in order to fulfill our potential for human progress, we unfortunately often risk our potential for enslavement, exploitation, and cruelty. For example, think of exploitation of Third World workers to produce technological devices and name-brand clothing. We use enslavement, exploitation, and cruelty in developing countries as a means to create human progress in developed countries. Because of this, there is debate as to whether our not our societal gains justify the means. What do you think?

CONCLUSION

If sociology is the study of the relationship between the individual and society, there is no question more central than how our statuses, roles, identities, and sense of self connect us to others. Our goal has been to discuss how sociologists have defined and thought about these concepts. We also sought to introduce readers to the types of sociological studies that these concepts have generated.

We started with structural functionalists, explaining the emphasis on statuses, roles, and the more or less predetermined role scripts attached to them. Symbolic interactionists, we went on to explain, reject a view of social actors as mere role players, stressing instead the agency that individuals exercise in deciding what roles to take on and how to play them.

This chapter has also reviewed various "sets" of people, including categories, networks, communities, groups, cliques, and organizations. Sets of people with a common sense of identity are typically called communities. Communities, whether urban or rural, real or virtual, are important because people are conscious of their membership and make personal investments to remain members. Formal organizations combine many of the features of networks, groups, cliques, and communities.

The main form of the large, powerful, and long-lived formal organization of the twentieth century is the bureaucracy. The goals of bureaucracy are maximum efficiency and productivity. Largely, bureaucracies achieve their desired goals in the expected ways, but they do so with unwanted side effects.

Finally, this chapter considered total institutions. All of them are organizations that have total control over those they administer, whether mental patients, nuns, convicts, soldiers-in-training, or addicts. Total institutions offer an extreme example of the bureaucratic organization and the bureaucratized society.

Questions for Critical Thought

1. Thinking about the connection between gender and role performance, can you describe how this relationship is shaped by cultural, political, and social contexts both in our society and elsewhere?
2. Can you recall a role you played—son, daughter, boyfriend, girlfriend—that has shifted in how you have played it over time? What prompted the change(s)?
3. According to *The Globe and Mail*, many Canadians who reported no Indigenous identity in the 2006 census declared themselves in the 2011 census to be First Nations, Inuit, or Métis. What do you think accounts for this change?
4. How might Internet communities, such as comment boards or chat rooms, resemble and affect *Gemeinschaft* and *Gesellschaft*?
5. Robert Bales (1950) discovered that in discussion groups, three roles regularly emerged: task leader, emotional leader, and joker. Was he right to infer that the groups "need" these roles to survive?
6. In what ways are bureaucracies rationally and irrationally designed? What kind of organizational system do you think would work more effectively than a bureaucracy?

Sociological Explorations

1. Think of five or six cliques that existed in your high school when you were a student there. What distinguished them from one another (e.g., ways of dressing, preferred activities, or ways of speaking)? In what ways were they similar (e.g., number of members, ways of dealing with teachers, or behaviour of leader)? On balance, were they more similar than different? If so, how would you explain that?
2. Sociologist Manford Kuhn believed that while we are responsive to others, we also have a core self that we carry into our interactions and that shapes those interactions. The stability of the core self, Kuhn argued, suggests the possibility

of measurement. Kuhn (Kuhn & McPartland, 1954) developed a test for this purpose. To take Kuhn's Twenty Statements Test, put the numbers 1 to 20 down the side of a page. Next to each number answer the simple question "Who am I?" Write the answers as they occur to you and answer as if you are answering for yourself, not for anyone else.

Recommended Readings

Crozier, M. (1964). *The bureaucratic phenomenon.* **Chicago, IL: University of Chicago Press.**
Crozier, a French sociologist, shows that bureaucracies can work differently in different societies and cultures despite their similar organization. Because societies vary—historically, socially, and politically—bureaucracies vary too.

Du Gay, P. (2005). *The values of bureaucracy.* **Oxford, UK: Oxford University Press.**
This book explores why bureaucracies are such successful, and therefore persistent, organizational structures. The book outlines the characteristics that make bureaucracies efficient in various settings.

Freeman, L.C. (2004). *The development of social network analysis: A study in the sociology of science.* **Vancouver, BC: Empirical Press.**
This book discusses social networks as vast webs of connections between nodes, with huge impacts on the lives of network members.

Goffman, E. (1959). *The presentation of self in everyday life.* **Garden City, NY: Doubleday.**
This is Goffman's classic statement on the dramaturgical approach. "Must" reading for anyone interested in identity work.

Hewitt, J.P. (2006). *Self and society: A symbolic interactionist social psychology* (10th edn). **Boston, MA: Allyn and Bacon.**
This is a good introduction to the central concepts of symbolic interactionism, filled with useful examples that make the perspective accessible to anyone reading about it for the first time.

Weinberg, T.S. & Newmahr, S. (Eds) (2015). *Selves, symbols and sexualities: An interactionist anthology.* **Los Angeles, CA: Sage.**
How we define others and ourselves sexually is a significant part of our selves. This collection of original papers explores various dimensions of our sexual selves, including the experiences of asexuals.

Recommended Websites

The Mead Project
www.brocku.ca/MeadProject
A useful inventory of documents by or about the founder of symbolic interactionism, George Herbert Mead, and other symbolic interactionists is available on this website.

Technology and Self
http://sherryturkle.com/
This is the website of Sherry Turkle, director of MIT's Initiative on Technology and Self, a centre for research on how technology affects our self-explorations and social encounters.

Self-Labelling and Identity
www.youtube.com/watch?v=pxbw7dDMX60
In this video, people who have had encounters with the mental-health system describe themselves, demonstrating many of the concepts discussed in this chapter.

Society for the Study of Symbolic Interaction
https://sites.google.com/site/ssinteraction/
This website includes news about a range of conferences related to symbolic interactionism, as well as a link to the journal *Symbolic Interaction*, which regularly publishes papers on self and identity.

Temple Grandin Website
www.templegrandin.com
This is the official website of Temple Grandin, an autistic woman whose life was depicted in an HBO movie of the same name. The movie offers a good example of identity work.

Community-Based Research
http://communityresearchcanada.ca/
This website contains resources for people who support and have an interest in *community-based research*.

Key Terms

category A set of people thought to share particular characteristics.

community A set of people who live in the same place; interact frequently; share many attitudes, interests, and goals; and, as a result, share a feeling of connection with others in that set.

group A set of people who know one another by name, interact frequently, and often share one or more common activities.

identity work The dynamics by which individuals, using appearance, behaviours, talk, and props of various kinds, present themselves and construct others.

identity What we announce ourselves to be, both to ourselves and to others.

impression management A process wherein actors try to shape how others will define them.

role conflict Incompatibility among roles corresponding to two or more statuses.

role The responsibilities, expected behaviours, and privileges connected with a given social position.

role performance The actual behaviour of individuals in the enactment of their roles.

role strain Incompatibility among roles corresponding to a single status.

self Our perception of ourselves, acquired by imagining how others see us.

status A particular social position that an individual holds.

status set The cluster of statuses held by any given individual at one time.

5 | Deviance

ALICIA D. HORTON AND VINCENT F. SACCO

INTRODUCTION

This chapter has three central objectives. First, it explains how the terms **deviance** and **social control** are used by sociologists. Next, it considers some of the major problems faced by researchers who empirically investigate deviance and social control. Finally, it focuses on the major theoretical questions that underlie the study of deviance and social control.

WHAT IS DEVIANCE?

Any discussion of the sociology of deviance and social control must begin with some consideration of what these terms mean. Formal sociological conceptualizations of deviance can be contrasted with more popular views that define deviance by illustration, statistics, and harm.

By Illustration

A typical approach to defining deviance is to list people or behaviours we think deserve the label. These lists could include criminals, child molesters, drug addicts, corrupt political officials, cult leaders, liars, and others. The major problem with these stand-alone lists is that they are incomplete and tell us nothing about inclusion criteria: who goes on the list and who does not is very much a function of who is doing the listing and when and where the list is created. For example, there is wide disagreement as to whether prostitution, abortion, and marijuana use, for example, should be considered deviant.

In Statistical Terms

Statistical rarity suggests a more explicit way to define deviance. It is intuitive to identify deviance by rarity, since many of the kinds of people, acts, and behaviours we think of as deviant do occur relatively infrequently. A major problem with statistical definitions of deviance is illustrated by Figure 5.1. The area between points X_1 and X_2 represents typical performance levels across some characteristic. The shaded area on the far left represents the minority of statistically rare cases that fall well below the average.

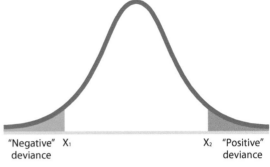

"Negative" X_1
deviance

X_2 "Positive"
deviance

FIGURE 5.1   The Normal Curve

Statistical definitions of deviance make it difficult to distinguish "negative" deviance from "positive" deviance.

For example, students who fail very badly on an examination would be represented here. We might tend to think of such people as deviants in the conventional sense of "inferior."

However, the shaded portion on the far right-hand side also suggests a statistically rare performance—but in the positive direction (Spreitzer & Sonenshein, 2004; Heckert & Heckert, 2015). It could represent students who show superior knowledge on an examination. Statistical definitions obscure distinctions between people who exceed and people who fall short of certain expectations.

As Harmful

Another familiar way of defining deviance is by equating it with action that produces destructive outcomes. Many of those who would appear on short-lists of deviants seem to be encompassed by this definitional criterion.

Graffiti is controversial: some call it art, and some call it property damage. What aspect of graffiti makes it, for some, a symbol of deviance?

Murderers, thieves, liars, sexual abusers, and wife-assaulters can all be said to be authors of real and tangible harm. However, like statistical rarity, equations of deviance with harm are fraught with difficulty because we also often disagree about that which causes harm, and because it is difficult to identify the supposed harm caused by many kinds of things and the people that might be considered deviant. For example, people with a mental-health problem may be treated as deviant, although it is difficult to ascribe harm to their differentness or document harm that they cause. In contrast, unethical politicians may be able to manage a socially benign image even though their actions might result in considerable harm to life and property. We tend to reserve the label of deviant for other categories of people (Simon, 2016).

DEVIANCE AS A SOCIOLOGICAL CONCEPT

Sociologists are interested in deviance as a product of **social interaction** and group structure; that is, we understand the study of deviance to be the study of people, behaviours, and conditions subject to *social control*—the myriad ways in which members of **social groups** express their disapproval of people and behaviour. These include name-calling, ridicule, ostracism, incarceration, and even killing. The study of deviance addresses ways of acting and ways of being that, within particular social contexts and in particular historical periods, elicit moral condemnation.

It is important to distinguish between the *objective* and the *subjective* character of deviance (Loseke, 2003b). The former refers to particular ways of thinking, acting, and being, the latter to the moral status accorded such thoughts, actions, and characteristics. From a sociological perspective, the deviant character of certain behaviours, world views, or physical features is not inherent in them, but conferred on them by society.

To be deemed deviant by a sociologist, a particular behaviour not only must hold the potential for being called deviant (e.g., unusual or rare behaviour) but also must be labelled as deviant by powerful others. Sociologists do not confuse the physical act of someone smoking marijuana with the designation of marijuana-smoking as a deviant act. Each suggests a distinct realm of experience, and each is an appropriate object of sociological attention, but why some people smoke marijuana and why others consider it deviant are indeed separate questions.

Additionally, not everything that could be labelled deviant is necessarily labelled deviant by society. Some people have greater access to resources to resist the efforts of others to consider them deviant. For example, although corporations engage in activities that undermine health or safety or weaken the economic well-being of many in society, they are able to define themselves as morally respectable by making donations to universities and hospitals or by launching public relations campaigns to promote a positive image.

> **TIME to REFLECT**
>
> Why do movies, television, and most other forms of popular culture seem so focused on deviant activities and deviant people?

RESEARCHING DEVIANCE

Research into the disvalued nature of people and behaviour often involves looking into the lives of the most vulnerable members of society. The problems discussed in this section represent challenges to all forms of social research, but special difficulties arise when the subject is deviance.

 When they embark on a study of deviant behaviour, it is crucial that sociologists choose the appropriate research method. See "Research Techniques," p. 22, in **Chapter 1**, "Sociological Theory and Research Methods," for more information on the methodological tools used in studying deviance and other sociological topics.

Safety

Researchers should take no action that could result in physical, emotional, mental, social, or economic harm to those who participate in the research. Guidelines such as these that govern research with human beings are detailed in the Tri-Council Policy Statement (TCPS2). In the case of one major survey of female victims of male violence, a safety concern arose with respect to the potential danger of abusers being present when a call was made to women and questions about violence were asked and answered (Johnson, 1996). Interviewers took several special precautions that heightened their sensitivity to stress cues.

Secrecy

Often people wish to keep their deviant behaviour a secret in order to protect themselves from social reactions. How do sociologists undertake **valid** research in a way that does not intrude excessively into the lives of those under study? One of the authors of this chapter undertook an ethnography of participants in a body modification practice called "flesh hook pulling" (Horton, 2013). This practice involves cheek skewering, sewing limes to one's back, and piercing the flesh of one's chest with hooks attached to ropes—and then pulling on them for some period of time. While highly deviant to outsiders, flesh hook pulling practitioners describe the practice primarily in terms of empowerment, spirituality, and ritual. The event is organized and carried out in secret so that the activities are shielded from public view. The researcher avoided deception and other ethical traps by collecting informed consent and respecting the group's need for secrecy by maintaining confidentiality.

Discovery of Reportable Behaviour

If research subjects confide in the researcher and reveal information about illegal or harmful circumstances, should the researcher report that wrongdoing to authorities? One the one hand, a researcher has a professional obligation to respect the confidentiality of information that research subjects divulge. On the other hand, one has a social and moral obligation to protect the safety of the public and research participants. The complexities involved in the discovery of reportable behaviour are exemplified in sociologist Sudhir Venkatesh's book *Gang Leader for a Day* (2008). The book describes how a rather standard piece of survey research in a high-crime, low-income neighbourhood led him to develop close personal friendships with local gang members and their families. As a result, Venkatesh became aware of many illegal and often violent activities in which the gang engaged.

> **TIME to REFLECT**
>
> Based on your reading, do you think that sufficient ethical safeguards are in place to protect the subjects of deviance research?

THE SOCIOLOGY OF DEVIANT BEHAVIOUR

We have defined deviance as ways of thinking, acting, and being that are subject to social control—in other words, as kinds of conditions and kinds of people that are viewed by most members of a society as wrong, immoral, disreputable, bizarre, or unusual.

Several theoretical problem areas can be identified. These include questions about causes and forms of deviant behaviour, the content and character of moral definitions, and issues that arise over deviant labels. Questions about why deviants do what they do have attracted most of the attention. However, the question "Why do they do it?" contains a number of important assumptions. It implies that most of us share a conformist view of the world in which the important thing to understand is why some deviant minority refuses to act the way "we" act, and that the moral status of deviant behaviour is never called into question. Most theoretical

OPEN FOR DISCUSSION

How Random Is Random Violence?

Mass media coverage of crime tends to focus a great deal of attention on random violence. After all, crimes such as serial murder, carjacking, robbery, home invasion, and child abduction are frightening to most people precisely because they involve elements of random threat. It is the strongly felt sense that such crimes could victimize us as easily as anyone else and that we are at risk whenever and wherever we find ourselves that makes news stories (and movies and television shows) about random violence so powerful and popular.

Despite public beliefs about the random nature of violence, sociologists have known for decades that the risks of becoming a victim of crime are anything but random. Like disease, accidents, and other kinds of negative life events, violence seems more likely to afflict some of us than others.

Sociological researchers have been able to document the "social structure of violence" through large-scale studies that ask a representative sample of the population about crimes they may have experienced during some defined period of time (e.g., the previous six months or the previous year). These studies allow the researchers to compare the profiles of victims and non-victims and therefore to identify the factors that seem to be associated with the risk of becoming a victim of violence.

In a 2014 Statistics Canada conducted a study of victimization experiences of Canadians over the age of 15 during the previous 12 months. In addition, the researchers collected a wealth of information about respondents' social, demographic, and lifestyle characteristics and about the circumstances of the crimes. Among the findings relating to the differential risk of violent victimization are the following:

- Younger Canadians were more likely than older Canadians to become victims of violence. People between the ages of 20 and 24 years are at the highest risk of violent victimization.

- With respect to marital status, single people were more likely than married people to be the victims of violence.

- Risk was also higher for those who self-identified as homosexual or bisexual than those who identify as heterosexual.

- Among persons who identified as Indigenous, rates of violent victimization far exceeded those of non-Indigenous people.

- Rates of violent victimization were lower for people who identified as a visible minority than for non-visible minorities. Rates of victimization were also lower for immigrants than for non-immigrants.

- Violent victimization was associated with higher levels of alcohol consumption.

- In about half of incidents of violent victimization (excluding violence between spouses) the victim and offender knew each other. (Statistics Canada, 2015f)

It should be noted that similar results have been produced by many researchers in many different countries. However, despite the consistency of many of these findings, they raise significant and controversial questions, which interested parties continue to debate. One such question concerns the reasons why such factors are related to an elevated risk of becoming a victim. A second question deals with the potential such research findings might have for blaming the victims for the crimes that befall them. In other words, when we start to focus on the reasons why some people rather than others are likely to be victimized, are we suggesting implicitly that they have done something to "invite" their victimization?

thought in this respect reflects the influence of functionalist perspectives. Three dominant ways of thinking about "why they do it" can be identified: strain theory, cultural support theory, and control theory (Cullen, Wright, & Blevins, 2007).

Strain Theory

Strain theory derives from the writings of the famous American sociologist Robert Merton (1938). Merton sought to understand why, according to official statistics, so many types of non-conformity such as crime, delinquency, and drug addiction are much more pervasive within lower socio-economic classes. Merton was interested in understanding the structure of society, rather than individual personalities, as the central explanatory mechanism.

The answer, he argued, resided in the mal-integration of the cultural and social structures of societies. Stated otherwise, the lack of fit between the *cultural goals* people are encouraged to seek and the *means* available to pursue these goals creates a social strain to which deviant behaviour is an adjustment. In Western societies, there is little recognition of the role that **class** barriers play in structuring social life. As a result, everyone is encouraged to pursue the goal of material success—and everyone is judged a success or a failure based on the ability to become materially successful.

When people steal money or material goods, it can be said that they are attempting to use "illegitimate means" to achieve the trappings of success. When they take drugs (or become "societal dropouts"), they can be interpreted as having withdrawn from the competition for stratification outcomes. For Merton, these problems are most acute in the lower social classes, where people are most likely to experience the disjuncture between the things to which they aspire and the things actually available (see Table 5.1).

Merton's argument has greatly influenced the way sociologists think about the causes of deviant behaviour (Laufer & Adler, 1994; Cloward & Ohlin, 1960).

Robert Agnew (1985, 2006) has theorized that in addition to the inability to achieve the things we want in life, a second source of strain involves an inability to avoid or escape some negative condition. For example, youths who cannot avoid abusive parents might use drugs, run away, or become aggressive as a way of coping with this strain. Strain can also result

Table 5.1 ► Robert Merton's Paradigm of Deviant Behaviour

Robert Merton argued that there are five ways of adjusting to a social structure that encourages large numbers of people to seek objectives that are not actually available to them.

	Attitude to Goals	Attitude to Means	Explanation/Example
Conformity	Accept	Accept	Most people accept as legitimate the culturally approved ways of achieving those goals. In Merton's example, most strive for material success by working hard, trying to get a good education, etc.
Innovation	Accept	Reject	The bank robber, drug dealer, or white-collar thief seeks success too but rejects the conventional means for achieving that success.
Ritualism	Reject	Accept	Some people seem to simply be going through the motions of achieving desired social goals. In large organizations, we use the term "bureaucrat" to describe people who are fixated on procedures at the expense of outcomes.
Retreatism	Reject	Reject	Some people adjust to strain by "dropping out" of the system. Such dropping out could include losing oneself in a world of alcohol or illegal drugs or adopting some unconventional lifestyle.
Rebellion	Reject/Accept	Reject/Accept	Rebellion includes acts intended to replace the current cultural goals (and means) with new ones. In this category we might include the radical political activist or even the domestic terrorist.

when individuals lose something they value. A child who is forced to move and thus leave important friendships might experience this type of loss strain. These arguments share an explanatory logic that focuses on how the organization of our social relations can create problems that require solutions. In this paradigm, the causes of deviant behaviour are located in patterns of social life that are external to but affect the individual.

Cultural Support Theory

According to **cultural support theory**, people behave in ways that reflect the cultural values to which they have been exposed and then internalize. Writing in the 1930s, sociologist Edwin Sutherland (1939, 1940) proposed that people become deviant as a result of exposure to learning experiences that make deviance more likely. People end up deviant in the same way that they end up as stamp collectors, saxophone players, and skateboarders—that is, as a result of exposure to influential learning experiences. According to Sutherland, an individual who becomes deviant must first learn to think about the deviant conduct as acceptable. For instance, we most commonly refrain from committing murder not because we do not know how but because we define such action as morally repugnant. For Sutherland, learning to accept or to value criminal or deviant action in a very real sense makes such action possible.

Sutherland's cultural insights help us to understand how people come to value actions the rest of a society might despise. Yet, society simultaneously condemns and supports deviant behaviour. Is it possible, then, both to believe in and to break important social rules? Most of us think that stealing is wrong but have also stolen something at some point. This is possible because we have learned to define certain deviant situations as ones to which the rules do not apply. When we steal a pen from work, we tell ourselves (and others) that we are underpaid

Behaviours such as excessive drinking are not always "deviant" from a statistical standpoint. Among young men, many risk behaviours (such as binge drinking) are celebrated as signs of masculinity and group conformity.

and deserve whatever fringe benefits we can get, or that employers expect people to steal and build this cost into their budgets. From this perspective, the broader culture both condemns deviance and makes available cognitive techniques for neutralizing the laws that prohibit deviant action (Maratea, 2015; Shigihara, 2013; Matza & Sykes, 1957).

Cultural arguments have been very influential in the sociological study of deviant behaviour (Akers & Jensen, 2003) and have proven more useful than strain arguments in making sense of so-called "respectable crimes" such as corporate crimes, music piracy, and hacking (Ingram & Hinduja, 2008; Chua & Holt, 2016). One may argue that **corporate crime**, at least to some extent, is rooted in a "culture of competition" that legitimates organizational wrongdoing (Calavita & Pontell, 1991). Cultural arguments can also illustrate how certain forms of "everyday" deviance are normalized in smaller-scale workplace thefts. For example, Shigihara (2013) recently conducted a study of theft among restaurant workers and found that many of the employees she interviewed drew on linguistic techniques to neutralize the deviance associated with stealing from employers. "Hooking up" friends and loyal restaurant patrons with free drinks to "keep them happy," for instance, suggests a dominant moral code that extends beyond the context of the restaurant (Shigihara, 2013, p. 501).

Control Theory

Advocates of **control theory** argue that people lie, cheat, and steal when and if they are free to do so and if these activities can be the fastest or easiest way of getting what they want. The important question is not "Why do some people break rules?" but "Why don't more people break rules?" For control theorists, deviant behaviour occurs whenever it is allowed to occur, so we can expect to find deviance when controls are weak or broken.

This idea can be traced to the writing of Émile Durkheim (1951 [1897]). In his classic study of suicide, Durkheim sought to explain variation in suicide rates among groups and across time. Catholics, he found, had lower suicide rates than Protestants, and married people had lower rates than single people. Suicide rates increased both in times of economic boom and during depressions. What is varying in all of these cases? Durkheim suggested that the crucial variable might be social regulation (or *social control*) that forces people to take others into account and discourages behaviours that are excessively individualistic. In short, suicide is more likely when people are disconnected from social regulation and left to their own resources.

Travis Hirschi (1969) attempted to use social control logic to explain the conduct of youthful offenders. For Hirschi, the problem of juvenile crime could be understood in reference to the concept of the bond to conventional society. Each of us, to a greater or lesser degree, has a connection to the world of conventional others. For youth, the world of conventional others is represented by parents, teachers, and members of the legitimate adult community. Hirschi reasoned that if youthful bonds to conventional others are strong, youths need to take these others into account when they act; if the bonds are weak, they are free to act in ways that reflect

much narrower self-interest. While theories of the bond have been eclipsed by later theoretical developments, the idea that deviance is a product of weak links to conventional society continues to attract attention (Church, Wharton, & Taylor, 2009; Ford, 2009).

In 1990 Hirschi collaborated with Michael Gottfredson to propose a general theory of crime and deviance (Gottfredson & Hirschi, 1990). This theory posits that crimes of all types tend to be committed by people who are impulsive, short-sighted, non-verbal risk-takers. The underlying social-psychological characteristic of such people is low self-control. These people are more likely to commit crime and to engage in a wide range of deviant practices (Weisner & Rab, 2015; Baron, 2003; Kerley, Xu, & Sirisunyaluck, 2008). For example, low self-control has been linked to many non-criminal forms of deviance including the provision of fictitious answers on survey questionnaires (Meldrum, Piquero, & Clark, 2013), use of profanity, "drunk dialling," and public flatulence (Reisig & Pratt, 2011).

TIME to REFLECT

Do you think that some explanations, such as strain theory, can be faulted for excusing deviant behaviour?

The Transactional Character of Deviance

Despite their sociological character, strain, cultural support, and social control arguments tend to focus attention on the individual.

Familiar explanations of murder focus on the murderous acts of the individual (see Figure 5.2 for homicide rates in Canada). Sociologists might try to understand how people who commit murder do so in response to social strain (Eriksson & Mazerolle, 2013; Levin & Madfis, 2009) or as a result of an affiliation with a culture of violence (Wolfgang & Ferracuti, 1967). Other theories encourage us to understand deviant behaviour—even murder—not as an individual outcome, but as a collective product that results from particular kinds of social interactions.

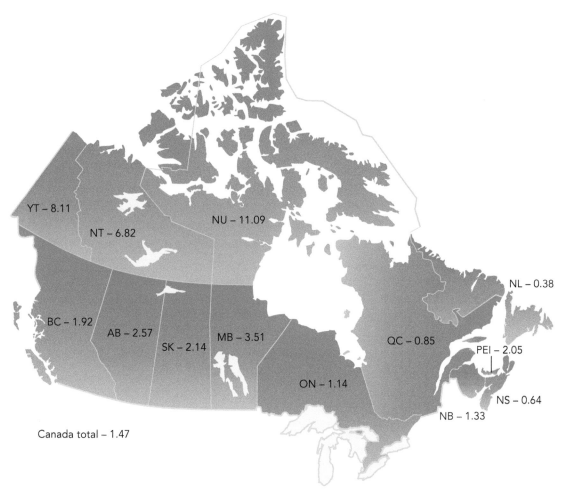

FIGURE 5.2 Provincial Variations in Rates of Homicide
(Number of Homicides per 100,000 population), 2014

For reasons that are not entirely clear, the rate at which the situated transaction we refer to as homicide occurs varies from province to province.

SOURCE: Statistics Canada 'Homicide offences, number and rate, by province and territory' 2014. http://www.statcan.gc.ca/tables-tableaux/sum-som/l01/cst01/legal12a-eng.htm

David Luckenbill (1977) has demonstrated that murder can in many cases be understood as a **situated transaction**, an interaction sequence between participants in a common physical territory. Based on a study of 70 homicides in California, Luckenbill identified six common stages of murder:

- *Stage 1*. The transaction starts when the eventual victim does something that the eventual offender could define as an insult or as an offence to "face." The victim might call the offender a liar,

refuse to share a cigarette, or make a sexually suggestive comment about the offender's partner.
- *Stage 2*. The offender defines what the victim has said or done as threatening or offensive.
- *Stage 3*. The offender makes a countermove intended to respond and save face. This could involve a verbal response or a physical gesture.
- *Stage 4*. The victim responds in an aggressive manner. A working definition of the situation as one that will require a violent

resolution seems to be emerging. The problems may be aggravated by onlookers who jeer the participants, hold their jackets, or block convenient exits.

- *Stage 5*. A brief violent exchange occurs. It may involve a fatal blow, stab, or gunshot.
- *Stage 6*. The battle is over; the offender flees or remains at the scene.

Luckenbill's work demonstrates how murder can be understood as a social product. This does not imply an absence of guilt or excuse for killing; rather, it shows that acts of deviance can involve complex and significant interactional dimensions.

Sociologist Randall Collins (2008) has addressed the role played by situational factors in the development of troublesome behaviour. He argues that in violent situations, people are tense and afraid of being hurt and hurting others. For example, researchers consistently find that many soldiers in battle do not fire their weapons but do exhibit signs of extreme trauma (Grossman, 2009). Because the driving force is much more emotional than rational, the eruption of violence depends on a variety of conditions that shape how people negotiate emotional tension.

According to Collins, one of the main pathways around confrontational tension and fear involves identifying and attacking a weak victim. This strategy applies across a wide range of situations, including military raids, violence during arrests, domestic violence, and bullying. Another strategy is making third parties the focus of emotional attention. In these situations observers play a key role in affecting the course of the violent exchange. For violence to be successful, it must turn emotional tension into emotional energy.

Considering these arguments, some suggest that it is more useful to think of murder and other forms of deviance as "social events" rather than the acts of individuals in isolation (Sacco & Kennedy, 2011). Crime as a social event implies much more than bad behaviour. The outcome of a homicide event is contingent not only on the "killer's" actions but on such factors as the actions of the bystanders, whether those involved are alone or with friends, and the response time of the police. For example, Kennedy and Forde have proposed a "routine conflict theory" of violent interactions which suggests that violent interactions can be understood as existing and emerging from everyday interactions. They argue that "incremental choices" are made during the course of our social interactions and that these series of choices can lead to either positive or negative outcomes, including violence (Kennedy & Forde, 1999).

From this perspective, much of violent crime can be understood as a collective product produced through social interaction as opposed to that which results from the intentions or motivations of a single party to deviant and criminal events.

TIME to REFLECT

Are theories of situated transaction guilty of victim-blaming?

MAKING SENSE OF THE "FACTS" OF DEVIANT BEHAVIOUR

Sociologists have repeatedly demonstrated that deviant acts are not randomly distributed in the population. Instead, people with certain social and demographic characteristics are much more likely to be involved in deviant behaviour than others. The task of sociologists of deviance is to explain these levels of differential involvement.

Sex and Age

Sex correlates closely with a wide range of deviant and other behaviours. Males and females differ in terms of the amount and types of disapproved behaviours in which they engage. Males are much more likely to be involved in criminal and

Table 5.2 ▶ Male and Female Involvement in Cases Completed in Adult Criminal Court (raw numbers and percentages), by Type of Crime, Canada, 2013–2014

	Female	Male
Violent Criminal Code violations	13,720 18%	63,445 82%
Property crime violations	21,326 28%	55,676 72%
Other Criminal Code violations	1,861 18%	11,684 86%
Total Criminal Code violations	58,080 20%	227,948 80%

SOURCE: Adapted from data in Table 4 of Ashley Maxwell, "Adult criminal court statistics in Canada, 2013/2014," Statistics Canada (2015), http://www.statcan.gc.ca/pub/85-002-x/2015001/article/14226-eng.pdf

socially disapproved behaviour (see Table 5.2). Males are more likely to consume both legal and illegal drugs (Health Canada, 2009), to commit suicide (see Table 5.3), and to use guns or explosives to do it (Langlois & Morrison, 2002). While there has recently been a narrowing in the gap between male and female offending, crime remains a male-dominated activity (Sacco & Kennedy, 2011).

Age is strongly associated with many kinds of deviant behaviour (Tanner, 2015). Crime rates are greatest during the late teens and early adulthood and decline very sharply after that (Sacco & Kennedy, 2011). For instance, in terms of domestic violence young husbands (those under 30) are much more likely than older husbands to treat their wives violently (Mihorean, 2005).

Table 5.3 ▶ Suicide Rates by Sex and Age (rates per 100,000)

All ages[1]	11.1	11.5	11.6	11.3	11.3
10 to 14	1.2	1.3	1.7	1.6	1.8
15 to 19	9.2	9.0	8.9	9.2	10.2
20 to 24	11.2	11.9	12.2	13.0	12.1
25 to 29	11.2	11.0	11.3	11.1	11.4
30 to 34	11.6	13.2	12.7	13.0	11.6
35 to 39	13.7	14.4	15.0	13.3	12.8
40 to 44	17.6	17.4	15.1	15.4	15.5
45 to 49	17.0	17.6	18.0	16.2	17.5
50 to 54	16.6	18.5	18.5	17.5	17.1
55 to 59	15.7	16.7	16.9	17.0	17.6
60 to 64	12.4	12.8	13.8	12.4	13.4
65 to 69	10.8	9.8	10.3	10.1	10.5
70 to 74	10.8	11.3	10.6	11.5	11.1
75 to 79	11.1	9.0	11.3	11.5	9.3
80 to 84	10.1	10.8	11.0	11.1	9.9
85 to 89	10.7	13.1	11.9	11.8	11.1
90 and older	10.9	9.3	8.6	5.0	8.1

[1.] "All ages" includes suicides of children under age 10 and suicides of persons of unknown age.
SOURCE: Statistics Canada, CANSIM, table 102-0551 'Suicides and suicide rate, by sex and by age group'. http://www.statcan.gc.ca/tables-tableaux/sum-som/l01/cst01/hlth66a-eng.htm

Class and Ethnicity

A great deal of sociological theorizing about the "causes" of deviant behaviour concerns how social and economic precariousness is related to deviant outcomes. Research indicates that poorer people and people from minority groups are more likely to be involved in many forms of crime and delinquency, use drugs and alcohol, and develop various kinds of mental illness. Minority-group status seems to be related to higher rates of crime in some cases—for example, with **First Nations** people—but lower in other groups such as Asian immigrants in British Columbia (Gordon & Nelson, 2000; Brzozowski, Taylor-Butts, & Johnson, 2006; Perreault, 2009). However, a consensus in the research literature does not exist regarding how we should measure concepts such as poverty, economic inequality, ethnicity, or minority-group status (Daley, Burton, & Phipps, 2015; Braithewaite, 1979; Wortley, 1999).

Still, we need to ask whether poorer or minority people more likely to be deviant, or are they just more likely to get caught and be labelled as deviant? Do our definitions of what constitutes crime and deviance themselves reflect class biases? Poor people, for instance, are less likely to commit many kinds of crimes, such as fraud and embezzlement, and even less likely to manufacture faulty products, engage in false advertising, profit from political corruption, or become involved in stock-market swindles. These observations suggest a need to ask questions about the subjective character of deviance. Why are some ways of thinking, acting, and being more likely than others to excite indignation and disapproval? Why do particular people become the objects of social control?

THE SOCIOLOGY OF DEVIANT CATEGORIES

The sociology of deviance is the study of moral stratification. To call something or someone "deviant" is to articulate a judgment that the thing or person is disreputable. An important set of issues in the sociology of deviance relates to the creation of deviant and non-deviant categories into which people and actions are sorted (Loseke, 2003b; Best, 2013).

We tend to treat categorical distinctions as common sense. The deviant qualities of people and acts, we convince ourselves, reside within the people and acts themselves. However, from the perspective of **social constructionism** (Miller & Holstein, 1993; Spector & Kitsuse, 1977), this logic is flawed. Acts and people are not inherently deviant but are defined as such by those with the power to do so. This perspective maintains that there is nothing self-evident or commonsensical about the deviant quality of people and their behaviour. Instead, the deviant quality assigned to people and behaviour is itself problematic and requires investigation.

Further, we need to recognize that the character of social condemnation changes over time (Curra, 2016). For example, a relatively short time ago being gay might have been considered in some contexts grounds for social exclusion, but in the contemporary mainstream it is seen as much less deviant. Similarly, many ways of acting or being that were once tolerated now seem to draw considerable disapproval. A clear example is cigarette-smoking (Bell et al., 2010; Evans-Polce et al., 2015; Stuber, Galea, & Link, 2008; Tilleczek & Hine, 2006). Only a few decades ago, people smoked in elevators, restaurants, around children—even in sociology classes. Today, smokers are the object of scorn, and their habit is the subject of a variety of forms of legal and extra-legal control (McNabola & Gill, 2009; Wigginton & Lee, 2013). Other examples of behaviour for which social tolerance has decreased are drinking and driving (Asbridge, Mann, & Flam-Zalcman, 2004) and sexual harassment (Lopez, Hodson, & Roscigno, 2009).

Deviance as a Claims-Making Process

Social constructionist writers understand the distinctions that people make between deviant and non-deviant behaviour as part of a **claims-making** process (Best, 2013; Spector & Kitsuse, 1977). This refers to the process by which groups assert grievances about the troublesome character of "other" people or behaviours. Claims-making can include many different sorts of activities, such as debating sexual practices on a daytime talk show, marching in protest, or providing expert testimony before a parliamentary committee. Claims-making promotes certain moral visions of social life. It is anything anybody does to propagate a view of who or what is deviant and what needs to be done about it (Loseke, 2003b).

Claims-making is directed toward three broad types of objectives:

(1) *Publicizing the problematic character of the people with the behaviour in question.* People generally need to be convinced that there is some tangible reason to regard others as troublesome. Claims-makers may endeavour to convince us that deviants are dangerous or irresponsible or that their behaviour is contagious (Best, 2013).

(2) *Shaping a particular view of the problem.* It matters greatly whether we see people as troubled or as troublesome (Gusfield, 1989). Generally, claims-makers want to convince us that certain people are a problem—and a problem of a particular type. Different constructions have very different implications for what it is we think needs to be done.

(3) *Building consensus around new moral categories.* Claims-makers endeavour to build widespread agreement about the correctness of a particular moral vision (Macek, 2006). This is accomplished by winning the support of the media, officialdom, and the general public (Best, 2013). As consensus is built, dissenting views are relegated to the margins of legitimate discourse, and deviant categories take on a common-sense character.

Illegal behaviours such as marijuana-smoking are common among young people. Some believe that marijuana use should be decriminalized, since non-enforcement of the law brings all law into disrepute.

Who Are Claims-Makers?

Howard Becker (1963) coined the term "moral entrepreneur" to describe claims-makers who "discover" and attempt to publicize deviant conditions. These are crusading reformers who are disturbed by some perceived evil and who will not rest until something is done about it.

In the early stages, definitions of deviance are often promoted by those with some direct connection to the problem. For instance, claims-making members of MADD (Mothers Against Drunk Driving) had a powerful emotional stake in initial efforts to criminalize drunk driving (Reinarman, 1996). Still, many involved in the construction of deviance have no vested interest in or emotional connection to the problem or outcome. Lawmakers, journalists, daytime talk-show hosts, and the producers of television drama frequently play a significant role in the promotion of particular designations of deviance (Sacco, 2005). Of course, the Internet has also shaped the nature of claims-making activity and arenas (Maratea, 2015).

What Are Claims?

When social constructionists speak of *claims*, they are talking about the actual message content that conveys a moral vision of deviance and non-deviance. Claims are communications intended to persuade audiences. Successful claims-making rhetoric demonstrates the gravity of a problem in several ways:

- *Using compelling statistics.* Statistics impress upon media consumers the size of a problem and its escalating severity (Best, 2013). Statistical estimates of this nature legitimate concern and provide compelling evidence of a problem's urgency.
- *Linking an emergent concern to problems already on the public agenda.* Familiar moral language can be used to provide reference points for emergent problems; new social problems can piggyback on more familiar constructions (Loseke, 2007). Addiction is widely recognized as a problem in North America and the term has been used in a very liberal way to convey problems of "pornography addicts," "gambling addicts," and "Internet addicts" (Butters & Erickson, 1999).
- *Using emotionally compelling examples to typify the seriousness and character of the threat posed by the behaviour* (see Bromley & Shupe, 1981; Loseke, 2009). For example, the 1999 Columbine High School killings are applied in a rhetoric to exemplify the problem of school violence, even though such incidents are extremely rare and most school crime in no way resembles this incident (Fox & Levin, 2001).

Deviance Ownership

As stated, claims-making is a matter not only of seeing particular types of people or behaviour as problems but of seeing them as particular *kinds* of problems (Gusfield, 1989). What is at stake is problem "ownership," and how a problem is framed determines who will be responsible for dealing with the problem (Sasson, 1995). For example, Liu and Blomley (2013) consider the way that news media frames the Downtown Eastside in Vancouver, British Columbia. The authors found the area is problematized in news media with criminalization, medicalization, and socialization frames. Each *frame* presents the Downtown Eastside as a particular type of problem requiring a particular group of people to provide a solution.

Vancouver's Downtown Eastside. What kind of "frame" of homelessness do you think this photo presents? How might middle-class people and homeless people try to frame the topic differently?

The criminalization frame implies that the area is "crime ridden," requiring intervention by criminal justice representatives and so on. Frames are important tools in the social construction of deviance because they persuade audiences to think about problems in certain ways and identify who should be responsible for solving problems.

Deviance and Social Conflict

Disagreement over who or what should be considered disreputable is reflected in the battle over abortion, the movement to legalize marijuana, and changing prostitution laws. Conservative and radical **conflict theories** suggest different ways of understanding the wider context of the claims-making process (Williams & McShane, 2013). Conservative conflict theorists view social conflicts regarding the moral meaning of conduct as emerging from diverse sources (Turk, 1976). As members of various ethnic, religious, professional, lifestyle, or cultural groups pursue their social interests, conflict can erupt over competition for scarce resources. From this perspective, the study of moral differentiation is the study of how some groups in society are able to influence systems of social control and more effectively compete in the struggle to achieve their goals.

In contrast, radical conflict theory draws on the Marxian understanding of society (Spitzer, 1975). It views the economic organization of society as the key to understanding moral stratification. The social construction of deviance must be understood as reflecting the economic realities of capitalism and the class exploitation it engenders. From this perspective, the internal logic of capitalism gives deviance both its objective and its subjective character. Capitalism requires a large pool of labour that can be exploited by keeping wages low. This means that there will always be more workers than jobs and some people will inevitably be marginalized. These populations have little stake in the system and are at greater risk of criminal labels and involvement.

TIME to REFLECT

In what ways does the study of claims-making reflect power dynamics between groups of people in society?

The Sociology of Deviant Stigma

A third key area of study in the sociology of deviance is **stigma** application and management (see, for example, Table 5.4). This body of research and theory focuses attention on the social interaction between those who exercise social control and those who are thought of as disreputable. In this respect, questions about the application and consequences of deviant stigma tend to be more micro- than macro-sociological.

The Process of Labelling

Deviant labels are charged with a great deal of emotion. Such labels sort through the thousands of acts in which a person has engaged and indicate that the person's identity is best understood in terms of the act according to which the label is affixed (Erikson, 1966).

Table 5.4 ▶ Types of Deviant Behaviour

Howard Becker (1963) suggested that once we recognize that deviant stigma is separable from deviant acts, it is possible to recognize at least four types of deviants. These types are created by the contrast between what people actually do (break rules or keep them) and how they are perceived (deviant or not deviant).

		Behaviour	
		Obedient	Rule-breaking
Perception	perceived as deviant	falsely accused	pure deviant
	not perceived as deviant	conforming	secret deviant

The assignment of stigma suggests what sociologists refer to as a **master status** or deviant label that overrides all other status considerations (Becker, 1963). Being known as a murderer trumps any other status characteristics the person might have (bright, interesting, poor, blonde, left-handed). Sociologists use the term **status degradation ceremony** to refer to the rituals during which the status of "deviant" is conferred (Garfinkel, 1956). Status degradation ceremonies, such as incompetency hearings, psychiatric examinations, and courtroom trials, mark the movement from one social position to another by publicly and officially acknowledging a shift in social **roles** and the emergence of a new, deviant identity.

Resistance to Labelling

The ability of some in society to confer the status of deviant on others reflects differentials in social power. People with access to power resources are able to more effectively negotiate the status of deviant (Pfuhl & Henry, 1993). One obvious method involves efforts to undermine social control through *evasion*. "Successful" deviants learn to engage in prohibited conduct in ways that decrease the likelihood of getting caught (Becker, 1963).

Others negotiate stigma through *performance* (Goffman, 1959). The dramatic roles we might perform when stopped by a police officer for speeding are part of a performance intended to neutralize the efforts of police to impose a deviant designation (Piliavin & Briar, 1964).

Deviant Careers and Deviant Identities

One potential consequence of the labelling process is *deviancy amplification*: the situation wherein the very attempt to control deviance makes deviance more likely (Lemert, 1951; Tannenbaum, 1938). Efforts to describe this usually distinguish between primary and secondary deviance (Wiley & Esbensen, 2013; Lemert, 1951). *Primary deviance* is that in which we all engage that has no real consequence for how we see ourselves or for how

other people see us. From time to time all of us might lie, cheat, or engage in some other prohibited behaviour. *Secondary deviance*, in contrast, suggests a deviant identity. While any of us might tell an occasional lie, most of us do not think of ourselves or are not thought of by others as liars.

Societal reaction to primary deviance leads to secondary deviance. One argument is that the ways in which agents of social control respond to initial acts of deviance—through stereotyping, rejection, and the degradation of status—can actually make future deviance more rather than less likely (Markin, 2005). One of the key intervening mechanisms in this process is the transformation of the **self**. Consistent with social-psychological theories, such as the one advanced by Charles Horton Cooley (1902), labelling theorists argue that individuals who are consistently stigmatized may come to accept others' definition of their deviant identity. To the extent that individuals increasingly come to see themselves as others see them, they may become much more likely to behave in ways that are consistent with the label of deviant. Individuals become committed to a life of deviance largely because others expected them to—deviance becomes a self-fulfilling prophecy (Tannenbaum, 1938).

Managing Stigma

Various strategies may be employed to control information about a deviant identity or to alter the meaning of stigma so as to reduce the significance of the deviance in a person's life (Durkin, 2009; Adler & Adler, 2015; Savio, 2016).

Canadian Sociologist Erving Goffman (1963) made an important distinction between the *discreditable* and the *discredited*. The former refers to people who might become discredited if their stigma were to become public. Conversely, discredited stigma is either evident or assumed to be known.

For the discreditable, stigma management involves a pressing need to control information others have about them. People with a hidden stigma face the constant worry that others they care about may reject them if information about this stigma becomes public (Elliot & Doane, 2015; James & Craft, 2002). For instance, those suffering from stigmatized diseases might keep this aspect of their life secret because they fear rejection (Rassin, 2011).

The discredited person's stigma tends to be apparent, so there is no need to keep it secret. Rather, the discredited attempt to restrict the stigma's relevance or try to change the way that other people treat them. They may attempt purification by trying to convince others that they have left a deviant identity behind (Pfuhl & Henry, 1993). One of our contemporary definitions of a hero is someone who has left a deviant stigma behind. Helen Keller and Terry Fox, for instance, were thought of as heroic largely because they rose above the stigmatizing character of physical conditions.

 For more discussion of stigma associated with disease or disability, see "Interpretive Theory," p. 207, in **Chapter 9**, "Families and Health Issues."

The discredited may also invoke collective stigma management by joining together to form associations intent on changing public perceptions of their disvalued character. Organizations intended to "undeviantize" behaviour include the National Organization for the Reform of Marijuana Laws (NORML); the National Association to Advance Fat Acceptance (NAAFA); and COYOTE (Call Off Your Old Tired Ethics), which promotes the rights of sex workers. Collective stigma management may involve attempts to influence media coverage of the group in question or the terms used to describe its members (Bullock & Culbert, 2002).

TIME to REFLECT

If deviance is a source of stigma, why are so many kinds of deviants in our society (e.g., gangsta rappers, misbehaving actors, and athletes) treated like celebrities?

Some cultural forms, such as drag and other forms of gender performance, occupy a changing or borderline status. Forms like these are stigmatized in some contexts but entirely acceptable in others; in any case, they do not yet conform to what the mainstream sees as "normal."

DEVIANCE AND POST-MODERNISM

Post-modernism suggests a more recent theoretical trend. Post-modernist theorists of crime and deviance study the way in which language works to marginalize and stigmatize people who come into contact with the criminal justice system or are otherwise labelled deviant. Language is a part of what post-modernists, and other theorists, call *discourse*—large, specialized units of knowledge (such as the scientific, legal, and medical languages) made up of any number of modes of communication.

For post-modern criminologists, that which is criminal or deviant can be understood as resulting from the capacity of powerful groups—such as lawmakers—to discursively control the behaviour of less powerful groups. Dominant discourses reflect the interests and values of those with the power to have their version of truth normalized or accepted. Normative modes of discourse inform popular notions of what is morally superior or true, while minority views go unheard.

When the meaning of language is taken for granted, it reflects the ability of one group to impose its will on others. By *deconstructing* or breaking down binaries created by language

RESEARCHERS IN ACTION ▶ Michael Atkinson

Michael Atkinson is a Canadian scholar whose contributions have addressed tattooing and body modification practices among other topics. His book *Tattooed: The Sociogenesis of a Body Art* (2003b) describes 10 years of work with tattoo enthusiasts in Canada. In it, Atkinson details how his interest evolved from a personal curiosity to an academic pursuit. Here, he recounts his experience receiving his first tattoo:

> . . .[it was the] first significant agreement I had ever made with my skin. . . . I felt exhilaration, nausea, and a recurring twinge of shame. But at the end, I was tattooed. . . . My first academic encounter with tattooing occurred . . . [during] a course in the sociology of deviance, [when] I read a piece from Clinton Sanders' well-known work, *Customizing the Body: The Art and Culture of Tattooing* (1989). . . . I eventually decided to pursue a small study of tattooing for a course in qualitative methodology during my Master's degree research. I quickly learned that sociologists, psychologists and the majority of cultural anthropologists writing on the subject had advanced no description of what Canadians were doing with tattoos. (Atkinson, 2003b, pp. vii–viii)

Since this initial observation, Atkinson has published numerous empirical articles that address Canadians' experiences with tattooing and deviance. His work shows how tattoo collectors celebrate this "difference" and how tattoos become part of a collective and individual response to negative social sanctioning. In particular, his work illustrates how tattooing is folded into stigma management strategies alongside linguistic techniques of disclosure and justification.

Atkinson's contributions highlight the importance of tattooing as a tool in stigma management and social problems work. A poignant example is found in his research on tattooing among members of the Straight-edge subculture in Canada, who reject what they perceive to be "hedonistic" body practices that characterize North American culture: promiscuity, substance use, and alcohol consumption. Straightedgers emphasize purity and bodily restraint as an alternative lifestyle and incorporate tattoos as signifiers of this resistance and commitment to a "clean" and "controlled" life. Atkinson's work reveals that "Straightedge corporeal resistance through tattooing is discursively arranged as a controlled and rationalized form of dissent" (2003a, p. 215).

The intersection between stigma, tattooing, and gender is a second important theme. Atkinson's article *Pretty in Ink: Conformity, Resistance and Negotiation in Women's Tattooing* (2002) raises interesting questions for the sociology of deviance in terms of how women use tattooing to signify association with an "established" or "outsider" construction of femininity. The paper reveals that Canadian women feel pressure to modify their bodies for the pleasure of men, and that many of their tattoo projects reflect either gender conformity or a negotiation that neither accepts nor rejects mainstream norms of femininity. He notes that "the flamboyantly tattooed woman's body tends to elicit negative responses from established others" (Atkinson, 2002, p. 233), yet some women challenge these reactions through their tattoo projects. This raises another important question for sociologists of deviance: "Does the campaign for resistance through tattooing further entrench these women into the status of the outsider?" (Atkinson, 2002, p. 233).

Michael Atkinson is a significant Canadian figure in the sociology of deviance in Canada because his work provides an example of the distinct ways in which sociologists think about deviant behaviour. Drawing our attention to struggles to define tattooing as deviant or conforming, his work reveals that "indelibly marking the body with ink . . . is a deeply individualistic yet highly social act" (Atkinson, 2003b, p. 215).

SOURCE: Atkinson, Michael. 2003b. Tattooed: The Sociogenesis of a Body Art. University of Toronto Press.

Some women try to challenge notions of mainstream femininity through tattooing, while others wonder if such challenges further reinforce the stigma surrounding a tattooed woman's body. What do you think?

UNDER THE WIRE — Deviance in Movies

Crime, delinquency, and deviance permeate movies, television, music videos, the Internet, and other arenas of popular culture. Films about serial killers, gangs, mental illness, or drug-trafficking, for example, speak to the nature of disvalued action by presenting images that morally evaluate people and behaviour. Because movies, television, and magazines play a significant role in defining deviance, it is crucial to consider how popular culture constructs certain groups and people as troubled or troublesome (Gusfield, 1989) and blameworthy or praiseworthy (Loseke, 2003a).

For instance, in films, prostitution is almost uniformly depicted as a dangerous, degrading, and devalued line of work that prostitutes ought to "escape." Prostitutes are depicted as routinely raped (*Leaving Las Vegas*), held captive and drugged (*Eastern Promises*), verbally abused (*Hustle & Flow, Deuce Bigalow: Male Gigolo, Pretty Woman*), cut with knives (*Unforgiven*), spat on (*Mysterious Skin*), and killed (*From Hell, The Dead Girl, Very Bad Things, Four Rooms*). In the movies, the problem of violence against prostitutes is often presented as an individual problem. In other words, the victimization that prostitutes are subjected to is constructed as originating with some personal deficiency that prevents them from leaving the trade. Characters who continue to prostitute end up being jailed, executed, or murdered (*Monster, The Dead Girl*), whereas others avoid repeat victimization by getting married, finding conventional, legitimate employment, or otherwise leaving prostitution (*Mighty Aphrodite, True Romance, Deuce Bigalow: Male Gigolo*).

Prostitutes' rights groups such as COYOTE argue that violence against prostitutes results from the legal prohibition of acts of prostitution in Canada, which implies that prostitutes are "bad women." They claim that the problem of violence against prostitutes is perpetuated by unsafe working conditions and negative cultural attitudes toward sex work. This problem is understood as originating with the legal prohibition of prostitution; thus, part of the solution is to change the law to make safer working conditions for sex workers and to apprehend those who perpetrate violence against them. Popular film, however, constructs this problem in a very different way. It tends to build a consensus around the problem of violence against prostitutes by implicitly claiming it is an individual problem that requires prostitutes to do something about their situation. It excludes explanations of the problem that shift responsibility to social institutions such as the legal system.

As you have learned in this chapter, what we perceive as the solution to a problem depends greatly on what type of problem we understand it to be. To be competent media consumers, we must learn to think critically about the taken-for-granted character of deviance and social problems in popular culture and the often one-dimensional nature of problems and solutions that it presents.

(such as male/female, rational/irrational, deviant/conforming), post-modernists illuminate the way in which categories privilege the truth claims of some groups over others by defining the behaviour of powerless groups as abnormal or criminal (Arrigo, 1999).

CONCLUSION

Our experience with deviance reflects the influence of the cultural context and the historical period in which we live. As times change, so do the categories of people and behaviour society finds troublesome. While gay and lesbian people were once viewed as deviants, today they are seen as less so. Drunk driving, wife assault, and cigarette-smoking were once regarded as normal; they are now viewed as highly deviant. Deviance is thus a dynamic process, and the future will present further permutations and innovations. By way of example, we need think only about the large number of newly constructed forms of deviance that we already associate with computer use, such as cyberporn, cyberstalking, and Internet addiction.

In the most general terms, the sociology of deviance is concerned with the study of the relationships between people who think, act, or appear in disvalued ways and those who seek to control them (Sacco, 1992). It seeks to understand the origins, character, consequences, and broader social contexts of these relationships. Deviance can be thought of as having objective and subjective dimensions. A comprehensive sociology of deviance needs to consider both elements; we want to know why some people rather than others act in ways that society forbids and why some ways of acting rather than others are forbidden.

Several major types of questions organize theory and research in the sociology of deviance. First, how do we understand the social and cultural factors that make prohibited behaviour possible? Strain theory argues that people engage in deviant behaviour because it is a form of problem-solving; cultural support theories focus on the ways in which people acquire definitions of deviant conduct that are supportive of such behaviour; and control theories maintain that deviance results when the factors that would check or constrain it are absent.

Second, what is and what is not viewed as disreputable is not obvious, and there is a need to explain the prevailing system of moral stratification. Definitions of deviance emerge from a process of claims-making. The establishment of consensus around such definitions gives categories of deviance a taken-for-granted quality.

We also need to ask questions about the application and management of deviant stigma. Being labelled deviant is a complex process that creates numerous problems for people subject to social control attention. Specifically, we need to be alert to who gets labelled, how they cope with social control, and the manner in which the imposition of labels can worsen the very problems that the application of social control is meant to correct.

Finally, we need to consider the role of language in the creation of categories of deviance and how these categories create power structures that privilege some ways of understanding crime and deviance over others.

Questions for Critical Thought

1. What images of crime and deviance dominate coverage in the local media in your community? What images do they create of troubled and troublesome people?
2. Why do some students plagiarize their assignments? How might this question be answered by proponents of strain, cultural support, and control theories?
3. Why are young males so much more likely than other groups to engage in a range of behaviours that many in society find troublesome?
4. What evidence do you see in your own social environment of the disvalued character of cigarette-smoking and smokers?
5. Can you suggest behaviours or conditions that have undergone a shift in moral status in the past few years? How would you account for these changes?
6. How might Marxian and more conservative conflict theorists differ in their interpretations of the legal and moral battle regarding the use of "soft" illegal drugs such as marijuana?
7. How might you explain to an interested layperson the difference between the ways in which sociologists and journalists think about deviance?
8. In your opinion, does it make sense to speak of something called "positive deviance"? Why or why not?
9. How do media sources such as movies, television, print news, and social media shape particular views of a problem?
10. What is the role of language in defining an action or behaviour as praiseworthy or blameworthy? What is the relationship between language, deviance, social control, and power?

Sociological Explorations

1. How we label behaviour matters a great deal in terms of whether people, behaviour, or actions are evaluated as problems. Consider the following pairs of binaries:
   - disabled/differently abled
   - terrorist/freedom fighter
   - prostitute/sex worker
   - alcoholic/drunk
   - cult leader/religious leader

   Pick an example of a behaviour, action, or person considered deviant. Create a list of competing terms used to describe the behaviour. What do the terms imply? Reflect on the kind of language you use to describe this problem.

2. Imagine you are a sociologist planning to conduct interview research with a stigmatized group of people. Describe your research goals. What kinds of interview questions will you ask your participants? How will you navigate ways to conduct the research ethically? For example, how will you deal with questions of secrecy and the discovery of reportable behaviour?

3. Pick an issue over which there is widespread public debate, for example the debate over marijuana use and distribution. Your task is to compare and contrast different sources of information that address this problem. You might consider social media sources, including news feeds on Facebook, Twitter, and so on; print news; radio interviews; or YouTube commentary. How is the problem framed differently across the sources? Who has ownership of the problem? What are some consequences of how the problem is framed?

Recommended Readings

Adler, P., & Adler, P. (2011). *The tender cut: Inside the hidden world of self-injury.* New York, NY: New York University Press.
This study employs a range of data sources in order to examine branding, cutting, and other forms of self-injury as a social phenomenon. The authors discuss the social meaning of this behaviour as well as comment on the future of the practice.

Best, J. (2013). *Social problems* (2nd edn). New York, NY: W.W. Norton.
This is a thorough and accessible introduction to the social constructionist approach to deviance and social problems. The author makes excellent use of practical examples in order to unravel the complex process by which people and behaviour come to be seen as troublesome.

Goffman, E. (1963). *Stigma: Notes on the management of spoiled identity.* Englewood Cliffs, NJ: Prentice Hall.
This is the classic discussion of how people who are defined as deviants manage stigma. The book was formative in the development of the sociology of labels of deviance.

Venkatesh, S.A. (2008). *Gang leader for a day: A rogue sociologist takes to the streets.* New York, NY: Penguin Books.
This is a fascinating first-person narrative in which the author tells of his experiences studying a high-crime neighbourhood on the South Side of Chicago. The book raises a large number of ethical and methodological questions.

Recommended Websites

Canadian Sociology Association
www.csa-scs.ca/
This website contains the rules, regulations, and principles relating to the ethics of professional sociological research.

Crime Theory
http://law.jrank.org/pages/824/Crime-Causation-Sociological-Theories.html
This site provides a very comprehensive discussion of deviance and crime theory for educational and research purposes.

Sex Professionals of Canada
http://spoc.ca

This site contains resources for professional sex workers and provides some interesting insights into how those involved in professional pursuits that others regard as deviant think about their own lives.

Society for the Study of Social Problems
www.sssp1.org

This is the main page for the Society for the Study of Social Problems (SSSP). The journal of the society, *Social Problems*, has been very influential in the development of the sociology of deviance.

Statistical Literacy
www.statlit.org

This is the website of an organization devoted to the promotion of statistical literacy. It is an invaluable resource for researching the various means by which statistics may be manipulated for political and social purposes.

Statistics Canada
www.statcan.gc.ca

This is the main page for Canada's national statistical agency, Statistics Canada. Many different sorts of reports, tables, and graphs relating to a variety of forms of deviance can be found at this site.

The Surveillance Project
www.sscqueens.org/

This page contains a wealth of information relating to the Queen's University Surveillance Project. The project is concerned with the study of the increasingly large number of technologies and social practices employed for the purpose of social control.

Key Terms

claims-making The social constructionist process by which groups assert grievances about the troublesome character of people or their behaviour.

class Inequality among groups of people based on the distribution of material resources and social capital.

conflict theory A theoretical paradigm linked to the work of Marx and Weber that emphasizes conflict and change as the regular and permanent features of society, because society is made up of various groups that wield varying amounts of power. Conflict theorists often stress the importance of status, economic inequality, and political power.

control theory A category of explanation that maintains that people engage in deviant behaviour when the various controls that might be expected to prohibit them from doing so are weak or absent.

corporate crime Crime committed on behalf of a corporation that victimizes consumers, competing businesses, or governments. It can lead to major social, financial, or physical harm, although often no criminal law has been violated.

cultural support theory A category of explanation that argues people become and remain deviant because the cultural environments in which they find themselves teach deviance and define such behaviour as appropriate.

deviance People, behaviours, and conditions subject to social control.

First Nations "Indians" in Canadian law; together with Métis and Inuit, they constitute Canada's Indigenous peoples.

master status A status characteristic that overrides other status characteristics in terms of how others see an individual. When a person is assigned a label of "deviant" (e.g., "murderer," "drug addict," "cheater"), that label is usually read by others as signifying the most essential aspects of the individual's character.

roles The specific behaviours, privileges, duties, and obligations expected of a person who occupies a specific status.

self In Mead's theory, an emergent entity with a capacity to be both a subject and an object and to assign meaning to itself, as reflected upon in one's own mind. In Goffman's dramaturgical theory, the self is a more shifting "dramatic effect," a staged product of the scenes one performs in.

sex Anatomical characteristics assigned at birth, such as male, female, and intersex.

situated transaction A process of social interaction that lasts as long as the individuals find themselves in each other's company. As applied to the study of deviance, the concept of the situated transaction helps us to understand how deviant acts are social and not just individual products.

social constructionism The sociological theory that argues that social problems and issues are less objective conditions than they are collective social definitions based on how they are framed and interpreted.

social control Various and myriad ways in which members of social groups express their disapproval of people, behaviours, and conditions. These include name-calling, ostracism, ridicule, incarceration, and even killing, among others things.

social groups A number of individuals, defined by formal or informal criteria of membership, who share a feeling of unity or are bound together in stable patterns of interaction; two or more individuals who have a specific common identity and who interact in a reciprocal social relationship.

social interaction The process by which people act and react in relationships with others.

status degradation ceremony The rituals by which formal transition is made from non-deviant to deviant status. Examples include the criminal trial and the psychiatric hearing.

stigma A symbol of disreputability. For the bearer, stigma often takes the form of a shameful label read by outsiders as a mark of discredit or spoiled identity.

strain theory A category of explanation that seeks to understand how deviant behaviour results as people attempt to solve problems that the social structure presents to them.

validity The accuracy of a measure, indicator, or study; many different dimensions to validity can be established through formal tests, logic, or depth of understanding.

Types of Inequality

Social inequality is a central area of inquiry in socio-logical research. As you will see from the chapters in Part III and throughout the book, inequality is pervasive, takes many forms, and can affect individuals and groups in very distinct ways. The study of social inequality is the study of relationships of power and of economic and political advantage. It involves the study of social status and privilege. It often incorporates a number of intersecting areas, including gender and sexuality, social class, and race, to name a few. Central to this area is the idea that there is an unequal distribution of resources and opportunities among individuals and social groups in any given society, and that this unequal distribution is neither random nor necessarily based on ability. Moreover, this inequality is often unfair and undermines rather than benefits society.

Many have come to question the notion that our society is a meritocracy—that the hardest-working reap the highest rewards. Most of us know people who work very hard but rarely are justly rewarded, and others who work very little yet are immensely and disproportionately rewarded. Today, many sociologists acknowledge these facts and research and write about how best to understand and disrupt these unjust and unproductive social realities. However, historically, the sociological study of social stratification has also included theories that helped to justify existing social inequalities by explaining the supposed functional values of and necessity for social inequality.

In Canada today, many who study social inequality look to the structural conditions that lead individuals and groups to succeed at the expense of others. They also focus on the discourse about inequality in formal laws, public policies, and media representations, which reflects the dominant values of a society that comes to normalize or reproduce inequalities.

In Chapter 6, "Class and Status Inequality," Sara Cumming and Ann Duffy help you to understand the important role that class inequality plays in the social construction of reality. They take you through the key historical events that changed economic and social inequalities in Canada. They also challenge you to examine and consider the menacing future that Canadians face in terms of economic and social inequalities.

Janet Siltanen, Andrea Doucet, and Patrizia Albanese introduce you in Chapter 7 to important concepts in sociological thinking about gender and sexuality. They also identify points of convergence and divergence between gender and sexuality. In these ways, they help you think sociologically about how gender and sexuality matter in your everyday life, and how they intersect with other dimensions of identity such as race, ethnicity, class, and age.

Similarly, in Chapter 8, Nikolaos Liodakis identifies the ethnic and racial hierarchies that exist in Canadian society. He begins his chapter with definitions of the terms "ethnicity" and "race." He shows how these concepts help clarify the processes behind the formation of social groups in Canadian society. His chapter also highlights how Canada has been shaped by the colonization of Indigenous peoples, capitalist economic development, and discriminatory immigration policies.

Taken together, these chapters demonstrate the importance of thinking carefully about inequalities that exist within our society, who benefits from them, and what can be done to make a difference. We are reminded that the often taken-for-granted and mundane forms of inequality are exceptionally powerful in normalizing and reinforcing unequal relations in both our personal lives and society at large.

6 Class and Status Inequality

SARA J. CUMMING AND ANN D. DUFFY

In this chapter you will:

▶ Understand the pivotal role that social and class inequality play in the social construction of reality

▶ Appreciate the centrality of class and status inequality in the development of sociological thought

▶ Learn some of the key historical and contemporary realities of economic and social inequalities in Canada

▶ Recognize the diverse ways in which social inequalities change through history

▶ Explore the contentious future that Canadians face in terms of economic and social inequalities

INTRODUCTION

One of the fundamental insights provided by sociology is that our lived realities are constructed socially. We become human through social processes, and our understanding of the world is forever framed by these social experiences. Consider this everyday occurrence: a new friend offers you a ride home. When you approach her car in the parking lot, you do not simply register the fact that here is a vehicle with four wheels and an internal combustion engine. Rather, you immediately and unconsciously run through a whole gamut of socially constructed meanings—meanings embedded in patterns of social inequality. The age, make, and upkeep of the car all are instantly noted. That your new friend drives a brand-new BMW evokes a whole range of social reactions and connections that are quite different from those you would experience if a rusty, dented Toyota Corolla were sitting there.

This example directly relates to the centrality of **class and status** inequalities in our day-to-day experiences. When we look at a car, we generally make assumptions about the relative class and standing of the individual who drives it. The BMW evokes, rightly or wrongly, an impression of wealth and economic well-being, while the rusty Toyota conjures up images of poverty and social marginalization. Clearly, among the most important sorting devices incorporated in our social construction of daily reality are these divisions between those who have and those who do not and, importantly, our relationship to them.

Of course, our responses to class inequalities vary; we may feel more "at home" with the rusty Toyota owner than the BMW owner. However, whatever our personal response, we likely are aware of a typical relationship between high economic class and **power**. Throughout history, individuals holding control over a community's assets—such as land and property (including BMWs)—also possess "power." Understood in the simplest terms, those at the top of the social hierarchy are typically in an excellent position to dictate what others do, and in this way they exercise control over the lives of those who are less well off.

Today in Canada many of these relationships between economic position and power are more nuanced and complex. Contemporary sociologists are likely to suggest that the power associated with social class is generally indirect and subtle (Lukes, 1974, 2005). Bill Gates, founder of Microsoft and one of the wealthiest individuals on the planet, is not only an employer who can require his many employees to perform specific tasks; he has also created a powerful public persona as a revered philanthropist and global activist. From this vantage point he is able to use his standing to promote specific beliefs and values globally. Instead of displaying simple coercive power, Gates has successfully mobilized his power indirectly.

The "celebrity" nature of Gates's status is, however, unusual in North America. In Canada, for example, those who are at the top of the economic hierarchy—the **economic elite**—are not public figures and their identities are typically obscured by their corporate connections. The power wielded by a globalized manufacturing conglomerate like General Motors may be widely recognized, but the individuals sitting on its corporate boards are not likely recognizable. When they decide to close a factory and thousands of workers become unemployed, their personal exercise of power over the lives of others tends to be rendered invisible as the mass media talk about "GM closings" rather than the actions of specific corporate executives.

Last, it is crucial to realize that not only are economic power relations often indirect and unclear, they are often further muddied by interconnections with intersecting inequalities. Various social factors—gender, ethnicity, race, age, disability, sexual orientation, and immigrant status—all interact. Some categories of individuals—women, ethnic and racial minorities, the disabled, recent immigrants, the elderly—are generally at greater risk of being economically disadvantaged and powerless. These complex intersections and interactions between economic and other inequalities—**intersectionalities**—must be kept in mind as we address class and status (McMullin, 2010).

TIME to REFLECT ●━━━ ▱▱▱▱

In what ways do social class, gender, ethnicity, and age intersect to support the political ascent of Prime Minister Justin Trudeau?

Keeping in mind these complexities, in this chapter we will explore social and economic inequalities in greater detail. Certainly, "social class" is a pivotal term in much historical and contemporary sociological thought. Given this centrality, it is not surprising that an understanding of Canadian society requires an appreciation of the patterns of class structure—especially the elites and the poor. As discussed below, these class divisions are sustained not only by various institutions, ranging from elite private schools to political parties, but also by popular ideologies that legitimize and perpetuate specific social class arrangements. Despite these supports, the history of Canadian society also reveals dynamic shifts in social class arrangements. Notably, social movements, public agencies, and government policies have addressed and changed the nature of economic inequalities. We conclude with a brief examination of future trends. Ominously, it appears that social and economic inequalities are on the brink of intensifying in Canada and in other industrialized countries.

CLASS AND STATUS INEQUALITIES IN SOCIOLOGICAL THOUGHT

A number of the key concepts in sociology emanate from concern with patterns of social inequality. Indeed, the term **social stratification** is one of the foundational issues in sociological inquiry. Social stratification affects almost every aspect of our lives—from where we live, our material possessions, and our level of education, to our health and well-being. Rather than focusing on individual circumstances, it stresses the

layering of groups of people, according to their relative privilege, into social classes. An individual's position within a social class is referred to as his or her social status. An individual's social status can be achieved or ascribed.

An ascribed status is typically assigned to a person at birth and is connected to many characteristics other than the income of parents—race, gender, disability/ability, age, and other factors that are not chosen or earned. In contrast, an achieved status is based primarily on earned accomplishments/achievements. If a person goes to university and successfully completes his or her PhD, that person has earned the title of "doctor." If an athlete performs well, he or she can potentially achieve the status of "professional athlete" and the corresponding high income.

Although most people would argue that a **meritocracy**, a system based upon achievement rather than ascribed status, is preferable, understanding individual social status and social class is far more complex than equating successes or failures to individual strengths or weaknesses. Not all positions within the hierarchy are based solely on merit. For instance, under a meritocracy, entrance into university should be based solely on a student's achieving the grades necessary for acceptance; in fact, the best predictor of university entrance is family income. Additionally, students who have university-educated parents are more likely to do well in university themselves. If social status were based primarily on earned achievement, we might expect to see a high degree of social mobility—the movement between classes; however, throughout their lifetime most people remain in the social class into which they were born (Western & Wright, 1994).

When we look beyond the borders of Canada, however, we find that compared to some other societies around the world, we appear to have a relatively open stratification system. It is possible in Canada for a person from a poor family to move up in class. A young person from a poor family can win a scholarship or can apply for a student loan to attend college or university. Through hard work and determination, the student may obtain a medical degree, for example, and become a practising physician, improving his or her socio-economic status dramatically. However, we also need to recognize the degree to which ascribed status limits opportunities for Canadians. As we discuss later, Indigenous people, visible minorities, recent immigrants, those with disabilities, and lone parents (especially lone mothers) experience disproportionate poverty.

Sociology and Social Stratification

Conflict Approaches to Social Stratification: Karl Marx

> The history of all hitherto existing society is the history of class struggles. . . . society is more and more splitting up into two great hostile camps, into two great classes directly facing each other—bourgeoisie and proletariat. (Marx and Engels 1985 [1848], 203–4)

In this famous quotation from the *Communist Manifesto*, Karl Marx (1818–1883) outlines the two issues that are central to his work on class: he argues that society is characterized by conflict (class struggles) and that a distinguishing feature of capitalism is the division of society into two central classes, the **bourgeoisie** and the **proletariat**. Marx maintained that society is divided into these classes on the basis of their relationship to the **means of production**—their access to the tools, factories, land, and investment capital used to produce wealth (Marx & Engels, 1985 [1848]). As the bourgeoisie, who owned the means of production, pursued their self-interest in the form of profit, they necessarily exploited the proletariat, who had little choice other than to sell their labour.

According to Marx, the drive for private property was primarily responsible for creating the two-class system. Under capitalism, everyone needed to have an income in order to obtain property and ensure survival. Those who existed outside this system—for example, the unemployed who lacked an income—served as a reserve army of labour ready to be called upon if the demand for labour increased or if current

workers complained about their exploitation. By paying workers low wages, capitalists were able to expropriate surplus wealth from the labour process. Given the absence of employment opportunities outside the industrial economy, workers had no choice but to exchange their labour for wages that were far below the value of the products they were producing for the owners. While working people were responsible for creating a surplus of wealth, they did not reap the benefits.

Marx maintained that the inequality this system produced was neither desirable nor inevitable (Lindsey & Beach, 2003). In fact, he held that class conflict between wage-labourers and the owners of the means of production would be historically inevitable as the inequality between these classes became ever more pronounced. As the proletariat class developed **class consciousness**—an awareness of workers' shared interests and their ability to act in those interests—Marx predicted a socialist revolution, the eradication of capitalist economies, and a new mode of production.

Structural Functionalist Approaches to Social Stratification

In contrast to Marx, other sociologists have emphasized the social functions played by social stratification.

Davis and Moore

Kingsley Davis and Wilbert Moore are best known for their 1945 publication "Some Principles of Social Stratification," which later became known as the Davis–Moore thesis. Davis and Moore argue that inequalities exist in all societies and thus must be necessary. In order to function properly, a society must somehow distribute its members into various social positions and persuade them to perform the duties of these positions. Not only are some positions more pleasurable than others, many require special training or talents and are viewed as more important. According to Davis and Moore, the positions that are rewarded with the highest economic gains and highest rank are those that have the greatest importance for society and those that require the greatest training or talent. In order to induce people to undertake a lengthy, expensive education, such as is required for becoming a medical doctor, the rewards must be high. Davis and Moore contend that this system is based on consensus and shared values, because members of society generally agree that the reward system is fair and just.

While the Davis–Moore thesis sounds like a remarkably reasonable and simple explanation for social stratification, their structural functionalist approach has been severely criticized. For example, while some difference in pay might be reasonable for people who spend long periods of time in school, the functionalist approach does not take into account that it is often people who can afford to attend school who do so, rather than those who are the most talented or gifted. Additionally, there are substantial differences—regardless of educational qualifications—in who gets into the highest-paid jobs, with minorities and women represented disproportionately at the lowest pay tiers. Furthermore, the social inequality between the top and bottom is extreme. Movie stars, bankers, and professional athletes bring home millions of dollars a year, while nurses, teachers, and daycare workers are paid significantly less. There is no doubt that many better-paying occupations require a great deal of training and education; however, this alone does not explain the inequality in our society, which is much greater than simple differences in effort and reward.

TIME to REFLECT •———————

Do you think class inequality is a functional and necessary part of society? Are higher rewards necessary in order to motivate people to fill certain positions?

Symbolic Interactionist Perspectives on Social Stratification: Thorstein Veblen

Symbolic interactionists take a different approach to social stratification. Rather than attempting to explain why stratification exists or how conflict is created because of class inequality, they are interested in how people interpret and represent inequality. As the term suggests, symbolic interactionists consider how meanings and symbols enable people to carry out uniquely human actions and interactions (Ritzer, 2000b, p. 357). In reference to social stratification, they pay particular attention to the use of **status symbols**.

In *Theory of the Leisure Class* (1899), Thorstein Veblen (1857–1929) suggests that there is a distinct difference between the productiveness of the manufacturing industry and the greed of business. Business, he argues, exists only to earn profits for a leisure class. Veblen maintained that the main activity in which the leisure class of his time engaged was **conspicuous consumption**—the purchasing of expensive goods and services primarily for the purpose of putting wealth on display. These purchases were status symbols—various signs that identified a particular social and economic status or position. Diamond tiaras, massive country estates, and large retinues of servants were all status symbols in Veblen's era. Not surprisingly, he not only drew attention to this conspicuous consumption, but given the dire poverty that characterized that period of US history, he also harshly criticized the waste and excess that accompanied conspicuous consumption.

Today, status symbols remain apparent everywhere, although they may manifest themselves differently depending on culture and location. Expensive houses, luxury cars and clothing, along with exotic vacations and elite sports, still communicate wealth and social position. Symbolic statements about wealth are visible throughout a typical university, with brands such as Michael Kors, Hunters, Yeezy, and Apple dotting the hallways even though similar, less inexpensive apparel is widely available.

Veblen's main contributions, then, were in highlighting the symbolic embodiment of social inequality through the practice of conspicuous consumption and in his contention that most people want to appear as though they live above their actual social location. Today, conspicuous

Photo by Viviane Moos/Corbis via Getty Images

Despite gains in education and job opportunities, women in traditionally female-dominated occupations, such as care workers or housekeepers, continue to be marginalized members of society.

consumption, even at the risk of indebtedness, has become an epidemic, as suggested by the multi-billion-dollar industries dedicated to helping millions of North Americans live beyond their means—industries ranging from payday loan companies to the credit card divisions of banks and credit unions.

Feminist Explanations for Social Stratification

Predictably, few theorists in the past included women in class analysis. Perhaps the breadwinner ideology (the assumption that a woman's role in the household was to provide unpaid work for her family while her husband provided the economic resources through his paid labour) excluded women as participants in the social class structures (Nakhaie, 2002). Certainly, stratification research has repeatedly been critiqued for being "malestream"—excluding women from research samples on the basis of their secondary relationship to the labour market, focusing

exclusively on class rather than incorporating gender inequality, and assuming that women's economic and social positions are derived from those of their husbands or fathers (Abbott & Sapsford, 1987). It has most often been assumed that "stay-at-home" wives take on their husband's social class, while women who earn a wage are included in what is assumed to be a gender-neutral class system (Acker, 1990).

 What is the economic value of women's unpaid household work? See "Social Reproduction," p. 257, in **Chapter 11**, "Work and the Economy."

Today, feminist scholars continue to press analysts to recognize that gender intersects in important and complex ways with social class. For example, because of the continued gender segregation of the labour force and women's traditional role in providing unpaid labour in the household, women have long been at greater risk of poverty. This **feminization of poverty** is important to an understanding of social class inequalities in Canada and globally. While there have been dramatic changes in women's status over the past 50 years, evidence suggests that women remain disadvantaged both in the world of paid work and in the home. As repeatedly documented in the Canadian census, many continue to undertake the lion's share of domestic labour in the home and must make the necessary adjustments (including less sleep) when they hold paid employment. Within the labour force, despite employment equity legislation, women continue to be ghettoized, not only into specific employment areas but also at the lower rungs of their work milieu and their professions—part-time rather than full-time, teachers rather than principals, and so on (Armstrong & Armstrong, 1994; Hochschild, 1997). In short, feminist analysts press for recognition of the complexities and contradictions embedded in class and status inequalities.

Class and Status Inequality in Canada

The Wealthy, Elites, and Super Rich

Often when social inequality is discussed, attention immediately turns to those who are deprived and marginalized. The poor, the homeless, and low-income earners seem the natural targets of analysis. However, the opposite end of the continuum—those who hold disproportionate financial and other assets—are at least as significant in understanding patterns of social inequality. Not surprisingly, the elites have long been of interest to sociologists.

One of the most prominent US sociologists of the twentieth century—C. Wright Mills (1916–1962)—played a key role in establishing elites as a topic worthy of social research and analysis. Most notably, his book *The Power Elite* (1956) challenged the then-dominant structural functional approach to social stratification—a viewpoint that suggested minimal class differences among Americans. Indeed, Mills proposed that the elites in US society were so powerful and so coordinated that they jeopardized democratic processes. This book triggered a wide variety of

studies examining the nature and implications of power discrepancies. Most notably in the US, G. William Domhoff (1936–) has produced a steady stream of books profiling the power elite and exploring "who rules America" (2013).

Canadian sociologists and social analysts have also studied the powerful. English Canada's pre-eminent sociologist of the twentieth century—John Porter (1921–1979)—authored *The Vertical Mosaic* (1965), which provides an eye-opening analysis of the concentration of corporate power in the hands of a few—mostly anglophone Canadian males. Wallace Clement (1951–) advanced Porter's work with his book *The Canadian Corporate Elite* (1975). Clement reveals that, in several respects, those holding economic power in Canada have become a more diverse (ethnically) group, but many of the traditional structures that bind the elite together—private schools, family relations, cultural and charitable organizations—persist.

More recently, popular commentators have joined with academic researchers in revealing the ways in which wealth and power are socially constructed and perpetuated in Canada. Journalists Peter C. Newman and Diane Francis played particularly important roles in drawing Canadians' attention to the key power-holders in our economy. Francis, for example, wrote *Controlling Interest: Who Owns Canada?* (1986) and *Who Owns Canada Now* (2008). Although she reported in 1986 that 32 families and five conglomerates were in control of 40 per cent of Canadian banking, business, and politics, her more recent work suggests that the elite is not becoming an increasingly closed circle, and she identifies new players who have entered these rarefied spheres. By 2007, "only 21% of the biggest 500 [companies] were family-controlled, by . . . 75 [families, rather than 32]; 30% of the country's biggest 500 [companies] were foreign owned, 8.5% [were] government owned [down from 22% in 1986]" (Francis, 2008, p. 16). Family control, while still centralized, has spread out, foreign ownership has increased, and government control has dropped precipitously in the era of privatization. The economic elite described by

Francis is a dynamic and shifting reality—but one that still plays a major role in society (2013).

Canadian social scientists have not, however, left the field to the mass media. Jamie Brownlee's *Ruling Canada: Corporate Cohesion and Democracy* (2005) pulls together much of the more recent information on the "ruling class"; he explores the various contemporary mechanisms—including conservative think tanks such as the Fraser Institute and overlapping memberships on various corporate boards—that serve to draw the Canadian corporate elite together into a self-conscious and integrated social force. Most notable among contemporary researchers is sociologist William K. Carroll. His *Corporate Power in a Globalizing World* (2004, 2010a) uses network analysis to document the social ties (from shared membership in elite clubs to corporate interlocks with universities) that integrate the elite into every facet of Canadian society while also creating the basis for elite solidarity.

In short, elite research has clarified the considerable gap that exists between the top and bottom of our economic hierarchy. Some of this is also communicated through Statistics Canada's income surveys. This analysis divides Canadians into deciles (one-tenths) and determines the average income for those occupying the wealthiest one-tenth all the way down to those at the bottom one-tenth. The latest data indicate that by 2013, the richest deciles were receiving on average $183,600 in after-tax income and the poorest, $9,200 (Statistics Canada, 2015d). Interestingly, despite the 2008 recession, the shares of income have remained fairly stable, with the poorest decile receiving 1.5 per cent of after-tax income in 2010 and 1.4 per cent in 2013, while the wealthiest received 27.4 per cent in 2010 and 27.6 per cent in 2013 (Statistics Canada, 2015d; Macdonald, 2015, p. 10). This distribution of wealth meant that 4.6 million Canadians (13.5 per cent) lived in households defined as "poor" (according to the after-tax Low-Income Measure [LIM-AT] discussed below) (Statistics Canada, 2015d, p. 3).

However, the issue here is not simply wealth inequality but also the presence of a very small number of Canadians who are extremely wealthy, and, often, powerful. In 2013, the wealthiest 1 per cent of Canadian tax filers held 10.3 per cent of the national total income—up considerably from the 7 per cent they held in the early 1980s (Statistics Canada, 2015g). To grasp these levels of wealth, consider Linda McQuaig and Neil Brooks's strategy: if one of Canada's wealthiest families—the Thomson family—started counting their wealth at one dollar per second and counted non-stop day and night, they would count it all in approximately 700 years (2010). This is wealth beyond the wildest imaginings of most Canadians. This is wealth that can be and is translated into endowments for universities, the creation of cultural institutions, and support for particular political parties. While some might see this pattern as benign, social critics question the desirability of small groups of individuals holding so much sway over the direction of Canadian society.

Further, the very wealthy, as Mills, Domhoff, Porter, Clement, Carroll, and others have pointed out, do not simply function as isolated individuals; they tend to be bonded together by important shared experiences. Many were themselves born into wealthy families. These families tend to live in exclusive neighbourhoods, vacation at elite resorts, belong to the "best" clubs, send their children to exclusive private schools, and join other wealthy families in participating in specific philanthropic and cultural events. In addition, out in the more public domain, they sit with one another on corporate boards, university governing councils, and political organizations. These shared experiences inevitably lend themselves to friendships, family intermarriage, and a common perspective on social issues. The elite are by no means a homogeneous, ingrown mass, but—to invoke the famous saying of F. Scott Fitzgerald—"They are different from you and me."

These social realities necessarily raise two concerns: What are the implications of this narrow consolidation of wealth and power for our democratic structures. How large a gap between haves and have-nots is desirable or acceptable in any society that wants to maintain a range of social mobility and open access?

TIME to REFLECT

What are the implications of the fact that the prime minister of Canada earned approximately $327,000 plus a housing and car allowance in 2014, while the highest-paid CEO in Canada in 2014 earned $89,715,019 in total compensation (Raj, 2014; Mackenzie, 2016, p. 9)?

Richard Levine / Alamy Stock Photo

During periods of high unemployment, many Canadians come to rely on support programs, such as food banks or soup kitchens, for their meals.

The Poor and Economically Marginalized

Who are the poor and marginalized in Canada? Is there something specific that determines who is poor and who is not? Do you have to be homeless? Jobless? Receiving social assistance? Are there status symbols that visibly mark the poor, such as worn-out clothing that lacks a brand name, a neglect of hygiene, criminal behaviour? Why are people poor? Is it because they are lazy? Drunks or drug users? Or is it because they cannot find employment or they have too many children? This next section will attempt to steer you through some of these much-reported myths about the poor and illuminate how poverty rates are determined in Canada (see Table 6.1).

The word "poverty" is often used as an all-encompassing term to describe situations in which people lack many of the opportunities

available to the average citizen (Levitas, 1998). There is no shortage of poverty measures. The Canadian federal government has developed five measures, while social planning councils, individual researchers, non-profit organizations, and others have developed their own measures (Statistics Canada, 2015h; deGroot-Maggetti, 2002). The most common distinctions between these definitions of poverty are the terms "absolute" and "relative." Definitions using "absolute" refer to a lack of basic necessities, while those using "relative" emphasize inadequacy compared to average living standards (Mitchell & Shillington, 2002; Sarlo, 1996). Teasing out the differences between absolute and relative definitions of poverty,

Table 6.1 ▶ Canadians Living in Low Income, after Tax, 2012

	Thousands—Persons in Low Income	% of All Persons—Persons in Low Income
All persons in low income	**4,682**	**13.8**
Persons under 18 years	1,100	16.3
In two-parent families	722	12.9
In female lone-parent families	314	44.5
Persons 18 to 64 years	2,976	13.3
In economic families	1,963	10.6
Unattached individuals	1,013	27.0
Persons 65 years and over	606	12.1
In economic families	228	6.2
Unattached individuals	378	28.5

SOURCE: CANSIM table 206-0003. http://www.statcan.gc.ca/daily-quotidien/141210/t141210a003-eng.htm

Ross and Shillington (1994) suggest that the first approach assumes that we can ascertain an absolute measure of poverty by calculating the cost of goods and services essential for physical survival. The relative approach is grounded in the belief that any definition of poverty should take social and physical well-being into account. This approach argues that someone who has noticeably less than the surrounding community will feel disadvantaged (Ross & Schillington, 1994, p. 4; Roberman, 2015).

Statistics Canada, which collects annual income data, relies on three measures to determine which Canadians are "poor" in that they live at or below low-income levels: the **Low Income Cut-Offs** (LICOs), the **Market Basket Measure** (MBM), and the **Low Income Measure** (LIM) (2015j). These are income-based measures that use formulas to calculate income "lines" with which analysts address low income and poverty. After-tax measures refer to levels of income after tax has been deducted. These after-tax measures include Low Income Cut-offs (LICO-AT) and Low Income Measures (LIM-AT).

Many analysts argue that poverty is an issue that extends far beyond income. Amartya Sen (2000) has made a significant intellectual contribution to poverty discourse with his assertion that an impoverished life is more than just the lack of money: "Income may be the most prominent means for a good life without deprivation, but it is not the only influence on the lives we can lead" (p. 3). Arguing for a relational understanding of poverty and deprivation, he suggests: "We must look at impoverished lives, and not just at depleted wallets" (2000, p. 3). For Sen, poverty is the lack of the capability to live a minimally decent life that, in turn, limits the ability to take part in the life of the community (2000, p. 4).

 Income inequality has a detrimental effect on one of the most important facets of life—health. See "The Social Determinants of Health," p. 214, in **Chapter 9**, "Families and Health Issues," to learn more.

Regardless of how we measure poverty, specific groups are particularly vulnerable, notably women (especially those in lone-parent families and seniors), unattached individuals, Indigenous people, persons with disabilities, recent immigrants and visible minorities, and the **working poor**.

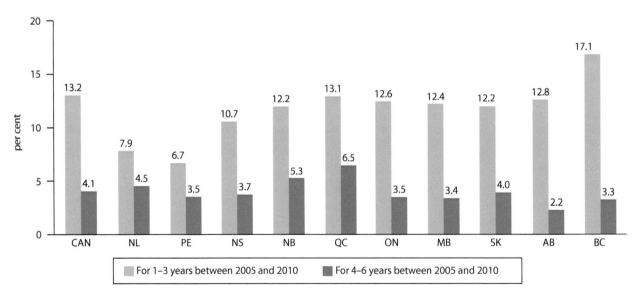

FIGURE 6.1 Canadians with Low Income over a 6-Year Period, by Region, 2005–2010 (%)[1, 2]

1. Years spent in low income are not necessarily consecutive.
2. Based on after-tax LICOs.
SOURCE: HRSDC calculations based on Statistics Canada, "Persistence of low income, by selected characteristics, every 3 years," CANSIM Table 202-0807 (2012)

Women

Women are the poorest of the poor, especially those raising children as lone parents and those living as unattached seniors. According to the most recently available census data, in 2011 there were 1,527,840 lone-parent families: 16 per cent of all families, which had increased by 5.5 per cent from 2006 to 2011 (Statistics Canada, 2012c). By 2014, lone-parent families accounted for one in five families with children under age 16 (up from one in ten in 1976) (Statistics Canada, 2015k). According to the 2011 National Household Survey, 59 per cent of lone-mother families and 28 per cent of lone-father families, both with children aged five and under, were living in low income, in contrast to 13 per cent of couples with children of the same age group (Milan, 2015, p. 16). It seems that when women are not protected by traditional marriage and family structures, they are more likely to be impoverished.

Gender wage inequities continue to contribute to women's high poverty rates. Although the Pay Equity Act, enacted in 1987, made it illegal to pay someone less for their work on the basis of gender, Canadian women continue to face "obstacles to employment and fair wages" (Lambert & McInturff, 2016, p. 2). Notably, inequities in the distribution of unpaid (household) work, the undervaluing of "'female'" paid work, the gender segregation of the workplace, and the male "premium" experienced in wages and promotions continues to put women at a disadvantage. While this gap has narrowed in recent years, it has by no means disappeared (Schirle, 2016). Problems continue to plague the female labour force, including growing precarity in the female-dominated service sector of the economy, the restructuring of women's employment through increased privatization and outsourcing, and a lack of child care limiting women's choices for employment. Even working full-time, women earn 20 per cent less than comparable men, and the inequity is greater for Indigenous, racialized, and immigrant women (McInturff with Lockhart, 2015). Even exceptional educational credentials do not eliminate the gender difference; in 2014, female university professors earned 93.6 per cent and female college instructors 86.4 per cent of the salaries of their male colleagues (CAUT Bulletin, 2016).

Unattached Individuals

In 2013, more than one in four individuals (27.8 per cent) not living in an economic family (unattached) were living in low income in contrast to one in ten (11 per cent) of those living in an economic family (LIM-AT). The income benefits of family structures are apparent when non-elderly and elderly Canadians are

---

RESEARCHERS IN ACTION ▶ Dr Julia Woodhall-Melnik

Although many sociologists worldwide are interested in issues of social inequality, relatively few academic researchers focus specifically on access to housing. Dr Woodhall-Melnik's research program comprises multiple projects that focus on housing instability and homelessness. She recently completed a community-based evaluation study which examined the impacts of a Housing First program for men in Hamilton, Ontario. Housing First programs provide rapid rehousing assistance to individuals experiencing chronic long-term or multiple episodes of homelessness. Generally speaking, these people live with a variety of complex needs (e.g. trauma related to early life neglect or abuse, poverty, substance addiction, gambling addiction, acquired brain injury, and so on). Traditional rehousing programs require sobriety and, for those with mental illness, medication compliance, but the Housing First model does not. In this sense, Housing First programs are considered "low-barrier," based on the ideology that supplying housing to individuals in crisis provides stability that can extend to other areas of their lives.

compared, despite slightly higher percentages of females in both categories experiencing low income. Between 2009 and 2013, there were slight increases in the low-income rates among both non-elderly and elderly unattached males and slight decreases for elderly females. Nonetheless, the overall patterns of low-income rates consistently suggest important economic disadvantages to living alone (Statistics Canada, 2015i).

Indigenous People

Most Canadians are well aware that poverty and economic deprivation are significantly higher among Indigenous people. A recent report (Arriagada, 2016) found, for example, that almost one in four (23 per cent) First Nations women and 18 per cent of Métis women lived in households experiencing **food insecurity**. A staggering 53 per cent of Inuit women living in Inuit Nunangat also experienced food insecurity. Predictably, this pattern often translates into hunger. Almost one in ten Indigenous women aged 15 and older reported being hungry in the previous 12 months because they could not afford enough food. Among women living in Inuit Nunangat, 25 per cent reported going hungry (Arriagada, 2016, p. 29).

Lower incomes and higher rates of unemployment help set the stage for poverty. In 2010, when average Indigenous incomes were $20,060, non-Indigenous people made $27,622. In 2011, the employment rate for Indigenous peoples aged 25 to 64 was 62.5 per cent, compared to 75.8 per cent for non-Indigenous (Statistics Canada, 2015a). A host of reasons combine to make Indigenous people particularly vulnerable to economic marginalization. Lack of necessary training and education, a shortage of jobs, and lack of work experience all undermine participation in the labour market. For example, while two-thirds (65 per cent) of non-Indigenous people aged 25 to 64 had a post-secondary qualification in 2011, only 48 per cent of Indigenous people were similarly qualified. The high school graduation rate for Indigenous peoples living off-reserve in northern communities is about 45 per cent lower than that of the rest of Canada (O'Gorman & Pandey, 2015).

 Many factors have contributed to Indigenous peoples' overall education levels being below national levels. See "Educational Opportunities and Inequalities" in **Chapter 10**, p. 240, for further information.

New Immigrants and Visible Minorities

Recent immigrants (especially those who have arrived within the preceding five years) have long been more vulnerable to living in poverty than other Canadians (Lightman & Gingrich, 2012). They are at greater risk of low income, unemployment, and lower wages than comparable Canadians, despite having significantly higher education and more potential earners per household (Morissette & Galaraneau, 2016; Hudon, 2015). In 2010 the poverty rate among new immigrants was 17.6 per cent, almost twice the overall rate for Canada and up by 5 per cent since 1981 (Citizens for Public Justice, 2013, p. 14). There has been a dramatic rise in the educational attainment of new immigrants due to changes to Canada's immigrant selection criteria in 1993. While this accounted for declining low-income

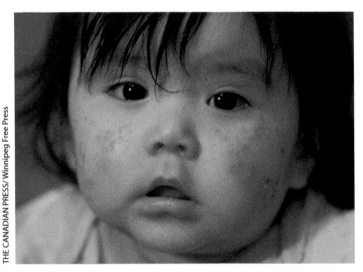

THE CANADIAN PRESS/ Winnipeg Free Press

Many First Nations reserves do not have access to running water. A multitude of health problems can arise from a lack of safe water, including gastrointestinal diseases and skin rashes, as suffered by Lyra Harper, who lives an hour outside of Winnipeg at Red Sucker Lake.

rates among immigrants over the 2000s, immigrant poverty persists as a social issue (Picot & Hou, 2014).

Complexly intersecting with recent immigrant status is visible-minority identity. Since over the past four decades, the overwhelming majority of Canadian immigrants have been visible minorities, there is often an overlap between these two elements. For example, there are higher rates of unemployment among visible-minority women, but this pattern appears to be significantly impacted by not only gender but also immigrant status. Analysis of stratification in the labour market shows that women are disadvantaged compared to men, visible-minority women are more disadvantaged than white women, and visible-minority immigrant women are even more disadvantaged than visible-minority Canadian-born women. These social facts clearly indicate that an intersectionality of gender, visible-minority, and immigrant status is at play. Similarly, visible-minority women have lower employment income and higher rates of low income when compared to non-visible-minority women. Again, immigrant status and age alter these patterns; notably, however, 26.3 per cent of visible-minority women aged 15 to 24 were living in low income compared to 15.8 per cent of same-aged women who were not visible minority (Hudon, 2016, pp. 30–31).

Relatively little research has focused on black families in Canada. A recent examination using the 2006 census data reports that disparities between household incomes of black (foreign and native-born) and non-black Canadians have only grown over the past two decades. While the proportion of Canadian children living in low-income households dropped from 22.4 per cent in 1986 to 18.6 per cent in 2006, the rate actually increased for black children from 33.3 per cent in 1986 to 35.3 per cent in 2006 (Livingstone & Weinfeld, 2015, p. 15).

People Living with a Disability

In 2012, 3.8 million Canadians (almost 14 per cent of the population) relied on disability supports in order to live independently in their communities

(Torjman, 2015a, p. 1). Despite these supports, almost one in five Canadians living with a disability live in low income (LICO-AT)(Crawford, 2013, pp. 10, 11; Citizens for Public Justice, 2013). Efforts to ensure access to education and employment have not eradicated the reality that persons with disabilities experience low rates of employment and high rates of reliance on government transfer payments, most notably social assistance (Crawford, 2013, p. 37). An estimated 500,000 Canadians with severe and prolonged disabilities rely on welfare payments—payments that lock them into low income (Torjman, 2015a, p. 13). As a result of inadequate supports, many Canadians living with a disability find themselves dependent on income-security programs that they "experience as restrictive, disrespectful, parsimonious and oppressive" (Crawford, 2013, p. 37). The aging of the Canadian population promises the intensification of these issues. By 2030, one-quarter of Canadians will be over age 65 and, according to current rates, 33 per cent of Canadians aged 65 and older will have some disability (Torjman, 2015b). In this context, concerns

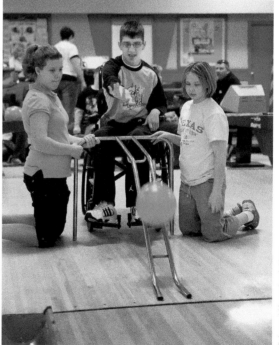

Enigma / Alamy Stock Photo

Simple solutions, like the bowling ball guide above, allow individuals with disabilities to take part in social activities that were previously inaccessible.

surrounding the societal integration of persons living with disabilities can only intensify.

The Working Poor

Although there are a number of definitions, the working poor are often defined as anyone who is between ages 18 and 64, is not a student, lives independently, has earnings of at least $3,000 a year, and has an income below the LIM-AT measure (Stapleton with Kay, 2015, p. 33). Contrary to impressions from the mass media, many of the poor are not unemployed and do not rely on government transfers. An individual working 40 hours a week at Ontario's minimum wage of $11.40 per hour (2016) for 50 weeks a year earns only $22,800 per year. This wage would marginally lift the single employable individual out of poverty, since a single person in Ontario needs to earn more than $20,160 to exceed the LICO-AT measure (Tweedle, Battle, & Torjman, 2015). But this wage will not lift a single parent with one child or a couple with two children above the LICO-AT in Ontario. A single parent in 2014 would need to earn more than $24,536 to exceed the LICO-AT and a couple with two children would need

$38,117. However, despite improvements in minimum wage, in 2014 the average minimum wage in Canada was only $8.20 per hour (rates vary across territories and provinces) (Battle, 2015, p. 28). Difficulties for minimum-wage workers are further compounded as the cost of living in heavily populated cities, such as Toronto, skyrocket in terms of child-care costs (up 30 per cent from 2008 to 2015), rental costs (up 13 per cent), and public transit (up 36 per cent) (Tiessen, 2015, p. 5). According to recent research, two parents with two young children would both need to earn $18.52 per hour and work 37.5 hours per week in order to afford "the basics of life" in Toronto (Tiessen, 2015, p. 5). By 2010, more than one-third of households where one person was employed were poor, and more than 10 per cent of households with two or more persons working for pay still were unable to lift themselves over the LICO-AT line (Citizens for Public Justice, 2013, p. 12). Low-income problems are further compounded by low-wage workers' lack of benefits, including limited or no dental-care plans, life and disability insurance, and pension plans (PEPSO, 2013).

UNDER THE WIRE — Technological Inequality

Poverty has wide-ranging consequences. Not the least of these is exclusion from many of the goods and services Canadian society can provide. For many Canadians, this pattern extends to access to modern technologies. There is much evidence that Canada is experiencing a digital divide, with various demographics not fully connected to the online world (Chapin, 2013). In a country that continually boasts of 99 per cent wireless coverage (Canadian Wireless Telecommunication Association [CWTA], 2013), over 20 per cent of its population could not access the Internet in the previous year (Chapin, 2013). Almost 100 per cent of the wealthy in Canada report having home Internet access, compared to just under 60 per cent of those who earn $30,000 or less (Harris, 2013). When poor people do spend on technology, the proportionate cost is nearly five times more of their annual income (8.4 per cent) than it is for wealthy Canadians (1.7 per cent) (Statistics Canada, 2014j).

The divide encompasses much more than just accessing new technologies: becoming a digital citizen is not just about affordability; it is about computer literacy (Chapin, 2013). Research shows us that many are simply overwhelmed with technology and do not know where to go or lack the time to learn about all that is available. Inequalities, notably in income, education, locale (i.e., rural vs. urban), immigration status, and age all affect the **digital divide** (Haight, Quan-Haase & Corbett, 2014). Predictably, many seniors have fallen furthest behind in terms of access and skill. This is increasingly problematic in a society that has moved most services online and creates a growing digital underclass.

UNDERSTANDING POVERTY

Many people believe that we all start out with the same chances of obtaining the "American Dream"—democracy promises prosperity. This belief system is grounded in **classism**—bias, prejudice, and discrimination on the basis of social class—and often results in blaming the victim rather than the system. Named by William Ryan (1971), **blaming the victim** is a view that holds individuals entirely responsible for any negative situations that may arise in their lives. Because there is an implicit understanding in Canada that individuals who work hard should be able to prosper, those who do not succeed are deemed at fault and are criticized as lacking motivation or being too weak to help themselves.

In a poverty "classic," anthropologist Oscar Lewis (1966) investigated the lives of the poor and argued that people who live in poverty are a subculture with different value systems from the rest of society. He maintained that those who live in this culture of poverty feel inferior and helpless and have a defeatist attitude, which then limits their ability to improve their situation. In this analysis, the responsibility for changing impoverished circumstances is placed squarely on the individual. Contemporary analysts argue that the classism and blaming-the-victim stance embedded in Lewis's analysis have contributed to "poor-bashing." Facts about poverty and the poor are ignored, and instead stereotypes are repeated. These stereotypes, in turn, may lead to both verbal and physical assaults on the poor.

This approach to the poor and poverty, of course, completely overlooks the facts that indicate poverty may be the result of institutional arrangements and even legislation. For example, a great deal of Canadian poverty would immediately disappear if legislation on welfare rates and minimum wages were improved. Moreover, this kind of individual-focused thinking about poor people—that they should transcend their social environment—"demands a higher standard of behaviour and sacrifice from people who are

poor than from people who are not" (Swanson, 2001, p. 3).

Michael Katz, a well-known poverty researcher in the United States, argues that poverty and inequality is not about specific people and their personal qualities; rather, it is about wealth distribution—some people receive a great deal more than others. He writes, "descriptions of the demography, behavior or beliefs [of people who are poor] can't explain inequality" (Katz, 1989, p. 7). Jean Swanson furthers this assertion and urges society to stop blaming individuals for their impoverished circumstances so that "we can expose the policies, laws, and economic system that force millions of people in Canada and around the world to compete against each other, driving down wages and creating more poverty" (2001, p. 8).

Katz and Swanson are employing a perspective often referred to as **blaming the system**. This is more consistent with a sociological view, since it recognizes the systemic discrimination that exists within society. People are poor for many reasons that are beyond their control. Many structural variables influence poverty levels, such as deindustrialization (the replacement of well-paid manufacturing jobs with lower-paid service-based jobs), rising costs of living, barriers to opportunities (such as increased tuition for education and training programs), limited access to affordable housing, inability to obtain credit, and so on.

TIME to REFLECT

What are the responsibilities of our governments to ensure that every Canadian has a reasonable quality of life?

POLICIES TO ADDRESS POVERTY

There is a very long tradition of efforts to "help" the poor. Initially driven by Christian and Jewish religious ethics, early charities in Canada provided food, clothing, and occasionally shelter for those who had fallen on "hard times." Then, as now, single mothers (often widows), orphaned children, seniors, and the disabled were routinely marginalized. In the absence of government-funded welfare programs, they were often forced to turn to private and religious agencies to beg for whatever support they could find. Reflecting the brutality of the times, many poor families had little recourse but to give up their hungry children. For example, in the nineteenth and early twentieth centuries, tens of thousands of poor children were brought to Canada from poorhouses and orphanages in England to work as servants and farm hands. Expected to receive only their room and board in return for their labours, they often experienced brutal living conditions. However, they were at least spared the hunger and malnutrition they had left behind on the streets of their native country.

After a tumultuous beginning to the twentieth century, including labour unrest in reaction to low pay and harsh working conditions, the Great Depression of the 1930s revealed most workers' profound vulnerability to impoverishment. Predictably, this constellation of events pushed social activists and politicians to formulate legislation that softened the harshest edges of the capitalist economy. In 1927, the Old Age Pensions Act was introduced, followed by unemployment insurance in 1940, the Family Allowance Act in 1944, and the first hospital insurance plan in 1947. Throughout the postwar period, particularly in the economically buoyant 1960s, much social legislation was passed—Canada and Quebec Pension Plans (1965), federal education grants (1976), and an improved Unemployment Insurance Act (1971). Many of these initiatives were funded by progressive income tax programs that taxed the well-to-do at a significantly higher rate than less well-off citizens. As a result, governments and their agencies were able to provide at least some assistance to the elderly, ill, and out-of-work.

This levelling of the economic playing field was then generally reversed throughout the 1980s and 1990s. Largely in response to the popularization of neo-liberalism by President Ronald Reagan in the US, Prime Minister Margaret Thatcher in the UK, and Prime Minister Brian Mulroney in Canada, legislators reduced the size of government and placed a greater burden directly on individuals and their families. Effectively, much of the "welfare state" was steadily dismantled. For example, unemployment benefits were increasingly restricted in terms of both eligibility criteria and the length of the benefit period. Similarly, the cash value of welfare benefits across the country was reduced, and **workfare** provisions (requiring many welfare recipients to accept any paid work or training in exchange for their benefits) were introduced.

As our understanding of the welfare state has changed over time, so too have social policy goals in Canada. Today, in most circles, the private market is understood as ineffective in ensuring an adequate "distribution of resources amongst citizens and the state is understood to have an important role in pursuing a number of policies and programs with redistributive and social minimum goals" (Hay, 2009, p. 6). Most currently, the election of a Liberal government led by Justin Trudeau in 2015 may signify a dramatic shift in social policies addressing redistribution and social inequality.

Historically, Canadians have been offered some level of security from living in dire circumstances throughout the life course. Canada offers a number of benefits for seniors: Old Age Security, the Canada Pension Plan, and private pensions and savings such as Registered Retirement Savings Plans. Social assistance programs are often available for residents of Canada who are in financial difficulty and who meet a needs assessment. These programs provide financial assistance to cover an individual's or family's basic living costs when all other means of financial support have been exhausted (HRSDC, 2010).

The Liberal government's 2016 budget announcement promised increased spending to help economically strained families. Many of the existing benefits are being overhauled, including child and family benefits. As well, a new tax-free child benefit will increase payments to most Canadians with children; families with low incomes will receive the maximum benefit of $6,400 per child. Canada's Employment Insurance (EI) program is also being reworked. EI offers financial assistance to unemployed Canadians who have lost their job involuntarily. Changes to EI are expected to include revision of the rules regarding the number of hours and weeks a person must work before being qualified to apply, which vary by province and region. At the maximum benefit level, EI offers a replacement income at about the level of the poverty line (LICO) for a single person in a large city (Mowat Centre, 2012).

Canada also offers a variety of subsidies for housing and child care for low-income families. While these services are often noted as the most helpful to low-income families, in most provinces the waiting lists for housing are long, and the housing is often poorly maintained and located in neighbourhoods with high crime rates. As discussed above, there are far too few regulated child-care spaces available across Canada, and the requirements for obtaining and maintaining the child-care subsidy are often burdensome.

In addition, almost every community across Canada has food banks, soup kitchens, and shelters to assist the economically marginalized.

The Alberta provincial government recently launched a school nutrition pilot program to be rolled out across 14 publicly funded school boards. School nutrition programs help mitigate child and youth hunger, but some might argue that they only indirectly address the effects of low income in Canadian communities.

Indeed, it is commonly remarked that there are more food banks in Canada than there are McDonald's franchises. While these help to ensure that the poor do not starve, they can offer only small quantities of food, often of limited nutritional value.

CONCLUSION: SOCIAL AND ECONOMIC INEQUALITIES—FUTURE TRENDS

Various indicators suggest that **economic polarization** in various countries is increasing. The incomes of average Canadians have tended to either stagnate or decline. Outside of the oil-boom provinces of Alberta, Saskatchewan, and Newfoundland and Labrador, average weekly earnings (inflation adjusted) grew by only 3 per cent between 2009 and 2014 (Rozworski, 2015). Meanwhile, in the past 25 years, the wealthiest 0.01 per cent of the Canadian population saw their incomes double, on average rising from $3.6 million to $8.4 million (McQuaig, 2009). The rich are getting richer. This trend is also reflected in the following figures: between 2008 and 2014, the industrial composite average weekly wage paid to full-time, all-year workers

Table 6.2 ▶ 2014 Yearly Rate of Social Assistance for a Single Mother with One Child

Province	Total Welfare Income
Newfoundland and Labrador	$21,254
Prince Edward Island	$18,562
Nova Scotia	$16,384
New Brunswick	$21,770
Quebec	$19,600
Ontario	$19,040
Manitoba	$15,480
Saskatchewan	$19,351
Alberta	$16,626
British Columbia	$17,277
Yukon	$28,586
Northwest Territories	$29,743
Nunavut	$13,223

SOURCE: A, Tweedle, K. Battle and S. Torjman. Canadian Social Report: Welfare in Canada 2014, Caledon Institute 2014: 50–53.

GLOBAL ISSUES

Economic Inequality

The World Economic Forum has recognized that economic inequality is rapidly increasing in most countries and identified this as a major risk to human progress. Some economic inequality is expected, and in some cases is considered necessary to drive progress through higher rewards for talent, skills, ambition, and innovation. However, extreme levels of wealth concentration essentially exclude hundreds of millions of people from realizing the benefits of their talents and hard work (Oxfam, 2014).

A 2015 Oxfam report (Elliott, 2016) indicated that

- more than half of the world's wealth is now owned by 62 individuals (down from 388 in 2010)
- the wealth of the richest 62 people increased to $1.76 trillion between 2010 and 2015 while the wealth of the poorest 50 per cent dropped by 40 per cent
- the wealth of the richest 1 per cent of people in the world is more than that of the other 99 per cent combined

Class polarization appears to be particularly alarming for the middle and working classes. Deindustrialization has meant the loss of numerous well-paid and secure manufacturing jobs. The manufacturing jobs that remain are primarily the purview of middle-aged males with long seniority rights, and even these jobs are in jeopardy because of plant closures. In their place are a variety of poorly paid, often precarious (part-time, contract, seasonal, temporary) jobs that do not afford job-holders, even in a dual-income family, the prospect of a secure middle-class existence. At the same time, many of the public sector jobs (for example, employment in the federal, provincial, or municipal governments) have also been eroded. **Neo-liberalism** and a penchant for deficit

reduction have meant not only that much of this work has disappeared but also that what work remains is increasingly part-time, contract, or obtained through employment agencies.

At the same time that well-paying, secure, full-time employment has become increasingly scarce, the economic pressures on middle-class and working-class families have grown dramatically. For example, Ontario undergraduate university tuition fees were $2,105 in 1992 and skyrocketed (in current dollars) to $9,231 in 2015; from 1990 to 2014 national average tuition fees increased (adjusted for inflation) by 155 per cent. At the same time, tuition for graduate and professional students increased even more (Canadian Federation of Students, 2015a; Burly & Awad, 2015). Predictably, more students are shouldering more debt. Between 2000 and 2010 the proportion of students graduating with $25,000 or more debt increased to 24 per cent for undergraduates (Canadian Federation of Students, 2015b). This is far from surprising, since youth unemployment and underemployment was 27 per cent in 2014 (Burly & Awad, 2015, p. 1).

Gilles_Paire /iStockphoto

Enabling communities to access resources in order to attain self-sufficiency is the goal of programs like Oxfam Unwrapped, which provides people with the necessary tools to build water pumps like this one in Burkina Faso.

rose 11 per cent; minimum wages rose 17 per cent; and compensation for the top 100 CEOs rose 22 per cent (MacKenzie, 2015, p. 8). Even when CEO earnings dropped from 2007 to 2008, they still averaged $7.35 million per year, and by 2014 the top 100 best-paid Canadian CEOs were

bringing home an average $8.96 million a year in total compensation (Mackenzie, 2015). To put it another way, in 2014 the average annual pay among the top 100 CEOs in Canada was 184 times more than the average wage of Canadians working full-year, up from 105 times in 1998

(Mackenzie, 2015, p. 11). Not surprisingly, research suggests that over the course of a lifetime, the wealthiest 10 per cent of Canadians are steadily accumulating much more wealth than those in the middle class, and, as a result, economic disparities are intensifying (Macdonald, 2015, p. 24). In the absence of significant government interventions and dramatic policy initiatives, it appears likely that this growing social gap will expand (Brennan, 2015).

Questions for Critical Thought

1. As you walk through your university campus, what kinds of social class messages are you confronted with?
2. Which theoretical paradigm best describes social inequality? Explain why.
3. What is the basis of the feminist critique of stratification theory?
4. Are there policies that could lessen the gap between the haves and the have-nots? What might some of these policies be, and how would they be funded?
5. If Canada is becoming less equal, what are the implications for the quality of Canadians' lives?
6. A policy currently being proposed in Ontario is a **guaranteed annual income**, which would assure every citizen a minimum living income whether they were employed or not. What are the benefits and drawbacks of this approach?

Sociological Explorations

1. Many analysts point out that "the poor pay more." In your community, check out the true economic costs of using "fast cash" outlets, at which economically marginalized people get short-term loans or cash their cheques. Similarly, examine rent-to-own operations (usually for appliances and other large household items) and calculate the actual costs of not being able to afford to pay upfront for such items or finance them in another way. Also, identify the specific drawbacks of not being able to stock up on items or buy them in bulk, and not being able to afford loyalty cards. Calculate the economic implications over the course of one year.
2. Calculate the wages needed for a family of four (two parents and two children) to afford the basics in your home community or neighbourhood.

Recommended Readings

Fleras, A. (2011). *Unequal relations: An introduction to race, ethnic and Aboriginal dynamics in Canada*. Toronto, ON: Pearson.
Fleras provides an overview of the vast inequalities faced by visible minorities in Canada.

Freeland, C. (2012). *Plutocrats: The rise of the new global super rich and the fall of everyone else*. Toronto, ON: Doubleday.
Freeland examines the dramatic economic rise of the world's wealthiest 0.01 per cent.

Grabb, E., Hwang, M., & Reitz, J. (Eds). (2016). *Social inequality in Canada: Dimensions of disadvantage (6th edition)*. Toronto, ON: Oxford University Press.
This edited book provides over 20 chapters discussing different elements of inequality in Canada.

Porter, J. (2015 [1965]). *The vertical mosaic: An analysis of social class and power in Canada (50th anniversary edn)*. Toronto, ON: University of Toronto Press.
This 1965 classic study was the first detailed analysis of class inequality in Canada.

Reiman, J., & Leighton, P. (2013). *The rich get richer and the poor get prison* (10th edn). New York, NY: Allyn & Bacon.
This popular text examines how the criminal justice system both is biased against the poor and serves the interests of the rich.

Zawilski, V. (Ed.). (2015). *Inequality in Canada: A reader on the intersections of gender, race and class.* Toronto, ON: Oxford University Press.
This edited book offers 23 chapters written by experts in their fields that address the ways in which inequality grows at the intersection of gender, race, and class.

Recommended Websites

Caledon Institute of Social Policy
www.caledoninst.org/about%20us/
Established in 1992, the institute is a charitable organization that undertakes research and analysis in order to ensure that public discussion of poverty and social policy is well informed. Their free publications provide up-to-date information on social welfare incomes and other poverty-related issues.

Canadian Centre for Policy Alternatives
www.policyalternatives.ca/
Founded in 1980, the CCPA is an independent, non-partisan research institute committed to progressive policies. Its website provides access to up-to-date reports, including free publications, ranging from detailed reports to fact sheets, on poverty and the growing gap between the rich and the rest of us. In addition, the website provides blogs and access to interactive tools providing a plethora of useful information, such as "The Pay Clock: CEO vs. Average Pay in Canada"; videos, such as "The Living Wage Movement," and audio presentations, such as "The Gender Wage Gap."

Campaign 2000: End Child and Family Poverty in Canada
www.campaign2000.ca

Founded in 1991, Campaign 2000 is a network of national, regional, and local partner organizations committed to ensuring that the Canadian government makes good on its 1989 promise to end child poverty in Canada. While the original 2000 deadline has come and passed, the organization seeks to improve public awareness of child/family poverty through publishing research on the topic and providing public education resources. Among the free resources available through their website are the national and provincial *Annual Report Card on Child Poverty*.

Who Rules America?
www2.ucsc.edu/whorulesamerica/
This site highlights the work of famed US sociologist G. William Domhoff. It provides free access to a wide variety of publications on class dominance and theories of power. In addition, it provides access to databases on members of the US power elite and guidance on undertaking research on elites. Finally, the site includes videotaped lectures by Domhoff on a variety of topics, including "The Triumph of the Corporate Rich" and "How They Succeed" (2015).

Key Terms

blaming the system Analyses that emphasize the structural and institutional sources of inequality. Unequal access to education would, for example, contribute to poverty patterns.

blaming the victim The tendency in popular prejudice to hold individuals entirely responsible for their own misfortunes. This form of poor-bashing is countered by analyses that point out that **blaming the system** may be more accurate.

bourgeoisie The term used by Marx to refer to the capitalist class—that is, the individuals who own the

means of production (factory owners), the merchant (economically dominant) or ruling class.

class and status "Class," also termed *socio-economic class*, refers to one's position within a society's economic hierarchy. Typical designations include upper, middle, and lower class. Finer distinctions, such as upper-middle class, also appear in the literature. In contrast, "status" refers to one's social position in terms of privilege and esteem. While often based in economic considerations, status suggests a broader lifestyle dimension. Status may be *achieved* (e.g., becoming a CEO) or *ascribed* (e.g., born an "untouchable").

class consciousness The sense of membership in a social class. For Marx, members of the working class would eventually (as a result of their concentration in factories and oppressive working conditions) recognize their common interests and act in concert to overthrow capitalism.

classism Akin to terms such as *racism* and *sexism*, the stereotypes and prejudices that surround social class.

conspicuous consumption The public consumption of specific expensive goods and services by which an individual is able to communicate his or her elite social position.

digital divide Inequalities in access to computers and/or the Internet. Sociologists usually see socio-economic status and social class as the basis for the digital divide, but gender and national origin are among other characteristics associated with these inequalities.

economic elite Men and women who hold economic power in a society. Contemporary researchers often operationalize this concept in terms of reported financial assets (wealth) and/or leadership positions on the boards of key (e.g., the 100 largest) corporations.

economic polarization Also referred to as *class polarization*, the growing gap (globally and nationally) between the very wealthy (sometimes referred to as the 1 per cent) and the remainder of the population.

feminization of poverty The fact that poverty rates among women, nationally and globally, tend always to be higher than those of their male counterparts.

food insecurity Insufficient access to the quantity or variety of food a person or household needs, due to poverty.

guaranteed annual income First popularized in the late 1960s and increasingly popular today, a policy approach to poverty reduction that proposes to provide all citizens a basic income, regardless of the recipient's income status. This would ensure a basic standard of living for all Canadians. Also known as *guaranteed minimum income* or *guaranteed basic income*.

intersectionalities The interweaving of social inequality factors, such as age, gender, visible-minority status, and so on, to either intensify or minimize the effect of each.

low income cut-offs (LICOs) Income thresholds below which a family will have to devote a larger share of the income on food, shelter, and clothing than the average family. Families who must spend 63 per cent or more of after-tax income on necessities are considered to be below the LICOs.

low income measure (LIM) A measure used most frequently in international comparisons referring to families living at 50 per cent below the median adjusted household income.

market basket measure (MBM) A measure of low income based on the cost of a specified basket of goods and services that represent a modest, basic standard of living.

means of production A term used by Marxists to refer to wealth-generating property such as land, factories, and machinery; the ways goods are produced for sale on the market, including all the workers, machinery, and capital such production needs.

meritocracy A form of social stratification that relies on differences in effort and ability rather than on ascribed statuses such as gender, age, or race.

neo-liberalism A popular ideology whose advocates argue that the "big" government and the welfare state are a drag on the free market and individual enterprise. It gained prominence in the 1980s and 1990s, the era of Ronald Reagan, Margaret Thatcher, and Brian Mulroney.

power In the classic formulation, the ability to exercise one's will, even in the face of opposition from others. In Marxist sociology, a social relationship that has a material base. Those who own the **means of production** have the power to exploit workers through the appropriation of their labour efforts. In Weberian sociology, power is more broadly defined and can reflect the capacity of individuals or groups to exert their will over others. Contemporary analysts point out that power may also involve a wide variety of indirect and subtle manifestations, including the ability to mobilize bias or define a situation in one's own interests.

proletariat A term used by Marx for individuals who provided the labour power to capitalism. Lacking property, the proletariat was forced to survive by selling its labour to the **bourgeoisie**, who in turn exploited workers' efforts in the pursuit of profit.

social stratification The structured patterns of inequality that often appear in societal arrangements. From a macrosociological perspective, it is possible to discern the hierarchical strata of social classes that characterize most contemporary societies.

status symbols A term, popularized by Thorstein Veblen, that refers to the social elements that confer higher social standing on their owner.

workfare Popularized along with neo-liberalism, a term referring to the practice of requiring welfare recipients to "work" for their welfare benefits.

working poor The many individuals who are poor and yet are part of the paid labour force.

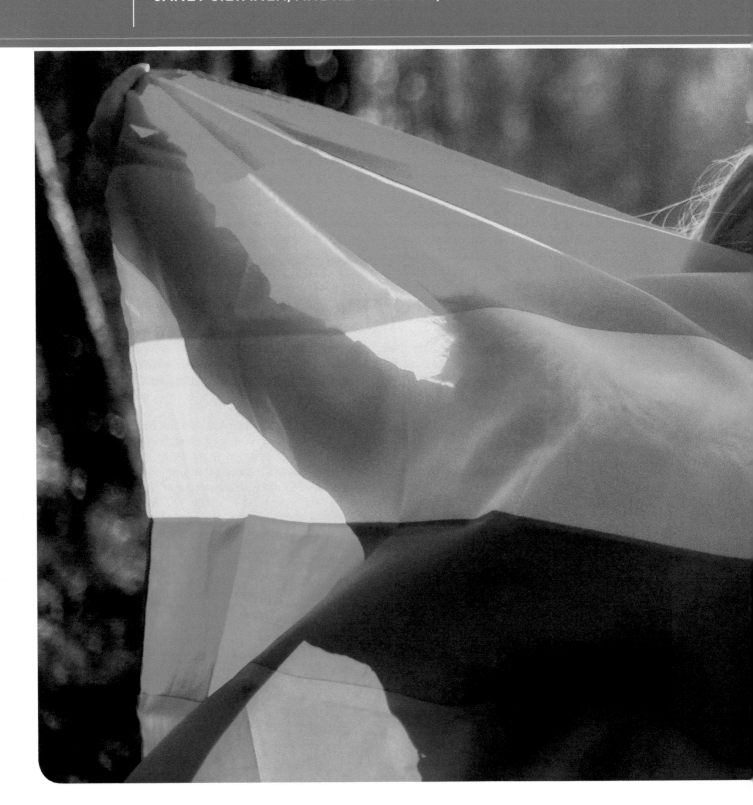

7 | Gender and Sexuality

JANET SILTANEN, ANDREA DOUCET, AND PATRIZIA ALBANESE

In this chapter you will:

▶ Learn some conceptual anchors in sociological thinking about gender and sexuality

▶ Understand the connections and disconnections between gender and sexuality

▶ Discover how the sociology of gender and sexuality is grounded in sites such as school, paid work, family, sexual violence, and the body

▶ Begin to think sociologically about how gender and sexuality matter in your everyday life and how they intersect with other dimensions of experience such as race/ethnicity, class, and age

INTRODUCTION: GENDER, SEXUALITY, AND YOU

If you were asked to describe yourself, what would first come to mind? Male or female? Straight or gay? Whatever descriptors you use, we hope you will discover in this chapter that we live in a society deeply structured by both gender and **sexuality**. Put differently, where you live, the families who raise you, the television shows you watch, the schools you go to, the computer games you play, and the friends you have are all shaped by gendered and **heteronormative** expectations. An aim of this chapter is to bring to your attention the many ways sociologists approach the study of gender and sexuality in order to understand both contemporary configurations as well as currents of change.

This chapter is guided also by the pedagogical principle that you will learn more meaningfully if you are able to link this material to your own life. We hope that you will be able to do this, and we also encourage you to look beyond your own experience to see patterns of social life that are both similar to and different from yours.

The first part of the chapter presents some core sociological ideas about gender and sexuality, namely that these are vantage points of critique, are social constructions, and involve relations of power and inequality.

The second part encourages you to examine your experiences sociologically by taking you through five sites where gender and sexuality are in play—education, sexual violence, work, family, and the body.

THINKING SOCIOLOGICALLY ABOUT GENDER AND SEXUALITY

Thinking sociologically about gender and sexuality means thinking about how to uncover and assess the social assumptions underlying particular configurations of gender and sexuality as structures and experiences. In what follows, we present three important insights in how sociologists think about gender and sexuality and discuss how they are used to analyze patterns of continuity and change.

Gender and Sexuality as Critical Vantage Points

The study of gender and sexuality is a central part of sociological study in Canada. Yet not so long ago, sociology was a **heterocentric**, male-centred discipline. This had two serious consequences. First, those who were *not* male and *not* heterosexual were invisible within the content of sociology. Second, they were also invisible within the profession of sociology.

Dorothy Smith (1987) and other pioneering feminist sociologists began to develop ways of not only including but also centring women's experiences within sociological research and theory. Gender has since become a key vantage point of sociological thinking. A vantage point enables us to see ourselves, the social institutions around us, and our social worlds in ways that include more experiences; it provides an angle to critique the status quo. This process of expanding our vision by adopting new vantage points is repeated within sociology for other dimensions of socially structured experience, including sexuality.

As a critical vantage point, sexuality studies almost always involve challenging fixed and often inaccurate ideas about human sexuality. Much of the early scientific research on sexuality focused on the biomedical aspects of sex and procreation. The development of sexology involved a shift in focus from reproductive processes to the study of sexual practices, but even then, studying sex and sexuality focused on heterosexual sex for procreation in marriage as normal and all other sexual activity and identities as deviant.

A pioneer in the scientific study of sexuality was Henry Havelock Ellis (1859–1939). Unlike others at the time, he tried to demystify sex and challenge many sexual norms of Victorian

England, famous for both its sexually repressive values and its abundance of clandestine erotic literature (see Kearney, 1982). For example, he assured his readers that masturbation did not lead to illness and that homosexuality was not a disease, vice, or amoral choice. Since then, the study of sexuality continues to challenge accepted norms and has shifted its focus to address more complex understandings of sexual identities. More recently, within sociology sexuality is typically studied and understood as intricately connected to cultural, economic, political, legal, moral, and ethical phenomena. Janice Irvine (2003, p. 431), for example, notes that from a sociological perspective, "sexuality is a broad social domain involving multiple fields of power, diverse systems of knowledge, and sets of institutional and political discourses."

Many feminist sociologists challenge, among other things, the social construction of sex and sexuality, the control of women's bodies and reproduction, the objectification of women, sexual double standards, the link between sex and power, and sexual abuse and oppression (Millett, 1969; Greer, 1984; Butler, 2006 [1990]; Weitz, 2002; Benkert, 2002). Sexuality is understood as both "an arena for women's liberation" and "a crucial vector of women's oppression" (Marcus, 2005, p. 193). Queer theory is yet another shift in this area, leading to a new vantage point.

The use of the term "queer" within the gay community began as a ploy to reclaim a slur and highlight the multiple ways that sexual practices, sexual fantasy, and sexual identity "fail to line up consistently" and "expresses an important insight about the complexity of sexuality" (Marcus, 2005, p. 196). Queer theory derives part of its philosophy from the ideas of Michel Foucault (1990), who saw homosexuality as a strategically situated marginal position from which it may be possible to see new and diverse ways of relating to oneself and others. More recently, "queer" has been used as a verb, where "to queer something" is to look critically

at its foundations, in order to explore its limits, biases, and boundaries. It means not settling for predefined categories, but instead creating new ones (Randazzo et al., 2015).

 Michel Foucault had a wide influence in many disciplines, and his work continues to shape sociological thought. See the Sociology in Action box, p. 18 in **Chapter 1**, "Sociological Theory and Research Methods," to learn more about his remarkable life.

Throughout the 1980s and 1990s, scholars such as the Canadian Blye Frank, the three American Michaels (Messner, Kimmel, Kaufman), the Australian Raewyn Connell, and others pioneered studies of men and masculinities. In doing so, they significantly developed a new direction in the sociological study of gender and sexuality. The study of masculinities is so active, it has produced specialized journals and conferences.

It is also important to note that gender itself has become a focus of critique. In Canada, women of colour and Indigenous women point to how the seemingly harmonious Canadian multicultural mosaic is marred by exclusion, discrimination, and violence. Examining the privileges of whiteness is an important feature of current studies of racialized understandings of gender and sexuality.

A further expansion of critical vantage points on gender and sexuality involves differences across generations. Younger generations of gender scholars mark out their own interests and issues. These include body image, **transgressive sexualities**, media-based violence against women, Internet pornography, and the anti-women iconography of video games. Younger generations of gender and sexuality scholars also work hard to shed light on the often invisible or stigmatized lives and experiences of members of **trans** communities (Taylor & Peter, 2011; Holtby et al., 2015; Peter et al., 2015). They point out that self-disclosure and visibility are not a risk-free endeavour given the tenacity of **transphobia** (Holtby et al., 2015).

Gender and Sexuality as Social Constructions

One of the earliest developments in thinking about gender in sociology was to challenge the notion that gender identities (e.g., masculinity and femininity) could be easily mapped onto biological identities (e.g., male and female). It was argued that ideas about masculinity and femininity have a social foundation independent of biology. *Gender* (socially produced differences, primarily of character, ambition, and achievement) was introduced as a term distinct from *sex* (biologically based differences, primarily related to chromosomes and reproductive functions). Sociology challenged ideas about sex and gender being dichotomous—two-part (male/female; masculine/feminine)—variables and thus being "natural" polar opposites. (Note that in the term "opposite sex," we are assumed to be sexually "drawn" to one another like magnets.)

Blue is for boys and pink is for girls, right? You may find it hard to believe, but this gender stereotype is relatively new. Prior to the 1940s, it was acceptable and even encouraged to dress boys in pink. So ingrained are these colour associations today that a baby boy dressed in pink would likely be mistaken for a female. This is one of many examples of how gender is socially constructed.

CaraMaria/iStockphoto

Inappropriate dichotomizing of sex and gender corresponds with an inappropriate dichotomizing of sexuality, sexual identity, and sexual orientation into heterosexual or **homosexual**. In fact sexuality, like gender, is considerably more complex.

Further, attributes and inequalities associated with being male and female came to be seen as socially created consequences of the way society is organized around gendered identities. Jeffrey Weeks (1993, p. 16) similarly notes that the meanings we give to sexuality are "socially organized, sustained by a variety of languages, which seek to tell us what sex is, what it ought to be—and what it could be." These languages of sex are then "embedded in moral treatises, laws, educational practices, psychological theories, medical definitions, social rituals, pornographic or romantic fictions, popular music and common sense assumptions."

The problem is that once people are packaged into boxes—male or female, masculine or feminine, heterosexual or homosexual—**sexism** (the subordination of one sex, usually female, and the perceived superiority of the other) and **homophobia** (an irrational fear of homosexuality) help to reinforce rigid boundaries and keep people "in their place." A young person who challenges traditional gender ideology or practices is likely to be teased and taunted, often harassed back into stereotypical behaviour. Children and youth learn to avoid ridicule by conforming to prescribed gender and sexual norms. As a result, we come to see certain types of behaviour as normal, natural, and inevitable—the core or **essence** of femininity or masculinity, heterosexuality or homosexuality—when in fact we may have been forced to suppress parts of our identities that cross the socially constructed gender and sexual divide. The decoupling of the sex–gender distinction from a division between the social and the natural also loosened the association of gender and sexuality and ushered in a torrent of research activity on sexuality as a socially constructed phenomenon that may or may not have a gendered form.

The trend now is to see a more dynamic relationship between identified features of sexed bodies and what these features come to mean in social situations and in personal identities. Thus, with the social construction of gender released from more limited notions of hetero-sexuality and reproduction, a greater range of challenged and accepted behaviours and identities emerge, which express a more varied relationship between sexual orientation, gender expression, and the gendered/sexed body.

Nevertheless, ideas about the necessity of gender are still strongly entrenched. The case of baby Storm is a good illustration of this. In May 2011, Torontonians Kathy Witterick and David Stocker sent an email to their friends and family, informing them that their baby Storm had been born. Unlike most birth announcements, it did not identify Storm as a boy or a girl. The email explained this as "a tribute to freedom and choice in place of limitation, a stand up to what the world could become in Storm's lifetime (a more progressive place)." When *The Toronto Star* (Poisson, 2011) heard this story, they interviewed the family and published a front-page piece on their gender non-conforming choice. The public reaction and the media frenzy that followed was overwhelming. Storm's parents faced a barrage of international media attention including invitations from NBC, *National Geographic*, *60 Minutes Australia*, Anderson Cooper, Dr. Phil, and the Oprah Winfrey Network. To quote *The Globe and Mail*, "this genderless baby story has connected with a deep level of anxiety out there" (Timson, 2011).

For their part, the parents of baby Storm resisted the media pressure, giving only one interview to CBC radio; Witterick also wrote to the *Toronto Star* and explained, "In not telling the gender of my precious baby, I am saying to the world, 'Please can you just let Storm discover for him/herself what s(he) wants to be?!.'" (Poisson, 2011). She also penned a book chapter challenging gender binaries in children and in child-rearing (Witterick, 2013).

The media frenzy finally fizzled out, but only after months of attention and debate in which international experts in gender and/or

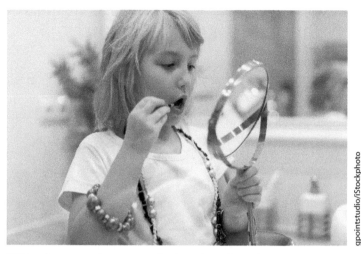

Children learn to conform to prescribed gender and sexual norms at a young age. Those who do not conform often face teasing and taunting when they break traditional gender boundaries.

gpointstudio/iStockphoto

child-rearing, journalists, bloggers, and parents weighed in on this family's choice. Suddenly the world seemed very interested in these ideas that sociologists have been studying and debating for many years. Why does gender matter? What would it mean to live in a society without gender? Is it possible to raise a gender-neutral child?

If gender and sexuality are socially constructed, they can be reconstructed and changed. Questions about **undoing** gendered and hetero-normative structures and assumptions are central to current sociological scholarship. Sociologists address matters of undoing from both a research and activist perspective. The work of Rachel Epstein, a post-doctoral fellow and adjunct professor of sociology at Brock University, is a great example.

Although at one point the separation of gender and sex was an important move forward, this development itself came under critical attention. As early as 1980, Canadian feminist sociologist Margrit Eichler voiced some of the analytical problems that emerge out of a separation of biological sex and social gender. One important problem is ignoring the extent to which biological sex is itself socially constructed. Today, there is more attention to the social construction of the so-called "natural" characteristics of biological sex, including, for example, investigations into the manipulation of bodily features (for example, changing the

RESEARCHERS IN ACTION ▶ Undoing: The Work of Rachel Epstein on LGBTQ2S Parenting

I am a long-time LGBTQ2S parenting activist, researcher and educator. In 1997, at a time when LGBTQ people were openly discouraged from parenting, midwife Kathi Duncan and I designed "Dykes Planning Tykes" (DPT), a 12-week course for lesbian/bisexual/queer women considering parenthood (see www.lgbtqpn.ca/dykes-planning-tykes-film). DPT has since spawned three other LGBTQ2S "family planning" courses for people across the LGBTQ spectrum (see www.lgbtqpn.ca/courses).

In 2001 I became the founding coordinator of the LGBTQ Parenting Network (PN), a community program that supports LGBTQ2S-led families. Here, I collaborated on community-based research projects exploring LGBTQ2S people's interactions with adoption and assisted reproduction systems, the experiences of queer spawn (children with LGBTQ2S parents) in schools, and the challenges faced by trans parents. These projects were defined by community concerns and were expressly conceived as advocacy initiatives. For example, the Creating Our Families (COF) project, based on interviews with 66 LGBTQ2S people about fertility clinics, produced an array of popular and academic writings, as well as theatre and video (see www.lgbtqpn.ca/ahr).

I completed my PhD dissertation at York University in 2014 and have combined community work with scholarly interests in a range of other publications, including the 2009 Canadian anthology *Who's Your Daddy? And Other Writings on Queer Parenting* (Epstein, 2009) and the Best Start Resource Centre's manual, *Welcoming and Celebrating Sexual Orientation and Gender Diversity in Families* (Best Start Resource Centre, 2012). I am currently a Banting post-doctoral fellow at Brock University, conducting research on LGBTQ2S family conflict.

Key to all this work is my desire to further recognition and support for a broad range of LGBTQ2S (and other) family configurations. My daughter, co-parent, and I were parties in the 2005 Charter challenge that resulted in provincial changes to birth registration procedures, and I recently worked with others to help shape the All Families Are Equal Act, which became law in Ontario in 2016, expanding the categories of people who are recognized as parents in Ontario.

SOURCE: Rachel Epstein

---

size of breasts and penises or the shape of labia and buttocks, or suppressing of menstruation), and greater acceptance of the fact that the "sex" of a human body is not adequately represented as an unambiguous natural binary.

As the appreciation of the complexity of gender and sexual identities developed, sociologists started to examine how some everyday practices work to reproduce and some to challenge existing understandings of what is "normal" or appropriate. There was particular interest in youth culture and experience. For example, was it possible to observe change in how young people negotiated their gender and sexuality?

TIME to REFLECT ●──▬▬

Do you think that young women and young men today are equally affected by "sexting"? How might the sociological vantage points of gender and sexuality help to answer this question?

A fascinating study by Jade Boyd (2010) reveals the pushes against and pulls toward conventional enactments of heterosexual masculinity and femininity. Examining Vancouver's entertainment district, Boyd argues that the "mainstream" produces, maintains, and reiterates the moral contours of heterosexuality within the city. Boyd shows that nightclubs, as spaces of hypermasculinity and hyperfemininity, offer a prime example of how **governmentality**, surveillance, and private enterprise work together in the maintenance and regulation of social and sexual conformity. Boyd explains that through heterosexual hegemony and heteronormativity, heterosexuality has been normalized and is understood as unproblematic and natural rather than revealed as constrained and produced by power relations. Like Adrienne Rich (2003 [1980]), Boyd argues that heterosexuality is a compulsory fiction and political institution, maintained and enforced through state practices. Like Judith Butler

(2006 [1990]) and Foucault (1990), she theorizes gender as performative in that it re-enacts meaning systems through the constant reiteration of heterosexual norms. Boyd (2010) argues that this works to conceal the instability and production of sex and gender, thus enabling gender inequality to remain unchallenged.

Young people in Boyd's study comment on the differences in gender dynamics between indie events in the East Side of Vancouver and mainstream events in "glossy bars" on the Granville Strip. As one young woman explains,

> Visually there's more hyper-females in mainstream clubs . . . more Barbie doll style. Not to say that they all look like Barbies. But they often have very long hair, they'll be wearing quite a lot of makeup, they'll be wearing very feminine clothes that show off their physical attributes like their boobs and their bum, their waist and hips and stuff. (Boyd, 2010, p. 182)

Boyd shows that hyper- and heterosexualized performance in Granville clubs reinforces hegemonic femininity and masculinity and heterosexual hegemony. In contrast, study participants note that the indie dance scene is more open to diverse sexualities than is the Granville scene (Boyd, 2010).

How does your own experience of gender and sexuality norms in public spaces compare to what Boyd discovered in her study? Have you encountered spaces that reproduce heteronormative identities? How about "alternative" spaces that challenge heteronormative identities? Considering these sorts of questions will help you to identify the social processes and interactions involved in the (de)construction of gender and sexuality identities.

Gender and Sexual Relations are Relations of Power and Inequality

A central sociological claim is that inequality in women's and men's life chances is a consequence of how society is organized and of the particular ways in which gender is created and sustained as a significant feature of social and personal life.

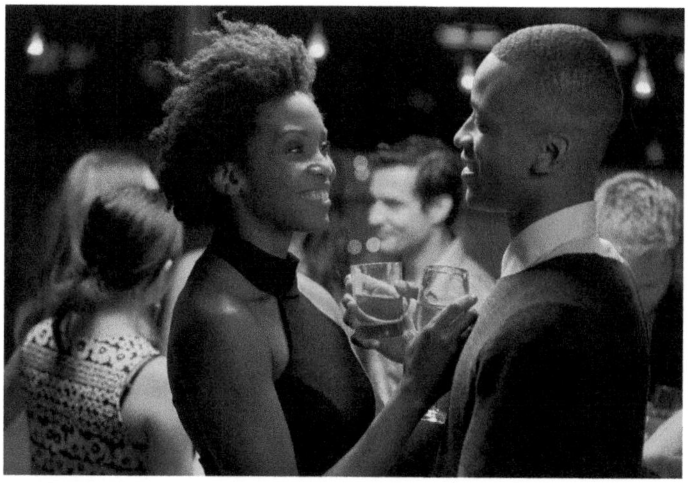

monkeybusinessimages/iStockphoto

Do your experiences at nightclubs and bars align with those expressed in Boyd's study? Why or why not?

In Canada, several streams of work develop this idea. One is focused on the organizational aspects of inequality, with an emphasis on inequalities in education, employment, income, and the amount and types of work that women and men do (we discuss this in more detail in the second part of this chapter). A second stream of research in Canada is concerned with larger systemic foundations of gender inequality, captured by analyses of capitalism, **patriarchy**, and what came to be called the sex/gender system. The work of sociologist Roberta Hamilton captures this trend in her well-known revision of Canadian sociologist John Porter's (1965) classic work on Canadian inequality as a vertical mosaic. The title of Hamilton's book refers to the "gendering" of the vertical mosaic (Hamilton, 2005 [1996]).

Beyond these foundational efforts, scholars of gender and sexuality increasingly began to attend to diversity, complexity, nuance, and fragmentation within earlier concepts and arguments. It was clear that context and circumstances mattered. For example, research and writing on intimate partner violence (IPV) began to look more closely at the way gender was essentialized in some explanations. There was a move away from seeing "men" as a homogeneous group of perpetrators and a more detailed analysis of which men are likely to commit IPV and in what circumstances (see CRIAW [n.d.] for further information). There was in general a move toward regarding the relevance, substance, and complexity of gender as questions for, and not assumptions of, research.

In Canada, the work of feminist sociologists Himani Bannerji and Sherene Razack stands out as drawing our attention to the multiple dimensions of inequality that interconnect with gender, and which at times have greater force. In their earlier work, both authors employ the evocative metaphor of the *gaze* to capture relations of oppression and resistance. Bannerji's *Returning the Gaze* (1993) and Razack's *Looking White People in the Eye* (1998) depict the active agency, response, and resistance of racialized women who stare back at and challenge injustices in Canadian society. Work with and by Indigenous women represents important efforts to recognize and address the gender struggles of the most marginalized individuals in our society. These efforts have helped to put on the sociological agenda the many forms of **racialization** in Canada and the way they intertwine with gendered and sexual hierarchies.

More recently, the words **interlocking** or **intersectional analysis** have come to dominate understandings of women's multiple identities as well as their location in multiple structures not only of gender and sexuality but also of dis/ability, class, and race. According to American sociologist Patricia Hill Collins, intersectionality "refers to particular forms of intersecting oppressions, for example, intersections of race and gender, or of sexuality and nation. Intersectional paradigms remind us that oppression cannot be reduced to one fundamental type, and that oppressions work together in producing injustice" (2000, p. 18).

While the terms seem to be shifting to capture increasing levels of diversity in our society, an important point to emphasize is that issues of difference and disadvantage need to be viewed as multifaceted and as both relational and structural phenomena. They operate at the level of identity or agency (i.e., "I feel discriminated against not just as a woman and not just as a racialized person but as a racialized woman"), and at the same time they are rooted in the ways

in which social institutions such as families, workplaces, and schools are set up and function.

A good example of an analysis highlighting the interlocking and intersecting dimensions of inequality is Rajiva and Batacharya's (2010) edited collection on the murder of 14-year-old Reena Virk in Victoria, BC, in 1997. They identify the purpose of these writings as an intervention in transforming how this tragic event has been framed and understood. Much of the media reporting identified this attack as a case of adolescent bullying and highlighted as the most shocking aspect the fact that all but one of the assailants were girls. Media reports generated what Barron and Lacombe (2010, p. 292) identified as a moral panic about the "nasty girl" with headlines such as "Girl violence reported on the rise," and "Girl-gang members more violent than boys, experts agree." As Rajiva and Batacharya (2010, p. 8) argue, this dominant narrative "obscured how race, gender, sexuality, class and other interlocking constructions of social difference and hierarchy constitute the material and discursive elements of this case." Further, they insist that reframing via an intersectional lens positions Reena Virk's murder as not an aberrant case, but another case of the high level of violence experienced by women of colour. This complex interlocking of inequality, with its underlying racism and misogyny, is also what underlies the distressing phenomenon of missing and murdered Indigenous women in Canada.

While intersectionality has been widely adopted, it has not been without controversy. Luft and Ward (2009) describe how the take-up of intersectionality in mainstream academic theory and research has obscured its grounding in black feminist activism and scholarship. This resonates with Bilge's (2013) observation of the dulling of the political edge of intersectionality by "disciplinary feminism." That said, the concept has brought attention to the multiple forms of inequality within which gender is embedded and has encouraged a more nuanced and complex understanding of how gender interacts with not only race but sexual orientation, disability, language, migration status, and many other factors to shape how inequalities permeate our lives.

GENDER AND SEXUALITY IN EVERYDAY LIFE

It would be difficult to identify any part of our everyday life that is free of expectations concerning gender and sexuality. Nevertheless, in certain sites of experience issues of gender and sexuality feature especially prominently. We discuss five—education, sexual violence, work, family, and the body.

Gender and Sexuality in School

Gender differences in schooling experiences and attainment have attracted sociological attention for many decades. Earlier on, the concern was that girls were losing out in education. Sociological research demonstrated that starting as early as elementary school and becoming more pronounced over time, classroom experiences, curriculum design, and measurements of student success highly favoured boys. After successful campaigns and educational changes, the tables seem to have turned. From the early 1980s onward, the enrolment of women in Canadian universities has exceeded that of men. Statistics Canada has reported that in 2011–2012, women made up close to 60 per cent of university and college enrolment, but less than half of enrolment in doctoral programs (Statistics Canada, 2011a, 2013h). Research (Abada & Tenkorang, 2009, p. 201) shows that the gender gap in attending and graduating from university also applies to children of immigrants to Canada, with young immigrant women "60 per cent more likely to have a university education" than their male counterparts. Slightly more than half of second-generation Canadian women aged 25–34 have at least 16 years of education, compared to roughly 45 per cent of second-generation men in the same age group (Aydemir, Chen, & Corak 2013, p. 109). For Indigenous youths, a slight gender gap favours women in completing a university education,

but the overall university completion rate for Indigenous youths is extremely low (Wilson & Macdonald, 2010).

What does this gender shift mean? Some have noted that this shift is happening within a pattern of gender continuity. They point, for example, to the fact that most students continue to be gender-segregated in terms of the programs and courses they take as undergraduates. Women have made significant inroads into professions such as law and medicine (now both roughly 50 per cent female) and now dominate some degree programs in which they were previously a minority (for example, pharmacology and veterinary medicine). However, overwhelming imbalances persist in traditionally female programs (nursing, social work, education, and fine arts) where roughly 66 per cent (or more) of the degrees are granted to women. Some male-dominated programs also seem very resistant to change. Women are particularly under-represented in engineering, physical sciences, and computer sciences in Canada (Shapiro & Sax, 2011), and make up only 26 per cent of students in mathematics and computer and information sciences, and 20 per cent of students in architecture, engineering, and related technologies (AUCC, 2011). As many note (Davies & Guppy, 2006, Powell, Dainty, & Bagilhole, 2011), these are programs (and areas of employment) where a long-standing male-focused culture presents a chilly climate to women daring enough to cross the gender divide.

Research shows the girls in school are caught between post-feminist discourses of achieved equality and everyday experiences of continued inequality (Pomerantz et al., 2013). Without a language to identify and name the experience of sexism in schools, girls are left to blame themselves for negative experiences. The chilly climate for those daring to be different, those whose gender expression or sexuality is not in sync with the majority, can be as severe as harassment and sexual violence. Grassroots organizations and women's and feminist groups continue to work to overcome marginalization and systemic prejudice (see Peter & Taylor [2011] and Egale's safe schools campaign [Egale, 2015] for statistics and details on homophobia, biphobia, and transphobia in schools).

Sexual Violence

The sexual domination of women is identified by Schippers (2007) as the cornerstone of **gender hegemony**. Building on Connell's formulation of **hegemonic masculinity**, Schippers develops a theory of gender hegemony that involves a relation of dominance between hegemonic masculinity and hegemonic femininity. She draws on Butler's idea of the heterosexual matrix, which makes the *relationship of difference* central to the concept of gender, and ties it to the hierarchical nature of heterosexual penetrative sex. The combination of difference and hierarchy is thus the "hegemonic scaffolding" (Schippers, 2007, p. 91) of the relational configuration of gender, which provides legitimation for the dominance of men. Challenging the sexual violence committed by men on women confronts these embedded notions of the legitimacy of male dominance and the assumed complicit relation of women to it.

 Violence against women can take many forms, but for more information on domestic violence, see "Intimate Partner Violence," p. 212, in **Chapter 9**, "Families and Health Issues."

Women's groups and feminists are quite ambivalent regarding the role of men in combating sexual violence. Some argue that "Take Back the Night" (www.takebackthenight.org) events should involve women only; others argue that men need to take part in these events, since sexual violence is not only a "women's issue." At the same time, men's groups have come up with their own male-centred approaches to ending sexual violence. The annual White Ribbon Campaign, started by Canadian sociologist Michael Kaufman, encourages men to wear a white ribbon as a symbolic pledge never to commit, condone, or remain silent about violence against women.

Bernard Weil/Toronto Star via Getty Images

Hundreds of men take part in the "Walk a Mile in Her Shoes" event to end violence against women. Do you think the walk, hosted by the White Ribbon Campaign in downtown Toronto, can succeed in changing attitudes?

OPEN FOR DISCUSSION
Sexual Assault on Campus | Elana Finestone

During my six years as a student at Queen's and Carleton, sexual assault posters captured my attention in women's bathroom stalls, the University Centre atrium, and the tunnel system on campus. I eyed posters for women's self-defence courses, offering to teach me how to protect myself from sexual assault. Another poster informed me that I should watch my drink at parties to lessen the risk of date rape.

These posters, like most of the sexual assault posters around campus, exclusively target women. They imply that if women fail to protect themselves from assault, they invite it. This message is not only victim-blaming for sexual assault survivors, but it completely ignores the role men can play in ending sexual assault.

Recently, Carleton University administration tried to target men in their sexual assault posters. Through focus groups with first-year Carleton University students, I learned that men did not feel targeted by these posters.

Most of the men *and* women I spoke with felt that men did not feel actively engaged because the posters portrayed all men as exhibiting central traits of hegemonic masculinity: aggressive,

emotionless, and slaves to their sex drive. For example, many men and women felt the poster with the catchphrase "Ask First: Any form of sexual activity without consent is sexual assault" talked down to all men as potential rapists.

While posters depicting hegemonic masculinity were unsuccessful, so too were posters depicting characteristics associated with femininity. For example, posters for events encouraging men to share their feelings were unsuccessful. Students' desire to differentiate masculine from feminine traits suggests they view gender as a dichotomy rather than a continuum.

My discussions with first-year students revealed the importance of sexual assault campaigns that target men in ways that recognize the multiplicities of masculinities and femininities. For example, a poster with the slogan "Being a friend means stopping him before he does something stupid: ... Rape is a man's issue too" was most effective for men. It redefined masculinity in positive ways by constructing men as part of the solution to sexual violence. Universities would do well to involve both genders in university-wide sexual assault prevention efforts.

It begins on 25 November, the International Day for the Elimination of Violence against Women, and ends on 6 December, Canada's National Day of Remembrance and Action on Violence against Women, the anniversary of the 1989 Montreal Massacre in which 25-year-old Marc Lépine shot and killed 14 female engineering students at Montreal's École Polytechnique.

While this sort of targeting of women students is extreme, there has been considerable outcry over other expressions of violence toward women in Canadian universities of a more everyday, but nevertheless highly destructive, character. As several recent events on Canadian campuses show, misogynistic attitudes and actions are explicitly or implicitly condoned to the point of university campuses being identified as sites of rape culture. Where such attitudes and actions have been challenged and addressed, the

inclusion of men in solution-focused activism is again a matter of debate. The MA research of Elana Finestone shows why and how a younger generation of women is seeking to include men in discussions of rape on campus.

Gender and Sexuality in Work

Although women are gaining ground in obtaining education credentials, they are less able to turn this educational advantage into dollars when they enter the labour market. This happens partly because gender segregation in university programs carries graduates into gender-segregated jobs. However, evidence shows that even within the same occupation, young men begin their careers at a higher starting salary (MacAlpine, 2005) and women continue to experience the glass ceiling (Livingstone et al., 2016).

Are you surprised that Canadian women continue to earn less than their male counterparts? See "Gendered Work," p. 260, in **Chapter 11**, "Work and the Economy," for a broader discussion on work participation, labour segregation, and the different experiences of racialized women.

But gendered experiences do not end there. A number of scholars argue that many workplace and organizational cultures play key roles in creating and maintaining inequalities focused on gender and sexuality (Welsh, 1999; Dellinger, 2002; Lance, Anderson & Croteau, 2010; Yoder & Mattheis, 2016). Dellinger suggests that instead of simply looking at sexuality as something individuals bring to work, we should examine how workplace customs and practices constitute a type of **organizational sexuality** or social practice that determines explicit and culturally elaborated rules of behaviour to regulate sexual identities and personal relationships. In other words, in different occupational cultures, different and specific social rules govern what constitutes "appropriate" or acceptable sexuality. Workplace norms about sexuality regulate who we say we are, who we "date," how we dress, and how we understand and experience sexual harassment in the workplace. Lance, Anderson, and Croteau (2010), for example, have written about *workplace sexual identity management*, or the wide range of actions taken by lesbian, gay, and bisexual workers to manage information concerning their sexual orientation.

Researchers note (Welsh, 1999; Newton-Francis & Young, 2015) that some organizations actually mandate the sexualization of their workers; as a result, in some sexually charged work cultures, degrading or sexualized behaviours become an institutionalized component of work. Consider, for example, a waitress at a Hooters restaurant (Newton-Francis & Young, 2015), who is required to wear short shorts and a top that shows cleavage—this is not, for the most part, considered sexual harassment. Given these highly sexualized workplace cultures, it is perhaps not surprising that researchers have found that waitresses' tips varied with age, increased with breast size, were higher for blondes, and decreased as body size increased (Lynn, 2009).

Workplace norms and organizational culture affect how sexuality is negotiated at work and, in part, determine what counts as sexual harassment.

TIME to REFLECT

In early 2016, a news headline read, "Restaurant dress codes: Sexy outfits for female staff may be discriminatory" (Sample, 2016). Think about a recent restaurant experience, as a diner or as an employee; how did the restaurant's dress code affect your experience? Is asking female employees to wear "sexy outfits" discriminatory or a form of sexual harassment?

Gender and Sexuality in the Family

Sociologists have known for some time that family experience and relations profoundly affect our sense of self—including our sense of ourselves as gendered and sexual beings. While in earlier decades sociologists were inclined to study the family as a "haven in a heartless world," recent attention focuses on inequalities running through families and their connection to gender and sexual hierarchies. Inequality within the family and the study of **gender divisions of domestic labour** are now burgeoning areas of research. While this is a large and diverse field of study, three features are noteworthy here.

First, it is important to see domestic labour and the care of children not as a small issue of concern only to women. How societies care, or do not care, for dependent others—both old and young—tells us a great deal about the social fabric, social institutions, and political priorities of that nation, province, territory, or city. For almost four decades, feminist social scientists have highlighted the economic, social, political, and personal costs to women of the gender imbalance in family-based care work. There is also increasing attention on how *not* caring for others affects men—including shorter lifespans and loneliness or isolation when they live without wives or partners.

A second point relates to something you may have seen in your own household: men doing more domestic work. While there are different interpretations of how much housework Canadian men are actually doing, there is a fairly strong consensus that *more* men are doing *more* housework than they did in previous generations and much of this increase is in child-care–related activities (Doucet, 2006, 2017).

A good indication of Canadian men's increasing involvement in child care is perhaps best revealed in two sets of statistics. The first concerns long-term stay-at-home fathers and the second, fathers taking parental leave. Statistics Canada (2011b) numbers indicate that the number of stay-at-home fathers (about 54,000 of them in 2010) has increased 25 per cent since 1976. In Canada, men were able to take parental leave to care for infants beginning in 1990. When total parental leave was extended from six months to one year in 2001, fathers' use of parental leave increased. While fathers tend to take less time off than do mothers, more and more fathers do take leave. According to Statistics Canada, in 2010 men took an average of 9 weeks of paid parental leave compared to 28 weeks for women; the number of eligible fathers taking leave increased from 12 per cent in 2004 to 29 per cent in 2011 (with most of the increase occurring in the province of Quebec, where there is more generous provision for fathers, including three to five weeks of paternity leave).

Third, families have always existed in diverse forms, but only recently have some families been allowed to legally "count" as families in the Canadian context. In 2000, the passing of Bill C-23 granted same-sex couples the same rights and obligations as common-law heterosexual couples. Then, in 2005, "equal marriage" legislation came into force with the passage of Bill C-315, the Civil Marriage Act, which recognized the right of same-sex couples to marry without legal discrimination. The 2011 census results reveal a growing number of same-sex families in Canada, which may also lead us to redefine and rethink the debate on the gender division of domestic labour.

Gender relations in the family are shifting as more men take on household responsibilities, such as child care and doing laundry.

Nick Kennedy / Alamy Stock Photo

While, as discussed above, young people are constantly negotiating gender relations and sexuality at school, at work, and within their families, they are also negotiating a wide range of gender and sexual identities in an increasingly globalized world.

TIME to REFLECT

Would you expect the division of household labour in same-sex couples to be similar to or different from that in heterosexual couples? Why?

The Body

A distinguishing aspect of the generational experience of gender negotiation for youth today is that it is being done in a relational context that is *globalized*. This means greater exposure to diverse images and practices of masculinity, femininity, and sexuality. However, it can also mean greater pressure toward homogenized, conservative, stereotyped, and, at the extreme, exploitative messages about what is "normal" and acceptable. The body is a site on and through which these tensions are worked out.

Research in Canada highlights how young people negotiate gender and sexual identities in contexts involving competing expectations. These clashes often include confrontations over how the body is used and displayed—such as choices in style of clothing, how much skin is exposed, hair style, hair colour, piercings, tattoos, and makeup—to name just a few areas of contention! Amita Handa (2003) tells of young South Asian girls "walking a tightrope" between saris and miniskirts in their attempts to meet and challenge the cultural expectations of their families, and Kelly et al. (2005) describe how "sk8ter girls" manoeuvre between the masculine culture of skateboarding and the "high heel" expectations of femininity.

Becoming oneself involves confronting the contours and power of hegemonic gender and sexual identities. This journey is complicated and made more challenging within a globalized context that includes the ubiquitous presence of Internet pornography, the stunning scale of sex tourism, and the increase in human trafficking for the sex trade. All of these are serious examples of gender, race, class, and historic processes of colonization and contemporary globalization colliding to produce extreme, exploitative versions of masculinity and femininity.

TIME to REFLECT •

Cabezas (2006) studied the eroticization of work and the role of race, class, and gender in Cuba's all-inclusive resorts. Using your sociological imagination, and given your own experiences at resorts or based on what you have heard from others, what might Cabezas have found?

Stereotyped presentations of gendered bodies are very familiar on television, in magazines, and on celebrity websites; there are many versions of the thin, tall, perfect-complexioned, young blonde woman and the "six-packed," clean-shaven young man with the dazzling white smile. Billions of dollars are spent every day on temporary and permanent body products and procedures, and this industry caters increasingly to men as well as to women.

Surgical modification to enhance and produce gendered standards of beauty is an expensive option, but as Zainab Amery explains, it is becoming a normalized practice in many places around the globe.

Although hegemonic expectations and pressures to conform to bodily norms are intense, sociologists know well that young people have a critical awareness. While recognizing youth culture as big business and full of marketing ploys, sociologists nevertheless see young people as capable of discernment in deciding how to shape their inner and outer selves. This awareness is expressed in campaigns, magazines, blogs, and websites that challenge dominant conceptions of the body as it relates to gender and sexuality. Leading the way in Canada are publications such as *Shameless*, initiatives like the Gender and Sexuality Alliance, and considerably smaller yet inspiring groups like the Toronto Queer Zine Fair Collective, a group of queer- and trans-identified

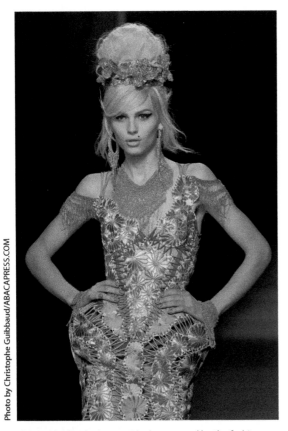

Photo by Christophe Guibbaud/ABACAPRESS.COM

This model fits the beauty ideals espoused by the fashion industry, right? Would you still agree if you found out this model was a man? Androgynous model Andrej Pejic has caused a sensation in the fashion world, successfully modelling for top fashion designers like Jean Paul Gaultier as both a man and a woman.

**Body Beautiful: Perfection under Construction |
Zainab Amery**

Who knew boob jobs and liposuction would be the top two surgical procedures in China and India, according to the 2010 survey of the International Society of Aesthetic Plastic Surgery? With the United States and Brazil taking first and second place as cosmetic surgery nations, China runs a close third, with India not too far behind. There are also reports that customers everywhere are getting younger, with cosmetic surgery becoming one way young women get ready for university.

But it is not about beauty alone: it is about the rewards that being beautiful can bring. Studies show that in the labour market, attractive people achieve more success than their less attractive competitors. In Brazil, where the body is worshipped and beauty means access to employment, government-run hospitals offer subsidized procedures for low-income people. In Asian countries, business is booming but is racialized, with many young people opting for double-eyelid

surgeries to become "Caucasian-looking" in order to get the best jobs.

However, it is Lebanon that takes the prize for the first cosmetic loan program. Billboards advertising the First National Bank's Plastic Surgery program read, "Beauty is no longer a luxury" beside an image of a Western-looking, Caucasian, blue-eyed, blonde woman. Astonishingly, the only stipulations are that the borrower be at least 17 years of age and make at least $600 a month. In a country where beauty is paramount for the purpose of getting (and staying) married, the perfect body can have high significance—especially since there is only one eligible male for every five women. The situation is so serious that mothers escort their daughters to surgeons to raise their odds of finding a husband. But the search for perfection is no longer solely a women's quest. Of the 1.5 million surgeries performed yearly in Lebanon, 30 per cent are on young men (Ajami, 2008), with a similar trend occurring globally.

writers, artists, and organizers seeking to make space for traditionally marginalized voices in the zine community.

CONCLUSION: ON TO THE FUTURE . . . GENDER RELATIONS AND SOCIAL CHANGE

Uncovering strategies and possibilities for change is an important focus of sociological investigations. This brings us to ask the question: how do we identify progress in the ways in which gender and sexuality are structured in society and negotiated in everyday lives? Is progress the eradication of differences themselves or the neutralization of the social, material, and political consequences of differences? Ideas about gender equality and sexuality change with the times, and we need to keep a constant watch on whether our understanding of and platforms for equality are keeping pace with social, economic, and political changes.

Youth are a key source of this energy for change. Many young people in Canada today

are involved in campaigns and other activist work to address gender and sexuality issues—from Femmetoxic (the campaign to remove toxic chemicals from women's beauty products) to the involvement of male youth in the White Ribbon Campaign to grassroots organizations like Egale Canada (which advocates for equality and justice for Canadian lesbian, gay, bisexual, and trans-identified people).

Equally ubiquitous are many people's efforts in their homes, workplaces, schools, neighbourhoods, and city streets to address gender inequality and homophobia in everyday relationships. The feminist insight that the personal is political continues to reverberate in contemporary gender and sexual relations.

While we have tried to write a sociology of gender and sexuality that speaks to you, at the end of the day, it is *you* who knows best how these ideas resonate with your everyday life. Where do these ideas fit your experience—where do they not? We urge you to bring your experiences and perspectives into a conversation with sociology. We believe that both you and the discipline of sociology will benefit from such an engagement.

Questions for Critical Thought

1. Thinking about your own life right now, where would you say gender *matters* the most? Can you think of areas of your life where gender does not seem to matter at all?
2. Feminists are deeply divided about the roles of pornography in promoting heterosexist institutions and relations. What role do you think pornography plays in our understanding of men's and women's sexuality? Has the Internet changed this? If so, how?
3. What evidence is there to support the idea that gender equality has been achieved? What evidence would suggest that this is not the case?

Sociological Explorations

1. Identify a popular video game and examine how it presents gender and sexuality.
2. Flip through a teen magazine at a store or library, or online. How do teen magazines discuss female and male sexuality? What are the similarities and differences? What messages are being conveyed about the benefits and costs of sexual experience to teen girls and boys?
3. Advertising is full of assumptions and messages about gender. Reflect on specific ads that you have seen on TV or the Internet, and consider what criteria you could use to determine whether advertising images are depicting hegemonic masculinity or hegemonic femininity. What about criteria that would identify a homophobic attitude?

Recommended Readings

Bauer, G.R., & Scheim, A.I. (2015). *Transgender people in Ontario, Canada: Statistics to inform human rights policy*. London, ON: Trans PULSE Project Team. http://transpulseproject.ca/wp-content/uploads/2015/06/Trans-PULSE-Statistics-Relevant-for-Human-Rights-Policy-June-2015.pdf
This report summarizes key results from the Trans PULSE project that are used in discussions, debates, and policy creation related to human rights in multiple jurisdictions in Canada.

Holtby, A., Klein, K., Cook, K., & Travers, R. (2015). To be seen or not to be seen: Photovoice, queer and trans youth, and the dilemma of representation. *Action Research*, *13*(4), 317–335.
Through the use of photovoice, this article sheds light on the ongoing negotiation of power imbalances and the dilemmas of visibility and representation in the lives of 15 queer and trans youths living in a small city in Ontario.

Siltanen, J., & Doucet, A. (2017). *Gender relations in Canada: Intersectionalities and social change* (2nd edn). Toronto, ON: Oxford University Press.
This book sets out major shifts in sociological thinking about gender and the contribution of intersectionality to understanding the complexities of gender inequality.

Spoon, R., & Coyote, I.E. (2014). *Gender failure*. Vancouver, BC: Arsenal Pulp Press.
Based on the live show of these two musicians and storytellers, a moving and often humorous account of their personal struggles to overcome the gender binary.

Connell, R. (2011). *Confronting equality: Gender, knowledge and global change*. Cambridge, UK: Polity Press.
This book weaves together theoretical insights on gender, sexuality, and social change with social justice concerns in global and local contexts.

Recommended Websites

Feminist Alliance for International Action (FAFIA) Canada
www.fafia-afai.org

FAFIA Canada is a coalition of over 75 Canadian women's equality-seeking and related organizations, with a mandate to further women's equality in Canada through domestic implementation of its international human rights commitments.

Egale Canada
www.egale.ca

Egale Canada is an organization that advances equality and justice for lesbian, gay, bisexual, and trans-identified people and their families across Canada.

The Passionate Eye, "Growing up Trans"
www.cbc.ca/passionateeye/episodes/
growing-up-trans

This CBC program examines the complicated and often controversial treatments now available to gender non-conforming and transgender children.

Native Women's Association of Canada
www.nwac.ca

An organization representing the interests and aspirations of Indigenous women and girls in Canada.

XY
www.xyonline.net

XY is a website focused on men, masculinities, and gender politics; it is a space for the exploration of men's and women's everyday lives, issues of gender and sexuality, and personal and social change.

Key Terms

essence/essentialism The idea that a "true" or core reality lies behind appearances, which makes something what it is and which, once identified, can establish its "truth."

gender division of domestic labour The identification of specific household tasks as appropriate for men (for example, painting, cutting the grass, putting out the garbage) and for women (for example, cooking, cleaning, child care).

gender hegemony A concept elaborated by Schippers (2007) to identify hegemonic masculinity and hegemonic femininity as a relation of dominance supported by the eroticization of difference, and the power imbalance in heterosexual sex.

governmentality A term coined by Michel Foucault to study the political rationalities underpinning power. Includes the study of the deliberate practices used by governments to produce compliant citizens.

hegemonic masculinity A dominant form of masculinity that may vary depending on the social context, but typically valorizes physical strength, economic power, heterosexuality, and the domination of women and subordinate men.

heterocentric Assessing social relations and structures by the norms of heterosexuality.

heteronormativity The assumption that heterosexuality is a universal norm, therefore making homosexuality invisible or "abnormal."

homophobia A term coined by George Weinberg in 1972 to refer to the psychological fear of homosexuality.

heterosexist A term referring to a set of overt and covert social practices in both public and private spheres that privileges heterosexuality over other sexual orientations.

homosexual Someone who has sex with and/or is attracted to a person of the same sex.

interlocking/intersectional analysis A way of understanding inequality that takes into account multiple, connecting dimensions. Used to understand gender inequalities as connected with and specified by race, class, dis/ability, sexuality, and so on.

organizational sexuality Social practices that determine explicit and culturally elaborate rules of behaviour to regulate sexual identities and personal relationships in the workplace.

patriarchy A society or family system in which some men have authority over women and other men.

racialization Social processes and practices whereby social relations are structured according to visible physical differences, to the advantage of those in the visible majority and to the disadvantage of those in visible minorities.

sexism Unfair discrimination on the basis of sex; it can be direct or indirect.

sexuality Defined by the World Health Organization (WHO) as a central aspect of being human, and encompasses sex, gender identifies and roles, sexual orientation, eroticism, pleasure, intimacy, and reproduction, experienced in thoughts, fantasies, desires, beliefs, attitudes, values, behaviours, roles, and relationships.

trans Someone whose gender identity or gender expression does not match societal conventions of their birth sex, and who may or may not experience same-sex attractions.

transgressive sexualities Involves transcending sexual binaries and boundaries to challenge cultural norms and explore new possibilities.

transphobia Antagonistic attitudes and feelings toward people who do not conform to society's gender expectations.

undoing The idea that what is socially constructed can be reconstructed and changed.

8 | Ethnic and Race Relations

NIKOLAOS I. LIODAKIS

In this chapter you will:

► Learn that the meanings of the terms "ethnicity" and "race" are historically specific and are important bases for the formation of social groups

► Understand that Canada has been shaped by the colonization of Indigenous peoples, the requirements of "nation-building," capitalist economic development, and discriminatory immigration policies

► Learn that multiculturalism and interculturalism are ideological frameworks within which government policies and programs attempt to manage ethnic and race relations and provide social cohesion

► Discover that ethnic and racial hierarchies exist in society

► Understand how culturalist and political economy approaches attempt to explain the economic inequalities among and within ethnic and racialized groups

INTRODUCTION

Canada is one of the most multicultural countries in the world. Except for Indigenous peoples, everyone is either an immigrant to this country or the descendant of one. As sociologists, we are interested in analyzing relations of power among individuals and social groups. Ethnicity and race are social relations, crucial for understanding Canadian society. We cannot appreciate the struggles of Indigenous peoples with Canadian governments over their land and self-determination without examining the legacy of colonization and its long-lasting effects on their cultural, economic, and social lives. We cannot explain the formation of Canada without reference to British–French conflicts. Our existing demographic makeup is a product of our history; it reflects Canada's immigration policies, even those before Confederation, many of which were blatantly discriminatory and racist at least until the mid-1960s.

Similarly, current problems in the economic, social, and political integration of minority groups may be attributed in part to **racism**. It is not surprising, then, that the field of ethnic and race relations has been central to and continues to grow within Canadian sociology. Let us begin by briefly examining how sociologists define the concepts of ethnicity and race and how we can approach the study of ethnic and race relations theoretically.

Children play street hockey in Inuvik, Northwest Territories, Canada.

A BRIEF HISTORY OF ETHNICITY AND RACE

Sociologists argue that the terms "ethnicity" and "race" are historically specific—i.e., they mean different things to different people at different times and in different places. Ethnicity and race are not static concepts but rather represent dynamic social relations in flux. Popular uses of the terms tend to differ from social scientific definitions (Miles & Torres, 1996). **Ethnicity** refers to social distinctions and relations among individuals and groups based on their cultural characteristics (language, religion, customs, history, and so on), whereas **race** refers to people's assumed but socially significant physical or genetic characteristics (Satzewich & Liodakis, 2017). The characteristics that have been used to classify human populations as races include skin colour, eye colour, hair type, nose shape, lip shape, body hair, and cheekbone structure (Driedger, 1996, pp. 234–235). The term "ethnicity" comes from the Greek word *ethnos* and means a large group of people. The ancient historian Herodotus, in the fifth century BCE, was the first to study **ethnic groups**. In his *Histories*, he described the languages, deities, customs, geography, history, politics, and economies of several groups, including Greeks, Persians, Arabs, Egyptians, Ethiopians, and Libyans (Herodotus, 1996, books 1–9). He documented that these ethnic groups shared a sense of "belonging together."

Émile Durkheim used the concept of **collective conscience** as a primary source of identity formation. In *The Division of Labour in Society* (1964 [1893]), he tried to explain what made pre-modern societies so cohesive by emphasizing the importance of group sentiments over individual ones. Social solidarity was based on sameness and the conformity of individual conscience to the collective. Sameness within the social group led members to differentiate and prefer their "own kind" over "others." This led to important "us" versus "them" sentiments, necessary in social group formation, reproduction, and maintenance (Durkheim, 1964 [1893], p. 60).

Lowell Georgia/Getty Images

Max Weber argued that social group formation is associated with practices of inclusion and exclusion, important for the production and distribution of scarce valuable resources such as goods, services, social status and status symbols, economic and political power, voting and human rights, autonomy, and so on. The practice of inclusion/exclusion constitutes the basis upon which decisions about rewards and sanctions are made. Common descent, tribe, **culture** (including language and other symbolic codes), religion, and nationality are important *ethnic markers* and determinants of ethnicity. Ethnicity is a subjective and presumed identity based on a "folk-feeling," not (necessarily) on objective blood ties (Weber, 1978 [1908]). Ethnic identity is often linked to people's "primordial attachment." Hard **primordialism** holds that people are attached to one another and to their communities because of blood ties, whereas soft primordialism holds that people's feelings of affinity, attachment, acceptance, trust, and intimacy for their "own kind" are not mediated by blood ties (Allahar, 1994).

For Weber, race denotes groups' common identity based on biological heredity (endogamy). Visible similarities and differences, however minor, serve as potential sources of either affection and appreciation or repulsion and contempt. He wrote, "Almost any kind of *similarity or contrast of physical type* and of habits can induce the belief that affinity or disaffinity exists between groups that attract or repel each other" (Weber, 1978 [1908], p. 386; emphasis added). This leads to **monopolistic closure**, i.e., to economic, political, and social processes and practices, often institutionalized, whereby members of the in-group ("we"/"Self") have access to the scarce valuable resources mentioned above, while members of the out-group ("they"/"Other") are excluded. Social boundaries, then, are set and reproduced over time (Weber, 1978 [1908], p. 386).

Today, sociologists use the term **racialization** to refer to social processes and practices through which relations among people are structured "by the signification of human biological characteristics in such a way as to define and construct differentiated social collectivities" (Miles & Brown, 2003, p. 99). Social group labelling creates hierarchical dichotomies by attributing negative intellectual, moral, and behavioural characteristics to subordinate groups and positive characteristics to dominant groups. Social *positions* of superiority and inferiority are thus created; a social order is built (Li, 1999).

"Race" as a term of categorizing human populations is historically linked to European colonization. Later, with the advent of capitalism, a new social dichotomy of "Self" and "Other" emerged. "Self" was seen as superior and referred to dominant European populations and cultures; "Other" referred to non-Europeans, who were seen as inferior and subordinate. Before capitalism the term "race" was used in a legal sense, often as a self-identification label reserved for the aristocracy. With the emergence of the bourgeoisie, it was used to define "Others" ("Negroes," "Arabs," "Asiatics," and so on). It became an externally imposed label. The classification of subordinate groups as races was coupled with negative evaluations of the biological and social characteristics of their members.

TIME to REFLECT

Do races exist? If so, how many races are there? Can all human populations be categorized in terms of inherited physical characteristics? Should they be?

"BUILDING THE NATION": CANADA'S DEVELOPMENT THROUGH IMMIGRATION

Until the 1960s, the image of Canada as a nation was based on the notion that the British and French peoples had founded this country. These two **charter groups**, by this thinking, built the country; everyone else "joined in" later. The "two founding nations" thesis endures even today but is historically inaccurate. The French and the British did not found Canada. They colonized and settled it at the expense of Indigenous peoples who lost their lands through colonization and deceitful treaties. Efforts to assimilate *them* into the dominant aspects of the British and French cultures (through Christianity, private property, and competitive individualism) left Indigenous peoples with long-lasting cultural trauma, deprived of the communal economies that had sustained them for centuries.

Immigration began around the time of Confederation. Nation-building required creating transportation infrastructures (roads, railways, canals) and developing commercial agriculture in western Canada and capitalist industry in major urban centres. For governments, these requirements necessitated a large influx of mostly northern- and central-European and American immigrants (except blacks), since **abocide** had devastated the populations of Indigenous peoples, who were seen as "uncivilized savages." It was also believed that Indigenous peoples did not have the necessary skills or could not adapt to the British or French "ways of doing things." Cultural compatibility was seen as *the* requirement for immigration to Canada. The offer of free land (stolen from Indigenous peoples) to European and American settlers resulted in the first large wave of immigration to Canada from 1896 to the beginning of World War I. The

Immigration Acts of 1906 and 1910 set the terms under which **entrance groups** were accepted. At the peak of this wave in 1913, 400,000 immigrants arrived in Canada. In contrast, during World War I, the Great Depression, and World War II, immigration almost ceased (see Figure 8.1).

Not everyone has always been welcomed in Canada. The **Immigration Act of 1910** prohibited the immigration of people who were considered "mentally defective," "idiots, imbeciles, feeble-minded, epileptics, insane, diseased, the physically defective, the dumb, blind, or otherwise handicapped" (McLaren, 1990, p. 56). Also, people with "dubious" political loyalties (communists) were excluded outright or, if already in Canada, were subject to deportation (Roberts, 1988, p. 19). Immigrants from China and India were of particular "concern" to xenophobic immigration authorities, since they were seen as unassimilable and thus unsuitable for permanent residence (see the Sociology in Action box). Until the liberalization of immigration in the 1960s, Canadian governments exercised exclusionary policies. Some groups were preferred (mostly northern and central Europeans and Americans). Others were labelled as "non-preferred" and were systematically excluded (Chinese, blacks, eastern and southern Europeans, and people

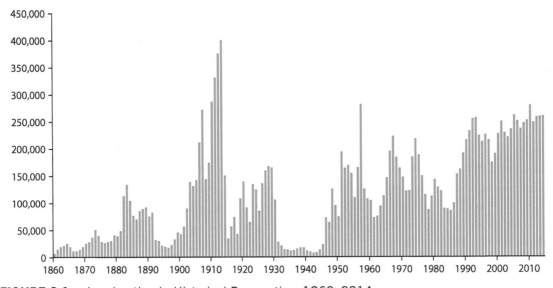

FIGURE 8.1   Immigration in Historical Perspective, 1860–2014

SOURCE: Citizenship and Immigration Canada, Facts and Figures—Immigration Overview—Permanent and Temporary Residents (2014).

Vancouver Public Library, Leonard Frank photo, Vancouver Public Library 6231

Sikh passengers aboard the *Komagata Maru*. The freighter ship was prohibited from landing at the Port of Vancouver in 1914, because it carried "unsuitable" prospective immigrants from India, and was eventually forced to return to Asia.

from India). Members of preferred groups were seen as good workers, law-abiding, and desirable future citizens, and "Others" as ethnoculturally or racially "unsuitable."

The end of World War II saw some minor improvements in immigration policy. **Discrimination** did not end—that process started slowly in the 1960s—but gradually, non-whites were allowed to immigrate. Small numbers of black women were admitted as domestic workers, typists, and nurses. It was not until 1962 that the government initiated the elimination of racist criteria in the immigrant selection process and not until 1967 that the points system was introduced, relying on more objective criteria by assigning more weight to each applicant's age, education, job skills, work experience, and language abilities rather than his or her **ascriptive characteristics**. In the late 1960s and early 1970s, family reunification provisions led to a large increase in the numbers of southern Europeans (Italians, Greeks, Portuguese, Spanish) and a moderate rise in non-white immigrants.

THE NEW MOSAIC: RECENT CANADIAN IMMIGRATION TRENDS

The "colour" of Canadian immigration has changed since the 1980s, with a remarkable shift in the geographical regions from which Canada admits immigrants. Until the 1950s, for example, the US, the United Kingdom, and continental Europe accounted for almost 90 per cent of all immigration to Canada; in 2014, they accounted for only 14.8 per cent. Immigrants from Asia and the Pacific region, Africa and the Middle East, and South and Central America accounted for 84.8 per cent—almost a total reversal of immigrants' origins (Citizenship and Immigration Canada, 2014).

 What would a non-white immigrant face in the job market upon arrival in Canada? See "Race and Racialized Work," p. 261, in **Chapter 11**, "Work and the Economy," for a broader discussion of the relationship between race, citizenship, and employment.

SOCIOLOGY ▬▬ IN ACTION — Is Canada So "Innocent"? Racist Immigration Policies toward Chinese Immigrants

Imagine that your ancestry is Chinese. Read the following carefully:

In the early 1880s, Chinese immigrants were allowed into Canada because of the growing demand for cheap and disposable labour to build the transcontinental railway. Approximately 16,000 Chinese immigrants arrived, mainly in British Columbia. Employers saw an opportunity to exploit them and called for increased Chinese immigration. Labour unions opposed the influx, since

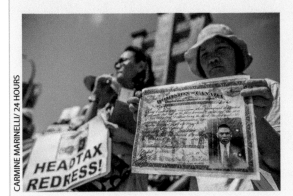

Head tax redress rallies have continued since Prime Minister Stephen Harper apologized in 2006 for the government's past discrimination against Chinese immigrants, with some arguing that the apology and subsequent compensation did not take into account the effects of family separation due to the Immigration Act.

increases in the supply of immigrant labour led to stiffer **labour market** competition and kept wages low. In 1885, the federal government imposed the **Chinese head tax**—a fee to be paid by each Chinese immigrant. It started at $50; it increased to $100 in 1890 and to $500 in 1903. Only those who could afford it could immigrate to Canada. Then, in 1923, Chinese immigration was almost completely prohibited.

There were exceptions, however. **Social class** and gender were important, since Chinese men who invested in or established businesses in Canada were exempt from the head tax and were allowed to immigrate even after 1923. Few Chinese women were permitted to enter Canada, since—it was feared—they would reproduce the "yellow peril" and lead to the propagation of "alien cultures and races," thus undermining Canada as a white settler society.

The federal government collected $23 million from the head tax (Satzewich & Liodakis, 2017). In today's dollars, this would amount to approximately $1.2 billion.

Using the Weberian concept of *verstehen* ("understanding"), and C. Wright Mills's sociological imagination, think about your reaction to Canadian immigration policies and practices of the past. How can these concepts assist you in understanding and explaining immigration and racism issues?

Table 8.1 lists the top 10 source countries of immigrants to Canada (2005 to 2014). In 2015, Canada admitted 271,847 immigrants, with 61 per cent coming from the top 10 source countries. The top source country was the Philippines (18.7 per cent), the second-highest was India (14.5 per cent), and the third was China (7.2 per cent). The UK, France, and the US are still found in the top 10, but their contributions are proportionately small (Citizenship and Immigration Canada, 2016).

Immigrants are divided into several classes: economic immigrants (skilled workers, business immigrants, investors, live-in caregivers, self-employed, etc.), the family class, refugees,

and others. In 2015, contrary to public misconceptions, the largest immigration class was economic immigrants (62.7 per cent of total immigration), usually mostly skilled workers, i.e., independent applicants who are admitted through the points system.

The family class—sponsored spouses or parents of immigrants—ranked second (24 per cent). After they arrive, they must be supported financially for three to ten years by their sponsors. Refugees (32,111 people) represented 1.8 per cent (Citizenship and Immigration Canada, 2016). Canada is a signatory to international treaties and is obliged by international

Table 8.1 ▶ Canada—Permanent Residents, Top 10 Source Countries, 2005–2014

Source Country	2005	2006	2007	2008	2009	2010	2011	2012	2013	2014
Philippines	18,139	18,400	19,837	24,887	28,573	38,617	36,765	34,315	29,545	40,035
India	36,210	33,848	28,742	28,261	29,456	34,235	27,509	30,933	33,087	38,341
People's Republic of China	42,584	33,518	27,642	30,037	29,622	30,391	28,502	33,024	34,130	24,640
Iran	5,837	7,480	6,974	6,475	6,580	7,477	7,479	7,534	11,291	16,781
Pakistan	14,314	13,127	10,124	8,994	7,217	6,811	7,468	11,227	12,603	9,128
United States of America	8,394	9,613	9,463	10,190	8,995	8,142	7,676	7,891	8,501	8,496
United Kingdom and colonies	7,258	7,140	8,216	8,979	8,876	8,724	6,204	6,195	5,827	5,764
France	4,429	4,002	4,290	4,532	5,051	4,646	4,080	6,280	5,623	4,717
Mexico	2,837	2,844	3,239	2,856	3,092	3,865	3,947	4,227	3,996	4,478
Republic of Korea	5,832	6,215	5,920	7,294	5,874	5,537	4,588	5,316	4,509	4,463
Total	262,242	251,640	236,753	247,244	252,170	280,687	248,747	257,903	259,023	260,404

SOURCE: Facts and figures 2014 – Immigration overview: Permanent residents Canada –Top-ten source countries, 2005-2014 http://www.cic.gc.ca/english/resources/statistics/facts2014/permanent/10.asp#figure77

law to provide asylum to people making demonstrably genuine refugee claims.

The geographical distribution of immigrants is particularly uneven. Ontario attracts 38.1 per cent of all immigrants; Quebec, 18 per cent; Alberta, 17.4 per cent; BC, 13.1 per cent; Manitoba, 5.5 per cent; and Saskatchewan, 4.6 per cent (Citizenship and Immigration Canada, 2016). Immigration to the rest of Canada is negligible. This uneven distribution variably influences our ethnic and racial makeup. In particular, there is a clear urban–rural divide. Immigrants are more attracted to urban centres where there are more economic opportunities and others from their own country. For example, most Torontonians were born outside Canada, whereas almost all the residents of Hérouxville, a small farming community in Quebec, are Canadian-born.

TIME to REFLECT

If you were to (re)design Canada's immigration policy, what criteria would you use for admitting immigrants? Why are your criteria important?

MULTICULTURALISM AND ITS DISCONTENTS

Canada may not now be as racist as in the past (Levitt, 1994), but evidence suggests that recent immigrants, mostly visible minorities, continue to face discrimination in the labour market (Galabuzi, 2006; Hum & Simpson, 2007). But what makes an individual a member of a visible minority? Why are Indigenous peoples not considered a visible minority? Are Indigenous peoples or the Québécois ethnic groups like any other? What defines your identity? Who is a "true" Canadian? In the 2011 National Household Survey, almost one in three respondents identified their *ancestry* as Canadian. Is "Canadian" an ethnic group? Who determines, defines, or sets the criteria? These are tough questions, so let us examine

some important aspects of the formation and meanings of ethnic and racial identities in the Canadian context of multiculturalism.

Prior to the advent of **multiculturalism** (1971), to which we are so accustomed today, Canadian society was characterized by **ethnocentrism**. There has always been sustained pressure on Indigenous peoples and minority-group newcomers to adopt the dominant British and French cultural values, customs, and symbols. **Assimilation** refers to sets of processes and social practices by which members of minority groups are "fused" into a dominant culture (Isajiw, 1999, p. 170). Sociologists distinguish between **behavioural assimilation** ("acquiring" the values of dominant groups) and **structural assimilation** (the integration of "Others" into socio-economic and political life). Behavioural assimilation was forceful and violent for Indigenous peoples, through **residential schools** and the banning of their languages, customs, and ceremonies (e.g., the thirst dance and the potlatch). Canadian government efforts to assimilate Indigenous peoples and non–charter group immigrants often resembled American **melting-pot policies**.

Multiculturalism refers to economic, political, and social practices which define boundaries and set limits to ethnic and racial group relations in order to either maintain social order or manage social change in Canada (Liodakis & Satzewich, 2003, p. 147). It has four interrelated dimensions (Fleras & Elliott, 1996, p. 325). First, multiculturalism is a demographic fact. Canada has never been culturally homogeneous and is now host to people of many diverse backgrounds. Second, as an ideology, it is part of cultural pluralism. It rests on **cultural relativism**, which promotes tolerance and diversity in order to achieve national goals (e.g., national unity, peaceful coexistence, and socio-economic progress) in ethnically and racially diverse societies. Third, multiculturalism is a terrain of competition among minority groups for valuable economic and political resources. Thus, it is used by governments as a mechanism for

GLOBAL
ISSUES

The Points System for Skilled Workers: Would You Make It?

Every year, millions of people from all over the world apply to enter Canada as **permanent residents**. Approximately 260,000 are approved annually. Would you qualify to immigrate to your own country? Test yourself. Read the **selection criteria** below to determine whether you qualify for admission as a skilled worker. For example, if at present your education consists of a secondary school diploma but no further diplomas, certificates, or degrees, you will receive 5 points in this category; under language, if you are completely proficient in English, you will get 16 points; total proficiency in French awards 8 additional points. You need at least 67 points (out of 100) to be admitted as a skilled worker. For the complete points system, visit the Immigration, Refugees and Citizenship website (http://www.cic.gc.ca/english/immigrate/skilled/apply-factors.asp).

The Points System for Skilled Workers

Selection Criteria	Points Awarded
Education	up to 25
Knowledge of official language(s)	up to 28
Work experience	up to 15
Age: Applicants 21–49 years of age receive maximum points. 2 points are deducted for each year under 21 or over 49, so that someone 16 or younger or 54 or older will receive no points.	up to 12
Arranged employment in Canada	up to 10
Adaptability	up to 10
Maximum points awarded	**100**
Minimum required to pass for skilled worker immigrants	**67**

SOURCE: Immigration, Refugees and Citizenship Canada. (2015a). Six selection factors—Federal skilled workers. http://www.cic.gc.ca/english/immigrate/skilled/apply-factors.asp

conflict management and resolution. Finally, multiculturalism refers to all government programs aimed at transforming its ideology into concrete forms of social intervention (Fleras & Elliott, 1996).

Multiculturalism emerged for several reasons (Fleras & Elliott, 1996, p. 335). First, during the 1960s immense political pressure was exerted on governments by "the other ethnic groups" (e.g., Ukrainians and Germans) for recognition of *their* contributions to Canada. Second, it became politically necessary for the federal government to counterbalance Western alienation and Quebec nationalism. Third, the Liberal Party of Canada needed greater electoral support from urban immigrants, and this was a tactical move in that direction.

As policy, multiculturalism was introduced by Liberal prime minister Pierre Elliott Trudeau in 1971. Ironically, it was not the legacy of racism, discrimination, and **prejudice** that the policy aimed to redress at first. Such issues did not figure at all in the initial policy framework. From 1971 to 1980, it was essentially folkloric (ethnic food, costume, and dance) and focused on "celebrating our differences" (Fleras & Elliott, 1996). The basic principles that guided multiculturalism were support for all of Canada's cultures, assistance to ethnic groups in overcoming cultural barriers for full participation in Canadian society, promotion of creative encounters and interchange among all cultural groups in the interest of national unity, and assistance to immigrants in learning at least one of the official languages in order to become full participants in Canadian society (Hawkins, 1988, p. 220).

The Multiculturalism Act (MA) was passed in 1988 by the Progressive Conservative government, which shifted emphasis away from "culture for culture's sake" toward an instrumentalist view of possible economic benefits from multiculturalism. The government strongly believed that multiculturalism meant increased business with the immigrants' countries of origin. Since the 1990s, however, the focus shifted to society-building. The development of "civic" multiculturalism rendered issues of socio-economic equality and political citizenship paramount (Fleras & Elliott, 1996, pp. 334–335). Governments have now moved away from the initial folkloric focus, withdrawing from certain programs (e.g., funding for cultural festivals).

Criticisms of Multiculturalism

Early criticisms of multiculturalism questioned the policy's inability to solve all the problems it set out to address. Critics argued that great emphasis was placed on depoliticized "song and dance" activities, non-threatening to British and French economic, political, and cultural hegemony. The identification of only "cultural barriers" to the full participation of minorities in Canadian society precluded the examination of racism and discrimination as barriers (Moodley, 1983; Bolaria & Li, 1988), and concealed more fundamental socio-economic inequalities based on labour market position, education, gender, age, etc. (Stasiulis, 1980, p. 34). Canadian society is characterized by race/ethnic- and gender-based class hierarchies and socio-political struggles not addressed by multiculturalism because such struggles challenge such hierarchies. It obfuscates these antagonisms and shifts the struggle to the cultural realm.

In the 1990s, critics claimed that multiculturalism reproduced ethnic stereotypes, undermined Canadian unity, ghettoized minority issues, and undermined the special claims of francophones and Indigenous peoples. Superficial "caravans" and "folk fests" are not serious cultural exchanges. Instead, they commodify cultures and reproduce cultural, ethnic, and racial stereotypes (Bissoondath, 1994, p. 83). Moreover, multiculturalism promotes cultural relativism and hence undermines "Canadian values" and social cohesion. After multiculturalism, focus has shifted to individual cultural choices, away from "*the* Canadian collective identity." We have ended up with a value system containing nothing *exclusively* Canadian. Multiculturalism has no future vision for Canada; it encourages division by ghettoizing people into ethno-cultural groups (Bibby, 1990).

CRITICIZING THE CRITICS: MULTICULTURAL POLICY AS A REFLECTION OF REALITY

These criticisms of multiculturalism share an appeal to the "national character of Canada," which is never defined. The implication is that the current system is somehow biased in favour of "non-whites" and "non-Europeans" and that it should not be. Critics seem silent or purposefully vague in describing what constitutes Canadian culture, the definition of what and who is or should be Canadian, or what Canadian values are. There is no definition of what constitutes *the* Canadian nation, culture, or character, and no indication of who would define them. Rhoda Howard-Hassmann (1999) points to a basic fault in the critiques of Bibby and Bissoondath: they both assume that Canadian multiculturalism calls for individuals to retain their ancestral identities. But the Canadian policy is liberal, not illiberal—that is, it does not impose the idea of maintaining

RESEARCHERS IN ACTION ▶ Dr Victor Nicholas Satzewich

Vic Satzewich is a renowned professor of sociology at McMaster University, in Hamilton, Ontario, past chair of its Sociology Department, and past president of the Canadian Sociological Association. He received his PhD at the University of Glasgow in 1988. His work, mainly in the area of race and ethnicity, is informed by both history and political economy. He has also done extensive research on a variety of topics including temporary agricultural workers in Canada; racism and social inequality; transnational migration and identity; capital accumulation and state formation; policing and minorities; Canada's First Nations; the Ukrainian Diaspora; and Canadian immigration policies.

Recently, he completed a research project titled "Immigration and Administrative Discretion in Canada," funded by the Social Sciences and Humanities Research Council. He is only the second Canadian researcher in 50 years to be granted access to Citizenship and Immigration Canada overseas posts in order to examine how its officers use their discretionary power to determine which people can join their spouses who have immigrated to Canada. Dr Satzewich visited 11 visa offices in Europe, the United States, the Middle East, South America, the Caribbean, Africa, and Asia between 2010

and 2012. He conducted 128 interviews with front-line officers and managers on their decision-making process.

Dr Satzewich analyzed how Canadian immigration officers abroad examine the spousal/partner relationships of visa applicants, in order to determine if they are "real" or "fake." He concluded that immigration officers do not make visa decisions to only *exclude* applicants; they actually determine which relationships are "real" in order to also *include* applicants and grant them permanent residence. They do not control the flow of applications from specific countries/regions but they must meet targets, so they must decide which applications are "deserving" or "undeserving." Variations from office to office exist, as expected, but there does not appear to be any hidden (racist) agenda by the Canadian state or its bureaucrats aiming to keep eligible applicants out of Canada.

You can read his article in the *Canadian Review of Sociology* (21 January 2014) or visit the journal's website (http://onlinelibrary.wiley.com/doi/10.1111/cars.12031/full). In 2015, the University of British Columbia Press published his work *Points of Entry: How Canada's Visa Officers Decide Who Gets In*, which details his research.

---

ethnic differences, nor does it force individuals to identify with ancestral cultural groups. In her view,

> Multiculturalism "normalizes" a wide range of customs and makes the enjoyment of such customs part of what it means to be a Canadian.... Liberal multiculturalism acknowledges the social need for difference, for smaller, more close-knit communities separated from the Canadian mainstream. But it does not mandate such difference. (Howard-Hassmann, 1999, p. 533)

Far from promoting disloyalty to Canada and things Canadian, multicultural policy has the seemingly ironic consequences of integrating immigrants, promoting national unity, and encouraging "a sense of connection with other Canadians" (Howard-Hassmann, 1999, p. 534). The rising number of people who identify their

ancestry as Canadian in recent censuses tends to support her argument.

Indigenous Peoples, Québécois, and Multiculturalism

Many argue that multiculturalism undermines the special claims of francophones and **Indigenous peoples** in Canada. In Quebec, multiculturalism is seen as an attempt by the federal government to weaken Quebec's aspirations for "nationhood." By severing culture from language, multiculturalism rejects the "two founding nations" metaphor of Canada and reduces the status of French Canadians from that of "founding people" to "just another ethnic group" (Abu-Laban & Stasiulis, 1992, p. 367). Multiculturalism "has bought allophone votes" in order to defeat Quebec separatism. Assimilationist French-language policies, directed toward allophones, can be understood in this context.

Successive Quebec governments have pursued a policy of **interculturalism**. According to Kymlicka (1998), interculturalism has three important principles: (1) it recognizes French as the language of public life; (2) it respects the liberal-democratic values of political rights and equality of opportunity for all; and (3) it respects pluralism, openness to and tolerance of the differences of others. These principles constitute a "moral contract" between the province of Quebec and immigrant groups. Interculturalism resembles the federal policy of multiculturalism, but there is one important difference: interculturalism promotes *linguistic assimilation*. The French language is seen as *the* indispensable condition for the creation of a common public culture and the cohesion of Quebec society.

Some suggest that interculturalism is an advanced form of pluralism (Karmis, 2004, p. 79), since it applies not only to ethnic/racialized groups but also to "lifestyle cultures," including gay, punk, environmental, feminist, and other non–ethnic-based identities. In principle, no cultural community is excluded from Québécois identity. In fact, **reasonable accommodation** in Quebec is based on the understanding that government policies and programs should not only tolerate but accommodate the cultural differences of new immigrants and of minority groups.

> **TIME to REFLECT**
>
> Would you prefer to live in a country without official multiculturalism or interculturalism? Would you rather live in the US, France, Belgium, or Germany? Why?

Canadian Indigenous peoples are also apprehensive. Multiculturalism reduces them to "just another minority group" and undermines their aspirations for self-government (Abu-Laban & Stasiulis, 1992, p. 376). They possess a distinct and unique set of rights—enshrined in the Constitution—that stem from their being the first inhabitants of Canada. Since Indigenous peoples do not consider themselves part of mainstream Canadian society but as distinct peoples, multiculturalism is seen as threatening their survival. They prefer to negotiate their futures in a bilateral framework with federal (and provincial) governments that recognizes their collective special status rights (Fleras & Elliott, 1996, p. 343). Today, more than 50 per cent of all Indigenous people in Canada live in big urban centres (Winnipeg, Edmonton, Vancouver, Toronto, and Calgary). Unfortunately, many Indigenous peoples with low socio-economic status still live in poverty; they experience high unemployment rates; they continue to face barriers to higher education and still endure low quality of life (Satzewich & Liodakis, 2017). The policy of multiculturalism does little to address these structural socio-economic issues.

Multiculturalism in a Changing World

Recent world events have led to renewed questions of multiculturalism. The terrorist attacks in New York and Washington in 2001, the 2004 Madrid and 2005 London bombings, and the 2015 Paris and 2016 Brussels attacks have put many Western governments on alert about threats that cultural and religious "Others" may pose to their peace and security. In the post-9/11 era of **Islamophobia** and "big brother" surveillance, two criticisms are prevalent: (1) multiculturalism encourages and tolerates the promotion of cultures and religions that are decidedly intolerant; (2) multiculturalism is a recipe for homegrown terrorism. Such critiques are often concealed forms of racism. No country has arrived at an ideal management of ethnic and racial conflicts. Canada's multicultural approach may not be perfect but many other, far more problematic approaches to diversity exist (e.g., US, UK, France, Germany, Belgium); we can be proud that we have avoided any serious problems, so far. Let us now turn, then, to unresolved issues of racism.

> **TIME to REFLECT**
>
> Are Indigenous Canadians and the Québécois just ethnic groups? If not, why not?

PREJUDICE AND RACISM

Racism is based on "othering" (Simmons, 1998). According to Stuart Hall, it is

> not a set of false pleas which swim around in the head ... not a set of mistaken perceptions. ... [Racist ideas] have their basis in real material conditions of existence. They arise because of the concrete problems of different classes and groups in society. Racism represents the attempt ideologically to construct those conditions, contradictions, and problems in such a way that they can be dealt with and deflected at the same moment. (in Li, 1999, p. 325)

Race problems often begin as labour problems (Bolaria & Li, 1988; Li, 1999). Competition for employment among workers from different ethnic/racialized groups keeps wages low and profits high. Workers usually participate in a **split labour market** in which more members of the dominant groups may have more secure, full-time, and high-paying jobs, whereas minorities may be found in insecure, part-time, low-paying, menial occupations. Expressions of working-class racism may be attributable to split labour market conditions (Dunk, in Satzewich, 1998).

These markets develop over long periods of time and are reproduced by prejudice and discrimination. Often, members of some groups are seen through the prism of stereotypes. Some are deemed hard-working, law-abiding, smart, moral, and so on. Others are seen as "lazy," "dirty," "stingy," "criminal," "promiscuous," "uncivilized," and the like (Driedger, 1996). Ethnic jokes, which might amuse us uncritically, are based on such stereotypes. Negative stereotypes are often reserved by the majority group for minority groups; positive stereotypes are related to dominant groups, although minority groups use positive *self*-stereotypes to resist racism. Stereotypes, discrimination, and prejudice maintain and reproduce racism.

Historically, Indigenous peoples have been treated unjustly by Canadian governments. Their lands have been taken away (through "treaties"), they have been forcefully segregated in reserves, and many children were sent to residential schools, depriving generations of their own cultural heritage. During the two world wars of the twentieth century, Germans, Italians, and Japanese were singled out for internment by Canadian authorities, and Russians, Ukrainians, and Jews were seen as harbouring communist political beliefs and often were not allowed to immigrate to Canada or, when they were involved in labour strife, were quickly deported. Canada accepted only a handful of European Jewish refugees escaping Nazism in the 1930s, and immigration policy in the first half of the twentieth century excluded Chinese and South Asians.

Today, a more subtle type of discrimination permeates Canadian life. Because it is covert, it is more difficult to combat. Canadian law prohibits overt discriminatory acts in employment, social services, and education, but the reality is that some members of minority groups face issues of **systemic discrimination**—impersonal, covert practices that penalize members of minorities. Carding, for example, is the controversial police practice that singles out for stopping and questioning members of visible-minority groups (e.g., young black males). Personal information, such as name, address, phone number, "perceived skin colour," weight, height, and so on is recorded by police officers and then entered in a massive database. Once in the system, individuals are "known

Supporters of the Black Lives Matter movement attend a rally at Toronto Police headquarters.

Steve Russell/Toronto Star via Getty Images

to police." This is an instance of racial profiling, where law enforcement authorities, under the guise of safety, security, or public protection, target minorities based on their physical characteristics—not their specific behaviour or personal actions—in order to single them out for greater scrutiny or differential treatment compared to whites.

The practices of racial profiling and carding do not help in improving relations between the police and minorities. Many minority community groups argue that there is no police accountability and that, increasingly, we are witnessing in Canada anti-black police brutality and often police impunity. In the summer of 2016, initially stemming from the deterioration of relations between police and minority groups in the US, including the alarming increase in shooting deaths of unarmed African Americans by police, the Black Lives Matter social movement emerged in Canada's major cities. Many protesters in Toronto, Vancouver, Montreal, Halifax, Ottawa, Edmonton, and Winnipeg took to the streets demonstrating against increased police surveillance and intrusions, racial profiling, carding, and racist violence, calling instead for greater police accountability and social justice.

In addition, **institutional racism**, operating in economic, educational, and political institutions, disadvantages minorities. For example, recent immigrants may be excluded from good jobs when government and employers require many years of "Canadian experience." Some minorities may be excluded from police or fire-fighting forces because of minimum height requirements (similar regulations have long kept many women out of these forces). Not recognizing educational credentials attained abroad (especially from developing countries) keeps large numbers of immigrants out of secure, well-paying jobs.

 To learn more about institutions that promote racism, see "Institutional Processes," p. 301, in **Chapter 13**, "Politics and Social Movements."

Henry and Tator (2010) argue that a peculiar form of racism exists in Canada: **democratic racism**. It is based not necessarily on old racist notions of the biological and social superiority of whites over racialized minorities, but rather on contradictions and conflicts over social values. For example, Canada is supposedly committed to justice, equality, and fairness, but these values coexist with differential treatment and discrimination against minorities. Democratic racism is an ideology and a mechanism for reducing the conflict inherent in maintaining a commitment to both liberal and non-egalitarian values. It permits and sustains the rationalization, justification, and maintenance of two apparently conflicting sets of values (liberal-democratic versus non-egalitarian) with regard to minorities.

Many dominant group members argue that they do not "see" colour. This claim of colour-blindness obfuscates the reality and the historical "baggage" of colour in our everyday lives—the policies, programs, and practices that continue to be racist. Just because we exalt tolerance of others through multicultural language and policies, these do not necessarily lead to equality or social harmony. Reasonable accommodation is not effective in combating racism (see the Open for Discussion box). Multiculturalism conceals the structural, economic, and political inequalities in Canada. The discourse of national identity tends to be racist, since it erases or silences minorities' contributions to Canadian identity.

Finally, there is a tendency to view racism as a binary opposition between white racists and the racialized. Racism is not found exclusively among members of dominant groups. There also exist intra- and inter-group racisms. For example, some minority-group members may exhibit racism toward other members of the same group because of regional, linguistic, religious, or political differences. Inter–minority-group racism is common. Some members of groups who are or have been marginalized in the past (for example, Irish, Greeks, and Italians) may

OPEN FOR
▬▬ DISCUSSION

Reasonable Accommodation, Xenophobia, and Islamophobia

"Reasonable accommodation" is the newest tune of Quebec interculturalism. It implies that government policies and programs aim not just to tolerate but also to accommodate the cultural differences of "Others." The debate over this policy continues; not all Quebecers agree with it. In fact, there is a clear urban–rural split: cities like Montreal are more diverse and more accepting of difference; rural areas are largely homogeneous and culturally

THE CANADIAN PRESS/Ryan Remiorz

Demonstrators take part in a protest against Quebec's proposed Values Charter in Montreal, in September 2013. The proposed charter resulted in numerous controversies, as it proposed to ban the wearing of any visible symbols indicating religious affiliation.

conservative, and their inhabitants would like to keep it that way.

In January 2007, Hérouxville, a small Quebec farming community of almost exclusively white, francophone, and nominally Catholic residents gained notoriety when its town council passed a resolution prescribing a code of conduct for potential immigrants. It set conditions under which they could be admitted. Specifically, immigrants who cover their faces, carry weapons to school, stone or burn women alive, or perform female genital mutilation were not welcome. A town councillor, André Drouin, argued that interculturalism and reasonable accommodation had gone too far, since, he claimed, that they allow "everything."

Then Premier Jean Charest suggested that Hérouxville's "measures" might be exaggerated, and not representative of Quebec society. In the spirit of understanding, a women's delegation from the Canadian Islamic Congress met with the town council and residents to discuss the issue. The Hérouxville resolution seemed directed against Muslims and people from northern Africa, the Middle East, and Asia. It was a concrete example of xenophobia and Islamophobia. The town resolution was eventually watered down, but the controversy remained and sparked debates across Canada.

identify today more with their skin colour than with their ethnic background and thus reproduce the racial dichotomy of "us" versus "them": they have changed from being "micks," "wops," or "macaronis" to being racists.

CULTURALISM AND POLITICAL ECONOMY: EXPLANATIONS FOR SOCIO-ECONOMIC INEQUALITIES

Broadly speaking, two major theoretical frameworks attempt to explain ethnicity and race as

socio-economic phenomena: **culturalism** and **political economy**. The central argument of culturalism is that ethnic and racial groups share common values, religion, beliefs, sentiments, ideas, languages, historical memories and symbols, and leadership, as well as a common past and often the same geographical territory. If we want to explain their differential achievements as groups, we must look into their cultures. Culture is the *explanans* (that which explains), not the *explanandum* (that which must be explained). Cultural values, often linked to biology, affect the psychological composition of group members and produce "differences in cognitive perception, mental aptitude, and logical reasoning" (Li, 1999, p. 10). Such differences are thought to affect subsequent educational and economic achievements. Thus, some groups, on average, are doing better than others in school and the labour market. Even if this theory holds, it cannot explain differing educational and economic achievements *within the same cultural group*.

From the political economy perspective, on the other hand, it is believed that social individuals are part of inherited structures that enable but also constrain their social positions and actions. These structures include those built on social relations of class, gender, race/ethnicity, age, sexual preference, physical ability, mental health/illness, and so on. Distributions of wealth, prestige, and power are unequal. The central concerns of political economy are who owns and controls what, and when, why, and how (Satzewich, 1998, p. 314). Race and ethnicity are seen as *relational* concepts. Social class, status, race, and ethnicity constitute an

> index of social standing or rank reflected in terms of criteria like wealth, education, style of life, linguistic capacity, residential location, consumptive capacity, or having or lacking respect. Status has to do with one's ranking in a social system *relative to the position of others*, where the ranking involves ... [positive] self-conception and (de)valuations of others. (Goldberg, 1993, p. 69; emphasis added)

Historically, entrance groups have been primarily associated with the lower classes because of the menial (yet highly important) jobs they have done upon arrival. In contrast, members of the charter groups have been associated with the upper classes and more prestigious occupations. There was, therefore, an overlap between lower-class membership and membership in a minority ethnic/racial group. John Porter, in *The Vertical Mosaic* (1965), argued that people's ethnic affiliation determined their social class and prevented the upward mobility of certain groups, partly because they had not *assimilated culturally* to the new conditions of Canadian capitalism. This is the **blocked mobility thesis**. We examine the economic dimensions of ethnic/racial inequalities below.

THE VERTICAL MOSAIC THEN AND THE COLOUR-CODED MOSAIC TODAY

Over the years, most research on social inequality in Canada has focused on the economic performance of ethnic and racialized groups to determine whether Canadian society is hierarchically structured (Agócs & Boyd, 1993, p. 337). Porter argued that immigration and ethnic affiliation were important factors in the process of social class formation, especially at the bottom and elite layers of the stratification system (Porter, 1965, p. 73). The charter groups (British and French) appropriated positions of power and advantage in the social, economic, and political realms and relegated "entrance status groups" to lower positions. Analyzing 1931, 1951, and 1961 census data, he found persistent patterns of ethnic economic inequality. The Canadian political elite was almost exclusively British and French. In the occupational structure, however, Jewish- and British-origin Canadians were over-represented in the professional and financial occupations (higher status and income) and under-represented in agricultural and unskilled jobs (lower status and income). Germans, Scandinavians, and the Dutch were closest to the British. Italians, Poles, and Ukrainians were next, with Greeks and the Portuguese at even lower positions (Porter, 1965, p. 90). The French were between the northern and southern Europeans. Indigenous peoples were at the bottom of the hierarchy. Comparing the charter groups, despite the considerable French Canadian influence on the political system and their access to high-status political positions and the media, the British, not the French, dominated economic life and were over-represented in elite positions (Porter, 1965, pp. 73–103, 201–308, 337–456, 520–559).

In the 1970s and 1980s questions were raised about Porter's findings. Since the mid-1960s, entrance groups had made considerable gains in education, occupations, and income. The **vertical mosaic** did not persist for certain European-origin non-charter groups. Regarding racialized groups, the 1984 Royal Commission on Equality in Employment found substantial income disparities between **visible minorities** and Indigenous peoples on one side, and non-visible groups on the other (Royal Commission on Equality in Employment, 1984, pp. 84–85). These were attributed to systemic discrimination in the workplace. Many visible minorities were denied access to employment because of unfair recruitment procedures and were more likely to be unemployed. Often, education credentials acquired outside Canada were not recognized in the labour market or by governments. Sometimes, Canadian experience was required unnecessarily (Royal Commission on Equality in Employment, 1984, pp. 46–51). For Indigenous peoples, the situation was even worse.

Today, it is claimed that the vertical mosaic persists, but in a *racialized*, not an ethnic form. Canada is now characterized by a **colour-coded vertical mosaic** (Galabuzi, 2006, p. 7). Lian and Matthews, analyzing 1991 census data, argued that race is now *the* fundamental basis of income inequality in Canada. The old ethnic vertical mosaic may be disappearing, but it is being replaced by a strong "coloured mosaic" (1998, p. 476). Similar findings were reported by Li (2003), using 1996 census data. Galabuzi (2006, p. 100) showed that in 2000 the average after-tax income for racialized persons was $20,627, which is 12.3 per cent less than the average after-tax income of $23,522 for non-racialized persons. Among university degree holders in 2000, after-tax income of racialized individuals was $35,617; that of their non-racialized counterparts was $38,919, an 8.5 per cent difference.

ECONOMIC INEQUALITIES WITHIN ETHNIC AND RACIALIZED GROUPS: THE ROLES OF CLASS, GENDER, AND PLACE OF BIRTH

Many analyses of economic inequality emphasize its "mosaic" dimension and only examine the earnings inequalities *among* ethnic and racialized groups. The "vertical" dimension is also worth examining to discover the earnings inequalities not only among, but also *within* them. Within each structural basis of inequality (race/ethnicity, gender, or class), the other two coexist. All classes have gender and ethnic/racialized segments. Gender groups have class and ethnic/racialized segments. All ethnic/racialized groups are permeated by class and gender differences. Ethnicity and race serve as sources of division within the broader class structure (Li, 1992). Inequality cannot be analyzed outside the class context (Li, 1988, 141; Nakhaie, 1999, 2000; Liodakis, 2002; Satzewich & Liodakis, 2017). Apart from a few exceptions (Li, 1988, 1992; Nakhaie, 1999, 2000; Liodakis, 2002), the class dimension of race/ethnic earnings inequalities has not been adequately examined.

Ethnic and racialized groups have internal hierarchies and are themselves stratified. They are not homogeneous; they are differentiated internally by religion, dialect, region of origin, time of arrival to Canada (Porter, 1965, pp. 72–73); social class (Li, 1988, 1992); gender (Boyd, 1992); age; and place of birth (Liodakis, 1998; 2002). The original vertical mosaic thesis and its colour-coded version should be questioned, not because we now have more ethnic or racial economic equality but arguably because economic inequality, both among and within groups, is also based on social class, gender, and place of birth.

> **TIME to REFLECT**
>
> Why do some people make more money than others? Do all members of the same ethnic/racialized group have the same income? What do you think causes income inequalities within ethnic and racialized groups?

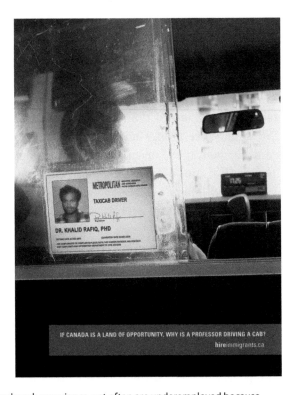

Increasing numbers of immigrants have impressive credentials and work experience, yet often are underemployed because their schooling and experience were gained abroad. These posters were part of a public awareness campaign for hireimmigrants.ca, mounted by the Toronto Region Immigrant Employment Council (TRIEC).

The colour-coded vertical mosaic thesis does not fully explain current patterns of earnings inequality in Canada. It is simplistic; it reduces the complexities of inequality to a two-tier system with non-visible groups at the top and visible minorities at the bottom of the hierarchy. It cannot account for the large class and gender earnings inequalities *within* racialized and ethnic groups. It overlooks many anomalies that undermine it. For example, much of the literature on inequality shows that southern European groups (Greeks, Portuguese, and, to a lesser extent, Italians) are not as well educated as the rest of the European groups and do not earn as much. Often their educational levels and income are exceeded by those of some visible-minority groups (Li, 1988, pp. 76, 78, 82, 84, 88, Tables 5.1–5.5). Boyd (1992) shows that non–visible-minority women of Greek, Italian, Portuguese, other European, and Dutch origin made less than the average earnings of all women, and often less than those of a visible-minority background.

Li's data from the 1996 census show that visible-minority Canadian-born women actually make more than their non-visible counterparts (Li, 2003). This pattern persists: some visible-minority groups (e.g., Chinese, Japanese) earn more than some non-visible groups (e.g. Portuguese, Greeks).

Research by Satzewich and Liodakis, using the 2001 and 2006 censuses, provides contemporary confirmation that ethnic and racialized groups differ greatly in terms of their class composition (heterogeneity *within*). There is no clear-cut visible/non-visible dichotomy in any class. Often, some non-visible groups are more likely to be found in the lower classes than visible minorities. For example, the Portuguese, Italians, Greeks, British, and French are more proletarianized than the Chinese. The Portuguese are more proletarianized than Caribbeans and South Asians (Satzewich & Liodakis, 2017). Indigenous peoples, as a group, are more likely to be working class and less likely to belong in the upper classes, although Indigenous women are less proletarianized than Indigenous and Portuguese men (Liodakis, 2009; Satzewich & Liodakis, 2017). In the class of professionals, the Chinese are well above the national average—above the Portuguese, Italians, Greeks, and charter groups (British and French), and second only to Jewish-origin Canadians. Filipinos, Caribbeans, and South Asians are above the Portuguese, who are not a visible-minority group. In fact, the percentage of Portuguese professionals is lower than that of Indigenous peoples. In the small-employer category, the Chinese are also over-represented, with all other visible groups being under-represented, along with the Portuguese, Greeks, and Indigenous peoples(Satzewich & Liodakis, 2017).

Class and gender variations in earnings *within* ethnic/racialized groups are usually greater than the average differentials in earnings *among* them (Liodakis, 2002; Satzewich & Liodakis, 2017). There are considerable differences in the earnings of classes *within* ethnic groups. Historically, the petite bourgeoisie and workers have had mean earnings below the national average, while small employers, professionals, and managers and supervisors earn considerably more (Li, 1988, 1992; Liodakis, 2002). In addition, women, on average, make less than men in all ethnic groups and in all social classes. In 2010, for example the male–female difference in median after-tax income was $9,354 ($32,434 – $23,080), or 29 per cent. The visible–non-visible difference in median after-tax income was $6,484 ($28,463 – $21,979), or 23 per cent (Statistics Canada, 2013g).

Data from the 2011 National Household Survey show that within Indigenous peoples, there is a marked difference of 31.6 per cent between the median total income of North American Indians ($17,903) and that of the **Métis** ($26,173). Within visible minorities, the Japanese are on top with $29,112 and Koreans on the bottom, with $16,408, or 44 per cent lower earnings (Statistics Canada, 2013g). Simply adding up the groups that make up the huge statistical categories of Indigenous peoples, visible minorities, and non–visible-minority groups

and then comparing their earnings is methodologically questionable, does not advance social science, and may be misleading.

Ethnic and racialized groups have different gender and nativity compositions also. For example, in terms of gender, the Caribbean and Filipino groups have more women than men in the paid labour market because of immigration patterns. In many visible-minority groups, the percentage of foreign-born exceeds 85 per cent, whereas in the non-visible category it is less than 50 per cent. Such differences affect the earnings inequalities that exist *within* them but remain concealed if we treat them as homogeneous entities (Satzewich & Liodakis, 2017).

The larger the immigrant component of an ethnic/racialized group, the more likely it is that the group will have below-average earnings. Three trends are discernible: First, immigrants make less than Canadian-born individuals. In 2010, the median total income of Canadian-born people was $31,085, whereas that of the foreign-born was only $26,691—a 14 per cent difference. Second, the earnings of recent immigrants were much lower than those of immigrants who had been in Canada longer than five years. 2010 data show 29 per cent higher median total income for those who had immigrated before 1981 ($30,964) compared to those who had immigrated between 2001 and 2009 ($21,975) (Statistics Canada, 2013g). It appears that the longer immigrants have been in Canada, the higher their earnings. Third, since the 1980s, recent-immigrant income has steadily declined compared to that of the Canadian-born. A close examination of Table 8.2 shows even greater differences. In general, there has been a steady deterioration of recent-immigrant earnings, irrespective of gender and university education. This is a troubling trend, given that most recent immigrants have higher educational credentials than those who immigrated to Canada before the 1980s. They earn less than Canadian-born people and face earnings volatility. Those initial differences in earnings tend to persist in later years, especially during times of economic recession, as we experienced in

Table 8.2 ▶ Median Earnings[1,2] of Male and Female Recent Immigrants[3] and Canadian-Born Earners, 1980–2005[4]

Year	Recent-Immigrant Earners				Canadian-Born Earners				Recent-Immigrant to Canadian-Born Earnings Ratio			
	With a university degree		With no university degree		With a university degree		With no university degree		With a university degree		With no university degree	
	males	females	males	females	males	females	males	females	males	females	males	females
	2005 constant dollars											
1980	24,541	24,317	36,467	18,548	63,040	41,241	43,641	24,463	0.77	0.59	0.84	0.86
1990	38,351	25,959	27,301	17,931	61,332	41,245	40,757	23,267	0.63	0.63	0.67	0.77
2000	35,816	22,511	25,951	16,794	61,505	43,637	39,902	25,622	0.58	0.52	0.65	0.66
2005	30,332	18,969	24,470	14,233	62,566	44,545	40,235	25,590	0.48	0.43	0.61	0.56

1. The numbers refer to all earners, whether or not they worked on a full-time basis for a full year. Individuals with self-employment income are included, and those living in institutions are excluded.
2. Medians are not available for counts of less than 250. Earnings are in 2005 constant dollars.
3. Recent immigrants in 2005 are those who immigrated between 2000 and 2004; recent immigrants in 2000 are those who immigrated between 1995 and 1999 and so on.
4. Unfortunately, no comparative 2010 summary data tables were available at the time of writing from the 2011 National Household Survey.

SOURCE: "Median earnings, in 2005 constant dollars, of male and female recent immigrant earners and Canadian-born earners aged 25 to 54, with or without a university degree, Canada, 1980 to 2005," adapted from "Income and earnings, 2006 Census," Statistics Canada Catalogue 97-563-XWE2006002, Table 8, www.statcan.gc.ca/bsolc/olc-cel/olc-cel?catno=97-563- XWE2006002&lang=end.

the 1990s (Ostrovsky, 2008, pp. 24–25). The recession that began in 2008 likely had negative effects on the earnings of all Canadian workers but especially on those of recent immigrants.

TIME to REFLECT •——————

Do you think that there is a link between a person's ethnic/racial background and his or her moral, intellectual, and behavioural characteristics? Can you think of specific examples, without resorting to stereotypes?

CONCLUSION: THE FUTURE OF RACE AND ETHNICITY

In this chapter, we have argued that ethnicity and race are social relations. As such, they are bases of economic, social, and political power among individuals and social groups. They are about domination and subordination; they are rooted in the history of colonialism and associated with the development of capitalism. Historical processes that have made some people "minorities" have led to and continue to inform and reproduce the formation of the social, political, and economic dichotomies of the "Self" and the "Other."

Canada's current socio-demographic makeup is linked to the historical (and ongoing) "othering" of Indigenous peoples, the usurpation of their lands, the destruction of their cultures, and government policies of forced assimilation. It is also intertwined with racist immigration policies that, for a long time, excluded "non-preferred" groups and visible minorities other from immigrating to Canada.

Race and ethnicity are bases of social inequality. They are inseparable from its class and gender dimensions. Canada has an official policy of multiculturalism that attempts to integrate minorities into the social fabric. But the policy does little to address economic inequalities and has not been very successful in combating racism or promoting the institutional integration of minorities. In Canada, some groups are doing better than others. If we consider ethnic and racial groups as homogeneous entities, there appears to be a binary social hierarchy based on visibility. When we examine the internal class and gender differences among groups, it is apparent that the colour-coded vertical mosaic thesis cannot fully explain differences among and within these groups. Social class, gender, place of birth and time of arrival in Canada greatly influence racial/ethnic earnings inequalities. In general, the Canadian-born, males, managers and supervisors, professionals, and small employers do better than the foreign-born, females, workers, and the petite bourgeoisie.

Recent efforts toward "reasonable accommodation" have sparked more debates. This is by no means an exclusively Canadian phenomenon. The wider global context is telling: in the post-modern, globalized world, the hegemonic economic, political, and cultural powers (e.g., the US, the European Union, Japan) have increasingly pushed for world economic integration through free trade, the free movement of capital across nation-states, the control and surveillance of international labour migration, the weakening of the role of the nation-state, as well as the rise of supranational organizations like the World Bank, the International Monetary Fund, and the World Trade Organization. A trend toward global cultural homogenization is partly attributable to the export of consumer popular culture to developing nations.

In the past three decades, the world has witnessed the disintegration of the Soviet Union, the triumph of capitalism, and the dominance of Western culture. And yet the world does not seem to be any more peaceful or egalitarian. Nor have ethnic/racial and cultural identities or racism disappeared. On the contrary, we have witnessed the rise of nationalisms; ethnic cleansing; a new racism, xenophobia, and Islamophobia (especially after 9/11); wars in the former Yugoslavia, Afghanistan, Iraq, Syria, and elsewhere; and a general thrust against the protection of individual and group rights and freedoms in all Western, liberal-capitalist democracies—all in the name of fighting "terrorism" and "exporting" what is claimed to be democracy. At the heart of all these matters are race and ethnicity, a major field of study within the social sciences, especially within sociology.

Questions for Critical Thought

1. What criteria would you use to differentiate human populations, and why?
2. What makes you a member of an ethnic and/ or racialized group? Should Ontarians be considered an ethnic group? Why or why not?
3. "The Canadian policy of multiculturalism is better than the American melting pot." Do you agree or disagree with this statement? Why?
4. With which criticisms of multiculturalism do you agree or disagree, and why?
5. Is multiculturalism alone able to solve the problems of racism and the attendant issues of minority-group integration into our political, social, and economic institutions?
6. What accounts for the earnings inequalities among various ethnic/racialized groups—cultural or structural differences? Assume, for the sake of argument, that all members of ethnic/racialized groups share the same cultural and behavioural characteristics. What would explain the marked economic inequalities *within* ethnic/racial groups?
7. Who decides what is reasonable in "reasonable accommodation"?
8. What explains (in non-racist terms) the rise of Islamophobia in the post-9/11 world of control and surveillance in the US, Canada, and Europe?

Sociological Explorations

1. In a magazine, select the first 10 ads that show human models. Try to identify each model's race and/or ethnicity. How do you determine which group each might belong to? What are the challenges in labelling the models? Do any patterns emerge in what you are seeing?
2. Look around at your classmates. What proportion do you think are immigrants? Can you

figure out who is a second- or third-generation Canadian? Assess your assumptions about the people around you when it comes to race, ethnicity, nationality, citizenship, and belonging.

3. Try to map out your family tree. What is the race, ethnicity, and nationality of each person on your tree? How diverse is the tree? How far back can you go?

Recommended Readings

Basok, T. (2002). *Tortillas and tomatoes: Transmigrant Mexican harvesters in Canada.* **Montreal, QC & Kingston, ON: McGill-Queen's University Press.**
This book examines the role of Mexican seasonal workers in Canadian agriculture and critiques the ways they have been treated by employers and the Canadian government.

Galabuzi, G.-E. (2006). *Canada's economic apartheid: The social exclusion of racialized groups in the new century.* **Toronto, ON: Canadian Scholars' Press.**
Galabuzi supports the view that Canada is characterized by a new colour-coded vertical mosaic and presents evidence of persistent income inequalities between racialized and non-racialized Canadians.

Henry, F., & Tator, C. (2005). *The colour of democracy: Racism in Canadian society* **(3rd edn). Toronto, ON: Thomson Nelson.**
This caustic critique of racism in Canadian policies and institutions points to the contradictions of multiculturalism and democratic racism in Canadian society.

Jablonski, N. (2006). *Skin: A natural history.* **Berkeley, CA: University of California Press.**
This nuanced work provides a fascinating and comprehensive account of the biological and cultural aspects of human skin. Jablonski begins with a look at skin's structure and functions and then tours its 300-million-year evolution, delving into such topics as how the skin reflects and affects emotions and how environmental conditions have influenced its colours.

Satzewich, V. (2015). *Points of entry: How Canada's visa officers decide who gets in.* **Vancouver, BC: University of British Columbia Press.**

This unique work examines the manner in which Canadian immigration officers abroad look at the spousal/partner relationships of visa applicants, in order to determine if they are "real" or "fake." Officers ultimately determine which relationships are "real" in order to approve applicants for immigration to Canada.

Satzewich, V., & Liodakis, N. (2017). *"Race" and ethnicity in Canada: A critical introduction* **(4th edn). Toronto, ON: Oxford University Press.**
This work summarizes theoretical approaches to the study of race and ethnicity, Canadian immigration policies, relations between Indigenous and non-Indigenous peoples, economic inequalities among and within ethnic groups, multiculturalism, racism, and transnationalism.

Steinberg, S. (1989). *The ethnic myth: Race, ethnicity, and class in America* **(2nd edn). Boston, MA: Beacon Press.**
The author argues that cultural "traits" often considered "ethnic" may be more directly related to class, locality, and other social conditions and provides a caustic commentary on the conditions of recent immigrants and a penetrating reappraisal of the black underclass in the United States. Also see his 2007 study, *Race Relations: A Critique* (Stanford, CA: Stanford University Press).

Synnott, A., & Howes, D. (1996). Canada's visible minorities: Identity and representation. In V. Amit-Talai & C. Knowles (Eds), *Re-situating identities: The politics of race, ethnicity and culture.* **Peterborough, ON: Broadview Press.**
Synnott and Howes question whether it makes sense to lump together many different groups, with different immigration histories and backgrounds, into a single category of dubious analytical value.

Recommended Websites

Assembly of First Nations
www.afn.ca
The national organization for status Indians site includes publications, policy information, and links to provincial and territorial organizations. Other Indigenous organizations are Inuit Tapiriit Kanatami (www.itk.ca) and the Métis National Council (www.metisnation.ca).

Canadian Heritage: Multiculturalism

www.canadianheritage.gc.ca/
eng/1266037002102

This site includes information on multicultural programs, definitions of "multiculturalism" and "diversity," news releases, publications, and links to numerous Canadian and international organizations.

Canadian Race Relations Foundation (CRRF)

www.crr.ca

The CRRF, established in 1991, is the lead government agency that seeks to eliminate racism. Its site outlines programs, includes publications, and has useful links.

Global Networks: A Journal for Transnational Affairs

http://onlinelibrary.wiley.com/
journal/10.1111/%28ISSN%291471-0374

The *Global Networks* journal, edited by world-renowned scholars Steve Vertovec and Robin Cohen, provides links to sites on transnational movements of goods and people and on globalization, as well as journal contents.

Greek Community of Toronto

www.greekcommunity.org

This site is representative of ethnic organizations in Canada. It provides information on Greek language lessons, dancing, theatre, social happenings, and politics of interest to the Greek community in Toronto.

International Organization for Migration

www.iom.ch

This intergovernmental organization, with 120 member countries, provides information on policy, research, international migration law, and UN resolutions. It believes that "humane and orderly migration benefits migrants and society."

Harvesting Freedom—Justicia for Migrant Workers (J4MW)

http://harvestingfreedom.org/

This is a Toronto-based political collective run by diverse volunteers (migrant workers, labour organizers, educators, researchers, students, and racialized youth). Justicia for Migrant Workers promotes the rights of migrant farm workers and farm workers without status in Canada.

Québec interculturel

www.quebecinterculturel.gouv.qc.ca/fr/index.html

This Quebec Ministry of Immigration and Cultural Communities site, in French, provides information on associations in Quebec, employment, the province's ethno-cultural diversity, and more.

Quebec Judge Wouldn't Hear Case of Woman Wearing Hijab

www.cbc.ca/news/canada/montreal/quebec-
judge-wouldn-t-hear-case-of-woman-wearing-
hijab-1.2974282

This CBC article reports the 2015 case in which Rania El-Alloul, a Muslim woman, was told by a judge that she would not be able to testify in court while wearing a hijab. The article includes comments in favour of allowing hijabs from El-Alloul and others.

Quebec Judge vs Muslim Woman Wearing Hijab

www.youtube.com/watch?v=ypqh7yquQv8

A video from Rebel Media that comments favourably on the Quebec judge's ruling against the wearing of a hijab in court and discusses other similar issues such as the niqab debate.

Key Terms

abocide A term referrring to the physical extermination of Indigenous people. Today it is used for criticizing Bill C-31, since it may lead to the legal "elimination" of status Indians if they marry non-Indians.

Indigenous peoples A term entrenched in Canada's Constitution that refers to all Natives, including status Indians, Inuit, and **Métis**.

ascriptive characteristics Social traits with which we are born, such as sex and skin colour.

assimilation Processes by which minority groups are forced to adopt the hegemonic culture of a society.

behavioural assimilation The acquisition of dominant group cultural values by minority groups.

blocked mobility thesis Porter's argument that **ethnic group** membership in **entrance groups** hinders opportunities for upward social mobility.

charter groups The so-called founding nations of Canada: the British and the French.

Chinese head tax A tax on Chinese immigrants introduced in 1885 by the federal government in order to exclude them from entering and staying in Canada permanently.

collective conscience Durkheim's concept of cohesion in pre-modern societies, based on sameness and conformity of individual thought and awareness to the group.

colour-coded vertical mosaic The argument that "race" or "visibility" has replaced ethnicity in the structure of social, economic, and political inequality in Canada.

cultural relativism The opposite of ethnocentrism; not evaluating other cultures with criteria derived from one's own culture.

culturalism A diverse body of literature that attempts to explain the differential socio-economic achievements of ethnic groups by examining their culture.

culture A set of dynamic social processes and practices; it is a collective response of groups of people to their ever-changing external conditions, largely determined by social structures.

democratic racism A new form of racism in Canadian society that is characterized by the conflict between the prevalent ideologies of democratic principles (justice, equality, fairness, etc.) on one hand, and their coexistence with negative feelings, attitudes, behaviours, prejudice, and discrimination against subordinate groups on the other.

discrimination A situation in which people are treated unfairly because of their membership in a particular group.

entrance groups The ethnic groups that immigrated to Canada after its founding by the British and the French.

ethnic group A social group formed around notions of common identity, culture, and (often presumed) common ancestry.

ethnicity and race "Ethnicity" refers to social distinctions and relations among individuals and groups based on their cultural characteristics (language, religion, customs, history, and so on), whereas "race" refers to people's assumed but socially significant physical or genetic characteristics.

ethnocentrism The opposite of cultural relativism; the evaluation of other cultures with criteria from one's own culture.

Immigration Act of 1910 A discriminatory act of Parliament that prohibited entrance to Canada for "the mentally defective," "the diseased," and the "physically defective."

institutional racism Prejudice and discrimination that is built into and permeates the structure and functions of economic, political, and social institutions.

interculturalism Quebec's version of multiculturalism, which discourages ethnic enclaves and promotes the linguistic assimilation of various cultures and minorities.

Islamophobia Fear of people who believe in Islam, based upon prejudice.

labour market A competitive arena in which labour power is sold by workers and bought by employers. Good jobs are found in the primary labour market; bad ones, in the secondary.

Métis A French term meaning "half-caste," used to describe the descendants of unions between male French Canadian fur-traders and Indigenous women in sixteenth- to seventeenth-century Canada.

melting-pot policies US policies that encourage immigrants to abandon their original identities and languages in favour of being "American."

monopolistic closure Weber's concept of social practices that exclude "others" from the distribution of scarce valuable resources such as wealth, high social status, and political power.

multiculturalism An ideology and a set of federal government programs that are used to maintain social order and manage ethnic and "racial" relations in poly-ethnic societies.

permanent residents Immigrants who have been given the right to live and work in Canada without limitations. They are eligible to apply for Canadian citizenship after a certain period of time in Canada. Also known as landed immigrants.

political economy A structural approach that attempts to explain socio-economic differences among and within social groups by analyzing social relations (class, gender, race/ethnicity, age, sexual preference, physical ability, mental health/illness, etc.).

primordialism *Hard primordialism* holds that people are attached to one another and to their communities because of objective blood ties; *soft primordialism* proposes that people's feelings of affinity, attachment, acceptance, trust, and intimacy toward their "own kind" are subjective, not mediated by blood ties.

race see ethnicity and race

racialization Processes by which, based on people's physical characteristics, human populations are categorized into different dominant and subordinate groups.

racism Prejudice and discrimination against people because of their ethnicity or race.

reasonable accommodation Quebec's pluralist notion that government policies and programs should not only tolerate but make allowances for the cultural differences of new immigrants and of minority groups.

residential schools A system of schools in which Indigenous children were placed by government educational authorities in order to assimilate them into the dominant culture.

selection criteria Standards set by immigration policy that are associated with different weights (points) such as prospective immigrants' education, work experience, age, knowledge of official languages, "adaptability," and so on.

social class The structural economic position of social individuals in relation to (a) ownership of money capital, (b) control of the physical means of production, and (c) control of the labour power of others.

split labour market A **labour market** split into (a) a primary one where more members of the dominant groups may have more secure, full-time, and high-paying jobs; (b) a secondary one where minorities may be found in more insecure, part-time, low-paying, menial occupations.

structural assimilation The integration of minority groups into the economic, social, and political life of the host country.

systemic discrimination Impersonal, covert practices that penalize members of minorities.

vertical mosaic Porter's metaphor about Canadian society implying that it comprises many ethnic groups (mosaic) but that there is an ethnic hierarchy with the British and the French on the top and all other groups at the bottom of social, economic, and political structures (vertical).

visible minorities Racialized groups defined by Statistics Canada as such. The categories are South Asian, Chinese, Black, Korean, Filipino, Latin American, Arab, Southeast Asian, West Asian, Korean, Japanese, visible minority not included elsewhere, and multiple visible minority.

Social Institutions

PART

IV

So much of what we do in our everyday lives—our written and unwritten rules, and our taken-for-granted assumptions and behaviours—are products of the social institutions that touch our lives. Social institutions are systems of densely interwoven and enduring relationships that function within society. Institutions order and structure our behaviour through the norms that they establish both formally and informally. One of the most obvious, common, and personal of these is the family in which we live.

In Chapter 9, Juanne Clarke and Patrizia Albanese introduce you to the sociological study of two important facets in our lives, families and health. In their chapter you will read about the diversity of family forms that have come to make up Canadian society. As the chapter unfolds, you will see that family, health, illness, and death are related to macrosociological issues of power, economics, and inequality.

Another important social institution connected to power and inequality is the educational system. According to the Organisation for Economic Co-operation and Development, Canada has one of the most highly educated populations in the world. However, Canada is also among the countries with the highest post-secondary tuition fees. In Chapter 10, Terry Wotherspoon helps you make sense of this and related issues. In his chapter you will gain a critical understanding of the theoretical perspectives that sociologists use to explain educational institutions, practices, and outcomes.

In Chapter 11, Pamela Sugiman introduces us to the sociological study of work and the economy. She walks us through the changing nature of work

to better understand the impact of the organization of work and economies on workers variously located within our gendered and racialized market-driven society. Sugiman shows that while at times challenging, stressful, and exploitative in nature, work is central to our existence: a place where individuals seek meaning in their lives.

In Chapter 12 Lori Beaman explores the definitions of religion and spirituality. She challenges us to think about the intersection of religion and the law, and about the gendered dimensions of religious participation. The chapter provides a sociological analysis of the changing religious demography of Canada. It also considers the impact of secularization and the rise of new religious movements and minority religious groups in Canada and internationally.

Internationally focused social research on politics can help illuminate the origin of social problems and point to possible solutions. Important actors in these systems are typically politicians, governments, and private, non-governmental, or intergovernmental institutions. Political sociologists examine the interactions of these different actors and social structures to understand outcomes that have national and international implications. In Chapter 13, Randle Hart, Howard Ramos, Karen Stanbridge, and John Veugelers introduce us to the sociological study of politics and social movements. Through the chapter you will see how political sociologists have analyzed politics in terms of contests over the control of material, cultural, social, and institutional resources. You will also be exposed to how social movements are studied sociologically.

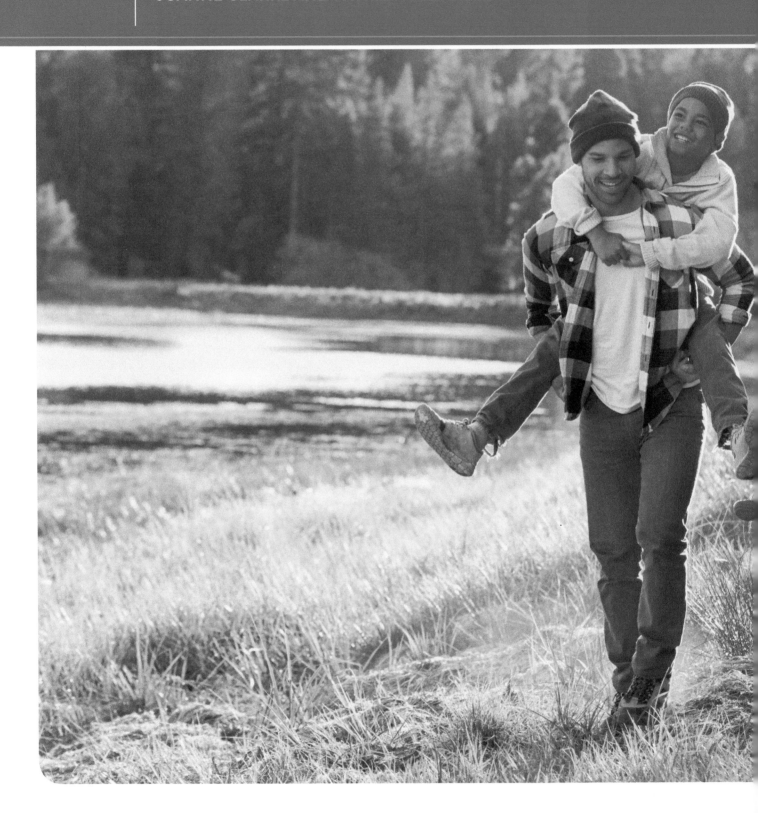

9 | Families and Health Issues

JUANNE CLARKE AND PATRIZIA ALBANESE

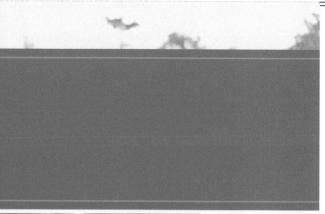

In this chapter you will:

▶ Learn about the diversity of family forms that have come to accompany what was once thought of as the "typical" Canadian family

▶ See how family life and health issues intersect throughout the life course, in a range of social-political contexts and situations

▶ Learn that family life, health, illness, disease, and death are related to sociological issues such as power, economics, and inequality

▶ Examine medicare as a system that embodies five principles: portability, universality, comprehensive coverage, public administration, and accessibility

▶ Consider how privatization is increasing in the Canadian medical system, and how this has affected family life today

INTRODUCTION

Canadian families come in an assortment of shapes, sizes, and configurations. As we will see in this chapter, they include a large range of experiences, yet increasingly face a number of similar challenges as they navigate through the life course (see Luxton, 2011). One similarity for all families is that they are expected to navigate through changing economic and political times. Canadian families have experienced an economic rollercoaster ride that includes a rise in **precarious employment** (amounting to economic insecurity) and an entrenchment of **neo-liberal** ideas and social policies, which favour the private sector. In particular this trend is clearly seen in families' interactions with health-related issues and the health-care system. In this chapter we will unpack some of these terms, trends, and changes. You will be challenged to think about how family life looks and feels and what it means to you and the many people around you. You will also be asked, What significant health and medical issues do you face today as a student, as a gendered person, as a member of a family, as a Canadian? This chapter will, among other things, introduce you to some sociological perspectives on such topics.

Health, like family life, is linked inextricably to the social order. Health's very definition, its many causes, and its consequences all are embedded in the social world. What is considered health or disease in one culture or society may be perceived differently in another. Both rates and understandings of disease and death vary across families, time, and place. Social classes differ in their definitions of good health. What a woman considers health may be different from a man's definition of health. Moreover, social class and gender differences lead to varying rates of **morbidity** (the frequency of disease) and **mortality** (the frequency of death).

The sociology of health is also about the various medical systems of diagnosis, prognostication, and treatment, which not all Canadians experience in the same way. Conventional modern medicine—sometimes called **allopathic medicine** (treatment with "opposites") is taken for granted in much of the Western world. However, naturopathic (treatment through "natural" remedies and procedures, such as herbs or massage), chiropractic (treatment through spinal adjustment), and homeopathic medicine (treatment with "similars") all are examples **complementary and alternative medicines** (CAM), and are of increasing importance in the Western world. In this chapter you will see how and when allopathic medicine and complementary and alternative medicines are used and experienced by Canadian families today.

We open the chapter with a review of recent trends in family forms and assess various definitions of "family" to determine which, if any, actually reflect the diversity that we see and experience. Then we review theories that help us understand and explain what is happening to, with, and in health, health care, and family life. Finally, we provide an overview of the changing health-care system and its impact on Canadian individuals and families.

FAMILY DIVERSITY AS NORM

The 2011 Canadian census counted 9,389,700 families, up 5.5 per cent from 8,896,840 in 2006 (Statistics Canada, 2012e; see Table 9.1). The proportion of married-couple families was still the largest (67.0 per cent), but the overall proportion of married-couple families in relation to other types families has decreased (from 68.9 per cent in 2006), since, for the first time, the 2011 census counted stepfamilies. In 2011, 7.4 per cent of couples with children were *simple stepfamilies* (in which all children were the children of only one of the spouses or partners); 5.2 per cent of couples with children were *complex stepfamilies* (comprising at least one child of both parents as well as one child of one parent only). In total, 10 per cent of children under the age of 14 lived in stepfamilies (Statistics Canada, 2012e). Since the 2006 census, the number of common-law couples

Families come in different forms and sizes. What unites families is what they do, rather than the form they take.

(now accounting for 16.7 per cent of all families) rose by 13.9 per cent, surpassing the number of lone-parent families (now accounting for 16.3 per cent of all families); lone-parent families increased by 8.0 per cent (male lone-parent families increased by 16.2 per cent, compared with 6 per cent for female lone-parent families; Statistics Canada, 2012e).

In 2005, for the first time in Canadian history, same-sex couples were entitled to legally marry. The number of same-sex married couples nearly tripled between 2006 and 2011, and the number of same-sex common-law couples rose 15 per cent. The 2011 census counted 64,575 same-sex couple families (21,015 were married and 43,560 were common-law). Over the same period a growing number of Canadian households included grandparents. In 2011, 4.8 per cent of children under the age of 14 lived in **multi-generational households (extended families)** that contained at least one grandparent. Of these children, 0.5 per cent lived in *skip-generation* families, which include grandparents but not parents (Statistics Canada, 2012e).

Behind some of these numbers are major changes in marriage rates, age at first marriage, cohabitation rates, age at which women have a first child, divorce rates, and remarriage rates. For example, a growing proportion of young women are postponing first marriages until well into their twenties and thirties (Statistics Canada, 2009b), and Canadian couples are increasingly choosing not to marry, deciding instead to cohabit or live common-law (Milan, 2015). At the same time, the proportion of first births occurring among women

Table 9.1 ▶ Distribution (number and percentage) and Percentage Change of Census Families by Family Structure, Canada, 2001–2011

Census Family	2001	%	2006	%	2011	%	% Change 2006–2011
Total census families	8,371,020	100.0	8,896,840	100.0	9,389,700	100.0	5.5
Couple families	7,059,830	84.3	7,482,775	84.1	7,861,860	83.7	5.1
Married	5,901,420	70.5	6,105,910	68.6	6,293,950	67.0	3.1
Common-law	1,158,410	13.8	1,376,865	15.5	1,567,910	16.7	13.9
Lone-parent families	1,311,190	15.7	1,414,060	15.9	1,527,840	16.3	8.0
Female parent	1,065,360	12.7	1,132,290	12.7	1,200,295	12.8	6.0
Male parent	245,825	2.9	281,775	3.2	327,545	3.5	16.2

SOURCE: Statistics Canada 2012

in their early thirties increased from 15 per cent in 1987 to 26 per cent in 2005 (Garner & Bushnik, 2008). While divorce rates stabilized after 1987 (a time of changes in the Divorce Act), the proportion of adults living in complex stepfamilies has grown from 39 per cent of stepfamily parents in 1995 to 42 per cent in 2001, 49 per cent in 2006, and 51 per cent in 2011 (Vézina, 2015).

Gazso and McDaniel (2015) point out that the timing and sequencing of life events or transitions (employment, marriage, childbirth, and so on) are no longer path-dependent. They explain that today, young adults can anticipate a life course marked by several jobs, continual educational upgrading (often postponing childbirth and marriage), and working past the age of 65, compared to the traditional *tripartite sequencing* of the life course that involved pursuing education that resulted in a lifelong career, then forming a family, and finally retiring—a sequencing far more typical of their parents or grandparents. This has also given rise to changes in our definition of families, particularly as we see shifts in who or what makes a family.

TIME to REFLECT

Imagine snapping a photograph of "your family," or crafting a composite of them. Who would that include? Who would you exclude? What makes someone a member of your family?

What Is a Family?

Given the variation in family forms and changing life transitions, a conventional definition of family is elusive. Most agree on the definition of a **nuclear family**, which typically includes a couple and their children sharing the same household, but increasingly this term is used to define a one-parent family with children. Today, through divorce and remarriage, we also see more **bi-nuclear families**—where children of divorced parents live in both households. In a growing number of extended families or multigenerational households, as we saw above, several generations or sets of kin—grandparents, aunts, uncles, cousins—share a household. Similarly, terms like **household** (any group of individuals who share a dwelling) and even "families by choice" are increasingly interchangeable with "family" (see the Researchers in Action box; Gazso & McDaniel, 2015).

In fact, at the level of individual families, there are likely as many definitions of "family" as there are families in this country, because the lived reality of each is quite different from the reality privileged through Canadian law and social policy. At the same time, individual-level explanations, like some more formal definitions, tend to stress the structural or compositional definition of the family (Gazso, 2009; Eichler, 1983). These definitions tend to focus on "Who makes up a family?" often missing the question, "What makes a family?" Pioneering feminist families researchers like Margrit Eichler (1983) have long stressed the importance of rethinking our definitions of "the family," to instead focus on the performative nature of family (the "doing" and exchanges that make a family), and more precisely on questions like "What makes a family?" The Vanier Institute of the Family definition reflects this:

Any combination of two or more persons who are bound together over time by ties of mutual consent, birth and/or adoption or placement and who, together, assume responsibilities for variant combinations of some of the following:

- Physical maintenance and care of group members
- Addition of new members through procreation or adoption
- Socialization of children
- Social control of members
- Production, consumption, distribution of goods and services
- Affective nurturance—love (Vanier Institute of the Family, 2016)

RESEARCHERS IN ACTION ▶ What Makes a Family? Doing Family among Families by Choice

Dr Susan McDaniel, a sociologist at the University of Lethbridge in Alberta, holds the Prentice Research Chair and is Director of the Prentice Institute in Global Population and Economy. Dr Amber Gazso is a professor of sociology at York University in Toronto. Her areas of research are sociology of the family and intimate relations, sociology of gender, poverty, and social policy. McDaniel and Gazso have worked on a number of projects together, including a recent one on the impact of economic insecurity on families and the creation of "families by choice."

Gazso and McDaniel (2015) note that globalization, individualization, and detraditionalization have transformed the character of family life in Canada. We have seen a rise not only in a diversity of family forms, but also in "families by choice" which include both kin and non-kin relations and are opportunistically created as a result of shared life events and daily needs. Through in-depth interviews, Gazso and McDaniel explore the support networks of a few families by choice. They pay particular attention to who constitutes each family, and how family and generational relations are practised and are constrained by the economic and social realities of Canadian society. They especially note that low-income families tend to increasingly rely on wide networks of support to supplement the limited (or absent) formal support from the state.

Gazso and McDaniel share the stories of eight families by choice. One is made up of Reanna (age 20), Jayla (18), and Shemeka (33). The three women

immigrated to Canada from the Caribbean, are Black, and are lone mothers. Reanna, our initial participant in Case 3, referred us to Jayla and her biological half-sister Shemeka as her family. Reanna initially met Jayla through a community organization that supports adolescent lone mothers. Reanna and Jayla both have children under the age of 2 years and are on social assistance. Both young women

live with traditional kin: Reanna shares a residence with her biological father and brothers; Jayla and Shemeka share an apartment. Shemeka is employed and has one child living with her in Canada and one child living with family in Jamaica. (Gazso & McDaniel, 2015, p. 380)

Jayla explained in her interview

that she loves Reanne's daughter like her own son. Reanne and Jayla's sense of each other as family is also informed by their exchanging of child care. Jayla confirmed: "[Reanne] doesn't have [subsidized] daycare so whenever she wants to do anything I'll keep her daughter and stuff for her." Jayla enhances her supportive relationship with Reanne by additionally relying on emotional and financial support from Shemeka. For example, on immigrating to Canada and finding herself pregnant, Jayla chose to live with Shemeka rather than with her father because she perceived that Shemeka, already a mother herself, could offer her more emotional support. As well, Shemeka's employment as a practical nurse enables her to help Jayla by paying rent and providing her with other necessary items like diapers. In return, Shemeka relies on Jayla to style her hair. (Gazso & McDaniel, 2015, p. 382)

For these women and others in the study, their sense of each other as family is intricately connected to their sharing of life events but also by their "doing" of things typically thought of as family practices. Gazso and McDaniel's research illustrates that both innovation and convention characterize contemporary family life, particularly for low-income people.

SOURCE: Gazso, Amber, and Susan McDaniel. 2015. "Families by Choice and the Management of Low Income Through Social Supports." Journal of Family Issues. 36(3): 371–395.

THEORETICAL PERSPECTIVES

Four theoretical paradigms may be considered the most significant approaches to understanding both families and health and medicine sociologically: structural functionalism, conflict theory, interpretive theory, and feminism/antiracism. To help develop your understanding of

the theories, we will focus primarily on how each applies to health. That said, they are equally used to help explain family life.

Structural Functionalism

From the structural functionalist perspective health, like the family, is necessary for the smooth running of the social system. Your university or college, for example, assumes your good health as it organizes its courses and exams—you probably have to get a letter from a doctor for exemption from writing an exam. In a stable society, all institutional forces work together to create and maintain good health for the population. For instance, societies are organized to support a population up to an average **life expectancy** and at a given level of health and ability. This normative standard of health and age at death are reinforced by political, economic, cultural, and educational policies. The age of mandated retirement and the timing of the funding of pensions are two examples of such policies.

Assertions about the interrelationships among institutions all fit within the structural functionalist theoretical perspective. A classic statement of this perspective is found in the work of Talcott Parsons (1951), in particular in his concept of the **sick role**. The sick role is to be thought of as a special position in society that prevents sickness from disrupting social life and provides a way of institutionalizing what might otherwise become a form of deviant behaviour. It does this by articulating two rights and two duties for those who claim sickness.

The rights are exemption from normal social roles and freedom from blame or responsibility for sickness. The duties are to want to get

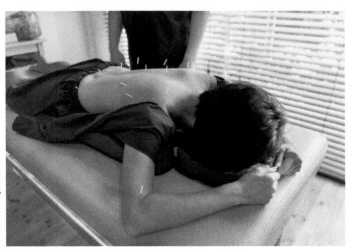

Many Canadians are choosing alternative health-care providers or CAM. Do rising rates in the use of CAM indicate changing attitudes toward conventional medicine? Why or why not?

andresr/iStockphoto

well and to seek and cooperate with technically competent help. However, these theoretically derived ideas do not always have empirical support. For example, it is well known that the right to be exempt from the performance of social roles depends in part on the nature of the sickness. A hangover, for instance, may not be considered a good enough reason to claim the sick role when proffering an excuse for an exam exemption. And with respect to duties, not everyone is expected to want to get well. Indeed, those with a chronic disease such as diabetes are expected to accept their condition and learn to live with it. Parsons assumes the dominance of allopathic medicine in asserting that a sick person is to get technically competent help. Today, however, many people believe that the best help does not always come from allopathic medicine, even though it is the type of medical care primarily supported by the state. Indeed, according to the Public Health Agency of Canada, about 70 per cent of Canadians use alternative health-care providers (CAM) (2008).

Conflict Theory

From the perspective of conflict theory, the frequency of health and ill-health results from inequitable and oppressive economic conditions. Questions driving this perspective include: Are the poor more likely to get sick? Is the **mortality rate** among the poor higher than among the rich? Does racism affect the **morbidity rate**? In this perspective, health may be seen as a commodity that is inequitably located across societies.

A classic statement of this position is found in the work of Friedrich Engels, who often wrote with Karl Marx. In *The Condition of the Working Class in England* (1994 [1845]), Engels demonstrates the negative health consequences of early capitalism. He describes how the development of capitalism advanced mechanization in agriculture and forced farm workers off the land and into the cities to survive. Urban capitalists sought profit regardless of the cost to the well-being of the workers. Owners maintained low costs through poor wages and long hours of backbreaking labour in filthy and noisy working conditions. Even children worked in these unhealthy circumstances.

As a consequence, poor labourers and their families lived exceedingly rough lives in shelters that offered scarce or no privacy, cleanliness, or quiet. They had very little money for food, and the quality of the foodstuffs available in the cities was poor. The slum-like conditions were perfect breeding grounds for all sorts of diseases, and because of the high density of living quarters, the lack of facilities for toileting and washing, and the frequent lack of clean drinking water, the morbidity and mortality rates in the slums were very high. Infectious diseases such as tuberculosis (TB), typhoid, scrofula, and influenza spread quickly and with dire results through these close quarters and malnourished populations.

Epidemics were almost common in nineteenth-century industrial cities, where overcrowding, overflowing cesspits, garbage piled all around, and unsafe water were the norm. It was only after discoveries in bacteriology showed that many of the worst diseases were spread by bacteria and viruses in the water, air, and food that governments enacted **public-health measures**. These new **prevention policies** included sewage disposal, garbage removal, cleaned and filtered drinking water, and hygienic handling of food. The death or mortality rates began to abate (Crompton, 2000).

The conflict perspective is useful for examining economic disparities and their corresponding health inequalities in Canada. Figure 9.1 demonstrates that if all neighbourhood income inequalities in Canada were eliminated, there would be a substantial increase in the equality of health outcomes. For example, if the lowest income quintile neighbourhood were equivalent to the most affluent neighbourhood in income there would be a 26 per cent decrease in health disparities in this quintile.

Interpretive Theory

Interpretation and meaning are the hallmarks of sociology within interpretive theories. What is the meaning, for example, of anorexia and bulimia? Are they medical or mental-health conditions? Are they the result of a moral choice? Or could they be considered "socio-somatic" conditions—that is, caused by society (Currie, 1988)? Various authors have attributed them to women's "hunger strike" against their contradictory positions, against culturally prescribed images, and against lack of opportunities in contemporary society. Are they a means "through

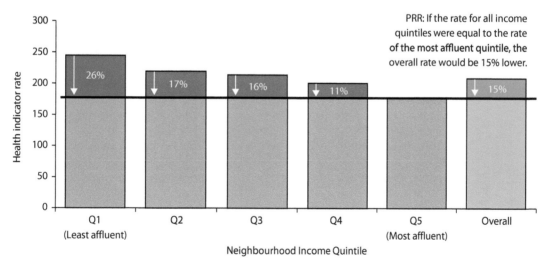

FIGURE 9.1 Neighbourhood Income Quintile as a Measure of Socio-economic Status

SOURCE: Canadian Institute for Health Information and Statistics Canada, Health Indicators 2013, 21

which women, both unconsciously and consciously, protest the social conditions of womanhood" (Currie, 1988, p. 208)?

One of the most useful concepts to derive from an interpretive theoretical paradigm is **stigma**. Its current use in sociology originated with Erving Goffman's 1963 book *Stigma: Notes on the Management of a Spoiled Identity*. The concept is still central to understanding how the negative repercussions of some illnesses are generalized beyond the disease to reflect negatively on the whole character of the person with the disease. In many cases the stigma of the disease may even exacerbate the suffering of the diagnosed person (Pescosolido, 2013).

Stigma is often attached to people with, among other diagnoses, HIV/AIDS, lung cancer, mental illness, inflammatory bowel disease, or fibromyalgia. Sometimes these diseases have connotations of immorality and lend an aura of blame or culpability to those diagnosed. In many ways, good health is often associated with being a good person.

TIME to REFLECT

Are obesity and overweight considered to be neutral medical conditions or are they stigmatized? Is this evident in any social policies of which you are aware?

OPEN FOR DISCUSSION — Interpreting "Disability"

The meaning or interpretation of "**disability**" is highly controversial and can lead to stigma. Many argue that the essence of "disability" lies not in the individual's differences of ability to engage in social, political, and economic life but rather in the lack of accessibility or social accommodations that would enable all to engage as actively as they wish. "Disability" in this view is determined not by individual disorder, pathology, or limitations but rather by society's failure to pursue the full human rights of all people by enabling equitable engagement through various social-structural, cultural, and environmental facilitators. With this view in mind, many people labelled or diagnosed with one "disability" or another may embrace their differences yet decry the lack of accommodation in society that, they argue, should encourage and allow their active involvement. One example is people diagnosed with autism or Asperger's syndrome (often considered a mild form of autism). Many people with such diagnoses make significant contributions to the world and lead satisfying and meaningful lives. Among them are accomplished inventors, artists, scientists, and philosophers such as Michelangelo, Glenn Gould, Albert Einstein, Bertrand Russell, Vincent van Gogh, and Andy Warhol (James, 2006).

A recent study addresses some of the paradoxes of stigma in respect to Asperger's syndrome. The study is based on a qualitative analysis of the blogs of people who self-identify as having Asperger's

(AS) and parents or caregivers of those thought to have the disorder (Clarke & Van Amerom, 2008). The findings indicate that these two groups held not only different but even oppositional views regarding AS. People who self-identified as having Asperger's rejected the popular but denigrating understanding of AS. They confidently called themselves Aspies and called others NTs or neurotypicals. They said they were proud of who they were and of the way they thought and communicated. Their major problems, they believed, were due not to the "disorder" or the "limitations" they suffered because of AS but to the stigma of AS and the way that others perceived and acted toward them. Parents and caregivers, on the other hand, expressed worry about their children's problems in schooling and in their social lives. They tended to accept the dominant and pathologizing view of AS, while the bloggers who self-identified as having AS expressed pride and mutual solidarity. The paper demonstrates the value of an "up-close and personal" investigation of the world views and meaning-making or interpretations of variously situated people, particularly those who are vulnerable to stigmatization or marginalization. It also points to the "**surplus suffering**" of people viewed as disabled (whether or not the disability is real), not because of their physical, emotional, cognitive, or other types of differences but because of the lack of societal and environmental conditions to enable integration and acceptance.

Feminism/Anti-Racism

Feminist and anti-racist health sociology recognizes the centrality of gender and racialization to social life. Feminist/anti-racist health sociology investigates whether, how, and why people who are racialized and gendered have different health and illness profiles, as well as different causes and average ages of death. It also considers such things as ethnicity, sexual preference, gender identity, and ability/disability as fundamental characteristics of social actors. These axes of inequality, therefore, are key in designing research, uncovering social injustice, and planning and making social change.

 Why do you think someone's ethnicity might matter when it comes to health outcomes? For more on economic inequalities among ethnic and racialized groups, see **Chapter 8**, "Ethnic and Race Relations."

One example of work within the feminist paradigm is Anne Kasper and Susan Ferguson's *Breast Cancer: Society Shapes an Epidemic* (2000), which suggests that among the reasons for the high **incidence** and **prevalence** of breast cancer is that it is an over-diagnosed (largely) women's disease that occurs in their highly sexualized breasts. Kasper and Ferguson's collection provides a thought-provoking look at one of the major causes of worry, sickness, and death among women in Canada. Despite the fact that both heart disease and lung cancer are more frequent causes of death for Canadian women, women in Canada fear breast cancer more and even think of their breasts as essentially flawed and vulnerable to disease. Some women even choose prophylactic breast removal as a way to circumvent the possibility of this diagnosis (as actor Angelina Jolie did after a positive genetic test of susceptibility). This is undoubtedly related to the enormous mass media attention the disease has received in the past 30 years or so. During this time, first in the United States and then in Canada, powerful groups of women activists founded highly successful breast cancer

Some think that corporate involvement in breast cancer awareness and fundraising could be a detriment to women's health. What do you think, and why?

advocacy coalitions, lobbied governments and corporations, and brought about substantially increased funding for research into the disease and its treatment (Klawiter, 2008). Samantha King, in *Pink Ribbons, Inc.*, also demonstrates how the focus on consumer activism, especially among white women in the breast cancer movement, "shaped as it is by an ideology of individualism and an imperative for uncomplicated, snappy marketing slogans, has allowed for the emergence of a preoccupation with early detection to the virtual exclusion of other approaches to fighting the epidemic (e.g., prevention) and a failure to address the barriers, financial or otherwise, to treatment" (King, 2006, pp. 117–118). She argues that the corporations involved in breast cancer awareness and fundraising benefit from their involvement, possibly to the detriment of women's health.

PUTTING THEORIES INTO PRACTICE: THE CASE OF PAID AND UNPAID WORK, FAMILY HEALTH, AND WELL-BEING

Between 1976 and 2014, the number of single-earner families with a stay-at-home parent declined from 1.5 million to 500,000. By 2014, couple families with one stay-at-home parent represented less than one-fifth of all couple families with children, down from over half of families in 1976 (Uppal, 2015). This may seem like cause for celebration if it simply reflects feminists' calls for the inclusion of more women in the paid labour force. In truth, it reflects a complex social and economic reality that has profound consequences for families, family health, and well-being.

Over the past few decades, Canada has been developing into what has been called a "post-industrial" society (Bell, 1973). Writing in the 1970s, Daniel Bell (1973, 1976) predicted that we would see a shift from the bulk of workers holding blue-collar, goods-producing (manufacturing) jobs that required less education,

to their holding white-collar, "clean," "smart," service-sector jobs, requiring higher levels of education and expertise, and paying higher incomes. His predictions have partially come true. With globalization, many manufacturing jobs are moving to other parts of the world where labour is cheaper. A growing proportion of workers in Canada have service-sector jobs (Statistics Canada, 2004). A recent labour-force survey revealed that while there were employment gains in professional, scientific, and technical services, the bulk of the gains were in accommodation and food services and in retail sales (Statistics Canada, 2013d).

The reality is that while some new jobs are highly skilled and knowledge based, most new jobs being created in Canada's "new economy" are low paid, low status, and part-time, often requiring non-traditional work hours—what some have colloquially termed "McJobs" (Albanese, 2009).

As a result of changing employment trends, family earnings instability and inequality have grown since the 1990s (Duffy, Corman, & Pupo, 2015; Morissette & Ostrovsky, 2005). According to Statistics Canada, in 1980, the ratio of household debt to personal disposable income was 66 per cent; by 2011, that ratio surpassed 150 per cent, meaning that households owed more than $1.50 for every dollar of their disposable income (Chawla & Uppal, 2012). We have also seen a rise in neo-liberal approaches to family life and social policies; as a society we are increasingly dependent on individual families providing income and care for their members, at a time when the state is expected to contribute less (Luxton, 2015).

A growing proportion of families find themselves relying on both parents working (see Table 9.2). While women's growing labour-force participation rates are partly due to their rising levels of education and women's greater desire for economic independence, families increasingly depend on women's incomes to make ends meet. By 2009, almost 73 per cent of women with children under the age of 16 living at home were in the workforce, as were

66.5 per cent of mothers with children under the age of 6 (Ferrao, 2010). Women, especially women with young children, rely upon (and want) paid work, yet not all can or do find jobs, at least not without assuming additional challenges related to securing non-parental care for their children. Because of the high cost of and limited access to child-care spaces (see Friendly & Prentice, 2009), some dual-earner families have resorted to using off-shift work arrangements—juggling complex shift-work schedules, despite the problems associated with shift work—to help manage work and care responsibilities (Pagnan, Lero, & MacDermid Wadsworth, 2011).

 Do you think that the domestic division of labour and care work has changed significantly in recent years? For more on the gender divisions of domestic labour, see **Chapter 7**, "Gender and Sexuality."

For most families with young children, when they do find adequate care, it remains one of the largest expenses when raising their child (Friendly & Prentice, 2009). (Some in Quebec, however, where the provincial government provides child care for $7 a day for families that need it, are spared this burden.) This expense affects family well-being and women's experiences when trying to balance paid work and family responsibilities (Fox, 2015).

While some men in heterosexual families are contributing more to housework and unpaid care work (Doucet, 2013), there continues to be a "resilient problem of gender differences in parental responsibilities" (Doucet, 2015, p. 238). Luxton (2015) adds that in providing this care work and household management—key tasks associated with social reproduction—women, and some men, are contributing to not only the

Table 9.2 ▶ Employment Status of Couple Families with at Least One Child under 16

	1976	2014	1976	2014
	Thousands		%	
Total couples	**2,825**	**2,753**	**100.0**	**100.0**
Dual earners[1]	**1,014**	**1,901**	**35.9**	**69.1**
Both working full-time	673	1,402	23.8	50.9
Husband full-time, wife part-time	329	422	11.7	15.3
Wife full-time, husband part-time	7	55	0.2	2.0
Both part-time	5	23	0.2	0.8
Single earners (SE)	**1,657**	**736**	**58.6**	**26.7**
SE working father	1,593	585	56.4	21.2
Mother unemployed	95	86	3.3	3.1
Mother not in the labour force	1,498	499	53.0	18.1
Permanently unable to work	3	12	0.1	0.4
Attending school	30	41	1.1	1.5
Staying home[2]	1,466	446	51.9	16.2
SE working mother	64	151	2.3	5.5
Father unemployed	33	70	1.2	2.5
Father not in the labour force	31	81	1.1	2.9
Permanently unable to work	6	11	0.2	0.4
Attending school	4	16	0.1	0.6
Staying home[2]	21	54	0.7	2.0
Non-earners	**154**	**116**	**5.4**	**4.2**

1. Excludes couples in the Armed Forces.
2. Defined as two-parent families with at least one child under 16 at home, with one non-working parent who is not in the labour force, excluding non-working parents who are unemployed, attending school or unable to work due to a disability.
SOURCE: Statistics Canada, Labour Force Survey, 1976 and 2014. Uppal, 2015, p. 4

well-being of their own households and families, but that of our society in general and of the Canadian economy. That said, this important and necessary work continues to be undervalued and unsupported by social and economic policies in this country (Bezanson, 2015).

TIME to REFLECT

Imagine the next 20 years of your life in 5-year increments. What do you expect to be doing at each point? Do you expect to do these things with a partner, or the same partner, for the entire 20 years? Will this include children? How do you expect to find time, money, and other resources to be able to do these things?

Some family scholars in Canada have therefore shifted their attention to what is known as **work–family conflict**, or the time-related stress arising from the competing demands of the different roles imposed on working parents (Tezli & Gauthier, 2009). Interestingly, Young (2015), using both census and individual-level data, examined how experiences of work–family conflict are affected by where families live. She found that those living in more disadvantaged neighbourhoods had more work–family conflict because those contexts both increased family stressors and reduced the availability of psychological resources that typically buffer those negative effects (Young, 2015). Women in particular were found to experience greater work–family conflict as a result of structural neighbourhood disadvantage (Young, 2015). This inevitably affects individual and family health and well-being.

Intimate Partner Violence

Another area deeply connected to family well-being and a point at which families and health intersect is intimate partner violence. According to the World Health Organization, intimate partner violence (IPV), committed by a former or current partner, is one of the most common forms of violence against women (WHO, 2012). It includes acts of physical violence, sexual violence, emotional (psychological)

abuse, and controlling behaviours, including isolating a person from family and friends; monitoring their movements; and restricting access to financial resources, employment, education or medical care (WHO, 2012).

According to Statistics Canada and results from the 2014 General Social Survey on Victimization, 4 per cent of Canadians with a current or former spouse or common-law partner reported having been physically or sexually abused by their spouse or partner during the preceding five years (Canadian Centre for Justice Statistics, 2016). Because of ongoing stigma related to this problem, the tenacity of patriarchal values, and the "private" nature of family life, this number likely under-represents the actual frequency of these assaults.

Both the causes and the negative effects of intimate partner violence on individual family members and communities are well-documented in a rich and growing body of research by Canadian feminist sociologists and Statistics Canada researchers (see Holtmann, 2016; Sinha, 2013a; Johnson & Dawson, 2011; Ursel, Tutty, & LeMaistre, 2008).

While rates of self-reported IPV seem to be on the decline, Canadian laws have nonetheless slowly changed to try to protect children, in particular, from the negative effects of IPV. For example, exposing a child to family violence is now grounds for intervention under provincial and territorial child protection laws and is considered a form of child maltreatment (Department of Justice, 2013).

THE SOCIOLOGY OF HEALTH, ILLNESS, DISEASE, AND SICKNESS

Comparative Analyses

The Changing Health of Canadians

Canadians generally live longer and healthier lives today than they did in the past. In the nineteenth century, infectious and communicable diseases such as cholera, typhoid, diphtheria, and scarlet fever were responsible for enormous suffering and death. Wound infections and septicemia were frequent results of dangerous and unhygienic working and living conditions and medical treatments. Puerperal fever killed many women during and after childbirth.

By 1920, the average life expectancy for Canadian men and women was 61 for women and 59 for men according to Statistics Canada (2012b). Today women can expect to live to 83, men to 79 (Statistics Canada, 2017). In the 1920s, the most common causes of death were heart and kidney disease, followed by influenza, bronchitis, and pneumonia, and the diseases of early infancy (see Table 9.3). Public-health improvements including better nutrition, hygiene through sanitation and water purification, and the availability of birth control, significantly increased life expectancy over the twentieth century, as did the widespread use of newly discovered vaccines and antibiotics; vaccines against diphtheria, tetanus, typhoid, and cholera were developed in the late nineteenth and early twentieth centuries, and antibiotics were introduced in the 1940s and 1950s (Crompton, 2000, p. 12). While heart disease remains an important cause of death, it has declined dramatically more recently as a result of lifestyle changes, such as reductions in smoking and dietary fat, and increased exercise, and better medical treatments. Lower infant death rates today result primarily from better nutrition and improved hygiene during pregnancy and birth and secondarily from medical and technological advances. For example, prematurity, a frequent cause of infant death in the past, is now often

Table 9.3 ▶ Leading Causes of Death, Canada, 1921–1925 and 2012

Cause of Death[1]	Rate per 100,000[2]
1921–5	
All causes	1,030.0
Cardiovascular and renal disease	221.9
Influenza, bronchitis, and pneumonia	141.1
Diseases of early infancy	111.0
Tuberculosis	85.1
Cancer	75.9
Gastritis, duodenitis, enteritis, and colitis	72.2
Accidents	51.5
Communicable diseases	47.1
2012	
All causes	670.1
Cancer (malignant neoplasms)	202.1
Heart disease	117.0
Cerebrovascular disease	33.4
Respiratory diseases (all)	45.0
Unintentional injuries	25.1
Influenza and pneumonia	11.7
Intentional self-harm (suicide)	10.2
HIV	1.2

1. Disease categories are not identical over time.
2. Rates are age standardized.

SOURCES: Adapted from Statistics Canada, Canadian Social Trends, Catalogue 11-008 (Winter 2000): 13; and Statistics Canada, CANSIM Table 102-0552 and Catalogue 840209X

prevented through educational programs, prenatal care, and effective management of birth in hospitals.

Significant health and health behaviour disparities still occur in Canada, however. One of the most fundamental is based on Indigenous status, as Table 9.4 illustrates. First Nations people

Table 9.4 ▶ Health Indicators by Indigenous/Non-Indigenous Status

	First Nations	Métis	Inuit	Non-Indigenous
One or more chronic conditions	60.4	58.9	46.7	53.3
Perceived mental health (very good or excellent)	64.2	66.2	65.8	74.5
Life satisfaction (satisfied or very satisfied)	88.1	89.2	92.0	92.0
Smoking	40.1	36.8	49.0	20.5
Heavy drinking	25.0	25.2	27.2	16.9

SOURCE: Canadian Institute for Health Information and Statistics Canada, Health Indicators 2013, 38, 44, 46

are more likely to have one or more chronic conditions, poorer (self-perceived) mental health, and lower life satisfaction. As well, they are more likely to smoke and drink heavily.

> **TIME to REFLECT**
>
> Should the HPV vaccine be mandated in Canada for preteen girls and/or boys? Why or why not?

Intra-Societal Analyses

The Social Determinants of Health

Affecting Indigenous and non-Indigenous Canadians alike, the degree of economic inequality has been increasing in Canada, especially in the last decade of the twentieth century and into the first decade of the twenty-first. A report for the Organisation for Economic Co-operation and Development (OECD) points out that Canada was, in fact, one of the two (out of 30) wealthy nations characterized by the largest growth in income inequality in the 1990s and 2000s (Mikkonen & Raphael, 2010). Consider the following statistics. Between 1984 and 2005, 30 per cent of Canadians had no net worth and over this time became more indebted. By comparison, the average net worth of the top 10 per cent increased over this period to $1.2 million (an increase of $659,000 in constant dollars) (Mikkonen & Raphael, 2010). Many people are aware of the widening gap between the rich and the poor, the "haves" and the "have-nots" in Canada. Less well known is the direct link between income inequality and health.

Shuey and Willson (2014) investigated how socio-economic conditions in childhood affect health later in life. They found that childhood poverty increases the risk of both disease in mid-life and the early onset of disease, while economic advantages during childhood reduces these risks. Clearly, poverty exacerbates health problems from birth onward. In 2012, the child poverty rate in Canada was 19.1 per cent (Campaign 2000, 2014, p. 3). About one-half of Indigenous children living on reserves funded by the federal government were living in poverty. Poor women are more likely to bear low-birth-weight babies. Low birth weight is associated with myriad negative health, disability, learning, and behavioural effects. People born in the poorest neighbourhoods in Canada (the lowest 20 per cent) live shorter lives, by 2 to 5.5 years. They also tend to spend more of these shorter lives with some degree of disability. Children at the lower end of the social hierarchy have a greater variety of health and developmental deficits than those higher up the socio-economic status ladder. It is also important to notice that these figures are situated in the context of medical care system funded by the federal and provincial governments. As well, the rate of childhood poverty in Canada is *higher* than in many other developed nations except for the United States and Italy (Conference Board of Canada, 2013, 1).

Table 9.5 portrays the differences in specific health-challenging events across the socio-economic spectrum as indicated by the average income of individuals and families in different

Table 9.5 ▶ Health Indicators by Neighbourhood Income Quintile, 2013

	Q1	Q2	Q3	Q4	Q5	Disparity Rate Ratio	Potential Rate Reduction
Hospitalized acute myocardial infarction event	243	216	212	201	179	1.36	15.0%
Injury hospitalization	613	531	520	514	488	1.26	8.5%
30-day acute myocardial infarction in-hospital mortality	8.1	7.2	7.1	7.3	6.6	1.22	9.0%
Self-injury hospitalization	101	73	63	59	50	2.01	27.4%

SOURCE: Canadian Institute for Health Information and Statistics Canada, Health Indicators 2013, 68, 69, 71, 72

HUMAN DIVERSITY · Health and Indigenous Canadians

One of the most troubling health issues facing Canadians today is the relatively poor health and shorter lives of Indigenous Canadians (See also Table 9.4). The average income of Indigenous men and women, at $21,958 and $16,529 respectively, was 58 per cent of the average income of non-Indigenous men and 72 per cent that of non-Indigenous women in 2001 (Mikkonen & Raphael, 2010). In the Northwest Territories, where more than half of the population is Indigenous, life expectancy is lower, by more than eight years, than that of non-Indigenous for both men and women, at 75 and 70 respectively (Helwig, 2000, p. 681). The infant mortality rate, one of the most sensitive indicators of the overall health of a people, is 1.5 times higher among First Nations people: 8 deaths per thousand, compared to 5.5 for all Canadians (Adelson, 2005). Moreover, the major causes of death among First Nations people include diseases of development and impoverishment, such as injury, poisoning, and respiratory disease, along with the causes more common among other Canadians such as heart disease and cancer. Suicide and self-inflicted injury are the chief causes of death among those aged 10 to 44. This is followed by motor vehicle accidents, drowning, and homicide. Violence, including physical abuse, sexual abuse, and rape, is also a significant problem. Indigenous people are three to five times more likely to suffer from diabetes (non-insulin-dependent diabetes mellitus). Tuberculosis is eight to ten times more frequent. HIV/AIDS is also increasing dramatically among this population: the rate of infection grew from 1 per cent in 1990 to 15 per cent in 2007 (Avert, n.d.).

First Nations people also do very poorly with respect to other social determinants of health, including employment rates, food security, education levels, and housing (Mikkonen & Raphael, 2010). This stems from the fact that most Indigenous Canadians live in the rural north of Canada, where there are fewer employment opportunities, as well as from "the complex interplay of job market discrimination, lack of education, cultural genocide, and loss of land and sovereignty that affects employment status, and, ultimately, the degree of poverty faced by those who are caught in a circle of disadvantage" (Mikkonen & Raphael, 2010). Indigenous Canadians also are more likely to live in inadequate and crowded housing. For instance:

1. Homes are twice as likely to need repair.
2. Houses are over 90 times more likely (9.4 per cent versus 0.1 per cent for all of Canada) to lack piped water.
3. Homes are five times more likely to lack bathroom facilities (3.2 per cent versus 0.6 per cent).
4. Households, on average, include four people. Three is the Canadian average today.

neighbourhoods across Canada, as well as the potential reduction in the health problems if inequalities were to be eliminated.

THE SOCIOLOGY OF MEDICINE

The sociology of medicine examines the medical care system. It includes study of the various health-care institutions such as hospitals, clinics, cooperatives, and home care, along with medically related industries and the training and work of medical and nursing professionals and other health-care providers today and in the past.

Because the history of medicine in the twentieth century is characterized by the increasing dominance of allopathic medicine and its spreading relevance to more and more of life (Zola, 1972), the term **medicalization** is an important conceptual framework for critical analysis.

The Canadian Medical Care System

Our present medical care system was first implemented in 1972 after a Royal Commission on Health Care (Hall, 1964–1965) under Justice Emmett Hall recommended that the federal government work with the provincial governments to establish a program of universal health care. While hospitalization and some medical testing had been covered before that, the new program would cover physicians' fees and other services not already covered under the Hospital Insurance and Diagnostic Services Act (1958).

Four basic principles guided the program. The first was universality: the plan was to be available to all residents of Canada on equal terms, regardless of prior health record, age, income, membership in a group (such as a union or workplace), or other considerations. The second was portability: individual benefits would travel with the individual across the country, from province to province. The third was comprehensive coverage: the plan was to cover all necessary medical services, including dentistry if it required hospitalization. The fourth was administration: the plan was to run on a non-profit basis.

The Canada Health Act of 1984 added a fifth principle, accessibility. The costs of the plan were to be shared by the federal and provincial governments in such a way that the richer provinces paid relatively more than the poorer provinces; thus, the plan would also serve to redistribute wealth across Canada. Doctors, with few exceptions (found mostly in community health clinics), were not salaried by the government. Instead, most were and continue to be private practitioners paid by the government on a fee-for-service basis.

Privatization

Despite universally available and government-supported medical care, there is considerable evidence of *privatization* (the tendency for more and more of health care to be provided by for-profit corporations) within the system. At present, approximately 70 per cent of the Canadian system is public and 30 per cent private (Mikkonen & Raphael, 2010, p. 38). The private aspects of the Canadian system are dominated by multinational corporations that deliver a variety of health-related goods and services, including medical insurance for treatments and services, such as drugs, medical devices, and home care, not covered by the public system, information technology services, food and laundry for hospitals, and long-term and other institutional care. The most important impetus for growth in the medical system is in the private sector, particularly in drugs and new (and very expensive) technologies such as MRI, CAT scan, and mammography machines and other increasingly popular diagnostic technologies.

Medicalization

Medicalization is the tendency for more and more of life to be defined as relevant to medicine. Irving Zola (1972) is one of the original social theorists who was critical of this process. He defined medicalization as including the following four components:

1. *An expansion of what in life and in a person is relevant to medicine.* This has grown from a narrow focus on the biomechanics of the human body to a broader concern by medicine with the "whole" person including aspects of behaviour and expression of feelings (through mental-health services as well as appearance, using, for example, cosmetic surgery).

2. *The maintenance of absolute control over certain technical procedures by the allopathic medical profession.* There are things that only doctors are allowed to do to the human body, including prescribing drugs and performing surgery and intentional radiation.

3. *The maintenance of almost absolute access to certain areas by the medical profession.* Doctors, through medicine, have transformed into medical problems areas of life such as pregnancy and aging that were formerly viewed as normal rather than pathological or medically relevant processes.

4. *The spread of medicine's relevance to an increasingly large portion of living.* Medicine increasingly has jurisdiction in areas formerly considered relevant to the criminal justice or religious systems, such as drug and alcohol addiction.

Do you think it is important for the backgrounds of physicians to reflect the cultural, ethnic, and other diverse features of Canada? Explain.

A GLOBAL CARE CRISIS? A CARE CRISIS IN CANADA?

In 2010, the United Nations noted that we are facing a global care crisis (UN Women, 2010; Luxton, 2015). To start, around the world there is, as we have seen, the expectation and the reality that women in families continue to do the bulk of the unpaid care work. At the same time women's growing participation in paid labour markets has reduced their ability to provide on-going, free, and reliable care for children, seniors, and others in need (Luxton, 2015). As we noted above, as health and other services are privatized, states withdraw support for care-based services at precisely the moment when women in families need it most. Mooney and Lashewicz (2014), for example, interviewed family caregivers who spoke about government agencies not meeting their needs and other challenges in navigating the current health-care system in order to find the services and supports their families needed.

Increasingly, families rely on intergenerational exchanges (older family members helping younger and vice versa; see Gazso & McDaniel, 2015). As well, more and more family members belong to the **sandwich generation**: people (usually women) who are caught between the demands of caring for both dependent children and aging parents. According to Statistics Canada, in 2012, about 8.1 million individuals, or 28 per cent of Canadians over the age of 15, cared for a family member or friend with a long-term health condition, disability, or aging needs (Sinha, 2013b). Over one-quarter of caregivers—28 per cent or 2.2 million Canadians—were "sandwiched" between caring for older family members (parents or parents-in-law) and raising young children. Most were women between the ages of 35 and 44 (Sinha, 2013b).

These elderly people maintain their energy and improve their health by participating in group exercise.

Mitchell's (2014) mixed-methods study of 236 parents from four cultural groups (Canadians of British, Chinese, southern European, and South Asian descent) similarly found that caregiving in the sandwich generation is highly gendered and is mediated by one's ethnocultural background and other work–family characteristics. Along the same line, after interviewing 873 caregivers in British Columbia, Chappell, Dujela, and Smith (2015), found that daughters and wives carried the highest caregiver burden in the sandwich generation, but daughters who were caregivers also registered the highest levels of self-esteem as a result of it.

While caregiving can be intrinsically rewarding, and experiences do differ depending on

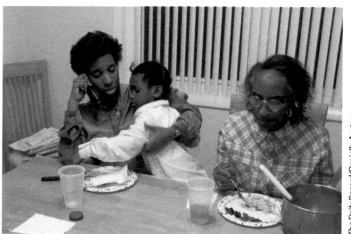

The sandwich generation.

families' specific situations (Boyczuk & Fletcher, 2016), Bachmann, Danuser, and Morin (2015) warn of the health risks, including vulnerability to depression, hypertension, and other diseases, for those of the sandwich generation.

TIME to REFLECT

Think back to the Time to Reflect box on page 212, that had you imagining the next 20 years of your life. How might that timeline be similar or different if you, your partner, your child, or your parent were diagnosed with a serious chronic illness 10 years into it?

CONCLUSION

In many ways, as we have seen, family life, health, and medical care issues are fundamentally social issues. We have seen that over the past several decades, with profound social change including globalization; the rise of neo-liberalism; and other major social, political, and economic shifts, families have taken on a plurality of forms. We have also seen that in the context of these profound transformations, family life and health issues intersect in important and interesting ways. In focusing on some of these intersections, we have tried to demonstrate that family life, health, illness, disease, and death are related to sociological issues such as power, economics, and inequality. We have provided an overview of the changing health-care system and its impact on Canadian individuals and families. Despite changes, we conclude by noting that most Canadians continue to expect and seek to develop loving, long-term, intimate relationships and most of us expect to do so in a society where our tax dollars continue to support a robust portable, universal, comprehensive, accessible, and publicly administered medicare system. Whether we continue to do so remains in our hands, as individuals, family members, and voting citizens.

Questions for Critical Thought

1. What are the three most important health or social policies that you would recommend the government establish to minimize the rate at which Canadians die from car accidents today?
2. Do you think that medical doctors hold too much power in Canada today? Explain.
3. What challenges to your health are evident in your school? In your answer, include threats from the physical plant, the organization of learning and testing, and the social life available to students.
4. In an ideal world, what kind of family life would you want as an adult? Given what you know, have experienced, have seen among your friends and family members, and have read in this chapter, what might your adult family life actually look like?
5. Imagine you have been hired to advise the federal government on the needs of families in navigating the health-care system. You decide to begin by doing research. What kind of research would you do? What kind of data would you collect? How would you collect it? What do you expect to find? What recommendations do you anticipate making to government and policy-makers? What challenges might you encounter in their implementation? How would you overcome them?

Sociological Explorations

1. Examine three magazines that you commonly read—for their health-related messages, perhaps—focusing on a particular subject such as depression or weight and appearance. Include both articles and advertisements (e.g., for anti-depressants) in your analysis. Consider the portrayal of issues such as gender, ethnicity, and social class in your discussion.

2. Think about a time you were ill. Describe the extent to which the sick role worked for you.

3. Plot out what you consider to be a typical family life course in Canada today. Now try to identify on that roadmap at what points families and the Canadian health-care system intersect in significant ways. What might that mapping look like to a parent of twins born with a significant respiratory illness? What might family life look like if we did not have a publicly funded medical system or if our current system deteriorated, became increasingly privatized, or both?

Recommended Readings

Doucet, A. (2015). Parental responsibilities: Dilemmas of measurement and gender equality. *Journal of Marriage & Family. 77*(1), 224–242.
This article uses cutting-edge methodologies to reveal a persistent problem of gender differences in parental responsibilities, but also argues for a conceptualization of parental responsibilities that shifts away from a measurement of time and tasks, toward assessing a set of practices that unfold relationally across time and diverse social spaces of parenting.

Ford, A.R. & Saibil, D. (Eds). (2010). *The push to prescribe: Women and Canadian drug policy.* Toronto, ON: Women's Press.
This edited collection of articles offers a critical analysis of the impact of pharmaceuticalization on the lives of women and men.

Hankivsky, O. (Ed.). (2011). *Health inequalities in Canada: Intersectional frameworks and practices.* Vancouver, BC: UBC Press.
This edited collection of articles examines health inequalities as the result of multiple forms of oppression and interrelated social conditions such as gender, class, race, and neighbourhood.

Horowits, A.V. & Wakefield, J.C. (2012). *All we have to fear: Psychiatry's transformation of natural anxieties into mental disorder.* Oxford, UK: Oxford University Press.
This book traces the process of medicalization through the social and evolutionary history of an expanding list of types of anxiety disorders.

King, S. (2008). *Pink Ribbons, Inc.: Breast cancer and the politics of philanthropy.* Minneapolis, MN: University of Minnesota Press.
King traces a development of the history of breast cancer from an individually and privately experienced disease to a highly successful marketing cause.

Luxton, M. (2011). *Changing families; New understandings.* Ottawa: Vanier Institute of the Family. http://vanierinstitute.ca/wp-content/uploads/2015/12/CFT_2011-06-00_EN.pdf.
Luxton, a pioneer in the feminist study of Canadian families, documents diversity in family forms and experiences. She argues that the way people understand families is central to how family practices are normalized or rejected, with important personal and social consequences.

Recommended Websites

Prostate Cancer Canada
www.prostatecancer.ca
Prostate Cancer Canada is a charitable organization that raises money to advance research, awareness, education, diagnosis, and treatment of prostate cancer.

Family Service Ontario
www.familyserviceontario.org/
This organization provides access to services and programs on a range of issues including relationship counselling, financial management, mental health and addictions, domestic violence and abuse, support for LGBTQ families, and so on.

Health Canada
www.hc-sc.gc.ca
Health Canada, a federal government department, provides health-related information.

Muriel McQueen Fergusson Centre for Family Violence Research (MMFC).
www.unb.ca/fredericton/arts/centres/mmfc/
Housed at the University of New Brunswick, the centre's focuses on conducting practice- and policy-relevant research on family violence and violence against women and children. Their aim is to develop and offer targeted educational programs.

Public Health Agency of Canada
www.phac-aspc.gc.ca
The Public Health Agency of Canada offers access to research and working papers on the social determinants of health, health promotion, and population health perspectives.

Statistics Canada
www.statcan.gc.ca
Statistics Canada is a federal government agency that produces statistics analysis to help us better understand Canada's population, resources, economy, and society.

Vanier Institute of the Family
http://vanierinstitute.ca/

The Vanier Institute of the Family is an independent, non-profit organization committed to doing and sharing national research and educational information about Canadian families today.

World Health Organization
www.who.int
The World Health Organization provides information, fact sheets, various reports, and news about health issues around the world. It also covers essential information regarding worldwide epidemics and news about outbreaks of various illnesses, including epidemic and pandemic alerts and responses.

Key Terms

allopathic medicine Part of conventional medicine, treatment by means of opposites, such as killing or cutting out germs, bacteria, or other disease processes through medication, surgery, or radiation.

bi-nuclear families A growing family type resulting from divorce and remarriage, in which children of divorced parents live in both households and move between them at regular intervals.

complementary and alternative medicines (CAM) Health-related philosophies and practices that fall outside conventional Western medicine, such as homeopathy and chiropractic.

disability A wide-ranging, disputed term referring to individuals' capacity or lack thereof to engage with all parts of society "normally."

extended family See **multigenerational household/ family.**

household A set of related and unrelated individuals who share a dwelling.

incidence The number of new cases (e.g., of a disease) in a year.

life expectancy The average length of life in a given population at a certain point in time.

medicalization The tendency for more and more of life to be defined as relevant to medicine.

morbidity The frequency of disease per a specified number of people over a particular period of time.

morbidity rate The number of cases of a particular illness in a given population over a specific period of time.

mortality The frequency of death per a specified number of people over a particular period of time.

mortality rate The number of deaths in a particular population over a particular period of time.

multigenerational household/family (or **extended family**) A family consisting of more than two generations living under the same roof.

neo-liberalism An approach to governance and the economy in which it is believed that control of economic factors should be shifted away from the public sector toward the private sector. It involves the belief that governments should reduce spending, open up markets to trade by limiting protectionism, privatize state-run businesses, and promote deregulation.

nuclear family A common family form which typically includes a couple and their children sharing the same household (increasingly this term has been used to describe a single parent with her or his children).

precarious employment A job that is poorly paid, insecure, unprotected, and typically cannot support a household. Also known as *non-standard employment/ work.*

prevalence The number of cases (e.g., of a disease) within a given population.

prevention policies Measures designed to prevent disease, including sewage disposal, garbage removal, cleaned and filtered drinking water, and hygienic handling of food.

privatization The tendency for health care to increasingly be delivered by for-profit corporations.

public-health measures Government-led efforts to promote health and prevent disease.

sandwich generation A term used to describe individuals (usually women) who are caught between the demands of caring for at least one dependent child and one or more aging parents.

sick role A special position in society that prevents sickness from disrupting social life and provides a way of institutionalizing what might otherwise become a form of deviant behaviour.

stigma An attribute, characteristic, or behaviour of an individual that is socially stereotyped in a denigrating manner.

surplus suffering Distress caused not by a health problem or disability but by the social arrangements that deal with it.

work–family conflict The time-related stress arising from the competing demands of the different roles imposed on working parents.

10 | Education

TERRY WOTHERSPOON

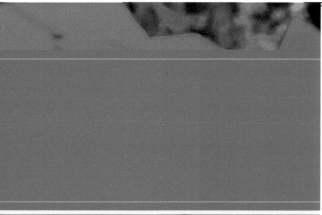

In this chapter you will:

▶ Understand how and why formal education has become a central social institution in Canada and in other nations

▶ Identify the main dimensions and challenges associated with the growth of formal education systems

▶ Gain a critical understanding of various forms of lifelong learning beyond formal education

▶ Understand the major theoretical perspectives and theories that sociologists employ to explain educational institutions, practices, and outcomes

▶ Understand the relationships between education and social inequality

▶ Critically evaluate contemporary debates and controversies over major educational issues

A century ago, schools were often segregated by social class and age. Here, young ladies are learning to sketch a live model—a skill that will give them cultural capital when they pass into adult social life.

INTRODUCTION

The United Nations Educational, Scientific and Cultural Organization (UNESCO, 2014, p. 9) recently observed that

> [w]e live in a rapidly changing and increasingly interdependent world where knowledge and innovation are major drivers of development. This means good quality education and learning are becoming even more important determinants of the well-being of individuals, the progress of countries and the quality of humanity's common future.

Few people would likely take issue with this statement.

In the context of what is often called the *knowledge* or *learning society*, education has been thrust into a central role as individuals, organizations, and nations struggle to keep pace with demands for new knowledge and credentials regarded as essential for jobs, career advancement, and economic and social development. We expect educational institutions to educate and prepare learners by instilling a wide range of technical, social, and personal competencies so that they can cope with changing, often uncertain futures. However, we also look to schools

to respond to the very diverse circumstances and needs of students and communities.

Sociologists are interested in several issues associated with educational processes and outcomes and in the environments within which education operates. This chapter examines several key questions that sociology addresses in its concern to understand education:

- Why is formal education so important in contemporary societies, and how did it get to be that way?
- What are the main dimensions of education and education systems in Canada and in other nations?
- How do sociologists explain the growth of education systems and the outcomes associated with education for different groups?
- What social factors are related to patterns of educational success and failure?
- What are the main educational experiences and outcomes for different social groups?
- What are the main challenges facing education systems in Canada and other nations?

THE CHANGING FACE OF EDUCATION

Education is generally understood as the formal learning that takes place in institutions such as schools, colleges, universities, and other sites that provide specific courses, learning activities, or credentials in an organized way, but it also includes informal learning processes. Both formal and informal education are part of the broader process that sociologists typically call **socialization**, which refers to all direct and indirect learning related to humans' ability to understand and negotiate the rules and expectations of the social world.

 For a broader discussion on how school is a socializing agent, see "Schools," p. 69, in **Chapter 3**, "Being Social."

Nearly all Canadians engage in formal education for extended periods of time. Just over a century ago, by contrast, many communities lacked schools or qualified teachers, many children did not go to school, and those who did attend typically left by their early teen years in order to work or pursue other activities (Guppy & Davies, 1998; Davey, 1978, p. 230). Today's students and teachers typically exhibit a far greater array of personal, stylistic, and cultural variation than was apparent a century ago, and they have access to many more learning and community resources. Education is a unique social institution that nonetheless represents characteristics that are integral to the society in which it operates.

TIME to REFLECT

What is the difference between education and socialization? How has the introduction of formal schooling influenced the relationship between these two phenomena?

Dimensions of Educational Growth

Table 10.1 provides an overview of the increasing educational attainment of Canadians since the mid-twentieth century. More than half of the population now hold post-secondary credentials, in stark contrast to the situation in 1951 when fewer than half continued beyond grade 9.

Growing emphasis on the importance of formal education and credentials is matched by three interrelated factors: the overall expansion of educational opportunities and requirements, increasing levels of educational attainment among people born in Canada, and recent emphasis on the selection of highly educated immigrants.

In the late nineteenth and early twentieth centuries, relatively few occupations required educational credentials. Early advocates of public **schooling** undertook a mission to convince the public, and especially members of influential groups, of the merits of the educational system (for examples, see Lawr & Gidney, 1973). They promoted schooling as an efficient enterprise that would serve the public or general interest, unlike narrow, more selective sites such as families, churches, and businesses.

By the mid-twentieth century, more and larger schools were required to accommodate growing educational demands. As credentials became more important for many jobs, people were more likely to extend their schooling into and beyond the high school years. The **baby boom** that occurred after World War II resulted in unprecedented sizes of cohorts of children entering and moving through the school system. By the end of the war in 1945, total enrolment in Canadian public elementary and secondary schools reached 2 million, about twice what it had been a half century earlier (about 1 million

Table 10.1 ▶ Educational Attainment in Canada by Percentage of Population Aged 15 and Over, Selected Years, 1951–2015

	Less than Grade 9	Grades 9–13	Some Post-secondary	Post-secondary Certificate or Diploma	University Degree
1951	51.9	46.1	–	–	1.9
1961	44.1	53.0	–	–	2.9
1971	32.3	45.9	11.2	5.8	4.8
1981	20.1	44.3	16.1	11.5	8.0
1991	14.4	43.8	8.8	21.9	11.4
2001	9.7	36.9	9.2	28.3	16.0
2011	6.3	33.0	8.0	31.2	21.5
2015	5.4	32.5	6.7	31.6	23.8

NOTE: Figures are rounded.
SOURCES: Compiled and calculated from Statistics Canada, census data (1951–81) and "Labour force survey estimates (LFS), by educational attainment, sex and age group, annual," Statistics Canada CANSIM Table 282-0004 (accessed 23 August, 2016).

in 1895), doubled again over the next decade and a half as it reached more than 4.5 million in 1963 and peaked at over 5.6 million in 1970 (Statistics Canada, 1983a, pp. W67–93). The average number of pupils per school in Canada was 66 in 1925–1926, but by the early 1970s it reached the current level of about 350 (Manzer, 1994, p. 131; CMEC, 2008, p. 8).

Although the school-age population has declined since the 1970s, formal education has expanded throughout the life course. Just over a century ago, it was not uncommon for children to begin their schooling at seven or eight years of age or even older. Today, most Canadian children attend compulsory kindergarten, sometimes beginning preschool or early childhood education programs as early as at two years of age, continuing their studies well past high school. More than a million students currently attend university programs in Canada, with the number of graduate students alone (over 150,000) now more than double total university enrolments of the early 1950s (Statistics Canada, 1983a, pp. W340–348; Statistics Canada, 2015j). There has also been significant growth in other post-secondary options since the introduction and expansion of the community college system in the 1960s and 1970s, offering students several pathways toward certification in specialized trades or vocations or toward university degrees.

Education in the Learning Society

The organization and nature of schooling across Canada vary. People typically encounter diverse education and work settings during the course of their lives. Elementary and secondary education is under the jurisdiction of the provinces in accordance with the Canadian Constitution, while other forms of education, including adult and post-secondary education and vocational training, are controlled, operated, or funded by a variety of governments (federal, provincial, and First Nations) and by private sources.

The growing popularity of terms such as "information society," "learning society," and **lifelong learning** signifies the central place that education holds within the context of what is commonly designated as the **new** or **knowledge-based economy**. "New economy" refers to the impact of rapidly changing information technologies and scientific advancements on business, workplaces, and education as well as other major spheres of social life. Learning is central to these emerging relationships for various purposes: training qualified personnel; researching for continuing innovation; developing, testing, and marketing new products and services; processing the vast quantities of new information being created; and enabling people to use new technologies at work and at home (Wolfe & Gertler, 2001). In this climate, what counts is not so much the knowledge that we acquire as our capacities to learn, innovate, and apply knowledge to emergent situations.

Over 6 million Canadians (about one-fifth of the entire population) are engaged in full-time schooling, and well over 500,000 more are involved in part-time studies. More than half of Canadians are involved in various forms of adult education, such as in-person, correspondence, or private courses; workshops; apprenticeships; or arts, crafts, or recreation programs. Levels of *informal learning* are even higher, as people seek knowledge outside formal schooling for work, personal, or community circumstances, such as learning a new language on one's own or with other people, learning computer skills or software programs, or gaining competencies that can be used for volunteer work or in family situations. Nearly all Canadians are involved in learning activities, although the more formal education they have, the more they are likely to be engaged in adult education and informal learning (Livingstone, 2012, pp. 54, 61; Desjardins et al., 2005, p. 89).

Canadians are not unique in their growing pursuit of education and training. Emphasis on credentials and lifelong learning is a phenomenon associated with **globalization** and competitiveness across national settings. Throughout the twentieth century, the degree to which a population was educated came to be recognized as a significant indicator of

GLOBAL ISSUES — Barriers to Educational Access

Canada has one of the most highly educated populations in the world, but educational qualifications are reaching unprecedented levels across the globe. Among a set of 17 priorities adopted by world leaders at a United Nations summit in 2015 is the objective to "Ensure inclusive and equitable quality education and promote lifelong learning opportunities for all" (UNESCO, 2015b, p. 5). Within OECD nations, 36 per cent of persons ages 25 to 64 held post-secondary credentials, while since 2000 post-secondary participation rates have accelerated rapidly in many developing nations (OECD, 2015, pp. 33, 39).

These trends contrast starkly with the realities for children and youth in many parts of the world, for whom access to schooling is highly constrained. While the world's media have focused on dramatic incidents like the armed kidnapping of over 200 girls from their school by extremists in northern Nigeria in 2014, many millions of children encounter barriers that make it difficult, if not impossible, for them to attend school. In 2015 it was conceded that a global agenda adopted in 2000 to achieve universal primary education for all of the world's children within 15 years had failed, and UNESCO (2015b, p. 8) projected that in low- and middle-income countries, as many as one in six children would not complete primary school. Among the most persistent barriers are

- inadequate funding and continuing budget cuts to education
- teacher shortages and too few people with teacher training in many nations
- lack of classrooms and inadequate facilities such as running water
- lack of textbooks and other learning materials
- exclusion of children with disabilities
- denial of schooling for girls because of work responsibilities, conflict, poverty, or discrimination
- war and other types of conflict
- distance from home to school
- hunger and poor nutrition
- high fees and other costs (McCormick, 2014)

While these conditions are most severe in the poorest nations, especially in sub-Saharan Africa and parts of south and west Asia, the lack of running water and other facilities in some northern communities in Canada illustrates how pervasive these problems can be.

modernization and development status. The more education one has, the higher one's chances of having a job, a better income, good health status, and many other factors positively associated with a high standard of living. Conversely, rates of poverty, unemployment, crime, serious illness and injury, and other less desirable characteristics rise when formal education is limited. Many nations are accelerating the pace of educational advancement as they undertake economic and human resource development strategies aimed at the production of new knowledge and a workforce better trained for knowledge-based activities and global competitiveness (Canadian Council on Learning, 2010, p. 10).

Despite this emphasis on learning, many people encounter significant barriers to educational access, achievement, and success. Educational disparities exist across Canada, but are even more evident on a global scale. Figure 10.1 illustrates that those living in the Americas, Europe, and parts of Asia and the Pacific regions can expect, on average, to complete much more formal schooling than those in other parts of the world. Educational attainment levels by girls and women in North America and Europe are nearly twice those in sub-Saharan Africa. Close to 58 million primary school–age children were out of school in 2012, many of whom are not expected ever to enrol in school (UNESCO, 2015a, pp. 77, 158). Girls and children living in impoverished nations or from low-income households are over-represented among those who will never go to school. In many parts of the world, shortages of qualified teachers and other problems restrict the quality of education for children who do attend school (UNESCO, 2015a, p. 197).

ALTERNATIVE ACCOUNTS OF EDUCATIONAL GROWTH AND DEVELOPMENT

There is no uniform way of understanding education. Various educational **ideologies** pose contrasting views about what kinds of education a society should have, who should control and pay for education, and what should be taught in schools. Sociological theories of education, by contrast, are more concerned with describing and explaining education systems, educational processes, and educational change. Two early influential theoretical perspectives (the structural functionalist approach and the symbolic interactionist–interpretive theories)

are contrasted below, followed by examination of two critical challenges (conflict and feminist theories) and more recent integrative orientations to the analysis of education.

Structural Functionalism

Structural functionalism is concerned primarily with understanding how different parts of the entire social system are interconnected in order to keep the system going. Structural functionalism examines education in terms of its contributions to social order and stability. Education gains importance in modern societies as an institution that provides participants with the core understandings, capabilities, and selection criteria necessary to enable them to fit into prescribed social and economic roles. As a society becomes more complex and specialized, educational institutions take on many of the functions previously managed by families, communities, and religious organizations to ensure that successive generations can make seamless **transitions** from early childhood and family life into schooling and eventually the labour force.

Émile Durkheim (1956 [1922], p. 123) described education as "the means by which society

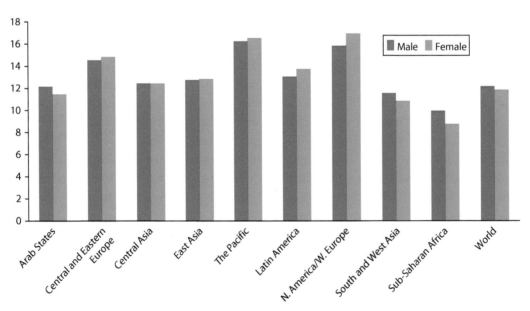

FIGURE 10.1 Average Years of Expected Schooling by Region, 2011

SOURCE: Based on data in UNESCO (2015a: 351).

perpetually re-creates the conditions of its very existence." Talcott Parsons (1959) later identified schools' two central functions within contemporary societies as selection (allocating individuals with appropriate skills and talents into necessary jobs and social positions) and socialization (providing people with aptitudes and knowledge required for adult roles and specific jobs). In the primary grades, schools partially resemble home environments where highly personal, emotional ties prevail, but as students proceed through successive grade levels, the schools are marked by progressively greater degrees of competition, merit, and instrumentality intended to prepare the individual for integration into work and other social settings. Schools and teachers cultivate characteristics essential for contemporary work and public life by reinforcing essential **norms** (Dreeben, 1968) related to independence, achievement, and individual merit. Structural functionalism attributes educational expansion to the growing complexity of the occupational structure, highlighting its increasing importance to citizenship in industrialized societies. A related form of analysis, *technical functionalism*, links educational growth to the increasing technical sophistication of jobs and knowledge production (Bell, 1973). Recent functional analysis has emphasized how education systems take on unique characteristics even as they are shaped through interactions with other social and economic systems in complex societies (Baker, 2011; Luhmann & Schorr, 2000).

Functionalist analysis typically assumes a broad social consensus about what should be taught in schools and how educational institutions should be organized. It tends not to question either the legitimacy of educational credentials to determine entry into specified labour market positions or the fairness of the way the education system operates. Describing liberal-democratic visions of what schools should be like rather than explaining how schooling came about, functionalism presents education as a meritocratic ideal, a means of enabling people to gain opportunities for social or economic success regardless of their social backgrounds. Societies require a careful fit among capability, talent, effort, training, and jobs as social tasks become more complex and specialized. Such claims have led to subsequent research into the definition and measurement of educational inequality, calling into question the degree to which educational realities match the needs of industrial democratic societies.

Human capital theory, an approach with some affinity to structural functionalism, emphasizes education's role as a critical tool for developing human capacities to create and apply new knowledge. The human being is regarded as an input, along with material and economic resources, that contributes to economic productivity and development. **Human capital** can be enhanced through adequate investment in the form of proper training, education, and social support; this approach has been used to justify the massive investment by governments that contributed to significant growth in postsecondary enrolment. Human capital theories have gained renewed currency as attention turns to the importance of advanced training and educational credentials in knowledge-based societies (Heckman & Krueger, 2004).

However, structural functionalism and human capital theory tend to ignore persistent

Modern universities are like factories in their efforts to mass-produce a product—educated graduates. Some believe that in this environment, people mainly learn how to submit to regimentation.

David R. Frazier Photolibrary, Inc. / Alamy Stock Photo

inequalities especially insofar as initial advantages contribute to ongoing educational and economic success. The theoretical emphasis on consensus limits consideration of differences in educational values, content, and practices; of how some things get incorporated into schooling while others do not; and of how these differences affect people from different social backgrounds. Alternative theoretical approaches to education attempt to address some of these issues.

Symbolic Interactionism and Microsociology

In contrast to structural functionalism's focus on education systems and institutional arrangements, *microsociology* or *interpretive theories* are concerned more with the ways in which people make sense of the world through their **social interactions**. **Symbolic interactionism** focuses on how meanings and **symbols** are integral to social activity, drawing attention directly to the lives and understandings of social participants.

Interpretive analysis of education examines such questions as how schooling contributes to the development of personality and **identity**, how some forms of knowledge and not others enter into the curriculum, and how students and teachers shape learning processes in and outside of the classroom. Willard Waller depicts schools as "the meeting-point of a large number of intertangled social relationships" which intersect with one another to "make the school what it is" (1965 [1932], p. 12). Schooling involves a series of **negotiations** among teachers, students, and parents, expressed in such phenomena as how pupils select the subjects they take, the role of humour and laughter in the classroom and staff room, and teacher reports on student progress (Woods, 1979). Teachers' backgrounds and other factors influence the construction of images of the ideal pupil, which in turn affect how students are treated and assessed (Becker, 1952).

For symbolic interactionists, societies and institutions are fluid rather than fixed entities. Institutional patterns are the result of recurrent daily activity and of people's capacities to shape, interpret, reproduce, and modify social arrangements through their social relations. *Ethnomethodology*, a variant of interpretive sociology, examines in detail the methods or approaches that people draw on to construct a sense of reality and continuity in everyday life. Understood this way, classrooms tend to resemble one another not so much because of a given model of schooling but more likely because people act in accordance with images about what is expected of them.

Symbolic interactionism and ethnomethodology offer interesting insights, but their focus on the details of ongoing social activity can restrict their ability to account for social structures and historical processes. Attention must be paid, as well, to educational policy, **power** structures, social change, persistent social inequalities, and other factors that strongly influence educational processes and outcomes.

Some researchers have combined interpretive sociology, with its insights into practical social activity, with other approaches that pay greater attention to the social contexts in which social action takes place. They are concerned with breaking down barriers between **micro-** and **macrosociology**. Educational knowledge and practices are socially constructed, but they are also shaped by wider relations of power and control as they become part of the taken-for-granted assumptions that guide the actions and understandings of teachers and other educational participants, including notions about "what it is to be educated" (Bernstein, 1977; Blackledge & Hunt, 1985, p. 290; Sadovnik, 1995).

TIME to REFLECT

How do symbolic interactionist theories differ from functionalist and conflict approaches to the study of education?

Conflict Theory

Conflict theory highlights inequalities and power relations among social actors, groups, or forces. This approach emphasizes how institutional structures and social inequalities are maintained or changed through conflict and struggle.

Samuel Bowles and Herbert Gintis, like structural functionalists, emphasize schools' role as mechanisms that select and prepare people for different positions in labour markets and institutional life. However, drawing from Marx, they see the labour market as conditioned more by capitalist interests than by general consensus about social values and needs. Claims that all students have a fair chance to succeed represent a democratic ideology that cannot be fulfilled. Bowles and Gintis (1976, p. 49) view education systems as mechanisms that reinforce social and economic inequalities by selecting people for positions within occupational hierarchies.

Conflict theorists emphasize the persistent barriers to opportunity and advancement created by deeply rooted relations of domination and subordination. This critical sociological orientation denies the functionalist and human capital theory accounts of educational expansion as being a result of the rising technical requirements of jobs. Different social groups are understood to employ education and educational ideologies as tools for pursuing their own interests. Employers rely on formal educational credentials—regardless of the skills demanded by the job—to screen applicants and assess a person's general attributes. Professions control access to education and certification as a way of preserving the status and benefits attached to their occupations. New knowledge and technological advancements in areas such as medicine, nursing, teaching, engineering, and information processing may appear to produce a demand for increasingly more advanced, specialized training. But more often, credential inflation occurs as occupations preserve special privileges by simultaneously claiming the need for superior qualifications and restricting entry into these kinds of jobs (Collins, 1979).

Technological developments are not necessarily accompanied by increasing skill requirements for many jobs. Machines and information technology often replace human input for routine technical operations or influence the content of "new jobs" in which people are required to do little but read gauges, respond to signals, or key in information. Schools may function more as warehouses for delaying people's entrance into the labour force and for dissipating their dissatisfaction with the economy's failure to provide a sufficient number of satisfying jobs than as places where effective learning and occupational training take place (Braverman, 1974, p. 440). **Capitalism**, in this view, has contributed less to skills upgrading through technological advancement than to processes that erode working skills, degrade workers, and marginalize youth.

 In "Revolutionary New Technology," p. 258, in **Chapter 11**, "Work and the Economy," the positive and negative effects of new technologies on employments opportunities and required skills are discussed in more detail.

Conflict theorists associate various forms of inequality with education. In post-secondary education, for instance, decreased government funding has led to rising tuition fees, which, accompanied by higher costs for textbooks and technology support, higher living expenses, and other factors, make it increasingly difficult for students without sufficient resources or who are unable or unwilling to take on significant student loans to attend colleges and universities. Conflict analysis also points to concern about the growing reliance of educational institutions on corporate donations and sponsorships to make up for shortfalls in government funding. More generally, processes of commercialization and **marketization**, in which educational institutions and practices become increasingly organized on the basis of consumer choice, competition, and profitability, reveal the continuing expansion of capitalist relations within a global context (Raduntz, 2005).

Conflict theories of education, in short, stress that expectations for schooling to fulfill its promise to offer equal opportunity and social benefits to all are unrealistic or unattainable within current forms of social organization. Barriers that exist at several levels—access to schooling, what is taught and how it is taught, ability to influence educational policy and decision-making, and differential capacity to convert education into labour market and social advantage—deny many individuals or groups the chance to benefit from meaningful forms and levels of education. Conflict theories offer varying assessments of what must be done to ensure that education can be more democratic and equitable. Some analysts stress that educational institutions and organizations themselves must be transformed, while others suggest that any kind of school reform will be limited without more fundamental social and economic changes to ensure that people will be able to use, and be recognized for using, their education and training more effectively.

Feminist Theories

Feminist analyses of schooling share some of the observations of other conflict theories, though with an explicit emphasis on the existence of and strategies to address social inequalities based on **gender**. Feminist theory stresses that social equity and justice are not possible as long as males and females have unequal power and status through **patriarchy** or gendered systems of domination. In the eighteenth century, Mary Wollstonecraft (1986 [1792]) saw access to education as a fundamental right for women;

RESEARCHERS IN ACTION ▶ Dorothy Smith

Dorothy Smith, one of the world's most eminent sociologists, spent much of her career at the Ontario Institute for Studies in Education before returning to the west coast (her first appointment in Canada was at the University of British Columbia), where she is currently an adjunct professor at the University of Victoria. In her early studies, her experience of having to balance household work and responsibilities for young children with academic work sensitized her to the importance of the ways in which people's standpoints, or their daily life circumstances, were shaped by and reflected the ways available to them to understand and approach social life. As reflected in the title of one of her most influential books, *The Everyday World as Problematic: A Feminist Sociology* (Smith, 1987), she drew from the ideas of Marx as well as ethnomethodology and other interpretative theorists in developing a unique analytical orientation dedicated to problematizing social life.

Her work highlights how the world is shaped by and reinforces "relations of ruling" as social life comes to be organized and framed in ways that reflect more the interests of dominant or privileged groups rather than with reference to people's daily life needs (Smith, 1990). Schools, universities, workplaces, and other institutional settings, as well as academic disciplines like sociology itself, are all implicated in the regulation of social life through the intersections of power, knowledge, and language. These relationships are analyzed by means of institutional ethnography, a research orientation that contrasts formal organizations and the rules and practices by which they are configured with the perspectives of the people who work in or encounter these institutions on a regular basis (Smith, 1992, 2005).

Her research is especially concerned with presenting an alternative understanding based on how women are able to see and understand the world in the context of their own experiences, seeking to present a "way of looking at things from the point of women, in the sense of how to make change: what do you need to know in order to begin to think about making change?" (cited in Carroll, 2010b, p. 21). Interviews with mothers of school-age children reveal, for instance, how discourses and expectations associated with mothering are shaped in conjunction with taken-for-granted middle-class standards of schooling. Thus, "What may properly be considered the work of parents (and mothers in particular) and the boundaries of school responsibility has been and continues to be negotiated within a discourse that presupposes middle-class resources and familial organization" that require commitments of time, knowledge, and other resources to which many working-class and other mothers do not have access (Griffith & Smith, 1987, pp. 99–100).

Integrating classical sociological tools with innovative insights applied to contemporary issues and concerns, Smith's work continues to provide a rich foundation for continuing research and analysis of social life in Canada and globally.

denied such a right historically, women were degraded as "frivolous" or a "backward sex." Later waves of feminism have continued to look to education as a central institution through which to promote women's rights, opportunities, and interests.

Various forms of feminism pose different questions for educational research and propose different explanations and strategies for change (Gaskell, 1993; Weiner, 1994; Smith, 1990). Feminist analysis has revealed how influential mainstream studies of schooling most often concentrated on the lives of boys and men, with little recognition that girls and women have different experiences and little chance to voice their concerns. Much research in the 1970s and 1980s focused on how such things as classroom activities, language use, images and examples in textbooks and curriculum material (including the absence of women and girls in many instances), treatment of students by teachers, and patterns of subject choice reflected gender-based stereotypes and perpetuated traditional divisions among males and females (Kenway & Modra, 1992).

Feminist analysis seeks to do more than simply demonstrate how these social processes contribute to inequalities; rather, it aims to change the conditions that bring these practices about. This focus has shifted as some aspects of the agenda on women's rights and issues have advanced successfully, while specific barriers continue to restrict progress on other fronts. For instance, school boards have policies, enforced through human rights legislation, to restrict sexist curricula and to prohibit gender-based **discrimination** in educational programs and institutions. The educational participation rates of and attainment by females have come to exceed those for males. Yet gender parity has not been achieved in several important respects. Female students remain highly under-represented in important fields such as information technologies, engineering, and some natural sciences, while gender-based barriers exist in other areas of schooling (see Table 10.2). Moreover, educational achievements do not always contribute equitably to successful social and economic outcomes.

Analysis of the feminization of teaching, as female teachers came to outnumber male teachers by the end of the nineteenth century, illustrates the relationship between education and changing gender relations. Teachers often lack the professional recognition that might otherwise accompany the demands and training their work involves. Teachers—and women teachers in particular—have been heavily regulated by governments and by school boards. During the early part of the twentieth century, guidelines often specified such things as what teachers could wear, with whom they could associate, and how they should act in public (Wotherspoon, 1995). Until the 1950s, legislation in many provinces required that women resign their teaching positions upon marriage. Although today's teachers have much greater personal and professional autonomy than those of the past, teachers' lives and work remain subject to various forms of scrutiny, guidelines, and informal practices that carry gender-based assumptions or significance. Female teachers predominate in the primary grades, while men tend to be over-represented in the upper grades and in post-secondary teaching positions, especially in the most senior teaching and educational administrative positions.

Feminist analysis increasingly has come to address interrelationships among gender, sexuality, and other social factors and personal characteristics. Gender-based identities, experiences, and opportunities are affected by race, region, social class, and competing expectations and demands that people face at home, in the workplace, and in other social spheres (Arnot, 2011; Dillabough, McLeod, & Mills, 2011). Students and teachers from different backgrounds encounter diverse experiences, concerns, and options even within similar educational settings, which in turn affect subsequent educational and personal options.

TIME to REFLECT

What are the main bases of inequality emphasized in conflict theories and feminist theories of education, respectively?

Table 10.2 ▶ University Degrees Awarded by Field of Study and Gender, Canada, 2013

Field of Study	Number of Graduates	Rank Order for Female Graduates	Female Graduates in Field as % of All Female Graduates	Females as % of All Graduates in Field	Rank Order for Male Graduates	Male Graduates in Field as % of All Male Graduates	Males as % of All Graduates in Field
Business, management, and public administration	65,463	2	20.5	54.0	1	25.6	46.0
Social and behavioural sciences and law	57,543	1	22.3	67.0	3	16.2	33.0
Health and related fields	36,912	3	16.2	75.6	5	7.7	24.4
Education	28,239	4	12.3	75.3	7	5.9	24.6
Architecture, engineering, and related technologies	25,002	8	3.4	23.2	2	16.3	76.7
Humanities	24,141	5	8.9	63.8	6	7.4	36.1
Physical and life sciences and technologies	21,087	6	6.8	55.2	4	8.0	44.7
Visual and performing arts and communications technologies	11,307	7	4.2	64.4	9	3.4	35.5
Mathematics, computer and information sciences	8,280	11	1.6	33.1	8	4.7	66.9
Agriculture, natural resources, and conservation	6,078	9	2.0	55.4	11	2.3	44.5
Other	6,210	10	1.9	52.9	10	2.5	47.1
All fields			100.1	59.5		100.0	40.5

SOURCE: Compiled with data from Statistics Canada, "Postsecondary graduates, by Pan-Canadian Standard Classification of Education (PCSCE), Classification of Instructional Programs, Primary Grouping (CIP_PG), sex and immigration status, annual (number)," Statistics Canada CANSIM Table 477-0020 (accessed 06 January 2016).

Emerging Analysis and Research in the Sociology of Education

Sociologists commonly employ insights from several models or orientations, acknowledging theory as a tool to help understand and explain phenomena and guide social action.

Critical pedagogy is one approach that draws from different theoretical positions, including conflict theory, feminist theory, and post-modernist challenges, both to explore how domination and power enter into schooling and personal life and to seek to change those aspects that undermine our freedom and humanity (Giroux, 1997; Darder, Baltodano, & Torres, 2003; McLaren & Kincheloe, 2007). Anti-racism education shares similar orientations, further stressing the ways in which domination builds on notions of racial difference to create fundamental inequalities among groups that are defined on the basis of biological differences or cultural variations (Dei, 1996).

Pierre Bourdieu (1997; Bourdieu & Passeron, 1979) has explored how **social structures** (the primary focus of structural functionalism and conflict theory) become interrelated with the meanings and actions relevant to social actors (the main concern of symbolic interactionism or interpretative sociology). Bourdieu, as a critical theorist, emphasizes that education contributes to the transmission of power and privilege from one generation to another as it employs assumptions and procedures that are to the advantage of some groups and the disadvantage of others. Educational access, processes, and outcomes are shaped through struggles by different groups to retain or gain advantages relative to one another. However, the mere fact that people hold varying degrees of economic, social, and cultural resources does not guarantee that these resources will be converted automatically into educational advantage. Competition for educational access and credentials increases as different groups look to education to provide a gateway into important occupational and decision-making positions.

Canadian research, influenced by Bourdieu's analysis and other integrative approaches such as life course theory, demonstrates the complex interactions among personal and social-structural characteristics that affect the pathways taken by children and youth through education and from schooling into work and other life transitions (Anisef et al., 2000; Taylor, 2005; Lehmann, 2007). Researchers are also especially interested in the complex ways in which education intersects with both local and global dimensions of cultural, economic, and social forces (Apple, Au, & Gandin, 2009; Spring, 2009). Sociological analysis draws attention to the multifaceted nature of schooling.

EDUCATIONAL PARTICIPANTS

Educational institutions are highly complex. Some colleges and universities exceed the size of small cities. Consequently, sociologists are interested in questions related to the changing nature of who attends and works in these institutions (with respect to gender, racial, ethnic, religious, and socioeconomic factors), what

positions they occupy, and what barriers and opportunities they encounter.

Educational diversity has increased amid social and demographic changes during a period in which more people continue schooling for longer periods. The educational participation of girls and women has increased significantly since World War II, especially at the post-secondary level. Immigration, rural-to-urban migration, labour market transitions, recognition of gender diversity and minority rights, inclusion of students with disabilities, and many other social changes have dramatically altered the composition of student populations.

Sociological interest extends beyond how formal curricula and structured activities affect learning and chances for success for different types of students. Educational organization, rules, expectations, and practices also contain a **hidden curriculum**: the unwritten purposes or goals of school life. Through the daily rhythm of school life, students are channelled into selected directions as they acquire taken-for-granted understandings about order, discipline, power relations, and other aspects of social life that favour students from some backgrounds to the detriment of others (Lynch, 1989). Schooling can also have limited connection with—and produce negative consequences for—the students and communities it is intended to serve (Dei et al., 2000; Stonechild, 2006).

How does this photo reveal evidence of a hidden curriculum in the classroom?

Practices known as *silencing* inhibit many students, often making students or parents uneasy about their own cultural backgrounds in relation to the authority represented by the school. These practices are often reinforced by a *banking model* of **pedagogy** (Freire, 1970) in which pre-established curricula are transmitted in one direction, from the educator to the student, working especially to the detriment of students from the least privileged backgrounds. Socio-economic status in particular remains a powerful determinant of student outcomes (Levin, 2007, pp. 75–76). Socially selective practices, though often unintended and sometimes resisted by teachers, are difficult to change as they become embedded within highly complex interactions between schooling and other features of social organization.

TIME to REFLECT

What does an understanding of the hidden curriculum tell us about the nature and purposes of schooling?

EDUCATIONAL POLICY, POLITICS, AND IDEOLOGIES

Educational policy is established and administered in quite different ways in other countries. Many nations, such as Sweden and Japan, have highly centralized systems of education. Canada and the United States, by contrast, do not have uniform or centralized education systems, contributing to what Paul Axelrod (1997, p. 126) describes as an "educational patchwork."

Canada's Constitution assigns primary responsibility for education to provincial and territorial governments, contributing to variations in many principal aspects of education systems, including how they are organized, the length of the school year, curriculum and graduation requirements, teacher qualifications and certification, and educational funding. The specific details related to setting and carrying out educational policies and operating schools are normally delegated to elected local school boards or similar regional bodies. In recent years, jurisdictions across Canada have undertaken a variety of initiatives that have modified the ways education is organized, administered, and delivered (CMEC, 2008).

Public education at elementary, secondary, and post-secondary levels has undergone significant financial changes since the early 1990s. Education spending has risen to levels exceeding $100 billion, but expressed as a proportion of Canada's gross domestic product (GDP, or total expenditures), current levels are about 6.4 per cent, below the rate it had reached in the early 1990s (OECD, 2013a, p. 191; Statistics Canada, 2014b, 2014e, 2014f, 2014g, 2014h, 2014i, 2014k, 2014l, 2014m, 2014n). Figures 10.2 and 10.3 reveal that in Canada, as in most other highly developed nations, education continues to be funded primarily by governments, but the share of educational spending from private sources, including tuition fees, is growing.

These trends suggest the risk of increased educational inequalities. As tuition fees, living expenses, and other educational costs increase, many students encounter substantial financial burdens including increased student debt (Berger, 2009, p. 185). Elementary and secondary schools also face difficult choices as they weigh the costs and benefits of seeking higher taxes to finance schools, increasing school fees, relying on corporate sponsors to cover educational expenses, cutting school programs and services, or fundraising to cover costs of school supplies and programs (Canadian Teachers' Federation, 2010). Teachers frequently pay for school materials and activities themselves, while parents or communities "are having to make up for programs that aren't paid for—so then it depends on where you live and who you are. . . . There is a growing concern about equity. There is a growing gap between the 'have' and 'have-not' schools" (Brown, 2002, pp. A1, A26).

Educational funding decisions are accompanied by growing concern over the extent to which education systems are able to prepare learners for contemporary economic and social conditions. There are competing viewpoints (often expressed through concerns

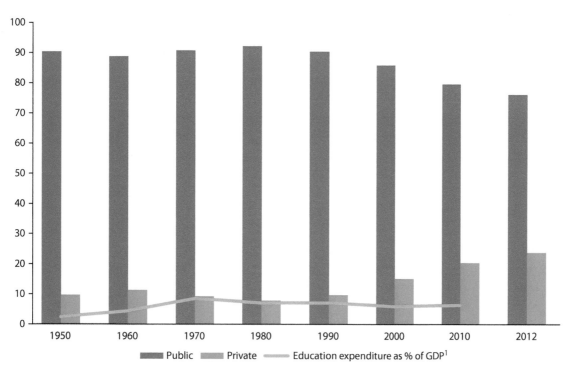

FIGURE 10.2 Total Education Spending in Canada: Relative Share of Public and Private Expenditure, Selected Years

[1] Figures for 1950 and 1960 are for gross national product, which results in slightly higher percentages than for gross domestic product.

SOURCES: Compiled from data in Statistics Canada (1983: W301-306 and W519-532); Statistics Canada, "Total expenditures on education, by direct source of funds and type of education, annual (dollars)," CANSIM Table 478-0001; and OECD, (2015: 234–235).

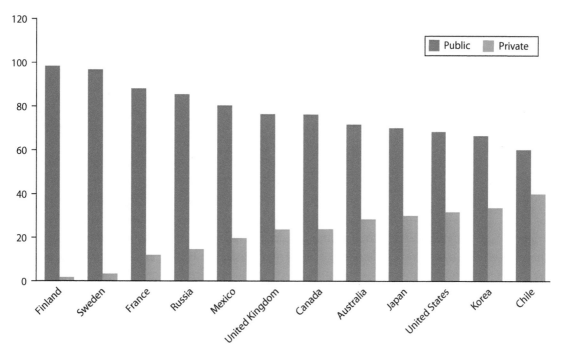

FIGURE 10.3 Public and Private Spending on Education: Relative Share of Public and Private Expenditure on Education in Canada and Selected Nations, 2012

SOURCES: Based on data from OECD (2015, 238 and Table B3.1).

about educational quality and excellence) about what role governments should play within this changing environment.

Neo-liberal critics promote the application of business or market-based principles to education and other social services. High-quality education is defined in terms of the excellence of educational "products," measured by such things as standardized test scores, parental choice, and public accountability. Parents and learners become "consumers" who should have the opportunity to approach education like decision-making about other purchases, with the added importance that humans, not some material object, require the options to make personal choices about educational futures.

Other observers draw attention to the dangers inherent in treating schooling like a market or reducing it to narrowly defined kinds of outcomes. Some suggest that inequality is likely to increase without a true commitment to community participation and high-quality education dedicated to the full range of activities and competencies that schools seek to foster (Osborne, 1999). Many initiatives that claim to increase choice and flexibility lead to the concentration of resources, control, and opportunities among a relatively small circle of agencies or participants (Gidney, 1999; Kachur & Harrison, 1999; Sears, 2003). Debate over education relative to other social priorities is likely to intensify as different forms of learning become increasingly more important for diverse social and economic objectives.

EDUCATION, WORK, AND FAMILIES

Changes in the nature and composition of learners' families and the varied demands from workplaces for particular kinds of qualified labour-force participants have made it even more crucial to understand how education systems interact with other institutions.

The nature of childhood and adolescence is changing profoundly as students and their families experience various life challenges. Few people experience "traditional" linear pathways from home to school to work. Periods of work and study often overlap, while family, work, and community responsibilities create multiple time demands on children as well as parents. Tensions sometimes spill over from one site of social life to another, expressed in public concern over phenomena such as bullying, violence, gang warfare, and "risk" among children and youth (although it is also important not to overemphasize the dangers while ignoring the positive experiences and contributions often associated with childhood and youth). Taking their cue from the market model of education, many parents view their children's education as an investment. Uncertainty about job futures heightens expectations on learners (seeking high performance to be competitive) and on teachers and educational administrators (in order to deliver a high-quality product that will yield the best results in the marketplace).

Parental education and expectations, along with emphasis on early reading and literacy skills, factor heavily as an influence on children's subsequent educational attainment and success (OECD, 2013b, pp. 13, 18). Parents and community members from diverse backgrounds frequently have differing expectations about the way education should be organized and delivered (Campey, 2002; Stonechild, 2006).

EDUCATION AND NEW TECHNOLOGIES

Education, like other institutions, has been significantly affected by the introduction of new information and communication technologies. In a few cases, information technology has revolutionized education. Some institutions have replaced traditional instructional settings with fully wired teaching/learning centres in which participants can not only communicate with each other but also draw upon material and interact with individuals on a global basis (Gergen, 2001). Web access and new technologies enable schools and learners in remote regions to gain access to varied learning resources and opportunities in both accredited and special education programs. Schools and universities are just beginning to explore fully the opportunities that new technologies make available to them (despite the origins of the World Wide Web as a tool to facilitate production and sharing of new knowledge among university-based researchers and other scientists).

New technologies and their use in and impact on education give rise to several important questions. Levin and Riffel raise the still relevant consideration for schools that "it may be that technology is not living up to its promise because it has been seen as an answer to rather than a reason to ask questions about the purposes of schools and the nature of teaching and learning" (1997, p. 114). Two issues are especially critical in this respect.

First, significant gaps remain between those who have access to computers and reliable electronic connections—and the skills and know-how to use and take advantage of new technologies—and those who do not. This "digital divide" is most commonly posed in global terms, distinguishing richer, more technologically developed nations from developing nations. However, even within Canada and other nations that have high rates of computer ownership and extensive Internet services, regular access to computers and mobile technology, along with the ability to use them productively, depend on such factors as a steady job, income and education levels, gender, area of residence and work, social class, and racial characteristics (Statistics Canada, 2010b; United Nations, 2009a, pp. 16–20).

Second, it is important to examine how and why new technologies are being adopted as tools and expectations in education. Clearly, information technology offers many advantages to users, contributes to important educational innovation, and may provide greater employment and economic opportunities outside of school. The rapid expansion of new technologies and applications—from text messaging, social networking, blogging, and communities involved in the dissemination of public

"When does the screen saver come on?"

How are new technologies and applications transforming the classroom and educational practices?

information resources such as Wikipedia, to gaming and electronic surveillance devices—is transforming everyday life for students and their families. However, students and teachers are not always equipped and supported sufficiently to use such technologies to their advantage or to fully understand their implications and limitations.

Issues related to the adoption of information technologies in education reflect more enduring concerns about the relationship of what happens in the classroom with structures and processes outside of schooling. Educational practices are strongly influenced by social, technological, and economic developments and innovations, although they also reveal their own peculiarities and rhythms. Demands for education to prepare people for the changing workplace sit side by side with parallel demands for producing better citizens and persons with multiple competencies to function in a global society.

TIME to REFLECT

What are the main ways in which the introduction of new technologies has influenced formal education?

EDUCATIONAL OPPORTUNITIES AND INEQUALITIES

Questions about the relationship of education to social inequality and opportunity structures have long been central to the sociological study of education. Education is closely related to social and economic advancement. As educational participation and attainment rates increase across populations, many traditional forms of inequality diminish. Data presented earlier in this chapter, for example, demonstrate that women's educational attainment levels now match or exceed those of men in Canada and in many other nations. Nonetheless, significant inequalities persist.

The shift in the gender balance of educational attainment has drawn attention to the complex interactions that occur among various socio-economic factors in relation to education. Findings from numerous surveys that girls have begun to outperform boys on a number of indicators, especially in areas like reading, have generated controversy over suggestions that gender inequality has reversed to the point that the education system is now "failing" boys (Bussière and Knighton, 2004, p. 38). However, major comparative studies from Canada and several other nations also demonstrate the complex nature of gender inequalities in education. For instance, in most provinces and in many dimensions of mathematics and science performance, relatively few pronounced gender differences appear, while in some instances boys outperform girls. Moreover, these surveys highlight how similarities and differences based on gender cannot be understood without reference to a broad array of other family, school, and individual characteristics, notably family socio-economic background and immigration status (OECD, 2013b, pp. 12–16).

Gender-related differences are often obscured through simple comparisons between boys' and girls' test results (Alloway, 2007). As Table 10.2 shows, although women outnumber men in post-secondary enrolment and graduation, strong gender differences persist across fields of study and programs.

These variations reflect a combination of personal choices and circumstances, institutional characteristics (such as cues or levels of comfort and discomfort that direct students into some areas and away from others or the compatibility between particular programs and responsibilities for the care of dependent children), and broader socio-economic factors (Arnot, 2011; Wotherspoon, 2000). Women's rising levels of education do not always translate fully into gains in labour market positions, incomes, and other equitable outcomes (Vosko, 2010).

Many educational differences between racial and ethnic groups also appear to have disappeared or diminished significantly in recent decades (Davies & Guppy, 2010, pp. 116–20). Canada's immigration policies emphasize the recruitment of immigrants with high educational credentials, contributing to increased numbers of immigrants from non-Western source countries. Many highly educated or professionally qualified immigrants place significant value on their children's educational advancement. Racial diversity has been accompanied by increasing sensitivity to the impact of racial discrimination and other mechanisms that have historically excluded or discouraged racial minority students from advancing through the Canadian education system.

To better understand the requirements skilled workers must meet to be accepted into Canada, see the Global Issues box, p. 181, in **Chapter 8**, "Ethnic and Race Relations."

As with gender inequalities, analysis of racial and ethnic inequalities in education reveals a complex series of interactions that do not lead to any straightforward conclusions. Davies and Guppy (2010), in common with many other commentators who have reviewed census data and education indicators over time, observe that Canadians in most categories (based on gender, race, region, age, class, and other factors) have benefited from the expansion of education systems. However, outcomes for specific groups, including Indigenous people, some immigrant and visible-minority populations, those from working-class backgrounds, and many persons with disabilities, continue to be less favourable relative to other groups. Social class has a strong impact on post-secondary attendance and educational attainment. These general trends are compounded by considerable variation in educational success and attainment within groups.

Research on education for Indigenous people is instructive in this regard. Many First Nations expressed their desire in the nineteenth-century treaty-making process to have access to formal education in order to keep pace with contemporary social and economic demands. However, subsequent developments, including the damaging legacy of residential schooling, lack of acceptance or discriminatory treatment in provincial schools, and other social, cultural, and economic factors, have left Indigenous people's overall education levels (especially those of registered Indians who live on reserve) well below national levels (Schissel & Wotherspoon, 2003). Despite continuing increases in the levels of educational attainment by Indigenous people, by 2011, Indigenous people aged 25 to 64 years were nearly 1.5 times less likely than non-Indigenous people to have a post-secondary degree or diploma and 2.7 times less likely to have graduated from university but 2.5 times as likely not to have completed high school (based on data in Statistics Canada, 2013e, p. 4).

Educational inequalities typically reflect a complex chain of interrelated cause-and-effect mechanisms. Increasing attention has been paid to the importance of early childhood development and to the family and social environments in which children are raised for the development of literacy and language skills, thinking

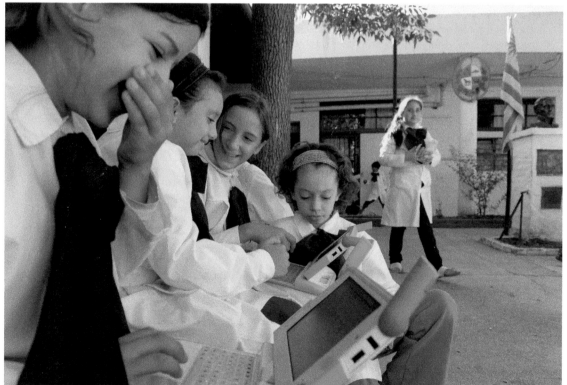

Joerg Boethling/Alamy Stock Photo

How do programs like One Laptop per Child succeed or fail at addressing educational inequalities?

processes, and other capacities that are central to educational success. These conditions, in turn, depend on the socio-economic circumstances of parents, the availability of support networks in the home and community, labour market opportunities for parents and students coming out of the education system, the extent to which people in particular communities or regions have access to high-quality educational programs and services, and numerous other factors. There are strong associations between social class or socio-economic background and educational attainment. Parents' education levels and household income are strong predictors, both independently and in combination with one another, of the likelihood that a person will continue into post-secondary education (Finnie, McMullen, & Mueller, 2010).

Educational institutions influence social opportunities and life chances in many ways with respect to informal practices and social relationships as well as to formal curricular matters. Social class and cultural differences are evident, for instance, in the grouping and **streaming** of students into specific educational programs that contribute, in turn, to diverse educational pathways.

There is general agreement, in the context of global economic developments that place a premium on knowledge and learning, that

HUMAN DIVERSITY   Education for Canada's Indigenous People

The educational experiences of Indigenous people in Canada help in understanding how education can both advance and restrict social and economic opportunities. Historical practices and inequities have contributed to a legacy of widespread failure, marginalization, and mistrust, but considerable optimism also accompanies many new initiatives.

Many Indigenous people in the late nineteenth century looked to schooling as a way of ensuring integration into contemporary societies. Tragically, while some education-related treaty promises were fulfilled, the residential school system and continuing problems with other forms of educational delivery had devastating consequences that many Indigenous communities and their members are still struggling to cope with. The report of the Royal Commission on Aboriginal Peoples (1996) endorsed the long-standing principle of First Nations control over education along with other measures to ensure that all educational institutions would provide more receptive schooling for Indigenous people.

In the two decades since that report, results have been mixed. The report of the Truth and Reconciliation Commission of Canada (2015b) underlines the damaging impact of residential schooling not only for those who attended such schools but also in the far-reaching consequences

they continue to have in the lives of many Indigenous people and their communities. While the Truth and Reconciliation process, combined with new initiatives across many Canadian school systems, has created new opportunities for education systems to become more receptive to Indigenous students and has promoted understanding about Indigenous issues, barriers continue to impede the road to success. Racial discrimination, for example, is expressed to such an extent that CBC News in late 2015 disabled the comments section in its reporting on Indigenous issues because so many comments were racially charged, hateful, or otherwise objectionable (CBC News, 2015).

Educational reform must also take into account considerable diversity among Indigenous populations and their educational options, aspirations, and circumstances. Several Indigenous communities and educators suggest that it is also important to reframe success in Indigenous learning in terms that are not restricted and not oriented to the measurement of learning deficits. Such a model would revitalize holistic notions of education as a lifelong process in which "Aboriginal learning is a fully integrated and potentially all-encompassing process that permeates all aspects of the learner's life and their community" (Canadian Council on Learning, 2009, p. 11).

Inuit students in Cape Dorset, Nunavut, demonstrate a leg-wrestling game. The degree of diversity within Indigenous populations makes it difficult to establish one-size-fits-all standards for educational attainment.

education is important for all people. The same consensus does not exist, however, with regard to how education should be arranged to fulfill its promise on an equitable basis.

CONCLUSION

This chapter has examined several dimensions of education and its relevance for sociological inquiry. It has highlighted the phenomenal growth of formal systems of education since the nineteenth century and the accompanying increases in general levels of education throughout the population. It has linked that growth to a strong degree of public faith in the ability of education both to contribute to individual development and to address social needs for knowledge, innovation, and credentials. Educational growth, processes, and outcomes have been understood from diverse theoretical perspectives: structural functionalism (focusing on education's contributions to dominant social and economic requirements); symbolic interactionism and microsociology (highlighting understandings and interactions of various participants within educational processes); conflict theories (emphasizing education's contributions to social inequality and power relations); feminist theories (drawing attention to gender-based educational differences); and integrative approaches (linking insights from diverse perspectives). The chapter has also addressed the changing significance of formal schooling to the experiences and social and economic opportunities of different social groups, particularly with respect to gender, race and ethnicity, and social class. All groups have benefited from educational expansion, though in varying degrees. Adequate sociological analysis of education requires an ability to integrate an understanding of what happens in and as a result of formal education with the social context in which education is situated.

Questions for Critical Thought

1. Why is education in most nations organized formally through schools and related institutional structures rather than through some other arrangement, such as families or community-based agencies? To what extent should education be a private as opposed to a public responsibility?

2. Explain how and why employers and other agencies have come to rely on formal educational credentials or qualifications as legitimate mechanisms for determining applicants' eligibility for positions in their organizations.

3. Compare and contrast schooling (formal education) with other major social institutions, including businesses, families, prisons, and religious organizations. Describe and explain the major similarities and differences.

4. What is the impact of emerging emphases on lifelong learning and economic productivity on education systems? What kinds of alternatives to formal schooling are being developed in response to increasing demands for lifelong learning? Explain and critically discuss the changes (or lack of change) you have identified.

5. Why have education levels increased across populations in Canada and in most other nations? Which theoretical perspectives offer the most adequate explanation of these trends?

6. To what extent and in what ways have educational institutions been influenced by new information technologies? Discuss the relative strengths and limitations of these changes in terms of schooling's ability to meet the needs of learners in contemporary societies.

7. To what extent has education in Canada fulfilled its promise to provide greater opportunities

for social and economic advancement to all social groups? Explain your response with reference to at least three different theoretical frameworks.

8. Whose interests are best served by formal education? Discuss with reference to how particular social groups (such as students, teachers, administrators, parents, policy-makers, corporations, or interest groups) have influenced educational decision-making and processes.

Sociological Explorations

1. Compare your own educational experiences with those of persons from previous generations in your family or community. What are the major differences? To what extent have these experiences contributed or been related to employment and other features of life for each generation?

2. Observe the characteristics of students (e.g., gender, age, ability status, race or ethnicity) in

your sociology class and compare these with students in one or more of classes in other disciplines. What patterns, if any, are evident and how might they be significant? Explore what these comparisons reveal about who participates in higher education and who may not be represented.

Recommended Readings

Ballantine, J.H., & Spade, J.Z. (Eds). (2015). *Schools and society: A sociological approach to education* **(5th edn). Thousand Oaks, CA: Sage.**
This collection integrates a comprehensive range of classical and contemporary contributions to the sociological analysis of education. Major theoretical frameworks are represented, as well as research methods and substantive areas such as student cultures, school organization, stratification, educational reform, and global issues.

Fennell, S. & Arnot, M. (Eds). (2009). *Gender education and equality in a global context.* **London, UK: Routledge.**
Contributors explore theoretical and policy dimensions associated with gender and education, drawing upon research from several nations. Feminist orientations are integrated with understandings of the ways in which gender inequality is intertwined with

poverty, culture, economic systems, and fundamental social conditions.

Guppy, N., & Davies, S. (2014). The *schooled society: An introduction to the sociology of education* **(3rd edn). Toronto, ON: Oxford University Press.**
The authors integrate their discussion of core concepts and theories in the sociological analysis of education with material drawn from sociological research and case studies. Both historical and contemporary issues and developments are covered.

Lauder, H., Brown, P., Dillabough, J., & Halsey, A.H. (Eds). (2006). *Education, globalization, and social change.* **Oxford, UK: Oxford University Press.**
A comprehensive analysis of education from various perspectives in sociology and other disciplines, containing influential chapters from different national settings that examine the impact of political

and economic changes on education, cultural diversity, new conceptions of knowledge and curricula, the reshaping of teaching, and the dynamics of inequality and exclusion in relation to formal education.

Livingstone, D.W., Mirchandani, K., & Sawchuk, P.H. (Eds). (2008). *The future of lifelong learning and work: Critical perspectives.* **Rotterdam, Netherlands: Sense Publishers.**
Contributors explore changing relations between learning and work in a knowledge-based economy with reference to different types of knowledge, workers, and employment circumstances.

Wotherspoon, T. (2014). *The sociology of education in Canada: Critical perspectives* **(4th edn). Toronto, ON: Oxford University Press.**
Various dimensions of Canadian education are explored from a critical orientation that emphasizes inequalities based on class, race, gender, region, and other factors. The book addresses contemporary aspects of Canadian education in the context of various theoretical perspectives and historical factors.

Recommended Websites

American Sociological Association, Section on Sociology of Education
www.asanet.org/sectioneducation/education.cfm
This site, though directed primarily to professionals and researchers, contains a summary description of the sociology of education. The homepage also has a tab connecting to many useful links to other databases and relevant sites.

Canadian Education Association
www.cea-ace.ca/
The Canadian Education Association offers information, resources, and services for anyone involved in or concerned about education issues, including parents, students, teachers, governments, researchers, and many others.

Canadian Teachers' Federation
www.ctf-fce.ca
This website provides an educator's perspective on important educational matters, ranging from facts on education systems and significant educational developments to position papers and analyses of pressing educational issues.

Council of Ministers of Education Canada
www.cmec.ca
The Council of Ministers of Education provides access to major reports and studies conducted through that organization as well as links to each of the provincial and territorial ministries of education and other important Canadian and international education bodies.

Educational Resources Information Center (ERIC)
www.eric.ed.gov
The ERIC database is a comprehensive collection of information (mostly abstracts of journal articles and reports) on various aspects of and fields related to education, including the sociology of education.

Organisation for Economic Co-operation and Development (OECD)
www.oecd.org
The OECD website provides useful and up-to-date information for major international comparisons and developments. It includes report summaries, statistics, and links to major documents on education and related thematic areas that highlight significant trends and issues for 34 member countries and several dozen other nations.

Statistics Canada
www.statcan.gc.ca
Statistics Canada provides a comprehensive body of data and information on education on its website and through its links with other sites.

United Nations Educational, Scientific and Cultural Organization (UNESCO)
www.unesco.org/new/en/unesco
UNESCO promotes dialogue, mutual respect, and improved living conditions for people around the world. Its website includes useful resources and information relevant to education as well as related social and cultural issues, including reports and programs on education in specific nations and on a comparative level.

Key Terms

baby boom The dramatic increase in birth rates in North America between the end of World War II and the mid-1960s.

capitalism An economic system characterized by a relationship of unequal economic exchange between capitalists (employers) and workers. Because they do not own the means of production, workers must sell their labour power to employers in exchange for a wage or salary. Capitalism is a market-based system driven by the pursuit of private profit.

conflict theory A sociological perspective influenced by Marx and Weber that emphasizes the role of power and conflict in maintaining social inequality and contributing to social change.

discrimination An action in which a person is treated differently (usually unfairly) because he or she is associated with a particular social category or characteristic.

education Processes (both formal and informal) through which human beings learn and develop capacities through understanding their social and natural environments.

feminism A theoretical perspective, as well as a social movement, that focuses on causes and consequences of inequality between men and women, especially patriarchy and sexism.

gender Socially recognized distinctions of masculinity and femininity.

globalization Social processes related to extension of resources, ideas, and people across national boundaries in increasingly extensive and complex ways.

hidden curriculum The tacit understandings (in relation to factors such as competition, hierarchy, or individualism) that students develop as a result of institutional arrangements and practices that occur within educational contexts.

human capital Recognition of the contributions made by education, skill development, and knowledge to innovation and productivity.

identity A person's sense of who they are based on their group membership(s) and interactions with others. It involves how we see ourselves and how others see us; it is a product of our history and of our interpretation of others' reactions to us. How others view us is termed "placement," and other people's reactions to our projections of ourselves is termed "announcement."

ideology A system of beliefs, ideas, and norms, reflecting the interests and experiences of a group, class, or subculture, that legitimizes or justifies the existing unequal distribution of power and privilege; ways of seeing and of understanding the world and its actors. Ideologies function by making the social appear natural or functional rather than constructed for partisan interests and advantage.

lifelong learning A focus on imperatives for people to develop new knowledge, skills, and capacities throughout their life, well beyond completion of their basic education.

macrosociology The study of social institutions, structures, and large social groups, focusing on societies or social systems as a whole.

marketization A process in which social relations and activities are determined increasingly through market relations through payment for services or other forms of commodity exchange.

microsociology A sociological approach that focuses analysis on small groups, face-to-face interactions, and everyday life activities.

negotiation A discussion intended to produce an agreement.

new (knowledge-based) economy A term used to describe the shift from manufacturing and other industrial activity toward a service-based economy driven by innovation, creativity, information exchange, and flexibility.

norms The rules and expectations of appropriate behaviour under various social circumstances. Norms create social consequences that have the effect of regulating appearance and behaviour.

patriarchy Social institutions or systems in which men have greater power and authority than women.

pedagogy Methods, practices, and processes associated with teaching and interactions within different teaching/learning situations.

power In the classic formulation, refers to the ability to exercise one's will, even in the face of opposition from others. In Marxist sociology, a social relationship that has a material base. Those who own the means of production have the power to exploit workers through the appropriation of their labour efforts. In Weberian sociology, power is more broadly defined and can reflect the capacity of individuals or groups to exert their will over others. Contemporary analysts point out that power may also involve a wide variety of indirect and subtle manifestations, including the ability to mobilize bias or define a situation in one's own interests.

schooling Processes that take place within formal educational institutions.

social interaction The process by which people act and react in relationships with others.

social structure Patterns of behaviour or social relationships developed and accepted through time in a given group, organization, or society.

socialization A lifelong interactive learning process through which individuals acquire a self-identity and the social skills needed to become members of society.

streaming Also known as tracking, a practice within education systems that places students in specific programs or groups over time. Groupings are typically based on performance on standardized aptitude tests, perceived personal preferences or qualities, or other social characteristics.

structural functionalism A theoretical paradigm that emphasizes the way each part of a society functions to fulfill the needs of society as a whole.

symbolic interactionism An intellectual tradition in sociology akin to interpretive theory, founded in the early twentieth-century work of Charles Horton Cooley and George Herbert Mead, although the term itself was not coined until years later by Herbert Blumer. Symbolic interactionism emphasizes the importance of understanding the meanings of social action and uses ethnographic methods to discover these meanings for individuals in an effort to explain human conduct.

symbols The heart of cultural systems, for with them we construct thought, ideas, and other ways of representing reality to others and to ourselves; gestures, artifacts, or uses of language that represent something else.

transitions The pathways that people follow through their lives as they move from family settings into various education programs, work experiences, and other major life course changes.

11 | Work and the Economy

PAMELA SUGIMAN

In this chapter you will:

▶ Be introduced to some of the main concepts that are used in the sociological analysis of work

▶ Examine ways in which work has been socially organized by employers

▶ Learn about some of the recent trends in the world of work

▶ Recognize the impact of the organization of work on workers variously located within a gendered and racialized market-driven society

▶ Come to understand the different types of paid and unpaid work that people do

▶ Highlight ways in which people experience work and sometimes resist

INTRODUCTION

Let us begin this chapter by making three key points. These assertions are the premises on which this chapter is based. First, most of us will spend the better part of our lives working because work is central to our economic well-being. Second, work is a social product and, as such, it is negotiable. Third, people seek meaning in the work that they perform; there is a close relationship between work, life, and **identity**. Let us look more closely at each of these points.

1. *Work is central to our existence.* What would it be like if you never held a job? Unless you are incredibly wealthy, unable to work as a result of an injury or disabling health condition, or willing (or forced) to live on social assistance or handouts on the street, it is unlikely that you could live without work. If you are like most people, you have no choice but to work in order to secure the basic necessities (food, clothing, a hospitable living environment). Most of us will spend a large chunk of our lives working; the majority will work for someone else, on another's terms. This holds true whether you wait tables, drive a truck, stock grocery shelves, trade on the stock exchange, or teach in a school. The very wealthy rely heavily on investment income for their economic well-being, and the extremely poor depend on social welfare (transfer payments). But the majority of people in the middle- and highest-income groups in Canada count on wages and salaries for their existence (Jackson & Robinson, 2000, p. 11). In 2008, close to 8 in 10 persons in Canada aged 15 to 64 participated in the paid labour force (Jackson, 2009, p. 3). Work has strong implication for how we will live our lives.

2. *Work is a social product.* Many Canadians view the work they perform as a given. Work is something that we either have or do not have (Gorz, 1999); that we go to every day or night; that we leave at the end of a career.

But it is important to understand that there is nothing inevitable about the way work is organized and experienced. Work is a social product. The way it is structured, the nature of jobs, and the rewards of work are all products of **social relationships** between groups of people. Over time and across cultures, work has taken varied forms. We need to critically examine the way in which it is currently organized, with the knowledge that it may be transformed.

3. *People seek meaning in their work.* Although most of us work in order to survive and live comfortably, we work for more than economic survival or comfort of living. The quality of work matters to us, young and old. According to a national work ethic study, when Canadian workers were asked what they would do if they won a million dollars, only 17 per cent said that they would never work again; 41 per cent of respondents claimed that they would keep their job, 17 per cent would embark on a different career, and 24 per cent would start their own business (Lowe, 2000, p. 52). Upon winning a lottery jackpot, no doubt many of us, over time, would quit our current jobs. But would we abandon work entirely? When faced with job loss and retirement, and even after voluntary early retirement, some Canadians express a desire to return to work. They report a loss of purpose and dignity and feelings of marginality. We have a strong attachment to our work.

In order to understand work fully, it is necessary to think about the economy in which it is situated. We may define the *economy* as a social institution in which people carry out the production, distribution, and consumption of goods and services. It is critical that we understand how economic systems function, for they have a bearing on how we live. The economy and our location in it shape the quality of health care, housing, diet and nutrition, consumer spending, and overall lifestyle. The economic system is linked to a nation's political system, to people's conceptions of democracy and citizenship, and to general measures of success and failure.

WORLD ECONOMIC SYSTEMS

Economic systems are not abstract and untouchable entities. They are structured, contested, and reshaped by the people who inhabit them. They further reflect relations of **power** and inequality. In Canada, we live in a society that is based on a system of **capitalism**, one in which there are blatant and subtle manifestations of inequality. We observe extremes of wealth and poverty every day. On the highway, a shiny new Porsche whirs by an old Kia Rio. A businessman rushing to pick up a $5,000 suit at Holt Renfrew walks quickly past a homeless person. A Filipina nanny on a temporary work permit spends her days taking care of someone else's children. At night, she returns, tired, to her small room in the basement of the family's well-appointed home. We live in a society in which economic inequalities are complexly wound up with inequalities based on *gender, race, ethnicity,* and *religion*.

The power of capitalism is so pervasive that we take for granted many of its central premises. Concerned about how we can individually climb up the capitalist hierarchy, we seldom stop to question the system itself. But by looking closely we can see how our society is the result of historical relationships based on conflict and struggle.

Capitalism

Unlike earlier economic systems, capitalism is based on private ownership of the **means of production**, an exchange relationship between owners and workers, an economy driven by the pursuit of profit, and competitive market relations.

Let us turn to the ideas of the classical social theorist Karl Marx. Marx (1976 [1867]) wrote about the profound changes he observed in nineteenth-century England. He witnessed a gradual but dramatic transition from a feudal agricultural society to an industrialized, capitalist economy. Under capitalism, the capitalist class (or bourgeoisie) owns the means of production, while the majority of people, the working class (or proletariat), does not. *Means of production* is wealth-generating property, such as land, factories, machines, and the capital needed to produce and distribute goods and services for exchange in a market. Capitalists and workers are engaged in a relationship of unequal exchange. Workers have no choice but to sell their labour to a capitalist employer in exchange for a wage. People are forced into this relationship because it is almost impossible to survive without money.

The capitalist class organizes production (work) with the goal of maximizing profits for personal wealth. It structures work in the most efficient way imaginable, pays workers the lowest possible wages, and extracts the greatest amount of labour from the worker. Finally, capitalism is based on a freely competitive market system and therefore a laissez-faire ("hands-off") government. The market forces of supply and demand are supposed to determine the production and distribution of goods and services, with no government interference.

Capitalism and Industrialization

While capitalism is a broad economic system, *industrialization* refers to a specific process that has consequences for the nature and organization of work as well as for the division of labour.

Industrialization involved the introduction of new forms of energy (steam, electricity) and of transportation (railroads), urbanization, and the implementation of new machine technology, all of which contributed to the rise of the factory system of production and the manufacture and mass production of goods. These changes greatly facilitated and heightened capitalist production. As well, they profoundly shaped the ways in which people worked and organized their lives.

The proliferation of factories led to the movement of work from homes and small workshops to larger, more impersonal sites, to the concentration of larger groups of workers under one roof, and to the introduction of *time discipline* (by the clock), in addition to a more specialized division of labour.

In industrial capitalism, economic inequalities became visible, and conflict between classes grew. While successful capitalists made huge amounts of money, working-class men toiled in factories or mines for a pittance, women combined long hours of domestic drudgery with sporadic income-generating activities, and children were sent to factories or domestic work. Many lived in poverty.

Family Capitalism

In the mid- to late nineteenth century, industrial capitalism was in its early stages. Throughout this period, a small number of individuals and families owned and controlled most of a country's wealth—major companies and financial institutions. Because wealth accrued from business enterprises was passed on within families over generations (for example, the Rockefellers in the United States and the Eatons in Canada), this era is termed *family capitalism*.

Corporate Capitalism

The economic development of the late nineteenth to mid-twentieth century is called *corporate* (or *monopoly*) capitalism. This phase witnessed the movement of ownership from individuals (families) to modern corporations and their shareholders. A *corporation* is a legal entity distinct from the people who own and control it. The corporation may enter into contracts and own property. This separation of enterprise from individuals has protected owners and chief executives from personal liability and debts incurred by the corporation.

Under corporate capitalism there is a growing concentration of economic power (power in the hands of a few large corporations). One way this happen is through mergers. By merging, large corporations are able to create situations of monopoly and oligopoly. A monopoly exists when one corporation has exclusive control over the market. Obviously, this situation is undesirable for consumers, since it restricts their market "choices."

An *oligopoly* is several companies controlling an industry. The insurance, newspaper, and entertainment industries are characterized by oligopolistic control. Increased revenue by way of mergers and acquisitions is desirable to corporate owners but may occur at the expense of industrial development and workers. In 2006, American corporate profits reached a record high of $785 billion. With the deflation of the credit bubble globally in 2008, US corporate profits plummeted to $98.6 billion. However, this economic crisis did not signify the dismantling of corporate capitalism. By 2009, the collective profits of US Fortune 500 companies had risen again to an outrageous $391 billion,

Family production was key to production in the earliest societies, and although work was differentiated by age and sex, it was shared by all in a familiar household setting.

Old Paper Studios/Alamy Stock Photo

Table 11.1 ▶ The 25 Largest Employers in Canada, 2011

Rank	Company (Year End)	Number of Employees	Location of Head Office	Revenue per Employee ($)	Profit per Employee ($)
1	Onex Corp. (De10)	238,000	Toronto, ON	$102,147	$–214
2	George Weston (De10)	155,000	Toronto, ON	$206,645	$2,916
3	Magna International (De10)ᵃ	96,600	Aurora, ON	$250,072	$10,072
4	Empire Company (My10)	90,000	Stellarton, NS	$172,747	$3,354
5	Royal Bank of Canada (Oc10)	72,126	Toronto, ON	$499,487	$72,415
6	Bank of Nova Scotia (Oc10)	70,772	Toronto, ON	$335,938	$59,897
7	Toronto-Dominion Bank (Oc10)	68,725	Toronto, ON	$369,720	$67,574
8	Bombardier Inc. (Ja11)ᵃ	65,370	Montreal, QC	$273,627	$11,550
9	Metro Inc. (Se10)	65,000	Montreal, QC	$175,157	$6,028
10	Canadian Tire (Ja11)	56,900	Toronto, ON	$157,974	$7,972
11	Thomson Reuters Corp. (De10)ᵃ	55,000	New York, NY	$239,964	$16,964
12	Alimentation Couche-Tard (Ap10)ᵃ	53,000	Laval, QC	$310,643	$5,715
13	Shoppers Drug Mart (Ja 11)	52,160	Toronto, ON	$198,928	$11,326
14	BCE Inc. (De10)	50,200	Verdun, QC	$362,689	$45,359
15	Garda World Security (Ja11)	45,000	Montreal, QC	$24,888	$634
16	CIBC (Oc10)	42,354	Toronto, ON	$353,591	$57,893
17	Extendicare REIT (De10)	38,000	Markham, ON	$54,694	$1,360
18	Bank of Montreal (Oc10)	38,000	Toronto, ON	$406,658	$73,947
19	Celestica Inc. (De10)ᵃ	35,000	Toronto, ON	$186,591	$2,309
20	Telus Corp. (De10)	34,800	Vancouver, BC	$281,149	$29,713
21	Power Corp. of Canada (De10)	33,087	Montreal, QC	$997,763	$27,413
22	Sears Canada (Ja11)ᵇ	31,470	Toronto, ON	$157,541	$4,760
23	Gildan Activewear (Oc10)ᵃ	28,000	Montreal, QC	$46,883	$7,080
24	Rogers Communications (De10)	27,971	Toronto, ON	$435,809	$54,628
25	CGI Group (Se10)	25,000	Montreal, QC	$149,475	$14,511

a. Company reports in US dollars.
b. Figures have been annualized in previous three through five years.
Figures for fiscal periods other than 12 months are annualized for rankings and calculating returns. Foreign currencies are converted into Canadian dollars at the end of the relevant period for balance sheet items and at the average exchange rate for the relevant period for earnings items.
SOURCE: Excerpted and adapted from "The top 1000," Globe and Mail Report on Business Magazine (23 June 2011), http://www.theglobeandmail.com/report-on-business/rob-magazine/top-1000/canadas-50-biggest-employers/article636152/.

over three times that of the previous year. Why did the corporate sector bounce back with such vigour? Economists tell us that the return was not the result of an increase in sales but the result of cost-cutting measures, largely at the expense of workers. In 2009, Fortune 500 firms eliminated 821,000 jobs, representing the largest job loss in their history (Carty, 2010). The corporate elite includes such employers as Walmart, Home Depot, and Target, all retailers known for offering low wages and few opportunities for training and advancement. Workers have not benefited from their growing wealth (Bivens & Mishel, 2015; see Table 11.1).

THE GLOBAL ECONOMY

Today, economic activity knows no national borders. Most large companies operate in a global context. These companies are called *transnational* or *multinational*. The head offices of transnational corporations are located in one

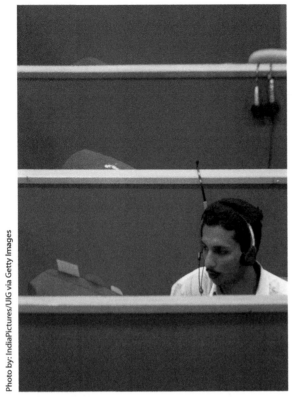

When you order a pizza or report a lost credit card, you may find yourself talking to someone in India—one consequence of the globalization of work and the export of Canadian jobs.

Time Warner owns over 1,000 movie screens outside the United States, the second-largest book publishing business in the world, cable and satellite operations, film and TV production/distribution companies, over 40 magazines (including *Time*, *People*, *Real Simple*, and *Fortune*), music labels, retail parks, and sports teams (Time Warner, 2010; Columbia Journalism Review, 2014). The power of transnational firms is immense.

Think about your own consumption of goods. What proportion would you say are connected to transnational firms? For a broader discussion on the globalization of trade and manufacturing that has occurred over the past several decades, see "Capital, Goods, and Services," p. 331, in **Chapter 14**, "Globalization and Social Change."

country (often the United States), while production facilities are based in others. We see the products of the global economy everywhere we turn. Look at the clothes you wear, the car you drive, the food you eat. Where are they from?

The goal of transnational corporations is profit. Capitalists move beyond national boundaries in an effort to secure the cheapest labour, lowest-cost infrastructure (power, water supply, roads, telephone lines), and production unencumbered by health and safety regulations, minimum-wage and hours-of-work laws, maternity provisions, and so on.

Critics point to the negative consequences of **globalization**. Some argue that globalization causes homogenization of **culture**. Media giants Time Warner and Disney, for instance, distribute many of the same cultural products (television shows, films, videos, books) to audiences around the globe. Among other holdings,

Global capitalism has an uneven impact on different groups of people around the world. Media exposés of, for example, children sewing Nike soccer balls in Pakistani sweatshops for the equivalent of six cents an hour brought worldwide attention to abuses in the garment and sportswear industries. More hidden, says the Maquiladora Solidarity Network, are the adolescent girls, often single mothers, who sew clothes in the maquiladora factories of Central America and Mexico for major retailers such as Walmart and The Gap (Kamel & Hoffman, 1999). We are seeing the intensification of divisions of labour, globally, along the lines of class, sex, and race.

These developments have direct consequences for the organization of work and for the collective power of working people in Canada as well. Many Canadians work under a threat of company relocation to lower-cost areas. This results in a weakening of the power of workers and unions, as many people in Canada have agreed to concessions (giving up past gains) such as pay cuts, loss of vacation pay, and unpaid overtime. The lingering threat of job loss affects the standard of living in Canada as a whole.

We are increasingly seeing the intensification of divisions of labour globally, along the lines of class, sex, and race.

THE CAPITALIST ECONOMY: WHERE PEOPLE WORK

Just as economies undergo change throughout history, so does our relationship to work. With the expansion of some economic sectors and contraction of others, our opportunities for jobs also change. There are four major economic sectors in which people find employment: primary and resource industries, manufacturing, the service sector, and social reproduction (see Table 11.2).

Primary Resource Industry

Decades ago, most Canadians worked in the primary (or resource) industry. Although not always for pay, Indigenous peoples have had an important history in the resource industry (Knight, 1996).

Work in the primary sector involves the extraction of natural resources from our environment. Primary-industry jobs may be found in agricultural production, ranching, mining, forestry, hunting, and fishing.

In the twentieth century the primary sector began to experience a dramatic decline. Many forces contributed to its contraction, notably the demise of family farms and independent fishing businesses, along with a corresponding rise in corporate farming (or "agribusiness") and large fishing enterprises. These developments result in dwindling opportunities for many people, and have especially devastated some towns (for example, Elliot Lake, Ontario) and entire regions (for example, Atlantic Canada).

Manufacturing

Into the twentieth century, many Canadians began to work in the *manufacturing* (or *secondary*) *sector*. Manufacturing involves the processing of raw materials into usable goods and services. If you make your living by assembling vans or piecing together the parts of Barbie dolls, you are employed in manufacturing.

The manufacturing sector in Canada has experienced a slower decline than primary industry. The decline in manufacturing began in the early 1950s. In 1951, manufacturing represented 26.5 per cent of employment in Canada, but by 1995, only 15.2 per cent (Jackson & Robinson, 2000, p. 11). By 2002, the sector entered a crisis phase: in the five previous years more than 30,000 manufacturing jobs were lost, due to plant closures and layoffs (a corporate drive to intensify productivity and increase outsourcing; Jackson, 2009, p. 262). Economist Andrew Jackson (2009, p. 262) notes that the job losses were greatest in the unionized manufacturing sector, among jobs that offered full-time employment with pensions and benefits.

The Service Sector

A massive number of new jobs have been created in the rapidly expanding *service* (or *tertiary*) *sector*. Studies demonstrate that employees who lost jobs in manufacturing were absorbed by the service industry. Indeed, like most other Canadians, many of you have service jobs (yours are likely to be part-time).

The rise of the service industry is linked to the development of a post-industrial, information-based economy and to the growth of a strong consumer culture. This results in a growing need for people to work in information processing and management, marketing, advertising, and servicing. Airline reservation agents, taxi drivers, teachers and professors, daycare staff, bank employees, librarians, and Starbucks baristas are all service workers.

The service sector embraces a wide range of jobs, with some being "good," high-skilled, well-paid jobs, but many others being "bad," poorly paid, dead-end jobs. Jobs in retail trade and food services are at the low end of the hierarchy, while those in finance and business, health, education, and public administration tend to be at the high end (Autor & Dorn, 2013). Much service employment involves both the physical

Table 11.2 ▶ Employment by Industry and Sex, 2013 (000s)

	Both Sexes	Men	Women
All industries	17,731.2	9,295.7	8,435.4
Goods-producing sector	3,883.4	23,060.0	823.4
Agriculture	314.6	222.7	92.0
Forestry, fishing, mining, oil and gas	367.4	300.2	67.2
Utilities	143.5	109.4	34.1
Construction	1,323.7	1,168.2	155.5
Manufacturing	1,734.2	1,259.5	474.7
Services-producing sector	13,847.7	6,235.7	7,612.0
Trade	2,705.2	1,386.4	1,318.8
Transportation and warehousing	863.2	650.4	212.9
Finance, insurance, real estate, and leasing	1,122.3	496.6	625.7
Professional, scientific, and technical services	1,347.7	767.9	579.9
Business, building, and other support services[1]	713.2	387.9	325.9
Educational services	1,289.0	430.8	858.2
Health care and social assistance	2,176.5	388.7	1,787.8
Information, culture, and recreation	782.8	422.7	360.1
Accommodation and food services	1,131.8	474.0	657.9
Other services	769.5	358.6	410.8
Public administration	945.8	471.7	474.0

1. Formerly "Management of companies, administrative, and other support services."
SOURCE: Statistics Canada, "Labour force survey estimates (LFS), by North American Industry Classification System (NAICS), sex and age group, annual (persons unless otherwise noted)," CANSIM Table 282-0008 (2013).

performance of a job and an emotional component. For example, service rests on a big smile and (artificially) personalized interactions. In *The Managed Heart* (1983), Arlie Hochschild explores the emotional work of flight attendants. Low-end service work is characterized by low-trust relationships. With the expectation that their workforce will have only weak loyalties to the company, managers attempt to control employees largely through close direction and surveillance (Pupo & Noack, 2010; Tannock, 2001). It is common practice for employers to use electronic equipment to monitor telephone conversations between employees and clients and to install security cameras to watch retail clerks. More common in the United States than in Canada is drug testing (urinalysis) of prospective employees. Such testing is standard, for example, at Walmart stores (Ehrenreich, 2001; Featherstone, 2004).

SOCIAL REPRODUCTION

The work discussed so far is conducted in what some call the *sphere of production*. Production typically occurs in the public world of factory, office, school, and store, and involves monetary exchange.

However, many people spend hours each day doing work that is not officially recorded as part of the economy. This labour is called **social reproduction**. Social reproduction involves activities for which there is no direct economic exchange. Often, this work is performed within family households by women. This includes hours spent buying groceries, planning and cooking meals, folding laundry, chauffeuring children, vacuuming, managing the household budget, caring for aging relatives, and supervising homework. The instrumental value of such activities is hidden; they are often deemed "labour[s] of love" (Luxton, 1980).

But what would happen if women and other family members no longer performed this labour? What would it cost if employers or the state had to ensure that workers were fed, clothed, nurtured, and counselled? Economist Marilyn Waring says breastfeeding, for example,

Many young Canadians are employed in the service sector today.

Jim West/Alamy Stock Photo

is "a major reproductive activity carried out only by women, and this thoroughly confuses statisticians' and economists' production models" (1996, p. 86) such that they have no means of measuring the economic value of the reproduction of human life. According to the Vanier Institute of the Family, family members in Canada spend 20 billion hours annually performing housework. Unpaid labour is valued at no less than $197 billion, or the equivalent of 10 million full-time jobs (cited in Nelson, 2010, p. 253).

The system of capitalism benefits tremendously from the performance of unpaid labour, yet for many years even sociologists did not consider this "work."

The Informal Economy

Also hidden from official growth figures is a range of economic activities that are not reported to the government. These activities make up the **informal** (or underground) **economy** and include, for example, jobs done for cash that have no paper trail, such as babysitting, cleaning homes, sewing clothes, doing people's income tax returns, peddling knock-off watches, and dealing drugs. In the downtown areas of major cities in Canada, you can see people of all ages trying to eke out a living in the informal sector.

We do not know the precise size of the underground economy. We have only estimates with much variation across the globe. According to the International Labour Organization (ILO), in developing countries the informal economy has been estimated to involve one-half to three-quarters of the non-agricultural labour force and is generally a larger source of employment for women than for men (Lapeyre, Ameratunga, & Possenti, 2012).

Increasingly, people are turning to "hidden work" in order to survive as opportunities in the formal economy become scarce. Unfortunately, most people who rely on the informal economy for a living face precarious, unstable "careers" in unregulated environments.

> **TIME to REFLECT**
>
> What examples of work in the informal economy can you observe in daily life? What social groups are most likely to work in the informal economy? Can you identify some of the benefits and constraints of working in this economic sector?

THE SOCIAL ORGANIZATION OF WORK TODAY

Revolutionary New Technology

Popular writers and scholars are talking about the emergence of a new world of work in a "knowledge society"—a world that offers more opportunity, more leisure time, and more enjoyable work than in the past. Are these assertions founded? Do people now have better jobs than their parents and grandparents did?

Most people agree that new technology can eliminate routine, repetitive tasks, thereby freeing people to perform more challenging work. Think, for example, about preparing a research paper without a computer or access to the Internet. Yet some sociologists argue that at the same time, technology has created new forms of inequality. While it has created new, more challenging jobs for some, many others have lost their jobs (or skills) as a result of technological change. In the **service economy**, for instance, employers rely extensively on computers and microelectronics to streamline work processes. In banking, the introduction of automated bank machines has made redundant

the work of thousands of tellers. In various industries, computers can effectively enforce productivity quotas and monitor workers (Fox & Sugiman, 1999; Lewchuk & Robertson, 2006).

Precarious Work

Some writers have extolled the benefits of new trends in management methods. Over the past few decades in business circles, one would hear buzzwords such as "workplace restructuring," "downsizing," and "lean production." These concepts belong to a managerial approach called *flexibility*. One popular practice, termed **numerical flexibility**, involves shrinking or eliminating the core workforce (in continuous jobs and full-time positions) and replacing them with workers in non-standard (or contingent) employment. **Non-standard (or precarious) work** describes various employment arrangements such as part-time work, temporary (seasonal and other part-year) work, contracting out or outsourcing (work that was previously done in-house), and self-employment. Non-standard work is far more tenuous than work of the past (Vosko, 2000, 2003, 2006).

Non-standard work arrangements now characterize most spheres of employment. We need look no further than the university or college for

"That's the one day we experimented with giving our employees guaranteed job security."

What are some effects of the rise of non-standard or precarious work?

examples. You may discover that many of your courses are taught by part-time or contract instructors, some of whom hold PhDs. The university pays them to teach on a course-by-course or session-by-session basis, and they seldom receive assurances of stable employment. Like Marx's "reserve army of labour," non-standard employees provide owners and managers with a ready supply of labour to "hire and fire" as the market demands. Employers invest minimally in these workers and offer them limited commitment. Corporations reduce labour costs through laying off permanent, full-time workers and replacing them with part-time, temporary, and contract labour (Cranford, Vosko, & Zukewich, 2006; Vosko, 2000, 2006; see Table 11.3).

Table 11.3 ▶ Full-Time and Part-Time Employment by Sex and Age Group, Canada, 2009–2013 (000s)

	2009	2010	2011	2012	2013
Both sexes					
Total	16,813.1	17,041.0	17,306.2	17,507.7	17,731.2
15–24 years	2,417.9	2,451.3	2,470.6	2,428.2	2,450.2
25–44 years	7,359.2	7,389.8	7,472.5	7,582.2	7,678.5
45 years and over	6,982.0	7,199.9	7,363.1	7,497.3	7,602.5
Full-time	13,578.9	13,736.7	13,995.0	14,212.9	14,380.2
15–24 years	1,312.9	1,274.3	1,299.0	1,279.5	1,282.2
25–44 years	6,447.7	6,460.3	6,543.6	6,652.6	6,740.5
45 years and over	5,818.3	6,002.1	6,152.4	6,280.8	6,357.5
Part-time	3,234.2	3,304.4	3,311.2	3,294.8	3,351.0
15–24 years	1,159.0	1,177.0	1,171.5	1,148.7	1,168.0
25–44 years	911.5	929.5	928.9	928.7	938.0
45 years and over	1,163.7	1,197.8	1,210.7	1,216.4	1,245.0
Men					
Full-time	7,707.2	7,830.9	7,979.5	8,101.2	8,177.0
15–24 years	752.0	736.2	747.3	737.4	739.9
25–44 years	3,615.7	3,648.6	3,695.5	3,763.4	3,845.6
45 years and over	3,339.6	3,446.1	3,536.7	3,600.4	3,126.2
Part-time	1,053.4	1,080.7	1,105.6	1,086.5	1,118.8
15–24 years	473.7	480.3	492.8	480.6	493.1
25–44 years	223.4	228.9	238.6	236.8	235.6
45 years and over	356.4	371.5	374.2	369.6	390.1
Women					
Full-time	5,871.7	5,905.8	6,015.6	6,111.7	6,203.2
15–24 years	560.9	538.1	551.8	542.1	542.4
25–44 years	2,832.1	2,811.7	2,848.1	2,889.2	2,948.6
45 years and over	2,478.7	2,556.0	2,615.6	2,680.4	2,712.2
Part-time	2,180.8	2,223.7	2,205.6	2,208.3	2,232.2
15–24 years	685.3	696.7	678.7	668.6	674.9
25–44 years	688.1	700.6	690.3	692.9	702.4
45 years and over	807.3	826.3	836.5	846.8	854.9

SOURCE: Statistics Canada, "Full-time and part-time employment by sex and age group," http://www.statcan.gc.ca/tables-tableaux/sum-som/l01/cst01/labor12-eng.htm.

Non-standard workers receive relatively low wages and few benefits. Consequently, many people in this type of work often resort to holding multiple jobs to make ends meet (Jackson, 2009, pp. 74–77; Lewchuk, deWolff, et al., 2006).

> ## TIME to REFLECT ●━━ ━━
>
> Have you ever worked at what could be termed a "McJob"? What do you think it is like to work at a "McJob" for the rest of your working life? In what ways do you think precarious employment is gendered, racialized, or both?

THE CHANGING FACE OF LABOUR: DIVERSITY AMONG WORKERS

Workplaces today are becoming increasingly diverse. Only a minority of families rely on a single paycheque. Indigenous Canadians and racialized people, some of whom are immigrants to this country, have a stronger-than-ever presence working in big cities such as Vancouver, Toronto, and Montreal. Social awareness and the public visibility of disabled workers from various social and cultural groups is slowly growing. As well, the workforce has become more highly educated and younger.

Gendered Work

In Canada, the participation of women in the paid labour force has increased steadily over the past four decades. In the mid-1970s, the labour-force participation rate of women aged 15 to 64 was slightly over one-half. By 2016, it was 71.3 per cent (OECD, 2016). Most striking is the growth in the employment rates of mothers of children under the age of six. The two-breadwinner (or *dual-earner*) family is now the norm.

Many people of university age today are unaware of the blatant sexual inequalities of the past. Women today are building their careers on a feminist foundation. If not for the challenges

---

HUMAN ▬▬ DIVERSITY   Offshore Migrant Farm Workers: A New Form of Slavery?

While they are not really slaves in the classical sense of the term, the 16,000 workers who come to Canada every year from the Caribbean and Mexico to work in Canadian agriculture are a form of unfree labour. "Slaves" may be too strong a term to describe them, but their condition of unfreedom does strongly resemble slavery.

These workers come to Canada under labour contracts that specify how long they can remain in the country and the conditions under which they must work. Workers are allowed to stay in Canada for three to eight months every year. When their contracts expire, or if they breach one of the terms of their contract, they must leave the country. Workers pay for a portion of their transportation and must pay their employers a portion of their accommodation costs. Workers may bunk five or six to a room and live in hot, overcrowded conditions. However, the main reason that they are considered unfree labourers is their inability to quit or change jobs in Canada without permission from their employer and a representative of the federal government. If they quit without permission, they are subject to deportation from Canada.

Why does this condition of unfreedom matter? After all, some people think that migrant workers are lucky to be here, compared to where they come from. They invariably make more money here than they would back home, so they should be grateful for the opportunity to come here to work, even temporarily. Yet even though no one is forcing them to come to Canada to work, it does matter that they are a form of unfree labour. Their lack of choice when it comes to whom they work for and their inability to find better-paying jobs in other sectors of the Canadian economy mean that farm employers have tremendous power over migrant workers. In many cases, workers are fearful of saying "no" when they are asked to do jobs that are dangerous and might harm their health. Employers who have a captive labour force do not have incentives to improve wages or working conditions.

—Vic Satzewich, McMaster University

mounted by women's rights activists, university lecture halls would be filled exclusively by men, women would not be permitted entry into the professions or management, and paid employment would not be an option after marriage.

But inequalities persist. In spite of increases in female labour-force participation, women and men are by no means equal in the labour market. The **social institution** of work is still a gendered one. Some women have made inroads in non-traditional fields, but the majority remain concentrated in female-dominated occupations such as retail salesperson, secretary, cashier, registered nurse, elementary school teacher, babysitter, and receptionist, while men are more commonly truck drivers, janitors, farmers, motor vehicle mechanics, and construction trade helpers, for example (Statistics Canada, 2008). Occupational segregation by sex has lessened somewhat over time, but more because of the entry of men into female-dominated occupations than the reverse.

As well, women (in addition to young people regardless of gender) are more likely than men to be employed on a part-time and temporary basis, making up approximately 70 per cent of the part-time workforce in Canada. We also see that self-employed men are more likely than self-employed women to hire others, with female-run businesses more likely to be in the less lucrative service sector (Kochhar, 2015, p. 10). Labour market segregation by sex and the over-representation of women in precarious employment contribute to gender-based differences in earnings.

In 2011, among full-time and part-time workers, we find that on average a woman earned 72 cents for every dollar earned by a man (Lambert & McInturff, 2016). The gap persists even when we control for education. While Canadian women posted better academic achievements than men, women with a post-secondary education still earn on average 71 per cent of the salary of men who possess similar qualifications (Williams, 2010.)

Immigrant women, women of colour (or racialized women), and Indigenous women bear the brunt of income and occupational polarization by sex. Statistics Canada reports that of those employed full-time, full-year in 2005, visible-minority women, for example, had average annual earnings of roughly $4,000 less than their "non-visible" equivalents (Chui & Maheux, 2011.)

Visibly racialized working-class women and some immigrant women have come to occupy job ghettos. Indeed, the labour of many visibly racialized working-class people is rendered invisible. Too often, private domestic workers and nannies, hotel and office cleaners, taxi drivers, health-care aides, and dishwashers—all performing indispensable labour—are treated as part of the backdrop (Arat-Koc, 1990; Das Gupta, 1996; Sherman, 2007).

 Why do you think visibly racialized working-class people have been rendered invisible? For more on discrimination and racialization, see **Chapter 8**, "Ethnic and Race Relations."

Today, many young women plan to both have a career and raise a family but are not quite sure how they will combine the two. Feminist researchers have demonstrated how the concept of "career" is gendered, built on a masculine model. Career success depends on the assumption of a wife at home—a helper who will pick up children from school, arrange dinner parties, and free the "breadwinner" to work late or on weekends and to travel out of town on business.

Feminist analysis calls attention to the complex link between paid and unpaid labour, employment, and family (Corman & Luxton, 2007; Eichler et al., 2010; Fox, 2009). With two breadwinners both spending increasing hours in their paid jobs, families are under enormous pressure. We see an intensification of (unpaid) family work, more stress, and growing tensions within families as people try to cope.

Race and Racialized Work

Barriers faced by the visibly racialized, Indigenous Canadians, and some immigrant groups are most often demonstrated in unemployment and earnings disparities. Indigenous people make up a tiny percentage of the working-age population, yet over the next 20 years will constitute a sizable share of new entrants to the labour force (Jackson, 2009, p. 146). Although one should be wary of making broad generalizations about the diverse group of people who identify as Indigenous, clearly, on the whole, they are disadvantaged in the labour market. Disadvantage is linked to systemic discrimination, in addition to low levels of education and geographic residence (Jackson, 2009, pp. 146–147).

The **unemployment rate** for Indigenous peoples is high compared to that for the Canadian population as a whole. In addition, more than half are in part-time, insecure employment and are concentrated in marginalized sectors of the economy. The economic prospects for those who live on reserves are even bleaker. Close to half of the on-reserve Indigenous population live in poverty (Jackson & Robinson, 2000, p. 71).

The category "visible racialized" is likewise quite diverse, containing notable differences according to class, education, and citizenship status. By 2031 in Canada, it is expected that one in three workers will be defined as being racialized (the official census term is "visible minority" and excludes Indigenous Canadians) (Malenfant, Morency, & Martel, 2011.) In 2011, 20.6 per cent of Canadians were foreign-born (Morency, Caron

Malenfant, & MacIsaac, 2017). According to the 2006 census, visible-minority workers aged 25 to 44 with a university degree earned 74.6 per cent of the median for the group as a whole, while "non–visible-minority" earners made 105 per cent of the median (Jackson, 2009, pp. 145–146). Typically, recent immigrants are younger than the labour force as a whole, but they also have more schooling. One problem is that foreign credentials are not always respected in Canada, contributing to a high concentration of racialized immigrants in low-wage jobs (Jackson & Robinson, 2000, pp. 69–70; see Table 11.4).

Because of racial and cultural differences, people experience work in distinct ways. In their classic study *Who Gets the Work*, Frances Henry and Effie Ginzberg (1985) found a striking incidence of discrimination directed at job seekers. For example, of the job seekers who made

Table 11.4 ▶ Median Annual Income of All Persons

	All	Men	Women
Not a visible minority	$31,286	$38,086	$25,589
Visible minority	$29,878	$36,211	$24,606

SOURCE: Statistics Canada, 2011 National Household Survey, Catalogue 99-014-X2011041 (2013).

inquiries by telephone, those who had accents (especially South Asian and Caribbean) were often quickly screened out by employers.

Youth

Today, youth (15–24 years old) constitute a much smaller share of the population than in past years. Nevertheless, the youth labour market is expanding at a significant rate. Young people today must confront harsh economic conditions, with the youth unemployment rate roughly 50 per cent higher than that of the population as a whole. Studies suggest that young people want high-quality work—work that is interesting and challenging and that provides a sense of accomplishment (Lowe, 2000). And youth have been increasing their human capital to acquire such jobs, especially through more education.

But while Canadian youth are better schooled on the whole than youth in some other parts of the world, they are also working less and in jobs for which they feel that they are overqualified. Young people are most likely to be employed in low-paying service-sector jobs such as fast-food restaurants, clothing stores, and grocery stores.

Some argue that the youth labour market is well suited to the new goals of managerial flexibility. Employers invest in the belief that young people will have a limited commitment to the firm and that they are in jobs temporarily as a stop-gap measure discontinuous with their adult careers and identities (Tannock, 2001). Stuart Tannock explains that youth themselves partially accept the popular **ideology** that positions them "as a separate class of workers who deserve less than adult workers do. Good jobs

OPEN FOR DISCUSSION — International Day of Persons with Disabilities

December 3rd is the International Day of Persons with Disabilities, a day when we celebrate the contributions of persons with disabilities in our communities, and commit to removing barriers and creating an inclusive and accessible society for all.

Canadians with disabilities commonly face severe challenges finding adequate and secure incomes. People with disabilities have lower employment rates and higher rates of underemployment than Canadians as a whole. They are at greater risk of living with low incomes than Canadians in general. The Daily Bread Food Bank's *Who's Hungry* report finds that the share of people with disabilities using food banks has nearly doubled since 2005 (from 17% to 28%), and the *HungerCount 2014* report reveals that nearly one in five households using food banks depends on disability-related benefits as their primary income source.

The structure of disability benefits compounds the problem: for instance, the Disability Tax Credit is a non-refundable tax credit, meaning that persons with disabilities need a certain level of income in order to benefit from the tax credit in the first place. The Canada Pension Plan (CPP) disability benefit requires that a disability be severe and prolonged, making it difficult for Canadians suffering from

fluctuating and episodic disabilities (like multiple sclerosis) to access the CPP disability benefit.

To make matters worse, the federal government has moved to make it harder for Canadians living with disabilities to access Canadian Pension Plan disability benefits.

CPP disability benefits, like CPP retirement benefits, are too low to enable Canadians to live in dignity in retirement. The maximum amount that a CPP disability beneficiary can receive is 75% of the retirement benefit they are entitled to, plus a flat amount ($457.60 in December 2014). For someone entitled to receive the average monthly CPP retirement benefit ($540.56 in October 2014), this works out to just $863.02 a month.

Canadian Labour Congress (CLC) is calling on the federal government to agree to a fully funded, phased-in doubling of future CPP benefits to achieve retirement security for all Canadians, including Canadians with disabilities. The labour movement's plan also aims to increase the Guaranteed Income Supplement, which would have a significant impact on people with disabilities who have had lower incomes or who have been unable to work.

SOURCE: http://www.canadianlabour.ca/news-room/statements/december-3rd-international-day-persons-disabilities

are predominantly the privilege of adulthood. Young workers must be content at first to spend their time in a tier of lower-quality service and retail employment. Dreams of meaningful work must be deferred" (2001, p. 109). Consequently, youth are more pliable and passive. Also, because their jobs are viewed as transient, youths are less likely to become unionized. All these features render them an exploitable source of labour.

Despite the popular view that young people are not especially concerned about their conditions of work, much evidence points to the contrary: "Teenagers and young adults working in these industries, who expect to have long lives ahead of them, worry that their jobs, which are supposed to be meaningless, stop-gap places of employment, will have lasting and detrimental effects on their bodies and future life activities" (Tannock, 2001, p. 54).

WORKERS' COPING AND RESISTANCE: THE STRUGGLE FOR DIGNITY AND RIGHTS

Finding Meaning in Work

Regardless of the differences among Canadian workers, most Canadians want work that is personally fulfilling (Lowe, 2000). People have a powerful desire to maintain dignity at work

Ontario teachers participate in a one-day strike action in Toronto, December 2012.

(Hodson, 2001). Some of us are fortunate to hold jobs that offer challenges, in which we can exercise autonomy and from which we can reap fruitful economic rewards. But even "good jobs" are not always meaningful, and many jobs are rarely rewarding.

Sociologists find that no matter how meaningless the job, people seek meaning in their work. People who have boring, routine jobs, for example, may make a game out of their work, varying repetitions, altering pace and intensity, imagining the lives of customers. As well, the social component of work (peer relations) is frequently a source of pleasure. Relationships with co-workers often make the job itself more bearable if not meaningful. Most people report that they are generally satisfied with their jobs (Lowe, 2000). On close examination, though, discontent brews near the surface. A majority of workers say that their jobs are somewhat or highly stressful, that they are not sufficiently involved, recognized, and rewarded, and that their talents are underutilized (Lowe, 2000). In addition, there are high rates of absenteeism, oppositional attitudes, shirking of duties, pilfering, and even destruction of company property. But in the face of a competitive job market, family responsibilities, consumer debt, and, for some, limited marketable skills, quitting a job is not always an option.

Faced with unfair, unsafe, and sometimes unchallenging work, workers will be discontented. They will find ways to make changes, to resist. The question is, how? Individual acts of coping and resistance may give workers the feeling of agency and control, but insofar as they are individual acts, they rarely result in a fundamental or widespread change in conditions of work. In order to effect large-scale change, people must resort to collective measures.

Professions and Negotiating Professional Control

Securing professional control is an option for middle-class people who possess formally recognized credentials and can claim expertise in an area. When we think of a *professional*, who comes to mind? Physicians, educators, psychiatrists, dentists, lawyers, engineers, accountants. Some sociologists (proponents of trait theory) have attempted to define professionals with reference to a checklist of characteristics (Freidson, 1970). This checklist includes possession of a body of esoteric or abstract knowledge, reliance on a specialized technical language or vocabulary, and membership in associations that control entry and membership in the occupation through licensing, accreditation, and regulation.

Critics argue that trait theory does not fully explain how and why some occupations come to be defined as professional while others do not. Rather than list a series of traits that define a profession, Terence Johnson (1972) highlights the resources available to different occupational groups. These resources have enabled physicians, psychologists, and lawyers to define themselves as distinct from other groups such as managers, clerical workers, and massage therapists. In focusing on the process of professionalization, critical theorists have noted that at the heart of the struggle to professionalize are relations of power and control. Feminist scholars have recently offered a more nuanced analysis of the ways in which *patriarchy* (a system of male dominance), too, structures the process of securing professional authority and control (Adams, 2000; Witz, 1992).

Labour Unions and Labour's Agenda

The struggle to professionalize is not one in which many Canadians will be engaged—it is largely an exclusive one. More people in Canada, and globally, turn to another form of collective action to secure their rights and dignity in the workplace: unionization. Just as campaigns to secure professional control are based in the middle class, the struggle to unionize in this country has traditionally been one of white men in blue-collar jobs. Increasing numbers of women, the visibly racialized, white-collar workers, and middle-class employees have joined the ranks of the labour movement.

When most of us think of unions, strikes come to mind. Some of us may view labour unionists as greedy, overpaid workers demanding higher wages and in the process disrupting our lives, transportation, communication—even our garbage collection. We may owe this perception to dominant media representations of unions.

The labour movement in this country goes far beyond this narrow and unfair characterization. The basic premise of the organized labour movement is taking collective action through the process of bargaining a contract. This *collective agreement* is the outcome of days, weeks, or even months of negotiations between two parties: worker representatives and company representatives. The contract is a legally binding document, signed by both the employer and the union. Only if the two parties cannot reach an agreement can there be a strike. The actual incidence of strikes in Canada is, in fact, low. Recently, throughout the entire country, there have only been 300 to 400 work stoppages per year, involving 100,000 to 400,000 workers. While one-third of all employees belong to unions, annual time lost due to strikes has typically been far less than one-tenth of 1 per cent of total working time (Jackson, 2009, p. 202). The strike is usually a measure of last resort. The vast majority of contracts that come up for renewal are settled without resorting to strike action. Workers in the nineteenth century first struggled to secure union representation in an effort to protect themselves against excessively long work days, extremely hazardous work environments, low pay, and blatant favouritism on the job. Today, labour–management conflict arises over a host of issues. Not only are wages an item of dispute, but companies and union representatives also negotiate benefits packages, job security, the implementation of technological change, outsourcing, concessions, and anti-harassment policies. Because of the struggles of union members, Canadian workers now have the right to refuse unsafe work, the right to participate in company-sponsored pension plans, and, in some cases, access to on-site daycare centres.

The gains of unionized workers have spilled over into the wider society. Both unionized and non-unionized workers now have employment standards, (un)employment insurance, a standard work day of eight hours, a five-day work week, overtime premiums, vacation pay, health benefits, and sick-leave provisions. Unions have been pivotal in lobbying governments to introduce worker-friendly legislation.

Union Membership

Unions represent roughly one in three workers (29.6 per cent in 2010) and 18.7 per cent of private-sector workers (Statistics Canada 2010c). Sex-based differences in union density (membership) have now disappeared. In fact, 2006 marked the first year in Canadian history in which women outnumbered men as union members (Jackson, 2009, p. 227). In part, growth in female membership reflects the high rate of unionization in the female-dominated public service (for example, in Crown corporations, education, and health care). It is also, in part, a result of union organizing drives in the 1990s in private service companies (Jackson & Robinson, 2000). As well, over the past several decades, the decrease in female union members has been less dramatic than that of men. The unionization rate for men has been dropping since the 1960s. This trend is largely attributable to a shrinking proportion of jobs in traditionally male-dominated and heavily unionized sectors, such as primary/resource, manufacturing, and construction (Jackson & Robinson, 2000).

The Union Advantage

There is no doubt that unionization benefits workers. Collective bargaining has secured advantages in wages, benefits, job security, and extended health plans. This has been called the *union advantage*. The union wage premium in particular is greatest for (traditionally disadvantaged) workers who would otherwise be low paid. Unionization tends to compress wage and benefit differentials, promoting an equalization of wages and working conditions among unionized workforces. In 2014, for example, average hourly earnings of unionized workers in Canada were $28.22, and for non-unionized workers, $23.03—a union advantage of 28.4 per cent

(Statistics Canada 2014d). The difference in wages between unionized and non-unionized women is even greater. In 2007, for example, the union advantage for women was $6.08 as compared to $3.18 for men (Jackson, 2009, p. 208).

> **TIME to REFLECT**
>
> Imagine you are employed in a non-unionized workplace, and a union organizer seeks to unionize it. Would you support this? What consequences would your involvement have for you and your co-workers? Do you think that youth around the world are reigniting movements for progressive social change?

CONCLUSION: WORK IN THE FUTURE, OUR FUTURE AS WORKERS

Workers and unions have limited powers. While newspaper headlines promote the "big" collective bargaining gains of the most strongly organized unions, most unionized workers across the country are still struggling to attain basic rights that others managed to secure years ago. Every day in small workplaces, employees (unionized and the unorganized) negotiate their rights. More often now than in the past, these are women, the visibly racialized, people with disabilities—not members of the dominant groups in this country.

These struggles continue to be difficult, particularly in the context of the current assault on unions. Powerful corporations such as Walmart and McDonald's effectively curb workers' rights to organize by simply closing down stores, mounting strong union decertification campaigns, or stalling when it comes time to bargain a first contract. The power of workers and their movements is even more severely circumscribed by the aggression of global capitalists, many of whom are openly supported by networks of governments in both developing and developed nations. Whether you work part-time at The Gap, labour a 60-hour week in a steel factory, freelance as a consultant, or find sporadic office employment through a temporary help agency, you face a challenge.

Regardless of theoretical perspective or political agenda, scholars today are debating the nature of the challenge of the transformation of work. Young people entering the labour market for the first time and middle-aged people confronting reconfigured jobs and refashioned workplaces both are part of this transformation. Workers, young and old, must work in order to survive, to nurture families, to participate in life. Therefore, it is crucial to know the debate, engage in it, and perhaps transform the world of work according to your own vision.

Questions for Critical Thought

1. If you are not currently employed, where do you plan to find work? How does this plan depart from your parents' and grandparents' work histories? What factors shape (or constrain) your work-related aspirations?

2. How would you describe the relationship between your formal education and the work you plan to do after graduating?

3. A prevailing view is that the youth today are merely "stop-gap" workers. As they mature, they will move on to better, more secure, and fulfilling employment. Thus, their conditions of work are not problematic. Why should sociologists bother writing about youths at work?

4. Do you believe that who you are (your age, gender, education, ethnic, racial and social class background, etc.) is an important indicator of the type of work you will perform? In what ways?

5. Many gender-based inequalities persist in employment. Identify some of these inequalities. What are some formal and informal barriers to equality between women and men in the labour market today? How would you confront them?

6. Some people would argue that today, union leaders and members face new challenges, perhaps more formidable than those of the past. Identify and discuss some of the new challenges that confront the labour movement in this country.

Sociological Explorations

1. Think about the work that you perform in a typical day. What proportion is paid and what is unpaid? Try to calculate the economic worth of the unpaid work that you do. How much should you be paid for it?

2. Open your closet and take an inventory of where your clothes are produced. Using the Internet, try to assess the cost of labour associated with your most prized article of clothing. How does that compare to what you actually paid for it?

Recommended Readings

Lehmann, W., & Adams, T. (2016). Labour markets, inequality, and the future of work. In E. Grabb, J.G. Reitz, & M. Hwang (Eds), *Social inequality in Canada: Dimensions of disadvantage* (6th edn). Toronto, ON: Oxford University Press.
This exemplary piece of Canadian scholarship looks at the important intersections of work, education, and social inequality.

Luxton, M., & Corman, J. (2001). *Getting by in hard times: Gendered labour at home and on the job.* Toronto, ON: University of Toronto Press.
Based on a series of interviews with women and men in families having one member employed at Stelco's manufacturing plant in Hamilton, Ontario, the authors demonstrate how working families are coping in the face of the economic restructuring that began in the 1980s.

Pupo, N.J., & Thomas, M.P. (Eds). (2010). *Interrogating the economy: Restructuring work in the 21st century*. Toronto, ON: University of Toronto Press.
This timely collection of articles based on Canadian research explores the many features that define work today in the context of economic and political change.

Sherman, R. (2007). *Class acts: Service and inequality in luxury hotels*. Berkeley, CA: University of California Press.
This engaging ethnographic study of the invisible and semi-visible workers in two luxury hotels makes a sobering comment on class relations and the normalization of inequality in the service industry in the United States.

Sugiman, P. (1994). *Labour's dilemma: The gender politics of auto workers, 1939–1979*. Toronto, ON: University of Toronto Press.
Sugiman explores the ways in which gender politics shaped the southern Ontario auto manufacturing industry and the Canadian Region of the United Auto Workers.

Recommended Websites

Unifor
www.unifor.org
Unifor is the largest public sector union in Canada, with over 300,000 members working in all major economic fields. It was formed in 2013 through a union of the Canadian Auto Workers Union (CAW) and the Communications, Energy and Paperworkers Union of Canada (CEP).

Canadian Centre for Policy Alternatives (CCPA)
www.policyalternatives.ca
The CCPA offers an alternative to the message that we have no choice about the policies that affect our lives, undertaking and promoting research on issues of social and economic justice.

Centre for Labour Management Relations (CLMR)
www.ryerson.ca/clmr
The CLMR is an initiative at Ryerson University and its website is a valuable resource for anyone interested in the latest developments in the study of paid employment.

International Labour Organization (ILO)
www.ilo.org
The ILO was founded in 1919 and is now an agency of the United Nations. Its mandate is to promote and realize standards, fundamental principles, and rights at work.

Labour/Le Travail
www.lltjournal.ca/index.php/llt
Labour/Le Travail is the leading journal for labour studies in Canada. In operation since 1976, it publishes historical and contemporary articles on all aspects of work in Canada.

LabourStart
www.labourstart.org
LabourStart is a Web-based news organization that provides information on a variety of labour-related issues around the globe. This site includes anything from job advertisements in Australia to information on strikes in the United Kingdom.

Key Terms

capitalism An economic system characterized by a relationship of unequal economic exchange between capitalists (employers) and workers. Because they do not own the means of production, workers must sell their labour to employers in exchange for a wage or salary. Capitalism is a market-based system driven by the pursuit of profit for personal gain.

culture At its broadest, the sum total of the human-produced environment (the objects, artifacts, ideas, beliefs, and values that make up the symbolic and learned aspects of human society), as separate from the natural environment; more often refers to norms, values, beliefs, ideas, and meanings; an assumption that different societies are distinguished by their shared beliefs and customary behaviours; the products and services delivered by a number of industries—theatre, music, film, publishing, and so on.

globalization A social process in which the constrains of geographic, economic, cultural, and social arrangements have receded and have been replaced by processes that extend beyond state boundaries.

identity How we see ourselves and how others see us. How we view ourselves is a product of our history and of our interpretation of others' reactions to us.

ideology A system of beliefs, ideas, and norms, reflecting the interests and experiences of a group, class, or subculture, that legitimizes or justifies the existing unequal distribution of power and privilege.

informal economy A wide range of legal and illegal economic activities that are not officially reported to the government.

means of production A term used by Marxists to refer to wealth-generating property such as land, factories, and machinery; the ways goods are produced for sale on the market, including all the workers, machinery, and capital that such production needs.

non-standard (precarious) work Jobs that are characterized by an increasingly tenuous or unstable relationship between employer and employee, including part-time employment, temporary employment, contract work, multiple job-holding, and self-employment; also termed "contingent work" and "casual work."

numerical flexibility Part of a general managerial approach that rests on flexibility in employment; it involves shrinking or eliminating the core workforce (in continuous, full-time positions) and replacing them with workers in non-standard employment.

power In the classic formulation, the ability to exercise one's will, even in the face of opposition from others.

service economy The economic sector in which most Canadians currently are employed. It is based on the provision of services rather than on a tangible product. Also called the "tertiary sector."

social institutions A stable, well-acknowledged pattern of social relationships that endures over time.

social relationships Interactions of people in a society.

social reproduction A range of unpaid activities that help to reproduce workforces daily and over generations.

unemployment rate The number of people who do not have a job but are actively looking for a job, divided by the labour force (which includes both the employed and unemployed), expressed as a percentage. Those who do not have a job and are not looking for one are considered not in the labour force.

12 | Religion in Canada

LORI G. BEAMAN

In this chapter you will:

▶ Explore definitions of religion and spirituality

▶ Learn about the changing religious demography of Canada and its potential impact

▶ Consider new religious movements and minority religious groups

▶ Examine the concept of secularization

▶ Explore the relationship between law and religion

▶ Think about the gendered dimensions of religious participation

INTRODUCTION

Religion is an important point of identity for many people in Canada. Almost daily, we hear or read about an aspect of someone's religious beliefs that bumps up against a regulation, law, or policy. Recently, hearings on the Quebec government's proposed "Charter of Values" took place before the National Assembly (National Assembly of Quebec, 2013). If passed, the Charter would have banned religious symbols such as **hijabs**, **kippas**, turbans, and visible crucifixes among public servants, including judges, police, teachers and school employees, and hospital workers. It garnered intense media attention and debate, reflected in newspaper and magazine articles, website postings, and letters to the editor (see Lefebvre, 2013; Friedman, 2013; Peritz, 2013; CBC News, 2014). At the same time, a controversy erupted at York University when a professor of sociology rejected a student's request to be excluded from group work with female classmates. The student said that his religion forbade him from having such close contact with women. A national discussion ensued that was framed largely in terms of competing rights to gender equality and freedom of religion (CBC News, 2014; Bakht et al., 2014; Elghawaby, 2014). No matter how one may feel about religion, it matters to a good many people. For social scientists, religion constitutes an important area of study in our pursuit to better understand social life.

Sociologists of religion do not question the veracity of particular sets of religious beliefs. In other words, we do not care, for example, whether gods exist or whether Raelians have really had contact with extraterrestrial beings. Rather, our concern is with how human beings act out their religious beliefs and practices, as well as how religious beliefs and social institutions intersect. How are certain sets of beliefs legitimized? What is constructed as being a "religion"? What are the power relations embedded in these processes? In other words, who gets to decide whether a religion is really a religion?

Marxist Influence

Until relatively recently, sociology—as a discipline—did not take the study of religion particularly seriously. There are a number of reasons for this. First, a good number of scholars accepted the popular wisdom that we live in a secular society. However, religion remains an important part of the Canadian social fabric and is likely to continue to do so.

Another reason for the lack of attention to religion within sociology is the strong Marxist tradition, particularly in Canadian sociology. Marx worried about the power of religion and in fact stated, "Religion is the sigh of the oppressed creature, the heart of a heartless world" (Marx, as cited in Raines, 2002, p. 167). While he recognized the ability of religion to offer solace in times of trouble, Marx worried that the happiness offered by religion was illusory and that it distracted people from seeking real happiness (which in Marx's view inevitably involved the transformation of economic arrangements and the end of capitalism). Marx concluded that "the abolition of religion as the illusory happiness of the people is the demand for their real happiness" (Marx, as cited in Raines, 2002, p. 167). Some sociologists understood this statement as a licence to minimize the importance of religion in society, to exclude religion as a variable from research, and to ignore its importance in theoretical work. This hardly reflects the spirit in which Marx wrote (one would think something deemed to be so powerful would need to be studied carefully) and has resulted in a paucity of research about religion and social life.

Moreover, some significant social movements have been grounded in a combination of religion and Marxism, most specifically liberation theology, which began in South and Central America in the 1960s and was based on the premise that part of the mission of Christianity is to bring "justice to the poor and oppressed, particularly through political activism" (Smith, 1991, p. 12). Its goal was to effect socio-economic change, and indeed, it became so sufficiently threatening that it was condemned by the Vatican. Several Latin American bishops were deposed for their continued fight for social and economic justice based on Marxist principles.

 For a more complete discussion of Karl Marx's theory and critique of the capitalist system, see "Karl Marx," p. 14, in **Chapter 1**, "Sociological Theory and Research Methods."

RELIGION IN PROFILE

What does religion in Canada look like from a demographic perspective? Mainstream Christianity has dominated Canada's historic landscape and, to some extent, continues to do so. Mainstream Christianity includes Roman Catholicism and Protestant groups such as the United Church of Canada and the Anglican Church of Canada. Groups outside of these two broad categories make up a relatively small proportion of the religious picture in Canada, but as we will see, that picture is rapidly changing. Generally, Canadians remain affiliated with the religion of their parents and grandparents, even if they do not actually attend church. Social scientists have realized that while church attendance is a measure of religious commitment or participation, it is only one measure

Table 12.1 ► Top 10 Religious Denominations, Canada, 2011

	Number	%
Roman Catholic	12,728,885	38.7
No religious affiliation	7,850,610	23.9
United Church	2,007,610	6.1
Anglican	1,631,850	5.0
Muslim	1,053,945	3.2
Baptist	635,840	1.9
Protestant	550,965	1.6
Hindu	497,960	1.5
Lutheran	478,185	1.4
Presbyterian	472,385	1.4

SOURCE: Statistics Canada, 2011 National Household Survey, Catalogue 99-010-X2011032 (2013)

and thus offers a fairly limited understanding of religion in Canada.

Statistically speaking, Canada is still dominated by Christianity (see Table 12.1). The 2011 Statistics Canada National Household Survey shows that 67.3 per cent of Canadians identify as Christian. Government data on religious affiliation dates back to the late 1800s, allowing us to formulate a longitudinal understanding of religious participation in Canada. These data also show the historical presence of Sikhs, Muslims, Buddhists, and Hindus. Moreover, we know that the Canadian Jewish community has roots that date back to the 1700s. Thus, while

SOCIOLOGY IN ACTION

Capturing the Complexity of Religious Participation and Non-participation

Despite the fact that participation in **organized religion** has declined in Canada, a majority of Canadians still identify with a religion, however sporadic their participation in the formal rituals of that tradition might be. Canadians are finding new and interesting ways to express their religious interests that do not necessarily manifest as participation in traditional religious groups. The increasing participation in yoga, for example, might arguably be a "religious practice." Think too about the creation of sacred space through **labyrinths** in the

past decade, such as the Toronto Public Labyrinth, which is adjacent to the Church of the Holy Trinity. The labyrinth is fully accessible to the public, and its creation was supported by the City of Toronto. Many people walk this labyrinth, some of whom are connected to faith communities, some not. Such forms of participation in sacred rituals do not fit into traditional measures of religious behaviour and thus remain undetected in research that measures religious participation (see http://www.labyrinthnetwork.ca/toronto-public-labyrinth).

we hear much about the increasing presence of religious groups who are not Christian, most of these religions have been present since the birth of Canada as a nation.

The data collected by Statistics Canada and researchers like Bibby (1993, 2002, 2006, 2011) provide invaluable resources for important information about religious beliefs and behaviours in Canada. However, we need more information about how Canadians are religious and spiritual. In other words, what do religion and spirituality look like in their daily lives? What is the nature of religious or spiritual practice at home? Unfortunately, statistical data gives us little information about these sorts of questions. Especially lacking are data that offer insight into minority religious communities as well as those who describe themselves as religious "nones," whose numbers have risen from 16.5 per cent in the 2001 census to 23.9 per cent in the 2011 National Household Survey (see Table 12.1; Statistics Canada, 2013c). "None" represents a complex amalgam of atheists, agnostics, humanists, and those who are simply indifferent to religion. Although there is an increasing literature on atheism, there is still very little social scientific data on this more narrowly defined subset of "nones."

Since 9/11 and subsequent attacks in the UK, Spain, Bali, and France, discussions about the link between religion and violence have become more frequent. Although this connection might seem recent, it has been present throughout history. We need only to examine Canada's history of violence against and violation of its Indigenous peoples to uncover a horrifying picture of the intertwining of religion, political goals, and power relations to understand the intersection of religion and violence. This history includes church-run residential schools (approximately 130 across Canada), whose goals included ridding students of their Indigenous cultural and religious/spiritual traditions. On 2 June 2015, the Truth and Reconciliation Commission of Canada released its final report on its investigation into residential schools, including 94 calls to action,

recommending that Canada respect "Indigenous peoples' right to self-determination in spiritual matters, including the right to practise, develop, and teach their own spiritual and religious traditions, customs, and ceremonies," and that the pope issue a formal apology for the Roman Catholic Church's role in facilitating the "spiritual, cultural, emotional, physical, and sexual abuse of First Nations, Inuit, and Métis children in Catholic-run residential schools" (TRC, 2015a, pp. 5, 7). If we look beyond Canada, the Christian crusades (the first was in 1095) provide another example in which the political and economic desires of kings and princes combined with religious ideology to justify a so-called holy war on Muslims, Jews, Orthodox Christians, and many other groups who fell outside of the then-mainstream definitions of Christian religion. More subtle forms of violence can be identified in the anti-condom messages of some Christian missions in an AIDS-ridden Africa.

Does religion cause violence? The answer to this question is not easy. Certainly religion can provide an ideological justification for violent acts or approaches that do violence to people or their culture in more subtle ways.

When we look at the power of religious ideology, we can begin to understand why it is important to have a better sense of the role of religion in the lives of Canadians. Religion can be a source of comfort, direction, and community. It can be both prescriptive, in that it offers people direction on important choices, and explanatory, in that it is a source of explanation for everyday events. It is often an important influence on how people think about issues such as same-sex marriage, abortion, and gender roles. It can influence how and why new Canadians feel welcome and a part of Canadian society or excluded and marginalized.

TIME to REFLECT

Think of some examples of the ways that religion is prescriptive and in which it is explanatory.

The religious demographic in Canada is changing. For example, between 1981 and 1991, the census data show a 144 per cent increase in the category of "other non-Christian religions" (Statistics Canada, 1993). There is growth in Jewish, Muslim, Sikh, Buddhist, and Hindu communities; at the same time, there is a decline in attendance and belonging among Christian communities. Intersecting with these trends are immigration policies, human rights legislation, and policies linked to the Canadian Multiculturalism Act. Religious identity is an important part of what people bring to their roles as employees and employers, their financial choices, their political involvement and decisions, and their conceptualizations of how society should respond to social issues. While religion is not the only factor in people's decisions, it is nonetheless important to understand the ways in which it informs people in their day-to-day lives.

Peter Beyer, head of the Religion and Immigrant Youth/Young Adults Research Team based at the University of Ottawa, situates a sociological understanding of religion in Canada in a global context. The team has spent the past 15 years examining the intersection of religion, youth, and Canadian culture. Participants self-identify as coming from a range of religious backgrounds (Christian, Sikh, Hindu, Muslim, Buddhist, none, and others), have at least one immigrant parent, and were born in Canada or arrived here as an immigrant before the age of 11. More than 550 youth and young adults have participated in the study, and a longitudinal extension of the project is now underway, allowing the team to re-interview participants 5 or 10 years after their initial participation. Results show that these youth locate their religious or spiritual quests in a complex web of family and cultural reference points. For them, spiritual definition is their own prerogative, and while they may rely on their parents and extended families to some extent for spiritual or religious information, they take responsibility

Gunter Marx/EV/Alamy Stock Photo

Despite the increasing numbers of people in Canada who indicate "No religion" when asked their denomination, people still celebrate a wide variety of religious traditions. Here, Sikh men march in the Vaisakhi Festival in Vancouver.

for their own spiritual and religious journeys. Certainly, they had experienced incidents of discrimination, but this was generally explained as a product of individual ignorance rather than a reflection of Canadian society (Beyer, 2008, 2012; Beyer & Ramji, 2013). For these youth, multiculturalism in Canada is a positive ideal that situates Canada as a progressive nation. Here is how one Muslim participant expressed this idea:

> Give it a couple of . . . generations for people to get . . . out of the shell of their own culture, to mix with the world. Because I believe what we have in Canada is an opportunity that a lot of the world doesn't have, I mean, don't get me wrong, there's a lot of blood on the hands of everybody who lives in this country. But we have an opportunity for people to start fresh. We have people from all different backgrounds, all over the world. We are a representation to the world. . . . There are certain points into staying and understanding your own culture and appreciating your own culture. But to be able to evolve and to move on with the times . . . we can show the world here how to live amongst people from all different backgrounds (MM26). (Beyer, 2008, p. 36)

TIME to REFLECT

In your opinion, why are many Canadians less tied to religious institutions than they were several decades ago? What are the potential impacts on micro and macro levels of society?

DEFINITIONS OF RELIGION

What do we mean when we use the word "religion"? Does it include spirituality? And what do we mean by "spirituality"? Sociologists face an ongoing challenge when they attempt to define religion. Meredith McGuire (2005) very simply categorizes definitions of religion into functional definitions and substantive definitions. In short, functional definitions focus on

what religion does for the social group and for the individual. The dominant theme running through most functional definitions is social cohesion—in other words, how religion offers a sense of connectedness to others and to a larger picture. Substantive definitions, on the other hand, examine what religion is and what does not count as religion, and attempt to define religion by examining its core elements, most typically a belief in a higher being, a set of prescribed beliefs and rituals, and so on.

TIME to REFLECT

Is hockey a religion?

Émile Durkheim (1965 [1912]) deserves some of the credit for the shape of functional definitions of religion, but his influence can be seen in substantive understandings as well. Durkheim was preoccupied with social cohesion, and thus viewed religion through this lens. For Durkheim, religion contributed to social cohesion in that it was fundamentally a reflection of the society in which it existed and it was, at its core, a social or group phenomenon. He argued that society divided the world into the sacred and the profane and that the former was the focus of religion. Durkheim's work had some powerful effects on how sociologists of religion define and think about religion. The binary between the sacred and the profane has limited conceptual resonance for some cultures, especially many Indigenous groups. Moreover, the emphasis on the social aspects of religion as they are highlighted by Durkheim has resulted in a denigration of sacred practices that are not communally oriented. Wiccans, for example, are often unconnected to a "faith community" in the traditional Christian sense of the word or in the sense that Durkheim thought was necessary for religious expression.

A contemporary application of Durkheim's functional ideas is reflected in the research of

Robert Bellah and his colleagues (1985) in the United States. They spent considerable time exploring the role of religion in social cohesion, or **civil religion**. This elusive and amorphous concept emerged in the American context and was most vocally defended as a "real" phenomenon by Bellah and his colleagues, who argued that it transcended any specific religious tradition and formed an ethical framework that existed apart from any one religion. However, the strong Christian presence in the United States might belie that claim. Perhaps the most important thing to remember about civil religion, its proponents argue, is that it forms an overarching framework that supports a cohesive society. Underlying this notion is the idea that society is based on and functions because of shared values and perspectives, something that is highly contested by many scholars. Much of Bellah's work focused on understanding how society has departed from those common ideals and the consequences of this, which they identify as largely negative.

Narratives of a cohesive society lost, such as that told by Bellah, return us to debates about the definitions of religion and spirituality. Many people neatly divide the two into religion as "organized religion" and spirituality as somehow representing something less institutional and more private. This division is arbitrary, and hidden behind the categorization are power sedimentations that create a hierarchy in which "religion" is privileged as what counts in terms of spiritual belief and practice. The implications of this are profound. Think about Wiccans, who are often sole practitioners or part of a very loosely organized group with broadly defined rituals and practices. Further, Canada's Indigenous peoples are largely excluded from these conceptualizations of religion. Linda Woodhead (2007) is especially critical of models that privilege religion over magic despite the fact that both are related to the sacred or transcendent. Woodhead also argues that "Religions look remarkably like what Christians think of as religion" (2007, p. 2). It is important that sociologists think carefully about

the work such categories do in the preservation of particular hierarchies of what "counts" as religion.

Substantive definitions focusing on content are equally vulnerable and are often characterized by a reliance on Christianity to form the basis of the determining criteria. Some important challenges to conventional thinking about definitions of religion have emerged both within sociology and from other disciplines, such as anthropology. Talal Asad (1993) calls into question the work that definitions of religion do. He argues that the separating out of religion as something distinct from everyday life is a decidedly Christian approach to thinking about spirituality and religion. As Asad states, "It is preeminently the Christian church that has occupied itself with identifying, cultivating and testing beliefs as a verbalizable inner condition of true religion" (1993, p. 48). By challenging definitions of religion, we also open the possibility of shifting the way religion is measured.

What might an alternative approach be? How would we think about people's involvement with the sacred if we were able to step outside of Christian thinking about religion? Meredith McGuire (2005) has proposed a methodological strategy for moving outside of the confines of Christianity. She asks us to attempt to bracket our assumptions about religion and to travel with a sociological imagination to the "past as another country." She uses this strategy to present the possibility of thinking in a time when there were "no tidy boundaries between the sacred and profane" (McGuire, 2005, p. 3). McGuire (2008) emphasizes the importance of **lived religion**, arguing that it is critical that sociologists pay attention to the ways in which people integrate and practise religion in their day-to-day lives. We will explore the idea of lived religion later in this chapter.

McGuire is also critical of another sociological heavyweight on religion, Max Weber. Although she shares his emphasis on the importance of conducting social scientific research through an understanding of the individual, she is critical of his argument that with moderniz-ation comes the disenchantment of the world. Weber argued that the rationalization that ac-companied modernity resulted in a decreased understanding of reality through magic and mystery. Yet, as McGuire shows in her research, this is not entirely accurate if we pay careful attention (as she does) to people's religious and spiritual practices in daily life. Weber is also known for his association of the ascetic practices of Calvinism with the rise of capitalism, a thesis too dense for detailed discussion here.

Canadian scholar William Closson James (2006) shares the view that we must find new and more nuanced ways to study religion. He argues that "as religion in Canada in the twen-tieth century becomes more highly personal and individual, we should expect it to continue to be characterized more by an eclectic spirit-uality cobbled together from various sources rather than a monolithic and unitary super-ordinating system of beliefs" (James, 2006, p. 288). If we only consider religion that looks a particular way (in the view of the scholars men-tioned above—that is, religion that looks like Christianity)—we will miss a great deal of the richness of Canadians' spiritual lives.

NEW RELIGIOUS MOVEMENTS

There are some very practical implications of decisions about what constitutes a religion.

Raelian founder and leader Claude Vorilhon.

Religious groups in many countries receive privileges simply because they are religious. In Canada, for example, there are certain tax exemptions for religions as charitable organ-izations. Thus, the determination of a group's status as a religion is not merely an academic discussion. In many countries, religions must register with a central state authority in order to be recognized for some benefits. Moreover, those who are not on official state lists are often persecuted through the harassment of group members, the denial of benefits, and the use of state apparatus such as the criminal jus-tice system to keep groups under close scru-tiny. Especially vulnerable are **new religious movements (NRMs)**.

The classic study on new religious move-ments is *The Making of a Moonie*, by Eileen Barker (1984). Barker was intrigued by the increasing frenzy around new religious movements, particularly the talk of "cults," "brainwashing," and "deprogramming" in the late 1970s and early 1980s. As a social scien-tist, she decided that she would investigate the workings of the Reverend Sun Myung Moon's Unification Church, also known as the Moon-ies. As it turned out, the mostly young adults who were joining the Unification Church were not brainwashed, deprived of sleep, or mal-nourished, as the hysterical discourse around their "conversion" had suggested. Rather, they were simply middle-class young adults who were seeking a spiritual or religious experience and a sense of community. Barker's research (1984, 2005, 2007) had profound implica-tions and triggered a debate that continues to this day.

TIME to REFLECT

Find an example of the use of "cult" language in news media coverage of a religious group. How does the article portray the group in question?

Susan Palmer is a Canadian researcher known for her research on new religious move-ments. She has studied a number of religious

UNDER THE WIRE

Religion on the Internet | Morgan Hunter

From an early presence in online newsgroups to current religiously focused social networking sites, religious communities have taken to Internet technology as quickly as it is developed. This use of technology is one more example of the dynamic nature of religion. These activities have come to the attention of scholars who seek to better understand how religion is manifested online. Christopher Helland is one such scholar who developed a schema to make sense of religious activities online. For him these activities exist along a spectrum between religion online, which he defines as websites dedicated to sharing information about largely offline religious organizations, and online religion, which is religious organizations that exist only on the Internet. It is easy to understand what religion online might look like (see, for example,

the Vatican website, which offers a great deal of information about the Roman Catholic Church). Online religion, however, is far more difficult to gauge. For religion to be considered an online religion, do all interactions have to take place online? Do rituals have to be virtual rituals, or can there be some offline components if the ritual is led by someone over the Internet? How many members have to be part of the community before it counts as an online religion? How active does the group have to be? Can there be solitary religious practice online? Does it still count as online religion if members tend to drop in and out? The difficulty of defining online religion reflects the debates about the very definition of religion itself.

SOURCE: Morgan Hunter.

groups, including the Raelians, the Quebec-based UFO **cult** that claimed that they had successfully cloned a human being. After 15 years of fieldwork with the Raelians, which involved attending their meetings, countless interviews with members and leaders, and examining video and written materials, Palmer wrote a book about Raelian culture. Her findings challenged some of the stereotypes associated with NRMs. She found that "Raelians with children make no effort to transmit the message to them, true to the Raelian ethic of individual choice" (Palmer, 2004, p. 139). Children cannot be baptized until at least age 15; even when they ask to be baptized as Raelian, they must pass a test "to prove that their choice was not due to parental influence or pressure" (Palmer, 2004, p. 139). As Palmer discovered, the Raelians have sometimes contradictory beliefs and, as with any social organization, there are power struggles and tensions. In her response to a journalist who wanted to know whether she had observed coercive or manipulative behaviour among the Raelians, Palmer stated: "Well, sure, but no more so than in my women's Bulgarian choir or my PTA

meetings. In any human organization you'll find people who try to control other people. Often they have to, just to get the job done" (2004, p. 6).

Unfortunately, new religious movements still suffer from a great deal of stigma. The language of cults and brainwashing used in the news media and in day-to-day conversation undergoes little critical examination of why it is that we are sometimes quick to marginalize such groups. After all, what is the difference between brainwashing and socialization? This is where questions of agency come into play. What we mean by "agency" is the capacity and ability of a human being to freely make decisions. This sounds simple enough, but ultimately none of us make decisions "freely" or without constraints. Whether it is the influence of parents, friends, economic constraints, or possibilities, our decisions are shaped by our social world and by social structure. Often, marginal religious groups are conceptualized as exerting "undue influence" on their members simply because the decisions those members make may be different from the choices we might make.

THEORIES OF RELIGION AND SOCIETY

Do we live in a secular society? We frequently hear this question as an affirmative statement with little explanation about what it means. To say a society is secular is to say that it is without religion in its public sphere. **Secularization** is the process by which religion increasingly loses its influence. Whether and how society is secular has occupied a great deal of time and energy among sociologists of religion. The narrative begins like this: Once upon a time, society was very, very religious—everyone participated in religious activity, and religion formed a sacred canopy of meaning over life for the vast majority of people. State and church were one and the same, with no separation between them and no perceived need for a separation. Then along came the Enlightenment, and gradually, science replaced religion (Berger, 1967).

To complicate the story, secularization theory developed some very sophisticated versions. In the midst of it all were contested notions of how religion should be defined. This debate is important because in order to determine whether religion is on the decline, we must first know what religion is. So if people stop attending church but take up yoga and engage in rituals such as meditative walks in labyrinths, can we say that we live in a more secular world? If we measure secularization as the decline in people's participation in the rituals and practices of organized religion, such as church attendance, marriage, and baptism, then yes, Canada has definitely secularized. But what happens if the population is increasingly made up of people for whom church attendance is not and has never been a measure of religious participation? How then do we think about secularization? So while one measure of secularization can be the level of individual participation in religious activities, we can see that this presents some interesting measurement challenges.

TIME to REFLECT

Do we live in a secular society?

Another measure of secularization exists at the level of institutions. As religion loses its influence, it has less and less presence in social institutions such as law, education, health care, and so on. And in this process, religion loses its influence as an important social voice. The overt involvement of religion in social institutions, to be sure, is different from what it was in other periods in Canadian history. But the religious voice cannot be discounted entirely. Think, for example, about the religious lobby against same-sex marriage legislation. The Supreme Court *Reference re Same-Sex Marriage* case was decided in 2004; the legislation passed, and the Civil Marriage Act was approved on 20 July 2005. The Court heard the opinions of a number of religious groups during the process. Some were vehemently opposed to the legislation, but some, like the Metropolitan Community Church of Toronto, were instrumental in ensuring that same-sex couples have the right to marry in Canada (see Dickey Young, 2012). Moreover, in some provinces, access to abortion is severely limited because of the insistence of religious lobby groups. In court, witnesses still swear to tell the truth on the bible. Public institutions close on Christian holidays such as Christmas and Easter. In some measure, religious beliefs are so embedded in our social institutions and form part of their histories that it is almost impossible for them to become completely secular or without religious influence.

José Casanova (1994) has done important work on secularization, employing a multi-level conceptualization. Casanova conducted a comparative study of religion using five case studies from two religious traditions (Protestantism and Catholicism) in four countries (Spain, Portugal, Brazil, and the United States).

He identified a trend of "deprivatization" of religion, arguing that beginning in the 1980s, religions began to reassert their intention to have a say over contemporary life. Casanova argues that secularization theory is actually made up of three interwoven strands of argument: (1) secularization as religious decline, (2) secularization as differentiation, and (3) secularization as privatization. While Casanova says that the idea that religion is differentiated (there is a secular and a sacred sphere) is a possible proposition, it does not follow that religion must be marginalized and privatized.

In Canada, we now have what British sociologist Grace Davie (1994) describes as **believing without belonging**, which means that while many Canadians still cite an affiliation with organized religion at census time, many of them do not have much, or any, contact with the churches to which they say they belong. Given current measures of religious life, it is difficult to determine the parameters of belief. Home-based religious practices remain largely invisible. Some scholars argue that such "private" religious behaviours do not really count when thinking about secularization or when measuring religious behaviour. This is a puzzling argument, because such thinking would exclude many religious groups who engage in religious practice almost exclusively in the realm of the so-called private. Also discounted by some scholars are "seekers," or people who may combine a variety of spiritual practices to create a pastiche of spiritual meaning. Thus, someone may engage in yoga, go to the Valentine's Day labyrinth walk at a neighbourhood church, and do a cleansing ritual of her living space to rid it of bad energy. Canada's Indigenous peoples present a complex blending of Christianity and Indigenous spirituality that is difficult to characterize. This blending of traditions remains outside the focus of much research on religion in Canada.

Understanding religion in complex ways can give us a rich picture of how people integrate religion and spiritual practices into their

One way theorists have measured secularization is by the closing of public institutions on Christian holidays such as Christmas and Easter. In what ways might this provide only a limited measure of secularization?

daily lives. One reason secularization theory seemed to have so much credibility is the problem of definition. If religion is conceptualized in narrow ways—church attendance, institutional involvement, and other so-called public measures—then without a doubt it has shown a decline of such proportions that it might be reasonable to conclude that it will eventually disappear. But alternative practices that are not measured form an important part of spiritual identity.

THE QUIET REVOLUTION

The province of Quebec deserves special mention in our consideration of secularization. If ever there was a classic story of secularization, Quebec seems to tell it. It had what we might consider an established church; historically, the Roman Catholic Church played an enormous role in the lives of Quebec citizens at a personal level as well as institutionally (Simpson, 2000, p. 276). Schools, hospitals, and much of public life were intertwined with the church. Public officials were Roman Catholic, as were most members of Quebec society.

In the late 1960s, it seemed that quite suddenly, the church pews were empty. The **Quiet Revolution** had happened. How this apparently abrupt shift came about remains a bit of a mystery, but the perceptions of the church as anti-modern, oppressive, and representative of an establishment with which the people of Quebec no longer wished to identify combined to create an impetus to abandon what had been a core part of identity in Quebec. David Seljak has argued that the Church did not give up its place in Quebec society; instead, it recreated its public role (2000, p. 135). Gregory Baum argues that the Quiet Revolution "initiated a gradual process of secularization" (2000, p. 151) in Quebec. What this means in practice is still unclear. The influence of the Roman Catholic Church in Quebec institutions has not been completely eliminated, and the relationship between the church and the citizens of Quebec remains complex.

Recently, a public debate about the role of religion in society has taken place in Quebec. That debate, in some measure prompted by the *Multani* case (discussed in detail in the next section), has been framed around the notion of "reasonable accommodation" and has focused primarily on the religious practices of immigrants, particularly Muslims (although some practices of Orthodox Jews have also attracted attention). As mentioned earlier, the most recent iteration of the debate was around a proposed "Charter of Values" that would have banned the wearing of religious symbols by public employees. The question of how much "accommodation" should be made for religious minorities has resulted in heated debate. For example, Solange Lefebvre notes that "when it comes to granting religious accommodations to members of minority religions, Quebeckers are reacting more strongly and publicly than people in other parts of North America" (Lefebvre, 2008, p. 179). To some extent, the impact of the debate and the 2008 report prepared by the Bouchard–Taylor Commission (a government-appointed commission to study the issue of accommodation), *Building the Future: A Time for Reconciliation*, is seen as largely confined to Quebec. However, we see similar debates arising all

across Canada. The issues discussed in the report remain largely unresolved and are likely to remain so as the religious demographics of Canada shift to include a greater percentage of people who practise minority religions.

The very language of accommodation leads us to another important issue raised by the public discussion around the Bouchard–Taylor report. "Accommodation" is often used interchangeably with the idea of "tolerance." But as Janet R. Jakobsen and Ann Pellegrini ask, "What does it feel like to be on the receiving end of this tolerance? Does it really feel any different from contempt or exclusion?" (2004, p. 14). If you think about it, there is a rather large difference between someone tolerating you and someone thinking that you are equal, and therefore worthy of respect, and your ideas worthy of protection. Understanding religious difference as something that is to be tolerated, dealt with, or managed is therefore problematic. Some people argue that if we eliminate these concepts, then we will be left with nothing, and that even these basic positions are better than nothing. We might think, although perhaps optimistically, that it is time to develop an approach to difference that is rooted in a deep understanding of equality rather than a teeth-gritting tolerance of those who are not like us. In summary, the debates that have been most intensely played out in Quebec raise issues that are crucial to all of us as we figure out what it means to live in an increasingly multicultural nation.

 To learn more about the debate surrounding reasonable accommodation in the context of Quebec, see "Indigenous Peoples, Québécois, and Multiculturalism," p. 183, in **Chapter 8**, "Ethnic and Race Relations."

RELIGION AND LAW

One important social institution that mediates the ways in which religious beliefs can be expressed through practice is law. For example, if you are a Sikh and wish to wear your **kirpan** (ceremonial dagger) to school, you may find yourself, as Gurbaj Multani did, arguing before the courts for your right to do so (*Multani v Commission scolaire Marguerite-Bourgeoys*, 2006). Law sets important boundaries on religious expression and provides a forum to which people can come to affirm their right to engage in certain religious practices. It is especially important for minority religious groups, whose practices are more likely to be called into question than those of majority religious groups.

Sections 2(a) and 15 of the Charter of Rights and Freedoms are the core sections dealing with the protection of religious beliefs in Canada:

2. Everyone has the following fundamental freedoms:
   a) of conscience and religion . . . ;

15. (1) Every individual is equal before and under the law and has the right to the equal protection and equal benefit of the law without discrimination and, in particular, without discrimination based on race, national or ethnic origin, colour, religion, sex, age or mental or physical disability.

Contrary to popular belief, mostly imported from the United States and France, both of which establish the separation of church and state in their founding constitutional documents, there is no separation of church and state in Canada. Separation of church and state means that the church has no authority over the state or political decisions. You can see, particularly in the United States, that this is more an ideal than a reality. Keep in mind, though, that while Canada does not have a strict separation of church and state, it also does not have an established church or a church that has authority over the state. So where does religion fit in Canada from a socio-legal perspective?

Since the Charter was enacted in 1982, the Supreme Court of Canada has attempted to find a workable definition of religion—employing both functional and substantive elements—that can be applied in its considerations of religious freedom. For example, in the *Syndicat Northcrest v Amselem* (2004) decision, the Court states the following:

> In order to define religious freedom, we must first ask ourselves what we mean by "religion." While it is perhaps not possible to define religion precisely, some outer definition is useful since only beliefs, convictions and practices rooted in religion, as opposed to those that are secular, socially based or conscientiously held, are protected by the guarantee of freedom of religion. Defined broadly, religion typically involves a particular and comprehensive system of faith and worship. Religion also tends to involve the belief in a divine, superhuman or controlling power. In essence, religion is about freely and deeply held personal convictions or beliefs connected to an individual's spiritual faith and integrally linked to one's self-definition and spiritual fulfillment, the practices of which allow individuals to foster a connection with the divine or with the subject or object of that spiritual faith. (at para 39)

Trying to define religion is no easy task. It becomes especially challenging as courts try to distill a very complex concept into a workable definition that acts as a gatekeeper for claims based on religious identity. Thus, courts are faced with the unenviable task of trying to capture a dynamic idea in a definitional box. Robert Orsi's (2003) work on lived religion offers important insight into the task of definitions and why it might prove especially difficult in law: "The study of lived religion is not about practice rather than ideas, but about ideas, gestures, imaginings, all as media of engagement with the world. Lived religion cannot be separated from other practices of everyday life, from the ways that humans do other necessary and important things, or from other cultural structures and discourses (legal, political, medical, and so on)" (Orsi, 2003, p. 172). In the definition quoted above, the Court says that religion is "a particular and comprehensive system of faith and worship." This raises the question of why a religion must be such a system. We might also ask whether that is a useful way to conceptualize religion, since the religious behaviour of the vast majority of Canadians does not actually seem to fit with this notion of "comprehensiveness." Belief in a divine, superhuman, or controlling power poses similar problems in that some religions do not have what we might call a central authority figure. How is it possible to determine whether a conviction is "deeply" held? These are the challenges posed by attempts to solidify religious behaviour into manageable definitions for law.

Although the Charter guarantees religious freedom and equality, the guarantees and rights are limited by section 1, which provides a balance of sorts between individual rights and interests and those of society more generally. This limitation means a court can find that rights have been violated but the offending legislation or policy can remain because it is a reasonable limit on religious freedom by the standards of section 1. Consider a Jehovah's Witness parent who wishes to refuse blood transfusions for her child's cancer treatment. A court may force the child to receive transfusions by assuming temporary custody and overriding the wishes of the parent (and possibly the child). While a court may find that such treatment constitutes a violation of the religious freedom provisions of the Charter, it may also find that such a violation is justifiable under section 1 as representing a societal interest (see Beaman, 2008).

To give this discussion a bit more context, let's consider one case in more detail. The *Multani* case (2006) provides an example of the subtleties of the process of defining religion and the meaning of religious freedom. In that case, "G" (the son) and "B" (the father) were fully observant Sikhs, or, as the Court described them, orthodox Sikhs. An arrangement was made to accommodate G's wearing of a kirpan

(an article of faith that resembles a dagger) to school; this agreement specified that it be kept under his clothing, in a sheath that was sewn shut. That agreement was overridden and the matter made its way through the courts. The Supreme Court upheld G's right to carry the kirpan at school under the agreed-upon conditions. We might see the carrying of a kirpan as an issue of safety, but given the extent of the provisions the Multanis made to keep the kirpan relatively inaccessible, this is not a viable argument and was not one that the Court accepted. We must ask, therefore, why the kirpan became an issue to the point that the family was forced to go to the Supreme Court to be able to exercise their religious beliefs. In part, we can identify the very narrow conceptualization we have of religion and the way it is practised. Fortunately, the Supreme Court was not so limited in its approach.

The naming and construction of the kirpan as a weapon is a discursive practice that relies on a socially constructed set of categories. Manjit Singh comments:

> Rather than go into a detailed explanatory meaning of the kirpan, I would like to talk about another weapon with origins in medieval Europe that has been adopted in Canada and Quebec as a symbol of public authority. I am talking about the mace that lies on a table in front of the speaker of the House of Commons in Ottawa as well as in the National Assembly in Quebec City. According to Webster's dictionary, a mace is "akin to a staff or club used especially in the Middle Ages for breaking armour" and "an ornamental staff borne as a symbol of authority before a public official or legislative body." It is clear from the above wording that a mace is a weapon. In the context of the two legislative chambers, however, it is a symbol of state authority. No one has ever questioned that some day, some member of one of these chambers, in a fit of rage, could use this weapon to attack a fellow member. The point of this discussion is that through mutual consent and historical tradition, this lethal

weapon has come to represent the authority of the state. (*Multani v Commission scolaire Marguerite-Bourgeoys* 2006, at para 39)

Singh's insightful commentary points to the constructed nature of religious symbols. James Beckford (2003) employs a moderate social constructionism, which acknowledges the culturally and socially situated position of religion as a concept and as a practice. Beckford notes the definition of religion as shifting throughout time and the link between those shifts and power relations: "What counts as 'really religious' or 'truly Christian' are authorized, challenged and replaced over time" (2003, p. 17).

Religious groups complicate issues around definition because they may disagree among themselves about who counts as a "real" member of their group. Adherents may challenge others who claim to be members of their group but who do not participate in particular rituals or adhere to specific beliefs. For example, some Anglicans support same-sex marriage while others are opposed to it. Some Muslims support the use of sharia law, others do not, and so on. These tensions can be confusing to those who are outside of the religious group trying to understand the group's religious identity. Some members of a religious group may claim to speak for all members. However, thinking that all members of a religious group believe and practise in the same way is misled at best. These identity issues frequently come before the courts, including in the case of *R v NS*, in which a Muslim woman wanted to wear her **niqab** while giving evidence in a sexual assault trial, and in *Loyola High School v Courchesne*, in which Roman Catholic parents argued that the Quebec Ethics and Religious Culture course forced their children "to attend lessons or instructions which are not in agreement with their religious beliefs" (at para 278). An interesting case is *Mouvement laïque québécois v Saguenay (City)* (2015), in which an atheist man argued that

Expressions of atheism and agnosticism can vary widely, raising complex questions about how to define religious practice. Sunday Assembly is a non-religious community gathering, started in England in 2013, that emulates many of the communal aspects found in religious services.

prayer before a municipal council meeting and religious symbols such as a crucifix in council chambers are inappropriate. The Supreme Court of Canada agreed. Debates over the presence of religion in the public sphere between "nones" and those who affiliate with a particular religious tradition are likely to increase as more people identify as non-religious. Such cases raise interesting and complex questions about religious practices and identity and the ways in which law should protect them.

RELIGION AND GENDER

Why is it important to talk about religion and gender? It matters because there are some decidedly gendered aspects to religious participation. Women tend to make up the bulk of religious congregations, and some argue that it is women's decisions to stop attending that have been the catalyst for the sharp decline in religious participation, at least among Christians. Gender roles are a flashpoint in contemporary conversations about the ways in which religion and society intersect.

A number of scholars, most notably Mary Daly (1985) and Naomi Goldenberg (2006), have argued that religion has been a key institutional site of women's oppression. Women have been excluded from positions of power within church structure. Some of these same debates are emerging in relation to Muslim women. Interpretations about wearing the hijab vary; some define it as a cultural rather than a religious symbol, while others see it as a symbol of women's agency or choice, and still others perceive it as a sign that a woman is oppressed by her religion. Perhaps most important, but sometimes overlooked in this discussion, are the voices of Muslim women themselves. Research reveals the complexity of this issue but, most significantly, clearly demonstrates that women's interpretations cannot be excluded from the interpretation of the meaning of a particular practice.

Homa Hoodfar's trailblazing research (2003) helps us to better understand the complex ways in which women interpret their own choice to wear a hijab. For many of the young women Hoodfar interviewed, the choice to wear the hijab created a newfound sense of freedom from strict parents. Suddenly, they were free to engage in activities that their parents had previously forbidden: "Parents seem to be relieved and assured that you are not going to do stupid things, and your community knows that you are acting like a Muslim woman, you are much freer" (Hoodfar, 2003,

The voices of hijab-wearing Muslim women illuminate the complexities behind the headscarf.

p. 21). Moreover, for some women it was a strategy to generate respect not only among fellow Muslims but also in the broader society: "I am telling them to see me otherwise. Do not think of my body, but of me as a person, a colleague and so on" (Hoodfar, 2003, p. 32). Many of the women interviewed were strategic in their choices to wear the hijab, weighing the advantages and disadvantages and often concluding that the advantages outweighed the negatives. Research since Hoodfar's continues to demonstrate the complex reasons for wearing the hijab, and the strategic approach many Muslim women take toward their choices (Bakht, 2012; Mossière, 2013).

Ultimately, there are a number of strategic choices involved in women's engagement with religion. Some, like Daly (1985), who is a former Roman Catholic nun, argue that religion is so patriarchal that there is no way that women can freely exercise agency within its confines and that women must therefore abandon traditional religion and create their own spheres for spiritual fulfillment. In part, this has been, if not the goal, the effect of some Wiccan groups, such as those researched by Wendy Griffin (2000).

Some strategies are less radical and call simply for a reshaping or reframing of religious teachings. For example, while evangelical Christians describe gender roles in rather particular ways (wives are taught to submit to their husbands), the exact ways in which these roles are interpreted are perhaps not as literal as one might think. Listen to Jane, an evangelical Christian woman who, while she says she is a "submissive" wife, tells the interviewer that all decisions in her marriage are made jointly:

I have had some discussions with women who have a real difficult time with that—wives submit to your husbands. Now, I don't have difficulty with that at all, because in the next breath it says, "Husbands, love your wives as Christ loved the church." In my mind, we've got the easy end of the job, they've got the hard one. I mean, they've got to love like Christ. (Beaman, 1999, pp. 30–31)

Jane's approach is representative of many women who are part of conservative religious traditions, who grow impatient with characterizations of them as having no choice or agency. While non-members tend to characterize them negatively, they often see themselves as benefiting from the demands of their religious traditions, which create rules for both men and women.

TIME to REFLECT

Does religion cause violence?

A heated area of discussion in relation to such teachings is violence against women. The relationship between teachings such as submission or male headship and violence against women is rendered even more complex by the valorization of family unity within faith communities (Alkhateeb & Abugideiri, 2007; Kroeger & Nason-Clark, 2010). This means that women from conservative faith communities—whether Christian, Muslim, or Jewish—are often especially hesitant to take action if they are abused by their husbands, for fear of disrupting the family unit. Thus, such women are "more likely stay in abusive relationships, more likely to return to abusive relationships after counseling, and tend to be more optimistic that abuse will stop if the abuser has some form of counseling" (Nason-Clark & Fisher-Townsend, 2007; Nason-Clark & Holtmann, 2013).

Violence against women within religious communities is made more complex by the fact that such communities are reluctant to admit the existence of violence within the family, perpetuating what Kroeger and Nason-Clark (2010) have called a "holy hush" of denial. To further muddy the waters, secular agencies for women are often reluctant to include religious resources in their strategies for helping

HUMAN DIVERSITY The Hutterites

For a small group of Hutterites in Alberta, having one's picture on one's driver's licence is a violation of religious teachings because it contradicts the second commandment, which prohibits making a graven image of oneself. For this group, posing for the picture on the driver's licence violates this teaching and is contrary to their religious beliefs. When the Alberta government revoked its exemption for the Hutterian Brethren in 2003 and insisted that they would need to have their pictures taken in order to obtain a valid driver's licence, the group took the matter to court, eventually going all the way to the Supreme Court of Canada, arguing that the new law violated their religious freedom. Unfortunately, the Supreme Court disagreed and found that the requirement for a photograph was a reasonable requirement that was necessary to protect the integrity of the Alberta system,

which was also directed at preventing identity theft. Not all of the judges agreed, however, with the majority decision. Justice Abella put the matter succinctly:

Unlike the severity of its impact on the Hutterites, the benefits to the province of requiring them to be photographed are, at best, marginal. Over 700,000 Albertans do not have a driver's licence and are therefore not in the province's facial recognition database. There is no evidence that in the context of several hundred thousand unphotographed Albertans, the photos of approximately 250 Hutterites will have any discernable impact on the province's ability to reduce identity theft. (*Alberta v. Hutterian Brethren of Wilson Colony*, 2009, at para 115)

abused women, thus excluding a resource that is important to abused women from faith communities.

The intersection of religion and gender often triggers interesting debates. The opposition of some religious groups to same-sex marriage was arguably a reaction to what they perceived to be shifting gender roles. Heather Shipley (2012, p. 170) notes that "Family has been constructed in media and public discourse as an ideological contract that justifies the (religious) institution of marriage for the purposes of procreation." Some groups argued that marriage was solely the terrain of opposite-sex couples and that it was inherently designed (by God) that way. In the case that went before the Supreme Court of Canada which decided the legality of same-sex marriage in 2000, the Evangelical Fellowship of Canada argued that "God instituted marriage for the express purposes of companionship, partnership in the task of procreation, for fulfilling a stewardly responsibility for the Earth, but fundamentally to mirror the intimate relationship which God desires to have with his people" (2000, p. 3). At the core of their arguments was a sense that there is a divinely mandated purpose to marriage. The Supreme Court rejected this argument, and same-sex marriage is now legal in Canada. However, the legislation allows for "the freedom of officials of religious groups to refuse to perform marriages that are not in accordance with their religious beliefs" (Canada 2005), thus offering an exemption for clergy who oppose same-sex marriage.

CONCLUSION

In this chapter we have considered the contemporary picture of religion in Canada and explored some of the issues that are of concern to sociologists of religion. We have seen that the religious demographic of Canada is in an interesting period of flux that may have a significant impact on Canadian society. Religious minorities in Canada play an important role in defining diversity in Canadian society. It is exciting to be a sociologist of religion in Canada in this time of rapid change.

We have already discussed to a great extent the limits of existing social scientific research on religion in Canada. Quantitative measures need to be more comprehensive to reflect Canada's shifting demographic. We need to understand how religious beliefs and practices fit into the day-to-day lives of Canadians and of those who have arrived in Canada more recently. We need definitional and measurement standards that are not based on Christian understandings of religion. In other words, our research needs to take an inclusive turn, extending beyond church attendance and Bible belief.

Research on religion in Canada is slowly becoming a priority. Sociology has a key role to play in the Canadian study of religion. No matter which theoretical tradition one uses, it brings tools that are invaluable to research. Ethnographic accounts of religious communities will provide insight that is as vital as more detailed survey work. Research into important intersections—like youth and religious practice and belief—is central to predicting the role that religion will play in Canada's future. Key, though, to understanding the role of religion in Canada's future are interdisciplinary approaches that seek to draw on the expertise and insights of various traditions of scholarly thought.

Students in the polygamist community of Bountiful in British Columbia. What does their mode of dress say about the community's social and gender values?

Questions for Critical Thought

1. Critically examine your own religious history. Where do you and your family fit in terms of believing and belonging? Are you part of a religious minority, a majority, or the "nones"?
2. Is Canada a secular nation? Are there some areas of life that are more or less removed from the influence of religion?
3. How is religion best defined? Explain your decision.
4. Should religious groups have a say in public policy issues?
5. Why do you think the language of "cults" and "brainwashing" persists?
6. The United States and France have a separation of church and state. What does this mean? Can you think of other examples of states that have such a separation? Are there states that have a merging of church and state, either now or historically?
7. Is yoga a religious or secular practice?
8. Should schools teach about religion?

Sociological Explorations

1. Given that almost a quarter of the Canadian population now identifies as "non-religious," constructing a survey that captures the diversity of people's responses to the question, "What is your religious or non-religious identity?" is difficult. Design a survey with the categories you think should be used to measure the range of religious and non-religious identities and ask your peers to fill it out.

2. Photo essays are an innovative tool that sociologists use to study religious diversity and the concept of lived religion. Go to the Linking Classrooms website (http://religionanddiversity.ca/en/projects-and-tools/projects/linking-classrooms/photo-essays/), choose a photo essay, and reflect on the images participants have chosen to share on their lived religious experiences.

Recommended Readings

Beckford, J. (2003). *Social theory and religion*. Cambridge, UK: Cambridge University Press.
Beckford presents an examination of religion by developing clear links between social theory and the social scientific study of religion. Relying on moderate social constructionism, his theory focuses on the ways in which religion is a complex and social phenomenon.

Beyer, P., & Ramji, R. (2013). *Growing up Canadian: Muslims, Hindus, Buddhists*. Montreal, QC: McGill-Queen's University Press.
Beyer and Ramji present a study based on data gathered from Canadian young adults of Muslim, Hindu, and Buddhist immigrant families. Research results are presented by the Religion and Immigrant Youth team members in a series of chapters

exploring various aspects of being an immigrant youth in Canada.

McGuire, M.B. (2008). *Lived religion: Faith and practice in everyday life*. Oxford, UK: Oxford University Press.
McGuire explores how the concept of lived religion can be used to understand the actual religious experiences and practices of people in everyday life.

Stahl, W.A. (2015). The church on the margins: The religious context of the New Atheism. In L.G. Beaman & S. Tomlins (Eds), *Atheist identities: Spaces and social contexts*. Dordrecht, Netherlands: Springer.
Stahl examines how narratives like secularization theory, and structural and cultural changes in social solidarity have been used to explain decline in church

membership, shaping the context for the New Atheism to emerge.

those who do not identify with any religion and never attend religious services (the "nones").

Thiessen, J. (2015). *The meaning of Sunday: The practice of belief in a secular age.* **Montreal, QC: McGill-Queen's Press.**
To evaluate the changing levels of Canadian religiosity, Thiessen presents research on the lived religion practices of three groups of people: those who actively attend religious services; those who attend religious services for holidays and rites of passage; and

Reimer, S., & Wilkinson, M. (2015). *A culture of faith: Evangelical congregations in Canada.* **Montreal, QC: McGill-Queen's University Press.**
Reimer and Wilkinson's study offers a look at evangelical Protestant congregations across Canada, finding the group retains high levels of institutional participation in the face of otherwise declining Canadian religiosity.

Recommended Websites

CBC Archives on Religion and Spirituality
www.cbc.ca/archives/categories/society/religion-spirituality/religion-spirituality.html
The CBC archive contains clips from radio and television coverage of religious issues in Canada over the past 60 years.

Centre for Studies in Religion and Society
http://csrs.uvic.ca
The Centre for Studies in Religion and Society, hosted by the University of Victoria, studies the intersection of religion and public life from an interdisciplinary perspective. The website offers information about religious research in Canada.

Religion and Diversity Project
www.religionanddiversity.ca
This University of Ottawa–based project brings together 37 researchers from Canada and other nations to research the contours of religious diversity and possible responses to the opportunities and challenges it presents.

Religion and Society Research Programme
www.religionandsociety.org.uk

The UK government–funded Religion and Society Research Programme supported 75 original research projects that were historical as well as contemporary in focus, and investigated international contexts in dealing with the knowledge and understanding of religion and society.

Statistics Canada: Guides to the latest information—Religion
www.statcan.gc.ca/search-recherche/bb/info/3000017-eng.htm
The Statistics Canada guide to the latest information on religion offers links to tables with data on religion in Canada and to the most recent Statistics Canada publications on religion.

Religion and Violence e-learning (RAVe)
www.theraveproject.com/index.php
Religion and Violence e-learning offers support and provides resources for women, clergy, and other service providers on the issue of violence against women. It is based on sociological research conducted by Nancy Nason-Clark and her research team.

Key Terms

believing without belonging The concept of religious belief that is not tied to traditional forms of religious practice or rituals.
civil religion The idea that religion plays a role in supporting social cohesion through shared values and perspectives.
cult A group typically composed of a small number of believers who are viewed as engaging in non-

traditional practices. More scientifically referred to as "new religious movements."
hijab A headscarf worn by some Muslim women.
kippa A skullcap worn by Jewish men in public or while praying.
kirpan A ceremonial dagger worn by some Sikhs.
labyrinth A maze-like structure used by some as a tool for meditation or spiritual practice.

lived religion A flexible and holistic lens focused on how religion is woven into individuals' everyday lives that reveals the fluidity of religious and non-religious identity.

new religious movements A religious or spiritual community that has come into being in modern times.

niqab A face covering worn by some Muslim women.

organized religion A traditional view of religion as institutionalized and involving formal practices.

Quiet Revolution A time of seemingly abrupt social change and secularization that took place in Quebec in the late 1960s.

secularization The contested notion that religion is increasingly losing influence in the public sphere.

In this chapter you will:

▶ Understand that power is relational and socially determined

▶ Discover that the state plays a focal role in the sociological analyses of politics because it shapes the ways that people and groups exercise and negotiate power

▶ Learn that political sociologists have analyzed politics in terms of control and contests over material, cultural, social, and institutional resources

▶ See how social movements are studied sociologically

▶ Review the theoretical approaches to the study of social movements

▶ Learn how social movements are embedded in national and international politics

INTRODUCTION

Politics is about *power* and its *contestation*—therefore, about political institutions and social and political movements. However, it is not only about the "suits" on Parliament Hill or the activists in the streets—it is also a part of all our daily lives. Sociologists understand politics as endemic to our social existence. It is not only about elections or the "red tape" of government, or protest signs and slogans, but instead it is also about how people negotiate their lives with family, friends, social groups, and institutions of all sorts. These too reflect power relations and challenges to them.

Sociologists use a much broader concept of politics than most of us are used to, one that sees politics playing out in realms of society that we normally consider outside of or unaffected by politics proper (Scott & Marshall, 2009). For this reason, the sociological conception of politics is complex and multifaceted. In this chapter, we will provide you with an overview of some of the key perspectives in political sociology that aim to identify and analyze how power is distributed in society and the sorts of factors on which it is based. We will also provide you with an overview of how sociologists approach power contests—that is, attempts to modify or overthrow existing power relations. We will focus here on **social movements** and their role in political life. When people lend time, energy, and material resources to a cause, their combined efforts create a social movement with a life and force of its own. Examples of present-day social movements include Indigenous, women's, LGBT (lesbian, gay, bisexual, and transgender), environmental, global social justice, ethnic, nativist, and regionalist movements.

We will begin by elaborating on the core concept of power and then consider the state and its central, but not exclusive, place in sociological analyses. From there, we will move on to the different ways that political sociologists have conceived of power, looking at who holds it and on what bases it is exercised. We will next look at the characteristics of social movements, consider theoretical approaches to social

Equality before and under law and equal protection and benefit of law

15. (1) Every individual is equal before and under the law and has the right to the equal protection and equal benefit of the law without discrimination and, in particular, without discrimination based on race, national or ethnic origin, colour, religion, sex, age or mental or physical disability.

Affirmative action programs

(2) Subsection (1) does not preclude any law, program or activity that has as its object the amelioration of conditions of disadvantaged individuals or groups including those that are disadvantaged because of race, national or ethnic origin, colour, religion, sex, age or mental or physical disability.(84)

Endnote 84:
(84)   Subsection 32(2) provides that section 15 shall not have effect until three years after section 32 comes into force. Section 32 came into force on April 17, 1982; therefore, section 15 had effect on April 17, 1985.

FIGURE 13.1 Section 15 of the Constitution Act, 1982

SOURCE: http://laws.justice.gc.ca/en/charter/1.html#anchorbo-ga:l_l-gb:s_15

movements, and then examine examples of social movements in Canada. The chapter ends with a discussion about social movements in today's transnational context.

POWER

Max Weber famously defined *power* as the capacity to realize one's will despite the resistance of others. It is the ability to do what you want, when you want, even in the face of opposition. Most people believe that one's condition is determined by one's own decisions, choices, and ambition despite circumstances. But sociologists have found that other factors influence people's capacities to pursue and achieve their goals, such as material wealth, cultural and social recognition, and access to institutions. These factors are defined by social structures that shape power relations and ultimately reward some people who possess or control them more than those who do not.

For example, people who have more money not only can buy more things but usually hold more power than those who have less money. Wealthy people often have more power to influence who owns and controls material resources, such as businesses or factories, and cultural and social resources, such as investing in art and leisure activities or belonging to elite clubs, and because of this, they often have preferred access to institutions of power, such as schools or governments that set standards for others in a society to follow. At first glance, many people think that merely having more money makes one powerful. However, the situation is not so straightforward.

Money is important because people agree that it is so and accept it as a payment for work and goods or services delivered. The power of money, then, is socially negotiated and only has value because people agree that it does. Because of this, it does not matter what money *is* but instead that people agree that it is valuable. It is in this sense that sociologists understand power as relational—a phenomenon that only manifests in human relationships—rather than intrinsic to its various representations.

 C. Wright Mills claimed that the elites in society are so powerful that they jeopardize democracy. Do you agree? Turn to "The Wealthy, Elites, and Super Rich," p. 139, in **Chapter 6**, "Class and Status Inequality," to read more on this topic.

Because power is relational, it is not fixed. It is a dynamic phenomenon that is under constant negotiation or challenge. Power is continually contested by people who oppose or disagree with its bases and defended by those who benefit from the status quo. For this reason, sociologists tend to treat power as a series of social or **political processes**. Power contests can result in new forms of power and modification of old power relations. Yet challenging and changing the bases of existing power relations is often difficult.

TIME to REFLECT

What reflects political power? Is it fixed and visible, or is it embedded within material, cultural, social, and institutional processes?

Political sociologists would argue that inequalities persist because people and groups who hold and exercise power in a society are generally not ready to give it up or even share it and so muster opposition to those seeking to eliminate old bases of power or generate new ones. Existing power-holders usually have material, cultural, social, and institutional resources at their disposal that their challengers do not. These resources are the mechanisms that shape the political process that sociologists try to understand. You will be introduced to some of them throughout this chapter.

THE STATE

Perhaps the greatest concentration of power in contemporary Western societies lies in the domain of the state. It is the only institution whose officials have the legal right to tax people, to assault them through the police and military, to permit or force people to commit murder when conscripted into military service, to legally detain people in prison, and, in places where capital punishment exists, even kill them. It is also the only institution that can set policies and laws governing personal behaviour, restrict the ways individuals conduct business and their personal and love relationships, authorize credentials, license professions' activities, and so on. Basically, states set the rules by which other social processes are ordered. And like all rule-makers, the leaders of states hold a lot of power to shape the capacities the rest of us have to realize our wills. But why do states hold so much power?

To answer this question we need to examine Western history. States emerged as one of the many transitions related to the **Industrial Revolution** and the emergence of modernity. As societies became larger and more urbanized and work became more specialized and mechanized, older forms of social order became unworkable. New urban middle classes formed in association with these changes and challenged the traditional authority of aristocracies, and the nature of negotiations around power began to change. Land ownership, for instance, which was once the epitome of material power, was replaced by capital and money as symbolic forms of material power. Divine and hereditary rights, which formed the fundamental bases for power in feudal societies, were questioned as new religions emerged and families began to marry outside of ethnic and religious lines. The dominance of churches and other religious institutions was also challenged by science and competing belief systems and their organizations. As the traditional foundations of power, knowledge, trust, and obligation weakened, new social configurations developed. They included new systems of governance, like the modern state, through which leaders managed the social conflicts that accompanied negotiations around the new foundations of power: capital over land, individual over hereditary rights, science and rationality over religion, and so forth.

A key development that accompanied the emergence of the modern state was bureaucracy. It is an organizational form that is ordered by criteria independent of the personal qualities of people holding positions of power. Whereas the authority of organizations of the old order flowed from the personal power of the people who occupied positions in them, bureaucracy enabled power to be exercised through a staff abiding by impersonal practices and procedures less susceptible to individual whims and preferences. This granted modern state leaders a very powerful tool through which they could manage conflicts and set rules around their negotiation.

 "Bureaucracy" is a commonly used term, but what does it mean to sociologists? See "Bureaucracies," p. 95, in **Chapter 4**, "Social Organization," for a clear explanation.

The state thus emerged as a key institution that accompanied the massive changes wrought by shifts in the primary bases of power that came with industrialization. Through its various branches, state leaders

today can shape all manner of social processes. Let us now examine three broad groupings of these processes—material, cultural and social, and institutional—and the different ways political sociologists have understood the effect of these processes on how power is exercised and challenged.

MATERIAL PROCESSES

Political sociologists who are concerned with why and how money operates as a source of power are part of a group of scholars who view the possession and control of material resources as central to politics. Material resources include money and other kinds of financial resources but also comprise things like property, technology, natural resources, and different means of communication, transportation, organization, and networking. Materialists generally maintain that the more material resources a person, group, institution, or state has, the greater their capacity to realize their will over others and to exercise and challenge power.

Certainly the most famous scholar to have made the argument that power is determined by possession of material resources is Karl Marx. He said that those who owned and controlled the means of production exercise the most power in human societies. Those who possessed the land to cultivate food, for example, held much power in agrarian societies and the feudal era; they controlled peasants' ability to provide for themselves and their families and dictated much of their daily lives. In the industrial era, those who owned machinery and factories, the bourgeoisie, wielded much power over the workers that kept them running, the proletariat. Again, owners governed, and continue to govern, workers' daily routines, setting their wages and determining the conditions under which they work.

For Marx, individuals' power is contingent on their class position or their relationship to the means of production. If they own the means of production, they hold power and can exercise it by influencing who has access to those means and how and for what purposes they are used. If they do not own the means of production, they are effectively powerless, compelled to submit to the owning class to gain access to the means they need to survive.

But for Marx, the power of the owning class, the dominant minority, went far beyond the manor estate or the factory. Other institutions that comprise a society, like the state, religion, family, and the education and legal systems—what Marx called the superstructure—also reflected and sustained the power of the dominant class.

The system Marx described was one in which the majority subordinate class was deceived by the dominant class into thinking that power inequalities reflected in and sustained by social institutions and the ideologies that sustained them were natural, commonsensical, or at best unchangeable. The subordinate class thus operated under a **false consciousness**, because these phenomena masked the true reason why elites held power, which was that they controlled or owned the means of production. It was for this reason, Marx argued, that the bourgeoisie was able to maintain its advantage over the working class.

Later writers critiqued Marx for reducing all politics to class politics. Without denying that significant power could be derived from one's ownership of the means of production and material wealth, Max Weber said that power also flowed from one's control over other sorts of assets, things like social status, professional skills, and institutions. These assets are related to material wealth, because they enhance a person's economic well-being, or "market situation." C. Wright Mills (1956) believed that material assets combine and overlap with other sorts of resources to affect how power is exercised in a society. He argued that the post–World War II United States was ruled by a higher circle of corporate, military, and political leaders. They held power because they controlled the massive and interlocking hierarchies of the economy, army, and state that made up the means of power.

POWER LUNCH

By 12:18pm on the first working day of the New Year, Canada's highest paid 100 CEOs will have already pocketed $48,636—what it takes the average full-time, full-year worker all year to earn.

Average pay of the 100 highest paid CEOs was $8.96 million, 184 times more than the average wage.

policyalternatives.ca/ceo2016

How does the difference between the earning power of CEOs and that of average workers illustrate Marx's concept of the bourgeoisie and the proletariat?

TIME to REFLECT

In what ways is Weber's conception of power closer than Marx's definition to what most of us understand to constitute class position?

John Porter (1965), a Canadian sociologist in the tradition of Weber and Mills, witnessed a hierarchical intersection between class, education, political standing, and ethnicity (see Helmes-Hayes 2009, 2002; Helmes-Hayes & Curtis, 1998; Satzewich & Liodakis, 2010). Porter described Canadian society as a vertical mosaic whose own *power elite* comprised political, economic, and cultural leaders from the charter groups. These were individuals whose heritage was linked to Canada's English and French "founders." Porter argued that these groups used their material and other advantages to sustain their power and held subsequent migrants to Canada in an *entrance status*. That is, non-charter groups earned lower incomes for their labour, held less prestigious positions, had fewer educational opportunities, and had less access to the state bureaucracy and political system. As a result, little had changed in the class and ethnic composition of the elites who controlled various power structures.

SOCIOLOGY ▰▰▰▰ IN ACTION

"Committing Sociology"

Because sociology seeks to understand the underlying social processes that shape societies and everyday life, it is not a discipline confined to an "ivory tower." Sociology does not distinguish between the academy and the "real world." Instead, it is a practice that analyzes social forces, offers insight on societies, and at times sparks widespread public debate that contributes to setting the political agenda.

Some years ago, Michael Burawoy (2004) challenged sociologists to practice "public sociology," a sociology that takes the insights of the discipline and applies them to everyday life, social policy, and social engagement. Although some sociologists have always done this, many more responded to his challenge. It is common to see sociologists making national headlines in major newspapers and commenting on significant social and cultural events. Take for instance Vic Satzewich's (2014) research on the "black box" of immigration decisions, or David Tindall's (2013) assessment of Indigenous rights and the environment, or Kathleen Rodgers and Willow Scobie's (2012) defence of the right to protest without fear of intimidation and legal sanctions.

Sociologists also "do" public sociology by contributing to social policy. They are invited to parliamentary standing committees as experts, contribute to the construction of surveys and data collection, and are relied upon to evaluate social programs and policies. Sociologists, however, are usually critical of the status quo, because they are trained to deconstruct the obvious and search for the latent causes of social problems. Such a perspective is evident in Elke Winter's (2014) questioning of Canada's reworking of its citizenship test requirements, Jeffrey Reitz and Rupa Banerjee's (2007) identification of racial inequality and the threat it poses for social cohesion, and Justin Piché's (2011) challenge of the efficacy of the "tough on crime" approach over restorative practices that seek justice through rehabilitation.

Because sociologists present insights that, at times, counter the interests of those who wield power, they are often the targets of political backlash. This happened in 2013 shortly after the Boston Marathon bombing. In the wake of the attack, Liberal leader Justin Trudeau cautioned that it was important not to respond rashly but to look to the "root causes" of such acts. Shortly after this a plot to blow up a VIA Rail train in Ontario was foiled. Reacting to these events, Prime Minister Stephen Harper took Trudeau to task for his "root causes" comment, framing it as a weak response to terror and retorting in a press conference that "this is not the time to commit sociology." Harper issued a similar comment about a year later when rejecting an inquiry into murdered and missing Indigenous women. In both instances Harper advocated an immediate, authoritative, and ideological approach, a response that he said was more effective than careful consideration of the circumstances underlying these events.

Harper's comments may have played well with his supporters, but they counter the research findings of sociologists who study terrorism and violence against Indigenous women. Robert Brym and Bader Araj (2006), for example, found that the suicide bombers they studied were not "crazy," but people who were reacting (albeit violently) to policies and actions that they perceived as excessively tough and repressive. Julie Kaye and Daniel Béland (2014) cited research by the UN and Statistics Canada to show that the many cases of missing and murdered Indigenous women in Canada had to be recognized not only as criminal, as Harper insisted, but also in light of the fact that Indigenous women were much more likely to be victims of violence that non-Indigenous women.

As these cases show, "committing sociology," or conducting sociological analysis, might just be what is needed to understand terrorist events and violence against Indigenous women, to perhaps prevent both from occurring in the future.

Sociology is not an ivory tower discipline but rather a tool to unearth the underlying patterns of the social world. Put differently, as Pierre Bourdieu (2000) once famously noted, ". . . sociology is a martial art, a means of self-defense. Basically, you use it to defend yourself, without having the right to use it for unfair attacks."

Porter's influence has been especially prominent in what has become known as the *political economy* perspective in Canadian scholarship. This tradition focuses on the politics around the acquisition and negotiation of material power within the economic, geographic, and social conditions characterizing the Canadian experience. The importance of Porter's thesis can be seen in its revisiting over the past 20 years (Helmes-Hayes & Curtis, 1998). Many of its tenets have been shown to still hold true but on racialized rather than ethnic grounds (cf. Agócs & Boyd, 1993; Helmes-Hayes & Curtis, 1998; Gosine, 2000; Galabuzi, 2006; Nakhaie, 2007). Visible minorities, rather than all non-charter ethnics, retain their entrance status in a colour-coded vertical mosaic.

We have come some way since Marx and his elaboration of the material bases of power. But while scholars after him have expanded upon and extended his ideas about how material resources configure power relations, his core claim—that control of material fundamentally determines the distribution of power in human societies—remains a key observation in political sociology. Let us now turn to some of the non-material processes of power that sociologists examine.

CULTURAL AND SOCIAL PROCESSES

Weber understood power as also stemming from sources other than material. One of these "other" sources was status, a person's social prestige. Social prestige is often connected to material advantage but not always, said Weber. He was one among many sociologists who recognized that cultural and social processes affect power relations in ways not captured by purely materialist perspectives.

One of the most notable social thinkers to have pondered how culture affects politics was Antonio Gramsci. He was an Italian Marxist of the early twentieth century who wondered why the working-class masses did not respond to Marxist calls for a class-based revolution. Gramsci reasoned that it was because elites "manufactured" the consent of the masses by communicating ideals supportive of the status quo. He argued that this was accomplished through political and cultural mechanisms like the state, schools, religious institutions, and media. He believed that to mobilize masses to contest power, **counter-hegemonic** positions had to be generated. These positions would lay claim to alternative cultural and social ideals

that would reconfigure and challenge the established **hegemonic** order. Gramsci called for "organic intellectuals" to communicate counter-hegemonic ideals through popular culture in ways that would resonate with average people. Max Horkheimer and Theodor Adorno (2006) wrote about similar ideas when they introduced the notion of the **culture industry** and the role cultural production played in the rise of fascism and later American consumer culture. However, they were less optimistic about the potential of organic intellectuals, or anyone for that matter, to challenge the cultural power of elites.

The sociologist who perhaps has gone the furthest in articulating how this works is Pierre Bourdieu. He coined what have become key terms in the field, **cultural capital** and **social capital**. Bourdieu's elaboration of these terms helped scholars to articulate how the different components of culture and other social practices operate in much the same ways as material resources. They act as sources of power and the bases of politics.

Simplifying somewhat, Bourdieu said that cultural capital is anything that reflects and facilitates cultural exchange between people. It includes how people see and understand the social world and the interactions that occur within it, as well as cultural symbols that help them do so, such as language, clothing, customs, and so forth. Social capital is a resource that fosters social relationships and the privileges and obligations that one can draw from them; it is derived from membership in groups. The number and nature of groups to which you belong thus affects the social capital you possess, which in turn can affect the power you are able to exercise over your life and others.

Bourdieu expanded upon Weber's insight by seeking to understand how different social dimensions, such as culture and social ties, overlap with material and economic well-being. He was interested in how each could be exchanged and how they influence social mobility. For Bourdieu (1984) there is a difference between elite and popular culture: the cultural and social capital of the most powerful, what some call highbrow culture, is exclusive and this is the source of its power. Others, such as Richard Peterson (1992, 2005), theorized that power comes with being a cultural **omnivore**, which is the ability to consume a wide range of cultural products and socialize with a broad set of people. Conversely, being a **univore**, or someone who has a narrow set of cultural habits and small social networks, is related to less power.

In Canada, Gerry Veenstra (2015) has used these ideas to map class position and musical tastes. In his analysis he found that musical omnivorism, that is, listening to a wide number of genres—from rap to country to classical to heavy metal—is not aligned to class differences. However, when people were pushed to pick their favourite musical genre and to speak about particular genres in depth, class differences emerged. In particular the upper-class omnivores were more likely to appreciate classical, jazz, opera, or world music, which were all less favoured by lower-class omnivores.

Although cultural and social processes can be used to understand how dominant groups sustain their power over subordinate masses, those same resources can be used to challenge existing power arrangements through political movements. Interestingly, some of the earliest and most influential work on how culture

HUMAN DIVERSITY   Food as a Source of Power

Can food be a source of power? We all need sustenance to do anything, of course, but can the *type* of food we consume allow us to exercise power over other people or challenge existing power arrangements?

A number of political sociologists have begun to explore the political implications of food choice, with some interesting results. Canadian consumers are increasingly interested in organic and fair trade products, as well as locally grown and processed produce. A few years ago, the CBC (2009) reported that organic food sales had increased by 20 per cent each year over the past decade. Canadian companies such as Just Us! Coffee Roasters Co-Op in Nova Scotia have seen their profits in fair trade coffee grow over the years, and more restaurateurs are embracing the principles of the "slow food" movement and the "100-mile diet" in response to demands from dining "locavores." Some Canadians are becoming small-scale farmers themselves, growing food and raising livestock in their backyards, even in urban areas.

How can we understand this trend in food consumption and production? Businesses that are part of the movement and their consumers often cite ethical, health, and environmental reasons for adopting these practices. But political sociologists have pondered some of the less obvious reasons that people engage with these trends. These scholars reveal that these "conscientious" businesses and consumers can end up either confirming or confronting the status quo, depending on how they take up the new food trends.

Emily Kennedy and Sara O'Shaughnessy (2010) found that many pursuing these trends understand themselves as activists of sorts by providing "alternative" examples to others in their communities. However, alternative food choices can also serve as a way to consolidate existing power, as Josée Johnston and Shyon Baumann (2009) contend. They observe that most people who embrace recent trends in organic/local/fair trade foods are white and affluent. Although they might deny that they are "food snobs," these "foodies" eschew food experiences they deem inauthentic, especially meals from chain restaurants, which the less affluent are more likely to patronize.

The result, say the authors, is that food choice becomes a means by which the privileged distinguish themselves from others, another status marker that signifies their belonging to an economic or cultural elite and differentiates them from less knowledgeable consumers.

Whether one's food choices represent a challenge to existing power arrangements or further evidence of one's privilege veils what is perhaps the most obvious inequity embedded in this discussion: that having any sort of "relationship" with one's food is in itself a marker of advantage—which is something to think about as we consume our burger or fair trade organic latte.

and social factors shape political movements was done by a sociologist who completed his doctoral work in the 1940s in Saskatchewan, Seymour Martin Lipset. Like many political sociologists, Lipset was interested in comparative analysis (Schwartz, 2007). One of his focuses was on the similarities and differences between Canada and the United States, especially with respect to unionism, values, and institutions. Lipset (1991, 1964, 1963) observed higher rates of union membership in Canada than in the US and said that the disparity was linked to value differences between the two populations (1990). Canadians tended to be more conservative and supportive of tradition and collective politics than Americans, he said, owing to Canada's history of commitment to loyalist traditions. The US was born of rebellion and revolution, a history that fostered a culture of individualism that discouraged collective responses such as unionism.

A number of prominent Canadian sociologists, however, have challenged Lipset's theory (Bowden 1989, 1990; Grabb & Curtis, 2002; Grabb, 1994; Baer, Grabb, & Johnston, 1987, 1990; Yates, 2008). Many found that Canadian attitudes are not significantly different from those of Americans, but rather that Canadian institutions are more supportive of unions than those in the United States. Lipset himself (1990) countered these challenges by asking *why* such institutions were more supportive in the first place, suggesting again that Canadian values have encouraged us to elect politicians who institute collective and union-friendly policies.

In challenging a purely materialist understanding of power relations, Max Weber and other political sociologists after him came up with concepts and identified means that have proven useful for analyzing how cultural and social processes are taken up and how they play into the negotiations that characterize politics in societies. While none of these thinkers would abandon the idea that material resources affect how power is exercised and challenged, they recognize that it alone cannot account for all forms of politics.

How do power and access to certain types of food limit choice in the food you consume? Does this have a healthy or unhealthy result?

INSTITUTIONAL PROCESSES

So far, we have seen how political sociologists have depicted power as shaped by differential ownership of material resources or cultural and social recognition. But some other sociologists say these approaches do not consider how institutions configure the circumstances in which people operate. Institutions set the bounds of social interactions, the "rules" and guidelines around how social relations unfold, and they delimit the choices and actions that are available to people to employ under different conditions. In this way, institutions may not determine political outcomes, but they shape them to a significant degree.

Sociologists understand **institutions** as patterns of behaviour that order people's lives in relatively predictable ways. They can be informal and flexible, like a group of friends regularly meeting for happy-hour drinks, or more formal, such as schools, business associations, or the state. Institutions shape social interactions because they exhibit *inertia* and *path dependence*. The first means that they are relatively stable and modified only with concerted effort. Institutions "push back" at attempts to change them by discouraging people from acting, or even thinking of acting, in other ways. The second means that once institutions are established, they affect decision-making down the road, encouraging people to proceed down certain "paths" of action instead of others.

Because of these tendencies, institutions can both help and hinder those engaged in the contestation of power. They help by providing a stable and predictable means through which people can exercise power. They hinder by channelling and delimiting the choices for action available to those who engage with and sustain them. Both can be a boon to power-holders, since it is often difficult, or at least bothersome, for others to change the procedures structuring the distribution of power. But institutions can help challengers too, because once they learn how things operate, challengers can formulate ways of changing the rules, getting around them, or mobilizing them on their own behalf.

The institution that political sociologists are most concerned with is the state. Certainly, many political sociologists analyze how institutions shape formal politics, such as elections, political attitudes, and political parties (see Grabb, 1994; Grabb & Curtis, 2002), but sociologists also recognize that state institutions influence the politics that happens outside this "official" sphere too. This is because state institutions shape other social processes, such as who is and is not considered a citizen. Your capacity to bring your interests to the fore and exercise power can be limited greatly if you are not recognized by state institutions.

Theda Skocpol is perhaps the best known institutionalist in sociology. In a comparative historical analysis of the revolutions in France, Russia, and China, she traced the impetus for revolution in each case to the incapacity of existing state structures to meet or resolve crises arising in the international realm, from war, or from economic troubles (Skocpol, 1979). Whichever powerful groups ended up exploiting these situations and fostering revolution depended on the relationships that had been conditioned by the state institutions in crisis. Although her subject matter may seem obscure, Skocpol's study was significant, because it reminded sociologists of the important role that state institutions play in configuring class and other antagonisms in different countries.

Michael Mann has elaborated on the capacity of state institutions to shape power relations. In his work on genocide, for example, Mann (1999, 2004) challenges popular explanations of genocide as terrible manifestations of rabid "tribal" racisms and points to democracy as spawning these atrocities. Democratic state institutions do not always foster peace by permitting everyone access to the state so that they can resolve group conflicts in an orderly manner, says Mann. In places inhabited by people with many ethnic backgrounds, they can result in the elite power-holding group defining who has legitimate citizenry in ethnic terms. As non-persons, members of subordinate groups and minorities can then be liable to persecution or, at worst, repression or mass murder.

An institutional perspective can, of course, also inform examinations of less violent events. In Canadian sociology, Daniel Béland (2005, 2006, 2008; Béland & Hacker, 2004) has explored how political "institutional legacies" in the US, Canada, Belgium, and other countries have shaped a range of social phenomena, including nationalism, fiscal policy, health and pension programs, and welfare regimes. Dominique Clément (2008) also offers an overview of how federal policy and funding interacted with and influenced the rise of what he calls Canada's "rights revolution"—that is, the expansion of civil liberty and human rights organizations during the course of the twentieth century. Subnational institutions also influence politics, as shown by Dominique Masson (2012) who researches the Quebec women's movement. She shows that it remains strong, despite federal cuts to funding during the last decade, in part because provincial structures link to the nationalist project. Others, such as Jane Jenson and Martin Papillon (2000), have used the notion of **citizenship regimes** to show how Indigenous peoples offer subnational governance structures and how they can use transnational institutions to fight for their rights when the dominant state refuses to.

TRANSNATIONALISM

So far, we have seen how political sociologists depict politics as encompassing contests around material resources, cultural and social factors, and institutions within states or as an attempt to create states. However, with the spread of global capitalism, many anticipate that we are entering a new era in which old notions of time and social space are collapsing (King, 1995; Appadurai, 1990) and states are losing their status as the dominant institutions in the world (Jenson & Saint-Martin, 2003). In fact, some surmise that as the world becomes increasingly integrated and political processes become globalized, we are witnessing a massive restructuring of societies rivalling that which accompanied the Industrial Revolution, the emergence of modernity, and the rise of the state. This restructuring, these scholars say, demands a new form of politics and, perhaps, a new kind of political sociology.

Malcolm Waters (1995) describes globalization as a social process in which the traditional constraints posed by geography, economic activity, culture, and social configurations have receded and have been replaced by processes that extend beyond state boundaries. He and other globalization scholars say that old ways of understanding politics and political movements are of little help today, considering that economies have become increasingly integrated; cultures, homogenized; networks, broadened; and state institutions, challenged. Such developments potentially undermine or at least introduce new and problematic twists to traditional perspectives on political processes.

Take material resources, for example. Globalization scholars note that economies have become increasingly integrated, in part because new technologies make it easier for people to engage in economic exchanges across national boundaries. This has repercussions for both elites and labourers within individual countries. Increasing foreign direct investment and trade across states, for example, generates new international flows of wealth that alter how national elites respond to and take up these resources. It

also fosters the development of new, sometimes more exploitive labour practices, such as the use of **export processing zones** (EPZs), which circumvent workers' ability to unionize and challenge power-holders.

If some sociologists say that the circumstances surrounding the distribution and exercise of material power are altered by globalization, others say that claims to power based on culture are also undermined. They argue that globalization is accompanied by cultural homogenization. As Hollywood films gain prominence in international movie theatres (Barber, 1995), for instance, and fast-food culture spreads to all corners of the globe (Watson, 1997), local cultures are swamped by a hegemonic consumer culture. The result is an overall reduction in the range of unique cultural resources to which people seeking power have access.

These scholars see even institutions as internationalizing. The past 30 years have witnessed a proliferation of international agreements that challenge the sovereignty of existing states. Take, for example, the emergence of the European Union (EU), which integrated most of the economies and governments of western Europe, or the implementation of the **North American Free Trade Agreement** (NAFTA) in Canada, the US, and Mexico. More recently the **Comprehensive Economic and Trade Agreement** (CETA) between Canada and the EU was negotiated and the **Trans-Pacific Partnership** (TPP) among 12 Pacific Rim countries was pursued. The prominence of these agreements and other international institutions, such as the United Nations, have led some to declare that a *world society* is arising in which the practices and procedures structuring people's lives and actions are becoming increasingly homogeneous (see Meyer et al., 1997).

Not all political sociologists agree, however, that globalization has changed the world as fundamentally as globalization theorists claim. Peter Urmetzer (2005), for instance, looking at the Canadian case, effectively questions whether or not states have lost control of their economies and the extent to which foreign direct investment is actually globalized. Most trade pacts, and for that matter international agreements, are bilateral, between just two states, rather than multilateral or global. With respect to communication, it is indisputable that we live in an era of unprecedented technological innovation, and for those with material wealth, increased travel and communication is indeed an option. Yet much of the world does not have access to those resources, and in a post-9/11 era, the securitization and monitoring of communication and travel is limited as never before, even for the most privileged populations. When it comes to cultural and social exchange, here too we find that much occurs among wealthy states and the wealthy people within them. Not everyone participates. If culture is becoming so cheerfully homogeneous, then why, as Benjamin Barber (1995) noted, do we at the same time see rising radicalism and nationalist groups seeking independence from, rather than integration into, the international community? Finally, although there has been a rise of international institutions, few have the force to challenge the will of powerful states. Take for instance the US ignoring UN resolutions when they do not fit that state's agenda, as it did when US leaders decided to launch a war against Iraq in 2003. United Nations secretary general Kofi Annan declared the war illegal and noted that

it was not sanctioned by the organization's security council and was not in accord with the UN's founding charter. For all these reasons, it is likely more accurate to acknowledge the rise of transnational processes or transnationalism between some states and thus pause before calling recent changes truly global.

The key difference between globalization and transnationalism is the scale of the processes. The former claims that the entire world is involved, whereas the latter makes a lesser claim, only that more than one state is involved in an interaction with at least one other state. Scholars of transnationalism want us to remember that, as Sidney Tarrow (2005) rightly cautions, it is still states that uphold international norms and implement laws, not international organizations. The ways in which state leaders exercise power, the issues with which they are concerned, and the institutions through which they work have indeed changed over time. But states are by no means withering away.

WHAT IS A SOCIAL MOVEMENT?

Social movements try to achieve change through the voluntary cooperation of those challenging power-holders. Participants may contribute financial or other material resources, recruit new members, or spread a counter-ideology. They may also participate in sit-ins, boycotts, flash mobs, prefigurative actions and alternative forums, spectacle, demonstrations, protest marches, violent action, or civil disobedience. Social movements aim to change attitudes, everyday practices, public opinion, or the policies and procedures of business, government, and even other social movements.

Social movements are easier to understand when compared and contrasted with other phenomena studied by sociologists (Diani, 1992). A *social trend*, for example, is simply a changing pattern of social behaviour, whereas a social movement is a cooperative effort to achieve social change from below. A *pressure group* is an organization that aims to influence large institutions,

International NGOs like the International Monetary Fund regulate much of the financial life of the planet, but most of us could not name the people on this stage at the IMF annual conference.

ZACH GIBSON/AFP/Getty Images

particularly the state. A social movement is one kind of pressure group. However, other pressure groups—known as *interest groups*—represent the concerns of specific sets of people. Prominent interest groups include the Canadian Labour Congress, the Canadian Medical Association, Canadian Manufacturers and Exporters, and the Consumers' Association of Canada.

Since social movements depend on voluntary participation, they are voluntary associations. However, not all voluntary associations seek deeper changes in the distribution of social goods. Some provide social or health services; others organize leisure activities or unite the followers of a spiritual doctrine. Voluntary associations that only help people to accept or enjoy the existing social system are not social movements.

Unlike social movements, political parties try to win and keep political power. In principle, a social movement becomes a political party when it fields candidates in elections. The Green parties in Canada, Germany, France, and Italy, for example, have grown out of environmental movements in these countries. However, traditional distinctions between mainstream politics and social movements are increasingly blurred, with each taking on the form of the other (Meyer & Tarrow, 1998; Ramos & Rodgers, 2015).

THEORETICAL APPROACHES

Many sociologists welcomed the movements of the 1960s against war, racism, sexism, pollution, bureaucracy, and the flaws in the educational system as positive signs of healthy protest against injustice and alienation. They led to an abundance of research on social movements that moved beyond earlier collective behaviour approaches that viewed social movements as deviant.

New Social Movements

In Europe *new social movement* (NSM) theorists (e.g., Melucci, 1989; Touraine, 1981) propose that structural changes in Western societies during the middle of the twentieth century fundamentally altered people's identities and cultures. These changes gave rise, they argue, to social movements that are distinct from older class-based movements. NSMs are interested in the politics of cultural recognition; they are concerned less with the redistribution of wealth and status than with securing rights to expressive freedoms, symbolic practices, or lifestyles. In this sense, the appearance of NSMs may be explained by a value shift (Inglehart, 1990). In North America, NSM scholars focus on how **collective identity** affects mobilization and organizational dynamics and have found these to be similar to the identity-based processes of the "old" class-based movements (Polleta & Jasper [2001] offer a review of the area).

The NSM perspective focuses largely on the relationship between culture and collective identity. It proposes that social movements are cultural laboratories where people try out new forms of social interaction (Melucci, 1989). For NSM activists, important struggles take place in civil society, the areas of social interaction that stand largely outside of the state and the market. In fact, theorists claim that NSMs have come about since the 1960s because state and economic practices have increasingly encroached on people's everyday lives. Slogans such as "the personal is political" are meant to express how everyday life is pervaded by government and corporate activities as well as by dominant cultural ideas that create inequality.

According to this approach, civil society offers greater chances for freedom, equality, and *participatory democracy*, a system of decision-making in which all members of a group exercise control over group decisions. Indeed, NSMs are, in part, characterized by institutional arrangements whereby their members try to organize according to the ideals of equal participation. This is what social movements are good at, and striving for other kinds of success risks perverting these ideals (Cohen, 1985).

Framing Theory

Framing theory explains the ways movements create and spread their understandings of the

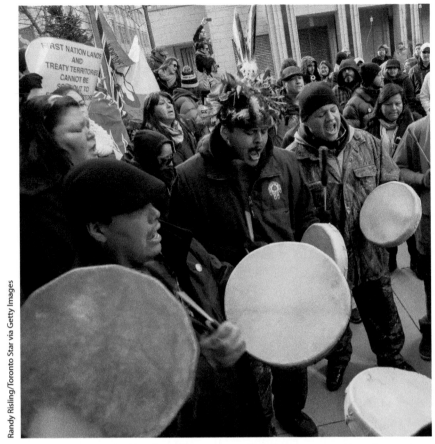

Randy Risling/Toronto Star via Getty Images

Social movements today, like Idle No More, are more likely than ever to combine reference to a particular demographic (e.g., First Nations people, women, disabled people) with reference to a particular social issue or disadvantage (e.g., poverty, mistreatment by police, ecological harm).

world and how these meanings help to form a sense of collective identity and common purpose.

Drawing on Erving Goffman's ideas, framing theorists define collective action frames as "action-oriented sets of beliefs and meanings that inspire and legitimate the activities and campaigns of a social movement organization" (Benford & Snow, 2000, p. 614). These communal understandings are used to identify and promote grievances.

According to framing theory, a social movement must succeed at three core framing tasks. First, an organization must articulate *diagnostic* frames that define social problems (or injustices) and their guilty agents. Second, *prognostic* frames must propose solutions to these social problems. Prognostic frames give meaning to specific strategies and are used to persuade potential recruits and members that these actions are the best way to solve or address particular

social problems. Third, since agreement with diagnostic and prognostic frames does not necessarily translate into participation, a social movement organization must provide compelling *motivational* frames that persuade people to join.

The process whereby individuals come to adopt the ideology and methods of a particular movement organization is called *frame alignment* (Snow et al., 1986). The alignment of interpretations is a necessary condition for maintaining participation. As Gamson suggests, "any movement that seeks to sustain commitment over a period of time must make the construction of collective identity one of its most central tasks" (Gamson, 1991, p. 27).

The Political Process Approach

The **political process approach** assumes that the **polity** can be characterized by its opportunities and constraints. Opportunities involve almost anything that provides reasons and resources for people to mobilize—as long as the political climate is not so oppressive that people cannot mobilize without fear or great difficulty. Political opportunities may include economic crises, laws ensuring the right to assemble, a history of previous collective action, even accidents that show the need for social change. Constraints include anything within the polity that may act as a barrier to the mobilization and survival of a social movement, including a repressive police state, inexperience with collective action, even a lack of communication among social movement participants. Opportunities and constraints go hand in hand: no polity is completely open or closed (Tarrow, 1988).

Fluctuations in the opportunities and constraints that influence the incidence of collective action create a cycle of contention. This can be illustrated by looking at contemporary Indigenous mobilization in Canada. Because much of it is in resistance to the colonial policies of the Canadian state significant events are often shaped by changes in federal policy. Take for instance the 1969 White Paper that aimed to eliminate Indian status and in turn sparked widespread protest across the country and led to the rebirth of Indigenous resistance. Another example can be seen around the 1982 patriation of the Constitution and Indigenous peoples' lobbying for formal incorporation in it, as well as splits among national organizations representing different Indigenous peoples—for instance the Métis, non-status Indians, and Indigenous women. Political opportunities and constraints also influenced Indigenous protest in 1990 which was marked by opposition to the Meech Lake Accord and later the 78-day armed standoff at Oka, Quebec, in the Kanesatake and Kahnawake communities, between Mohawks and the Canadian army, which triggered nationwide protest among communities in solidarity (Wilkes, 2001). The standoff arguably sparked a new generation of Indigenous activists and left many iconic images of resistance to colonization (Wilkes & Khel, 2014). Similar changes in

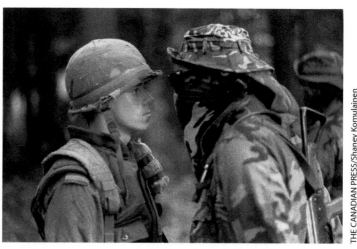

This famous image of Mohawk warrior Brad Laroque and Canadian soldier Patrick Cloutier from the 1990 Oka standoff is known as "Face to Face." Rima Wilkes and Michael Kehl (2014) examined how it shaped multiple nationalist discourses of colonization and resistance to it.

political opportunity are linked to the rise of the Idle No More movement and widespread national protest in late 2011 and early 2012 in reaction to an omnibus Bill, C-45, which threatened environmental protection and Indigenous rights as well as ongoing attention and protest to gain an inquiry into the disproportionately high number of missing and murdered Indigenous women (MMIW) in the country.

The political process model also looks at mobilizing structures, which include levels of informal and formal organization (McCarthy, 1996). An example of informal organization is a friendship network. When the cycle of contention is at its lowest point—when there are relatively few (or no) active social movement organizations—the network of friendships among demobilized movement participants keeps the spirit of collective action alive. These latent networks explain why social movements arise when political opportunities appear and when constraints are eased. Although informal communication alone cannot give rise to a social movement, it can become an important resource for mobilization.

The analysis of formal organization looks at the inner dynamics of social movements, which include leadership structures, flows of communication, the entry and exit of members, and the means of identifying, obtaining, and utilizing resources. The study of social movement organizations also includes inter-organization dynamics, such as movement coalitions, which result when two or more social movement organizations share resources. Coalitions can be temporary or enduring, and they can bridge different types of movements. Environmental, feminist, gay and lesbian, labour, peace, and anti-poverty organizations in British Columbia, for example, have formed coalitions based on shared understandings of social injustice (Carroll & Ratner, 1996).

THE ANALYSIS OF SOCIAL MOVEMENTS

Why do some movements succeed while others fail? To help answer this question, we will briefly examine two social movements in Canada: the women's movement and the separatist movement in Quebec.

Unity and Diversity in the Canadian Women's Movement

The first wave of feminism in Canada began in the late nineteenth century and effectively ended in 1918 when women gained the right to vote in federal elections. During this period, women formed organizations for the protection and education of young single women, such as the Anglican Girls Friendly Society and the Young Women's Christian Association (YWCA). Women's groups also protested against child labour and poor working conditions and pressed for health and welfare reforms.

Feminists of the first wave differed in their religious, class, and ethnic backgrounds. While many were Protestant, others were not. Anglo-Saxon women from the middle and upper classes predominated, especially among the leadership, while language divided anglophone and francophone feminists. Moreover, women's organizations had diverse goals. But the battle for women's voting rights unified the movement.

As with many other social movements, success led to decline. The fight for voting rights had given the movement a common goal. When this goal was attained, the movement lost unity

and momentum. Certainly, women did not stop pushing for change. Some worked within the labour movement; others continued to fight for social reform or female political representation. Yet after 1918, the Canadian women's movement became fragmented, and four decades would pass before it regained strength (Wilson, 1991).

The second wave rose out of the peace, student, and civil rights movements of the 1960s. In some cases, organizations advanced the women's cause by branching out. For example, a Toronto organization called the Voice of Women (VOW) was founded in 1960 as a peace group but gradually adopted other women's issues, and by 1964 it was promoting the legalization of birth control.

As a distinct women's movement emerged in the late 1960s and early 1970s, so did internal diversity. Some members were revolutionary Marxists while others were socialists, liberals, or radical feminists. At times, those who favoured grassroots activism criticized those who worked through high-profile official committees such as the Canadian Advisory Council on the Status of Women. The specific concerns of lesbian, non-white, immigrant, or Native women often were ignored or marginalized by mainstream women's groups. Finally, issues of language and separatism split women's organizations in Quebec from those in the rest of Canada.

Still, the movement found bases for unity. In 1970, a cross-Canada caravan for the repeal of the abortion law attracted publicity. Other coalitions formed around the issues of daycare, violence against women, labour, and poverty. Women's groups also worked together on International Women's Day celebrations.

To better represent their interests, in 1972 Canadian women formed the National Action Committee on the Status of Women (NAC). NAC grew and by the late 1980s had become an umbrella organization for more than 575 women's groups. At the same time, however, debate over the use of assisted reproductive technologies was growing. These technologies include cloning, surrogacy, assisted insemination, in vitro fertilization, embryo research, and prenatal diagnosis techniques. During a first round of consultations about these technologies with the federal government (1989–1993), NAC adopted a position that dissatisfied many of its members. Leaders of the women's organization argued that reproductive technologies were being developed not to meet the needs of ordinary women but to further the interests of the scientific community and the biotechnology industry. These technologies, claimed NAC, "represent the values and priorities of an economically stratified, male-dominated, technocratic science" (NAC, 1990, quoted in Montpetit, Scala, & Fortier, 2004, p. 145). Many within NAC disagreed with this position, which was seen as too simple and out of touch with concerns at the grassroots. Those offended included lesbians and infertile women who wished to bear children.

Between 1993 and 1997, therefore, NAC adopted a more open approach to the question. Discussions within the women's organization allowed ample room for the expression of diverse views. NAC now argued that assisted reproductive technologies were acceptable when they reduced inequalities between women.

The Canadian women's movement has organized around many issues. The diversity of its concerns and perspectives not only reflects the many faces of gender inequality but also promotes a diffusion of the movement's ideas and its survival in the face of changing social conditions. Internal arguments may exhaust activists, however. Although factions permit the coexistence of different constituencies, they draw attention and energy away from common interests that unify. When the time for action comes, a movement may lose effectiveness if its factions do not set aside their differences. As with all social movements, the success of the women's movement depends on balancing the trade-offs between diversity and unity (Briskin, 1992).

TIME to REFLECT

In what ways, if any, do you believe the women's movement has altered your life and your attitudes about gender? Has the environmental movement had a greater or lesser effect on you than the women's movement?

UNDER THE WIRE   G20 Protests in Toronto

In June 2010, world officials met in Toronto to discuss the global economy and to negotiate financial plans. Ever since the 1999 protests in Seattle, security has been strong at these economic summits, and Toronto police and private security firms had planned for months on how to deal with both peaceful and potentially riotous protests. Activists from Canada and around the world came to Toronto for a week of organized activity to help publicize their issues and grievances: worldwide poverty and growing inequality, the expansion of corporate power, colonialism and Indigenous rights, women's undervalued global labour, environmental degradation, food security, financial deregulation, and so on. How did so many people get involved in protesting financial summits? Why has protest activity now become expected by activists and police forces alike?

The answer is simple: the Internet and the ease of worldwide communication. Now that protest is fully "wired," activists can maintain a strong sense of collective identity and collective efficacy by staying in contact with one another, by reliving their triumphs and sorrows on YouTube, by recruiting and staying in touch through Facebook and Twitter, by organizing and participating in online activist forums, or simply by subscribing to a listserv, electronic newsletter, or blog.

Following more than 900 arrests in Toronto, activists used online communication technologies to help raise money for legal fees and to publicize what some take to be police brutality or government repression. Toronto police use modern technologies too as they comb through footage of rioters and use advanced face-recognition software to identify those culpable for damages to property and for endangering public safety.

The Separatist Movement in Quebec

What came to be known as the Easter Riots began on 28 March 1918 when police in Quebec City arrested a young man for avoiding conscription. As he was escorted to the police station, the suspect was followed by a group of angry sympathizers. Soon the police released him, but by then a crowd of some 2,000 people had gathered. Instead of dispersing, they stormed the police station and beat several officers. Next day, about 8,000 people attacked the offices of two pro-conscription newspapers before setting fire to the office of the registrar for conscription.

Authorities in Quebec City and Ottawa responded quickly, partly because they feared a repeat of recent revolution and civil war in Mexico, South Africa, Ireland, and Russia. Bolstered by hundreds of English-speaking troops from Ontario and western Canada, over the next few days the army patrolled the streets of Quebec City, guarding key government buildings such as the Legislative Assembly, the Dominion Arsenal, and the Dominion Rifle Factory. This did not prevent a series of violent clashes that left up to 10 civilians dead and dozens of soldiers and civilians wounded (Auger, 2008).

Other episodes of collective action for the French Canadian cause followed, but until the 1960s they were sporadic. What was then known as French Canadian "nationalism" was conservative. Its goal was to preserve the identity of the French by insulating them from outside influences: not just the English language but the world of politics, business, and the mass media.

Social change accelerated after the Asbestos Strike of 1949, a bitter labour dispute overlaid with ethnic tensions, because the miners who walked off the job for four months were mostly francophone while their managers tended to be English-speaking and the owners of mining companies were American. Through advances in communication—the spread of

radio, telephone, and television—the world outside Quebec became ever harder to ignore during the 1950s. This encouraged comparison, self-scrutiny, and awareness that more social change was inevitable. Families relying on agriculture were disappearing, and most of the population was now urban. During the Great Depression, citizens had sought help from the Canadian state, whose reach expanded greatly during the two world wars. French Canadians could not escape modernity. Why not therefore assert control over its direction (Balthazar, 1992)?

The 1960s and 1970s witnessed a sharp rise in collective action on behalf of the French in Quebec. In 1962, demonstrators in Montreal protested against the absence of any French speakers on the board of directors of Canadian National Railways. Queen Elizabeth's 1964 visit to Quebec City spurred anti-royalist, anti-British protests. When Prime Minister Pierre Trudeau visited Montreal for the annual Saint-Jean-Baptiste Day parade in 1968, hundreds of hostile and sometimes violent protesters voiced their opposition to the Liberal party and Canadian federalism. That same year, the school board for Saint-Léonard (a Montreal neighbourhood with a significant Italian minority) decided to limit the language of instruction in local schools to French. Immigration to Montreal was increasing, and the school board wanted to halt a trend—the adoption of English by newcomers—that threatened the importance of French. In what came to be known as the Saint-Léonard Crisis, unruly demonstrations continued as backers of Quebec's collective right to protect the French language confronted those who believed parents had a right to choose the language of instruction for their children (Hewitt, 1994).

The October Crisis of 1970 is etched in our collective memory. Members of the Front de libération du Québec (FLQ) kidnapped a British diplomat in Montreal, James Cross, and then the provincial Minister of Labour, Pierre Laporte, who was murdered by his captors. This was the peak of contentious nationalist politics in Quebec. Since its founding in 1963, the FLQ and allied groups had bombed property and monuments associated with the federal government, big business, and British colonialism. The extremism of the FLQ alienated the majority of Quebecers, however, and indeed can be taken as a sign of its political weakness (Breton, 1972; Hewitt, 1994). The events of 1970 were the culmination of a wave of contention that subsided quickly thereafter.

Looking back on the period since the October Crisis of 1970, it is difficult to discern a separatist *movement* in Quebec. This raises some provocative questions. If political parties are now its main promoters, has separatism become tamed? As organizations that work within the political system, today the Parti Québécois and the Bloc Québécois push less for the independence of Quebec than for the decentralization of power in Canada. Around the globe, moreover, citizens are turning to social movements as they search for grassroots alternatives to parties. What political options does this leave for those in Quebec who are nationalists yet have no separatist movement to join and believe that the Parti Québécois and the Bloc Québécois are no different from other parties—remote, bureaucratic, and unable to fulfill their promises to voters?

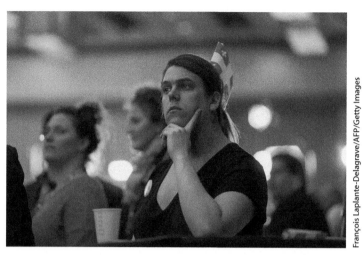

François Laplante-Delagrave/AFP/Getty Images

Parti Québécois supporters watch the provincial vote results in Montreal, 2014. After nine years in opposition, the Parti Québécois had won the provincial election in September 2012. However, with some controversial items on the agenda, such as the proposed Charter of Values, Quebec ended up voting out the separatist government in 2014.

> ### TIME to REFLECT
>
> Given what you have learned about the cyclical nature of social movement activity, what do you think the future holds for the separatist movement in Quebec? Can you justify your ideas with any particular social movement theory?

Is the Future of Social Movements Global?

Will globalization change the potential for social movement formation? Not all sociologists agree that globalization has created a fundamentally new political reality. Leslie Sklair (1994) argues that global politics are very much like national politics, simply on a larger scale. For Sklair, organizations such as Greenpeace International mirror the organizational structures of transnational corporations. He suggests that the global environmental movement consists of transnational environmental organizations whose professional members make up a global environmental elite. This elite plays an ideological game with the transnational corporate and governmental elite: each side attempts to have its version of the environmental reality accepted as the truth. For Sklair, this is politics as usual.

Sociologists also question whether the rise of supranational organizations, such as the European Union, will bring about new forms of collective action that link activists across national boundaries. Although the EU does constitute a new political terrain, collective action in Europe remains strongly rooted within the nation-state. While Europeans have many grievances against the EU, most protest against it is domestic rather than transnational. This may simply indicate that activists have yet to develop new transnational strategies and linkages. Nevertheless, domestic politics remains a viable political arena for voicing concerns about the EU (Imig & Tarrow, 2001).

Today, the world is more intricately connected than in the past. A variety of new social issues have arisen as a result, and there are now social movements that attack globalization. Each has to identify guilty institutions and actors, however, and states and corporations remain the best choice, because they are largely responsible for the policies and practices that promote globalization.

Generally, three factors are needed for a social movement to be truly global. First, a social movement must frame its grievances as global grievances. By framing environmental risks as global risks, the environmental movement hopes to demonstrate that environmental degradation affects everyone. Second, to be global, a social movement needs to have a worldwide membership and organizational structure. On a global scale, membership and frame alignment probably are supported by communication technologies such as email and the World Wide Web. Alternatively, a global movement can arise through a long-term coalition or network of movement organizations. For example, Indigenous peoples across North and South America, Australia, and New Zealand have united against the ongoing effects of colonialism and to ensure that the rights of Indigenous populations are recognized. Third, collective identity has to be a globalized identity. Global activists throughout the world would have to see each other as serving the same, common goal. Each would also have to identify cognitively and emotionally with that goal, as well as with other global activists and movement organizations.

CONCLUSION

In this chapter, we have highlighted a number of key perspectives to help you grasp how sociologists understand politics. In doing so, we noted that, unlike many other social sciences and vernacular understandings of politics and political movements, sociologists see these processes as being inherently linked to the negotiation of power. Sociologists, moreover, understand power as a relational concept that involves the overt and hidden interactions of individuals and groups, organizations, and institutions. We also highlighted that the state plays a prominent role in political sociology, because it remains a key force in structuring political processes and shaping political resources. Throughout the chapter, we illustrated this by looking at material, cultural, social, and institutional resources to understand how they are used to maintain power as well as launch challenges to it through political movements.

Early forms of collective action were poorly organized and relatively sporadic. Often their grievances were tied to local affairs, and usually their targets were local elites. With the rise of nation-states, however, new kinds of social movements appeared. These movements were highly organized and often identified social issues that stemmed from structural conditions such as economic inequality and narrow political representation. They also routinized protest activities: different social movements learned to apply similar methods of protest, such as the mass demonstration. The rise of NSMs in the second half of the twentieth century marks another change. These movements are more concerned with gaining cultural recognition than with the redistribution of social goods. So even though NSMs tend to use traditional forms of protest, they are more concerned with the politics of everyday life (the politics of recognition) than with the traditional politics of governance (the politics of redistribution).

The success of collective action is always linked to the social and political climate. Social and political changes can create opportunities for social movements, or they can impose constraints. According to a theory developed by Herbert Kitschelt (1993), present conditions in Canada have created opportunities that may lead to an increase in social movement activity. Support for social movements usually rises when political parties and interest groups fail to channel citizens' demands. Social movements can then mobilize support, attract resources, and forge alliances among protest groups. According to Kitschelt, however, this surge in social movement activity peaks as resources dwindle, as political parties begin to take up citizens' concerns, and as people's interest in collective mobilization wanes. Social movement activity then falls, only to rise again the next time organizers capitalize on frustration with parties and interest groups. In other words, the short-term pattern of movement activity is cyclical.

The long-term trend, by contrast, is toward an increase in the number of social movements. In the wealthy capitalist democracies, social movement activity has grown steadily since the 1960s. Established parties and politicians have proved increasingly incapable of providing satisfactory solutions to such issues as nuclear power, toxic waste disposal, resource management, and equal rights. Many Canadians now share a distrust of established politicians, political parties, and interest groups. Clearly, the extent of citizen discontent should not be exaggerated: federal elections show that established parties still attract much support. Nevertheless, many burning public questions—around gender; citizen participation; and environmental, ethnic, and Native rights issues—often elude both parties and interest groups. The current climate in Canada, therefore, favours an expansion of social movement activity. Whether organizers will actually exploit this situation remains to be seen. The outcome will depend on social movement leaders and on the political establishment's ability to co-opt them.

Questions for Critical Thought

1. We do not usually think of our capacities to pursue our interests in terms of the *power* we hold relative to others. In what ways is your capacity to "realize your will" or do what you want *enabled* or *curtailed* by your access to material, cultural and social, or institutional resources?

2. Does the Canadian state influence how you go about your daily life? How does it affect your power, your rights, and your ability to challenge authority?

3. What can account for Quebec nationalism in the 1970s, 1980s, and 1990s? Why have Indigenous peoples been active in resisting the colonizing efforts of the Canadian government?

4. With regard to the worldwide economic problems that began in 2008, does economic prosperity encourage or hinder the formation of protest movements? Would you expect more protest or less as a result? Which countries do you think will be more likely to experience social movement action? Which would be less likely? Can you draw on social movement theory to justify your answers to these questions?

5. Many people today believe that social movements offer better prospects for democratic participation than political parties or interest groups. However, Roberto Michels's "iron law of oligarchy" says that organization discourages democratic participation because resources, expertise, and status tend to flow to leaders (Michels 1962 [1911]). If you were organizing a social movement, what kind of safeguards would you put in place to prevent its leaders from dominating a movement organization? Are there lessons to be learned from the women's movement about decentralized decision-making or participatory organizational forms?

6. Why do you think that some social issues provoke social movement campaigning while other issues are hardly addressed by social movement activities? Do you think that these "orphan" issues have something in common that does not resonate with Canadian (or global) society? How might an activist frame an issue to increase the chances that people will pay attention?

7. What features of social movements make them similar to—or different from—business

organizations? Are social movements like firms: led by political entrepreneurs, do they compete against other suppliers in trying to find and expand the market for a product they want to sell? Do some important features set business firms and social movements apart?

8. In the 1940s, psychologist Abraham Maslow (1943) elaborated a theory of the hierarchy of needs. According to this theory, people have ranked needs: before they can turn to fulfilling their human potential, they need (1) physical well-being, (2) safety, (3) love, and (4) a sense of belonging. What social conditions render a re-arrangement of Maslow's hierarchy of needs more likely? Specifically, can social movement activism upset his ranking of needs: can belonging to a social movement that opposes a perceived injustice change the order of Maslow's hierarchy (e.g., belonging to a movement becomes more important than love, safety, well-being, or self-fulfillment)?

Sociological Explorations

1. Follow the coverage of a political protest in a local, a national, and an international news outlet for one week. This can be done through news archives (such as Factiva), by constructing a Google alert, or by tracking specific news sites. Identify the key frames covering the protest, the tactics used, and who is involved. In doing so, compare and contrast the coverage at the different levels (local, national, international).

2. Find political polling on key issues or parties on the websites of polling firms (e.g., Environics or Pew Research Center) or through blogs (e.g., FiveThirtyEight.com or ThreeHundredEight.com). Analyze the polls to identify the trends on specific parties, issues, and debates and look for underlying patterns that drive them across time.

3. Choose a politician in the news and research his or her biography, political career, and positions on public issues. Pretending that you are Max Weber, identify the source(s) of their power. Is their power a function of their class, their social status/prestige, the party to which they belong, or some combination of these? Perform the same analysis for another politician and then compare your results.

Recommended Readings

Baer, D. (Ed.). (2002). *Political sociology: Canadian perspectives.* **Don Mills, ON: Oxford University Press.**
This introductory text presents an overview of Canadian scholarship in political sociology and includes the work of many of the area's key luminaries.

Davenport, C., Johnston, H., & Mueller, C. (Eds). (2005). *Repression and mobilization.* **Minneapolis, MN: University of Minnesota Press.**
A collection of essays on state responses to collective action, this is a must-read for students of social movements.

della Porta, D., Andretta, M., Mosca, L., & Reiter, H. (2006). *Globalization from below: Transnational activists and protest networks.* **Minneapolis, MN: University of Minnesota Press.**
Challenging the idea that global social movements are merely coalitions of local movements, the authors argue that the global movement against neo-liberalism is a form of collective action that represents important changes in tactics, collective identities, and patterns of organization.

Fligstein, N., & McAdam, D. (2012). *A theory of fields.* **New York, NY: Oxford University Press.**
Destined to become a classic, Fligstein and McAdam formulate a novel theoretical framework for explaining political and collective action.

Lachmann, R. (2010). *States and power.* **Cambridge, UK: Polity Press.**
This text offers an overview of how states emerged and how they have come to dominate contemporary

political processes. It introduces students to key perspectives on theories of the state.

Nash, K., & Scott, A. (Eds). (2001). *The Blackwell companion to political sociology.* **Malden, MA: Blackwell.**
An encyclopedia of North American political sociology, this book is a one-stop resource that covers the main debates and innovations in this area of sociology.

Ramos, H., & Rodgers, K. (2015). *Protest and politics: The promise of social movement societies.* **Vancouver, BC: UBC Press.**
A collection of essays largely by Canadian social movement scholars, *Protest and Politics* problematizes the conceptual divides between political sociology and the study of social movements.

Snow, D., Soule, S.A., & Kriesi, H. (Eds). (2004). *The Blackwell companion to social movements.* **Oxford, UK: Blackwell.**

This is a comprehensive examination of the state of social movement research and what remains to be studied and theorized. Chapters are written by well-known movement scholars.

Staggenborg, S., & Ramos, H. (2015). *Social movements* **(3rd edn). Don Mills, ON: Oxford University Press.**
Staggenborg and Ramos provide a thorough introduction to major social movement theories as well as a comprehensive account of the history of important Canadian social movements.

Stanbridge, K., & Ramos, H. (2012). *Seeing politics differently: A brief introduction to political sociology.* **Don Mills, ON: Oxford University Press.**
Stanbridge and Ramos provide an introduction to political sociology by challenging the common assumption that people can be "not that into" politics. It looks at much Canadian scholarship and provides examples to illustrate points.

Recommended Websites

AlterNet
www.alternet.org
AlterNet is an award-winning Web magazine dedicated to issues of social justice and the promotion and amplification of alternative voices.

Assembly of First Nations
www.afn.ca
This very comprehensive site contains detailed information about social issues pertaining to Canada's First Nations.

Canadian Centre for Policy Alternatives
www.policyalternatives.ca
The Canadian Centre for Policy Alternatives is an independent non-profit organization committed to presenting counter-hegemonic information.

Canadian Lesbian and Gay Archives (CLGA)
www.clga.ca
This site provides information that relates to lesbian, gay, bisexual, and transgender movements. Its focus is mostly Canadian, but the archive also provides plenty of information from around the world.

Canadian Race Relations Foundation
www.crrf-fcrr.ca/en/
The Canadian Race Relations Foundation's primary goal is to end race- and ethnic-based discrimination

in Canada. This website provides information about current issues and research.

Charter of Rights and Freedoms
http://laws-lois.justice.gc.ca/eng/Const/page-15.html#h-39
The Department of Justice provides the text of the Canadian Charter of Rights and Freedoms, which is the freestanding first 34 sections of the Constitution Act, 1982.

Independent Media
www.independentmedia.ca
This website offers a directory of non-corporate journalism. It lists many news sources that are not widely disseminated or are missed by mainstream audiences.

Mobilizing Ideas
https://mobilizingideas.wordpress.com/
Produced by The University of Notre Dame's Center for the Study of Social Movements, *Mobilizing Ideas* presents scholarly debates and news on the study of collective action.

Yoruba Richen, TedTalk: What the Gay Rights Movement Learned from the Civil Rights Movement
www.ted.com/talks/yoruba_richen_what_the_gay_rights_movement_learned_from_the_civil_rights_movement

Film director Richen explains how social movements inspire not only more collective action but innovation in tactics.

Sarah Hunt, Ted^x:Victoria: In Her Name: Relationships as Law

https://youtu.be/XmJZP2liqKI
Sarah Hunt (First Nations and Indigenous Studies Program, University of British Columbia) speaks on activism, colonial violence, and missing and murdered Indigenous women.

Key Terms

citizenship regimes Institutions, rules, and understandings that define who is a citizen, who is not, and what rights and protections come with citizenship.

collective identity As opposed to someone's sense of individual Self, an activist's feeling or awareness that other members of their movement think and feel similarly about the movement, the social movement organization (SMO), and each other. The development of collective identity is crucial to the recruitment and retention of SMO members.

Comprehensive Economic and Trade Agreement (CETA) A trade agreement between Canada and the European Union.

counter-hegemony The ability to launch oppositional views that challenge existing power-holders. See also **hegemony**.

cultural capital A term coined by Pierre Bourdieu for cultural and linguistic competence, such as prestigious knowledge, tastes, preferences, and educational expertise and credentials, that individuals possess and that influences the likelihood of their educational and occupational success.

culture industry The political economy involved in the production of norms, meanings, values, mores, knowledge, and customs of a society through media, art, literature, and entertainment. A term associated with the work of Max Horkheimer and Theodor Adorno, who argued that the modern culture industry was homogenizing culture, lowering artistic and intellectual standards, and undermining the political consciousness of the working class.

export processing zone (EPZ) Special area within a state where its tariff restrictions, laws, and labour practices are not fully enforced and goods are produced for export to other countries. Such zones usually house foreign companies that exploit local workers. The *maquiladoras* along Mexico's northern border with the US are an example of an EPZ.

false consciousness A person's misunderstanding of his or her lot in life and the wider social structure and relationships that shape power and politics. A term coined by Karl Marx as a label for ignorance or delusion about one's objective class position.

framing theory The process by which people develop a particular conceptualization of an issue or change their thinking about an issue. Any issue can be viewed from a variety of perspectives and be construed as having implications for multiple values or considerations. According to Goffman, frames are definitions of a situation that are built up in accordance with social principles of organization that govern them and our subjective involvement in them. Frame analysis is concerned with the organization of experience.

hegemony The dominance of ideology and culture by an elite group to the point that few alternatives exist or can be imagined.

Industrial Revolution A period of rapid social and political transition from feudal to modern forms of governance beginning in the eighteenth century in western Europe.

institutions Patterns of behaviour that order people's lives in relatively predictable ways. Institutions comprise norms and social practices that have calcified to the extent that they create a predictable pattern or map of behaviours that people will usually follow.

North American Free Trade Agreement (NAFTA) Signed in 1992 by the US, Canada, and Mexico, the "model" of trade liberalization that the most powerful in the world were hoping to extend to the rest of the world. Under NAFTA, capital flows and investments as well as trade have been liberalized. Under Chapter 11 of the accord, private entities (companies) are entitled to sue governments if their interests are jeopardized by legislation on issues such as labour rights or the environment.

omnivore A cultural omnivore is a person able to consume a wide range of cultural products and to interact comfortably with people across the social hierarchy.

political process approach An approach that assumes that political constraints and opportunities influence the rise and fall of social movements as well as their institutional organization.

political processes The dynamic contestation of power among dominant elites and subordinate challengers. It is also associated with a branch of social movement theory.

polity A sovereign political unit.

social capital The power that is derived from ties to social networks; a concept widely thought to have been developed by American sociologist James Coleman in 1988 but discussed by Pierre Bourdieu in a similar way in the early 1980s.

social movements The social form taken by collective actors engaged in struggles against dominance relations; the coordinated, voluntary action of non-elites (people with no control over major resources) for the manifest purpose of changing the distribution of social goods. The outcomes of these struggles are often difficult to grasp. To what extent social actors contribute to social change or toward participating in system regulation remains an open question.

Trans-Pacific Partnership (TPP) An attempted trade agreement between Canada and 11 other countries of the Pacific Rim.

univore A cultural univore is someone with narrow cultural tastes whose social networks are restricted to people with less power.

Canadian Society and the Global Context

PART

V

We are living in a time of rapid globalization. Globalization has many definitions, but in respect to culture, it refers to a process of international integration that results from a growing interchange of world views, products, ideas, and other aspects of culture. From an economic standpoint, it refers to the sped-up cross-national flow of capital investment, labour power, immigrants, goods, and services. While globalization is not new, the rapid expansion of sophisticated information technology has made the instant exchange of ideas, goods, and services the norm. We do not need to physically cross borders to gain access to products, news, and views from around the world. Rapidly expanding information technology has also made the study of events around the globe and international relationships relatively easy and common, as we will see in the chapters in this section.

To begin, in Chapter 14, on globalization and social change, author Liam Swiss helps you explore different theoretical perspectives on globalization and how they account for social change. In this chapter, you will examine various types of global flows of capital, goods, and people to gain a better understanding of how globalization affects all of us every day in a variety of ways. You will also begin to appreciate the tensions between centralization or convergence (globalization's power to unite and homogenize us) and divergence (globalization's power to divide us) and how these globalizing processes contribute to social change.

Cheryl Teelucksingh's chapter (Chapter 15) on population, urbanization, and the environment similarly focuses on large-scale, macro forces that shape our lives and contribute to social change. Teelucksingh's chapter begins by looking at how social forces influence human population growth. It then considers the impact of industrialization (and deindustrialization) on social inequality in Canadian cities. All these processes inevitably affect the environment and opportunities for sustainable development, as you will see as you read on. Population growth and urbanization almost always have environmental impacts—and even environmental damage. Teelucksingh challenges you to think critically about population growth, industrialization, sustainability, urban environments, urban sprawl, and, more broadly, humanity's place in the environment.

Today, technology, and the Internet in particular, has opened up opportunities for us to become more aware of and more socially engaged in social struggles that are taking place in our neighbourhoods and communities as well as in distant parts of the globe. In Chapter 16, David Young and Anabel Quan-Haase introduce us to a number of perspectives that sociologists use to analyze technology and the media. They also tackle sociological issues such as power, control, inequality, and conflict as they pertain to media and technology in Canadian society. This chapter will help you think sociologically about how technology and the media affect our everyday lives, including notions of the self and performativity. In fact, technology and media affect every part of our society, including culture, socialization, organization, deviance, and everything else we have discussed in this book.

14 | Globalization and Social Change

LIAM SWISS

In this chapter you will:

▶ Explore different theoretical perspectives on globalization and how they account for social change

▶ Examine various types of global flows of capital, goods, and people to gain a better understanding of how globalization affects us all

▶ Learn more about competing global networks of groups actively trying to shape the globalization agenda

▶ Appreciate the tensions between convergence and divergence associated with globalization and how these processes contribute to social change

INTRODUCTION

How is globalization affecting your daily life? How is it changing the world around you? Do we witness and critically engage with the effects of globalization, or do we take them for granted? These questions underline the contradictory nature of globalization in most lives. It is at once implicated everywhere and in everything and simultaneously can be overlooked by many in society. Past discussions of globalization have viewed it as a primarily economic process. Indeed, it is often regarded as a homogenizing economic force within global society. Economic policies and development processes lead to an increasingly similar world where you can just as easily buy an Apple iPhone in suburban Vancouver as you can in central Lagos or Jakarta. Emerging global similarities—like the Apple iPhone—and the effects of neo-liberal economic policies are signs of globalization's impact on our world; however, to confine our understanding of globalization to a narrow economic interpretation is to ignore other facets of globalization that have political, cultural, and social implications for us all.

Apart from the homogenizing effects of globalization that can promote convergence of different societies toward similar products, policies, and perspectives, we must equally assess globalization's power to divide and further differentiate societies and communities at the global and, indeed, national levels. This tension between convergence and divergence has been a central question of the sociology of globalization and will frame this chapter's exploration of globalization(s) and the various sociological views on them.

First, we will examine concepts of convergence and divergence to assess the evidence of both processes of social change at the global level. Next, the chapter outlines how globalization has been conceptualized economically, socio-culturally, and politically. The tension between convergence and divergence will be interpreted through three key sociological approaches to understanding globalization: the

world system perspective, the world society perspective, and a range of perspectives on space and time. These theoretical vantage points conceive of globalization in differing yet interrelated ways and allow sociologists to engage with globalization as a complex set of processes leading to social change. Globalization processes involve a variety of flows and connections that make globalization apparent in everyday life in concrete ways. By examining these flows and the networks of actors involved in enacting and facilitating them through the lens of the various sociological perspectives on globalization, the chapter concludes by weighing the evidence for convergence and divergence and arguing that globalization's role in social change is a contradictory one that continually both levels and divides societies, states, and people.

Convergence vs. Divergence

There are many ways in which globalization promotes social change. One ongoing debate surrounding globalization and social change of great interest to sociologists is the question of convergence versus divergence. These are opposing trends in global social change. Convergence makes people, societies, and states more similar, uniform, or homogenous. Divergence, on the other hand, makes the world more unequal, differentiated, or diverse. Can globalization lead to both of these changes? Possibly. Are they mutually exclusive? If we consider them as absolutes, yes. If we consider the possibility that we might witness convergence and divergence operating simultaneously, then the social change resulting from globalization will be more complex and multidirectional than we might think at first. In the remainder of this chapter, as we explore different sociological perspectives on globalization, the global flows associated with the process, and the key actors involved, be mindful of the following questions:

(1) How does globalization promote convergence?
(2) How does globalization promote divergence?
(3) Can globalization lead to convergence and divergence simultaneously?

Blueplanet2/iStockphoto

Does this photo from China provide evidence of an increasingly similar world or one in which traditional values continue to survive?

SOCIOLOGICAL APPROACHES TO GLOBALIZATION

Globalization is evident in our daily lives in many ways, so it is not surprising that sociologists have devised a variety of theoretical perspectives on what globalization is and how it works. These perspectives address different facets of the globalization phenomenon. This chapter introduces you to three perspectives that have influenced the way that sociologists interpret globalization and social change: the *world system perspective*, the *world society perspective*, and a number of perspectives on space and time. Although each perspective offers a unique take on what globalization is and why it happens, sociologists may use all of them to help understand different aspects of globalization.

The World System Perspective

When we consider globalization as a process, the first thing that probably comes to mind is its economic dimension. The world system perspective offers one lens through which to view economic globalization, but it does contradict some widespread popular beliefs about the globalization process. In particular, while some see globalization as a relatively recent phenomenon, supporters of the world system approach argue that economic globalization today is simply a continuation of a series of long economic cycles in the capitalist world system (Arrighi, 1994; Chase-Dunn & Grimes, 1995; Chase-Dunn, 1998; Wallerstein, 1976, 1979b).

Emerging initially in the 1970s as a refinement of the dependency theories of economic development and a rejection of the earlier modernization theories, the world system perspective rejects the concept of "national" development and instead emphasizes that the only development that can be observed is within the capitalist world system (Chase-Dunn & Grimes, 1995; Wallerstein, 1979a, 1979b). The need to view the system as a global whole, acknowledging that states are simply smaller parts of the world system, is one of the main arguments of this perspective.

This focus on the capitalist world system breaks down its component states into three categories: a developed core, the semi-periphery, and an underdeveloped periphery. Capital accumulation flows from periphery to core as a consequence of the overall workings of the world system and the unequal power hierarchy of core and periphery (Chase-Dunn & Grimes, 1995). Countries in the periphery can only benefit from the interaction of globalization and economic development through increased integration of the periphery into the world economy in a more competitive fashion (Portes, 1997). As the world economy expands, states that are better integrated within it will stand a greater chance of benefiting from global economic expansion (Wallerstein, 1979a). Considering each of the three categories in turn will give us a better sense of the roles they play in the globalization process.

Core countries are those at the centre of economic and political power on the global stage. Economic production in the core depends on skilled, high-wage labour and requires significant amounts of capital (Chase-Dunn, 1998). The core accumulates capital through appropriating the surpluses or profits of the capitalist world system. Through this control of resources, the core is able to evolve more complex modes of production and maintain its global political and military supremacy. Unsurprisingly, the core countries identified in the map in Figure 14.1 align very closely with the countries defined as "high income" by the World Bank.

In contrast, the **periphery** is that part of the world where we would expect to find labour-intensive economic production, often linked to resource extraction but relying on low-skilled and low-wage labour (Chase-Dunn, 1998). The periphery accumulates little of the global capitalist surplus and therefore has few resources on which to develop or expand its share of global wealth and power. Similarly, peripheral countries tend to be on the margins of global political and military power, lacking the power that dominant core countries possess. Figure 14.1 shows that the periphery aligns with the countries in the Global South defined by the World Bank as members of the low-income group.

 We live in a society in which economic inequalities are complexly related to a range of inequalities. For more on world economic systems see **Chapter 11**, "Work and the Economy."

Not surprisingly, the **semi-periphery** comprises countries that show a mix of both core and peripheral characteristics. This third category is a necessary feature of the world system, preventing overt conflict between core and periphery, with the semi-periphery as "both exploited and exploiter," thus emphasizing the

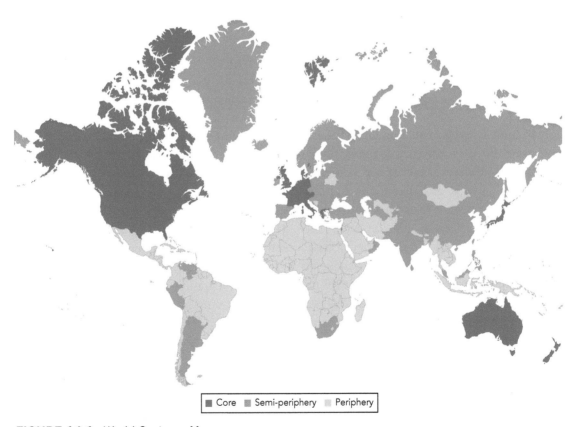

Core   Semi-periphery   Periphery

FIGURE 14.1 World Systems Map

SOURCE: Map created by author using data from Jason Beckfield, 2003, "Inequailty in the world polity: The structure of international organization." *American Sociological Review* 68 (3): 401–24, and author's own coding.

dual nature of such countries (Wallerstein, 1979b, p. 23). It is a buffer between the two extremes of core and periphery, and as the map in Figure 14.1 indicates, it is composed mainly of countries with longer histories of independence as well as a number of the former members of the Soviet bloc.

> ### TIME to REFLECT
>
> Where do you think Canada fits into the scheme of core, semi-periphery, and periphery? Can you think of arguments to place it in another category?

This single global division of labour underpins the capitalist world system, but it is not based on any one centre of power. Certain core countries may become dominant or hegemonic in various periods, but this hegemony can shift. In the colonial era of the nineteenth century, Britain held a position of dominance in the world system. After World War II, a period of American hegemony succeeded British dominance (Chase-Dunn, 1998). Signs of American decline were becoming apparent to world system researchers in the 1990s, but no new hegemon has emerged within the core. Some speculate about a coming period of Asian hegemony, corresponding to the recent rise of China as an economic superpower, as possibly the next evolution in the world system (Arrighi, 1998). Still others suggest that China is unlikely to jump from semi-periphery to core status and instead is more likely to become the site of a proxy battle by other core powers and the interests of multinational corporations (Petras, 2006).

This underlines one of the main contentions of the world system perspective: it is very difficult for societies/states to move between the three categories of core, semi-periphery, and periphery. Much more likely is movement within categories as countries ebb and flow in terms of economic and political importance. Globalization and social change from the world system perspective thus reflects the evolution of the capitalist world economy as it cycles through periods of expansion and contraction linked to capital accumulation, innovation, political competition, and other power struggles (Arrighi, 1994). These systemic cycles of global capitalism, rather than any truly novel form of economic organization, are what we have come to recognize as economic globalization in recent years. The integration of economies into the global capitalist system is not a new phenomenon and indeed simply supports world system arguments that the capitalist world system should be sociologists' chief concern when considering globalization.

If we consider the implications of the world system perspective in the context of our question of convergence and divergence, we can see within the core–periphery divide a very clear argument in favour of globalization as a divergent force. Global capitalist accumulation requires the exploitation of the periphery by the core. While the core benefits and advances economically and politically, the periphery, if not falling further behind, at least experiences relatively persistent levels of deprivation compared to the core and semi-periphery (Chase-Dunn, 1998). Globalization from this perspective is primarily an economic manifestation of capitalist exploitation leading to the aggrandizement of the core at the expense of others. With this focus on a narrow interpretation of global capitalism, the world system perspective lens offers a unique view of economic globalization but does little to address some of the other forms of globalization that surround us. To add to our understanding of these other forms, the next two sections explore alternative sociological viewpoints on globalization: the world society and space–time perspectives.

The World Society Perspective

Looking around the global community, you might take for granted that states appear to share very similar structures and practices. These similarities might include things like central banks, education systems, environmental regulations, and human rights frameworks. Rather than taking this similarity for granted, sociologists have asked, "Why *do* states and other organizations so closely resemble one another despite their widely varying histories?" This is the question at the crux of the world society perspective popularized by a group of sociologists associated with John W. Meyer of Stanford University. Meyer and his students argue that the striking similarities we witness in terms of policies, structures, and other institutions of the state arise from a common set of "world cultural" norms, scripts, and models adopted and implemented by states (Meyer, 2007; Meyer et al., 1997). Such norms and models spell out what is expected of a legitimate state or other organization in the global community. They arise because of the efforts of international non-state actors like non-governmental organizations, intergovernmental bodies, and networks/communities of experts globally (Boli & Thomas 1997; 1999). These organizations compose what "world society" is and create, spread, and refine these common models and scripts at the global level.

States enact these scripts in order to be deemed legitimate by their peers, citizens, and the others (non-state actors) of world society. This leads to the striking similarities seen globally among states, something sociologists have identified as **institutional isomorphism**: the similarity of organizational structure emerging from imitation, coercion, or pressures of legitimacy (DiMaggio & Powell, 1983). Because states enact similar scripts—the structuring of legal systems to protect human rights, for instance—we begin to see state structures closely resemble one another despite diverse contexts.

What drives states and other actors to enact these scripts? World society researchers have highlighted the influence of two key factors that promote the diffusion of world cultural models among states: (1) embeddedness: the extent to which a state is tied to the rationalized others of world society through global networks of ties, memberships, and treaty adoptions; and (2) model density: the extent to which previous adoption of a model by other states or organizations influences other states to act similarly (Hughes et al., 2009; Swiss, 2009, 2012; Yoo, 2011).

Embeddedness, simply put, involves the influence of NGOs, experts, and global treaties and conferences on states. Model density, on the other hand, represents influence exerted by the actions of other states. Described sometimes as a **contagion** or demonstration effect, we can see density either as a form of peer pressure or as evidence that various models and institutions are worth adopting. The combination of embeddedness and model density has indeed been shown to affect the adoption of world models as varied as women's rights (Paxton, Hughes, & Green, 2006; Swiss, 2009; Wotipka & Ramirez, 2008), environmental protection (Frank, Longhofer, & Schofer, 2007; Schofer & Hironaka, 2005), and education (Schofer & Meyer, 2005).

If these models are so influential, why do we not see institutional isomorphism everywhere and an international community composed of nearly identical states? Evidence suggests that a key feature of the world society perspective is what has been described as either a loose or a complete decoupling of model implementation and intent (Clark, 2010; Drori et al., 2003; Swiss, 2009). This accounts for the great variation we see in implementation of world-level models within local contexts and explains the persistent divergence in the global community. One example is states signing on to treaties intended to protect human rights or to reduce greenhouse gas emissions but then failing to protect such rights or cut emissions.

The gap between democracy in intent and democracy in application in many states of the Global South is also evidence of persistent decoupling in the global community. Despite elections held to promote the appearance of free, fair, and accountable government, the actual practices of democracy often fall far short of what we might in Canada deem free or fair. Loose coupling is linked to a number of causes. For instance, Clark (2010) argues that less wealthy, non-Western, and conflict-prone states are more likely to experience loose coupling in the area of human rights. These causes of decoupling suggest that the application of world society models can be very uneven globally, and indeed, other research suggests that world society's reach is unequal and can exclude parts of the Global South in significant ways (Beckfield, 2003, 2008).

TIME to REFLECT ●━━━━ ━━━━

How does Canada's past track record on its international commitments to cut greenhouse gas emissions demonstrate decoupling?

A final feature of the world society perspective is the extent to which the models and norms that world society promotes are not static or fixed. Instead, they evolve and are refined as norms become institutionalized by various actors. In this sense, world culture is dynamic and subject to contestation and change. States and other organizations implementing certain models and scripts draw upon their experience of enacting such scripts as they collaborate further with international non-governmental and intergovernmental organizations to tweak and alter the content of world cultural scripts.

In the world society perspective, the focus is squarely on institutions and how they appear increasingly similar on the global level. Particular attention is paid to the relationship of states to a world society consisting of international organizations, networks of experts, and other actors that shape world cultural institutional scripts and models. The world society perspective, in this respect, is likely best equipped to explain and characterize questions of political globalization and aspects of global governance. In contrast, it is less equipped to account for economic globalization than is the world system perspective, nor can it explain cultural forms of globalization as readily as we might expect, given its focus on "world cultural models." As we will see in the next section, a group of other perspectives offers a better lens through which to examine the cultural effects of globalization.

Space–Time Perspectives

In contrast to the relatively unified world system and world society perspectives discussed above, the range of views labelled here as space–time

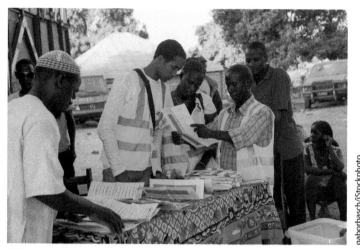

Helping make sure the general election is fair, an international election observer examines a polling station and ballot boxes in rural Guinea-Bissau. This election in 2014 was the first since a coup overthrew the government in 2012.

perspectives encompass a number of attempts to describe and understand globalization by examining how the world is becoming increasingly connected through changes in the way that society interacts with space and time. These changes can be seen in societies abandoning conventional relationships with time and space (Giddens, 1990), increased global awareness as a result of greater interconnectedness (Robertson, 1992, 1995), global networks underpinned by new technologies (Castells, 2000), and changing concepts of locality (Sassen, 2007). As we will see, this sort of lens on globalization enables us to go beyond the purely economic or institutional globalizations treated by the world system and world society perspectives and provides a means for examining other social and cultural shifts associated with globalization.

Anthony Giddens defined globalization as the "intensification of worldwide social relations which link distant localities in such a way that local happenings are shaped by events occurring many miles away and vice versa" (1990, p. 64). This intensification of relations leads to greater interconnectedness globally both in the linking of distant places and in the extent to which events elsewhere work to shape events in any particular locality. Roland Robertson echoes this notion that what goes on elsewhere in the world matters more to us than it did in the past. He defines globalization as "the compression of the world and the intensification of consciousness of the world as a whole" (Robertson, 1992, p. 8). Both definitions emphasize the idea that the world is becoming more interconnected and that a process of intensification or compression is at play, connecting localities through both events and awareness in an unprecedented way.

Giddens argues that this process of intensification is linked to increases in the level of time–space *distanciation* experienced in society. This concept refers to the ways in which "time and space are organised so as to connect presence and absence" (Giddens, 1990, p. 14). With increased levels of time–space distanciation, we see greater global interconnectedness emerge by "fostering relations between 'absent' others, locationally distant from any given situation of face-to-face interaction" (Giddens, 1990, p. 18). This change in the notion of space and place closely parallels a similar concept described as time–space compression, which refers to processes that change the way we view time and space, compressing or accelerating time and shrinking distances through technologies associated with communication or travel (Harvey, 1990). These changes in the social functioning of time, facilitated by technologies and emerging networks, have gone so far as to encourage operation of business and social relations globally in "real time" outside of the traditional linear conceptions of time, something Castells refers to as timeless time (2000). These changing social notions of time and space contribute to the shrinking of the world that Robertson identifies and, in turn, help to make individuals more aware of the global.

TIME to REFLECT

How have technological advances and other global networks changed the way people relate to one another in your lifetime?

Building upon notions of space–time compression and the intermixing of global and local, other thinkers in the space–time perspective have emphasized the importance of understanding globalization as building links or networks across borders and societal boundaries, altering traditional notions of place, and breaking down the conventional sense of local (Castells, 2000; Sassen, 2007). With their emphasis on the networks and spatiality of globalization, both Castells and Sassen echo the notions discussed above of a compressed world, with boundaries between local and foreign blurred. Castells emphasizes, alongside his notion of timeless time, the idea of the space of flows, which refers to the manner in which space has become less connected to actual physical places and is now connected to the flows of ideas, communication, and relations fostered by the network society and underscoring the global economy. Sassen's work on global cities also examines how changing notions of space and the definition of "local" are resulting in new ways of working, communicating, and living in the globalized world. She highlights the important ways in which boundaries and borders that had once separated place and space are now being transformed as a result of globalization, leading to the emergence of global cities and corresponding transnational communities of financial and economic activity (Sassen, 2001). These cities exist at the nexus of global and local and reflect the extent to which local cultures are being reshaped to incorporate global concerns as a result of the changed context of space and place in the global era. Many global cities, like New York, Tokyo, and Shanghai, have now reached "megacity" status, exceeding 10–15 million in population. Still other megacities across the Global South, such as New Delhi, Sao Paulo, and Mexico City, continue to grow by drawing migrants from rural areas in search of greater economic opportunity in the global economy. Megacities face unique challenges of globalization linked to population pressure, environmental degradation, and resource shortages. Despite these challenges, the number of megacities in the Global South is predicted to grow sharply in the next 50 years.

Global cities, like Toronto, Montreal, and Vancouver, are a crucial part of the global economic system. For an extended discussion of global cities, turn to the Global Issues box, p. 360 in **Chapter 15**, "Population, Urbanization, and the Environment."

Robertson also draws attention to the overlooked place of culture and identity within the globalization context and argues that the "intensification of consciousness of the world as a whole" led to emerging similarities in social structure and identity, because these things were more often being defined relative to others globally (1992). This process of relativization is an important feature of this view of globalization, since it implies that all features of the global community (states, humankind, individuals, and so on) are constantly being shaped relative to all others. This relativization is a significant indicator of the global awareness Robertson identifies.

Even though states, societies, and individuals might shape their identities relative to others globally, this does not mean that we should expect to see a uniform world emerging. Instead, Robertson suggests that we should instead see the interpenetration of both the universal and

Bolivian dancers celebrate International Migrants Day in Sao Paulo, Brazil. In recent years, many Bolivian immigrants have come to megacity Sao Paulo to work in the international textile industry.

the particular as a result of this relativization. This contradiction of convergence and divergence (universal versus particular) is evident in the ways that globalized identities, commodities, and structures are adapted or modified in local practice. Robertson labels this mixing of global and local as **glocalization**, reflecting the mixing of global and local whether strategically or organically (Robertson, 1995). Others have referred to this mixing of convergence and divergence as a form of cultural hybridization in which we see emerging out of the globalization

GLOBAL ISSUES
Globalization and the Maharaja Mac

What is glocalization, and how does it function? We might think that it would be difficult to see the effects of the mixing of global and local, but we do not have to look much further than the McDonald's restaurants that are so often a major referent of the Americanization of the world associated with globalization.

In India, for instance, the Big Mac has been replaced on the McDonald's menu by the "Maharaja Mac." Originally based on goat or lamb meat, all McDonald's burgers in India are now vegetable- or chicken-based. Why would we see a change to such an American staple? Not surprisingly, the double beef patties of the original Big Mac do not go over well in a country where the majority of the population follows the Hindu faith, revere the cow

as sacred, and do not eat beef. Moreover, some customers might mistake lamb for beef. Thus, the Maharaja Mac was born out of a process of glocalization that still enables Indian customers to partake in the McDonald's experience but in a way that caters to local tastes. Other glocalized items on the McDonald's menu in India include items such as the "McSpicy Paneer" (a battered, deep-fried patty composed of the Indian curdled milk cheese, paneer) or the "McAloo Tikki" (a potato and pea-based patty in a burger bun with typical burger trimmings, representing a McDonald's version of the traditional "Aloo Tikki" snack common throughout north India). These examples demonstrate the concept of glocalization but provide clear evidence of the mixing of cultures at work in the globalization of fast food.

process cultures that reflect mixtures of global and local traits and have a relationship to place very different from the way that relationship is conventionally interpreted as fixed and static (Pieterse, 1994). This notion of globalization as at once converging and diverging is an important counterpoint to views of globalization that would argue for uniformity as a chief outcome of globalization.

Though less cohesive than either the world system or world society perspectives, the space–time perspective grapples with an equally important aspect of how society is changing in the era of globalization. Through examination of how time and space are reshaped by technological advances and increasing global awareness, this perspective offers a number of convincing models that explain why we see altogether different forms of social relations

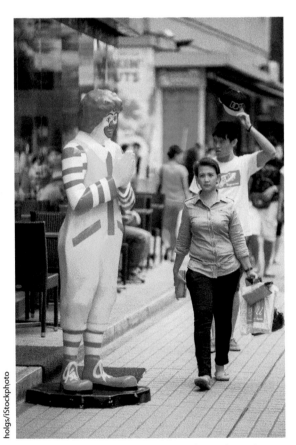

Ronald McDonald welcomes visitors with a traditional greeting at a McDonald's restaurant in Bangkok, Thailand. The success of McDonald's in foreign markets like Thailand relies on the food chain's adaptability to local customs and environments.

emerging in the realms of economics, politics, and culture. This move away from conventional relationships to time and space can be seen in the increased flows of ideas, communication, capital, and people throughout the increasingly compressed global community. At once connecting peoples and societies, and removing national boundaries and barriers, and at the same time encouraging hybrid forms of glocal cultural interpretation to emerge, this perspective can simultaneously support arguments for both convergence and divergence—a contradiction we will examine in the following sections.

Globalization in Perspective

What do these perspectives tell us about globalization as a whole? Each perspective has strengths and highlights key features of the globalization process. These highlights are captured in Table 14.1.

What do these perspectives tell us about convergence and divergence? Table 14.1 suggests support for both trends. The capitalist world system suggests convergence in the way that it encompasses all societies globally, but its sharp cleavages between core and periphery reflect divergence. Likewise, the world society perspective explains convergence emerging around world cultural models and the way they are enacted by states. Simultaneously, however, divergence from these models appears in the form of decoupling between intent and implementation—often with the weakest states being most likely to fall short of these models in practice. Finally, the space–time perspective suggests we are seeing a converging world with instant, real-time communication and the building of communities or places over great distance; however, if we consider the exclusion of people in the Global South from these technological and social changes, these changes can be seen as a form of divergence. This mixed evidence of convergence and divergence in all three perspectives suggests that we need to look instead at how globalization manifests itself in various global flows—economic, social, cultural, and political.

Table 14.1 ▶ Summary of Sociological Perspectives on Globalization

Perspective	Key Thinkers	Key Features	Strengths	Convergence vs. Divergence
World system	– Wallerstein – Chase-Dunn – Arrighi	– Core – Periphery – Semi-periphery – Capitalist world system	– Explains persistent global inequality and exploitation	– Convergence in encompassing all societies globally – Divergence between core and periphery
World society	– Meyer	– World cultural models – World society composed of international organizations and actors	– Explains institutional isomorphism and common policy models	– Convergence around world cultural norms – Divergence in decoupling of policy from practice
Space–time	– Giddens – Robertson – Harvey – Castells – Sassen	– Changing social roles for space and time – Effect of global networks and recent technological changes	– Explains increasing global interconnectedness – Explains mixing of global and local: hybridity	– Convergence in shifting relationships to time and place – Divergence in ways that glocalization promotes local adaptation

GLOBAL FLOWS

In each of the perspectives on globalization explored above, a common feature is the centrality of global interconnectedness manifested through the flow of various things, ideas, and people throughout the global community. By examining global flows, we can learn how globalization does matter in our daily lives and how it is related to processes of convergence and divergence associated with social change. This section looks at three types of flows: (1) capital, goods, and services; (2) transportation and information/communication technologies; and (3) people. Looking at each of these flows, we will examine what patterns have developed in recent decades and what they indicate about globalization and its effects on social change.

Capital, Goods, and Services

Given that globalization is frequently conflated with economics, it is worth considering its economic manifestations through various economic flows. You can identify such flows concretely by simply looking at the manufacturer's tag in your jeans or considering where the banana you ate for breakfast came from. If you are reading this in Canada, it is highly unlikely that those jeans or that banana originated there. This reflects the globalization of trade and manufacturing over the past several decades. Figure 14.2, which shows what proportion of global gross domestic product (GDP) is linked to trade, illustrates the growth in trade over the past four decades. In 1970, trade amounted to just over 27 per cent of global GDP. Twenty years later, trade's share of GDP had jumped to almost 39 per cent. By 2013, trade accounted for over 59 per cent of global income. With the share of global income linked to trade more than doubling in just 40 years, we can see direct evidence of the increased flows of goods and services globally. Bear in mind, though, that these figures represent the global average. For Canada alone during this period, the share of trade as percentage of GDP jumped from about 41 per cent in 1970 to an unprecedented level of nearly 85 per cent in 2000, then fell to hover around 64 per cent in 2014 (World Bank, 2016). These sharp increases in trade are paralleled by similar increases in global flows of capital investment, both in stock markets (portfolio investment) and directly in capital in foreign countries (foreign direct investment).

These figures tell a story of accelerated flows of goods, services, and capital in recent years, something that has its roots in the exploitation and resource extraction economics of the colonial era but has been influenced more

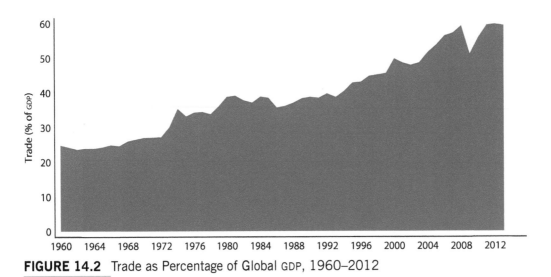

FIGURE 14.2 Trade as Percentage of Global GDP, 1960–2012

SOURCE: Graph created by author using data from World Bank, *World Development Indicators*, http://data.worldbank.org/products/wdi
(Washington: World Bank 2015).

recently by neo-liberalism as a dominant economic model. The neo-liberal economic model is based on concepts of free-market libertarianism, rational choice, and the belief that the state should interfere as little as possible in the market economy. To foster economic growth, advocates of neo-liberalism support free trade, privatization of state enterprise, widespread deregulation, the free flow of capital, and austerity measures to curtail government spending (Portes, 1997). Neo-liberalism was adopted by both the World Bank and the International Monetary Fund in the 1980s, which led to the implementation of austerity measures, or "structural adjustment programs," in many countries of the developing world (Bradshaw et al., 1993; Portes, 1997; Sen, 1999; Stiglitz, 2002).

These programs and the neo-liberal agenda have been sharply criticized by many social scientists, particularly for the disproportionate negative impact they have on disadvantaged groups in many countries where they have been applied, leading to criticism even from the former chief economist of the World Bank (Stiglitz, 2002). For neo-liberal theorists, economic growth is governed by the market and free access to trade and investment by firms both nationally and internationally. Only by adopting competitive economic and fiscal policies can states hope to gain from their

participation in the global market economy, and thus states compete in offering lucrative incentives to attract foreign capital and investment. Neo-liberal economic growth as a function of globalization is thus primarily an economic process, with an overriding belief that the social benefits of economic growth and development will "trickle down" from economic processes. Sadly, many examples suggest that this trickle-down process very rarely happens (Bradshaw et al., 1993; Stiglitz, 2002).

With neo-liberalism influencing most global economies and encouraging increased flows of goods and investment, we have seen the emergence of globalized patterns of production in recent decades. This is evident in the significant shift of manufacturing from the high-income economies of North America and Western Europe to regions with lower costs of manufacturing, wages, and labour standards. The result is a pattern of global production and consumption whereby goods are produced at the lowest possible cost by multinational corporations to be sold in high-income countries for maximum profit. Tied to the neo-liberal principles of free trade and foreign investment, this globalized pattern of production and consumption feeds the Western appetite for clothing, electronics, and other goods, while at the same time taking advantage of low-cost labour in the Global South. Recalling the world system perspective and exploitation of the periphery, we can see how such a pattern can reinforce global inequality. It also raises a set of ethical concerns, including questions about the treatment of workers, the exploitation of natural resources, and the environmental hazards of labour-intensive export-oriented manufacturing in the Global South.

> **TIME to REFLECT** ●━━━
>
> Consider a product you are wearing or using today that was produced in the Global South. What are the ethical implications of your purchase of this product?

Along with the spread of neo-liberal ideology, technological changes in transportation and communication over the past century underpin many of these economic flows. The next section examines the impact of these changes on how globalization affects our daily lives.

Transportation and Information Technologies

Technological change has created a greater sense of interconnectedness around the world. Advances in transportation, for example, have made it easier than ever to move people and objects from point A to point B in a fraction of the time it would have once taken.

In the mid-nineteenth century, a transatlantic crossing via ship would have taken approximately two weeks. With improving maritime technology, that same trip was reduced to about five days by the end of the century (Hugill, 1995). Today, we can board an airplane in any major Canadian city and arrive in Europe in less than 10 hours.

How have these technological advances in transportation shaped global flows? If we consider parts a and b of Figure 14.3, we can see how

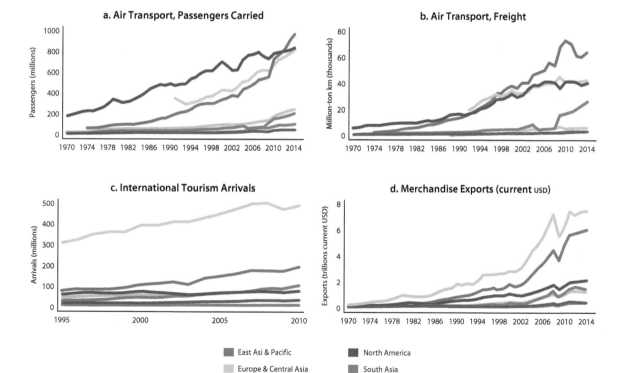

FIGURE 14.3 Assorted Global Flows by Region, 1970–2014

SOURCE: Graph created by author using data from World Bank, *World Development Indicators,* http://data.worldbank.org/products/wdi (Washington: World Bank 2015).

the expansion of air transportation has shaped the growth in the flow of both people and freight between 1970 and 2010. Broken down by major world regions, the graphs show significant increases across the board in both total numbers of passengers carried and total freight carried. Not all of this carriage was transnational, but the numbers do indicate the extent to which transportation advances have facilitated a changing relationship of societies to space and time, even in some of the more marginalized regions of the world. For instance, while the number of passengers carried in North America rose from about 173.7 million in 1970 to more than 838 million in 2014—a more than four-fold increase—there was an even larger increase in air passenger traffic in regions like East Asia and the Pacific (over 17 times more traffic in 2014 than in 1974) and in Latin America (over 14 times more traffic in 2014 than in 1970). Similarly, sub-Saharan Africa experienced a nearly ten-fold increase in air passenger travel during this period. These patterns suggest that the changes associated with technological advances in transportation are widespread globally, even though the sheer numbers of air passenger traffic are concentrated in the high- and upper-middle-income regions of the world (North America, Europe, and East Asia). Figure 14.3b, showing trends in air freight traffic, also indicates a sharp increase over the same period, illustrating

the extent to which advances in transportation have facilitated significant flows of goods within and between countries. This increasing flow of goods is also evident in Figure 14.3d, which shows the growth in merchandise exports over the same 40-year period. The pattern evident in the graphs on air passenger and air freight traffic is repeated here, showing an increase in merchandise exports, with the bulk of the exports from Europe, East Asia, and, to a lesser extent, North America.

More recently, we have witnessed significant innovation in information and communication technologies. The changes brought about by these innovations have been studied by sociologists from the space–time perspective (Castells, 2000; Sassen, 2007), and a critical factor is the comparative access to these technologies around the world and over time. Figure 14.4 traces trends in the use of telephone (landline) service, mobile phones, and the Internet regionally and globally from 1990 to 2010. In each regional chart, we can see two corresponding patterns: (1) sharp increases in mobile phone subscription and, to a lesser degree, Internet use; and (2) relative stagnation or even decline in use of conventional fixed telephone lines. In 2014, for instance, the global average of mobile phone subscriptions per 100 people was 96.2, meaning nearly one mobile phone subscription per person on the planet. With regional averages ranging from 71.1 per 100 in sub-Saharan Africa to 126.1 per 100 people in Europe and Central Asia, the growth in the availability of mobile phones has been astounding. These 2014 figures far outstrip the level of mobile phone subscription even 14 years earlier in 2000, when the global average was only 12.1 per 100 people and a region like sub-Saharan Africa had an average of less than two subscriptions per 100 people. This massive jump in the number of mobile phone subscriptions is fundamentally altering communication in many developing countries, since the availability of mobile phones has enabled many countries to significantly expand their telecommunication networks in ways that were not possible with

Trevor Snapp/Bloomberg via Getty Images

Pedestrians pass a giant mobile phone advertisement in Nairobi, Kenya.

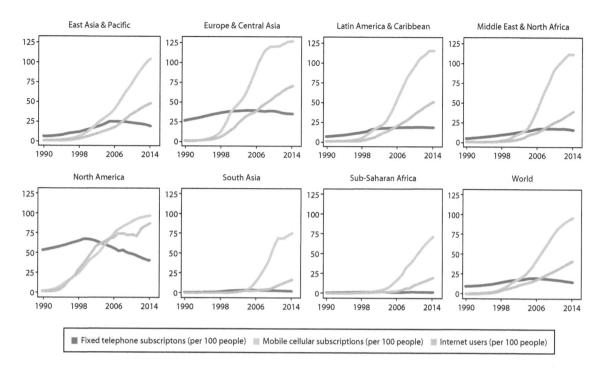

FIGURE 14.4 Information and Communication Technology Use and Availability, 1990–2014

SOURCE: Graph created by author using data from World Bank, *World Development Indicators,* http://data.worldbank.org/products/wdi (Washington: World Bank 2015).

a landline telephone infrastructure. Greater access to mobile wireless services has resulted in significant innovations in many countries, including widespread use of electronic banking and money transfers previously unavailable to many rural residents.

With the wider availability of new computing technologies and network infrastructure, Internet use has also grown in the period reflected in Figure 14.4. The global average number of Internet users per 100 people grew from less than 1 in 1995 to more than 40 in 2014. Regional averages also show significant increases during this period. For instance, North American Internet use grew from fewer than 9 users per 100 people in 1995 to more than 87 per 100 in 2014. In contrast to the expansion of mobile phone use, however, Internet use has grown more slowly in many of the regions of the Global South. For example, in sub-Saharan Africa, Internet users are estimated at just under 19 per 100 people in contrast to the 71 mobile phone subscriptions per 100 people estimated in 2014. In South Asia, with the massive combined populations of

India, Pakistan, and Bangladesh and some of the largest pockets of absolute poverty in the world, Internet use rose from less than 0.5 users per 100 people in 2000 to just over 8 per 100 in 2010, and then doubled to over 16 per 100 by 2014.

These increases represent a significant technological change in society; more importantly, along with the other changes in information technology, the Internet directly facilitates the changing social meanings of space and time discussed earlier in this chapter. Further, these advances, not unlike the earlier advances in transportation technology, mediate increased flow of information and communication in revolutionary ways. Email communication, text messaging, video conferencing, the availability of massive amounts of information on the Web: all of these innovations in the way societies communicate lead to increased flows of knowledge and information among people.

One corollary of the increased flow of information and communication is the spread and diffusion of shared ideas, norms, and institutions—and these flows are related to the world society perspective. For example, researchers have demonstrated that international telecommunication networks can act as a means through which support for human rights discourse can diffuse through the global community (Clark & Hall, 2011). Other research argues that communication using key Internet and mobile phone technologies and platforms (Twitter, Facebook, YouTube) played a critical role in fostering the pro-democracy movements associated with 2011's "Arab Spring" in countries like Tunisia and Egypt (Howard, et al. 2011). The same technologies also played a part in the spread of similar protest movements in other countries in the Middle East and North Africa, including Libya, Syria, and Yemen.

This diffusion of a common protest model points to the density or contagion effects often referred to in the world society perspective. It also highlights how new, rapid flows of information over transnational networks can play an important part in the spread of political ideology across diverse societies.

Increasing interconnection via information and communication technologies reflects a convergence process whereby more and more commonly accessible information and the means to communicate it rapidly are fundamentally altering social relations among those plugged in. But these technologies might also contribute to divergence, given what has often been labelled the "digital divide"—the gap between people who can neither afford nor are sufficiently educated to access the new means of bridging time and space and those who can and are. The former are thus excluded from the direct flows

---

SOCIOLOGY ▬▬ IN ACTION   Is Your Phone Contributing to Rape in the Congo?

One of the deadliest wars in recent history, which has received relatively little attention in the West, is the prolonged conflict in the Democratic Republic of the Congo (DRC). International estimates suggest that upward of 5 million people died as a result of the conflict between 1997 and 2007. At the same time, the DRC has experienced one of the highest rates of conflict-related rape ever reported, with estimates suggesting that on any given day in 2006–2007, more than 1,150 women aged 15 to 49 were raped (Peterman, Palermo, & Bredenkamp, 2011). Conflict in the DRC is directly connected to these rapes, with combatants on both sides using rape as a means of dominating and destroying local communities (Baaz & Stern, 2009).

How is the phone in your pocket contributing to this use of rape as a weapon of war? The ongoing conflict in the eastern DRC is largely perpetuated by various armed groups and the Congolese national armed forces competing over control of the significant resource wealth in this area. One mineral in particular has garnered interest from these groups: an ore called coltan. This mineral is mined and processed to produce the element tantalum, which is highly sought-after because of its ability to store electrical charges. Tantalum capacitors are a key component in mobile phones and other electronics. Although the DRC's global share of tantalum production is not overly large, coltan mining is still a significant part of the local economy. Control of the export and sale of this mineral have a direct effect on the conflict in the DRC and, consequently, on the use of rape in that conflict (Whitman, 2012).

The United Nations and other organizations have drawn attention to the role played by coltan and other minerals in the conflict, and this has spurred other actors globally to campaign against the use of "blood coltan" in the manufacture of electronics. Groups like The Enough Project (www. enoughproject.org) have launched awareness and fundraising initiatives to combat sexual violence in the conflict in the Congo. They have also set their sights on educating consumers in the West about the role played by coltan and other minerals in fostering the conflict. Online campaign videos encourage consumers to commit to buying conflict-free electronics and to pressure major electronics manufacturers to eliminate conflict coltan from their products. Still, these conflict-free options have yet to materialize in your neighbourhood electronics store, which suggests that few of us are asking whether our phones are contributing to rape in the Congo.

of globalization that the new technologies facilitate. In this respect, many of the flows we have discussed in this section are beyond the reach of many of the poorest or most geographically isolated members of most societies, whether in the West or in the Global South. Even in Canada, there are sharp disparities in the availability of wireless and high-speed Internet access between urban and rural areas, a problem further compounded in extremely isolated northern or Indigenous communities that have little infrastructure and are far from major cities.

TIME to REFLECT

Should broadband Internet access be considered a basic right of all Canadians? Why or why not?

People

Along with that of goods, services, information, and ideas, the movement of people transnationally is another key flow linked to globalization. This flow has deep historical roots. Indeed, migration of peoples is a phenomenon dating from prehistoric times. More recently, in the colonial era, the phenomenon of settler colonialism saw the Americas, Southern Africa, and parts of the Asia-Pacific region colonized by European nations to the detriment of Indigenous groups. The devastating (and ongoing) effects of colonization on Indigenous peoples in Canada and the elsewhere had a dire impact on

their culture and livelihoods and established exploitative and often genocidal colonial institutions which persist to the present day. In this respect, the flow of peoples has never been a politically neutral process and it remains a contentious phenomenon.

Still, as we noted in the discussion of air passenger traffic, more people than ever before are crossing national boundaries for either temporary or permanent stays in foreign countries.

In terms of transnational temporary stays, Figure 14.3c indicates that international tourist travel increased significantly from 1995 to 2014. During that period, international tourist arrivals globally more than doubled, from approximately 550 million annually to more than 1.12 billion. Figure 14.3c also shows that the global growth in tourist flows was not necessarily concentrated in the wealthiest countries or regions, but that more countries are welcoming international visitors, no doubt as a result of more available travel options in recent years.

More permanent flows of people involve migrants settling in a country other than that of their birth. Figure 14.5 gives a global estimate of the total stock of international migrants (all the individuals permanently residing in a country other than that of their birth, as estimated by national census data). It shows that international migration has been increasing since 1960, although as a percentage of worldwide population, the growth has not been extreme.

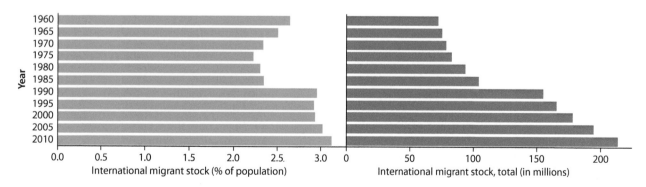

FIGURE 14.5 Global Migration Trends, 1960–2010

SOURCE: Graphs created by atuhor using data from World Bank, *World Development Indicators*, http://databank.worldbank.org/ddp/home. do?Step=12&id=4&CNO=2

Still, with some 213 million migrants in 2010, compared to approximately 72 million in 1960, the sheer number of migrants nearly tripled during this period. Some of these migrants move by choice, while others are forced into migration as refugees by natural disaster, conflict, or political or cultural repression. When we consider that more than 3 per cent of the world's population reside in countries other than that of their birth, it is clear that the role of migrant and diaspora groups in shaping other global flows is significant. For example, the World Bank estimates that the more than 250 million migrants worldwide in 2016 will send more than US$601 billion in remittances to communities and family members in their home countries, with more than $441 billion of that total sent to developing countries (World Bank, 2015). The role

of these remittances cannot be discounted in terms of promoting development and economic well-being in the countries of origin, and the World Bank cautions that the amount of global remittance is probably much larger than these official estimates, because a larger proportion of remittances go unreported. In this way, the flow of people globally is closely linked to the economic and other flows we have already discussed. Furthermore, research suggests that migrants play a key role in helping to promote support for international norms such as human rights (Clark & Hall, 2011). Such "social remittances" that accompany the financial variety include the diffusion of ideas, attitudes, behaviour, and even various forms of social capital from migrants back to their home countries and communities (Levitt, 1998).

OPEN FOR DISCUSSION — Syrian Refugees: A Global Crisis

The Syrian Civil War began in 2011 following pro-democratization protests similar to those witnessed elsewhere in the so-called "Arab Spring." The regime of President Bashar al-Assad in Syria responded harshly to protests, and fighting soon broke out, which spiralled rapidly into a humanitarian crisis with multiple actors involved in the conflict. The targeting of civilians by the Syrian armed forces and militant groups has prompted one of the largest refugee crises in recent history. The United Nations High Commissioner for Refugees (n.d.) reported that by mid-2016, more than 4.75 million Syrians had registered as refugees, with more than 1.1 million applying for asylum in Europe, while others fled to Syria's neighbours. Nearly one-quarter of Syria's pre-war population has been forced into migration as refugees and another estimated 6 million are internally displaced persons remaining within Syria.

Refugees fleeing the conflict have gone to extremes to reach safety and seek new lives for their families. Millions are fleeing to neighbouring countries; others attempt to reach Western Europe over land and by sea, often in perilous conditions. Thousands of would-be refugees from Syria and other parts of the Middle East and

North Africa have died while fleeing—the International Organization for Migration (n.d.) estimating that more than 3,500 people died in the Mediterranean Sea in the first 10 months of 2016 alone. What started as a civil war in Syria quickly became a complex humanitarian crisis affecting many other nations.

Canada, following the election of the Liberal government led by Justin Trudeau in late 2015, pledged to resettle 25,000 Syrian refugees. Giving priority to families, the Canadian government and private sponsors across Canada (mostly community groups and organizations) resettled nearly 32,000 Syrian refugees between November 2015 and early October 2016. Although this is only a small portion of the vast population of Syrian refugees, Canada has done more than many other countries to offer permanent residence to refugees fleeing the Syrian conflict. This example demonstrates how the global flow of people is a key aspect of current globalization, and how even a distant humanitarian crisis can have great significance to Canadians. Should all countries have legal obligation to permanently resettle refugees in response to humanitarian crises? A moral obligation?

AP Photo/Petros Giannakouris

Syrian refugees wait at the port of Lesbos Island, Greece, to board a ferry to Athens.

CONCLUSION: CONVERGENCE, DIVERGENCE, AND SOCIAL CHANGE?

This chapter has demonstrated how globalization is a critical transnational process of social change. Theorists have laid out the various ways in which globalization has reshaped economic, social, and political relations worldwide. A complex set of processes linked to capitalism, institutional isomorphism, and changes in our relationships to time and space, globalization has the potential to promote *both* convergence and divergence.

We see more global flows than ever before, which are linking societies and states in increasing uniformity. The availability of common sets of goods, services, information, and technologies erases some of the social, political, and cultural differences that earlier differentiated the regions of the world. At the same time,

some areas of the world are excluded or exploited by the same processes of globalization that promote convergence. In this respect, divergence is unavoidable for many in the globalization era. Impoverished, marginalized, and otherwise excluded from the potential benefits of globalization, they are outside of the mainstream of globalization. In this respect, the ever increasing similarities and connections we see emerging around us are linked inextricably to aspects of divergence elsewhere. The aspects of globalization that at once bring the world together can simultaneously further differentiate and promote global inequalities. Social change stemming from globalization thus, can be seen to have a dual nature: convergence for some, divergence for others. With contestation over how globalization *should* look, it remains to be seen whether the current form of globalization will maintain its ability to simultaneously unite and divide in the future or be replaced by another form less rife with contradictions.

Questions for Critical Thought

1. Which of the sociological perspectives on globalization discussed in this chapter appeals most to you? Why?
2. How do different global flows affect your everyday life?
3. How have the flows associated with globalization intensified over time?
4. What evidence do you see of convergence promoted by globalization?
5. What evidence do you see of divergence?
6. How could globalization processes be changed to promote greater equality around the world?
7. How are Canadians affected favourably by globalization? Negatively?
8. What role do international organizations play in the globalization process?

Sociological Explorations

1. Access the World Bank's World Development Indicators website (http://databank.worldbank.org/data/reports.aspx?source=world-development-indicators) and find one indicator that shows growing divergence between world regions. Chart or map the data using the site's built-in data visualization tools to analyze trends over time. Repeat the exercise to look for evidence of convergence.

2. Survey your classmates to see what proportion are wearing clothes made in Canada. For more detail, collect information on where your classmates' clothes are manufactured. Graph or map the survey results to get a sense of the global textile manufacturing economy.

Recommended Readings

Meyer, J.W., Boli, J., Thomas, G.M., & Ramirez, F.O. (1997). World society and the nation-state. *American Journal of Sociology, 103,* 144–181.
This article succinctly summarizes the world society perspective and highlights the key features of how states relate to world society and how this relationship promotes the adoption of common norms, policies, and structures in states and other organizations.

Smith, J. (2008). *Social movements for global democracy.* Baltimore, MD: Johns Hopkins University Press.
This book highlights the composition, aims, and efficacy of two networks promoting competing visions of globalization on the world stage.

Stiglitz, J.E. (2002). *Globalization and its discontents.* New York, NY: W.W. Norton.
This book, by a former chief economist of the World Bank, is a condemning account of the policies of neo-liberalism promoted by the bank and its counterpart, the IMF.

Recommended Websites

Gapminder World
www.gapminder.org/world
This website offers an online tool for examining data about global social, economic, and political trends.

World Bank
http://data.worldbank.org
The World Bank website is the source for much of the data on various global flows and development indicators used in this chapter.

World Economic Forum
www.weforum.org
This site outlines the aims, programs, and structures of the World Economic Forum.

International Organization for Migration
http://missingmigrants.iom.int
This site explores the phenomenon of missing migrants and tracks estimated numbers of migrant deaths globally.

Key Terms

contagion The diffusion of a norm or model linked to the spread of similar institutional models within a region or in neighbouring countries.

core The countries at the centre of economic and political power on the global stage.

glocalization The process through which globalized identities, commodities, and structures are adapted or modified in local practice.

institutional isomorphism The similarity of organizational structure emerging from imitation, coercion, or pressures of legitimacy.

periphery Countries with labour-intensive, resource-extractive economies, which accumulate little wealth and are on the margins of global political and military power.

semi-periphery Countries which show a mix of both core and peripheral characteristics.

15 | Population, Urbanization, and the Environment

CHERYL TEELUCKSINGH

In this chapter you will:

▶ See how social forces influence human population growth

▶ Consider the impact of industrialization/deindustrialization and social inequality on urban sociology perspectives of cities

▶ Examine the dynamics of population trends in Canadian cities

▶ Learn about cities' relationships to the environment, including concerns for sustainable development and climate change

▶ Think critically about some solutions to urban sprawl, including attempts to address contemporary concerns about the urban environment

INTRODUCTION

While siting in a car on a hot, humid, smog filled-day, have you ever wondered how cities change to accommodate population growth or whether cities and social life have an impact on physical environment? Globally and across Canada, more people now live in cities than ever before (United Nations, 2014; Statistics Canada, 2015b). High population concentrations in urban centres coupled with human-induced stresses on the environment, such as air pollution, are causing unprecedented social concerns related to health, housing, and transportation. For millennials, those born since 1990, population growth, urban life, and the environment are some of the most pressing issues that affect their decisions related to everything ranging from the type of employment that seems best or where to buy their first condominium.

The Population Division of the Department of Economic and Social Affairs of the United Nations provides projections of world population growth and urban and rural populations for all countries. According to the 2015 revision of the *World Population Prospects*, between 2015 and 2050 the world's population is expected to increase by 2.4 billion, from 7.3 billion to 9.7 billion. Urban areas globally are expected to carry the burden of this population increase; *World Urbanization Prospects* (United Nations,

2014) projects that urban populations will rise from 3.9 billion in 2014 to 6.3 billion in 2050. As argued in this report, higher levels of urbanization, which centralize populations particularly in the developing countries, will improve the delivery of services such as health care and education as well as provide a wide range of economic opportunities for residents. However, these benefits of urbanization must be weighed against the costs associated with mounting urban problems, including deteriorating urban infrastructure, stress on limited energy and water reserves, and urban poverty.

This chapter examines the interrelated issues of population, cities, and the environment from the perspective of Canada and Canadian cities. Examining demography, or human population characteristics, and historical changes is essential to examining how cities evolve over time and to considering cities' dynamic relationships to the natural environment. Cities have become a principal form of settlement as an alternative to living in rural areas. The majority of Canada's population now live in urban areas, which has a major impact on the Canadian way of life, economy, and environment. This is a significant transformation when one considers that in 1851, only 13 per cent of what was then Canada was urbanized (Statistics Canada, 2009a).

We begin this discussion by reviewing the demographic indicators and theories of demographic change, including Thomas Malthus's controversial theory of population and **demographic transition** theory. Malthus's work engages with the question, "Are there too many people in the world?" An overview of the development of Canadian cities and urbanism provides a framework for considering the theories of urbanism presented by the early European urban sociologists, the Chicago School, and the new urban sociology. These are different perspectives for explaining the shift from rural living to urban living and the new problems that arise when social life is based in cities. Particular attention is paid to contemporary urban issues related to deindustrialization and globalization. Since many urban issues in the twenty-first century

Andrew Francis Wallace/Toronto Star via Getty Images

Condo development continues rapidly in many of Canada's major urban centres.

are increasingly about assessing the limits of urbanism in the context of potential environmental problems, we also examine the dominant perspectives on urban environmental sociology. We look at the challenges posed by urban sprawl in many metropolitan Canadian cities in order to return to critical questions about unregulated urban development.

DEMOGRAPHIC INDICATORS

Demography is the study of the causes and consequences of population growth. To examine the social consequences of population, demographers consider factors such as the size, composition, and geographical variations of population over time. They also study changes in birth rate, infant mortality rate, death rate, **growth rate**, and migration. Demographic trends can inform policies related to health care, immigration, the labour market, and urban planning, in addition to providing comparable quantitative measures to assess Canada's well-being relative to other nations. In Canada, the census, or the counting of the population every five years, provides a wealth of demographic statistics at different geographic scales. **Birth rates** are an indicator of the reproductive patterns of women of child-bearing age. Demographers usually measure the **crude birth rate**, which represents the number of live births in a given year for every 1,000 people in a population. In 2011, the crude birth rate in Canada was 10.28 (CIA, 2013). Canada's crude birth rate is stable, and as indicated in Table 15.1, is consistent with the crude birth rate in the United States but much lower than that of many developing countries (CIA, 2013). In 2011, the total fertility rate in Canada was 1.61 children per woman. This is low relative to the **replacement fertility rate**, the average number of children per woman of one generation needed to maintain the population size, which is estimated at 2.1 children per woman (Statistics Canada, 2015e). Differences in crude birth rates and fertility rates globally highlight differences in the status of women around the

world. Women's freedom to choose at what age they will have their first pregnancy, the number of children they will have, and the frequency of childbirth are tied to a number of factors, including access to education and birth control and female labour market participation, as well as religious and cultural values.

 As discussed in **Chapter 7**, "Gender and Sexuality," gender relations and gender division of domestic labour are socially constructed and differ according to context.

TIME to REFLECT

In July 2010, in response to some Canadians' concerns about personal privacy, the Canadian federal government decided to make completion of the long census form voluntary rather than mandatory. However, in November 2015, the mandatory long-form census of 2016 was reinstated. From the perspective of demographers, why is the reinstating of the long-form census significant?

Table 15.1 ▶ Comparative Crude Birth Rates for Selected Countries, 2013

	Births/1,000 population
Japan	7.93
Germany	8.47
Canada	10.28
Norway	12.14
United Kingdom	12.17
France	12.38
China	12.49
United States	12.49
India	19.55
Pakistan	22.58
Philippines	24.27
Afghanistan	38.57
Uganda	43.79
Mali	44.99
Niger	45.45

SOURCE: Central Intelligence Agency. 2013. The World Factbook 2013-14. Washington, DC: Central Intelligence Agency. https://www.cia.gov/library/publications/the-world-factbook/index.html Accessed on January 28, 2016.

The death rate is normally measured in terms of the **crude death rate**, which represents the number of deaths in a given year per 1,000 people. According to Statistics Canada (2015e), the crude death rate in Canada in 2011 was 7.0 per 1,000 people for all ages and sexes. The crude death rate, as an indicator, is affected by the age distribution. An aging population such as Canada's will translate into a slow increase in the crude death rate. Statistics Canada defines the **infant mortality rate** as the number of deaths of children less than one year of age per 1,000 live births in the same year. In 2011, the infant mortality rate at the national level for both sexes was 4.8 per 1,000 live births (Statistics Canada, 2015e). The death rate and infant mortality rates are indicators of health-care quality and access as well as living conditions. Life expectancy is the median number of years that a person can expect to live. In 2011, **life expectancy at birth** in Canada reached 79.3 years for males and 83.6 years for females (Statistics Canada, 2015e). Death rates, infant mortality rates, and life expectancies in Canada are

A new Canadian family poses for the camera after a citizenship ceremony in a government courtroom.

DayOwl/Shutterstock

similar to those in the United States (National Vital Statistics Report, 2014).

Net migration is the difference between the number of immigrants and the number of emigrants between two dates. Immigrants are those entering Canada from international locations, while emigrants are those leaving Canada. Since Confederation, immigration has contributed to the growth in Canada's population. Since 1993, net migration has been the main source of population growth in Canada. In 2013/2014, net migration accounted for 66.5 per cent of the population growth in Canada, which is a significant increase from 43.6 per cent in 1994/1995 (Statistics Canada, 2015b). Net migration rate is the difference between the number of immigrants and the number of emigrants during the year per 1,000 persons. The net immigration rate allows demographers to compare the contribution of migration to population change. In 2013, Canada's net immigration rate was 5.66 in comparison to 3.86 in the United States or 2.54 for the United Kingdom for the same year (CIA, 2013).

The **natural growth rate** is the difference between the crude birth rate and the crude death rate, not taking into account migration or the movement of people into and out of a specific geographical area. At the national level, Canada's population grew by 5.0 per cent between 2011 and 2016, including migration. This is a slight decrease from the previous census period (2006 to 2011), when population grew by 5.9 per cent (Statistics Canada, 2017). As indicated in Figure 15.1, Canada's population growth from 2011 to 2016 was the highest among G7 countries (Statistics Canada, 2017). Between 1984 and 2014, all provinces except for Prince Edward Island saw population increases with strong increases in the combined populations of Western provinces and territories. In 2014, four provinces, Ontario (38.6 per cent), Quebec (23.2 per cent), British Columbia (13.0 per cent), and Alberta (11.6 per cent) were home to more than 85 per cent of Canadians, with the strongest growth population growth, 72.2 per cent, between 1984 and 2014 taking place in Alberta (Statistics Canada, 2015b).

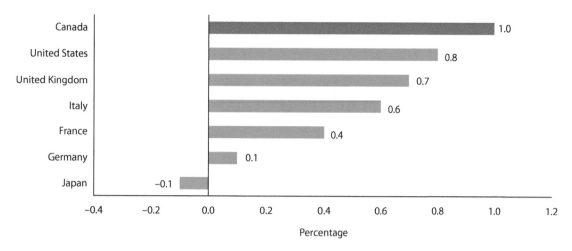

FIGURE 15.1 Average Annual Population Growth Rate (%) of the G7 Countries, 2011–2016

1. With latest data available. The annual rates for the United Kingdom and Italy are from 2011 to 2015.
SOURCE: Statistics Canada. (2017). Population size and growth in Canada: Key results from the 2016 Census. Ottawa: Statistics Canada.
http://www.statcan.gc.ca/pub/91-215-x/2014000/ct002-eng.htm

These demographic statistics are aggregates, applicable to the whole of Canadian society, and therefore do not highlight the variations within the population—for example, from the perspective of lower-income people, racial minorities, or Indigenous people. Beyond the statistics, demography asks questions about the effects and consequences of population change. We cannot begin to develop innovative strategies to solve environmental, social, and economic problems, such as how to get urban dwellers to leave their cars at home and take public transit, unless we are equipped with an understanding of human populations and their structure.

Malthus's Population Explosion and Marx's Response

Concerns about possible limits to population growth have existed for some time. Debates among theorists stem from their differences in interpreting the demographic trends and the social dynamics that explain the trends. In 1798, the Reverend Thomas Robert Malthus, an economist, in his book, *Essay on the Principle of Population* (1970 [1798]), outlined an influential theory of human population growth. Malthus's theory starts with the recognition of two constants: people eat, and they reproduce. Based

on his analysis, Malthus concluded that while the food supply increases arithmetically over time, population increases exponentially. For Malthus, this scenario would result in an eventual catastrophe, with insufficient resources to enable people to survive. To prevent this crisis, Malthus recommended population control. Because of his religious convictions, Malthus rejected the idea of birth control but instead suggested that men postpone marriage until later in life, when they would be better able to provide for their families. From his perspective, Malthus could not anticipate the gains in food production, the drop in the European birth rate because of the introduction of various forms of birth control, and longer life expectancy because of improvements in health care.

Karl Marx (1967 [1867]) criticized Malthusian arguments about the relationship between the food supply and population growth. By focusing on economic systems in society, Marx believed that as the population grew, wealth would also expand, but not hunger. The expansion of wealth associated with overpopulation would lead to greater social inequality and the uneven distribution of resources, including fewer people owning and controlling private property, as discussed in Chapter 1. Since

HUMAN DIVERSITY

Youth Boom in India

In contrast to Canada and most Western nations, which are experiencing the consequences of an aging population, in India almost 30 per cent of the population is between the ages of zero and 14 (CIA, 2012). It is estimated that India's population is growing at a rate of 1.4 per cent per year, exceeding China's rate of 0.7 per cent (Bloom, 2011). At this pace, India's population will surpass China's by 2030.

India's baby boom is an outcome of a rapid population growth coupled with declines in mortality rates and increased household incomes. The baby boom can also be seen as the beginning of a demographic transition, because India also experiences declining fertility, since fewer births are needed to maintain family needs. India's population pyramid or age structure diagram, below, shows the distribution of its population by age and sex. India and other developing countries have a pyramid-shaped age structure, and in future decades as the population ages, the base of the pyramid will become smaller with an increase in the number of working-age individuals (Bloom, 2011).

Initially, a young population increases the amount of economic expenditures, because a greater proportion of children and youth in a population means that more resources are needed in terms of food, shelter, and education. However, what is widely anticipated in India is an increased economic growth capacity as the young population becomes of working age within the next couple of decades (Bloom, 2011). The younger cohort is expected to be more urbanized, healthier, and better educated than previous generations.

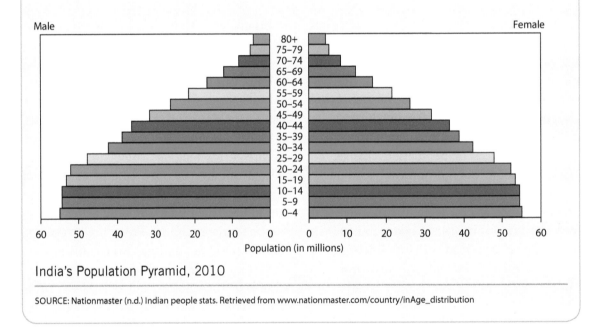

India's Population Pyramid, 2010

SOURCE: Nationmaster (n.d.) Indian people stats. Retrieved from www.nationmaster.com/country/inAge_distribution

Malthus first proposed his theories, they have been adopted by neo-Malthusians (Ehrlich & Ehrlich, 1990) to support a wide range of population control arguments. Some neo-Malthusians have attributed the blame for the population increase on people living in the Global South, where the growth rates are higher than in the Global North. Based on this claim, many neo-Malthusians have advocated birth control and other efforts to curtail further population growth. Neo-Malthusian sentiments have also been re-ignited by fears about global limits to oil supplies and access to clean water. Those on the other side of the debate, drawing on neo-Marxian perspectives, question the legitimacy of blaming the Global South when those in the Global North consume far more food, fuel, and other resources per capita and create more pollution and waste.

Demographic Transition Theory

Warren Thompson's demographic transition model, originally conceived in 1929, provides a more complex explanation for demographic change than Malthus's argument. The demographic transition theory distinguishes Western nations, such as Europe, the United States, and Canada, from less industrialized nations. Thompson's (1929) original model of the transitions from high birth rates and high death rates to low birth rates and low death rates, starting in the eighteenth century in Western nations, included three periods of transition: pre-industrial, early industrial, and modern industrial. Recent revisions to this model of population growth in Western societies have been revised to include a further, fourth stage (see Figure 15.2):

- *Stage 1.* Pre-industrial (high birth rates; high death rates; slow population growth)
- *Stage 2.* Early industrial and urbanization (fall in death rates; high birth rates continue; rapid population growth)
- *Stage 3.* Mature industrial (low birth rates; low death rates; slow population growth)
- *Stage 4.* Post-industrial (low birth rates; low death rates; total population is high; slow population growth)

Critics of the demographic transition model argue that the model is an oversimplification

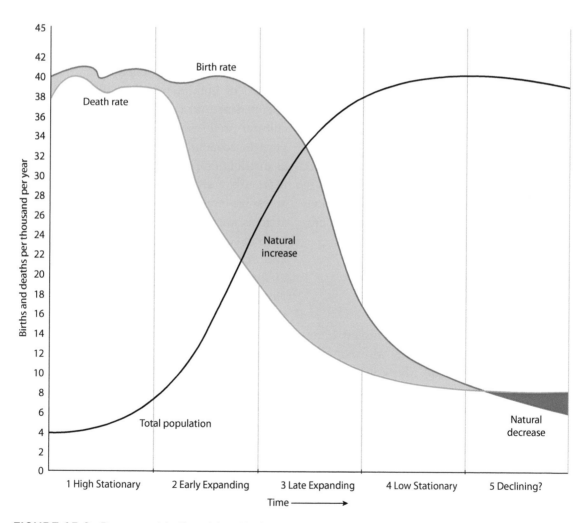

FIGURE 15.2 Demographic Transition Model

SOURCE: Anthony Bennett www.internetgeography.net

(Hauser & Duncan, 1959). For example, political and economic contexts that affect population growth, such as economic recessions and the move toward globalization, are not accounted for in the model. Another limitation is that the time periods corresponding to the transitions in the stages vary depending on the Westernized nation considered. The impact of immigration is also not incorporated into the model. As explained above, while Canada's natural population growth rate has slowed as a characteristic of stage 4, immigration to Canada has led to significant population growth.

While a more sophisticated theory to explain population change is useful, the demographic transition theory, when considered critically, suggests one monolithic path to development, with a strong emphasis on technology as the instrument to control the natural population growth. Across the model, technology takes various forms, including birth control, medical science, industrialization, and modern infrastructure. The model assumes that technology is universally adopted in the same way by all Westernized nations. However, gender relations, class, and culture also affect how technology is adopted, as we saw above regarding global differences in birth rates. Macro-level structural explanations of population change must be sensitive to micro-level differences and contexts.

DEVELOPMENT OF CANADIAN CITIES

Urban histories of cities, such as Toronto, Montreal, and Vancouver, often start with European settlement. Freeman (2010), who writes about **settler colonialism** in early Toronto, argues that the place of Indigenous peoples in Canadian cities has been forgotten in our collective memories and that it is important to acknowledge this gap in urban histories. Urban development is influenced by demographic, economic, ideological, and technological changes at the national and international levels (Bunting & Filion, 2006; Stelter & Artibise, 1984). Bunting, Filion, and Walker (2010, pp. 19–34) identify five distinct epochs of urban development in Canada. In summarizing

these five stages, we emphasize the evolution of urbanism in Canada. Urbanism is the process by which a society is transformed from one organized around rural activities to one organized around urban activities, such as transportation, housing, and economic activity.

The earliest stage was the mercantile era (1600–1800) when populations were limited. Small settlements, starting in Quebec, originated as colonial outposts for the **staple economy** and the export of natural resources back to France and, later, Britain. Early mercantile settlements in Quebec City, Montreal, Halifax, and St John's were also administrative or military centres (Artibise & Stelter, 2012). During this stage, Quebec City and Montreal were the largest cities.

The second period, urban development (1800–1850), was associated with weaker colonial ties to Britain and an increase in commercial production and consumption. Rural settlements experienced increased population growth as a result of immigration from Europe and accelerated natural growth. In response to agricultural production in rural settlements, cities grew in economic importance as markets and as distribution points (Bunting & Filion, 2006). Most urban settlements were still located near accessible waterways, because transportation systems were limited. Toronto, founded in 1793 by John Graves Simcoe, grew in size and importance relative to early Kingston, in part because of Toronto's location close to the agricultural regions of southern Ontario and its military location in relationship to the United States.

At the time of Canada's Confederation in 1867, Canada's population was approximately 3 million people, with about 18 per cent of the population urbanized (Macionis, 1997, p. 575). The building of railways and increased industrialization drove urban growth during the third stage from 1850 to 1945. The Canadian Pacific Railway, completed in 1885, propelled settlement westward to Calgary and Vancouver and other locations along the railway line. Industrialization accelerated in Canada in the latter part of the nineteenth century with the opening of many American branch plants (Foster, 1986). Many of the industries were concentrated within the Quebec City to Windsor corridor.

Corresponding to the locations of economic activity, urbanization grew faster in southern Ontario and parts of Quebec than in western Canada and the Maritimes (Bunting & Filion, 2006).

The redistribution-oriented government interventions, such as family allowance, public health care, and subsidized housing, that characterized the fourth epoch following World War II up to 1975 helped to stimulate demographic and economic growth. Urbanization, in the postwar context, involved the spatial expansion of cities to suburban regions, facilitated by the widespread accessibility of cars and home ownership to the middle class. The city cores and outlying suburban regions formed the metropolitan areas as we know them today. The growth of corporations across all sectors of the economy allowed for a concentrated economic base in cities (Artibise & Stelter, 2012).

In response to a range of factors, including the oil crisis in the early 1970s and the post-1970 recessions, **deindustrialization** from 1975 to the present signalled the unravelling of the assembly-line approach to industrialization and an end to many well-paying blue-collar jobs associated with the previous period of transition.

This fifth epoch was also marked by a political shift toward neo-liberalism, with a reduction in government spending on interventions and a shift toward deregulation (Bunting & Filion, 2006). Reviewing the five stages of urbanization reveals that cities and city life have changed over time in response to political and economic forces.

 See "Capital, Goods, and Services," p. 331, in **Chapter 14**, "Globalization and Social Change," for more on neo-liberalism.

Urban growth is now predominately concentrated in the metropolitan areas, such as Vancouver, Calgary, Edmonton, Toronto, Ottawa, and Montreal, that are able to draw and employ immigrants (Bunting & Filion, 2006). In 2014, almost 70 per cent of Canadians lived in metropolitan areas (Statistic Canada, 2015c). More recently, Calgary and Saskatoon are increasingly able to draw international migrants and migrants within Canada because of the boom in Western economies and declines in the manufacturing sector in other central cities, such as Windsor and Sudbury. Calgary and Edmonton have grown in response to economic opportunities in the oil and gas sector and its spin-off industries. As Table 15.2 reveals,

Table 15.2 Top 10 Census Metropolitan Areas, 2016 and 2011 Censuses, Canada

Geographic Name	Population, 2016	Population 2011	Population, % Change	Population Density per Square Kilometre, 2016	National Population Rank, 2016	National Population Rank, 2011
Toronto	5,928,040	5,583,064	6.2	1,003.8	1	1
Montreal	4,098,927	3,824,221	4.2	890.2	2	2
Vancouver	2,463,431	2,313,328	6.5	854.6	3	3
Calgary	1,392,609	1,214,839	14.6	272.5	4	5
Ottawa–Gatineau	1,323,783	1,236,324	5.5	195.6	5	4
Edmonton	1,321,426	1,159,869	13.9	140.0	6	6
Quebec	800,296	765,706	4.3	234.8	7	7
Winnipeg	778,489	730,018	6.6	146.7	8	8
Hamilton	747,545	721,053	3.7	544.9	9	9
Kitchener–Cambridge–Waterloo	523,894	477,160	5.5	480.1	10	10

SOURCE: Statistics Canada. 2017. Population and dwelling counts, for census metropolitan areas, 2016 and 2011 censuses (table). Population and Dwelling Count Highlight Tables. 2016 Census. Statistics Canada Catalogue no. 98-402-X2016001. Ottawa. Released February 8, 2017. Retrieved from: http://www12.statcan.gc.ca/census-recensement/2016/dp-pd/hlt-fst/pd-pl/Tables/File.cfm?T=205&SR=1&RPP=100&PR=0&CMA=0&CSD=0&S=3&O=D&Lang=Eng&OFT=CSV (accessed May 15, 2017)

Calgary and Edmonton have experienced population increases of 14.6 per cent and 13.9 per cent, respectively, since 2011 (Statistics Canada, 2017). Other metropolitan areas are attempting to restructure economically to attract globally oriented "new economy" industries that require highly skilled and educated employees. Much of the settlement during this period has been in the suburban areas of cities. As shown in Figure 15.3, smaller urban centres are now in decline, except for those within commuting distance to metropolitan areas (Artibise & Stelter, 2012).

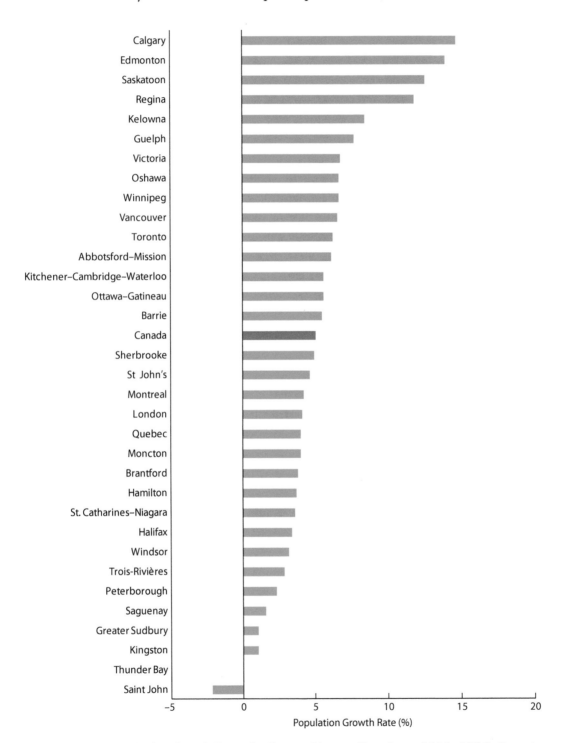

FIGURE 15.3 Population Growth Rates by Census Metropolitan Area, 2011–2016, Canada

SOURCE: Population size and growth in Canada: Key results from the 2016 Census. Ottawa: Statistics Canada. Census of population, *Highlight Tables* (98-402-X2016001). Retrieved from: http://www.statcan.gc.ca/daily-quotidien/170208/cg-a003-eng.htm

TIME to REFLECT

Population growth in the Montreal census metropolitan area has been only 4.2 per cent since the 2006 census. What do you think accounts for this relatively low growth?

SOCIOLOGICAL PERSPECTIVES ON CITIES

Different approaches to explaining how society works can also be applied to understanding the transition toward urbanism and its impact on social relations. The perspectives reveal that cities present great opportunities and challenges at the same time.

Functionalism: Urbanism and the Industrial City

Early European urban sociology emerged in response to conditions created by the Industrial Revolution during the late nineteenth and early twentieth centuries. Sociologists were concerned about the movement of people from rural settings into cities and the potential impact of the demographic shift on social life. The transformation toward urban life and industrialization signalled the disappearance of one kind of human association and its replacement by another (Gusfield, 1975).

Many of the early urban sociologists adopted a structural functionalist approach, with its concern for social order and stability, which they applied to the move toward city life. German sociologist Ferdinand Tönnies (1957 [1887]) developed the rural/urban typology, or classification, to contrast the two types of social life. The term *Gemeinschaft* referred to a rural or pre-industrial community based on agriculture or a primitive mode of production. Social bonds and relationships existed for their own sake and focused around kinship and neighbourhood. Human motivation for action was natural, and community was assumed to have greater stability. The *Gesellschaft*, in contrast, was the industrial urban community, which involved superficial associations based on contract or exchange. There was less emphasis on the family, and the human motivation for action was rational rather than natural. Lack of social cohesion resulted in social problems. From today's perspective, Tönnies's distinction is useful for explaining, at the structural level, why people might feel isolated in cities, but the *Gemeinschaft* is a crude categorization and the past is over-idealized.

Émile Durkheim (1964 [1893]) provided a rural/urban typology that was much more optimistic about cities. Durkheim classified communities as having either "mechanical solidarity" (rural) or "organic solidarity" (urban). The mechanical solidarity of rural life derived from social relationships based on common bonds. Individuals in a rural community were bound to each other without having any choice in the matter. In the city, relationships were based on specialization. The greater division of labour in cities gave the individual freedom and new forms of cohesion. Consistent with structural functionalism and its views on social integration, everyone had a function but was still independent. In cities, people did not have to engage in all forms of labour. For example, if you want, you can hire someone to clean your house. The division of labour in cities can make individuals dependent on strangers; however, they can also have more free time. But when people or organizations do not perform their expected function, chaos may occur.

Georg Simmel explored the meaning of urban life from a micro-level, or social-psychological, perspective in his work "The Metropolis and Mental Life" (2002 [1903]). For Simmel, the early industrial city created conditions that predisposed individuals to repress their emotional involvement and to focus on formal interactions with others. In the city, there was an intensification of stimuli and an emphasis on market relations. Simmel suggested that in the urban context, individuals were forced to protect themselves and to become detached and reserved (McGahan, 1995). Simmel's work provides a valuable perspective on the urban way

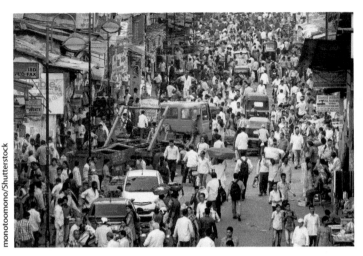

Toronto is Canada's largest and most densely populated city, with 2,650 people per square kilometre. But it does not come close to Mumbai, India, which has 29,650 people per square kilometre (City Mayors, n.d.).

of life. However, his writings do not offer a systematic theoretical model. Simmel's regard for urban culture and how people act and behave in cities influenced the Chicago School theorists in North America in the 1920s and 1930s.

The Chicago School of Sociology

Urban sociology in North America took root at the University of Chicago early in the twentieth century. As a collective, the Chicago School of Sociology tended to be more systematic about its insights than were other perspectives in the past. In addition to industrialization and its impact on cities, a central question for the Chicago School theorists was the effect of diversity on the social order as Chicago expanded with an influx of immigrants.

Louis Wirth's (1938) essay "Urbanism as a Way of Life" presents a formal theory of urbanism that is still relevant to how we understand cities and urbanism today. Wirth's definition of the city as "a relatively large, dense and permanent settlement of heterogeneous individuals" (1938, p. 1) highlights social processes in the city and city living. Deriving from this definition, size, density, and heterogeneity are the three criteria that determine the degree of urbanism. A city is larger than a rural settlement, which facilitates segregation. However, a city is much more than its mere size. The higher the

density in a city, or the more people per square kilometre, the greater the division of labour.

Heterogeneity in cities provides people with the opportunity to pursue a variety of interests and have regular contact with a wide range of people. For Wirth, population size, density, and diversity present opportunity for urbanites. A weakness of Wirth's definition of a city is that it does not take into account the need for an administrative centre responsible for governance to deal with the ways that differences associated with heterogeneity affect people living in proximity.

The Chicago School of Sociology, led by Robert Park, developed two approaches to empirically studying the city based on the view that the city represented a sociological laboratory (Lindner, 1996). First, drawing on Simmel's earlier work, ethnography was adopted to examine detailed descriptive accounts of lived experience in the city. Field research was used to construct detailed case studies, based on participant observation and life histories, to identify patterns of social bonding and everyday experiences of people in their natural settings. Many ethnographies profiled the lives of the marginalized, underprivileged, and criminals. One controversial element was that researchers often gained access to the people they were studying by "breaching"—attempting to pass as members of the communities they were studying. Ethnographic narratives such as *The Gang* (Thrasher, 1927) and *The Hobo* (Anderson, 1923) had popular mass market appeal (McGahan, 1995).

The human ecology approach (often called the ecological perspective) was the second empirical approach, developed by Robert Park, Ernest Burgess, and Roderick McKenzie (1967[1925]) to examine the social organization of the city in order to understand city processes at the macro level. Drawing on components of biology and ecology, human ecology conceives of cities as social organisms. People, like species, exist with a division of labour that allows for a balance within society. The city has its own spatial division of labour, but all the parts fit together (McGahan, 1995). In this sense, cities grow not randomly but rather in an orderly fashion in response to features of the environment. Competition in the city determines the optimal distribution of land and people (Park, Burgess, & McKenzie, 1967 [1925]; McKenzie, 1967 [1925]). From the perspective of heterogeneity, each social group (i.e., each income group or each immigrant group) has its place in the city, which allows for stable social relations. Competition leads to expansion of the city outward. Invasion and ecological succession is the process whereby one segment of the population takes possession of the urban territory from another population.

The concentric zone model, envisioned by Park and Burgess in 1925, provides a visual model for the human ecology perspective. The model emphasizes function and balance, indicating that every social group and land use has its place. Figure 15.4 shows the five major zones radiating out from the core of the city. These zones are described in terms of housing and social characteristics.

Burgess (1967 [1925]) characterizes the zones as follows:

- Zone I is the central business district or commercial heart and centre of the city, consisting of department stores and office buildings. The outer portion of zone I is occupied by industrial enterprises that need a centralized location. This is the most valuable zone in the city.
- Zone II is the "zone in transition." It includes old residential areas surrounding the commercial core, rundown housing, and rental housing for the poorest populations, including recent immigrants, minorities, and other urban undesirables. This area is characterized by competition between commercial and lower-end residential uses along with high levels of crime. Access to better jobs and money enables the residents of zone II to move to the better housing in outer zones.
- Zone III is the "zone of working-class homes," which are inexpensive semi-detached homes.

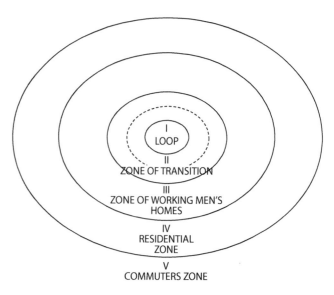

FIGURE 15.4 Concentric Zone Model

SOURCE: N. Brown. (2001). Robert Park and Ernest Burgess: Urban ecology studies, 1925. CSISS *Classics*, Center for Spatially Integrated Social Science. www.csiss.org/classics/content/26

- Zone IV consists of better residential single-family detached homes.
- Zone V, labelled the "commuter zone," includes the more expensive detached homes for upper-middle-class and upper-class households. Zones IV and V are associated with economic and social uniformity. Those living in zone V can afford cars to commute to work in the inner zones.

The concentric zone theory was one of the earliest theories to explain the spatial organization of industrial cities. It had great influence on Canadian urban research (e.g., Balakrishnan & Kralt, 1987; Anderson, 1991). However, the model has a number of weaknesses that limit its applicability, as a general predictive tool, outside of Chicago in the 1930s. For example, in contemporary Canadian cities affected by globalization and deindustrialization, developments such as competition, invasion, and succession are also occurring in the parts of the city, such as zone II, that the model conceptualizes as undesirable. Many inner zones are experiencing **gentrification** as more affluent people move into previously low-income neighbourhoods.

Further, the model assumes that the shape of the city is radial, whereas grid patterns exist in many North American cities. Suburbanization has led to more than one zone I, or central business district area, in many metropolitan cities as companies locate in the suburbs. Lower-income areas are often no longer concentrated but dispersed throughout cities. The model, oriented to explaining structural processes, also gives little attention to the role of individual choice, government regulation, and cultural preferences in settlement (McGahan, 1995).

The limitations of the concentric zone theory have been taken up by other theorists, including Homer Hoyt (1939) in his sector theory, which conceived of the city as sectors with different economic activities. Harris and Ullman's (1945) multiple nuclei theory conceived more advanced stages of urbanization in which there could be multiple centres within a larger city. More contemporary approaches to examining the organization of cities attempt to explore the importance of ethnic bonds and lifestyle and the overall significance of the political and economic context. Modelling today often uses geographical information systems to map demographic and land-use variables of interest in terms of the spatial organization of cities.

 For more on the importance and role of ethnic bonds see **Chapter 8**, "Ethnic and Race Relations," p. 172.

Conflict Approach: Urbanization and Globalization

Starting in the late 1960s, many urban sociologists, influenced by conflict theory, responded to the lack of consideration of power relations in human ecology and in urban sociology grounded in a functionalist orientation. For the new urban sociology theorists, the political and economic context is the driving force for urban activity (Feagin, 1998; Gottdiener & Hutchison, 2000; Harvey, 1985; Zukin, 1980). Much of the sociological work in this approach converges with the work of urban theorists in urban planning, political science, and geography. The

political economy orientation raises questions about inequalities in urban power rooted in capitalist relations, including uneven distributions in wealth. Urban space itself is a commodity that embodies political interests and conflicts. The large urban cities are seen as instrumental sites for the **global economy**.

Joe Feagin (1998), one of the major contributors to defining the new urban sociology, has summarized the central assumptions of the approach. Cities are part of a global system oriented around profit, or capitalist accumulation. The new urban sociology is concerned with power inequalities in urban politics and how cities are defined by decision-making processes that are locally defined in each city. This critical perspective on urban processes attempts to highlight the links between capitalism and the workings of racism and patriarchy.

The different political and economic interests of powerful players in cities are central to John Logan and Harvey Molotch's (1987) portrayal of cities as machines fuelled by a drive to grow. Real estate investors, bankers, developers, and corporate officials are examples of the powerful elite in cities who push a pro-growth and pro–urban development mentality. Urban growth leads to competing tensions between community groups and more powerful stakeholders. Those with the most economic and political power are able to position urban development as being good for the whole city. Logan and Molotch (1987) argue that the growth machine influences the workings of municipal governments, which become focused on creating the kind of city that can attract industry and investors, with less attention to community needs.

Critical urban sociological perspectives have also been applied to the role of the city in the transformation from industrialization (or de-industrialization) toward globalization (Harvey, 1985; Kipfer & Keil, 2002; Sassen, 1991). Broadly defined, globalization is the internationalization of the market economy, leading to the global exchange of capital. Under industrialization, large-scale manufacturing, such as clothing factories, was predominantly located in one particular city. Starting in the 1980s, with the global expansion of multinational corporations, the production of goods and services could take place in any or several locations where profit could be maximized. With deindustrialization, there has been a restructuring of the economy and creation of a "new economy," which relies on information- and technology-driven jobs. In the same way that industrialization had a significant impact on the growth and expansion of cities, deindustrialization and globalization also affect cities. According to global cities theory, cities provide the necessary infrastructure for global control (Kipfer & Keil, 2002). Global cities, including Vancouver, New York, London, and Tokyo, act as command points for centralizing finance, telecommunications, and access to labour markets. Increasingly, global cities are centres for culture as well (Sassen, 1991).

As a global city, Toronto has become central in coordinating the international division of labour, which, on one level, involves multinational corporations with various locations of production and distribution and the global movement of financial capital. The head offices of many top Canadian corporations and foreign-owned corporations are now located in Toronto. On another level, the division of labour on both local and global scales results in the uneven development of marginalized communities and people. Since the liberalization of Canadian federal immigration policy in the late 1960s, large numbers of new immigrants were drawn to Toronto from developing nations. These new waves of immigrants facilitated the division of labour between the highly skilled and highly paid professional classes and the low-skilled and poorly paid service-sector classes (Sassen, 1991). For Sassen (1991), global political-economic restructuring affects the spatial organization of the city, as gentrification of inner-city neighbourhoods accommodates professional classes and groups with capital. Meanwhile, the less-skilled classes are relegated to less desirable areas. The notion of the global city, as conceived by Sassen (1991), links global economics, social divisions of labour, and urban spatial

changes. A critical urban sociological perspective draws attention to the fact that culture in the global city is commodified and consumed. The marketing and branding of global cities is seen to be more important than valuing culture, including artists and diverse communities, for their own value. Culture is valued to meet larger political and economic objectives rather than to address the specific needs of local communities.

CITIES AND PERSPECTIVES ON THE ENVIRONMENT

Environmental sociology, as a distinct area of sociology, emerged in response to growing concern over environmental problems. Environmental sociology recognizes the close relationship between humans and their biophysical environments. As Dunlap and Rosa (2010, pp. 1–2) state, the biophysical environment and human populations are linked in three essential ways: (1) the environment provides resources that maintain human life; (2) in the process of consuming resources, humans generate waste that the environment must absorb; and (3) the environment provides a habitat or home for humans and all living species. In light of this close relationship, environmental problems such as pollution, resource scarcity, and overcrowding or overpopulation can result.

In the twenty-first century, cities have become a focal point for concerns about the environment because of their unrestricted economic growth and the fact that they are sites for the large-scale consumption of goods and services, resulting in high levels of waste and pollution. Canadian cities face a wide range of environmental problems. Air pollutants from automobile exhaust and other toxic emissions increase the levels of ambient air particles. Frequent "smog days" are now a reality of city living. The resulting health problems cause many deaths every year, in spite of the impact of deindustrialization and government controls to reduce urban airborne pollutants. In part because of the lessons learned from the *E. coli* bacteria contamination of the municipal water supply in Walkerton, Ontario, in 2002, maintaining water quality in urban areas has become a priority. This water crisis resulted from both individual and structural causes. But even so, it was estimated in 2005 that 18 per cent of Canadian cities still did not have adequate sewage treatment for wastewater (Canadian Environmental Grantmakers' Network, 2005, p. 11), and Canadians were second only to the United States in the production of solid waste per capita (2005, p. 12). Near Toronto and Montreal, landfill space is limited, and concern about the risk of land contamination makes it difficult for municipalities to locate new landfill sites. Rising concern about climate change has led to calls for residents of Canadian cities to reduce their use of energy, particularly fossil fuels, and to be open to forms of renewable energy. But energy conservation and energy production are topics of contentious debate in Canada. In cities such as Calgary and Edmonton, with economies largely driven by the oil and natural gas industries, energy efficiency is less an urgent priority than in most other Canadian urban centres, which are consumers rather than producers of energy and thus feel the pinch of rising energy prices.

CLIMATE CHANGE AND CITIES

One of the most challenging of all environmental problems to understand and the one that may create the most confusion is climate change (Harper & Fletcher, 2011). Climate change and its possible effects are highly contested even though the science has existed to provide evidence for many decades (Farmer & Cook, 2013). Human activities related to the burning of fossil fuels—natural gas, petroleum, and coal—increase the concentrations of carbon dioxide. Carbon dioxide gases in the atmosphere play a heat-trapping role, which causes the **greenhouse effect,** which is ultimately characterized by extreme weather, including global warming and changes in precipitation patterns. Over time, climate change will disturb ecosystems; compromise health outcomes; decrease air, water, and soil quality;

damage infrastructure; and create food security issues dues to reduced agricultural yields. All these effects are magnified in urban centres, where population is heavily concentrated.

Through the Intergovernmental Panel on Climate Change, scientists began widely discussing the problem of climate change in 1988. Yet, people in cities and throughout more developed countries depend on fossil fuels to heat homes, power cars, and run economies. Plenty of everyday evidence, such as increasingly warmer summers, seems to indicate that climate change is taking place but still doubt persists. There is uncertainty about the magnitude and timing of the problem, how to prevent or mitigate the effects of climate change and the associated costs, and the ability of scientists to predict the course of climate change (Harper & Fletcher, 2011). In addition, many economic arguments tend to run counter to the logic of acknowledging and addressing climate change.

The climate justice movement, which is closely tied to the environmental justice movement discussed below, recognizes the differential impacts of climate change. Lower-income communities, both in Canada and globally, bear the largest burden of the problems associated with climate change, despite being the least responsible for high levels of carbon emissions. The politics of climate change links high carbon dioxide emissions to the economic and social organization of developed countries and examines the power dynamics related to fossil fuel extraction. For example, many Indigenous communities in Canada have challenged the extraction of bitumen from the Alberta tar sands due to the proximity of vast extraction operations to Indigenous communities, the lack of consultation with affected communities, and the pollution that results from extraction (D'Arcy et al., 2014).

Amid the confusion and politics related to climate change, many initiatives aim to reduce carbon emissions. Cities are starting to embrace a mix of energy systems that do not produce harmful emissions, including renewable energy sources such as solar, wind, and biofuel. Many cities are expanding and changing their public

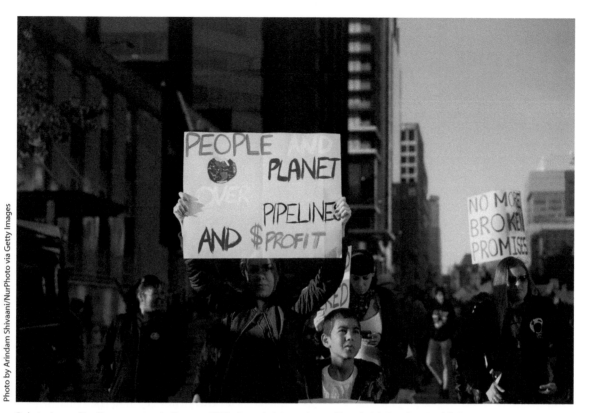

Dakota Access Pipeline protesters in Toronto, 2016, show their intention to "Stand with Standing Rock." They oppose a proposed oil pipeline that threatens the main water supply for the Standing Rock Sioux Tribe in North Dakota.

transportation systems to use these alternative energy systems. At the 2015 United Nations Climate Change conference in Paris, participants recognized the greater responsibility of richer countries in reaching carbon reduction targets. Canadian delegates also pushed for the recognition of Indigenous rights and a just transition that takes into account the needs of workers displaced from manufacturing jobs in the shift to green jobs (Perry, 2015). **Green jobs** are those oriented to reducing carbon outputs within the existing economy (Teelucksingh & Zeglen, 2016). The future of green jobs and addressing climate change depends on our ability to understand humans' impact on the natural environment.

The concept of ecological footprints, developed by Canadian William Rees (1992), is a numerical indicator of our lifestyles' impact on the planet in terms of the scarcity of land, fuel, and natural resources. A population's ecological footprint represents how much land and water are used to produce the resources that the population consumes and to absorb the subsequent

waste produced (Rees, 2010; Wilson & Anielski, 2005). The footprint takes into account the population size, the standard of living, "the productivity of the land/water base (whether local or 'imported' in trade goods), and the efficiency of resource harvesting, processing, and use" (Rees, 2010, p. 74). Ecological footprint analysis calculates a population's biocapacity, or natural capital, which is the amount of natural resources for food, energy, and other materials that a population requires relative to the supply of natural resources available.

It is estimated that 7.25 hectares of land and water resources from throughout the world is needed to sustain Canada's level of consumption per capita (Wilson & Anielski, 2005). Across Canadian cities footprints vary between 6.87 in Greater Sudbury to 9.86 in the Calgary metropolitan area, reflecting different levels of energy used to sustain consumption needs. Canada has higher levels of natural capital because of its abundance of natural resources; however, some Canadian cities are consuming beyond

GLOBAL ■■■ ISSUES — The Global City and the Knowledge-Based Economy

A global city, also known as a world city, is a "command and control centre" in the global economy (Sassen, 1991, 2001). In Canada, Vancouver, Toronto, and Montreal play a complex networking role at the global level by connecting global processes of production, consumption, and distribution. With globalization, business activity is no longer tied to one particular location or city. Rather, in many cases raw materials are extracted at one location; fabrication takes place in another location; and distribution, financing, and marketing, in yet another. However, activity in spatially dispersed locations must be linked and coordinated (Shin & Timberlake, 2000). Global cities, as conceived by Saskia Sassen (1991), are the few cities at the top of a hierarchy of cities that centralize banking and other specialized services, including finance, culture, and ideology, for a transnational marketplace (Shin & Timberlake, 2000). Increasingly, these specialized services are associated with the knowledge-based economy: the union of globalization and the trend toward greater reliance on knowledge and high skill levels in response to businesses' needs for quick information. Global cities fuel the knowledge-based economy by providing educated, skilled workers and

the information infrastructure that together foster innovation, such as advances in telecommunication and international transfers of knowledge and capital.

Global cities, as transnational focal points, are sites of innovation, growth, and trade in part because they attract well-educated migrants who drive the knowledge-based economy (Courchene, 2007). Richard Florida (2008) argues that knowledge-based economy workers, whom he calls the "creative class," are drawn to cities with a dynamic culture as an indicator of a city's commitment to risk-taking, diversity, and innovation. For Florida, the culture in global cities is reflected in museums, art galleries, and street festivals as well as multicultural populations and grassroots movements that challenge the status quo. Thus, many policies of Canadian global cities are intended to entice globally oriented professional workers and businesses. Critical urban sociology perspectives raise important questions about what happens to local communities and locally defined needs if global cities favour the dictates of the knowledge-based economy, including international players and agendas.

the world's ecological means. Canada has the seventh-largest ecological footprint among 130 nations, with nearly half of this footprint resulting from carbon emissions from fossil fuels (World Wildlife Fund, 2010).

The ecological footprint is also a tool for measuring a population's progress toward sustainability. Sustainable development has been defined as "development which meets the needs of the present without compromising the ability of future generations to meet their own needs" (Brundtland, 1987, p. 43) and involves an attempt to balance concerns for the three E's: environment, economy, and equity. On one level, sustainable development, as a mandate, means seeking to reconcile the objectives of economic growth and development with the world's resource limits. While this approach to environmentalism has been widely endorsed by various

actors, including municipal governments, businesses, and non-governmental organizations, the definition of environmental sustainability has been broadly interpreted to suit specific actors' own economic and political interests. For some, sustainable development involves recycling programs or new "green" product lines or initiatives. Other actors have pursued a complete restructuring of their objectives, focusing equally on all components of environment, economy, and equity.

Urban sustainability, when adopted, involves a commitment to using the natural resources of a city within its capacity to sustain its social, economic, and natural significance. Goals associated with urban sustainability are related to improving the quality of life in the city without stealing resources from future generations. Under urban sustainability mandates, some municipalities, such as Toronto, have installed solar generation panels and wind turbines. In other contexts, city planning and development staff have become sensitive to the importance of green space, increasing the density of urban developments, and improving public transportation and facilitating cycling in the city.

Functionalist Perspectives on the Environment

Cities are often seen as incompatible with notions of nature. Discussions of urbanization can mistakenly relegate the natural environment to the rural context where agriculture-based subsistence is seen as closer to nature (Rees, 2010). Technological innovations associated with industrialization and globalization tend to blind urbanites to the connection between nature and their own dependence on food, fuel, and other natural resources. Thus, the challenge for sociologists and others is to conceive of cities as biophysical forms and to consider the impact of urban environments on shaping social structure and processes.

William Catton and Riley Dunlap (1978) were among the first to criticize sociologists for their lack of consideration of the biological and environmental. They called this dominant sociological world view the human exemptionalist paradigm (HEP). The HEP assumes that humans, because of their use of culture, are distinct from other biological beings; thus, it is possible to reject the significance of biology and the physical in social processes (Harper & Fletcher, 2011). Catton and Dunlap (1978) encouraged sociologists to adopt the new ecological paradigm (NEP) that situates humans within an interdependent ecosystem. NEP's world view recognizes that while humans' use of culture and technology allows for some control over the environment, the carrying capacity of the environment is a reality that cannot be ignored (Catton & Dunlap, 1978). With the new paradigm, Dunlap and Catton could merge an understanding of ecological processes with the structural functionalist perspective's regard for stability and order.

The Bixi bike program in Montreal provided the first unstaffed bicycle rental stations of their kind in Canada, and the network now boasts 5,120 bikes at 411 stations. The bikes offer a sustainable and affordable alternative to other modes of transport.

Arguments that recognize the city's biophysical orientation are, in part, reminiscent of components of the Chicago School's human ecology perspective, which conceived of the city as a living organism that grows in a natural and orderly manner. However, the new ecological paradigm (Catton & Dunlap, 1978; Dunlap & Catton, 1983) situates cities and their populations as belonging to ecosystems or as ecosystems in themselves. "An ecosystem is an interacting set of living organisms (animals and plants) and their nonliving environment (air, land, water) that are bound together by a flow of energy and nutrients (e.g., food chains)" (Dunlap & Rosa 2010, p. 2). Humans, as only one component of ecosystems, should not disrupt the inherent balance by overusing other components.

Despite growing awareness of environmental problems, Canadians' ecological footprints, and the need for urban sustainability, some scientists, policy-makers, and environmentalists continue to turn to technocratic solutions to manage urban environments. For example, scientific and technological innovations have made it possible to produce more energy-efficient "smart cars" and hybrid cars. Science is also coming up with ways to address the limits of natural resources by developing alternatives to fossil fuels and finding ways to reduce ozone depletion. Counting on the possibility that technology can resolve environmental problems, some policy-makers continue to pursue policies aimed at urban growth rather than encouraging reduced consumption and slower growth.

The Conflict/Political Economy Approach to the Environment

The conflict approach to environmental sociology, conceived by British theorists such as James O'Connor, highlights the role of power inequalities in struggles over resources. These theorists rework Marxist analysis to examine the intersection between the oppression of labour and the oppression of the environment within the capitalist production process (Gould, Schnaiberg, & Weinberg, 1996; O'Connor, 1996). In this sense, environmental degradation—both resource depletion as a result of production processes and pollution as a result of the output of these processes—leads to social consequences that are differentially experienced (Schnaiberg & Gould, 1994). By connecting marginalized environments and communities through capitalism and, by extension, processes of globalization, it is possible to identify why threats to the ecosystem require changes to status quo social relations, not just temporary technological solutions.

In the current context of rising neo-liberalism and the demands of the global economy on cities, many new theorists, under the interdisciplinary label of urban political ecology, focus on cities as sites where new forms of social and environmental inequalities are emerging from inter-related social, ecological, and political conflicts (Keil & Bourdeau, 2006; Heynen et al., 2007). Some urban environmental issues that these urban political ecologists engage with include debates around the privatization of water and utilities (Young & Keil, 2007) and deregulation of environmental protection (Overton, 2009).

Environmental justice is a sub-theme of urban political ecology. It emerged in sociology in the 1980s in the United States in response to the popular environmental justice movement and the recognition that distributive injustices were resulting from the disproportionate burden of environmental degradation and polluting industries borne by poor communities and communities of colour (Bullard, 1990; Cole & Foster, 2001). In Canada, the undesirable land uses in the former black community of Africville in Halifax and the environmental health problems on many Indigenous peoples' reserves across Canada point to the link between the oppression of marginalized people and their environment (Gosine & Teelucksingh, 2008; Agyeman et al., 2009). Environmental justice research and activism in Canada has emerged more slowly and without the same grassroots and political commitment that characterized the US movement (Agyeman et al., 2009; Haluza-DeLay, 2007). However, many experiences of environmental injustice, while not specifically named and labelled as such, have an enormous impact on the lives of Indigenous and racialized communities in Canada and contribute to these communities' marginalized status vis-à-vis the Canadian state (Haluza-DeLay et al., 2009). And environmental justice research is being applied in Canadian cities to better understand uneven development, environmental health risks, and racialization of minorities and new Canadians.

Urban Sprawl

Urban sprawl is one of the most significant environmental and social problems affecting many larger cities in Canada. It involves decentralization or the shifting of economic activity and residential patterns away from the central city toward peripheral areas. Urban sprawl is often associated with uncontrolled growth in urban centres as previous suburban regions become extended over time. For example, steady population growth, and the corresponding growth in residential housing and business expansion, account for Calgary's urban sprawl (Carter-Whitney, 2008). It can be seen in large-scale, low-density development that poses serious threats to the natural environment, agricultural land, energy resources, and human health and quality of life. There is now greater

---

SOCIOLOGY ■ IN ACTION   Brownfields Redevelopment

Trendy lifestyle-oriented advertising beckons young professionals to come work, live, and play in the modern metropolis. Normally, gentrification is associated with upscaling existing lower-income, inner-city neighbourhoods. However, urban renewal in Toronto currently targets underused and virtually abandoned industrial brownfield sites. In downtown Toronto, brownfield sites have become hot properties, especially those close to the downtown commercial and financial centre and the coveted Lake Ontario waterfront. This instant form of gentrification (Rose, 2004, p. 7) involves the claiming of previously undesirable industrial spaces by the middle class and upwardly mobile. Tension over scarce resources in downtown Toronto is positioning those on the side of capital (developers, real estate agents, and potential middle-class residents) against the subsistence needs of marginalized groups and marginalized land uses.

Cheryl Teelucksingh, an environmental sociologist in Toronto, used the issue of brownfields redevelopment to examine important environmental justice and citizenship questions, such as who has claims to space in the city and who belongs in the city. Teelucksingh's (2009) research considered how universal and egalitarian rights to the city are threatened when stakeholders with fewer resources become vulnerable to environmental inequalities.

The study involved an analysis of various stakeholders' perspectives (e.g., people living near brownfields, affluent residents, and public- and private-sector interests) on brownfields redevelopment in light of competing needs emerging from post-industrialization and shifts toward neo-liberal agendas in Toronto. Based on this analysis, the study found that brownfields gentrification is a unique form of gentrification that has the potential to isolate lower-income and ethno-racial groups within limited neighbourhoods in downtown Toronto, to minimize the focus on creating affordable housing for Toronto's growing population, and, ultimately, to tarnish Toronto's image as the ideal Canadian multicultural urban centre that includes mixed-income neighbourhoods in the downtown core. The development of brownfields in downtown Toronto is resulting in social and environmental inequalities as well as new forms of resistance, such as demonstrations in support of the rights of the homeless and those living in poor-quality housing.

---

awareness of the social and environmental costs associated with urban sprawl, which seems all the more ominous given that the demographic trend is toward smaller families and larger, predominately suburban houses.

Larger housing lots and ease of commuting to the central city often draw residents to suburban communities. However, not only are suburbanites less likely to know and interact with their neighbours, but many suburban communities are class-segregated because of the way new housing developments are designed. Social segregation in low-density communities means less diverse neighbourhoods, which does not foster racial tolerance. As part of urban sprawl, decentralization of economic activity results in the dispersal of workplaces and makes it difficult for those living in the central city to get to work. As people spend more time commuting, their social isolation increases.

One of the most significant environmental consequences of urban sprawl is its threat to farmland. To lessen the threat, some cities, like Portland, Oregon, in 1979, have established a **greenbelt** to contain the sprawl (Carter-Whitney, 2008). Suburbanization and urban sprawl also require construction of more highways. Greater reliance on cars translates into increased fuel consumption and pollution. In many suburban neighbourhoods, public transit options are few, because extensive sprawl makes it difficult to establish and maintain cost-effective transit systems. This disadvantages lower-income people who either live or work in suburban areas.

In an effort to address urban growth in a manner that does not further contribute to urban sprawl, municipalities and developers are increasingly adopting "smart growth" as a development strategy (Eidelman, 2010). Smart growth is an approach to urban development that seeks to make more efficient use of existing inner-city infrastructure by creating higher-density communities. Making better and more efficient use of existing urban space and infrastructure is the alternative to new greenfield development. Some smart-growth initiatives in Toronto and Vancouver (Girling, 2010) involve the creation of urban villages where people do not need to use their cars to meet their everyday needs. Stores, entertainment, daycare centres, and, ideally, workplaces are all within walking distance or a short public transit ride away. However, many smart-growth developments in the form of high-density condominiums, lofts, and townhouses are economically and socially oriented toward young urban dwellers and older "empty nesters," which limits the ability of people with lower incomes or larger families to benefit from such options.

Vancouver, Calgary, Hamilton, and Toronto are all experiencing urban renewal in the form of gentrification (Ley & Dobson, 2008; Behan, Maoh, & Kanaroglou, 2008; Eidelman, 2010; Meligrana & Skaburskis, 2005). As discussed earlier in the chapter, gentrification involves the upscaling of formerly lower-income or working-class neighbourhoods. Like smart-growth developments, gentrification is breathing new life into many inner-city neighbourhoods that have desirable access to employment, public transit, and

various amenities and offer an alternative to urban sprawl development. However, drawing from conflict approaches to both urbanization and the environment, critics of gentrification point to the displacement of lower-income residents as inner-city neighbourhoods become unaffordable and the fact that the racial and class diversity that once characterized mixed-income neighbourhoods can be lost (Meligrana & Skaburskis, 2005).

TIME to REFLECT

Based on the arguments presented, is some level of gentrification desirable in lower-income communities? If so, how can gentrification occur without displacing lower-income residents?

CONCLUSION

Social forces related to changes in the labour market, the family, health care, immigration, and urban planning have all contributed to Canada's current demographic trend toward low fertility rates, an aging population, and a continued reliance on immigration. In this chapter, we have considered demography as the starting point for examining how cities evolve in Canada and the relationship of Canadian cities to their natural environment.

Similarly, we have seen how theoretical perspectives on urbanism and the environment have developed and responded to social transformations. Late nineteenth- and twentieth-century industrialization led early European and later Chicago School of Sociology theorists to consider the impact of cities on social relations and social order. The Chicago School was instrumental in providing urban sociology with a definition of urbanism and systematic methods for studying the city. Subsequent conflict perspectives on urbanism applied the political economy approach to understanding urban inequalities stemming from capitalism and globalization.

22DigiTal/Alamy Stock Photo

Do you think Calgary has an urban sprawl issue greater than that of other Canadian cities? Why or why not?

As sites for large-scale consumption and high levels of waste and pollution, cities are now central to the drive toward sustainability and a more nuanced regard for humans' place in interdependent ecosystems. It is impossible to predict how today's social and environmental actions will influence future demographic trends and patterns of urbanism. As explained in this chapter, functionalist approaches to urbanism and the environment focus on maintaining urban growth and development by using science and technology to come up with sustainable solutions. But in the context of heightened inequalities caused by globalization and neo-liberalism, conflict perspectives on urbanism and the environment emphasize the uneven distribution of benefits and costs in current urban development strategies such as suburbanization and gentrification.

Questions for Critical Thought

1. Demography helps us to predict population change. From the perspective of Canada and Canadian cities, what are some demographic trends that Canadians will be responding to in the future?
2. What are some social benefits and challenges associated with the shift from rural settlements to urban settlements?
3. Why are current environmental problems more critical today than in the past?
4. Sustainable development attempts to balance concerns for environment, economy, and equity. Can these three components exist together, or is sustainable development an unattainable goal?

Sociological Explorations

1. Walk around a neighbourhood in your city that is currently undergoing urban renewal. Drawing on the conflict approach to urbanization and globalization, critically examine the changes taking place in this neighbourhood. Will the changes in housing stock, businesses, or infrastructure draw different types of people? Who will be displaced as a result of these changes?
2. Visit the downtown in your city and consider Georg Simmel's observation (as discussed on page 353) that urban life forces us to be detached and reserved. Simmel made this claim reflecting on early industrial cities in Europe; is it still applicable in our cities today? List the different types of social groups or urban "noises" that you encounter as an urbanite and note which items on the list you were more inclined to directly engage with and those from which you were more detached.
3. Watch the film *This Changes Everything* (2015), which you can stream through iTunes (directed by Avi Lewis and written by Naomi Klein). The film profiles the devastating impact of climate change and different communities' efforts to build a climate movement. Use concepts like sustainable development in considering some of the major social barriers that the film presents.

Recommended Readings

Filion, P., Moos, M., Vinodrai, T., & Walker, R.C. (2015). *Canadian cities in transition: Perspectives for an urban age* (5th edn). Don Mills, ON: Oxford University Press. This book examines major transformations taking place in urban Canada.

Ehrlich, P.R., & Ehrlich, A.H. (1990). *The population explosion.* New York, NY: Simon and Schuster. The authors examine recent Malthusian perspectives and concerns about population growth.

Hannigan, H. (2014). *Environmental sociology* (3rd edn). New York, NY: Routledge. This book reviews the major narratives in environmental thinking over the last 40 years.

LeGates, R., & Stout, F. (Eds). (2003). *The city reader* (3rd edn). London, UK; New York, NY: Routledge. This anthology includes the best publications on the city, with chapters on globalization, information technology, and urban theory.

Recommended Websites

"Global Population Growth Box by Box": TED Talk with Hans Rosling
www.ted.com/talks/hans_rosling_on_global_population_growth
Hans Rosling presents compelling arguments and data related to global population growth and its implications.

World Wildlife Fund Footprint Calculator
http://footprint.wwf.org.uk
The footprint calculator estimates land and ocean area required annually to sustain your consumption patterns and absorb your wastes.

United Nations, Department of Economic and Social Affairs, Population Division
http://esa.un.org/unpd/wup/index.htm
This site gives estimates and projections of the urban populations of all countries in the world and their major urban agglomerations, including country profiles, interactive data, and maps.

Key Terms

birth rate The number of live births in a given year.
crude birth rate The number of live births in a given year for every 1,000 people in a population.
crude death rate The number of live births in a given year for every 1,000 people in a population.
deindustrialization The withdrawal of investment in factories.
demographic transition The process whereby a country moves from high birth and death rates. The shift in fertility rates is often referred to as the fertility transition, while the complementary change in death rates is referred to as the mortality transition. The epidemiological transition theory is a complementary theory to the demographic transition theory.
demography The study of population. Demographers examine changes in birth rates, infant mortality rates, death rates, growth rates, and migration, considering factors such as the size, composition, and geographical variations of populations over time.
gentrification The process whereby more affluent households purchase and upgrade housing that was previously occupied by lower-income residents.
global economy A connection of the world's businesses and markets worldwide.
green job A job oriented to reducing carbon outputs within the existing economy.
greenbelt An area around a city where no development is permitted.
greenhouse effect The result of carbon dioxide and other gases in the atmosphere trapping heat, which creates extreme weather effects.

growth rate The difference between births and deaths, taking into account the difference between immigrants and emigrants.

infant mortality rate The number of deaths of children less than one year of age per 1,000 live births in the same year.

life expectancy at birth The median number of years that a person can expect to live.

natural growth rate The difference between the crude birth rate and the crude death rate, not taking into account migration (the movement of people into and out of a specific geographical area).

net migration The difference between the number of immigrants and the number of emigrants in a given period.

net migration rate The difference between the number of immigrants and the number of emigrants per 1,000 persons in a given period.

replacement fertility rate The average number of children per woman of one generation needed to maintain the population size.

settler colonialism The process whereby Indigenous populations are displaced by invading settlers.

staple economy A reliance on natural resources, such as fish, fur, lumber, agricultural products, and minerals, that are exported to support the economy.

urban sprawl Decentralization or the shifting of economic activity and residential patterns away from the central city toward peripheral areas of the city.

urban sustainability A commitment to using the natural resources of a city within its capacity to sustain its social, economic, and natural significance. Goals associated with urban sustainability are related to improving the quality of life in the city without robbing resources from future generations.

Media and Technology

DAVID YOUNG AND ANABEL QUAN-HAASE

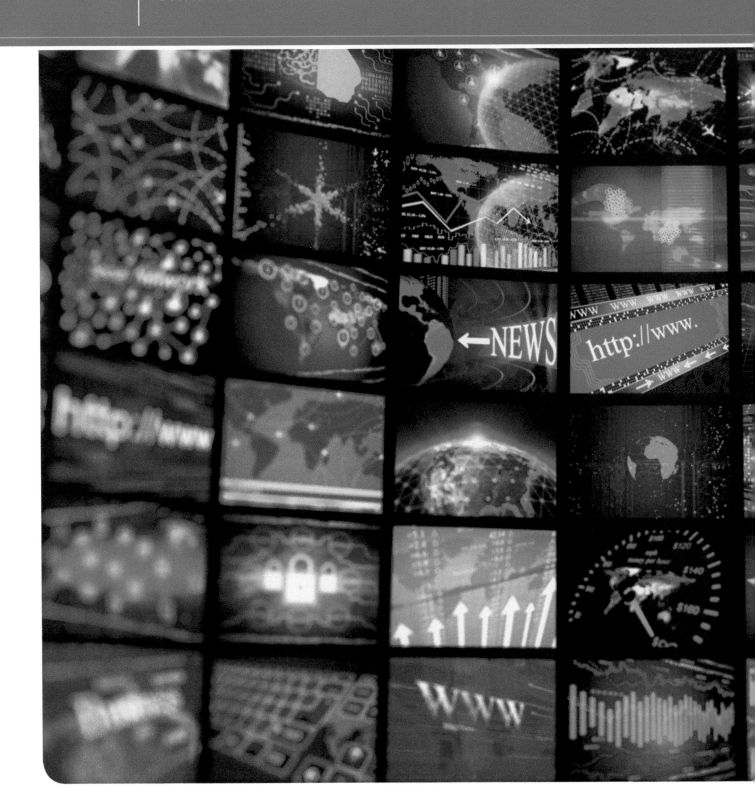

In this chapter you will:

▶ Learn about perspectives sociologists have used to analyze technology and the media

▶ Grasp sociological issues such as power, control, inequality, and conflict as they pertain to technology and the media

▶ Learn about changes in the conceptualization of the digital divide and its relevance to Canadian society

▶ Learn about how technology and the media affect our everyday lives, including notions of the self and gender performativity

INTRODUCTION

This chapter examines various perspectives sociologists have used to analyze **technology** and the media. The study of technology and the media is increasingly relevant to Canadians as our reliance on technology and the media continues to increase. Canadians integrate technology and the media into their daily routines and practices by checking the weather on their mobile devices, seeking health information online, and communicating with friends and family via Skype and cellphones (Haight, Quan-Haase, & Corbett, 2014). In fact, Canada is highly connected; the London-based agency *We are Social* reports that Canada is a world leader in Internet penetration (Kemp, 2014). The agency reports that as many as 93 per cent of Canadians have Internet access and 56 per cent have a profile on a social media account. Not only is Canada among the countries with the highest numbers of Facebook users, but it is also at the forefront of mobile usage (Oliveira, 2014). Facebook reports that about 19 million Canadians access the site at least once a month and 14 million log into their account daily. Canadians are also connected to Facebook on the go, as 15 million Canadians access their account from a mobile device at least once a month (Oliveira, 2014). Technology and the media have become such a central part of daily life

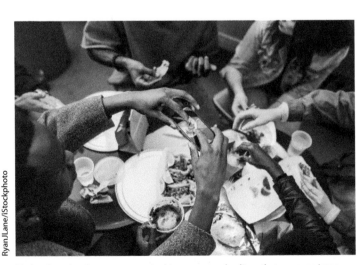

Technology has become so central to our everyday lives that we even interrupt conversations at mealtime to photograph the food.

RyanJLane/iStockphoto

that many Canadians no longer read the news in print; rather, they obtain their news from sites such as *The Huffington Post*, *Buzzfeed*, and online versions of *The Globe and Mail*, the *National Post*, and global media such as CNN and the *New York Times* (Quan-Haase, Martin, & Schreurs, 2016). Many activities are now conducted online for convenience, such as banking transactions and looking for health information; even background checks for employment are often done through Google, LinkedIn, and Facebook.

The move toward a digital society has brought about many social transformations and as a result daily life today is much more commodified. Our cellphones suggest products we may like, and our friends' online behaviours serve as a means to predict our own consumer behaviour. Technology has also changed our social interactions and social ties. Facebook, Twitter, and Instagram have all facilitated the formation of large, dispersed, and loosely bound networks that can span the globe (Chayko, 2016). Because of easy computer-mediated communication, there is less need to meet face to face. Sherry Turkle (2011) warns that even when young people meet face to face today, technologies like the cellphone, tablet, and "phablet" stand in the way and become disruptive. She claims that these technologies take people away from their in-person interactions, make them lonely, and lead to new forms of social interaction, which she calls "alone together." That is, people are collocated, but instead of engaging with one another, they check text messages, comment on Facebook, and post status updates.

In this chapter, we also examine how technology and the media can serve to establish new power dynamics. New media are creating alternative venues for the dissemination of information, the establishment of what is newsworthy, and the reproduction of wealth. New media companies that bring together a massive, global audience are supplanting companies that were gatekeepers in the past, such as print media (Yang, Quan-Haase, & Rannenberg, 2016). This demonstrates the relevance of grasping such sociological concepts as power, control, inequality, and conflict as they pertain to technology and the media.

DEFINITIONS AND PERSPECTIVES

Understanding Technology

Technology is a complex and multifaceted concept, as there is no one single way of defining it. Historically, the study of technology started in the technical fields, such as engineering, where research focused primarily on creating tools to increase efficiency and reduce human error. In this context, technology was primarily defined as a collection of technical components that exist outside of the social realm (Feist, Beauvais, & Shukla, 2010). The technical fields were less interested in the social side of technology development, implementation, and use, as they were not concerned with the social consequences of technological inventions on our social world and how technology affects various social groups in different ways. It was only when technology had left its mark on the social world that sociologists realized the study required a strong social component. It became evident that it is highly relevant to examine the close interplay between social processes and technological developments and to discern the nature of social change resulting from technological advances (Quan-Haase, 2016).

To better reflect the social aspects of technological development, many definitions try to encompass the social world. Renowned Canadian scientist Ursula Franklin in her 1992 book *The Real World of Technology* talks about technology not as "the sum of the artifacts" (1992, p. 2), that is, the integration of a complex set of mechanical components, but as a "system" involving organization, procedures, symbols, new worlds, and most importantly, a mindset. She views technology as not limited to the apparatus, to the material substance itself, that which makes a machine work. Her unique perspective focuses our attention on how technology becomes embedded and contained in our everyday activities. She does not, however, see technology's effect on daily life as necessarily positive; her view is rather dystopian in that the "real world of technology seems to involve an inherent trust in machines and devices ('production is under control') and a basic apprehension of people" (Franklin, 1992, p. 25). Franklin criticizes the way that society depicts technology as a solution for all human problems; she argues that people see themselves as unpredictable and unreliable, while machines are viewed as providing the solutions to problems and being always controllable. Hence, technologies are idealized; any problems they cause can be easily blamed on the people who designed, produced, or consumed a given technology. Franklin's definition and view of technology are important because they allow us to see technology from different angles, instead of focusing only on the positive effects of technological advances. For example, current discussions of climate change stress the importance of understanding how cars, factories, and many industrial operations leave a lasting and negative effect on human societies.

Similarly, Quan-Haase (2016, p. 9) in her definition of technology demonstrates the coming together of technical components and social aspects. For her, technologies are a part of social systems, and often are invisible since they are so fully integrated into our activities. Think of your reliance on your smartphone: it is used as a flashlight, alarm clock, and a communication device, and for countless other functions.

> Technology is an assemblage [or configuration] of material objects, embodying and reflecting societal elements, such as knowledge, norms, and attitudes that have been shaped and structured to serve social, political, cultural, and existential purposes. (Quan-Haase, 2016, p. 9)

In this particular definition, the social and the technological are linked through multiple processes and shape one another. Taking an approach that carefully considers social processes is important for sociologists because it allows for the study of the social system in relation to technology, regardless of whether one views technology as having a positive or negative impact on society.

Understanding Media

Technology is crucial to analysis of the media, a point that is evident in the work of Raymond Williams. In his book *Television: Technology and Cultural Form*, Williams (1975) is critical of technological determinism (a concept that ignored the social context while holding that technologies themselves shape the development of society). Williams argues that the impact of media technologies must be seen in the political, economic, and cultural context of the society that produced the technologies.

Williams's work draws attention to political economy and cultural studies. These perspectives offer a critical and sociological analysis of the media. Political economy considers private corporations and the state in relation to media production/distribution. Cultural studies analyze ideology in media content. Both perspectives address conflicts over the media (between powerful and less powerful groups). Adapting the themes that Mosco (1989) associated with political economy and cultural studies, we will now examine these two perspectives.

MEDIA AND SOCIETY

Political Economy of Media

While emphasizing historical analysis, researchers who specialize in the political economy of media devote particular attention to several issues. The main issues are ownership, policy, and globalization in relation to the media.

Forms of Media Ownership

We can distinguish between public and private media ownership as well as various types of ownership that are private.

Public ownership—ownership of media by the government—has a long history in Canada. Examples of public media in this country include the National Film Board (NFB), the Canadian

Broadcasting Corporation (CBC), and the educational television broadcasters operated by some provincial governments (e.g., TVOntario). The goal of these organizations is to provide a public service and meet social objectives (by offering media that are freely available to citizens, using the media for educational purposes, and ensuring a Canadian voice in the media). Public media organizations are often supported by government funding, but additional funding may come from advertising.

TIME to REFLECT

How much time do you spend with public media? In your view, how important is it to have public media ownership?

Private ownership refers to ownership of the media by commercial firms, and it too has a long tradition in Canada. Most media in Canada are privately owned; the largest private companies include Bell Media, Rogers Communications, and Shaw Communications. The goal of private media organizations is "survival and growth in a marketplace driven by profit" (Lorimer & Gasher, 2001, p. 223).

Critical researchers argue that the pursuit of profit through private ownership has significant implications for media content. The interests of private media companies mean that media content "is regarded by their management not as a public service, but as a business cost to be met as inexpensively as possible" (Hackett, Pinet, & Ruggles, 1996, p. 260). For example, the private television network CTV can purchase the rights to broadcast American shows for approximately one-tenth the cost of producing a Canadian series (Taras, 2001).

There are several different types of private media ownership. Horizontal integration exists when one company owns media organizations in different locations that are doing the same type of business. For instance, one firm might own newspapers across Canada. Vertical integration exists when one company owns media enterprises that link production, distribution, and exhibition (or retail). Quebecor is an example; it owns the French-language television broadcaster TVA as well as Vidéotron, a cable company in Quebec that carries TVA. Cross-ownership involves one company holding organizations associated with different types of media content. Bell Media, for instance, owns properties in television (such as CTV) and radio (including TSN Radio). Finally, conglomerate ownership entails one company holding both media and non-media enterprises. The Irving Group—a conglomerate based in the Maritimes—has had interests in oil, agriculture, shipbuilding, newspapers, and other businesses (Lorimer & Gasher, 2001).

Critical scholars express concerns about the implications of these different ownership forms and the resulting **ownership concentration**. For example, if a company acquires several newspapers through horizontal integration, it could cut costs by using some news stories across the chain and thus reduce the number of journalists at each newspaper (Hackett & Gruneau, 2000). Since vertical integration enables a firm to control production of content *and* access to content, it can result in content from other sources being shut out (Croteau & Hoynes, 2000). Cross-ownership has certain advantages for a company, including the opportunity to share resources among media outlets, but it can limit the diversity of media messages (Hackett, Pinet, & Ruggles, 1996). News media held under conglomerate ownership may be required to carry promotional material for other parts of the conglomerate, and news stories could be suppressed if they contain negative information about other aspects of the corporate empire (Hackett & Gruneau, 2000).

The State and Media Policy

In Canada, the **state** encompasses all levels of government; the administration (e.g., regulatory agencies); parliamentary assemblies; the armed forces and police; intelligence agencies; the legal system; prisons; and organizations associated with public education, public health care, and public media (Cuneo, 1990).

 The state has been a topic of study in a good number of disciplines, especially political science. How might a sociological approach to the study of the state differ from that found in political science or other disciplines? For more on the state, see **Chapter 13**, "Politics and Social Movements."

While the state includes public media, other parts of the state have implications for both public and private media. As prepared by governments and passed by parliamentary assemblies, laws set out requirements for media organizations. For example, the Broadcasting Act indicates what is expected of organizations that provide public and private radio or television in Canada. The legislation makes it clear that these organizations must provide Canadian programming. Regulatory agencies are also components of the state that have consequences for media organizations. Historically, Canada has had two independent broadcasting regulators. The Board of Broadcast Governors (BBG) was established in 1958 and replaced in 1968 by the Canadian Radio-television and Telecommunications Commission (CRTC). The CRTC ensures that media organizations comply with media legislation by setting specific rules for the organizations to follow. For example, in relation to the Broadcasting Act, the requirement to provide Canadian programming is reflected in Canadian content regulations which stipulate that Canadian broadcasters must air a certain percentage of Canadian content.

Analysis of media policy is often based on a key point in Marxist theories of the state. As Gold, Lo, and Wright (1975, p. 31) note, "Marxist treatments of the state begin with the fundamental observation that the state in capitalist society broadly serves the interests of the capitalist class." The state in Canada serves the interests of private media companies, as the CRTC's regulatory process illustrates. According to Mosco (1989, p. 57), "this formal regulatory process generally serves the interests of communications companies and large corporate users of communications systems." For instance, since the CRTC has taken "a permissive attitude to industry mergers" (Mosco, 1989, p. 212), the agency has given regulatory approval to ownership concentration. The state also serves the interests of the capitalist class by practising **neo-liberalism**. Neo-liberalism is an economic doctrine favoured by private companies, and it has been adopted by governments around the world since the 1970s. The doctrine supports free trade between countries, cuts in social spending, and measures such as deregulation or privatization. Deregulation means that regulatory agencies reduce or eliminate rules they had previously imposed on organizations, whereas privatization involves organizations under public ownership being transferred to private ownership. Both have had an impact on the Canadian media; the CRTC has relaxed requirements for private media companies, and the Alberta government sold its educational television broadcaster to a private firm in the 1990s.

Globalization and the Media

Globalization involves the flow of goods, services, media, information, and labour between countries. There are different types of globalization. *Economic globalization* concerns worldwide production and financial transactions. *Cultural globalization* refers to "the transmission or diffusion across national borders of various forms of media and the arts" (Crane, 2002, p. 1).

 Globalization is driven by a mixture of factors—see the discussion in **Chapter 14**, "Globalization and Social Change," p. 320.

Some factors are technological; while the emergence of a transnational financial system and global production have been facilitated by information technologies, communication technologies have enabled media content to spread around the world (Nash, 2000). It is also important to recognize economic factors, such as deepening ownership concentration across national borders and the international impact of free trade. These economic factors are tied to political factors, including international treaties such as the North American Free Trade

Agreement (NAFTA) and the emergence of the World Trade Organization (WTO), an international body that enforces trade rules for member countries (Karim, 2002). Such developments have led critical media sociologists to be concerned about globalization.

In relation to cultural globalization, critical researchers are concerned about the worldwide impact of media industries. Consider the global dominance of the US film industry. By 1939, it was already supplying 65 per cent of the films shown in theatres worldwide. Hollywood was providing more than 80 per cent of the world's films by the 1990s (Miller et al., 2001). In Canada, American films accounted for 86.7 per cent of box-office revenues in 2014 (Canadian Media Producers Association et al., 2015). The historical growth and influence of the motion picture industry in the United States has cultural implications for Canada and other countries.

With regard to economic globalization, critical researchers are concerned about the emergence of an *international division of labour*. Multinational corporations, including those with holdings in media and information industries, have spread their production operations around the world. The standard view of this process suggests that it involves shifting jobs from developed, rich countries (such as the United States) to developing, poor countries (such as India). Although the trend is certainly in the direction of moving jobs to the developing world, Mosco (2005, p. 52) has pointed to "an increasingly complex international division of labour involving far more than simply the transfer of service jobs from high- to low-wage nations." This is illustrated by the fact that several developed countries, especially Canada and Ireland, have gained many jobs through outsourcing and offshoring in the media and information industries. *Outsourcing* occurs when a company shifts a portion of its production to a locally owned firm in another country. *Offshoring* exists when a company has one of its own foreign holdings handle the production. Although developing countries offer cheaper labour and other advantages, multinational corporations maintain some outsourcing or offshoring in developed countries because they need certain jobs to be filled by workers with higher levels of skill or education (Mosco, 2005). Due to favourable currency exchanges and wage rates in these developed countries, multinationals can still keep production costs lower than in the United States. These factors explain the existence of so-called "runaway" film and television productions. Hollywood studios have moved a number of productions from Los Angeles to Canadian cities to cut costs while utilizing the expertise of Canadian companies and production crews (Elmer & Gasher, 2005).

Conflicts over Ownership, Policy, and Globalization

Capitalist interests in ownership, policy, and globalization have generated conflicts between private companies and subordinate groups. Although the state serves the interests of the capitalist class, Marxist theory suggests that the state makes some concessions to the working class and its allies. Consequently, despite the power of corporate capital and its influence on the state, subordinate groups have occasionally won victories through their resistance.

This point can be illustrated through reference to some historical conflicts. With regard to media ownership, the early 1930s were marked by "a struggle between the popular forces in Canada fighting for public service broadcasting and those seeking private profit" (Smythe, 1981, p. 165). Trade unions, women's organizations, educational leaders, and others mounted strong opposition to the desire of existing private broadcasters and corporate advertisers to establish an entirely privately owned broadcasting system. As a result of this opposition, the federal government made public ownership an important aspect of the broadcasting system and eventually created the CBC (while still allowing private broadcasting to exist). Other examples of successful resistance appeared during the 1950s and 1960s in relation to media policy on Canadian content. Private broadcasters were interested in maximizing audiences and advertising revenues by offering popular American content. A different position was taken by Canadian nationalists as well as unions representing actors, musicians, and other workers in Canadian media industries. They argued (quite successfully) that regulations were required to force private broadcasters to air Canadian content (thereby providing jobs for Canadian artists and protecting Canadian culture). This led the BBG to establish Canadian content regulations for television in 1960, and the CRTC followed with similar regulations for radio in 1970. However, debate continues about whether Canadian content regulations are still needed—a debate that is especially fierce in relation to radio (Young, 2013).

In recent years, much conflict associated with the media has been connected to globalization. This is most obvious in the protests against economic and cultural globalization held by social movements at meetings of the WTO or other international bodies, but conflict over globalization also takes other forms. For example, trade unions for media workers in the United States have resisted the loss of jobs to other countries (Mosco, 2005).

Cultural Studies of Media

While political economy examines media production/distribution, the perspective of cultural

Opponents of Canadian content regulations, especially private broadcasters, claim that CRTC regulations are an attack on the freedom of broadcasters.

UNDER THE WIRE The Surveillance Society

Hirst, Harrison, and Mazepa (2014, p. 269) argue that we are living in a "surveillance society." This society features "state surveillance" (Hirst et al., 2014, p. 286), such as the use of closed-circuit television in public spaces and cyberspace

Do drones make for a safer society or are they a dangerous violation of privacy? Do high-quality cameras flying ever-longer distances improve our lives or worsen them?

monitoring by intelligence agencies to protect citizens from crime or terrorism. While many people are aware of and even accept such surveillance, critical scholars contend that it is too extensive and violates privacy (Hirst et al., 2014). Similar concerns are raised about corporate surveillance, which is driven by the pursuit of profit. Corporate surveillance includes surveillance of the workplace (e.g., using video cameras and data from computers to monitor employee productivity). It also entails surveillance of the market. Information about individual consumers is recorded and tracked (e.g., through "cookies" created by websites or through loyalty cards associated with purchases). This information is used by private companies to manipulate consumers through targeted advertising. Personal information about consumers and their buying habits is even sold to other companies (Hirst et al., 2014). Shaped by the political-economic context of capitalist society, the "surveillance society" has worrying social implications.

studies addresses media content (see Chapter 2). It considers the content of mainstream media and how the ideology in this content may be interpreted or resisted.

Representation in Mainstream Media

Mainstream media include the newspapers, magazines, radio stations, or television channels that most people are exposed to every day. These means of communication are owned by private companies or the government. Mainstream media present *texts* (such as newspaper articles or television shows) that convey certain messages about society and groups in society. Critical media sociologists argue that these messages reflect the **dominant ideology**. In other words, the messages express the viewpoints of the capitalist class or other powerful groups. Capitalist, patriarchal, or racist ideologies are specific

forms of the dominant ideology that have been embedded in media texts.

We can investigate aspects of the dominant ideology by considering representation of the working class, women, and ethno-racial minorities in mainstream media. These groups have little power and receive poor representation in media content; members of less powerful groups experience *under-representation* (since they are usually not seen in the media as frequently as they actually exist in society) as well as *misrepresentation* (because they are often portrayed in ways that are stereotypical and negative).

Some research has been done on representation of the working class, and this is strikingly illustrated by analysis of domestic situation comedies (family sitcoms). Examining all domestic situation comedies that appeared on American television between 1946 and 1990, Butsch (1992) identified the class position of the family in each show through the occupation of the lead male character. The family was categorized as working class if the husband/father was a blue-collar, clerical, retail, or service worker. It was categorized as middle class if he was a professional or manager. Not all family sitcoms fell into these two categories, but Butsch found that 71 per cent of the sitcoms were about a middle-class family and only 11 per cent centred on a working-class family. In earlier research, Butsch and Glennon (1983) noted that similar findings were out of line with the existence of both classes in American society; since working-class households are actually in the majority rather than the minority, the working class was under-represented in family sitcoms. Furthermore, the men in working-class comedies were generally represented negatively. Emphasis was placed on their "ineptitude, immaturity, stupidity, lack of good sense, or emotional outburst" (Butsch, 1992, p. 391). As Butsch (1995) pointed out, this was the case with the lead male characters in various working-class comedies from the 1950s to the 1980s. Consider *The Honeymooners* (Ralph Kramden), *The Flintstones* (Fred Flintstone), *All in the Family* (Archie Bunker), and *The Simpsons* (Homer Simpson). In contrast, Butsch found that middle-class men often received positive representation. They were portrayed as being "intelligent, rational, mature, and responsible" (Butsch, 1992, p. 391). Examples of such middle-class comedies from the 1950s to the 1980s include *Father Knows Best*, *My Three Sons*, *The Brady Bunch*, and *The Cosby Show* (Butsch, 1992). Updating his work, Butsch (2005) found that the representational patterns for both classes were still evident in family sitcoms produced during the 1990s and 2000s. Butsch argued that these patterns are significant because they ideologically justify class inequality: "Blue-collar workers are portrayed as requiring supervision, and managers and professionals as intelligent and mature enough to provide it" (1995, p. 404).

The representation of women has been the subject of much research, and some of this work has focused on motion pictures. Dole (2000) examined the representation of women as law enforcers in American motion pictures that were released during the 1980s and 1990s. She argued that the women in these films had "types of power culturally coded as masculine" (Dole, 2000, p. 11). The women had power because they occupied the position of law enforcer and because they carried a gun (two characteristics socially defined as "masculine" within our culture). Dole saw the genre of women cop films as emerging in two phases. The earlier films (1987–1991), such as *Blue Steel* and *Impulse*, often imitated the violence of male action films by showing the women using their guns. Because many of these films were commercially unsuccessful, the later films (1991–1995) took a softer approach. These films, including *The Silence of the Lambs* and *Copycat*, were more inclined "to privilege intellectual over physical power" (Dole, 2000, p. 12). Rather than using their guns, the female law enforcers in the later films relied on their sleuthing skills. Several other techniques were employed to play down "the threatening image of Woman with a Gun" (Dole, 2000, p. 16). These techniques included *domestication* (portraying the female cops as mothers or at least as women who have "maternal instincts"); *infantilization* (representing the women as being dependent, vulnerable, helpless, or in need of rescue); and *sexualization* (emphasizing the physical attractiveness of the women). Finally, the films that focused on intellectual power utilized what Dole called *splitting strategies*. Splitting strategies distribute among multiple characters the power that would otherwise be concentrated in one character. Through the use of splitting strategies, the power of the female law enforcer is reduced. This can be illustrated by *The Silence of the Lambs*. In that film, intellectual power was split between Clarice Starling (Jodie Foster) and Hannibal Lecter

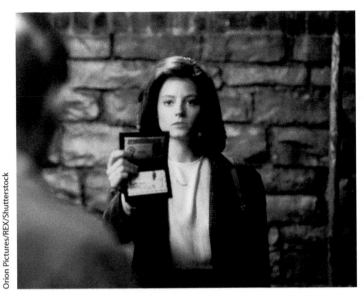

Orion Pictures/REX/Shutterstock

FBI agent Clarice Starling, played here by Jodie Foster, holds up her badge in the movie *The Silence of the Lambs* (1991). Dole (2000), citing films including this one, argues that Hollywood has preferred to show women cops using their wits and being dependent on males. Has this state of affairs changed since 1991, when *The Silence of the Lambs* was released?

(Anthony Hopkins). Although Starling was intelligent, she needed male assistance in the form of Lecter (Dole, 2000, p. 16). The ideological message was that a woman is incapable of solving the case and catching the killer on her own. Although female cop films gave women more representation than most movies (because they occupied central rather than peripheral roles), the stereotypical and patriarchal misrepresentation of women was still quite evident in these films.

Especially in Canada, much research also addresses the representation of ethno-racial minorities. Canadian studies document the under-representation of francophones, blacks, Indigenous peoples, and other groups in advertisements, magazines, news, television series, and even the nationally televised Juno Awards ceremony for the Canadian music industry (Fleras & Kunz, 2001; Mahtani, 2001; Young, 2006). The general absence of ethno-racial minorities in media content (relative to their existence in the actual population) means that their contributions to Canadian society are trivialized and their roles as Canadian citizens are devalued (Mahtani, 2001). Along with under-representation, misrepresentation of these groups is a problematic issue in Canadian media. To the extent that they are seen, ethno-racial minorities are frequently portrayed in stereotypical and negative ways. In the news media, this often takes the form of identifying them as social problems; ethno-racial minorities are depicted as "having problems or creating problems in need of political attention or costly solutions" (Fleras & Kunz, 2001, p. 145). They are seen to be participating in illegal activities, clashing with police, cheating on welfare, creating difficulties for immigration authorities, or having other undesirable effects. Specific groups—including Indigenous peoples, Asians, blacks, and Muslims—are often singled out. For instance, Karim (2008) demonstrated that editorials and columns opposing multiculturalism have appeared in Canadian English-language newspapers after news reports about the arrests of Muslim men on terrorism-related charges.

How can we explain the under-representation or misrepresentation of the working class, women, and ethno-racial minorities? First, we must reject the notion that there is a conspiracy by powerful groups against less powerful groups. The circumstances are far more complicated than that, and we must return to the concept of the dominant ideology to understand why. According to Hall (1980), the dominant ideology is woven into media texts through *encoding*. This is a complex process, and it involves meanings or ideas becoming embedded in media content unintentionally as a result of various factors. For instance, members of less powerful groups often do not occupy important positions associated with media production. This is certainly the case with women in the film industry; women made up only 17 per cent of all directors, producers, executive producers, writers, cinematographers, and editors who worked on the top-grossing American films in 2014 (Lauzen, 2015). Such exclusion from the process of media production can have a substantial impact on media content. Butsch (1995) makes this clear when he notes that the under-representation of the working class in domestic situation comedies, along with the negative representation of working-class men, can partially be explained by the middle-class background of most producers and writers; middle-class people develop shows based on what is familiar to them, and when they occasionally focus on working-class characters, they rely on the negative stereotypes of the working class that circulate in our culture as part of the dominant ideology.

Interpreting and Resisting Mainstream Media

We have seen that the dominant ideology of powerful groups is embedded in the content of mainstream media through encoding, but it is also important to consider the *decoding* of this content by audience members. As part of his encoding/decoding model, Hall (1980) argues that the dominant ideology is inscribed as the *dominant* or *preferred meaning* within media content. Since Hall recognizes that audience members may not always adopt this meaning when they interpret media messages, he identifies three possible ways of decoding (reading) media texts. A *dominant-hegemonic* reading involves taking the preferred meaning, while an *oppositional* reading involves rejecting a message by interpreting it through an alternative ideological framework. A *negotiated* reading contains a mixture of the dominant-hegemonic and oppositional readings and is therefore contradictory. In a seminal study of these approaches to decoding, Morley (1980) investigates how groups interpreted the British current affairs television series *Nationwide*. He demonstrates that decoding is affected by class position; working-class groups produce more oppositional and negotiated readings than middle-class groups. However, Morley (2006) suggests that decoding can also be affected by other types of social position (such as gender, race/ethnicity, and age).

Photo by Dominic Chan

Alanis Obomsawin (left) with Inuit filmmaker Alethea Arnaquq-Baril, who won the Alanis Obomsawin Best Documentary Award at the imagineNATIVE film and media arts festival in Toronto 2016. Festivals like imagineNATIVE can be found all across Canada promoting the work of artists who are often under-represented or misrepresented in mainstream media.

TIME to REFLECT

Can you think of ways in which your class position, gender, race/ethnicity, or age might affect your decoding of media content?

Decoding involves resistance when there are oppositional readings of mainstream media, but further resistance (and more direct conflict with powerful groups) can occur through **alternative media**. Alternative media are forms of communication used by subordinate groups or social movements to present messages that challenge the dominant ideology and existing social conditions. Many types of alternative media are employed by groups or movements committed to social change. In Canada, community broadcasting plays a particularly important role. This is illustrated by Vancouver Co-operative Radio, a non-commercial station owned and run by its members. According to its website (www.coopradio.org), the station is "a voice for the voiceless that strives to provide a space for under-represented and marginalized communities." Other types of alternative media are also utilized by relatively powerless groups. Carroll and Ratner (1999) find that social movements in Vancouver produce magazines, videos, monthly newspapers, and other media to distribute their oppositional messages.

The Internet: Extending Political Economy and Cultural Studies

The critical perspectives of political economy and cultural studies have long been utilized to study so-called "old media" like newspapers, motion pictures, and television. However, these perspectives can also help us understand the "new media" of digital communication such as the Internet (an interconnected computer network) and the World Wide Web (interconnected documents accessible through the Internet).

The Internet can be seen through long-standing issues in political economy. For instance, the state was crucial to the origins of the Internet. The Internet had its beginnings in the 1950s when the US Department of Defense established the Advanced Research Projects Agency (ARPA). ARPA developed a means to interconnect computers in such a way that an attack on one server or one part of the network would not knock out other servers or the rest of the network (Cuneo, 2002). While the Internet began with the state, growing access to it has been tied to private ownership; most of us connect to the Internet through private companies such as Bell Canada or Rogers Communications. Since the Internet contributes to spreading communication and information across national borders, we should also note that it plays a crucial role in globalization.

Key issues associated with cultural studies also provide a basis for thinking about the Internet and the World Wide Web. In many ways, the Web represents an extension of mainstream media and the content provided by powerful groups. Mainstream media content and the dominant ideology it conveys have spread onto the Web. Recorded music, motion pictures, and television shows are available for download. The advertising that is crucial for supporting many mainstream media now appears on websites. Newspapers and television news channels have websites where they can reproduce news stories. While it has qualities of mainstream media, the Web is also a new form of alternative media that subordinate groups or social movements use to challenge the dominant ideology through their own content and messages. This form of resistance on the part of less powerful groups was solidified when the website of the Independent Media Centre (Indymedia) was established just before a meeting of the WTO in Seattle in 1999. The purpose of the website was to provide news coverage of the meeting which countered that offered by the corporate-dominated mainstream media (Downey & Fenton, 2003). Through the website, independent journalists broke stories about the brutality of the police toward anti-globalization demonstrators. The website had more than 1 million hits during the WTO meeting, and its success spawned other Indymedia websites around the world (Pickard, 2006).

TECHNOLOGY AND SOCIETY

Two central theoretical approaches in sociology—conflict theory and feminism—help us understand the close interlink between technology and society.

Conflict Theory

Conflict theory uncovers and describes inequalities in society based on class, gender, race, and religious background, with the aim of eliciting social change that will benefit those who are oppressed. Those in power control the means of production, the machines, and equipment that allow for the production of goods, the computers and mobile devices, that create digital content.

How can we best understand discrepancies in technology ownership among social groups? A central aspect of inequality in the twenty-first century is systematic differences in access to and use of information and communication technologies (ICTs). This phenomenon has been called the **digital divide**. Figure 16.1 shows changes between 2000 and 2012 in the proportion of Canadians who have access to the Internet.

In 2000, 51 per cent of Canadians were online, with this number increasing to 84 per cent in 2012 (Statistics Canada 2010a, 2012a). More recent data suggests that up to 93 per cent of Canadians now have access to the Internet (Kemp, 2014). Even though this statistic seems high, with nine out of ten Canadians online, careful analysis of the data shows a continuous gap in access along key demographic variables. For instance, the percentage of Canadians reporting an Internet connection in 2012 drops considerably in Canada's northern regions. A combination of factors, including the low population density of the North and the difficulty of placing fibre optic and other cables in permafrost makes it expensive and challenging to provide Internet access in these remote regions. Canadians living in urban areas are often surprised to learn that in rural areas the Internet is not reliable or broadband, or that high-speed Internet access is not available at all, precluding such online activities as playing video games, streaming video and movies, and engaging in Skype sessions (Brodkin, 2015).

It is important that sociological work not focus exclusively on access. Recent work by sociologists emphasizes a need to go beyond this simple dichotomization—being online versus not being online. The argument is that in addition to examining who is online, it is crucial also to take a closer look at an individual's **digital skills**, often referred to as the skills divide. Digital skills are "a person's ability to perform tasks effectively in a digital environment" (Jones & Flannigan, 2006, p. 9). Understanding the range of activities a person performs online is important because it can help users take full advantage of the Internet for locating information, getting a job, and connecting with friends and family (Hargittai, 2002; Hargittai & Hinnant, 2008; Wellman et al., 2001). In the Human Diversity box, we look at Canada as an example of a developed nation that struggles with digital inequality, as specific subgroups of its population either remain disconnected from the Internet altogether or lack the necessary skills to fully engage.

 Social class affects many parts of our lives. For more on class inequality and its impact on Canadians, see Chapter 6, "Class and Status Inequality."

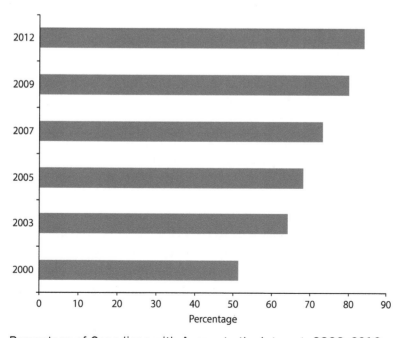

FIGURE 16.1 Percentage of Canadians with Access to the Internet, 2000–2012

SOURCE: M. Haight, A. Quan-Haase, and B. Corbett, "Revisiting the digital divide in Canada: The impact of demographic factors on access to the Internet, level of online activity, and social networking site usage," Information, Communication & Society 17, 4 (2014): 503–519.

HUMAN DIVERSITY — Challenges to Digital Adoption and Inclusion

Not all Canadians have equal access to the Internet. One demographic variable that predicts differences in Internet access is immigration. In the United States, Ono and Zavodny (2008) observe lower rates of computer ownership and Internet access among immigrants than among those born in the United States. Does Canada have similar trends? This is an important question as recent data show that in some of Canada's largest cities as much as half the population is foreign born (City of Toronto, 2006). Helping recent immigrants adapt to their new home also includes helping them access online services to find health resources, obtain government information, and participate in Canada's digital economy. These questions are of even greater societal relevance with the arrival in Canada of over 35,000 Syrian refugees in 2015 and 2016 (Friesen, 2017).

Understanding the role of digital technologies in the lives of recent refugees is of the outmost importance. A study by Haight, Quan-Haase, and Corbett (2014) found that in Canada, individuals' access to the Internet and levels of online activity vary based on demographic factors. In the study, they distinguish between respondents born in Canada and those who immigrated during or prior to 2004. This study showed that recent immigrants to Canada, those who arrived in Canada during or after 2005, are significantly less likely to have Internet access, even after controlling for socio-economic differences. That is, variations in financial status across recent immigrants do not predict Internet access alone. Respondents who had been residing in Canada for more than five years were 74 per cent more likely to have Internet access than recent immigrants, who had been in Canada for five years or less (Haight, Quan-Haase, & Corbett, 2014).

This finding shows that policy initiatives need to specifically target new immigrants and refugees to help them bridge the digital divide. The use of ICTs seems particularly relevant for this population, as they need to stay in touch with family and friends back home and to learn about the culture, history, and language of their new home country. Moreover, connectivity to their home country may be particularly important in the first few years of immigration, when social, emotional, and economic support is needed the most. So, providing access to the Internet for this population is central; also important is understanding any barriers that they may encounter, including language, technical skills, and computer ownership.

The findings around immigration not only are critical in the Canadian context, but are also relevant to other countries:

> ...as other countries—the US, Germany, and Singapore—also experience comparable levels of immigration, the findings from the present study will provide a baseline for comparative research and future analysis on immigration and the digital divide, an as yet much neglected topic. (Haight, Quan-Haase, & Corbett, 2014, p. 505)

Class inequality, as discussed in Chapter 6, also concerns addressing issues around the digital divide and therefore needs to be a key policy initiative in Canada for at least two reasons. First, access to technology can either overcome or exacerbate existing inequalities (Chen, 2013; Witte & Mannon, 2009). Norris (2001) identifies early the need for digital inclusion and states that digital networks can particularly benefit remote areas and poor neighbourhoods. Second, innovation, economic development, and capital investment are all moving online. Hence, nations that cannot take full advantage of the new global digital markets will fall behind.

Clearly, a significant shift is taking place, with job applications, government services, and education more frequently requiring access to the Internet, with consequences for those not yet able to fully participate in the digital society (DiMaggio, Hargittai, Neuman, & Robinson, 2001; Wellman et al., 2001). A recent United Nations report suggests that access to the Internet should be considered a basic human right, highlighting the importance of this technology in contemporary society (La Rue, 2011). The significance of access to the Internet will only grow in the future, making it important to foster equitable access in schools and other key institutions. By understanding the groups that are lagging behind we can begin to develop innovative and comprehensive strategies to close the gaps (Haight et al., 2014). Along with equitable access

TIME to REFLECT •

To what extent has Internet connectivity increased in Canada? What barriers exist to connectivity? What policy needs to be developed to address concerns around the digital divide, in particular around discrepancies among social groups in terms of their level of digital skills? An interesting example of addressing problems of access in Canada is the First Mile program (http://firstmile .ca/) (McMahon, Hudson, & Fabian, 2014). In this initiative First Nations are coming together to build a broadband infrastructure to facilitate connectivity, share resources, and make important information available to the community by the community itself.

to the Internet, training and skill development ought to be a central focus of any policy aimed at addressing this growing and pressing issue.

Feminism

Feminism is related to conflict theory in that it examines power imbalances in society. It explores how power imbalances result from gender differences and how these play out in everyday life. Modern forms of feminism go beyond looking at differences between men and women and examine *intersectionality*, which looks at how multiple dimensions and characteristics of an individual, including gender, sexual orientation, race/ethnicity, class, and religious background, together explain inequality, prejudice, and disadvantage through, for example, sexism, homophobia, racism, classism, and religious intolerance. In particular, the work of Kimberlé Williams Crenshaw (Crenshaw et al., 1995) has been instrumental in opening up the discussion around how feminism can be more inclusive and incorporate a wider range of concerns beyond the exclusive focus on gender. That is, a person's identity can be understood only by looking at the person as a whole instead of isolating a single characteristic.

One stream of feminism critically investigates how technology affects the lives of men and women differently and how it may lead toward social change. Wajcman (2013) proposed two views that outline the relation between women and technology:

1. *Women's liberation view.* Technology is perceived to have a positive impact, in that it can liberate women by supporting various fertility choices, easing the burden of daily household work, and facilitating alternative, flexible work environments well suited to women.
2. *Women's oppression view.* Technology is perceived to have a negative impact in that it will enslave women through technological advances on which they will become dependent, women will have fewer choices in their lives, and they will become more reliant on various technologies.

Let's look more carefully at these two perspectives and how they apply to specific technologies. The debate surrounding reproductive technology illustrates the tension between the liberation and oppression views. Reproductive technology includes such matters as birth control, fetal monitoring, and infertility programs (Stanworth, 1987). Reproductive technologies are presented as empowering women by allowing them to take control over their bodies. While it is true that reproductive technologies allow for more open debates around women's bodies, they are also contested and impose certain dominant values on women. Advances in reproductive technology are often also contested because they are perceived to be part of the overarching patriarchal structure, further enabling the male domination of women and their bodies (Wajcman, 2013). What is missing from discussions around reproductive technologies is women's struggles for self-determination and the active role women can play in shaping how technologies affect them.

To further examine how technology can function to either further oppress women or liberate them, it is useful to look at modern technologies, such as social media. Social media uptake in North America has grown rapidly. For young people, creating **user-generated content** and engaging with others' content are a daily practice. User-generated content is that created or posted by a user and can include images, tweets, "likes," retweets, or videos. As of June 2015, Facebook had 1.49 billion monthly active users, who collectively every minute post 510,000 comments, provide 293,000 status updates, and upload 136,000 photos (Zephoria, 2015). The Pew Research Center reports that about 52 per cent of Americans have adopted more than one social media platform (Duggan, Ellison, Lampe, Lenhart, & Madden, 2015). Social media make it easy, exciting, and rewarding to create and share user-generated content as friendships are build and maintained through these practices (boyd & Ellison, 2007). This makes it an important topic for sociologists to investigate and consider more closely with regards to issues of gender and equality.

Feminist scholars have long been interested in the link between the portrayal of women's

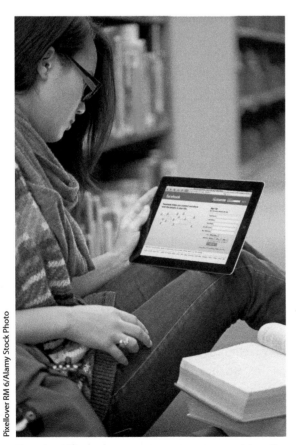

Pixellover RM 6/Alamy Stock Photo

Does the ability to generate our own content on social media liberate us or oppress us? Why?

bodies in mass media and the perception of girls and women of their own bodies. Recently, medical professionals have also expressed concerns that these images of "ideal" body types may be helping to pattern anorexic and bulimic practices (Burke, 2006). Studies show that even seemingly insignificant concerns about one's body can lead to harmful eating habits such as bingeing and vomiting, as well as other unhealthful practices (Grogan, 2010). While most studies focus on the way in which media representations affect girls' and women's body image, recent studies also find similar issues among boys and men (Kim & Chock, 2015; Grogan, 2010).

The "ideal" body type presented in mass media for both females and males is generally tall and thin, with low body fat, and muscular for males (Kim & Chock, 2015). But it goes beyond body mass index to promote an overall ideal of beauty/handsomeness that is increasingly rooted in a gendered and racialized type. Female features should be "delicate," while male features should be "strong" (Tait, 2007, p. 126). Indeed, with the wide range of body-altering techniques and technologies available today—from diet and exercise regimens to teeth whitening and plastic surgery—it is easier than ever to achieve the "ideal." In an era of radical individualism, efforts to expose the ways in which society "constructs and pathologizes" (Tait, 2007, p. 132) different body images are drowned out.

Our growing use of social media is adding fuel to the fire. There has been a recent explosion in the number of images that are circulating online, with the "selfie" being a particularly prominent form of **self-presentation**. Within this emerging digital visual culture, selfies are a "genre unto themselves, with their own

TIME to REFLECT ●━━━━┫

To what extent do digital media such as Instagram, Snapchat, and even Facebook give women more control in terms of how the female body is represented? Do we see more diversity in terms of body shape, ethnicity, and beauty? Or, are these digital media further circulating images of an "ideal" female body type?

visual conventions and clichés" (Marwick, 2015, p. 141) meant to delight a networked audience and grab their attention.

Social media can open the debate as to what femininity and masculinity are and how to move away from traditional, stereotypical depictions of beauty and the ideal female and male bodies. This debate becomes particularly poignant in the context of selfies, which are often heavily manipulated, whether they are of celebrities or lesser-known Internet users. In the Sociology in Action box, we look at the work of prominent sociologist Judith Butler and see how her theory of performativity helps us understand the circulation of selfies on digital media.

Butler's work provides the framework to examine how gender affects performativity on social media. On the one hand, similarities exist between how both genders express themselves and craft an online self; on the other hand, the evidence suggests that gender stereotypes persistently circulate online, as does the pressure to conform to an ideal body type. For Burns (2015), selfies reflect contemporary social norms and anxieties, and put new pressures on young women to perform a visual kind of

---

SOCIOLOGY IN ACTION

Gender Performativity on Social Media

American scholar Judith Butler contends that there is nothing natural or innate about gender. Most influential have been her two books *Gender Trouble: Feminism and the Subversion of Identity* (1990) and *Bodies that Matter: On the Discursive Limits of Sex* (2006), in which she describes her theory of gender performativity. For her, gender is a performance: it is produced through everyday acts that we do over and over again. An individual displays gender-specific behaviours, attitudes, and preferences, not because these are innate or biologically determined, but rather because they are learned through social interaction and based on societal norms around the expectations imposed on different genders. Moreover, these vary by culture and context. The conventions of "masculinity" and "femininity" that guide these acts are themselves brought into being through language, that is, by naming an act "masculine" or "feminine." They create the illusion of contained and coherent gender definitions, but Butler sees gender as being much more fluid and argues for imagining and considering gendered and sexual practices beyond what is possible within a binary notion of gender.

Butler's work can be applied to examine gender performativity on social media sites such as Snapchat, Instagram, and Facebook. Self-presentation is "motivated by a desire to make a favorable impression on others, or an impression that corresponds to one's ideals" (Herring & Kapidzic, 2015, p. 146). Photoshop, Picasa, and automatic photo editing tools on smartphones give users renewed control of their appearance in digital photography,

allowing them to, for example, remove blemishes, lighten the image, and smooth sections, which positions the selfie at the edge of immediacy and alterability (Hand, 2017). This places new pressure on the body, as it is "increasingly subject to scrutiny and 'improvement'" (Hand, 2017). Teens' online self-presentations reflects a desire for gender conformity. In a study of Facebook use among young women and men, Kim and Chock (2015, p. 335) found a "significant and positive correlation" between participants' use of Facebook and a desire for thinness. Importantly, they found that mere exposure had no significant impact, but rather it is the interaction—visiting others' profiles, commenting, "liking," etc.—that is having an impact on people's body image. Other studies have found correlations between positive endorsements (comments and "likes") on an individual's posts and dissatisfaction with one's body. Indeed, selfie takers are routinely subject to social regulation, particularly young women (Burns, 2015). Burns argues that selfies have been gendered as "feminine" when discursively framed as "trivial" and embodying a "devalued femininity." Celebrities contribute as well to how gender is depicted in selfies. For instance, Kim, Kourtney, and Khloé Kardashian use their celebrity status to promote recognizable and stereotypical depictions of the female body and beauty. This not only serves purposes of personal branding, but also promotes stereotypical reflections of femininity. Alternative depictions of gender in selfies include those posted by celebrity Miley Cyrus, whose hashtag #InstaPride has drawn global attention.

Table 16.1 ▶ Two Central Sociological Approaches to Understanding Technology

Theory	Main Ideas
Conflict theory	• Inequalities exist in how individuals use digital technology. • Digital inequality can further disadvantage those who are already at the fringes. • Digital inequality has real consequences for people's well-being, their ability to gain employment, and their means to participate in public debate on news outlets, social media, and public-interest websites.
Feminist theory	• Gender influences how we adopt, use, and make sense of technology and its impact. • Inequality between men and women stems from the encoding of patriarchal values into technology. • While new forms of performativity exist online, new media largely continue showcasing gender-stereotypical representations.

femininity. Burns argues that a selfie contains "patriarchal authority and maintains gendered power relations by perpetuating negative feminine stereotypes that legitimize the discipline of women's behaviors and identities" (2015, p. 1716). These stereotypical representations are found in various social media platforms, suggesting that social media does not function as a space for breaking with traditional gender roles and presenting greater gender diversity.

CONCLUSION

In this chapter, we have adopted a sociological approach to understanding media and technology. Such an approach stands in contrast to many definitions of technology, which fail to see that technology embodies and reflects societal elements. It also stands in contrast to the concept of technological determinism, which similarly strips technology out of a social context while focusing on the impact of the technology itself. A sociological approach makes it possible for us to examine the political, economic, cultural, and social conditions that influence the emergence, uses, and effects of media and technology.

Through this approach, we have seen how media and technology are connected to important sociological issues. For instance, in the political and economic context of capitalist society, we have seen that *control* over media production/distribution is largely held by private companies or governments. Furthermore, we have seen that media content primarily reflects the perspectives of those who hold *power* in society. Through different aspects of the digital divide, we have seen that there is *inequality* with regard to media and technology. Finally, we have seen that there is a great deal of *conflict* over media and technology as subordinate groups struggle against groups or organizations that have power and exercise control.

Questions for Critical Thought

1. Do we need Canadian content regulations for radio and television broadcasting? Why or why not?
2. In your view, what might be some advantages and disadvantages of cultural globalization (which involves the transmission of media and the arts across national borders)?
3. Review the discussion of domestication, infantilization, and sexualization in the media representation of women. Are these aspects of representation problematic? Why or why not?
4. Consider websites that you visit often. In what ways might they involve an extension of mainstream media and the content provided by powerful groups?
5. How does Ursula Franklin view technology and its relation to the everyday experiences of individuals? What are the strengths and weaknesses of her perspective?
6. Why is it relevant to look at the digital divide in terms not only of access to the Internet, but also

of a person's skill level? Why are digital skills relevant to how people use the Internet?

7. Contrast the women's liberation and women's oppression views. How does each approach

contribute to our discussion of the role of reproductive technologies in the lives of women?

8. How are women represented in selfies, and what social pressures are present in this performativity?

Sociological Explorations

1. Find a newspaper article that reports on a regulatory decision of the CRTC about radio or television. Does the CRTC's decision favour powerful or less powerful groups? What do sociological ideas about the state suggest about the reasons for the CRTC's decision?

2. Visit your Instagram or Snapchat account and examine your 10 most recent interactions with friends or family. To what extent did you use emoji to help you convey your message? What emoji did you use and what do they mean to you?

Search online for the meaning of each of the emoji that you used in these interactions. Are you surprised at all about how they are described online? Our digital culture relies heavily on emoji for communication and we have developed shared understandings around what they mean and social norms as to how they should be used. Has anyone in your social circle ever used emoji in an unexpected way? What does this say about our understanding of digital communication?

Recommended Readings

Boyd, d. (2014). *It's complicated: The social lives of networked teens.* **New Haven, CT: Yale University Press.**
The author explores many different factors that are relevant to understanding the dynamic of teens on the Internet and social media, such as identity, privacy, addiction, bullying, and inequality.

Greenberg, J. & Elliott, C. (Eds). (2013). *Communication in question: Competing perspectives on controversial issues in communication studies* **(2nd edn). Toronto, ON: Nelson Education.**
Greenberg and Elliott present opposing position papers that Canadian researchers have prepared on a number of media topics. This thought-provoking book gives students a sense of the various issues and debates in Canadian media studies.

Hackett, R.A., & Carroll, W.K. (2006). *Remaking media: The struggle to democratize public communication.* **New York, NY: Routledge.**
Hackett and Carroll use interviews with media activists and case studies of social movement organizations in the United States, Britain, and Canada to identify key issues involving the use of media by social movements and the struggles of movements to challenge the mainstream media.

Klein, N. (2000). *No logo: Taking aim at the brand bullies.* **New York, NY: Picador.**

In this very readable book, Klein examines issues associated with brands and logos (such as the Nike swoosh). She discusses the expansion of branding by companies, the role of corporations in relation to globalization, and forms of resistance to these developments.

Quan-Haase, A. (2016). *Technology and society: Inequality, power, and social networks* **(2nd edn). Don Mills, ON: Oxford University Press.**
Various aspects of the intersection between technology and society are explored, focusing on such themes as the digital divide, technology-mediated relationships, and communities in the network society. This book addresses the changing nature of technology and encourages readers to draw upon their own experiences to make sense of the link between technology and society.

Rainie, L. & Wellman, B. (2012). *Networked: The new social operating system.* **Cambridge, MA: MIT Press.**
This book examines how the constant connectivity of daily life provides new opportunities for learning and decision-making through weak ties, which need to be maintained and balanced effectively. The authors present the idea of "networked individualism" as a way of emphasizing the empowering potential of technology on social capital.

Recommended Websites

Alliance of Canadian Cinema, Television, and Radio Artists (ACTRA)
www.actra.ca
ACTRA is a labour union that represents Canadian media workers, and its website will help you to see issues from the perspective of these workers.

Association of Internet Researchers (AoIR)
www.aoir.org/
AoIR is an international, interdisciplinary scholarly association of researchers with an interest in the advancement of Internet studies. The association hosts an open-access mailing list, has a website with extensive resources, and organizes an annual conference.

Berkman Klein Center for Internet and Society
http://cyber.law.harvard.edu/
The Berkman Klein Center is located at Harvard University and is dedicated to exploring cyberspace, specifically examining issues of governance, social activism, and politics.

Canadian Radio-television and Telecommunications Commission (CRTC)
www.crtc.gc.ca/eng/home-accueil.htm
The CRTC's website enables you to learn more about this federal regulatory agency and its various policies.

Independent Media Center
www.indymedia.org/
You can find out more about Indymedia through this website, which also provides links to Indymedia websites in various areas of the world.

Pew Research Center: Internet, Science & Tech
www.pewinternet.org
The Pew Research Center is an American non-profit organization; in its Internet and American Life Project it conducts empirical research of how Americans use the Internet and the impact it has on their lives. The website is comprehensive, including reports, press releases, and statistics.

Key Terms

alternative media Types of communication that subordinate groups and social movements use to present their own messages, which often challenge existing conditions in society.

digital divide Discrepancies between social groups in access to, use of, and empowerment by networked computers and other digital tools, such as cell phones, personal digital assistants (PDAs), and MP3 players. The term also can encompass differences in skill level and knowledge about digital artifacts.

digital skills The ability to understand and use a range of digital devices including personal computers, Web browsers, smartphones, and tablets to fulfill a person's individual needs.

dominant ideology The ideas and viewpoints held by the capitalist class or other powerful groups in society. Specific forms of the dominant ideology include capitalist, patriarchal, and racist ideology.

neo-liberalism An economic doctrine that supports free trade between countries, cuts in social spending, and measures such as deregulation and privatization.

ownership concentration The process by which media properties fall under the control of fewer and fewer companies.

self-presentation The idea that a user's profile on social media and other online environments can represent the virtual self. This digital curation occurs through the use of images, text, and icons and takes place over time.

state Institutions associated with governing a specific territory as well as establishing and enforcing rules within that territory. The state in a number of countries (including Canada) also provides various public services.

technology An assemblage of material objects, embodying and reflecting societal norms, expectations, and attitudes that are shaped and structured to serve social, political, cultural, and existential purposes.

user-generated content Any kind of digital content such as images, text, "likes," retweets, and videos that an individual creates or posts to an online system or platform.

GLOSSARY

abocide A term referring to the physical extermination of Indigenous people. Today it is used for criticizing Bill C-31, since it may lead to the legal "elimination" of status Indians if they marry non-Indians.

agency The human capacity to interpret, evaluate, choose, and act accordingly.

AGIL An analytical paradigm developed by Talcott Parsons. He said that in order for social stability to be achieved, the system must adapt (A), seek out and obtain its goals (G), integrate (I) its lived and material components, and sustain its latent (L) pattern, a cultural system or template.

allopathic medicine Part of conventional medicine, treatment by means of opposites, such as killing or cutting out germs, bacteria, or other disease processes through medication, surgery, or radiation.

alternative media Types of communication that subordinate groups and social movements use to present their own messages, which often challenge existing conditions in society.

Americanization The idea that American culture victimizes other cultures through its dominance of media and other important global institutions.

anomie The condition of modern society in which there are too few moral rules and regulations to guide people's conduct.

anticipatory socialization The informal adoption and rehearsal of norms and behaviours appropriate to a future aspired role or status.

ascriptive characteristics Social traits with which we are born, such as sex and skin colour.

assimilation Processes by which minority groups are forced to adopt the hegemonic culture of a society.

baby boom The dramatic increase in birth rates in North America between the end of World War II and the mid-1960s.

back-stage See **front-stage and back-stage**

base/superstructure In Marxist theory, the base is the relations of production such as workers and owners, and the superstructure includes culture, institutions, and power structures that depend on that base.

behavioural assimilation The acquisition of dominant group cultural values by minority groups.

believing without belonging The concept of religious belief that is not tied to traditional forms of religious practice or rituals.

bi-nuclear families A growing family type resulting from divorce and remarriage, in which children of divorced parents live in both households and move between them at regular intervals.

biologically determined The idea that our social acts are determined by biological needs such as reproduction.

birth rate The number of live births in a given year.

blaming the system Analyses that emphasize the structural and institutional sources of inequality. Unequal access to education would, for example, contribute to poverty patterns.

blaming the victim The tendency in popular prejudice to hold individuals entirely responsible for their own misfortunes. This form of poor-bashing is countered by analyses that point out that **blaming the system** may be more accurate.

blocked mobility thesis Porter's argument that **ethnic group** membership in **entrance groups** hinders opportunities for upward social mobility.

bourgeoisie The term used by Marx to refer to the capitalist class—that is, the individuals who own the **means of production** (factory owners), the merchant (economically dominant) or ruling class.

capitalism An economic system characterized by a relationship of unequal economic exchange between capitalists (employers) and workers. Because they do not own the means of production, workers must sell their labour power to employers in exchange for a wage or salary. Capitalism is a market-based system driven by the pursuit of private profit for personal gain.

category A set of people thought to share particular characteristics.

charter groups The so-called founding nations of Canada: the British and the French.

Chinese head tax A tax on Chinese immigrants introduced in 1885 by the federal government in order to exclude them from entering and staying in Canada permanently.

citizenship regimes Institutions, rules, and understandings that define who is a citizen, who is not, and what rights and protections come with citizenship.

civil religion The idea that religion plays a role in supporting social cohesion through shared values and perspectives.

claims-making The social constructionist process by which groups assert grievances about the troublesome character of people or their behaviour.

class Inequality among groups of people based on the distribution of material resources and social capital.

class and status "Class," also termed *socio-economic class*, refers to one's position within a society's economic hierarchy. Typical designations include upper, middle, and lower class. Finer distinctions, such as upper-middle class, also appear in the literature. In contrast, "status" refers to one's social position in terms of privilege and esteem. While often based in economic considerations, status suggests a broader lifestyle dimension. Status may be *achieved* (e.g., becoming a CEO) or *ascribed* (e.g., being born an "untouchable").

class consciousness The sense of membership in a social class. For Marx, members of the working class would eventually (as a result of their concentration in factories and oppressive working conditions) recognize their common interests and act in concert to overthrow capitalism.

classism Akin to terms such as *racism* and *sexism*, the stereotypes and prejudices that surround social class.

collective conscience Durkheim's concept of cohesion in pre-modern societies, based on sameness and conformity of individual thought and awareness to the group; the shared system of beliefs that provide our basis for solidarity.

collective identity As opposed to someone's sense of individual Self, an activist's feeling or awareness that other members of their movement think and feel similarly about the movement, the social movement organization (SMO), and each other. The development of collective identity is crucial to the recruitment and retention of SMO members.

colour-coded vertical mosaic The argument that "**race**" or "**visibility**" has replaced ethnicity in the structure of social, economic, and political inequality in Canada.

communitas A term popularized in 1969 by Victor Turner to describe a **ludic**, egalitarian social space that is found in places of festival and dance, for example. Because people gather to have fun, there is less direction, less governance, and more equality than in participants' daily lives.

community A set of people who live in the same place; interact frequently; share many attitudes, interests, and goals; and, as a result, share a feeling of connection with others in that set.

complementary and alternative medicines (CAM) Health-related philosophies and practices that fall outside conventional Western medicine, such as homeopathy and chiropractic.

Comprehensive Economic and Trade Agreement (CETA) A trade agreement between Canada and the European Union.

compulsory heterosexuality A term coined by Adrienne Rich (1978) to explain that heterosexuality is a politically reinforced value in patriarchal society.

concept An abstract idea that cannot be tested directly. Concepts can refer to anything, but in social research they usually refer to characteristics of individuals, groups, or artifacts or to social processes. Some common sociological concepts include religiosity (strength of religious conviction), social class, and alienation.

conflict theory A theoretical paradigm or sociological perspective linked to the work of Marx and Weber that emphasizes conflict and change as the regular and permanent features of society, because society is made up of various groups that wield varying amounts of power. Conflict theorists often stress the importance of status, economic inequality, and political power, and the role of power and conflict in maintaining social inequality and contributing to social change.

consensus theory A term used to describe functionalism in the 1960s.

consensus General agreement within a population.

conspicuous consumption The public consumption of specific expensive goods and services by which an individual is able to communicate his or her elite social position.

contagion The diffusion of a norm or model linked to the spread of similar institutional models within a region or in neighbouring countries.

control theory A category of explanation that maintains that people engage in deviant behaviour when the various controls that might be expected to prohibit them from doing so are weak or absent.

core The countries at the centre of economic and political power on the global stage.

corporate crime Crime committed on behalf of a corporation that victimizes consumers, competing businesses, or governments. It can lead to major social, financial, or physical harm, although often no criminal law has been violated.

counter-hegemony The ability to launch oppositional views that challenge existing power-holders. See also **hegemony**.

critical turn The paradigm shift in the social sciences and humanities which began in the early 1980s. The turn is marked by a destabilization of the concept of the "other" and the recognition that objective reality is impossible because the measures we use to see it are socially constructed. Also called the *post-modern turn*.

crude birth rate The number of live births in a given year for every 1,000 people in a population.

crude death rate The number of live births in a given year for every 1,000 people in a population.

cult A group typically composed of a small number of believers who are viewed as engaging in non-traditional practices. More scientifically referred to as "new religious movements."

cultural capital A term coined by Pierre Bourdieu for cultural and linguistic competence, such as prestigious knowledge, tastes, preferences, and educational expertise and credentials, that individuals possess and that influences the likelihood of their educational and occupational success.

cultural diversity A way to explain how different cultures meet people's material and immaterial needs in different ways.

cultural evolution The idea that cultures evolve to meet the biological requirements of human societies, a notion sometimes linked to social Darwinism.

cultural hegemony A concept developed by Marxist theorist Antonio Gramsci, describing how, in culturally diverse societies, powerful social classes dominate others through their ownership and dominance of culturally powerful institutions, making their vision of the social world seem normal; as a result, class distinctions persist.

cultural imperialism The idea that by controlling popular culture and economies, a powerful culture can dominate others. See also **Americanization**.

cultural relativism The opposite of **ethnocentrism**; not evaluating other cultures with criteria derived from one's own culture.

cultural support theory A category of explanation that argues people become and remain deviant because the cultural environments in which they find themselves teach deviance and define such behaviour as appropriate.

cultural universals Those elements shared by all cultures, such as beliefs and practices about birth and death, shelter, and food.

culturalism A diverse body of literature that attempts to explain the differential socio-economic achievements of **ethnic groups** by examining their culture.

culture industry The political economy involved in the production of norms, meanings, values, mores, knowledge, and customs of a society through media, art, literature, and entertainment. A term associated with the work of Max Horkheimer and Theodor Adorno, who argued that the modern culture industry was homogenizing culture, lowering artistic and intellectual standards, and undermining the political consciousness of the working class.

culture of dissent A term used by Drache (2008) to explain how a global sense of disenfranchisement and political activism is uniting people into transnational, often Web-supported, cultures of activism.

culture A set of dynamic social processes and practices, which is a collective response of groups of people to their ever-changing external conditions, largely determined by social structures; at its broadest, the sum total of the human-produced environment (the objects, artifacts, ideas, beliefs, and values that make up the symbolic and learned aspects of human society), as separate from the natural environment; more often refers to norms, values, beliefs, ideas, and meanings; an assumption that different societies are distinguished by their shared beliefs and customary behaviours; the products and services delivered by a number of industries—theatre, music, film, publishing, and so on; the set of beliefs, values, and practices that help people establish their places and carry out their roles in webs of significance, or society.

culture-jamming A term for anti-capitalist, anti-consumerist activists taking over advertising billboards and other symbolic tools used by powerful organizations and replacing those symbols with the activists' own ideas. An example would be an ad on a bus saying, " Corporate advertising is bad."

defiant publics Those people united by their political activism into cultures of dissent.

deindustrialization The withdrawal of investment in factories.

democratic racism A new form of racism in Canadian society that is characterized by the conflict between the prevalent ideologies of democratic principles (justice, equality, fairness, etc.) on one hand, and their coexistence with negative feelings, attitudes, behaviours, prejudice, and discrimination against subordinate groups on the other.

demographic transition The process by a country moves from high birth and death rates. The shift in fertility rates is often referred to as the fertility transition, while the complementary change in death rates is referred to as the mortality transition. The epidemiological transition theory is a complementary theory to the demographic transition theory.

demography The study of population. Demographers examine changes in birth rates, infant mortality rates, death rates, growth rates, and migration, considering factors such as the size, composition, and geographical variations of populations over time.

deviance People, behaviours, and conditions subject to social control.

digital divide Discrepancies or inequalities between social groups in access to, use of, and empowerment by networked computers and other digital tools, such as cell phones, personal digital assistants (PDAs), and MP3 players. The term also can encompass differences in skill level and knowledge about digital artifacts. Sociologists usually see socioeconomic status and social class as the basis for the digital divide, but gender and national origin are among other characteristics associated with these inequalities.

digital skills The ability to understand and use a range of digital devices including personal computers, web browsers, smartphones, and tablets to fulfill a person's individual needs.

disability A wide-ranging, disputed term referring to individuals' capacity or lack thereof to engage with all parts of society "normally."

discourses Powerful stories usually supported by dominant institutions and powerful people to force a vision of the world on others.

discrimination A situation or action in which a person is treated differently (usually unfairly) because of his or her membership in a particular group or because he or she is associated with a particular social category or characteristic.

dominant ideology The ideas and viewpoints held by the capitalist class or other powerful groups in society. Specific forms of the dominant ideology include capitalist, patriarchal, and racist ideology.

dramaturgical approach The idea of a stage (Goffman, 1963) to explain how people act, as if it were a performed drama.

economic elite Men and women who hold economic power in a society. Contemporary researchers often operationalize this concept in terms of reported financial assets (wealth) and/or leadership positions on the boards of key (e.g., the 100 largest) corporations.

economic polarization Also referred to as *class polarization*, the growing gap (globally and nationally) between the very wealthy (sometimes referred to as the 1%) and the remainder of the population.

education Processes (both formal and informal) through which human beings learn and develop capacities through understanding their social and natural environments.

Enlightenment An era in the 1700s when theorists believed that human reason could be the instrument of perfecting social life; emotions had to be controlled, and the role of religion, custom, and authority was criticized.

entrance groups The **ethnic groups** that immigrated to Canada after its founding by the British and the French.

essence/essentialism The idea that a "true" or core reality lies behind appearances, which makes something what it is and which once identified, can establish its "truth."

ethnic group A social group formed around notions of common identity, culture, and (often presumed) common ancestry.

ethnicity and race "Ethnicity" refers to social distinctions and relations among individuals and groups based on their cultural characteristics (language, religion, customs, history, and so on), whereas "race" refers to people's assumed but socially significant physical or genetic characteristics.

ethnocentrism The opposite of **cultural relativism**; the evaluation of other cultures with criteria from one's own culture.

eugenics A moral position that advocated sterilization and murder of persons or entire "races" deemed genetically defective.

export processing zone (EPZ) Special area within a state where its tariff restrictions, laws, and labour practices are not fully enforced and goods are produced for export to other countries. Such zones usually house foreign companies that exploit local workers. The *maquiladoras* along Mexico's northern border with the US are an example of an EPZ.

extended family See **multigenerational household/family**.

false consciousness A person's misunderstanding of his or her lot in life and the wider social structure and relationships that shape power and politics. A term coined by Karl Marx as a label for ignorance or delusion about one's objective class position.

feminism A theoretical paradigm or perspective, as well as a social movement, that focuses on causes and consequences of inequality between men and women, especially patriarchy and sexism.

feminization of poverty The fact that poverty rates among women, nationally and globally, tend always to be higher than those of their male counterparts.

First Nations "Indians" in Canadian law; together with Métis and Inuit, they constitute Canada's Indigenous peoples.

food insecurity Insufficient access to the quantity or variety of food a person or household needs, due to poverty.

framing theory The process by which people develop a particular conceptualization of an issue or change their thinking about an issue. Any issue can be viewed from a variety of perspectives and be construed as having implications for multiple values or considerations. According to Goffman, frames are definitions of a situation that are built up in accordance with social principles of organization that govern them and our subjective involvement in them. Frame analysis is concerned with the organization of experience.

front-stage and back-stage The two realms of human behaviour in Goffman's dramaturgical approach. The front-stage is how we present ourselves based on socially acceptable public conventions. The back-stage is the realm of our private selves.

gender division of domestic labour The identification of specific household tasks as appropriate for men (for example, painting, cutting the grass, putting out the garbage) and for women (for example, cooking, cleaning, child care).

gender hegemony A concept elaborated by Schippers (2007) to identify hegemonic masculinity and hegemonic femininity as a relation of dominance supported by the eroticization of difference, and the power imbalance in heterosexual sex.

gender Socially recognized distinctions of masculinity and femininity.

gender-role socialization The process of learning the societal and cultural norms and expectations associated with being a male or a female.

generalized other This developmental stage of the self signifies how individuals become consistent and predictable in their behaviour and how people learn to view themselves from the perspective of others.

gentrification The process whereby more affluent households purchase and upgrade housing that was previously occupied by lower-income residents.

global economy A connection of the world's businesses and markets worldwide.

globalization A social process in which the constrains of geographic, economic, cultural, and social arrangements have receded and have been replaced by processes that extend beyond state boundaries; social processes related to extension of resources, ideas, and people across national boundaries in increasingly extensive and complex ways.

glocalization The process through which globalized identities, commodities, and structures are adapted or modified in local practice.

governmentality A term coined by Michel Foucault to study the political rationalities underpinning power, and to describe how neo-liberal states cause people to self-govern according to discourses of which they rarely are aware. Includes the study of the deliberate practices used by governments to produce compliant citizens.

green job A job oriented to reducing carbon outputs within the existing economy.

greenbelt An area around a city where no development is permitted.

greenhouse effect The result of carbon dioxide and other gases in the atmosphere trapping heat, which creates extreme weather effects.

group A set of people who know one another by name, interact frequently, and often share one or more common activities.

growth rate The difference between births and deaths, taking into account the difference between immigrants and emigrants.

guaranteed annual income First popularized in the late 1960s and increasingly popular today, a policy approach to poverty reduction that proposes to provide all citizens with a basic income, regardless of the recipient's income status. This would ensure a basic standard of living for all Canadians. Also known as *guaranteed minimum income* or *guaranteed basic income*.

hegemonic masculinity A dominant form of masculinity that may vary depending on the social context, but typically valorizes physical strength, economic power, heterosexuality, and the domination of women and subordinate men.

hegemony The dominance of ideology and culture by an elite group to the point that few alternatives exist or can be imagined.

heterocentric Assessing social relations and structures by the norms of heterosexuality.

heteronormativity (heteronormative) The assumption that heterosexuality is a universal norm, therefore making homosexuality invisible or "abnormal."

heterosexist A term referring to a set of overt and covert social practices in both public and private spheres that privileges heterosexuality over other sexual orientations.

heterotopia A term coined by Foucault (1984) to describe spaces where people take part in or act out in ways that are different from their daily activities. These spaces are real and representative. For example, one can go to the theatre or to a cemetery and experience other ways of being without acting or dying oneself.

hidden curriculum The tacit understandings (in relation to factors such as competition, hierarchy, or individualism) that students develop as a result of institutional arrangements and practices that occur within educational contexts.

hijab A headscarf worn by some Muslim women.

homophobia A term coined by George Weinberg in 1972 to refer to the psychological fear of homosexuality.

homosexual Someone who has sex with and/or is attracted to a person of the same sex.

household A set of related and unrelated individuals who share a dwelling.

human capital Recognition of the contributions made by education, skill development, and knowledge to innovation and productivity.

hypotheses Testable statements composed of at least two variables and how they are related.

ideal culture The way a culture presents itself in its mores and norms or prescriptions for social action. It rarely achieves this status.

identity A person's sense of who they are based on their group membership(s) and interactions with others. It involves how we see ourselves and how others see us; it is a product of our history and of our interpretation of others' reactions to us. How others view us is termed "placement," and other people's reactions to our projections of ourselves is termed "announcement."

identity work The dynamics by which individuals, using appearance, behaviours, talk, and props of various kinds, present themselves and construct others.

ideology A powerful system of knowledge supported by dominant institutions that rationalizes different perceptions about social justice and order; a system of beliefs, ideas, and norms, reflecting the interests and experiences of a group, class, or subculture, that legitimizes or justifies the existing unequal distribution of power and privilege; ways of seeing and of understanding the world and its actors. Ideologies function by making the social appear natural or functional rather than constructed for partisan interests and advantage.

immanent transcendence The misguided belief held by the Frankfurt School that society contained the potential and destiny to transcend capitalist exploitation.

immaterial/material elements The intangible and tangible aspects of culture, such as ideas and technology.

Immigration Act of 1910 A discriminatory act of Parliament that prohibited entrance to Canada for "the mentally defective," "the diseased," and the "physically defective."

impression management A process wherein actors try to shape how others will define them.

incidence The number of new cases (e.g., of a disease) in a year.

Indigenous peoples A term entrenched in Canada's Constitution that refers to all natives, including status Indians, Inuit, and **Métis**.

Industrial Revolution A period of rapid social and political transition from feudal to modern forms of governance beginning in the eighteenth century in western Europe.

infant mortality rate The number of deaths of children less than one year of age per 1,000 live births in the same year.

informal economy A wide range of legal and illegal economic activities that are not officially reported to the government.

institutional isomorphism The similarity of organizational structure emerging from imitation, coercion, or pressures of legitimacy.

institutional racism Prejudice and discrimination that is built into and permeates the structure and functions of economic, political, and social institutions.

institutions Patterns of behaviour that order people's lives in relatively predictable ways. Institutions comprise norms and social practices that have calcified to the extent that they create a predictable pattern or map of behaviours that people will usually follow.

interculturalism Quebec's version of **multiculturalism**, which discourages ethnic enclaves and promotes the linguistic assimilation of various cultures and minorities.

interlocking/intersectional analysis A way of understanding inequality that takes into account multiple, connecting dimensions. Used to understand gender inequalities as connected with and specified by race, class, dis/ability, sexuality, and so on.

intersectionalities The interweaving of social inequality factors, such as age, gender, visible minority status, and so on, to either intensify or minimize the effect of each.

intersubjectivity The notion that we adjust our behaviour according to the back-and-forth interpretation of what we think is on others' minds; for example, what I think *you* think of me.

Islamophobia Fear of people who believe in Islam, based upon prejudice.

kippa A skullcap worn by Jewish men in public or while praying.

kirpan A ceremonial dagger worn by some Sikhs.

labour market A competitive arena in which labour power is sold by workers and bought by employers. Good jobs are found in the primary labour market; bad ones, in the secondary.

labyrinth A maze-like structure used by some as a tool for meditation or spiritual practice.

LGBTQ(S) An acronym for lesbian, gay, bi(sexual), trans, queer and straight alliances that work together to fight gender discrimination.

life expectancy at birth The median number of years that a person can expect to live.

life expectancy The average length of life in a given population at a certain point in time.

lifelong learning A focus on imperatives for people to develop new knowledge, skills, and capacities throughout their life, well beyond completion of their basic education.

liminal A term used to described the transitional moments that people go through during rites of passage.

lived religion A flexible and holistic lens focused on how religion is woven into individuals' everyday lives that reveals the fluidity of religious and non-religious identity.

low income cut-offs (LICOs) Income thresholds below which a family will have to devote a larger share of the income on food, shelter, and clothing than the average family. Families who must spend 63 per cent or more of after-tax income on necessities are considered to be below the LICOs.

low income measure (LIM) A measure used most frequently in international comparisons referring to families living at 50 per cent below the median adjusted household income.

ludic A term describing essentially unmonitored, unrestricted acts of fun. Anthropologist Victor Turner (1969) refers to fun festivities as ludic spaces that make **communitas** possible.

macrosociology The study of social institutions and large social groups; the study of the processes that depict societies or social systems as a whole and of the social-structural aspects of a given society.

market basket measure (MBM) A measure of low income based on the cost of a specified basket of goods and services that represent a modest, basic standard of living.

marketization A process in which social relations and activities are determined increasingly through market relations through payment for services or other forms of commodity exchange.

mass media The technologies, practices, and institutions through which information and entertainment are produced and disseminated on a mass scale.

master status A status characteristic that overrides other status characteristics in terms of how others see an individual. When a person is assigned a label of "deviant" (e.g., "murderer," "drug addict," "cheater"), that label is usually read by others as signifying the most essential aspects of the individual's character.

matrix of domination Complex structures of power within which people live and in which various forms of oppression intersect, such as colour, gender, poverty, ability, and health; these must be resisted simultaneously.

means of production A term used by Marxists to refer to wealth-generating property such as land, factories, and machinery; the ways goods are produced for sale on the market, including all the workers, machinery, and capital such production needs.

mechanical and organic solidarity Durkheim's terms for understanding how social integration occurs in simple and complex social groups.

medicalization The tendency for more and more of life to be defined as relevant to medicine.

melting-pot policies US policies that encourage immigrants to abandon their original identities and languages in favour of being "American."

meritocracy A form of social stratification that relies on differences in effort and ability rather than on ascribed statuses such as gender, age, or race.

Métis A French term meaning "half-caste," used to describe the descendants of unions between male French Canadian fur-traders and Indigenous women in sixteenth- to seventeenth-century Canada.

microsociology A sociological approach that focuses analysis on small groups, face-to-face interactions, and everyday life activities.

mode of production A Marxist term for how the economy works (e.g., agriculture vs. industry).

monopolistic closure Weber's concept of social practices that exclude "others" from the distribution of scarce valuable resources such as wealth, high social status, and political power.

morbidity rate The number of cases of a particular illness in a given population over a specific period of time.

morbidity The frequency of disease per a specified number of people over a particular period of time.

mores The legalized forms of norms.

mortality rate The number of deaths in a particular population over a particular period of time.

mortality The frequency of death per a specified number of people over a particular period of time.

multiculturalism An ideology and a set of federal government programs that are used to maintain social order and manage ethnic and "racial" relations in poly-ethnic societies; Canada's official political and inclusive disposition toward race and ethnicity.

multigenerational household/family (or extended family) A family consisting of more than two generations living under the same roof.

narrative inevitability The idea that discourses impact social action by making people expect certain outcomes from certain situations.

natural growth rate The difference between the crude birth rate and the crude death rate, not taking into account migration (the movement of people into and out of a specific geographical area).

negotiation A discussion intended to produce an agreement.

neo-liberalism A form of liberal-democratic politics where the state decreasingly serves its social function and increasingly leans toward economic initiatives; a popular ideology whose advocates argue that the "big" government and the welfare state are a drag on the free market and individual enterprise, which gained prominence in the 1980s and 1990s, the era of Ronald Reagan, Margaret Thatcher, and Brian Mulroney; an approach to governance and the economy in which it is believed that control of economic factors should be shifted away from the public sector toward the private sector, and which involves the belief that governments should reduce spending, open up markets to trade by limiting protectionism, privatize state-run businesses, and promote deregulation; an economic doctrine that supports free trade between countries, cuts in social spending, and measures such as deregulation and privatization.

net migration rate The difference between the number of immigrants and the number of emigrants per 1,000 persons in a given period.

net migration The difference between the number of immigrants and the number of emigrants in a given period.

new (knowledge-based) economy A term used to describe the shift from manufacturing and other industrial activity toward a service-based economy driven by innovation, creativity, information exchange, and flexibility.

New Left A radical social and political movement with roots in conflict theory that emerged among mostly privileged students in the 1960s seeking liberation from oppressive social conditions and influencing a generation of young, critical academics in the 1970s and beyond.

new religious movements A religious or spiritual community that has come into being in modern times.

niqab A face covering worn by some Muslim women.

non-standard (precarious) work Jobs that are characterized by an increasingly tenuous or unstable relationship between employer and employee, including part-time employment, temporary employment, contract work, multiple job-holding, and self-employment; also termed "contingent work" and "casual work."

norms The rules and expectations of appropriate behaviour under various social circumstances; values that tend to be repeatedly expressed or practised such that they seem normal. Norms create social consequences that have the effect of regulating appearance and behaviour.

North American Free Trade Agreement (NAFTA) Signed in 1992 by the US, Canada, and Mexico, the "model" of trade liberalization that the most powerful in the world were hoping to extend to the rest of the world. Under NAFTA, capital flows and investments as well as trade have been liberalized. Under chapter 11 of the accord, private entities (companies) are entitled to sue governments if their interests are jeopardized by legislation on issues such as labour rights or the environment.

nuclear family A common family form which typically includes a couple and their children sharing the same household (increasingly this term has been used to describe a single parent with her or his children).

numerical flexibility Part of a general managerial approach that rests on flexibility in employment; it involves shrinking or eliminating the core workforce (in continuous, full-time positions) and replacing them with workers in non-standard employment.

objective Something completely unaffected by the characteristics of the person or instrument observing it. "Objective" observations were used in the past to establish the truth of scientific theories until it became clear that completely objective observations are impossible.

omnivore A cultural omnivore is a person able to consume a wide range of cultural products and to interact comfortably with people across the social hierarchy.

operationalization The translation of abstract theories and concepts into observable hypotheses and variables. Once abstract ideas are operationalized, they can be tested in a study.

organization A set of people connected by regular relationships that conform to shared norms and values.

organizational sexuality Social practices that determine explicit and culturally elaborate rules of behaviour to regulate sexual identities and personal relationships in the workplace.

organized religion A traditional view of religion as institutionalized and involving formal practices.

ownership concentration The process by which media properties fall under the control of fewer and fewer companies.

patriarchy (patriarchal) A culture, society, or family system in which men have greater power authority than women, where males are granted privilege, or where some men have greater power over other men as well as women.

pedagogy Methods, practices, and processes associated with teaching and interactions within different teaching/learning situations.

periphery Countries with labour-intensive, resource-extractive economies, which accumulate little wealth and are on the margins of global political and military power.

permanent residents Immigrants who have been given the right to live and work in Canada without limitations. They are eligible to apply for Canadian citizenship after a certain period of time in Canada. Also known as landed immigrants.

political economy A structural approach that attempts to explain socio-economic differences among and within social groups by analyzing social relations (class, gender, race/ethnicity, age, sexual preference, physical ability, mental health/illness, etc.).

political process approach An approach that assumes that political constraints and opportunities influence the rise and fall of social movements as well as their institutional organization.

political processes The dynamic contestation of power among dominant elites and subordinate challengers. It is also associated with a branch of social movement theory.

polity A sovereign political unit.

post-modernism An intellectual trend that became current in the arts and social theory in the 1980s and that opposes and deconstructs the dominant ideologies of rationality, progress, science, social democracy, and social regulation.

post-structuralism A social theory that became current in the late twentieth century and that depicts the construction of social life as complex, diverse, interconnected, multi-dimensional, undetermined, interpretive, and ultimately fragile.

power In the classic formulation, the ability to exercise one's will, even in the face of opposition from others. In Marxist sociology, a social relationship that has a material base. Those who own the **means of production** have the power to exploit workers through the appropriation of their labour efforts. In Weberian sociology, power is more broadly defined and can reflect the capacity of individuals or groups to exert their will over others. Contemporary analysts point out that power may also involve a wide variety of indirect and subtle manifestations, including the ability to mobilize bias or define a situation in one's own interests.

precarious employment A job that is poorly paid, insecure, and unprotected, and typically cannot support a household. Also known as *non-standard employment/work*.

prevalence The number of cases (e.g., of a disease) within a given population.

prevention policies Measures designed to prevent disease, including sewage disposal, garbage removal, cleaned and filtered drinking water, and hygienic handling of food.

primary agent of socialization The most important transmitter of societal and cultural norms, typically the family.

primordialism *Hard primordialism* holds that people are attached to one another and to their communities because of objective blood ties; *soft primordialism* proposes that people's feelings of affinity, attachment, acceptance, trust, and intimacy toward their "own kind" are subjective, not mediated by blood ties.

privatization The tendency for health care to increasingly be delivered by for-profit corporations.

proletariat A term used by Marx for individuals who provided the labour power to capitalism. Lacking property, the proletariat was forced to survive by selling its labour to the **bourgeoisie**, who in turn exploited workers' efforts in the pursuit of profit.

public-health measures Government-led efforts to promote health and prevent disease.

queer theory A number of approaches oriented toward social justice by abandoning traditional theories about normal identities in favour of inclusive and fluid categories of sexual, psychological, social, and other experience.

queering A way of looking at traditional ideas, such as rules for using public space or the meaning of marriage, and turning them inside out to allow for other perceptions.

Quiet Revolution A time of seemingly abrupt social change and secularization that took place in Quebec in the late 1960s.

race see **ethnicity and race**.

racialization Social processes and practices by which, based on people's physical characteristics, human populations are categorized into different dominant and subordinate groups and by which social

relations are structured according to visible physical differences, to the advantage of those in the visible majority and to the disadvantage of those in visible minorities.

racism Prejudice and discrimination against people because of their ethnicity or race.

real culture The way culture actually happens, despite what **ideal culture** would imply.

reasonable accommodation Quebec's pluralist notion that government policies and programs should not only tolerate but make allowances for the cultural differences of new immigrants and of minority groups.

reciprocal socialization The idea that socialization is not unidirectional, but a two-way process that can occur simultaneously, for example, between a parent and a child.

replacement fertility rate The average number of children per woman of one generation needed to maintain the population size.

residential schools A system of schools in which Indigenous children were placed by government educational authorities in order to **assimilate** them into the dominant culture.

resocialization The unlearning of old behaviours so that new behaviours, roles, and statuses can be acquired and adopted.

Rites of passage A term coined by Arnold Van Gennep in his 1908 study of culture and folklore to describe rituals performed when a person enters a more advanced status in a cultural group, such as graduating from college or getting married.

role The responsibilities, expected behaviours, and privileges connected with a given social position; the specific behaviours, privileges, duties, and obligations expected of a person who occupies a specific status; the kinds of things we do as social beings such as being a wife, mother, sister, teacher, and so on.

role conflict Incompatibility among roles corresponding to two or more statuses.

role performance The actual behaviour of individuals in the enactment of their roles.

role strain Incompatibility among roles corresponding to a single status.

sample The group of people or objects drawn from the whole population that will be studied. In quantitative research, a great deal of time and effort is devoted to the selection of truly random samples, while in qualitative research, samples are often selected on the basis of the theoretical importance of the people or objects.

sandwich generation A term used to describe individuals (usually women) who are caught between the demands of caring for at least one dependent child and one or more aging parents.

Sapir–Whorf hypothesis A theory that helps us to understand how gender values permeate the structure of language.

schooling Processes that take place within formal educational institutions.

secondary socialization The transmission of societal and cultural norms through the second-most important agents of socialization (after the family), such as the school, the mass media, religion, the workplace, and peer groups.

secularization The contested notion that religion is increasingly losing influence in the public sphere.

selection criteria Standards set by immigration policy that are associated with different weights (points) such as prospective immigrants' education, work experience, age, knowledge of official languages, "adaptability," and so on.

self Our perception of ourselves acquired by imagining how others see us. In Mead's theory, an emergent entity with a capacity to be both a subject and an object and to assign meaning to itself, as reflected upon in one's own mind. In Goffman's dramaturgical theory, the self is a more shifting "dramatic effect," a staged product of the scenes one performs in.

self-help A term that refers to the idea that individuals are responsible for their own well-being. The idea of self-help is different from self-conduct or self-governing. The latter two concepts are very old and refer to codes often enshrined in religious and civil codes, and as such refer to moral and ethical behaviour. Self-help is popularized under neo-liberalism such that those who are ill, for example, must pay for medical care on their own, thus releasing the state from financial responsibility for people's well-being.

self-presentation The idea that a user's profile on social media and other online environments can represent the virtual self. This digital curation occurs through the use of images, text, and icons and takes place over time.

semiotics A perspective on how language is constructed to establish powerful meanings.

semi-periphery Countries that show a mix of both core and peripheral characteristics.

service economy The economic sector in which most Canadians currently are employed. It is based on the provision of services rather than on a tangible product. Also called the "tertiary sector."

settler colonialism The process whereby Indigenous populations are displaced by invading settlers.

sex Anatomical characteristics assigned at birth, such as male, female, and intersex.

sexism Unfair discrimination on the basis of sex; it can be direct or indirect.

sexuality Defined by the World Health Organization (WHO) as a central aspect of being human, and encompasses sex, gender identifies and roles, sexual orientation, eroticism, pleasure, intimacy, and reproduction, experienced in thoughts, fantasies, desires, beliefs, attitudes, values, behaviours, roles, and relationships.

sick role A special position in society that prevents sickness from disrupting social life and provides a way of institutionalizing what might otherwise become a form of deviant behaviour.

significant others Those persons who are of sufficient importance to influence an individual's sense of self, emotions, and behaviours.

situated transaction A process of social interaction that lasts as long as the individuals find themselves in each other's company. As applied to the study of deviance, the concept of the situated transaction helps us to understand how deviant acts are social and not just individual products.

social capital The power that is derived from ties to social networks; a concept widely thought to have been developed by American sociologist James Coleman in 1988 but discussed by Pierre Bourdieu in a similar way in the early 1980s.

social class The structural economic position of social individuals in relation to (a) ownership of money capital, (b) control of the physical means of production, and (c) control of the labour power of others.

social constructionism (constructionist) The sociological theory that argues that social problems and issues are less objective conditions than they are collective social definitions based on how they are framed and interpreted.

social control Various and myriad ways in which members of social groups express their disapproval of people, behaviours, and conditions. These include name-calling, ostracism, ridicule, incarceration, and even killing, among other things.

social groups A number of individuals, defined by formal or informal criteria of membership, who share a feeling of unity or are bound together in stable patterns of interaction; two or more individuals who have a specific common identity and who interact in a reciprocal social relationship.

social institutions A stable, well-acknowledged pattern of social relationships that endures over time.

social interaction The process by which people act and react in relationships with others.

social movements The social form taken by collective actors engaged in struggles against dominance relations; the coordinated, voluntary action of non-elites (people with no control over major resources) for the manifest purpose of changing the distribution of social goods. The outcomes of these struggles are often difficult to grasp. To what extent social actors contribute to social change or toward participating in system regulation remains an open question.

social relationships Interactions of people in a society. Because people share culture and a sense of collective existence, these interactions are to some extent recurrent and predictable.

social reproduction A range of unpaid activities that help to reproduce workforces daily and over generations.

social stratification The structured patterns of inequality that often appear in societal arrangements. From a macrosociological perspective, it is possible to discern the hierarchical strata of social classes that characterize most contemporary societies.

social structure Patterns of behaviour or social relationships developed and accepted through time in a given group, organization, or society.

socialization A lifelong interactive process of learning the social skills needed to become a capable, functioning member of society and through which individuals acquire a self-identity. This process is shaped by institutions such as the family, peer groups, schools, and the mass media.

socially constructed The idea that nothing is innate or natural and that all social truths are the result of humans acting toward ideas produced by culture.

society A group of people living in a certain and sharing a culture, or otherwise sharing mechanisms for establishing webs of significance.

sociobiology A contentious paradigm that argues that human behaviour is the result of social and cultural evolution that reflects universal biological tendencies.

split labour market A **labour market** split into (a) a primary one where more members of the dominant groups may have more secure, full-time, and high-paying jobs; (b) a secondary one where minorities may be found in more insecure, part-time, low-paying, menial occupations.

staple economy A reliance on natural resources, such as fish, fur, lumber, agricultural products, and minerals, that are exported to support the economy.

state Institutions associated with governing a specific territory as well as establishing and enforcing rules within that territory. The state in a number of countries (including Canada) also provides various public services.

status A particular social position that an individual holds; the kind of prestige or relative power attributed to one's possessing an important role or economic power; a way of understanding one's social place relative to another (boss vs. worker, single vs. married).

status degradation ceremony The rituals by which formal transition is made from non-deviant to deviant status. Examples include the criminal trial and the psychiatric hearing.

status set The cluster of statuses held by any given individual at one time.

status symbols A term, popularized by Thorstein Veblen, that refers to the social elements that confer higher social standing on their owner.

stigma A symbol of disreputability; an attribute, characteristic, or behaviour of an individual that is socially stereotyped in a denigrating manner. For the bearer, stigma often takes the form of a shameful label read by outsiders as a mark of discredit or spoiled identity.

stigmatized Discriminated against based on a negatively perceived personal attribute (from the word "stigma").

strain theory A category of explanation that seeks to understand how deviant behaviour results as people attempt to solve problems that the social structure presents to them.

stratified Hierarchically ordered; in relation to power, stratification occurs when some groups control more material, cultural and social, and institutional resources than others and block others from challenging their control or gaining access to them.

streaming Also known as tracking, a practice within education systems that place students in specific programs or groups over time. Groupings are typically based on performance on standardized aptitude tests, perceived personal preferences or qualities, or other social characteristics.

structural assimilation The integration of minority groups into the economic, social, and political life of the host country.

structural functionalism A theoretical paradigm that emphasizes the way each part of a society functions to fulfill the needs of society as a whole.

sub-cultures Groups of people, such as religious sects or fetishists, who establish their own webs of significance and social practices that set them apart from the larger society in which they live.

subjective The opposite of "objective"; refers to the observer's mind, to perceptions, intentions, interpretations, and so on that affect how she or he acts in the world.

surplus suffering Distress caused not by a health problem or disability but by the social arrangements that deal with it.

surplus That part of the value of goods produced by working people that is taken by the dominant class and used to maintain social inequalities; a measure of the exploitation of the working class.

symbolic interactionism An intellectual tradition in sociology akin to interpretive theory, founded in the early-twentieth-century work of Charles Horton Cooley and George Herbert Mead, although the term itself was not coined until years later by Herbert Blumer. Symbolic interactionism emphasizes the importance of understanding the meanings of social action and uses ethnographic methods to discover these meanings for individuals in an effort to explain human conduct.

symbols The heart of cultural systems, for with them we construct thought, ideas, and other ways of representing reality to others and to ourselves; gestures, artifacts, or uses of language that represent something else.

systemic discrimination Impersonal, covert practices that penalize members of minorities.

technology An assemblage of material objects, embodying and reflecting societal norms, expectations, and attitudes that are shaped and structured to serve social, political, cultural, and existential purposes.

Tinguian of Austronesia A group of tribal people who do not kiss for any reason.

total institutions Any group or organization that has an almost complete, continuous control over the individual.

trans Someone whose gender identity or gender expression does not match societal conventions of their birth sex, and who may or may not experience same-sex attractions.

transgression The usually deliberate violation of social rules. In post-structuralism, this is the only viable, liberating, and non-oppressive strategy of personal and social change

transgressive sexualities Involves transcending sexual binaries and boundaries to challenge cultural norms and explore new possibilities.

transitions The pathways that people follow through their lives as they move from family settings into various education programs, work experiences, and other major life course changes.

Trans-Pacific Partnership (TPP) An attempted trade agreement between Canada and 11 other countries of the Pacific Rim.

transphobia Antagonistic attitudes and feelings toward people who do not conform to society's gender expectations.

undoing The idea that what is socially constructed can be reconstructed and changed.

unemployment rate The number of people who do not have a job but are actively looking for a job, divided by the labour force (which includes both the employed and unemployed), expressed as a percentage. Those who do not have a job and are not looking for one are considered not in the labour force.

univore A cultural univore is someone with narrow cultural tastes whose social networks are restricted to people with less power.

urban sprawl Decentralization or the shifting of economic activity and residential patterns away from the central city toward peripheral areas of the city.

urban sustainability A commitment to using the natural resources of a city within its capacity to sustain its social, economic, and natural significance. Goals associated with urban sustainability are related to improving the quality of life in the city without robbing resources from future generations.

user-generated content Any kind of digital content such as images, text, "likes," retweets, and videos that an individual creates or posts to an online system or platform.

validity The accuracy of a measure, indicator, or study; many different dimensions to validity can be established through formal tests, logic, or depth of understanding.

values Central beliefs that underlie the way people perceive justice or injustice in social situations. For example, freedom and autonomy are key values in North America.

variable The operational or observable equivalent of concepts. Many concepts require more than one variable for proper operationalization. The key characteristic of variables is that there must be a range of different values that can be observed.

vertical mosaic Porter's metaphor about Canadian society implying that it comprises many ethnic groups (mosaic) but that there is an ethnic hierarchy with the British and the French on the top and all other groups at the bottom of social, economic, and political structures (vertical).

visible minorities Racialized groups defined by Statistics Canada as such. The categories are South Asian, Chinese, Black, Korean, Filipino, Latin American, Arab, Southeast Asian, West Asian, Korean, Japanese, visible minority not included elsewhere, and multiple visible minority.

webs of significance A term for a way of looking at culture. These are our social and other ties with people who share a similar understanding of the world and who, therefore, do things similarly enough that together we form a culture.

work ethic A Western value that places the need to work and reach economic solvency above other needs and values.

work–family conflict The time-related stress arising from the competing demands of the different roles imposed on working parents.

workfare Popularized along with neo-liberalism, a term referring to the practice of requiring welfare recipients to "work" for their welfare benefits.

working poor The many individuals who are poor and yet are part of the paid labour force.

REFERENCES

Abada, T., & Tenkorang, E. (2009). Pursuit of university education among immigrant youth in Canada: The roles of parental human capital and social capital. *Journal of Youth Studies, 12*(2), 185–207.

Abbott, P., & Sapsford, R. (1987). *Women and social class.* London, UK: Tavistock.

Abu-Laban, B., & Stasiulis, D. (1992). Ethnic pluralism under siege: Popular and partisan opposition to multiculturalism. *Canadian Public Policy, 27*(4): 365–386.

Acker, J. (1990). Hierarchies, jobs, and bodies: A theory of gendered organizations. *Gender and Society, 4*, 139–158.

Adamic, L., & Adar, E. (2005). How to search a social network. *Social Networks, 27*, 187–203.

Adams, T.L. (2000). *A dentist and a gentleman: Gender and the rise of dentistry in Ontario.* Toronto, ON: University of Toronto Press.

Adelson, N. (2005). The embodiment of inequity: Health disparities in Aboriginal Canada. *Canadian Journal of Public Health, 96*, S45.

Adler, P., & Adler, P. (2015). *Constructions of deviance: Social power, context, and interaction.* Boston, MA: Cengage Learning.

Adler, P.A., & Adler, P. (2011). *The tender cut: Inside the hidden world of self-injury.* New York, NY: New York University Press.

Adorno, T. (1985). The sociology of knowledge and its consciousness. In A. Arato & E. Gebhardt (Eds). *The essential Frankfurt School reader* (pp. 452–466). New York, NY: Continuum.

Agnew, R. (1985). A revised strain theory of delinquency. *Social Forces, 64*(1), 151–167.

Agnew, R. (2006). General strain theory: Current status and directions. In F.T. Cullen, J.P. Wright, & K.R. Blevins (Eds), *Taking stock: The status of criminological theory.* New Brunswick, NJ: Transaction.

Agócs, C., & Boyd, M. (1993). The Canadian ethnic mosaic recast for the 90s. In J. Curtis, E. Grabb, & N. Guppy (Eds), *Social Inequality in Canada: Patterns, Problems, Policies* (2nd edn, pp. 330–352). Scarborough, ON: Prentice Hall Canada.

Agócs, C., & Boyd, M. (1993). The Canadian ethnic mosaic recast for the 90s. In J. Curtis, E. Grabb, & N. Guppy (Eds), *Social inequality in Canada: Patterns, problems, policies*

(2nd edn, pp. 330–352). Scarborough, ON: Prentice Hall Canada.

Agyeman, J., Cole, P., Haluza-DeLay, R., & O'Riley, P. (2009). *Speaking for ourselves: Environmental justice in Canada.* Vancouver, BC: University of British Columbia Press.

Ahn, J. (2016). "Don't cry, you're not a baby!": Emotion, role and hierarchy in Korean language socialisation practice. *Children and Society, 30*, 12–24. doi: 10.1111/chso.12125

Ajami, L. (2008, 2 May). Nose job nation—In Lebanon, surgical bandages are something to flaunt. *NOW.* Retrieved from www.nowlebanon.com/News ArchivesDetails.aspx?ID = 40594#ixzz) y6RszOKO

Akers, R.L., & Jensen, G.F. (2003). *Social learning theory and the explanation of crime: A guide for the new century: vol. 11, Advances in criminological theory.* New Brunswick, NJ: Transaction.

Albanese, P. (2009). $7/day, $7/hour, 7 days a week: Juggling communities, shift work and child care in a changing ("new") economy. In J. Klaehn (Ed.), *Roadblocks to Equality* (pp. 26–40). Toronto, ON: Black Rose Books.

Albas, D., & Albas, C. (1988). Aces and bombers: The post-exam impression management strategies of students. *Symbolic Interaction, 11*(2), 289–302.

Alberta v. Hutterian Brethren of Wilson Colony. 2009. SCC 37, [2009] 2 S.C.R. 567.

Alkhateeb, M.B., & Abugideiri, S.E. (2007). *Change from within: Diverse perspectives on domestic violence in Muslim communities.* Great Falls, VA: Peaceful Families Project.

Allahar, A. (1994). More than an oxymoron: The social construction of primordial attachment. *Canadian Ethnic Studies, 16*(3): 15–63.

Alloway, N. (2007). "Swimming against the tide: Boys, literacies, and schooling: An Australian story." *Canadian Journal of Education* 3 (2): 582–605.

Anderson, K. (1991). *Vancouver's Chinatown: Racial discourse in Canada, 1875–(1980).* Montreal, QC & Kingston, ON: McGill-Queen's University Press.

Anderson, N. (1923). *The hobo: The sociology of the homeless man.* Chicago, IL: University of Chicago Press.

Anisef, P., Axelrod, P., Baichman-Anisef, E., James, C., & Turritin, A. (2000). *Opportunity and uncertainty: Life course experiences of the class of '73.* Toronto, ON: University of Toronto Press.

Anthony, A.K., & McCabe, J. (2015). Friendship talk as identity work: Defining the self through friend relationships. *Symbolic Interaction, 38*(1), 64–82.

Appadurai, A. (1990). *Disjuncture and difference in the global cultural economy.* Durham, NC: Duke University Press.

Apple, M.W., Au, W., & Gandin, L.A. (Eds). (2009). *The Routledge international handbook of critical education.* New York, NY: Routledge.

Arat-Koc, S. (1990). Importing housewives: Non-citizen domestic workers and the crisis of the domestic sphere in Canada. In M. Luxton, H. Rosenberg, & S. Arat-Koc (Eds), *Through the kitchen window: The politics of home and family* (2nd edn, pp. 81–103). Toronto, ON: Garamond.

Armstrong, P., & Armstrong, H. (1994). *The double ghetto: Canadian women and their segregated work* (3rd edn). Toronto, ON: McClelland and Stewart.

Arnot, M. (2011). *Gender and education.* New York, NY: Routledge.

Arriagada, P. (2016). *First Nations, Metis and Inuit women.* Catalogue no. 89-503-X. Ottawa, ON: Statistics Canada.

Arrighi, G. (1994). *The long twentieth century: Money, power, and the origins of our times.* London, UK: Verso Books.

Arrighi, G. (1998). Globalization and the rise of East Asia. *International Sociology, 13*(1), 59–77.

Arrigo, B.A. (1999). Can students benefit from an intensive engagement with postmodern criminology? In J.R. Fuller & E.W. Hickey (Eds), *Controversial issues in criminology* (pp. 149–156). Boston, MA: Allyn and Bacon.

Artibise, A.F., & Stelter, G.A. (2012). Urbanization. *The Canadian Encyclopedia/ Historica Canada.* Retrieved from http://thecanadianencyclopedia. com/articles/urbanization

Asad, T. (1993). *Genealogies of religion: Discipline and reasons of power in Christianity and Islam.* Baltimore, MD: Johns Hopkins University Press.

Asbridge, M., Mann, R.E., & Flam-Zalcman, R. (2004). The criminalization of impaired driving in Canada: Assessing the deterrent impact of Canada's first per se law. *Journal of Studies in Alcohol, 65*(4): 450–9.

Association of American Geographers. (2012). The demographic transition model. Retrieved from http://cgge.aag. org/PopulationandNaturalResources1e/ CF_PopNatRes_Jan10/CF_PopNatRes_ Jan105.html

Atkinson, M. (2002). Pretty in ink: Conformity, resistance, and negotiation in women's tattooing. *Sex Roles, 47*(5–6), 219–235.

Atkinson, M. (2003a). The civilizing of resistance: Straightedge tattooing. *Deviant Behavior, 24*(3), 197–220.

Atkinson, M. (2003b). *Tattooed: The sociogenesis of a body art.* Toronto, ON: University of Toronto Press.

Atkinson, M. (2016). Masks of masculinity: (Sur)passing narratives and cosmetic surgery. In D. Waskul & P. Vannini (Eds), *Body/embodiment: Symbolic interaction and the sociology of the body* (2nd edn, pp. 247–262). New York, NY: Routledge.

Atkinson, P., Coffey, A., Delamont, S., Lofland, J., & Lofland, L. (2007). *Handbook of ethnography.* London: Sage.

AUCC. (2011). *Trends in higher education: Vol. 1. Enrolment.* Ottawa, ON: Association of Universities and Colleges of Canada.

Auger, M.F. (2008). On the brink of civil war: The Canadian government and the suppression of the 1918 Quebec Easter riots. *Canadian Historical Review, 89*(4), 503–40.

Auster, C.J., & Mansbach, C.S. (2012). The gender marketing of toys: An analysis of color and type of toy on the Disney Store website. *Sex Roles, 67*, 375–388.

Autor, D.H., & Dorn, D. (2013). The growth of low-skill service jobs and the polarization of the US labor market. *American Economic Review, 103*(5), 1553–1597.

Avert. (n.d.). Canada HIV & AIDS statistics. Retrieved from http://www.avert.org/canada-hiv-aids-statistics.htm

Axelrod, P. (1997). *The promise of schooling: Education in Canada, 1800–1914.* Toronto, ON: University of Toronto Press.

Aydemir, A., Chen, W.-H., & Corak, M. (2013). Intergenerational education mobility among the children of Canadian immigrants. *Canadian Public Policy, 39*, S107–S122.

Baaz, M.E., & Stern, M. (2009). Why do soldiers rape? Masculinity, violence, and sexuality in the armed forces in the Congo (DRC). *International Studies Quarterly, 53*(2), 495–518.

Babbie, E.R. (1988). *The sociological spirit: Critical essays in a critical science.* Belmont, CA: Wadsworth.

Bachmann, A.O., Danuser, B. & Morin, D. (2015). Developing a theoretical framework using a nursing perspective to investigative perceived health in the "sandwich generation" group. *Nursing Science Quarterly, 28*(4), 308–318.

Baer, D., Grabb, E., & Johnston, W.A. (1987). Class, crisis, and political ideology in Canada: Recent trends. *Canadian Review of Sociology, 24*(1), 1–22.

Baer, D., Grabb, E., & Johnston, W.A. (1990). The values of Canadians and Americans: A critical analysis and reassessment. *Social Forces, 68*(3), 693–713.

Baker, D.P. (2011). The future of the schooled society: The transforming culture of education in postindustrial society. In M.T. Hallinan (Ed.), *Frontiers in sociology of education* (pp. 11–33). Dordrecht, Netherlands: Springer.

Bakht, N. (2012). Veiled objections: Facing public oppositions to the niqab. In L.G. Beaman (Ed.), *Reasonable accommodation: Managing religious diversity* (pp. 70–108). Vancouver, BC: University of British Columbia Press.

Bakht, N., Bullock, K., Kanji, A., Kanji, S., & Siddiqui, S. (2014, 23 January). The misplaced moral panic at York University. *TheStar.com.* Retrieved from http://www.thestar.com/opinion/commentary/2014/01/23/the_misplaced_moral_panic_at_york_university.html

Balakrishnan, T.R., & Kralt, J. (1987). Segregation of visible minorities in Montreal, Toronto and Vancouver. In L. Driedger (Ed.), *Ethnic Canada: Identities and inequalities.* Toronto, ON: Copp Clark Pitman.

Bales, R.F. (1950). A set of categories for the analysis of small group interaction. *American Sociological Review, 15*(2), 257–263.

Balthazar, L. (1992). L'évolution du nationalisme québécois. In G. Daigle & G. Rocher (Eds), *Le Québec en jeu: comprendre les grands défis* (pp. 647–667). Montreal, QC: Presses de l'Université de Montréal.

Banerjee, S. (2016). Canadian professor held in Iranian jail indicted on unknown charges. *Toronto Star,* 11 July.

Bannerji, H. (1993). *Returning the gaze: Essays on feminism, racism and politics.* Toronto, ON: Sister Vision Press.

Barber, B. (1995). *Jihad vs. McWorld.* New York, NY: Ballentine Books.

Barker, E. (1984). *The making of a Moonie: Choice or brainwashing?* Oxford, UK: Blackwell.

Barker, E. (2005). New religions and cults in Europe. In L. Jones (Ed.), *The encyclopedia of religion.* New York, NY: Free Press.

Barker, E. (2007). How do modern European societies deal with new religious movements? In P. Meusburger, M. Welker, & E. Wunders (Eds), *Knowledge and Space: Clashes of Knowledge,* 154–71. Heidelberg: Springer.

Barnes, M.W. (2015). Anticipatory socialization of pregnant women: Learning fetal sex and gendered interactions. *Sociological Perspectives, 58*(2), 187–203.

Baron, S.W. (2003). Self-control, social consequences and criminal behavior: Street youth and the general theory of crime. *Journal of Research in Crime and Delinquency, 40*(4), 403–425.

Barron, C. & Lacombe, D. (2010). Moral panic and the nasty girl. In M. Rajiva & S. Batacharya (Eds), *Reena Virk: Canadian Perspectives on a Canadian Murder.* Toronto, ON: Canadian Scholars Press.

Battle, K. (2015). *Minimum wage rates in Canada: 1965–2015.* Ottawa, ON: Caledon Institute.

Baudrillard, J. (1998 [1970]). *The consumer society: Myths and structures.* Thousand Oaks, CA: Sage.

Baum, G. (2000). Catholicism and secularization in Quebec. In D. Lyon & M. Van Die (Eds), *Rethinking church, state and modernity: Canada between Europe and America* (pp. 149–66). Toronto, ON: University of Toronto Press.

Beach, F.A., & Ford, C.S. (1951). *Patterns of sexual behaviour.* New York, NY: Harper and Brothers.

Beaman, L.G. (1999). *Shared beliefs, different lives: Women's identities in evangelical context.* St Louis, MO: Chalice Press.

Beaman, L.G. (2008). *Defining harm: Religious freedom and the limits of law.* Vancouver, BC: University of British Columbia Press.

Becker, H. (1952). Social class variations in the teacher–student relationship. *Journal of Educational Sociology, 25*, 451–465.

Becker, H. (1963). *Outsiders: Studies in the sociology of deviance.* New York, NY: Free Press.

Beckfield, J. (2003). Inequality in the world polity: The structure of international organization. *American Sociological Review, 68*(3), 401–424.

Beckfield, J. (2008). The dual world polity: Fragmentation and integration in the network of intergovernmental organizations. *Social Problems, 55*(3), 419–442.

Beckford, J.A. (2003). *Social theory and religion.* Cambridge, UK: Cambridge University Press.

Behan, K., Maoh, H., & Kanaroglou, P. (2008). Smart growth strategies, transportation and urban sprawl: Simulated futures for Hamilton, Ontario. *Canadian Geographer/Le Géographe Canadien, 52*(3), 291–308.

Béland, D. (2005). Ideas and social policy: An institutionalist perspective. *Social Policy and Administration, 39*(1), 1–18.

Béland, D. (2006). The politics of social learning: Finance, institutions, and pension reform in the United States and Canada. *Governance, 19*(4), 559–83.

Béland, D. (2008). *Nationalism and social policy: The politics of territorial solidarity.* Oxford, UK: Oxford University Press.

Béland, D., & Hacker, J.S. (2004). Ideas, private institutions, and American welfare state "exceptionalism": The case of health and old-age insurance, 1915–1965. *International Journal of Social Welfare, 13,* 42–54.

Bell, D. (1973). *The coming of post-industrial society: A venture in social forecasting.* New York, NY: Basic Books.

Bell, D. (1976). Welcome to the post-industrial society. *Physics Today, 28* (2), 46–49.

Bell, K., Salmon, A., Bowers, M., Bell, J., & McCullough, L. (2010). Smoking, stigma and tobacco "denormalization": Further reflections on the use of stigma as a public health tool. *Social Science and Medicine, 70*(6), 795–799.

Bellah, R., Madsen, R., Sullivan, W.M., Swidler, A., & Tipton, S.M. (1985). *Habits of the heart: Individualism and commitment in American life.* Berkeley, CA: University of California Press.

Benford, R.D., & Snow, D.A. (2000). Framing processes and social movements: An overview and assessment. *Annual Review of Sociology, 26,* 611–39.

Benkert, H. (2002). Liberating insights from a cross-cultural sexuality study about women. *American Behavioral Scientist, 45*(8), 1197–207.

Bennett, T. (2007). "Making culture, changing society: The perspective of cultural studies." *Cultural Studies, 21,* 4–5.

Berger, J. (2009). Student debt in Canada. In J. Berger, A. Motte, & A. Parkin (Eds), *The Price of Knowledge: Access and Student Finance in Canada* (4th edn, pp. 182–205). Montreal, QC: Canada Millennium Scholarship Foundation.

Berger, P.L. (1963). *Invitation to sociology.* New York, NY: Anchor Books.

Berger, P.L. (1967). *The sacred canopy: Elements of a sociological theory of religion.* Garden City, NY: Doubleday.

Berger, P.L., & Luckmann, T. (1966). *The social construction of reality: A treatise in the sociology of knowledge.* New York, NY: Anchor.

Berlin, I. (1963). *Karl Marx: His life and environment.* New York, NY: Oxford University Press.

Bernstein, B. (1977). Class and pedagogies: Visible and invisible. In J. Karabel & A.H. Halsey (Eds), *Power and Ideology in Education* (pp. 511–34). New York, NY: Oxford University Press.

Best Start Resource Centre. (2012). *Welcoming and celebrating sexual orientation and gender diversity in families: From preconception to preschool.* Toronto, ON: author.

Best, J. (2013). *Social problems* (2nd edn). New York, NY: W.W. Norton.

Beyer, P. (2008). From far and wide: Canadian religious and cultural diversity in global/local context. In L.G. Beaman & P. Beyer (Eds), *Religion and Diversity in Canada* (pp. 9–40). Leiden, Netherlands: Brill.

Beyer, P. (2012). Religion and immigration in changing Canada: The reasonable accommodation of "reasonable accommodation"? In L.G. Beaman (Ed.), *Reasonable accommodation: Managing religious diversity* (pp. 13–31). Vancouver, BC: University of British Columbia Press.

Beyer, P., & Ramji, R. (2013). *Growing up Canadian: Muslims, Hindus, Buddhists.* Montreal, QC: McGill-Queen's University Press.

Bezanson, K. (2015). Return of the nightwatchman state? Federalism, social reproduction and social policy in a conservative Canada. In K. Strauss & K. Meehan (Eds), *Precarious worlds: Contested geographies of social reproduction* (pp. 25–44). Athens, GA: University of Georgia Press.

Bibby, R. (1990). *Mosaic madness.* Toronto, ON: Stoddart.

Bibby, R. (1993). *Unknown gods: The ongoing story of religion in Canada.* Toronto, ON: Stoddart.

Bibby, R. (2002). *Restless gods: The renaissance of religion in Canada.* Toronto, ON: Stoddart.

Bibby, R. (2006). *The boomer factor: What Canada's most famous generation is leaving behind.* Toronto, ON: Bastion Books.

Bibby, R. (2011). *Beyond the gods & back: Religion's demise and rise and why it matters.* Lethbridge, AB: Project Canada Books.

Bilge, S. (2013). Intersectionality undone: Saving intersectionality from feminist intersectionality studies. *Du Bois Review, 10,* 405.

Binder, A.J., Davis, D.B., & Bloom, N. (2016). Career funneling: How elite students learn to define and desire "prestigious" jobs. *Sociology of Education, 89*(1), 20–39.

Bissoondath, N. (1994). *Selling illusions: The cult of multiculturalism.* Toronto, ON: Penguin.

Bivens, J., & Mishel, L. (2015, September). Understanding the historic divergence between productivity and a typical worker's pay—Why it matters and why it's real. Economic Policy Institute briefing paper #406. Retrieved from http://www.epi.org/publication/understanding-the-historic-divergence-between-productivity-and-a-typical-workers-pay-why-it-matters-and-why-its-real/

Blackledge, D, & Hunt, B. (1985). *Sociological interpretations of education.* London, UK: Routledge.

Bloom, D.E. (2011). Population dynamics in India and implications for economic growth. In C. Ghate (Ed.), *The handbook of the Indian economy.* Oxford, UK: Oxford University Press.

Blumer, H. (1969). *Symbolic interactionism: Perspective and method.* Englewood Cliffs, NJ: Prentice Hall.

Bolaria, B.S., and Li, P. (1988). *Racial oppression in Canada* (2nd edn). Toronto, ON: Garamond.

Boli, J., & Thomas, G.M. (1997). World culture in the world polity: A century of international non-governmental organization. *American Sociological Review, 62*(2), 171–190.

Boli, J., & Thomas, G.M. (1999). *Constructing world culture: International non-governmental organizations since 1875.* Stanford, CA: Stanford University Press.

Boltanski, L. (2011). *On critique: A sociology of emancipation.* Cambridge, UK: Polity.

Bourdieu, P. & Passeron, J.-C. (1979). *The inheritors: French students and their relations to culture.* Richard Nice (Trans.). Chicago, IL: University of Chicago Press.

Bourdieu, P. (1984 [1979]). *Distinction: A social critique of the judgement of taste.* R. Nice (Trans.). London, UK & Cambridge, MA: Routledge & Harvard University Press.

Bourdieu, P. (1997). The forms of capital. R. Nice (Trans.). In A.H. Halsey, H. Lauder, P. Brown, & A.S. Wells (Eds), *Education: Culture, economy, and society* (pp. 46–58). Oxford, UK: Oxford University Press.

Bourdieu, P. (2000). *La sociologie est un sport de combat.* Film. P. Carles (Dir.).

Bourgois, P. (1995). *In search of respect: Selling crack in El Barrio.* New York, NY: Cambridge University Press.

Bourgois, P. (2001). Culture of poverty. In D. Levinson (Ed.), *The encyclopedia of homelessness.* Thousand Oaks, CA: Sage.

Bourgois, P., & Schonberg, J. (2009). *Righteous dopefiend.* Los Angeles, CA: University of California Press.

Bowden, G. (1989). Labour unions in the public mind: The Canadian case. *Canadian Review of Sociology, 26*(5), 123–42.

Bowden, G. (1990). From sociology to theology: A reply to Lipset. *Canadian Review of Sociology, 27*(4), 536–539.

Bowles, S., & Gintis, H. (1976). *Schooling in capitalist America: Education reform and the contradictions of economic life.* New York, NY: Basic Books.

Boyczuk, A. & Fletcher, P. (2016). The ebbs and flows: Stresses of sandwich generation caregivers. *Journal of Adult Development, 23*(1), 51–61.

Boyd, D., & Ellison, N.B. (2007). Social network sites: Definition, history, and scholarship. *Journal of Computer-Mediated Communication, 13,* 210–230. http://doi.org/10.1111/j.1083-6101.2007.00393.x

Boyd, J. (2010). Producing Vancouver's (hetero)normative nightscape. *Gender, Place and Culture: A Journal of Feminist Geography, 17*(2), 169–189.

Boyd, M. (1992). Gender, visible minority, and immigrant earnings inequality: Reassessing an employment equity premise. In V. Satzewich (Ed.), *Deconstructing a nation: Immigration, multiculturalism and racism in '90s Canada* (pp. 279–321). Halifax, NS: Fernwood.

Bradshaw, Y.W., Noonan, R., Gash, L., & Sershen, C.B. (1993). Borrowing against the future: Children and Third World indebtedness. *Social Forces, 71*(3), 629–656.

Braithewaite, J. 1979. *Inequality, crime and public policy.* London, UK: Routledge and Kegan Paul.

Braverman, H. (1974). *Labor and monopoly capital: The degradation of work in the twentieth century.* New York, NY: Monthly Review Press.

Brennan, J. (2015). *Ascent of Giants: NAFTA, Corporate Power and the Growing Income Gap.* Ottawa, ON: Canadian Centre for Policy Alternatives.

Breton, R. (1972). The socio-political dynamics of the October events. *Canadian Review of Sociology and Anthropology, 9*(1), 33–56.

Briskin, L. (1992). Socialist feminism: From the standpoint of practice. In M.P. Connelly & P. Armstrong (Eds), *Feminism in action: Studies in political economy* (pp. 267–93). Toronto, ON: Canadian Scholars' Press.

Brodkin, J. (2015, 2 December). Town that has no cell phone service loses its primary Internet provider. *Ars Technica.* Retrieved 8 March 2016 from http://arstechnica.com/business/2015/12/town-that-has-no-cell-phone-service-loses-its-primary-internet-provider/

Bromley, D.G., & Shupe, A.D., Jr. (1981). *Strange gods: The great American cult scare.* Boston, MA: Beacon.

Brown, L. (2002, 31 May). Two-tier grade schooling feared. *Toronto Star,* A1, A26.

Brown, N. (2001). Robert Park and Ernest Burgess: Urban ecology studies, 1925. *CSISS Classics.* Center for Spatially Integrated Social Science. www.csiss.org/classics/content/26

Brownlee, J. (2005). *Ruling Canada: Corporate cohesion and democracy.* Halifax, NS: Fernwood.

Brundtland, G.H. (1987). *Our common future.* Oxford, UK: Oxford University Press.

Brym, R.J., & Araj, B. (2006). Suicide bombing as strategy and interaction: The case of the second intifada. *Social Forces, 84*(4), 1969–1986.

Bryman, A., Teevan, J.J., & Bell, E. (2009). *Social research methods* (2nd Cdn edn). Toronto, ON: Oxford University Press.

Brzozowski, J.A., Taylor-Butts, A., & Johnson, S. (2006). Victimization and offending among the Aboriginal population in Canada. *Juristat, 26*(3).

Bullard, R. (1990). *Dumping in Dixie: Race, class and environmental quality.* Boulder, CO: Westview.

Bullock, C.F., & Culbert, J. (2002). Coverage of domestic violence fatalities by newspapers in Washington State. *Journal of Interpersonal Violence, 17,* 475–499.

Bunting, T., & Filion, P. (Eds). (2006). *Canadian cities in transition: Local through global perspectives* (3rd edn). Don Mills, ON: Oxford University Press.

Bunting, T., Filion, P., & Walker, R. (Eds). (2010). *Canadian cities in transition: New directions in the twenty-first century* (4th edn). Don Mills, ON: Oxford University Press.

Burawoy, M. (2004). Public sociologies: Contradictions, dilemmas and possibilities. *Social Forces 82*(4), 1603–1618.

Burgess, E.W. 1967 [1925]. The growth of the city: An introduction to a research project. In R.E. Park, E.W. Burgess, & R.D. McKenzie (Eds), *The city* (pp. 47–62). Chicago, IL: University of Chicago Press.

Burke, E. (2006). Feminine visions: anorexia and contagion in pop discourse. *Feminist Media Studies, 6*(3), 315–330.

Burly, G., & Awad, A. (2015). *The impact of student debt.* Ottawa, ON: Canadian Federation of Students.

Burns, A. (2015). Self(ie)-discipline: Social regulation as enacted through the discussion of photographic practice. *International Journal of Communication, 9,* 1716–1733.

Bussière, P., & Knighton, T. (2004). Measuring up: Canadian results of the OECD PISA Study: The performance of Canada's youth in mathematics, reading, science and problem solving, 2003. First Findings for Canadians Aged 15. Ottawa, ON: Minister of Industry.

Butler, J. (1990). *Gender trouble: Feminism and the subversion of identity.* New York, NY: Routledge.

Butler, J. (2006 [1990]). *Gender trouble: Feminism and the subversion of identity.* New York, NY: Routledge Classics.

Butler, J. (2006). *Bodies that matter: On the discursive limits of "sex."* (2nd edn). New York, NY: Routledge.

Butsch, R. (1992). Class and gender in four decades of television situation comedy: Plus ça change. . . . *Critical Studies in Mass Communication, 9,* 387–399.

Butsch, R. (1995). Ralph, Fred, Archie and Homer: Why television keeps recreating the white male working-class buffoon. In G. Dines & J.M. Humez (Eds), *Gender, race and class in media: A text-reader* (pp. 403–412). Thousand Oaks, CA: Sage.

Butsch, R. (2005). Five decades and three hundred sitcoms about class and gender. In G.R. Edgerton and B.G. Rose (Eds), *Thinking outside the box: A contemporary television genre reader* (pp. 111–135). Lexington, KY: University of Kentucky Press.

Butsch, R., & Glennon, L.M. (1983). Social class: Frequency trends in domestic situation comedy, 1946–1978. *Journal of Broadcasting, 27*(1), 77–81.

Butters, J., & Erickson, P. (1999). Addictions as deviant behaviour: Normalizing the pleasures of intoxication. In L.G. Beaman (Ed.), *New perspectives on deviance: The construction of deviance in everyday life* (pp. 67–84). Toronto, ON: Prentice Hall Allyn and Bacon.

Cabezas, A.L. (2006). The eroticization of labor in Cuba's all-inclusive resorts: Performing race, class and gender in the new tourist economy. *Social Identities, 12*(5), 507–521.

Calavita, K., & Pontell, H.N. (1991). "Other people's money" revisited: Collective embezzlement in the savings and loan insurance industries. *Social Problems, 38*(1), 94–112.

Campaign 2000. (2014). *2014 Report card on child and family poverty in Canada.* Family Service Toronto. Retrieved from http://www.campaign2000.ca/anniversary report/CanadaRC2014EN.pdf

Campey, J. (2002). Immigrant children in our classrooms: Beyond ESL. *Education Canada, 42*(3), 44–7.

Canada. (2005). *Civil Marriage Act.* Statutes of Canada 2005, c 33.

Canadian Centre for Justice Statistics. (2016). Family violence in Canada: A statistical profile, 2014. *Juristat.* Catalogue no. 85-002-X. Ottawa, ON: Statistics Canada. Retrieved from http://www.statcan.gc.ca/pub/85-002-x/2016001/article/14303-eng.pdf

Canadian Council on Learning. (2009). *The state of Aboriginal learning in Canada: A holistic approach to measuring success.* Ottawa, ON: Canadian Council on Learning.

Canadian Council on Learning. (2010). *State of learning in Canada 2009–2010:*

A year in review. Ottawa, ON: Canadian Council on Learning.

Canadian Environmental Grantmakers' Network (CEGN). (2005). *Urban environmental issues: A summary of issues and approaches*. Toronto, ON: CEGN.

Canadian Federation of Students. (2015a). An overview of tuition fees in Canada—Fact sheet. Ottawa, ON: Canadian Federation of Students.

Canadian Federation of Students. (2015b). *Private student debt in Canada: Ten year trends from 2000–2010*. Ottawa, ON: Canadian Federation of Students.

Canadian Institute for Health Information & Statistics Canada. (2013). *Health Indicators 2013*. Retrieved from https://secure.cihi.ca/free_products/HI2013_Jan30_EN.pdf, 38, 44, 46

Canadian Labour Congress (2014, 2 December). International Day of Persons with Disabilities. http://www.canadianlabour.ca/news-room/statements/december-3rd-international-day-persons-disabilities

Canadian Media Producers Association, l'Association québécoise de la production mediatique, the Department of Canadian Heritage, Telefilm Canada, and the Nordicity Group Ltd. (2015). *Profile 2015: Economic report on the screen-based media production industry in Canada*. Retrieved from http://www.cmpa.ca/sites/default/files/documents/industry-information/profile/PROFILE-2015-ENG.pdf

Canadian Research Institute for the Advancement of Women (CRIAW). (n.d.) *Fact Sheet: Violence against women in Canada*. Retrieved September 2016 from http://www.cwhn.ca/sites/default/files/CRIAW%20FACTSHEET%20Violence%20against%20women%20-%20short%20version.pdf

Canadian Teachers' Federation. (2010). Fundraising. *Commercialism in Canadian schools: Who's calling the shots?* CTF Fact Sheet. Retrieved from www.ctf-fce.ca/documents/Resources/en/commercialism_in_school/en/CISCKitFundraising%28R6%29.pdf

Canadian Wireless Telecommunication Association (CWTA). (2013). Facts and figures 2013. Retrieved January 2014 from http://cwta.ca/facts-figures/

Carroll, W.K. (2004). *Corporate power in a globalizing world: A study of elite organization*. Don Mills, ON: Oxford University Press.

Carroll, W.K. (2010a). *Corporate power in a globalizing world* (Rev. edn). Don Mills, ON: Oxford University Press.

Carroll, W.K. (Ed.). (2010b). "You are here": Interview with Dorothy E. Smith. *Socialist Studies, 6*(2), 9–37.

Carroll, W.K., & Ratner, R. (1996). Master framing and cross-movement networking in contemporary social movements. *The Sociological Quarterly, 37*, 601–625.

Carroll, W.K., & Ratner, R.S. (1999). Media strategies and political projects: A comparative study of social movements. *Canadian Journal of Sociology, 24*(1), 1–34.

Carter-Whitney, M. (2008). Cinching sprawl: Worldwide experience with greenbelts can help Calgary protect its near-urban land. *Alternatives Journal, 34*(3), 17.

Carty, D. (2010, 15 April). Fortune 500 cuts record 821K jobs in 2009. CBS News. Retrieved from http://www.cbsnews.com/news/fortune-500-cuts-record-821k-jobs-in-2009/

Casanova, J. (1994). *Public religion in the modern world*. Chicago, IL: University of Chicago Press.

Casey, E.S. (1993). *Getting back to place: Toward a renewed understanding of the place-world*. Bloomington, IN: Indiana University Press.

Castells, M. (2000). *The rise of the network society*. Oxford, UK: Blackwell.

Caton, C. (1990). *Homeless in America*. New York, NY: Oxford University Press.

Catton, W., Jr, & Dunlap, R. (1978). Environmental sociology: A new paradigm. *American Sociologist, 13*, 41–49.

CAUT (Canadian Association of University Teachers). (2016). By the numbers: Women's salaries as a percentage of men's salaries. *CAUT Bulletin, 63*(3), A2.

CBC News, Office of the GM and Editor in Chief. (2015, 30 November). Uncivil dialogue: Commenting and stories about Indigenous people. Editor's Blog, CBC News. Retrieved 15 December 2015 from http://www.cbc.ca/newsblogs/community/editorsblog/2015/11/uncivil-dialogue-commenting-and-stories-about-indigenous-people.html

CBC News. (2009). Going organic: Growing demand, tougher regulations. Retrieved from www.cbc.ca/consumer/story/2008/05/07/f-food-organic.html

CBC News. (2014, 22 January). Secular "values" charter hearings continue in Quebec City. Retrieved from http://www.cbc.ca/news/canada/montreal/secular-values-charter-hearings-continue-in-quebec-city-1.2506305.

Central Intelligence Agency (CIA). (2012). *The world factbook*. Retrieved from https://www.cia.gov/library/publications/the-world-factbook/fields/2054.html

Central Intelligence Agency (CIA). (2013). *The world factbook 2013–14*. Washington, DC: CIA. Retrieved 28 January 2016 from https://www.cia.gov/library/publications/the-world-factbook/index.html

Chapin, A. (2013, 14 November). Digital divide: Canada's poorest sacrifice basic needs to get connected. *Huffington Post*. Retrieved January 2014 from http://www.huffingtonpost.ca/2013/11/14/digital-divide-canada-poor_n_4269171.html

Chappell, N., Dujela, C., & Smith, A. (2015). Caregiver well-being: Intersections of relationship and gender. *Research on Aging, 37*(6), 623–645.

Charon, J.M. (1979). *Symbolic interactionism: An introduction, an interpretation, an integration*. Englewood Cliffs, NJ: Prentice Hall.

Chase-Dunn, C.K. (1998). *Global formation: Structures of the world-economy*. Lanham, MD: Rowman and Littlefield.

Chase-Dunn, C.K., & Grimes, P. (1995). World-systems analysis. *Annual Review of Sociology, 21*, 387–417.

Chawla, R. & Uppal, S. (2012). Household debt in Canada. *Perspectives on Labour and Income, 24* (2), 1–15.

Chayko, M. (2016). *Superconnected: The Internet, digital media, and technosocial life*. Thousand Oaks, CA: Sage.

Chen, W. (2013). The implications of social capital for the digital divides in America. *The Information Society, 29*(1), 13–25. doi: 10.1080/01972243.2012.739265

Chomsky, N. (1973). Preface. In A. Schaff, *Language and Cognition*. New York, NY: McGraw-Hill.

Christakis, N.A., & Fowler, J.H. (2007). The spread of obesity in a large social network over 32 years. *New England Journal of Medicine, 357*(4), 370–379.

Christakis, N.A., & Fowler, J.H. (2008). The collective dynamics of smoking in a large social network. *New England Journal of Medicine, 358*(21), 2249–2258.

Chua, Y.T., & Holt, T.J. (2016). A cross-national examination of the techniques of neutralization to account for hacking behaviors. *Victims & Offenders, 11*(4), 1–22.

Chui, T., & Maheux, H. (2011). *Visible minority women. Women in Canada: A gender-based statistical report*. Statistics Canada Catalogue 89-503-X. Retrieved from http://www.statcan.gc.ca/pub/89-503-x/2010001/article/11527-eng.pdf

Chung, D., DeBuys, B.D., & Nam, C.S. (2007). Influence of avatar creation on attitude, empathy, presence, and para-social interaction. Lecture Notes in Computer Science, *Proceedings of the 12th International Conference on Human-Computer Interaction: Interaction Design and Usability, Beijing, China*. Berlin, Germany: Springer-Verlag.

Church, W.T., II, Wharton, T., & Taylor, J.K. (2009). An examination of differential association and social theory: Family systems and delinquency. *Youth Violence and Juvenile Justice, 7*(1), 3–15.

Citizens for Public Justice. (2013). Poverty trends highlights: Canada 2013. Retrieved from http://www.cpj.ca/poverty-trends-highlights-canada-2013

Citizenship and Immigration Canada. (2015). *Facts and Figures 2014—Immigration Overview—Permanent Residents.* http://www.cic.gc.ca/english/resources/statistics/facts2014/permanent/index.asp#figure1

Citizenship and Immigration Canada. (2016). Permanent resident admissions. Retrieved from http://open.canada.ca/data/en/dataset/ad975a26-df23-456a-8ada-756191a23695

City Mayors. (n.d.) Statistics. Retrieved from www.citymayors.com/statistics/largest-cities-density-125.html

City of Toronto. (2006). *Toronto's racial diversity.* Retrieved from http://www.toronto.ca/toronto_facts/diversity.htm

Clark, R. (2010). Technical and institutional states: Loose coupling in the human rights sector of the world polity. *Sociological Quarterly, 51*(1), 65–95.

Clark, R., & Hall, J. (2011). Migration, international telecommunications, and human rights. *Sociological Forum, 26*(4), 870–896.

Clarke, J.N., & Van Amerom, G. (2008). The differences between parents and people with Asperger's. *Social Work in Health Care, 46* (3), 85–106.

Clément, D. (2008). *Canada's rights revolution: Social movements and social change, 1937–82.* Vancouver, BC: University of British Columbia Press.

Clement, W. (1975). *The Canadian corporate elite.* Toronto, ON: McClelland and Stewart.

Clifford, J., & Marcus, G.E. (1986). *Writing culture: The poetics and politics of ethnography.* Berkeley, CA: University of California Press.

Cloward, R.A., & Ohlin, L.E. (1960). *Delinquency and opportunity: A theory of delinquent gangs.* New York, NY: Free Press.

CMEC (Council of Ministers of Education Canada). (2008). *The development of education: Reports for Canada.* Ottawa, ON: Council of Ministers of Education Canada.

Cohen, J.L. (1985). Strategy or identity: New theoretical paradigms and contemporary social movements. *Social Research, 53,* 663–716.

Cole, F.-C. (1915). The Tinguian: Social, religious and economic life of a Philippine tribe." *Field Museum of Natural History Publication 209,* Vol. XIV.

Cole, L.W., & Foster, S.R. (2001). *From the ground up: Environmental racism and the rise of the environmental justice movement.* New York, NY: New York University Press.

Collins, P.H. (2000). *Black feminist thought: Knowledge, consciousness, and the politics of empowerment* (2nd edn). New York, NY: Routledge.

Collins, R. (1979). *The credential society: An historical sociology of education and stratification.* New York, NY: Academic Press.

Collins, R. (2008). *Violence: A micro-sociological theory.* Princeton, NJ: Princeton University Press.

Columbia Journalism Review. (2014). Who owns what: Time Warner Inc. Retrieved from http://www.cjr.org/resources/?c=timewarner

Comte, A. (1974). Positivist philosophy. In S. Andreski (Ed.), *The essential Comte.* London, UK: Croom Helm.

Conference Board of Canada. (2013). Income Inequality. Retrieved January 2014 from http://www.conference-board.ca/hcp/details/society/income-inequality.aspx

Connell, R.W. (1996). Teaching the boys: New research on masculinity and gender strategies for schools. *Teachers College Record, 98,* 206–235.

Cooley, C.H. (1902). *Human nature and social order.* New York, NY: Scribner.

Cooley, C.H. (1962 [1909]). *Social organization: A study of the larger mind.* Glencoe, IL: Free Press.

Corman, J., & Luxton, M. (2007). *Getting by in hard times: Gendered labour at home and on the job.* Toronto, ON: University of Toronto Press.

Courchene, T.J. (2007). Global futures for Canada's global cities. *IRPP Policy Matters, 8*(2).

Crane, D. (2002). Culture and globalization: Theoretical models and emerging trends. In D. Crane, N. Kawashima, & K. Kawasaki (Eds), *Global culture: Media, arts, policy, and globalization* (pp. 1–25). New York, NY: Routledge.

Cranford, C.J., Vosko, L.F., & Zukewich, N. (2006). The gender of precarious employment in Canada. In V. Shalla (Ed.), *Working in a global era: Canadian perspectives* (pp. 99–119). Toronto, ON: Canadian Scholars' Press.

Crawford, C. (2013). *Looking into poverty: Income sources of poor people with disabilities in Canada.* Toronto, ON: Institute for Research and Development on Inclusion and Society (IRIS) and Council of Canadians with Disabilities.

Crenshaw, K.W., Gotanda, N., Peller, G., & Thomas, K. (Eds). (1995). *Critical race theory: The key writings that formed the movement.* New York, NY: New Press.

Crompton, S. (2000). Health. *Canadian Social Trends, 59,* 12–17.

Croteau, D., & Hoynes, W. 2000. *Media/society: Industries, images, and audiences* (2nd edn). Thousand Oaks, CA: Pine Forge.

Crozier, M. (1964). *The bureaucratic phenomenon.* Chicago, IL: University of Chicago Press.

Cullen, F.T., Wright, J.P., & Blevins, K.R. (Eds). (2007). *Taking stock: The status of criminological theory.* Edison, NJ: Transaction.

Cuneo, C. (1990). *Pay equity: The labour-feminist challenge.* Toronto, ON: Oxford University Press.

Cuneo, C. (2002, 31 January). Globalized and localized digital divides along the information highway: A fragile synthesis across bridges, ramps, cloverleaves, and ladders. 33rd Annual Sorokin Lecture, University of Saskatchewan.

Curra, J. (2016). *The relativity of deviance.* Sage.

Currie, D. (1988). Starvation amidst abundance: Female adolescents and anorexia. In B.S. Bolaria & H.D. Dickinson (Eds), *Sociology of health care in Canada* (pp. 198–215). Toronto, ON: Harcourt Brace Jovanovich.

Curtiss, S. (1977). *Genie: A psycholinguistic study of a modern day wild child.* New York, NY: Academic Press.

D'Arcy, S., Black, T., Weis, T., & Russell, J.K. (Eds). (2014). *A line in the tar sands: Struggles for environmental justice.* Toronto, ON: Between the Lines.

Daley, A., Burton, P., & Phipps, S. (2015). Measuring poverty and inequality in northern Canada. *Journal of Children and Poverty, 21*(2), 89–110.

Daly, K. (2004). *The changing culture of parenting.* Ottawa, ON: Vanier Institute of the Family.

Daly, M. (1985). *Beyond God the Father: Towards a philosophy of women's liberation.* Boston, MA: Beacon Books.

Darder, A., Baltodano, M., & Torres, R.D. (Eds). (2003). *The critical pedagogy reader.* New York, NY: Routledge Falmer.

Das Gupta, T. (1996). *Racism and paid work.* Toronto, ON: Garamond.

Davey, I.E. (1978). The rhythm of work and the rhythm of school. In N. McDonald & A. Chaiton (Eds), *Egerton Ryerson and his times* (pp. 221–253). Toronto, ON: Macmillan.

Davie, G. (1994). *Religion in Britain since 1945: Believing without belonging.* Oxford, UK: Blackwell.

Davies, S., & Guppy, N. (2006). *The schooled society: An introduction to the sociology of education.* Toronto, ON: Oxford University Press.

Davies, S., & Guppy, N. (2010). *The schooled society: An introduction to the sociology of education* (3rd edn). Toronto, ON: Oxford University Press.

Davis, K. & Moore, W. (1945). Some principles of stratification. *American Review of Sociology, 10*(2), 242–249.

De Tarde, G. (1903). *The laws of imitation.* New York, NY: H. Holt.

Dean, M. (1991). *The constitution of poverty.* New York, NY: Routledge.

Dean, M. (2010). *Governmentality, power and rule in modern society* (2nd edn). London, UK: Sage.

deGroot-Maggetti, G. (2002). *A measure of poverty in Canada: A guide to the debate about poverty lines.* Ottawa, ON: Citizens for Public Justice.

Dei, G., James, I.M., Karumanchery, L.L., James-Wilson, S., & Zine, J. (2000). *Removing the margins: The challenges and possibilities of inclusive schooling.* Toronto, ON: Canadian Scholars Press.

Dei, G.J.S. (1996). *Anti-racism education: Theory and practice.* Halifax, NS: Fernwood.

Delanty, G. (2011). Varieties of critique in sociological theory and their methodological implications for social research. *Irish Journal of Sociology, 19*(1), 66–92.

Dellinger, K. (2002). Wearing gender and sexuality "on your sleeve": Dress norms and the importance of occupational and organizational culture at work. *Gender Issues, 20* (1), 3–25.

DeLong-Bas, N. (n.d.). The new social media and the Arab Spring. *Oxford Islamic Studies Online.* Retrieved 3 September 2016 from http://www.oxfordislamicstudies.com/Public/focus/essay0611_social_media.html

Department of Justice. (2013). About family violence. Retrieved from http://www.justice.gc.ca/eng/cj-jp/fv-vf/about-apropos.html

Desjardins, R., Murray, S., Clermont, Y., & Werquin, P. (2005). *Learning a living: First results of the Adult Literacy and Life Skills Survey.* Ottawa, ON and Paris, France: Statistics Canada and OECD.

Diani, M. (1992). The concept of social movement. *Sociological Review, 40,* 1–25.

Dickey Young, P. (2012). It's all about sex: The roots of opposition in some Christian churches to gay and lesbian marriages. In L.G. Beaman (Ed.), *Religion and Canadian society: Contexts, identities, and strategies* (2nd edn, pp.

145–156). Toronto, ON: Canadian Scholar's Press.

Dill, K.E., & Thill, K.P. (2007). Video game characters and the socialization of gender roles: Young people's perceptions mirror sexist media depictions. *Sex Roles, 57,* 851–864.

Dillabough, J., McLeod, J., & Mills, M. (Eds). (2011). *Troubling gender in education.* New York, NY: Routledge.

DiMaggio, P., Hargittai, E., Neuman, W.R., & Robinson, J.P. (2001). Social implications of the Internet. *Annual Review of Sociology, 27,* 307–336.

DiMaggio, P., & Powell, W. (1983). The iron cage revisited: Institutional isomorphism and collective rationality in organizational fields. *American Sociological Review, 48*(2), 147–160.

DiProperzio, L. (2013). Should you raise a gender-neutral baby? Retrieved 23 September 2016 from http://www.parents.com/parenting/gender-neutral-parenting/

Dole, C.M. (2000). Woman with a gun: Cinematic law enforcers on the gender frontier. In M. Pomerance & J. Sakeris (Eds), *Bang bang, shoot shoot! Essays on guns and popular culture* (2nd edn, pp. 11–21). Needham Heights, MA: Pearson Education.

Domhoff, G.W. (2013). *Who rules America? The triumph of the corporate elite.* Boston, MA: McGraw-Hill.

Doucet, A. (2006). *Do men mother? Fathering, care and domestic responsibilities.* Toronto, ON: University of Toronto Press.

Doucet, A. (2013). A "choreography of becoming": Fathering, embodied care, and new materialisms. *Canadian Review of Sociology, 50*(3), 284–305.

Doucet, A. (2015). Parental responsibilities: Dilemmas of measurement and gender equality. *Journal of Marriage & Family, 77*(1), 224–242.

Doucet, A. (2017). The ethics of care as practice, relational ontology, and social justice: The radical potential of fathers "home alone on leave." In M. O'Brien & K. Wall (Eds), *Comparative perspectives on work-life balance and gender equality: Fathers on leave alone.* New York, NY: Springer.

Downey, J., & N. Fenton. (2003). New media, counter publicity and the public sphere. *New Media and Society, 5*(2), 185–202.

Downs, E., & Smith, S. (2010). Keeping abreast of hypersexuality: A video game character content analysis. *Sex Roles, 62,* 721–733.

Drache, D. (2008). *Defiant publics: The unprecedented reach of the global citizen.* Cambridge, UK: Polity.

Dreeben, R. (1968). *On what is learned in school.* Reading, MA: Addison-Wesley.

Driedger, L. (1996). *Multi-ethnic Canada: Identities and inequalities.* Toronto, ON: Oxford University Press.

Drori, G.S., Meyer, J.W., Ramirez, F.O., & Schofer, E. (2003). Loose coupling in national science: Policy versus practice. In G.S. Drori, J.W. Meyer, F.O. Ramirez, & E. Schofer (Eds), *Science in the modern world polity: Institutionalization and globalization* (pp. 155–173). Stanford, CA: Stanford University Press.

Duffy, A., Corman, J., & Pupo, N. (2015). Family finances: Fragility, class, and gender. *Canadian Review of Sociology, 52*(2), 222–31.

Duggan, M., Ellison, N.B., Lampe, C., Lenhart, A., & Madden, M. (2015). *Social media update 2014.* Pew Research Center. Retrieved from http://www.pewinternet.org/files/2015/01/PI_SocialMediaUpdate20144.pdf

Dukes, R.L. & Stein, J.A. (2014). Evidence of anticipatory socialization among tattooed, wannabe, and non-tattooed adolescents: Differences in attitudes and behaviour." *Sage Open Journal* (April–June), 1–12.

Dunlap, R., & Catton, W., Jr. (1983). What environmental sociologists have in common (whether concerned with "built" or "natural" environments). *Sociological Inquiry, 53*(2/3), 113–115.

Dunlap, R., & Rosa, E.A. (2010). Environmental sociology. In E.F. Borgatta & R.J.V. Montgomery (Eds), *Encyclopedia of sociology* (2nd edn, pp. 1–7). New York, NY: Macmillan Reference USA (Gale Group).

Durkheim, É. (1951 [1897]). *Suicide: A study in sociology.* J.A. Spaulding & G. Simpson (Trans.). New York, NY: Free Press.

Durkheim, É. (1956 [1922]). *Education and society.* Sherwood W. Fox (Trans.). Glencoe, IL: Free Press.

Durkheim, É. (1964 [1893]). *The division of labor in society.* New York, NY: The Free Press.

Durkheim, É. (1965 [1912]). *The elementary forms of the religious life.* London, UK: Allen & Unwin.

Durkheim, É. (1982 [1895]). *Rules of sociological method.* London, UK: The Free Press.

Durkheim, É. (2001 [1912]). *The elementary forms of the religious life.* C. Cosman (Trans.). New York, NY: Oxford University Press.

Durkin, K.F. (2009). "There must be some kind of misunderstanding, there must be some kind of mistake": The deviance disavowal strategies of men arrested in

Internet sex stings (2008 presidential address). *Sociological Spectrum, 29*(6), 661–676.

Ebaugh, H. (1988). *Becoming an ex: The process of role exit.* Chicago, IL: University of Chicago Press.

Egale. (2015). Gay–straight alliance (GSA). myGSA.ca

Ehrenreich, B. (2001). *Nickel and dimed: On (not) getting by in America.* New York, NY: Henry Holt.

Ehrlich, P.R., & Ehrlich, A.H. (1990). *The population explosion.* London, UK: Hutchinson.

Eichler, M. (1983). *Families in Canada today: Recent changes and their policy consequences.* Toronto, ON: Gage.

Eichler, M., Albanese, P., Ferguson, S., Hyndman, N., Liu, L.W., & Matthews, A. (2010). *More than it seems: Household work and lifelong learning.* Toronto, ON: Women's Press.

Eidelman, G. (2010). Managing urban sprawl in Ontario: Good policy or good politics? *Politics and Policy, 38*(6), 1211–1236.

Elghawaby, A. (2014, 28 January). Lost in the York U furor: Accommodation isn't a trump card. *Globe and Mail.* Retrieved from http://www.theglobeandmail.com/globe-debate/lost-in-the-york-u-furor-accommodation-isnt-a-trump-card/article16540869/

Elliott, L. (2016). Richest 62 people as wealthy as half of world's population, says Oxfam. *Canadian Dimension, 50*(1). Retrieved 25 March 2016 from https://canadiandimension.com/articles/view/richest-62-people-as-wealthy-as-half-of-world's-population/

Elliott, M., & Doane, M.J. (2015). Stigma management of mental illness: Effects of concealment, discrimination, and identification on well-being. *Self and Identity, 14*(6), 654–674.

Elmer, G., & Gasher, M. (Eds). (2005). *Contracting out Hollywood: Runaway productions and foreign location shooting.* Lanham, MD: Rowman and Littlefield.

Engels, F. (1968 [1893]). *Gestamtausgabe: Marx and Engels correspondence.* D. Torr (Trans.). New York, NY: International.

Epstein, R. (Ed.). (2009). *Who's your daddy? And other writings on queer parenting.* Toronto, ON: Three O'Clock Press.

Eribon, D. (1991 [1989]). *Michel Foucault.* B. Wing (Trans.). Cambridge, MA: Harvard University Press.

Erikson, E. (1963). *Childhood and society.* New York, NY: Norton.

Erikson, E. (1982). *The life cycle completed: A review.* New York: W.W. Norton.

Erikson, K.T. (1966). *Wayward puritans: A study in the sociology of deviance.* New York, NY: Wiley.

Eriksson, L., & Mazerolle, P. (2013). A general strain theory of intimate partner homicide. *Aggression and Violent Behavior, 18*(5), 462–470.

Evangelical Fellowship of Canada. (2000, 2 March). Submission to the Standing Committee on Justice and Human Rights on Bill C-23, An Act to Modernize the Statutes of Canada in Relation to Benefits and Obligations.

Evans-Polce, R.J., Castaldelli-Maia, J.M., Schomerus, G., & Evans-Lacko, S.E. (2015). The downside of tobacco control? Smoking and self-stigma: a systematic review. *Social Science & Medicine, 145,* 26–34.

Fairbanks II, R.P. (2004). *Communal re-appropriation of blighted spaces: Governmentality and the politics of everyday life in the Kensington Recovery House movement.* PhD dissertation, University of Pennsylvania.

Farmer, G. T., & Cook, J. (2013). *Climate change science: A modern synthesis.* New York, NY: Springer.

Feagin, J.R. (1998). *The new urban paradigm: Critical perspectives on the city.* Lanham, MD, & Boulder, CO: Rowman and Littlefield.

Featherstone, L. (2004). *Selling women short: The landmark battle for workers' rights at Wal-Mart.* New York, NY: Basic Books.

Featherstone, M. (1990). *Consumer culture and postmodernism.* London, UK: Sage.

Feist, R., Beauvais, C., & Shukla, R. (2010). Introduction. In R. Feist, C. Beauvais, & R. Shukla (Eds), *Technology and the changing face of humanity* (pp. 1–21). Ottawa, ON: University of Ottawa Press.

Ferrao, V. (2010). Paid work. *Women in Canada: A Gender-Based Statistical Report.* Catalogue no. 89-503-X. Ottawa, ON: Statistics Canada. Retrieved from http://www.statcan.gc.ca/pub/89-503-x/2010001/article/11387-eng.pdf

Finnie, R., McMullen, K., & Mueller, R. (2010, 29 April). New perspectives on access to postsecondary education. *Education Matters: New Insights on Education, Learning and Training in Canada, 7* (1). Retrieved from www.statcan.gc.ca/bsolc/olc-cel/olc-cel?catno=81-004-X&chropg=1&lang=eng

Firestone, S. (1970). *The dialectic of sex: The case for feminist revolution.* New York, NY: Bantam Books.

Fleras, A., & Elliott, J.L. (1996). *Unequal relations: An introduction to race, ethnic and Aboriginal dynamics in Canada.* Toronto, ON: Prentice Hall.

Fleras, A., & Kunz, J.L. (2001). *Media and minorities: Representing diversity in a multicultural Canada.* Toronto, ON: Thompson Education.

Florida, R. (2008). *Who's your city?: How the creative economy is making where to live the most important decision of your life.* New York, NY: Basic Books.

Force, W.R. (2009). Consumption styles and the fluid complexity of punk authenticity. *Symbolic Interaction, 32*(4), 289–309.

Ford, J.A. (2009). Nonmedical prescription drug use among adolescents: The influence of bonds to family and school. *Youth and Society, 40,* 336–352.

Foster, J.B. (1986). *The theory of monopoly capitalism: An elaboration of Marxian political economy.* New York, NY: Monthly Review Press.

Foucault, M. (1969). *The archeology of knowledge.* A.M.S. Smith (Trans.). New York, NY: Pantheon.

Foucault, M. (1979 [1975]). *Discipline and punish: The birth of the prison.* A. Sheridan (Trans.). New York, NY: Random House.

Foucault, M. (1984). Of other spaces: Utopias and heterotopias. *Diacritics, 16,* 22–27.

Foucault, M. (1990). *The history of sexuality: An introduction.* New York, NY: Vintage Books.

Foucault, M. (1991). Governmentality. R. Braidotti (Trans.), C. Gordon (Rev.). In G. Burchell, C. Gordon & P. Miller (Eds), *The Foucault effect: Studies in governmentality* (pp. 87–104). Chicago, IL: University of Chicago Press.

Fox, B. (2001). The formative years: How parenthood creates gender. *Canadian Review of Sociology and Anthropology, 38,* 373–90.

Fox, B. (2009). *When couples become parents: The creation of gender in the transition to parenthood.* Toronto, ON: University of Toronto Press.

Fox, B. (Ed.). (2014). *Family patterns, gender relations* (4th edn). Toronto, ON: Oxford University Press.

Fox, B. (2015). Feminism on family sociology: Interpreting trends in family life. *Canadian Review of Sociology, 52*(2), 204–221.

Fox, B., & Sugiman, P. (1999). Flexible work, flexible workers: The restructuring of clerical work in a large telecommunications company. *Studies in Political Economy 60,* 59–84.

Fox, J.A., & Levin, J. (2001). *The will to kill: Making sense of senseless murder.* Boston, MA: Allyn and Bacon.

Francis, D. (1986). *Controlling interest: Who owns Canada.* Toronto, ON: Macmillan.

Francis, D. (2008). *Who owns Canada now: Old money, new money and the future of Canadian business.* Toronto, ON: HarperCollins.

Francis, D. (2013). *Merger of the century: Why Canada and America should become one country*. Toronto, ON: Harper Collins.

Frank, D.J., Longhofer, W., & Schofer, E. (2007). World society, NGOs and environmental policy reform in Asia. *International Journal of Comparative Sociology, 48*(4), 275–295.

Franklin, U.M. (1992). *The real world of technology*. Concord, ON: Anansi.

Freeman, V. (2010) "Toronto has no history!" Indigeneity, settler colonialism, and historical memory in Canada's largest city. *Urban History Review, 38*, 2, 21–35.

Freidson, E. (1970). *The profession of medicine: A study in the sociology of applied knowledge*. New York, NY: Harper and Row.

Freire, P. (1970). *Pedagogy of the oppressed*. Myra Bergman Ramos (Trans.). New York, NY: Herder and Herder.

Freud, S. (1938). *The basic writings of Sigmund Freud*. A. Brill (Trans., Ed.). New York, NY: Modern Library Press.

Friedan, B. (1963). *The feminine mystique*. New York, NY: W.W. Norton.

Friedman, M. (2013, 13 September). Dear Madame Marois. *Undefended Border*. Retrieved from http://undefendedborder.com/2013/09/13/dear-madame-marois/

Friendly, M., & Prentice, S. (2009). *About Canada: Childcare*. Winnipeg, MB: Fernwood.

Friesen, J. (2017, 5 January). Syrian exodus to Canada: One year later, a look at who the refugees are and where they went. *The Globe and Mail*. Retrieved from http://www.theglobeandmail.com/news/national/syrian-refugees-in-canada-by-the-numbers/article33120934/

Galabuzi, G.-E. (2006). *Canada's economic apartheid: The social exclusion of racialized groups in the new century*. Toronto, ON: Canadian Scholars' Press.

Gamson, W. (1991). Commitment and agency in social movements. *Sociological Forum, 6*, 27–50.

Gara, T. (2012). Highlights from the gender-neutral Swedish Toys "R" Us catalog. Retrieved 21 July 2016 from http://blogs.wsj.com/corporate-intelligence/2012/11/29/highlights-from-the-gender-neutral-swedish-toys-r-us-catalogue

Garfinkel, H. (1956). Conditions of successful status degradation ceremonies. *American Journal of Sociology, 61*, 420–424.

Garner, R., & Bushnik, T. (2008). The children of older first-time mothers in Canada: Their health and development. *Children and Youth Research Paper Series*. Catalogue no. 89-599-MWE2008005. Ottawa: Statistics Canada. Retrieved from http://www.statcan.gc.ca/pub/89-599-m/89-599-m2008005-eng.htm

Garrett-Petts, W.F., Hoffman, J., & Ratsoy, G. (Eds). 2014. *Whose culture is it anyway? Community engagement in small cities*. Vancouver, BC: New City Books.

Gaskell, J. (1993). Feminism and its impact on educational scholarship in Canada. In L.L. Stewin & S.J.H. McCann (Eds), *Contemporary educational issues: The Canadian mosaic* (2nd edn, pp. 145–60). Toronto, ON: Copp Clark Pitman.

Gazso, A. (2009). Reinvigorating the debate: Questioning the assumptions about and models of "the family" in Canadian social assistance policy. *Women's Studies International Forum, 32*(2), 150–162.

Gazso, A. (2014). Parenting young children: decisions and realities. In D. Cheal & P. Albanese (Eds), *Canadian families today: New perspectives* (3rd edn, pp. 65–84). Toronto, ON: Oxford University Press.

Gazso, A., & McDaniel, S. (2015). Families by choice and the management of low income through social supports. *Journal of Family Issues, 36*(3), 371–395.

Geertz, C. (1973). *The interpretation of cultures*. New York, NY: Basic Books.

Gergen, K. (2001). From mind to relationship: The emerging challenge. *Education Canada, 41*(1), 8–11.

Giddens, A. (1990). *The consequences of modernity*. Stanford, CA: Stanford University Press.

Gidney, R.D. (1999). *From hope to Harris: The reshaping of Ontario's schools*. Toronto, ON: University of Toronto Press.

Girling, J.L. (2010). *Capital and power: Political economy and social transformation*. Abingdon, UK: Routledge.

Giroux, H. (1997). *Pedagogy and the politics of hope: Theory, culture, and schooling: A critical reader*. Boulder, CO: Westview.

Globe and Mail. (2011, 23 June). The top 1000. *Report on Business Magazine*. Retrieved from http://www.theglobeandmail.com/report-on-business/rob-magazine/top-1000/canadas-50-biggest-employers/article636152/.

Goffman, E. (1959). *The presentation of self in everyday life*. Garden City, NJ: Doubleday-Anchor.

Goffman, E. (1961). *Asylums: Essays on the social situation of mental patients and other inmates*. New York, NY: Doubleday.

Goffman, E. (1963). *Stigma: Notes on the management of spoiled identity*. Englewood Cliffs, NJ: Prentice Hall.

Gold, D.A., Lo, C.Y.H., & Wright, E.O. (1975). Recent developments in Marxist theories of the capitalist state. *Monthly Review, 27*, 29–43.

Goldberg, D.T. (1993). *Racist culture: Philosophy and the politics of meaning*. Oxford, UK: Blackwell.

Goldenberg, N. (2006, July). What's God got to do with it? A call for problematizing basic terms in the feminist analysis of religion. Paper presented at the biannual meeting of the Britain and Ireland School of Feminist Theology, Edinburgh.

Gordon, R.M., & Nelson, J. (2000). Crime, ethnicity, and immigration. In R.A. Silverman, J.J. Teevan, & V.F. Sacco (Eds), *Crime in Canadian society* (6th edn). Toronto, ON: Harcourt Brace.

Gorz, A. (1999). *Reclaiming work: Beyond the wage-based society*. C. Turner (Trans.). Cambridge, UK: Polity Press.

Gosine, A., & Teelucksingh, C. (2008). *Environmental justice and racism in Canada: An introduction*. Toronto, ON: Emond Montgomery.

Gosine, K. (2000). Revisiting the notion of a "recast" vertical mosaic in Canada: Does a post secondary education make a difference? *Canadian Ethnic Studies, 32*(3), 89–104.

Gottdiener, M., & Hutchison, R. (2000). *The new urban sociology* (2nd edn). Boston, MA: McGraw-Hill.

Gottfredson, M., & Hirschi, T. (1990). *A general theory of crime*. Stanford, CA: Stanford University Press.

Gould, K., Schnaiberg, A., & Weinberg, A.S. (1996). *Local environmental struggles: Citizen activism in the treadmill of production*. New York, NY: Cambridge University Press.

Grabb, E. (1994). Democratic values in Canada and the United States: Some observations and evidence from the past and present. In J. Dermer (Ed.), *The Canadian Profile: People, Institutions, and Infrastructure* (pp. 113–139). Toronto, ON: Captus Press.

Grabb, E., & Curtis, J. (2002). Comparing central political values in the Canadian and American democracies. In D. Baer (Ed.), *Political Sociology: Canadian Perspectives* (pp. 37–54). Don Mills, ON: Oxford University Press.

Gramsci, A. (1971). *Selections from the prison notebooks*. New York, NY: International.

Granovetter, M.S. (1974). *Getting a job: A study of contacts and careers*. Cambridge, MA: Harvard University Press.

Gray, G., & Guppy, N. (2008). *Successful surveys: Research methods and practice* (4th edn). Toronto, ON: Nelson Thomson.

Greer, G. (1984). *Sex and destiny: The politics of human fertility*. London, UK: Martin Secker and Warburg.

Griffin, W. (2000). The embodied goddess: Feminist witchcraft and female divinity. In S.C. Monahan, W.A. Mirola, & M.O. Emerson (Eds), *Sociology of religion: A reader*. New York, NY: Prentice Hall/Penguin Putnam.

Griffith, A.I., & Smith, D.E. (1987). Constructing cultural knowledge: Mothering as discourse. In J. Gaskell & A. McLaren (Eds), *Women and education: A Canadian perspective* (pp. 87–103). Calgary, AB: Detselig.

Grogan, S. (2010). Promoting positive body image in males and females: Contemporary issues and future directions. *Sex Roles, 63*(9–10), 757–765.

Grossman, D. (2009). On killing: The psychological cost of learning to kill in war and society. New York, NY: Back Bay Books.

Grover, C., & Piggott, L. (2013). Disability and social (in)security: Emotions, contradictions of "inclusion" and employment and support allowance. *Social Policy and Society, 12*, 369–380.

Gunter, B. (2014). *Media and the sexualization of childhood*. New York: Routledge.

Guppy, N., & Davies, S. (1998). *Education in Canada: Recent trends and future challenges*. Ottawa, ON: Statistics Canada.

Gusfield, J.R. (1975). *Community: A critical response*. New York, NY: Harper and Row.

Gusfield, J.R. (1989). Constructing the ownership of social problems: Fun and profit in the welfare state. *Social Problems, 36*, 431–441.

Hackett, R.A., & Gruneau, R. (2000). *The missing news: Filters and blind spots in Canada's press*. Aurora, ON: Garamond.

Hackett, R.A., Pinet, R., & Ruggles, M. (1996). News for whom: Hegemony and monopoly versus democracy in Canadian media. In H. Holmes & D. Taras (Eds), *Seeing ourselves: Media power and policy in Canada* (2nd edn, pp. 257–272). Toronto, ON: Harcourt Brace Canada.

Haight, M., Quan-Haase, A., & Corbett, B. (2014). Revisiting the digital divide in Canada: The impact of demographic factors on access to the internet, level of online activity, and social networking site usage. *Information, Communication & Society, 17*(4), 503–519.

Hall, E. (1964–1965). *Report of the Royal Commission on Health Services*. Ottawa: Queen's Printer.

Hall, S. (1971). *Deviancy, politics and the media*. Birmingham, UK: Centre for Contemporary Cultural Studies.

Hall, S. (1980). Encoding/decoding. In S. Hall, D. Hobson, A. Lowe, & P Willis (Eds), *Culture, media, language: Working papers in cultural studies, 1972–79* (pp. 128–138). London, UK: Hutchinson.

Haluza-Delay, R. (2007). Environmental justice in Canada. *Local Environment, 12*(6), 557–564.

Haluza-Delay, R., O'Riley, P., Cole, P., & Agyeman, J. (2009). Introduction. In J. Agyeman, P. Cole, R. Haluza-DeLay, & R. O'Riley (Eds), *Speaking for ourselves: Environmental justice in Canada* (pp. 1–26). Vancouver, BC: University of British Columbia Press.

Hamilton, R. (2005 [1996]). *Gendering the vertical mosaic: Feminist perspectives on Canadian society* (2nd edn). Toronto, ON: Pearson.

Hand, M. (2017). Visuality in social media: Researching images, circulations and practices. In L. Sloan & A. Quan-Haase (Eds), *Handbook of social media research methods*. London, UK: Sage.

Handa, A. (2003). *Of Silk Saris and Mini-Skirts: South Asian Girls Walk the Tightrope of Culture*. Toronto, ON: Women's Press.

Hankivsky, O. (2014). *Intersectionality 101*. Simon Fraser University, Burnaby, BC: Institute for Intersectionality Research and Policy.

Hargittai, E. (2002). Second-level digital divide: Differences in people's online skills. *First Monday, 7*(4). http://firstmonday.org/htbin/cgiwrap/bin/ojs/index.php/fm/article/view/942/864 doi:http://dx.doi.org/10.5210%2Ffm.v7i4.942

Hargittai, E., & Hinnant, A. (2008). Digital inequality: Differences in young adults' use of the Internet. *Communication Research, 35*(5), 602–621. doi:10.1177/0093650208321782

Harley, D.A., Gassaway, L., & Dunkley, L. (2015). Isolation, socialization, recreation, and inclusion of LGBT elders. In D.A. Harley & P.B. Teaster (Eds), *Handbook of LGBT elders* (pp. 563–581). New York, NY: Springer.

Harper, C.L., & Fletcher, T.H. (2011). *Environment and society: Human perspectives on environmental issues* (Canadian edn). Toronto, ON: Pearson Canada.

Harris, C.D., & Ullman, E.L. (1945). The nature of cities. *Annals of the American Academy of Political and Social Science, 242*(1), 7–17.

Harris, M. (2013, 21 March). Digital divide persists in Canada, both in access and internet fluency. *Financial Post*. Retrieved January 2014 from http://business.financialpost.com/2013/03/21/digital-divide-persists-in-canada-both-in-access-and-internet-fluency/?__lsa=35d4–238f#Scene_1

Harvey, D. (1985). *The urbanization of capital: Studies in the history and theory of capitalist urbanization*. Baltimore, MD: Johns Hopkins University Press.

Harvey, D. (1990). *The condition of postmodernity: An enquiry into the origins of cultural change*. Oxford, UK: Blackwell.

Hauser, P.M., & Duncan, O.D. (1959). *The study of population: An inventory and appraisal*. Chicago, IL: University of Chicago Press.

Hawking, S. (Writer). (2010). *Into the universe with Stephen Hawking*. Television mini-series. Darlow Smithson Productions.

Hawkins, F. (1988). *Canada and immigration: Public policy and public concern* (2nd edn). Montreal, QC & Kingston, ON: McGill-Queen's University Press.

Hay, D.I. (2009). *Poverty reduction policies and programs*. Social Development Report Series. Ottawa, ON: Canadian Council on Social Development.

Health Canada. (2009). Canadian alcohol and drug use monitoring survey. www.hc-sc.gc.ca/hc-ps/drugs-drogues/cadums-esccad-eng.php

Heckert, D.M., & Heckert, D.A. (2015). Positive deviance. In E. Goode (Ed.), *The handbook of deviance* (pp. 80–100). Hoboken, NJ: Wiley-Blackwell.

Heckman, J.J., & Krueger, A.B. (2004). *Inequality in America: What role for human capital policies?* Cambridge, MA: MIT Press.

Helmes-Hayes, R. (2002). John Porter: Canada's most famous sociologist (and his links to American sociology). *American Sociologist, 33*(1), 79–104.

Helmes-Hayes, R. (2009). *Measuring the mosaic: An intellectual biography of John Porter*. Toronto, ON: University of Toronto Press.

Helmes-Hayes, R., & Curtis, J. (Eds). (1998). *The vertical mosaic revisited: Social inequality and social justice in Canada, 1965–1995*. Toronto, ON: University of Toronto Press.

Helwig, D. (2000). NWT residents are accident prone, live shorter lives. *Canadian Medical Association Journal, 162*, 681–682.

Henry, F., & Ginzberg, E. (1985). *Who gets the work: A test of racial discrimination in employment*. Toronto, ON: Urban Alliance on Race Relations and Social Planning Directorate.

Henry, F., & Tator, C. (2010). *The colour of democracy: Racism in Canadian society* (4th edn). Toronto, ON: Thomson Nelson.

Herodotus. (1996). *Histories*. G. Rawlinson (Trans.). Hertfordshire, UK: Wordsworth.

Herring, S.C., & Kapidzic, S. (2015). *Teens, gender, and self-presentation in social media*. In J.D. Wright (Ed.), *International Encyclopedia of the Social & Behavioral Sciences* (2nd edn.). Oxford, UK: Elsevier. http://doi.org/10.1016/B978-0-08-097086-8.64108-9

Hewitt, C. (1994). The dog that didn't bark: The political consequences of separatist violence in Quebec, 1963–70. *Conflict Quarterly, 14*(1), 9–29.

Heynen, N., McCarthy, J., Prudham S., & Robbins, P. (2007). Introduction: False promises. In N. Heyman, J. McCarthy, S. Prudham, & P. Robbins (Eds), *Neoliberal environments: False promises and unnatural consequences* (pp. 1–21). New York, NY: Routledge.

Hirschi, T. (1969). *Causes of delinquency*. Berkeley, CA: University of California Press.

Hirst, M., Harrison, J., & Mazepa, P. (2014). *Communication and new media: From broadcast to narrowcast* (Cdn edn). Don Mills, ON: Oxford University Press.

Hochschild, A. (1983). *The managed heart: Commercialization of human feeling*. Berkeley, CA: University of California Press.

Hochschild, A. (1997). *The time bind: When work becomes home and home becomes work*. New York, NY: Metropolitan Books.

Hodson, R. (2001). *Dignity at work*. Cambridge, UK: Cambridge University Press.

Holtby, A., Klein, K., Cook, K., & Travers, R. (2015). To be seen or not to be seen: Photovoice, queer and trans youth, and the dilemma of representation. *Action Research, 13*(4), 317–335.

Holtmann, C. (2016). Christian and Muslim immigrant women in the Canadian Maritimes: Considering their strengths and vulnerabilities in responding to domestic violence. *Studies in Religion/Sciences Religieuses*. doi: 10.1177/0008429816643115

Hoodfar, H. (2003). More than clothing: Veiling as an adaptive strategy. In S.S. Alvi, H. Hoodfar, & S. McDonough (Eds), *The Muslim veil in North America: Issues and debates*. Toronto, ON: Women's Press.

Hopper, K., & Baumohl, J. (2004). Liminality. In D. Levinson (Ed.), *Encyclopedia of homelessness* (pp. 354–356). Thousand Oaks, CA: Sage.

Horkheimer, M. (1985). The end of reason. In A. Arato & E. Gebhardt (Eds), *The essential Frankfurt School reader* (pp. 26–49). New York, NY: Continuum.

Horkheimer, M., & Adorno, T. (2006). The culture industry: Enlightenment as mass deception. In M.G. Durham & D.M. Kellner (Eds), *Media and cultural studies: Key works* (rev. edn). Malden, MA: Blackwell.

Horton, A.D. (2013). Flesh hook pulling: Motivations and meaning-making from the "body side" of life. *Deviant Behavior, 34*(2), 115–134.

Howard, P.N., Duffy, A., Freeion, D., Hussain, M., Mari, W., & Mazaid, M. (2011). Opening closed regimes: What was the role of social media during the Arab Spring? In *Project on Information Technology and Political Islam Working Paper*, University of Washington, Dept of Communication.

Howard-Hassmann, R. (1999). "Canadian" as an ethnic category: Implications for multiculturalism and national unity. *Canadian Public Policy, 25*(4), 523–537.

Hoyt, H. (1939). *The structure and growth of residential neighborhoods in American cities*. Washington, DC: Federal Housing Administration.

Hudon, T. (2015). *Immigrant women*. Catalogue no. 89-503-X. Ottawa, ON: Statistics Canada.

Hudon, T. (2016). *Visible minority women*. Catalogue no. 89-503-X. Ottawa, ON: Statistics Canada.

Hughes, E. (1945). Dilemmas and contradictions of status. *American Journal of Sociology, 50*, 353–9.

Hughes, E.C. (1971) [1962]). *The sociological eye: Selected papers*. New Brunswick, NJ: Transaction Books.

Hughes, M.M., Peterson, L., Harrison, J.A., & Paxton, P. (2009). Power and relation in the world polity: The INGO network country score, 1978–1998. *Social Forces, 87*(4), 32.

Hugill, P.J. (1995). *World trade since 1431: Geography, technology, and capitalism*. Baltimore, MD: Johns Hopkins University Press.

Hum, D., & Simpson, W. (2007). Revisiting equity and labour: Immigration, gender, minority status, and income differentials in Canada. In S. Hier & B.S. Bolaria (Eds), *Race and racism in 21st century Canada*. Peterborough, ON: Broadview.

Human Resources and Skills Development Canada (HRSDC). (2010). *Social assistance statistical report: 2007*. Catalogue number HS25-2/2007E-PDF. Ottawa, ON: HRSDC.

Imig, D., & Tarrow, S. (2001). Mapping the Europeanization of contention: Evidence from a quantitative data analysis. In D. Imig & S. Tarrow (Eds), *Contentious Europeans: Protest and politics in an emerging polity* (pp. 27–49). New York, NY: Rowman and Littlefield.

Immigration, Refugees and Citizenship Canada. (2015a). Six selection factors—Federal skilled workers. Retrieved from http://www.cic.gc.ca/english/immigrate/skilled/apply-factors.asp

Immigration, Refugees and Citizenship Canada. (2015b). Facts and figures 2014—Immigration overview: Permanent residents by top source countries, 2005–2014. Retrieved from http://www.cic.gc.ca/english/resources/statistics/facts2014/permanent/10.asp#figure7

Inglehart, R. (1990). Values, ideology, and cognitive mobilization in new social movements. In R.J. Dalton & M. Kuechler (Eds), *Challenging the political order* (pp. 23–42). New York, NY: Oxford University Press.

Ingram, R.J., & Hinduja, S. (2008). Neutralizing music piracy: An empirical examination. *Deviant Behavior, 29*(4), 334–366.

International Organization for Migration (n.d.) Missing migrants project. Retrieved from http://missingmigrants.iom.int/mediterranean

Irvine, J. (2003). "The sociologist as voyeur": Social theory and sexual research, 1910–1978. *Qualitative Sociology, 26*(4), 429–456.

Irwin, Sarah, & Elley, S. (2012). Parents' hopes and expectations for the children's future occupations. *The Sociological Review, 61*, 111–130.

Isajiw, W. (1999). *Understanding diversity: Ethnicity and race in the Canadian context*. Toronto, ON: Thompson Educational Publishing.

Jackson, A. (2009). *Work and labour in Canada: Critical issues* (2nd edn). Toronto, ON: Canadian Scholars' Press.

Jackson, A., & Robinson, D. (2000). *Falling behind: The state of working Canada, 2000*. Ottawa, ON: Canadian Centre for Policy Alternatives.

Jakobsen, J.R., & Pellegrini, A. (2004). *Love the sin: Sexual regulation and the limits of religious tolerance*. New York, NY: Beacon Press.

James, D.L., & Craft, E.A. (2002). Protecting one's self from a stigmatized disease . . . once one has it. *Deviant Behavior, 23*: 267–299.

James, I. (2006). *Asperger's Syndrome and high achievement: Some very remarkable people*. London, UK: Jessica Kingsley.

James, W.C. (2006). Dimorphs and cobbles: Ways of being religious in Canada. In L.G. Beaman (Ed.), *Religion and Canadian society: Traditions, transitions and innovations* (pp. 119–131). Toronto, ON: Canadian Scholars' Press.

Janis, I.L. (1982). *Groupthink: Psychological studies of policy decisions and fiascoes*

(2nd edn). Boston, MA: Houghton Mifflin.

Jenson, J., & Papillon, M. (2000). Challenging the citizenship regime: The James Bay Crees and transnational action. *Politics and Society, 28*(2), 245–264.

Jenson, J., & Saint-Martin, D. (2003). New routes to social cohesion? Citizenship and the social investment state. *Canadian Journal of Sociology, 28*(1), 77–99.

Joanisse, L. (2005). "This is who I really am": Obese women's conceptions of self following weight loss surgery. In D. Pawluch, W. Shaffir, & C. Miall (Eds), *Doing ethnography: Studying everyday life* (pp. 248–259). Toronto, ON: Canadian Scholars' Press.

Johnson, H. (1996). *Dangerous domains: Violence against women in Canada*. Toronto, ON: Nelson.

Johnson, H., & Dawson, M. (2011). *Violence against women in Canada: Research and policy perspectives*. Toronto, ON: Oxford University Press.

Johnson, T. (1972). *Professions and power*. London, UK: Macmillan.

Johnston, J., & Bauman, S. (2009). *Foodies: Democracy and distinction in the gourmet foodscape*. New York, NY: Routledge.

Jones, B.R., & Flannigan, S.L. (2006). Connecting the digital dots: Literacy of the 21st century. *EDUCAUSE Quarterly, 29*(2), 8–10.

Joyce, J. (1968 [1922]). *Ulysses*. Harmondsworth, UK: Penguin.

Kachur, J.L. & Harrison, T.W. (1999). Introduction: Public education, globalization, and democracy: Whither Alberta? In T.W. Harrison & J.L. Kachur (Eds), *Contested classrooms: Education, globalization, and democracy in Alberta* (pp. xiii–xxxv). Edmonton, AB: University of Alberta Press and Parkland Institute.

Kamel, R., & Hoffman, A. (1999). *The maquiladora reader: Cross-border organizing since NAFTA*. Philadelphia, PA: American Friends Service Committee.

Karim, K.H. (2002). Globalization, communication, and diaspora. In P. Attallah & L.R. Shade (Eds), *Mediascapes: New patterns in Canadian communication* (pp. 272–294). Scarborough, ON: Thomson Nelson.

Karim, K.H. (2008). Press, public sphere, and pluralism: Multiculturalism debates in Canadian English-language newspapers. *Canadian Ethnic Studies, 40*(1), 57–78.

Karmis, D. (2004). Pluralism and national identity(ies) in contemporary Quebec: Conceptual clarifications, typology, and discourse analysis. In A.-G. Gagnon (Ed.), *Quebec: State and society* (pp. 69–96). Peterborough, ON: Broadview.

Kasper, A.S., & Ferguson, S.J. (Eds). (2000). *Breast cancer: Society shapes an epidemic*. New York, NY: St Martin's.

Katz, M. (1989). *The undeserving poor*. New York, NY: Pantheon.

Kaye, J., & Béland, D. (2014, 22 August). Stephen Harper's dangerous refusal to "commit sociology." *Toronto Star*. Retrieved from http://www.thestar.com/opinion/commentary/2014/08/22/stephen_harpers_dangerous_refusal_to_commit_sociology.html

Kearney, P. (1982). *A history of erotic literature*. Hong Kong: Parragin Books.

Keil, R., & Boudreau, J.-A. (2006). Metropolitics and metabolics: Rolling out environmentalism in Toronto. In N. Heynen, M. Kaika, & E. Swyngedouw (Eds), *In the nature of cities: Urban political ecology and the politics of urban metabolism* (pp. 41–62). London, UK & New York, NY: Routledge.

Kelly, D.M., Pomerantz, S., & Currie, D. (2005). Skater girlhood and emphasized femininity: "You can't land an ollie properly in heels." *Gender & Education, 17*, 129.

Kemp, S. (2014). *Social, digital, & mobile in the Americas*. Retrieved from http://wearesocial.com/blog/2014/06/social-digital-mobile-americas

Kennedy, E.H., & O'Shaughnessy, S. (2010, 31 May). *Relational activism: Gender and environment reconsidered*. Presentation to the Canadian Sociological Association.

Kennedy, L.W., & Forde, D.R. (1999). *When push comes to shove: A routine conflict approach to violence*. Albany, NY: State University of New York.

Kenway, J., & Modra H. (1992). Feminist pedagogy and emancipatory possibilities. In C. Luke & J. Gore (Eds), *Feminisms and critical pedagogy* (pp. 138–66). London, UK: Routledge.

Kerley, K.R., Xu, X., & Sirisunyaluck, B. (2008). Self-control, intimate partner abuse, and intimate partner victimization: Testing the general theory of crime in Thailand. *Deviant Behavior, 29*(6), 503–532.

Killingsworth, B. (2006). "Drinking stories" from a playgroup: Alcohol in the lives of middle-class mothers in Australia." *Ethnography, 7*(3), 357–384.

Kim, J.W., & Chock, T.M. (2015). Body image 2.0: Associations between social grooming on Facebook and body image concerns. *Computers in Human Behavior, 48*, 331–339.

Kim, S.Y., & Hou, Y. (2016). Intergenerational transmission of tridimensional cultural orientations in Chinese American Families: The role of bicultural socialization. *Journal of Youth and Adolescence*. doi: 10.1007/s10964-016-0423-4

King, A. (1995). Globalization, modernity and the spatialization of social theory: An introduction. In M. Featherstone, S. Lash, & R. Robertson (Eds), *Global modernities*. Thousand Oaks, CA: Sage.

King, S. (2006). *Pink ribbons, inc.* Minneapolis, MN: University of Minnesota Press.

Kipfer, S., & Keil, R. (2002). Toronto Inc? Planning the competitive city in the new Toronto. *Antipode, 34*(2), 227–264.

Kitschelt, H. (1993). Social movements, political parties, and democratic theory. *Annals of the American Academy of Political and Social Science, 528* (July), 13–29.

Klawiter, M. (2008). *The biopolitics of breast cancer: Changing cultures of disease and activism*. Minneapolis, MN: University of Minnesota Press.

Knight, R. (1996). *Indians at work: An informal history of native labour in British Columbia, 1858–1930*. Vancouver, BC: New Star.

Kochhar, R. (2015, 22 October). Three-in-ten U.S. jobs are held by the self-employed and the workers they hire. Washington, DC: Pew Research Center. Retrieved from http://www.pewsocialtrends.org/2015/10/22/three-in-ten-u-s-jobs-are-held-by-the-self-employed-and-the-workers-they-hire/

Kohlberg, L. (1969). Stage and sequence: The cognitive-development approach to socialization. In D.A. Goslin (Ed.), *Handbook of socialization: Theory and research* (pp. 347–380). Chicago, IL: Rand McNally.

Kohlberg, L. (1975). Moral education for a society in moral transition. *Educational Leadership, 33*, 46–54.

Koontz, D. (2007). *The darkest evening of the year*. New York: Dell Bantam.

Kroeger, C.C., & Nason-Clark, N. (2010). *No place for abuse: Biblical and practical resources to counteract domestic violence* (2nd edn). Downers Grove, IL: InterVarsity Press.

Kuhn, M.H. & McPartland, T.S. (1954). An empirical investigation of self-attitudes. *American Sociological Review, 19*, 68–76.

Kymlicka, W. (1998). The theory and practice of Canadian multiculturalism. *Canadian Federation of the Social Sciences and Humanities, 23*(Nov.), 1–10. Retrieved from www.fedcan.ca/english/fromold/breakfast-kymlicka1198.cfm

La Rue, F. (2011). *Report of the special rapporteur on the promotion and* protection of the right to freedom of opinion and expression, Frank La Rue. New York, NY: United Nations.

Lambert, B. & McInturff, K. (2016). *Making women count: The unequal economics of women's work*. Ottawa, ON: Canadian Centre for Policy Alternatives, Retrieved from https://www.policyalternatives.ca/sites/default/files/uploads/publications/National%20Office/2016/03/Making_Women_Count2016.pdf

Lance, T., Anderson, M., & Croteau, J. (2010). Improving measurement of workplace sexual identity management. *Career Development Quarterly, 59*(1), 19–26.

Landecker, H., & Panofsky, A. (2013). From social structure to gene regulation and back: A critical introduction to environmental epigenetics for sociology. *Annual Review of Sociology, 39*, 333–357.

Langlois, S., & Morrison, P. (2002). Suicide deaths and suicide attempts. *Health Reports, 13*(2), 9–22.

Lapeyre, F., Ameratunga, S., & Possenti, S. (2012). Addressing informality for rural development. *Rural Development through Decent Work*. Rural Development Briefs. International Labour Organization. Retrieved from http://www.ilo.org/wcmsp5/groups/public/---ed_emp/documents/publication/wcms_182737.pdf

Laufer, W.S., & Adler, F. (1994). *The legacy of anomie theory: Advances in criminological theory*. New Brunswick, NJ: Transaction.

Lauzen, M.M. (2015). The celluloid ceiling: Behind-the-scenes employment of women on the top 250 films of 2014. Retrieved from http://womenintvfilm.sdsu.edu/files/2014_Celluloid_Ceiling_Report.pdf

Lawr, D., & Gidney, R. (Eds). (1973). *Educating Canadians: A documentary history of public education*. Toronto, ON: Van Nostrand Reinhold.

Lefebvre, S. (2008). Between law and public opinion: The case of Québec. In L.G. Beaman & P. Beyer (Eds), *Religion and diversity in Canada*. Leiden, Netherlands: Brill.

Lefebvre, S. (2013, 3 September). Libre opinion–Laïcité et valeurs: des positions inconciliables? *Le Devoir*. Retrieved from http://www.ledevoir.com/politique/quebec/386479/laicite-et-valeurs-des-positions-inconciliables

Lehmann, W. (2007). "I just didn't feel like I fit in": The role of habitus in university drop-out decisions. *Canadian Journal of Higher Education, 37*(2), 89–110.

Lemert, E. (1951). *Social pathology: A systematic approach to the theory of sociopathic behavior*. New York, NY: McGraw-Hill.

Levin, B. (2007). Schools, poverty, and the achievement gap. *Phi Delta Kappan, 89*(1), 75–6.

Levin, B., & Riffel, J.A. (1997). *Schools and the changing world: Struggling toward the future*. London, UK: Falmer.

Levin, J., & Madfis, E. (2009). Mass murder at school and cumulative strain: A sequential model. *American Behavioral Scientist, 52*(9), 1227–1245.

Lévi-Strauss, C. (1966) [1962]). *The savage mind*. Chicago, IL: University of Chicago Press.

Levitas, R. (1998). *The inclusive society? Social exclusion and new labour*. Basingstoke, UK: Macmillan.

Levitt, C. (1994). Is Canada a racist country? In S.F. Zerker (Ed.), *Change and impact: Essays in Canadian social sciences* (pp. 304–316). Jerusalem, Israel: Magnes Press, Hebrew University.

Levitt, P. (1998). Social remittances: Migration driven local-level forms of cultural diffusion. *International Migration Review, 32*(4), 926–948.

Lewchuk, W., deWolff, A., King, A., & Polanyi, M. (2006). The hidden costs of precarious employment: Health and the employment relationship. In L. Vosko (Ed.), *Precarious work in Canada*. Montreal, QC & Kingston, ON: McGill-Queen's University Press.

Lewchuk, W., & Robertson, D. (2006). Listening to workers: The reorganization of work in the Canadian motor vehicle industry. In V. Shalla (Ed.), *Working in a global era: Canadian perspectives* (pp. 53–73). Toronto, ON: Canadian Scholars' Press.

Lewis, O. (1966). *La vida: A Puerto Rican family in the culture of poverty*. New York, NY: Random House.

Lewis, O. (1996) [1966]). The culture of poverty. In G. Gmelch & W. Zenner (Eds), *Urban life*. Longrove, IL: Waveland Press.

Ley, D., & Dobson, C. (2008). Are there limits to gentrification? The contexts of impeded gentrification in Vancouver. *Urban Studies, 45*(12), 2471–2498.

Li, P. (1988). *Ethnic inequality in a class society*. Toronto, ON: Thompson Educational Publishing.

Li, P. (1992). Race and gender as bases of class fractions and the effects on earnings. *Canadian Review of Sociology and Anthropology, 29*(4), 488–510.

Li, P. (Ed.). (1999). *Race and ethnic relations in Canada* (2nd edn). Toronto, ON: Oxford University Press.

Lian, J.Z., & Matthews, R. (1998). Does the vertical mosaic still exist? Ethnicity and income in Canada, 1991. *Canadian Review of Sociology and Anthropology, 35*(4), 461–81.

Lightman, N., & Gingrich, L. (2012). The intersecting dynamics of social exclusion: Age, gender, race and immigrant status in Canada's labour market. *Canadian Ethnic Studies, 44*(3), 121–145.

Lindner, R. (1996). *The reportage of urban culture: Robert Park and the Chicago School*. Cambridge, UK: Cambridge University Press.

Lindsey, L., & Beach, S. (2003). *Essentials of sociology*. Upper Saddle River, NJ: Prentice Hall.

Liodakis, N. (1998). The activities of Hellenic-Canadian secular organizations in the context of Canadian multiculturalism. Études helléniques/Hellenic Studies, 6(1), 37–58.

Liodakis, N. (2002). *The vertical mosaic within: Class, gender and nativity within ethnicity*. PhD dissertation, McMaster University.

Liodakis, N. (2003). *Destination Canada: Immigration debates and issues*. Toronto, ON: Oxford University Press.

Liodakis, N. (2009). The social class and gender differences within Aboriginal groups in Canada: 1995–2000. In D. Beavon & D. Jetté (Eds), Journeys of a generation: Broadening the Aboriginal wellbeing policy research agenda. *Canadian Issues Journal* (Winter): 93–7. Montreal: Association for Canadian Studies.

Liodakis, N., & Satzewich, V. (2003). From solution to problem: Multiculturalism and "race relations" as new social problems. In W. Antony & L. Samuelson (Eds), *Power and resistance: Critical thinking about Canadian social issues* (3rd edn, pp. 145–168). Halifax, NS: Fernwood.

Lipset, S.M. (1963). The value patterns of democracy: A case study in comparative analysis. *American Sociological Review, 28*(4), 515–531.

Lipset, S.M. (1964). Canada and the United States: A comparative view. *Canadian Review of Sociology, 1*(4), 173–185.

Lipset, S.M. (1990). *Continental divide: The values and institutions of the United States and Canada*. New York, NY: Routledge.

Lipset, S.M. (1991). Canada and the United States: The great divide. *Current History, 90*(560), 432–437.

Liu, S., & Blomley, N. (2013). Making news and making space: Framing Vancouver's Downtown Eastside. *The Canadian Geographer/Le Géographe Canadien, 57*(2), 119–132.

Livingstone, A.-M. & Weinfeld, M. (2015). Black families and socio-economic inequality in Canada. *Canadian Ethnic Studies, 47*(3), 1–23.

Livingstone, D.W. (2012). Probing the icebergs of adult learning: Comparative findings and implications of the 1998, 2004, and 2010 Canadian Surveys of Formal and Informal Learning Practices. *The Canadian Journal for the Study of Adult Education, 25*(1), 47–71.

Livingstone, D.W., Pollock, K., & Raykov, M. (2016). Family binds and glass ceilings: Women managers' promotion limits in a "knowledge economy." *Critical Sociology, 42*(1), 145–166.

Logan, J., & Molotch, H. (1987). *Urban fortunes: The political economy of place.* Berkeley, CA: University of California Press.

Lomax, A. (1966). *The folk songs of North America.* London, UK: Cassell.

Lopez, S.H., Hodson, R., & Roscigno, V.J. (2009). Power, status, and abuse at work: General and sexual harassment compared. *Sociological Quarterly, 50*(1), 3–27.

Lorimer, R., & Gasher, M. (2001). *Mass communication in Canada* (4th edn). Toronto, ON: Oxford University Press.

Loseke, D.R. (2003a). Constructing conditions, people, morality and emotion: Expanding the agenda of constructionism. In J.A. Holstein & G. Miller (Eds), *Challenges and choices: Constructionist perspectives on social problems* (pp. 120–129). New York, NY: Aldine de Gruyter.

Loseke, D.R. (2003b). *Thinking about social problems: An introduction to constructionist perspectives.* New York, NY: Aldine de Gruyter.

Loseke, D.R. (2007). *Thinking about social problems: An introduction to constructionist perspectives* (2nd edn). New Brunswick, NJ: Transaction.

Loseke, D.R. (2009). Examining emotion as discourse: Emotion codes and presidential speeches justifying war. *Sociological Quarterly, 50*(3), 497–524.

Lowe, G.S. (2000). *The quality of work: A people-centred agenda.* Toronto, ON: Oxford University Press.

Lowry, W.R. (2008). Can bureaucracies change policy? *Journal of Policy History, 20*(02), 287–306.

Luckenbill, D.F. (1977). Criminal homicide as a situational transaction. *Social Problems, 25,* 176–186.

Luft, R., & Ward, J. (2009). Toward an intersectionality just out of reach: Confronting challenges to intersectional practice. In D. Vasilikie & M.T. Segal (Eds), *Perceiving gender locally, globally and intersectionally.* Bingley, UK: Emerald Group.

Luhmann, N., & Schorr K.-E. (2000). *Problems of reflection in the system of education.* Rebecca A. Neuwirth (Trans.). Münster, Germany: Waxmann.

Lukes, S. (1972). *Émile Durkheim: His life and work.* New York, NY: Harper and Row.

Lukes, S. (1974). *Power: A radical view.* London, UK: Macmillan.

Lukes, S. (2005). *Power: A radical view* (2nd edn). New York, NY: Palgrave Macmillan.

Luxton, M. (1980). *More than a labour of love.* Toronto, ON: Women's Press.

Luxton, M. (2011). *Changing families, new understandings.* Ottawa, ON: Vanier Institute of the Family.

Luxton, M. (2015). Feminist scholarship and family sociology: New ways of thinking, outstanding questions. *Canadian Review of Sociology, 52*(2), 212–221.

Lynch, K. (1989). *The hidden curriculum: Reproduction in education, a reappraisal.* London, UK: Falmer.

Lynn, M. (2009). Determinants and consequences of female attractiveness and sexiness: Realistic tests with restaurant waitresses. *Archives of Sexual Behavior, 38*(5), 737–745.

MacAlpine, K. (2005). *Ask and you shall receive: An exploration of salary expectations and the gendered earnings gap in Canada.* Unpublished MA thesis, Dalhousie University, Halifax.

Macdonald, D. (2015). *The wealth advantage: The growing gap between Canada's affluent and the middle class.* Ottawa, ON: Canadian Centre for Policy Alternatives.

Macek, S. (2006). *Urban nightmares.* Minneapolis, MN: University of Minnesota Press.

Macionis, J.J. (1997). *Society: The basics* (4th edn). Upper Saddle River, NJ: Prentice Hall.

Mackenzie, H. (2015). *Staying power: CEO pay in Canada.* Ottawa, ON: Canadian Centre for Policy Alternatives.

Mahtani, M. (2001). Representing minorities: Canadian media and minority identities. *Canadian Ethnic Studies, 33*(3), 99–133.

Malenfant, C.E., Morency, J.-D., & Martel, L. (2011). Projected trends to 2031 for the Canadian labour force. *Canadian Economic Observer.* Ottawa, ON: Statistics Canada. Retrieved from http://www5.statcan.gc.ca/olc-cel/olc.action?ObjId=11-010-X201100811537&ObjType=47&lang=en

Malthus, T.R. 1970 [1798]. *An essay on the principle of population.* Harmondsworth, UK: Penguin.

Mann, M. (1999). *The dark side of democracy.* Cambridge, UK: Cambridge University Press.

Mann, M. (2004). *Fascists.* Cambridge, UK: Cambridge University Press.

Manzer, R. (1994). *Public schools and political ideas: Canadian educational policy in historical perspective.* Toronto, ON: University of Toronto Press.

Maratea, R.J. (2015). Online claims-making: The NRA and gun advocacy in cyberspace. *Qualitative Sociology Review, 11*(2), 144–159.

Marcus, S. (2005). Queer theory for everyone: A review essay. *Signs, 31*(1), 191–218.

Marcuse, H. (1964) [1941]). *Reason and revolution: Hegel and the rise of social theory.* New York, NY: Arc.

Markin, K.M. (2005). Still crazy after all these years: The enduring defamatory power of mental disorder. *Law and Psychology Review, 29,* 155–185.

Martineau, H. (1838). *Retrospect of western travel.* London, UK: Saunders and Otley.

Marwick, A.E. (2015). Instafame: Luxury selfies in the attention economy. *Public Culture, 27*(1 75), 137–160.

Marx, K. (1967 [1867]). *Capital: A critical analysis of capitalist production.* F. Engels (Ed.). London, UK: Lowry.

Marx, K. (1976 [1867]). *Capital* (Vol. 1). Harmondsworth, UK: Penguin.

Marx, K., & Engels, F. (1985 [1848]). *The communist manifesto.* New York, NY: Penguin.

Maslow, A.H. (1943). A theory of human motivation. *Psychological Review, 50*(4), 370–396.

Masson, D. (2012). Changing state forms, competing state projects: Funding women's organizations in Quebec. *Studies in Political Economy, 89,* 79–103.

Matza, D., & Sykes, G. (1957). Techniques of neutralization: A theory of delinquency. *American Sociological Review, 5,* 1–12.

Maxwell, A. (2015). Adult criminal court statistics in Canada, 2013/2014. Table 4. Statistics Canada. http://www.statcan.gc.ca/pub/85–002-x/2015001/article/14226-eng.pdf

McCarthy, J.D. (1996). Constraints and opportunities in adopting, adapting, and inventing. In D. McAdam, J. McCarthy, & M. Zald (Eds), *Comparative perspectives on social movements* (pp. 141–151). New York, NY: Cambridge University Press.

McCormick, M. (2014, 2 June). Ten barriers to education around the world. *Global Citizen.* Retrieved 24 August 2016 from https://www.globalcitizen.org/en/content/10-barriers-to-education-around-the-world-2/

McGahan, P. (1995). *Urban sociology in Canada* (3rd edn). Toronto, ON: Harcourt Brace.

McGuire, M. (2005). *Rethinking sociology's sacred/profane dichotomy: Historically contested boundaries in western*

Christianity. Paper presented at SISR/ ISSR, Zagreb.

McGuire, M. (2008). *Lived religion: Faith and practice in everyday life*. Oxford, UK: Oxford University Press.

McInturff, K., with Lockhart, C. (2015). *The gender gap in Canada's 25 biggest cities*. Ottawa, ON: Canadian Centre for Policy Alternatives.

McLaren, A. (1990). *Our own master race: Eugenics in Canada, 1885–1945*. Toronto, ON: McClelland and Stewart.

McLaren, P., & Kincheloe, J.L. (Eds). (2007). *Critical pedagogy: Where are we now?* New York, NY: Peter Lang.

McMahon, R., Hudson, H., & Fabian, L. (2014). The First Mile Connectivity Consortium and digital regulation in Canada. *The Journal of Community Informatics, 10*(2).

McMullin, J. (2010). *Understanding social inequality: Intersections of class, age, gender, ethnicity and race in Canada*. Don Mills, ON: Oxford University Press.

McNabola, A., & Gill, L.W. (2009). The control of environmental tobacco smoke: A policy review. *International Journal of Environmental Research and Public Health, 6*(2), 741–758.

McQuaig, L. (2009, 20 October). Ever upward trend for bankers' pay. *Toronto Star*, A19.

McQuaig, L., & Brooks, N. (2010). *The trouble with billionaires*. Toronto, ON: Viking Canada.

Mead, G.H. (1934). *Mind, self, and society from the standpoint of a social behaviorist*. Chicago, IL: University of Chicago Press.

Meldrum, R.C., Piquero, A.R., & Clark, J. (2013). Does low self-control predict fictitious drug use and untruthfulness? *Deviant Behavior, 34*(3), 242–254.

Meligrana, J., & Skaburskis, A. (2005). Extent, location and profiles of continuing gentrification in Canadian metropolitan areas, 1981–2001. *Urban Studies, 42*(9), 1569–1592.

Melucci, A. (1989). *Nomads of the present: Social movements and individual needs in contemporary society*. Philadelphia, PA: Temple University Press.

Merton, R.K. (1938). Social structure and anomie. *American Sociological Review, 3*, 672–682.

Merton, R.K. (1957). *Social theory and social structure*. Glencoe, IL & New York, NY: Free Press.

Meyer, D.S., & Tarrow, S. (Eds). (1998). *The social movement society: Contentious politics for a new century*. Lanham, MD: Rowman and Littlefield.

Meyer, J.W. (2007). Globalization: Theory and trends. *International Journal of Comparative Sociology, 48*(4), 261–273.

Meyer, J.W., Boli, J., Thomas, G.M., & Ramirez, F. (1997). World society and the nation state. *American Journal of Sociology, 103*(1), 144–181.

Michels, R. (1962 [1911]). *Political parties: A sociological study of the oligarchical tendency of modern democracy*. New York, NY: Free Press.

Mihorean, K. (2005). Trends in self-reported spousal violence. In K. AuCoin (Ed.), *Family violence in Canada: A statistical profile*. Ottawa, ON: Canadian Centre for Justice Statistics, Statistics Canada.

Mikkonen, J., & Raphael, D. (2010). *Social determinants of health: The Canadian facts*. Toronto, ON: York University, Health Policy and Management. Retrieved from www.thecanadianfacts.org

Milan, A. (2015). *Families and living arrangements. Women in Canada: A gender-based statistical report*. Catalogue no. 89-503-X. Ottawa, ON: Statistics Canada. http://www.statcan.gc.ca/pub/89-503-x/2015001/article/14235-eng.pdf

Miles, R., & Brown, M. (2003). *Racism* (2nd edn). London, UK: Routledge.

Miles, R., & Torres, R. (1996). Does "race" matter? Transatlantic perspectives on racism after "race relations." In V. Amit-Talai & C. Knowles (Eds), *Re-situating identities: The politics of race, ethnicity and culture* (pp. 24–46). Peterborough, ON: Broadview.

Miller, G., & Holstein, J.A. (1993). *Constructionist controversies: Issues in social problems theory*. New York, NY: Aldine de Gruyter.

Miller, T., Govil, N., McMurria, J., & Maxwell, R. (2001). *Global Hollywood*. London, UK: British Film Institute.

Millett, K. (1969). *Sexual politics*. New York, NY: Doubleday, Avon.

Mills, C.W. (1940). Situated actions and vocabularies of motive. *American Sociological Review, 5*(6), 904–913.

Mills, C.W. (1956). *The power elite*. New York, NY: Oxford University Press.

Mills, C.W. (1959). *The sociological imagination*. New York, NY: Oxford University Press.

Mitchell, A., & Shillington, R. (2002). *Poverty, inequality and social inclusion. Perspectives on Social Inclusion* (Working Paper Series). Toronto, ON: Laidlaw Foundation.

Mitchell, B.A. (2012). *Family matters: An introduction to family sociology in Canada* (2nd edn). Toronto, ON: Canadian Scholar's Press.

Mitchell, B.A. (2014). Generational juggling acts in midlife families: Gendered and ethnocultural intersections. *Journal of Women & Aging, 26*(4), 332–350.

Monahan, T., & Fisher, J.A. (2015). Strategies for obtaining access to secretive or guarded organizations. *Journal of Contemporary Ethnography, 44*(6), 709–736.

Montpetit, E., Scala, F., & Fortier, I. (2004). The paradox of deliberative democracy: The National Action Committee on the Status of Women and Canada's policy on reproductive technology. *Policy Sciences, 37*, 137–157.

Moodley, K. (1983). Canadian multiculturalism as ideology. *Ethnic and Racial Studies, 6*(3), 320–331.

Mooney, L., & Lashewicz, B. (2014). Voices of care for adults with disabilities and/or mental health issues in Western Canada: What do families and agencies need from each other? *Health & Social Care in the Community, 22*(2), 178–186.

Morency, J.-D., Caron Malenfant, É. & MacIsaac, S. (2017). *Immigration and diversity: Population projections for Canada and its regions, 2011 to 2036*. Catalogue no. 91-551-X. Ottawa: Statistics Canada.

Morissette, R., & Galarneau, D. (2016). *Labour Market Participation of Immigrant and Canadian-born Wives, 2006 to 2014*. Catalogue no. 11-626-X-No. 055. Ottawa, ON: Statistics Canada.

Morissette, R., & Ostrovsky, Y. (2005). *The Instability of Family Earnings and Family Income in Canada, 1986 to 1991 and 1996 to 2001*. Catalogue no. 11F0019MIE, No. 265. Ottawa, ON: Statistics Canada, Analytical Studies Branch Research Paper Series.

Morley, D. (1980). *The "Nationwide" audience*. London, UK: British Film Institute.

Morley, D. (2006). Unanswered questions in audience research. *Communication Review, 9*, 101–121.

Mosco, V. (1989). The payper society: Computers and communication in the information age. Toronto, ON: Garamond.

Mosco, V. (2005). Here today, outsourced tomorrow: Knowledge workers in the global economy. *Javnost—The Public, 12*(2), 39–55.

Mossière, G. (2013). *Converties à l'islam. Parcours de femmes au Québec et en France*. Montreal, QC: Presses de l'Université de Montréal.

Mouvement laïque québécois v Saguenay (City), 2015 SCC 16, 2 SCR 3.

Mowat Centre (2012). *Annual report*. Retrieved from http://mowatcentre.ca/mowat-centre-annual-report-2012-13/

Muir, N., & Bohr, Y. (2014). Contemporary practices of traditional aboriginal child rearing: A review. *First Peoples Child and Family Review, 9*(1), 66–79.

Multani v. Commission scolaire Marguerite-Bourgeoys, 2006 SCC 6, 1 SCR 256.

Murdoch, G. (1945). The common denominator of culture. In R. Linton (Ed.), *The science of man in the world crisis*. New York, NY: Columbia University Press.

Nakhaie, M.R. (Ed.). (1999). *Debates on social inequality: Class, gender and ethnicity in Canada*. Toronto, ON: Harcourt Canada.

Nakhaie, M.R. (2000). Ownership and management position of Canadian ethnic groups in 1973 and 1989. In M.A. Kalbach & W. Kalbach (Eds), *Perspectives on ethnicity in Canada*. Toronto, ON: Harcourt Canada.

Nakhaie, M.R. (2002). Class, breadwinner ideology and housework among Canadian husbands. *Review of Radical Political Economics, 34*(2), 137–157.

Nakhaie, M.R. (2007). Universalism, ascription, and academic rank: Canadian professors 1987–2000. *Canadian Review of Sociology, 44*(3), 361–386.

Nash, K. (2000). Contemporary political sociology: Globalization, politics, and power. Oxford, UK: Blackwell.

Nason-Clark, N., & Fisher-Townsend, B. (2007). Women, gender and feminism in the sociology of religion: Theory, research and social action. In T. Balsi (Ed.), *American Sociology of Religion Histories* (pp. 203–221. Leiden, Netherlands: Brill.

Nason-Clark, N., & Holtmann, C. (2013). Thinking about cooperation and collaboration between diverse religious and secular community responses to domestic violence. In W.F. Sullivan & L.G. Beaman (Eds), *Varieties of Religious Establishment* (pp. 187–200). Farnham, UK: Ashgate.

National Assembly of Quebec. (2013). Bill 60, *Charter affirming the values of State secularism and religious neutrality and of equality between women and men, and providing a framework for accommodation requests*, 1st Session, 40th Legislature, Quebec.

National Defence and the Canadian Armed Forces. (n.d.). Organizational structure. Retreived from http://www.forces.gc.ca/en/about-org-structure/index.page

National Vital Statistics Report (2014, 6 November). *United States Life Tables 2010, 63*(7).

Nationmaster. (n.d.). India people stats. Retrieved from www.nationmaster.com/country/in/Age_distribution

Native Women's Association of Canada. (2007). *Revitalization of matrilineal/matriarchal/egalitarian systems*. Issue paper for the National Aboriginal Women's Summit. Cornerbrook, NL.

Nelson, A. (2010). *Gender in Canada* (4th edn). Toronto, ON: Pearson.

New York Times. (2015, 23 November). Meet some of our top commenters. Retrieved from http://www.nytimes.com/interactive/2015/11/23/nytnow/23commenters.html

Newman, D.M. (2006). *Sociology: Exploring the architecture of everyday life*. Thousand Oaks, CA: Pine Forge Press.

Newton, M. (2002). *Savage girls and wild beasts: A history of feral children*. New York, NY: St Martin's.

Newton-Francis, M., & Young, G. (2015). Not winging it at Hooters: Conventions for producing a cultural object of sexual fantasy. *Poetics, 52*, 1–17.

Norris, P. (2001). *Digital divide: Civic engagement, information poverty, and the Internet worldwide*. New York, NY: Cambridge University Press.

O'Connor, J. (1996). The second contradiction of capitalism. In T. Benton (Ed.), *The greening of Marxism*. New York, NY & London, UK: Guilford Press.

O'Gorman, M., & Pandey, M. (2015). Explaining high school attainment in northern Aboriginal communities: An analysis of the Aboriginal People's Surveys. *Canadian Public Policy, 41*(4), 297–308.

Occhionero, M.F. (1996). Rethinking public space and power. *International Review of Sociology, 6*, 453–464.

Organisation for Economic Co-operation and Development (OECD). (2013a). *Education at a glance 2013: OECD indicators*. Paris: OECD.

OECD. (2013b). *PISA 2012 results in focus: What 15-year-olds know and what they can do with what they know: Key Results from PISA 2012*. Paris: OECD.

OECD. (2015). *Education at a glance 2015: OECD indicators*. Paris: OECD.

OECD. (2016). Labour force participation rate (indicator). Retrieved 13 October 2016 from https://data.oecd.org/emp/labour-force-participation-rate.htm. doi: 10.1787/8a801325-en

Oliveira, M. (2014, February 19). 10 million Canadians use Facebook on mobile daily. *The Globe and Mail*. Retrieved from http://www.theglobeandmail.com/technology/10-million-canadians-use-facebook-on-mobile-daily/article16976434/

Ono, H., & Zavodny, M. (2008). Immigrants, English ability and the digital divide. *Social Forces, 86*(4), 1455–1479.

Orsi, R. (2003). Is the study of lived religion irrelevant to the world we live in? *Journal for the Scientific Study of Religion, 42*(3), 169–174.

Osborne, K. (1999). *Education: A guide to the Canadian school debate: Or, who wants what and why?* Toronto, ON: Penguin.

Ostrovsky, Y. (2008). *Earnings inequality and earnings instability of immigrants in Canada*. Analytical Studies, Research Paper Series no. 309. Catalogue no. 11F0019M. Ottawa, ON: Statistics Canada.

Overton, J. (2009). Privatization, deregulation, and environmental protection: The case of provincial parks in Newfoundland and Labrador. In L. Adkin (Ed.), *Environmental conflict and democracy in Canada* (pp.159–173). Vancouver, BC: University of British Columbia Press.

Oxfam. (2014). *Working for the few: Political capture and economic inequality*. Retrieved from http://www.oxfam.org/sites/www.oxfam.org/files/bp-working-for-few-political-capture-economic-inequality-200114-en.pdf

Pagnan, C., Lero, D., & Wadsworth, S.M. (2011). It doesn't always add up: examining dual-earner couples' decision to off-shift. *Work & Family, 14*(3), 297–316.

Palmer, S. (2004). *Aliens adored: Rael's UFO religion*. New Brunswick, NJ: Rutgers University Press.

Park, R.E., Burgess, E.W., & McKenzie, R.D. (Eds). 1967 [1925]. *The city*. Chicago, IL: University of Chicago Press.

Parsons, T. (1951). *The social system*. New York, NY, & Glencoe, IL: Free Press.

Parsons, T. (1959). The school class as a social system: Some of its functions in American society. *Harvard Educational Review, 29*, 297–318.

Paul, A.M. (2010, 21 March). How to be brilliant. *New York Times Book Review*, 19.

Paxton, P., Hughes, M.M., & Green, J.L. (2006). The international women's movement and women's political representation, 1893–2003. *American Sociological Review, 71*, 898–920.

PEPSO (Poverty and Employment Precarity in Southern Ontario). (2013). *It's more than poverty: Employment precarity and household well-being*. Hamilton, ON & Toronto, ON: McMaster University Social Sciences/United Way.

Peritz, I. (2013, 20 September). How is the controversial charter of values going over in the Quebec heartland? *Globe and Mail*. Retrieved from http://www.theglobeandmail.com/news/national/how-is-the-controversial-charter-of-values-going-over-in-the-pq-heartland/article14439565/#dashboard/follows/

Perreault, S. (2009). The incarceration of Aboriginal people in adult correctional services. *Juristat, 29*(3).

Perry, E. (2015, December). COP21, Just Transition, and Canadian Reaction. Work and Climate Change Report. Toronto, ON: York University, Adapting Canadian Work and Workplaces to Respond to Climate Change. Retrieved 13 October 2016 from https://workandclimatechangereport.org/2015/12/

Perry, S.L. (2015). Pornography consumption as a threat to religious socialization. *Sociology of Religion, 76*(4), 436–458.

Pescosolido, B. (2013). The public stigma of mental illness: What do we think; what do we know; what can we prove? *Journal of Health and Social Behavior, 54* (1), 1–21.

Peter, T., & Taylor, C. (2011). *Every classroom in every school. Final report on the first national climate survey on homophobia, biphobia, and transphobia in Canadian schools.* Toronto, ON: Egale Canada Human Rights Trust. Retrieved from http://egale.ca/wp-content/uploads/2011/05/EgaleFinalReport-web.pdf

Peter, T., Taylor, C., Ristock, J., & Edkins, T. (2015). Pride and prejudice: Factors affecting school attachment among lesbian, bisexual, and heterosexual girls. *Journal of Lesbian Studies, 19*(2), 249–273.

Peterman, A., Palermo, T., & Bredenkamp, C. (2011). Estimates and determinants of sexual violence against women in the Democratic Republic of Congo. *American Journal of Public Health, 101*(6), 1060–1067.

Peterson, R.A. (1992). Understanding audience segmentation: From elite and popular to omnivore and univore. *Poetics, 21*, 243–258.

Peterson, R.A. (2005). Problems in Comparative Research: The Example of Omnivorousness. *Poetics, 33*, 257–282.

Peterson, R.A., & Anand, N. (2004). The production of culture perspective. *Annual Review of Sociology, 30*, 311–334.

Petras, J. (2006). Past, present and future of China: From semi-colony to world power? *Journal of Contemporary Asia, 36*(4), 423–441.

Pew Research Center. (2016, 5 January). Parents, teens, and digital monitoring. Retrieved 24 September 2016 from http://www.pewinternet.org/2016/01/07/parents-teens-and-digital-monitoring/pi_2016-01-07_parents-teens-digital-monitoring_2-03

Pfuhl, E.H., & Henry, S. (1993). *The deviance process* (3rd edn). New York, NY: Aldine de Gruyter.

Piaget, J. (1932). *The moral judgement of the child.* London, UK: Routledge and Kegan Paul.

Piaget, J. (1950). *The construction of reality in the child.* London, UK: Routledge and Kegan Paul.

Piché, J. (2011). Standing Committee on Public Safety and National Security. Number 58, 3rd Session, 20th Parliament.

Pickard, V.W. (2006). Assessing the radical democracy of Indymedia: Discursive, technical, and institutional constructions. *Critical Studies in Media Communication, 23*(1), 19–38.

Picot, G., & Hou, F. (2014). Immigration, Low Income and Income Inequality in Canada: What's New in the 2000s? Catalogue 11F0019M, No. 364. Ottawa, ON: Statistics Canada.

Pieterse, J.N. (1994). Globalisation as hybridisation. *International Sociology, 9*(2), 161–184.

Piliavin, E., & Briar, S. (1964). Police encounters with juveniles. *American Journal of Sociology, 70*, 206–214.

Poisson, J. (2011, 21 May). Parents keep child's gender secret. *Toronto Star.*

Polletta, F., & Jasper, J. (2001). Collective identity and social movements. *Annual Review of Sociology, 27*, 283–305.

Pomerantz, S., Raby, R., & Stefanik, A. (2013). Girls run the world?: Caught between sexism and postfeminism in school. *Gender & Society, 27*(2), 185–207.

Porter, J. (1965). *The vertical mosaic: An analysis of social class and power in Canada.* Toronto, ON: University of Toronto Press.

Portes, A. (1997). Neoliberalism and the sociology of development: Emerging trends and unanticipated facts. *Population and Development Review, 23*(2), 229–259.

Powell, A., Dainty, A., & Bagilhole, B. (2011). A poisoned chalice? Why UK women engineering and technology students may receive more "help" than their male peers. *Gender and Education, 23*(5), 585–599. doi:10.1080/09540253.2010.527826

Pruit, J.C. (2015). Preschool teachers and the discourse of suspicion. *Journal of Contemporary Ethnography, 44*(4), 510–534.

Public Health Agency of Canada. (2008). Complementary and alternative health. Retrieved from http://www.phac-aspc.gc.ca/chn-rcs/cah-acps-eng.php

Pupo, N., & Noack, A. (2010). Dialling for service: Transforming the public-sector workplace in Canada. In N.J. Pupo & M.P. Thomas (Eds), *Interrogating the new economy: Restructuring work in the 21st century* (pp. 111–128). Toronto, ON: University of Toronto Press.

Quan-Haase, A. (2016). *Technology and society: Social networks, work, and inequality* (2nd edn). Don Mills, ON: Oxford University Press.

Quan-Haase, A., Martin, K., & Schreurs, K. (2016). Interviews with digital seniors: ICT use in the context of everyday life. *Information, Communication & Society, 4*(5). http://doi.org/http://dx.doi.org/10.1080/1369118X.2016.1140217

Raby, R. (2009). School rules, bodily discipline, embodied resistance. In C. Levine-Rasky (Ed.), *Canadian perspectives on the sociology of education.* Don Mills, ON: Oxford University Press.

Raduntz, H. (2005). The marketization of education within the global capitalist economy. In M.W. Apple, J. Kenway, & M. Singh (Eds), *Globalizing education: Policies, pedagogies, and politics* (pp. 231–45). New York, NY: Peter Lang.

Raines, J. (Ed.). (2002). *Marx on religion.* Philadelphia, PA: Temple University Press.

Raj, A. (2014). How much do Canadian MPs and senators make? *Huffington Post.* Retrieved 20 March 2016 from http://www.huffpost.com

Rajiva, M., & Batacharya, S.,(Eds). (2010). *Critical perspectives on a Canadian murder.* Toronto, ON: Canadian Scholar's Press.

Ramos, H. (2006). What causes Canadian Aboriginal protests: Examining resources, opportunities, and identity, 1951–2000. *Canadian Journal of Sociology, 31*(2), 211–234.

Ramos, H., & Rodgers, K. (Eds). (2015). *Protest and politics: The promise of social movement societies.* Vancouver, BC: UBC Press.

Randazzo, R., Farmer, K., & Lamb, S. (2015). Queer women's perspectives on sexualization of women in media. *Journal of Bisexuality, 15*(1), 99–129.

Rassin, M. (2011). Tactics of concealment among people living with HIV. *Deviant Behavior, 32*(2), 101–114.

Razack, S. (1998). *Looking white people in the eye: Gender, race and culture in courtrooms and classrooms.* Toronto, ON: University of Toronto Press.

Rees, W.E. (1992). Ecological footprints and appropriated carrying capacity: What urban economics leaves out. *Environment and Urbanization, 4*, 120–30.

Rees, W.E. (2010). Getting serious about urban sustainability: Eco-footprints and the vulnerability of twenty-first century cities. In T. Bunting, P. Filion, & R. Walker (Eds), *Canadian cities in transition: New directions in the twenty-first century* (4th edn, pp. 70–86). Don Mills, ON: Oxford University Press.

Reinarman, C. (1996). The social construction of an alcohol problem. In G.W. Potter & V.E. Kappeler (Eds), *Constructing crime: Perspectives on making news and social problems* (pp. 193–220). Prospect Heights, IL: Waveland.

Reisig, M.D., & Pratt, T.C. (2011). Low self-control and imprudent behavior revisited. *Deviant Behavior, 32*(7), 589–625.

Reitz, J.G., & Banerjee, R. (2007). Racial Inequality, Social Cohesion, and Policy Issues in Canada. In K. Banting, T.J. Courchene, & F.L. Seidle (Eds), *Belonging? Diversity, recognition and shared citizenship in Canada* (pp. 489–545).

Montreal, QC: Institute for Research on Public Policy.

Rich, A. (1978). *The dream of a common language: Poems 1974–1977*. New York, NY: W.W. Norton.

Rich, A.C. (2003 [1980]). Compulsory heterosexuality and lesbian existence. *Project Muse—Journal of Women's History, 15*(3), 11–48.

Ritual. (n.d.) *Merriam-Webster Dictionary*. Retrieved from https://www.merriam-webster.com/dictionary/ritual

Ritzer, G. (2000a). *The McDonaldization of society* (3rd edn). Thousand Oaks, CA: Pine Forge.

Ritzer, G. (2000b). *Sociological theory* (5th edn). New York, NY: McGraw-Hill.

Roberman, S. (2015). Not to be hungry is not enough: An insight into contours of inclusion and exclusion in affluent western societies. *Sociological Forum, 30*(3), 743–763.

Roberts, B. (1988). *Whence they came: Deportation from Canada, 1900–1935*. Ottawa, ON: University of Ottawa Press.

Robertson, R. (1992). *Globalization: Social theory and global change*. London, UK: Sage.

Robertson, R. (1995). Glocalization: Time-space and heterogeneity–homogeneity. In M. Featherstone, S. Lash, & R. Robertson (Eds), *Global modernities*. Thousand Oaks, CA: Sage.

Rodgers, K., & Scobie, W. (2012, 16 May). Intentions of anti-mask bill must be revealed. *Ottawa Citizen*. Retrieved 5 February 2014 from http://www2.canada.com/ottawacitizen/news/archives/story.html?id=04df0e2a-989d-4067-9459-9512199cc502&p=2

Rose, D. (2004). *The uneasy cohabitation of gentrification and "social mix": A case study of infill condominiums in Montreal*. Working paper. Montreal, QC: Institut National de la Recherche Scientifique (INRS), Urbanisation, Culture et Société.

Rose, N. (1999). *Powers of freedom: Reframing political thought*. New York, NY: Cambridge University Press.

Ross, D., & Shillington, R. (1994). *The Canadian fact book on poverty*. Ottawa, ON: Canadian Council on Social Development.

Royal Commission on Aboriginal Peoples (RCAP). (1996). *Report of the Royal Commission on Aboriginal Peoples*. Ottawa: RCAP.

Royal Commission on Equality in Employment. (1984). *Report*. Ottawa, ON: Supply and Services Canada.

Rozworski, M. (2015, 25 March). Stagnant wages for over 80 percent of Canadian workers. *Education for Workers*.

Winnipeg, MB: Canadian Centre for Policy Alternatives.

Ryan, W. (1971). *Blaming the victim*. New York, NY: Pantheon.

Rymer, R. (1993). *Genie: Escape from a silent childhood*. London, UK: Michael Joseph.

Sacco, V.F. (1992). An introduction to the study of deviance and control. In V.F. Sacco (Ed.), *Deviance: Conformity and control in Canadian society* (pp. 1–48). Scarborough, ON: Prentice Hall.

Sacco, V.F. (2005). *When crime waves*. Thousand Oaks, CA: Sage.

Sacco, V.F., & Kennedy, L.W. (2011). *The criminal event: An introduction to criminology* (5th edn). Scarborough, ON: Thomson.

Sadovnik, A.R. (Ed.). (1995). *Knowledge and pedagogy: The sociology of Basil Bernstein*. Norwood, NJ: Ablex.

Saïd, E. (1978). *Orientalism*. New York, NY: Pantheon.

Sample, L. (2016, March 4). Restaurant dress codes: Sexy outfits for female staff may be discriminatory. *CBC News*. Retrieved from http://www.cbc.ca/news/business/marketplace-gender-specific-dress-codes-1.3474289

Sanders, C., & Vail, D.A. (1989). *Customizing the body: The art and culture of tattooing*. Temple University Press.

Sandstrom, K.L., Lively, K.J., Martin, D., & Fine, G. (2013). *Symbols, selves and social reality: A symbolic interactionist approach to social psychology and sociology*. New York, NY: Oxford University Press.

Sapir, E. (1921). *Language: An introduction to the study of speech*. New York, NY: Harcourt, Brace.

Sarlo, C. (1996). *Poverty in Canada* (2nd edn). Vancouver, BC: The Fraser Institute.

Sassen, S. (1991). *The global city: New York, London, Tokyo*. Princeton, NJ: Princeton University Press.

Sassen, S. (2001). *The global city revised: New York, London, Tokyo*. Princeton, NJ: Princeton University Press.

Sassen, S. (2007). *A sociology of globalization*. New York, NY: W.W. Norton.

Sasson, T. (1995). *Crime talk: How citizens construct a social problem*. Hawthorne, NY: Aldine de Gruyter.

Satzewich, V. (Ed.). (1998). *Racism and social inequality in Canada*. Toronto, ON: Thompson Educational Publishing.

Satzewich, V. (2014). Canadian visa officers and the social construction of "real" spousal relationships. *Canadian Review of Sociology, 51*(1), 1–21.

Satzewich, V. (2015). *Points of entry: How Canada's visa officers decide who gets in*. Vancouver, BC: University of British Columbia Press.

Satzewich, V., & Liodakis, N. (2010). *"Race" and ethnicity in Canada: A critical introduction* (2nd edn). Toronto, ON: Oxford University Press.

Satzewich, V., & Liodakis, N. (2017). *"Race" and ethnicity in Canada: A critical introduction* (4th edn). Don Mills, ON: Oxford University Press.

Savio, G. (2016). Organization and stigma management: A comparative study of dumpster divers in New York. *Sociological Perspectives*. doi: 0731121416632012

Schippers, M. (2007). Recovering the feminine other: Masculinity, femininity, and gender hegemony. *Theory and Society, 36*(1), 85–102.

Schirle, T. (2016). The gender wage gap in the Canadian provinces, 1997–2014. *Canadian Public Policy, 41*(4), 309–319.

Schissel, B., & Wotherspoon, T. (2003). *The legacy of school for Aboriginal people: Education, oppression, and emancipation*. Toronto, ON: Oxford University Press.

Schnaiberg, A., & Gould, K.A. (1994). *Environment and society: The enduring conflict*. New York, NY: St Martin's Press.

Schofer, E., & Hironaka, A. (2005). The effects of world society on environmental protection outcomes. *Social Forces, 84*(1), 25–47.

Schofer, E., & Meyer, J.W. (2005). The worldwide expansion of higher education in the twentieth century. *American Sociological Review, 70*(6), 898–920.

Schwartz, M. (2007). Remembering Seymour Martin Lipset. *Canadian Journal of Sociology Online* (March-April). Retrieved from www.cjsonline.ca/soceye/lipset.html

Scott, J., & Marshall, G. (2009). Political sociology. In J. Scott & G. Marshall, *A dictionary of sociology*. Oxford, UK: Oxford University Press.

Scott, S. (2011). *Total institutions and reinvented identities*. London, UK: Palgrave Macmillan.

Scott, S. (2015). *Negotiating identity: Symbolic interactionist approaches to identity*. Oxford, UK: John Wiley and Sons.

Sears, A. (2003). *Retooling the mind factory: Education in a lean state*. Aurora, ON: Garamond.

Seljak, D. (2000). Resisting the "no man's land" of private religion: The Catholic church and the public politics in Quebec. In D. Lyon & M. Van Die (Eds), *Rethinking Church, State and Modernity: Canada between Europe and America* (pp. 131–148). Toronto, ON: University of Toronto Press.

Sen, A.K. (1999). *Development as freedom*. New York, NY: Knopf.

Sen, A.K. (2000). *Social exclusion: Concept, application, and scrutiny*. Social

Development Papers 1. Manila, Philippines: Asian Development Bank.

Shaffir, W. (1991). Conversion experiences: Newcomers to and defectors from Orthodox Judaism (*hozrim betshuvah* and *hozrim beshe'elah*). In Z. Sobel & B. Beit-Hallahmi (Eds), *Tradition, Innovation, Conflict: Jewishness and Judaism in Contemporary Israel* (pp. 173–202). Albany, NY: State University of New York Press.

Shapiro, C.A., & Sax, L.J. (2011). Major selection and persistence for women in STEM. *New Directions for Institutional Research, 2011*(152), 5–18. doi:10.1002/ir.404

Shenk, D. (2010). *The genius in all of us: Why everything you've been told about genetics, talent, and IQ is wrong.* New York, NY: Doubleday.

Sherman, R. (2007). *Class acts: Service and inequality in luxury hotels.* Berkeley, CA: University of California Press.

Sherman, S.Y. (2014). *In search of purity: Popular eugenics and radical uplift among new Negroes 1915–1935.* PhD dissertation, Department of History paper 68, University of Nebraska.

Shigihara, A.M. (2013). It's only stealing a little a lot: Techniques of neutralization for theft among restaurant workers. *Deviant Behavior, 34*(6), 494–512.

Shin, K.-H., & Timberlake, M. (2000). World cities in Asia: Cliques, centrality, and connectedness. *Urban Studies, 37* (12), 2257–2285.

Shipley, H. (2012). One of these things is not like the other: Regulating sexual difference. In L.G. Beaman (Ed.), *Reasonable accommodation: Managing religious diversity* (165–86). Vancouver, BC: UBC Press.

Shpiegelman, C.-N., & Gill, C.J. (2014). How do adults with intellectual disabilities use Facebook? *Disability and Society, 29*, 1601–1616.

Shuey, K., & Willson, A. (2014). Economic hardship in childhood and adult health trajectories: An alternative approach to investigating life-course processes. *Advances in Life Course Research, 22*, 49–61.

Simbürger, E. (2014). The forbidden discipline: The impact of the Pinochet dictatorship on Chilean sociology and sociologists. Presented at the Eighteenth World Congress of Sociology, 13–19 July.

Simmel, G. 2002 [1903]. The metropolis and mental life. In G. Bridge & S. Watson (Eds), *The Blackwell city reader* (pp. 11–19). Oxford, UK & Malden, MA: Blackwell.

Simmons, A. (1998). Racism and immigration policy. In V. Satzewich (Ed.), *Racism and social inequality in Canada.* Toronto, ON: Thompson Educational Publishing.

Simon, D. (2016). *Elite deviance* (10th edn). Boston, MA: Pearson.

Simpson, J.H. (2000). The politics of the body in Canada and the United States. In D. Lyon & M. Van Die (Eds), *Rethinking church, state and modernity: Canada between Europe and America* (pp. 263–282). Toronto, ON: University of Toronto Press.

Sinha, M. (2013a). Measuring violence against women: Statistical trends. *Juristat.* Catalogue 85-002-X. Ottawa, ON: Statistics Canada.

Sinha, M. (2013b). Portrait of caregivers, 2012. *Spotlight on Canadians: Results from the General Social Survey.* Catalogue no. 89-652-X, No. 1. Ottawa, ON: Statistics Canada.

Skinner, B.F. (1953). *Science and human behaviour.* Oxford, UK: Macmillan.

Sklair, L. (1994). Global sociology and global environmental change. In M. Redclift & T. Benton (Eds), *Social theory and the global environment* (pp. 205–227). London, UK: Routledge.

Skocpol, T. (1979). *States and social revolutions: A comparative analysis of France, Russia, and China.* Cambridge, UK: Cambridge University Press.

Smith, C. (1991). *The emergence of liberation theology: Radical religion and social movement theory.* Chicago, IL: University of Chicago Press.

Smith, D. (1987). *The everyday world as problematic: A feminist sociology.* Boston, MA: Northeastern University Press.

Smith, D. (1990). *The conceptual practices of power: A feminist sociology of knowledge.* Toronto, ON: University of Toronto Press.

Smith, D. (1992). Sociology from women's experience: A reaffirmation. *Sociological Theory, 10*(1), 88–98.

Smith, D. (2005). *Institutional ethnography: A sociology for people.* Walnut Creek, CA: AltaMira Press.

Smith, J.M. (2013). Creating a godless community: The collective identity work of contemporary American atheists. *Journal for the Scientific Study of Religion, 52*(1), 80–99.

Smythe, D.W. (1981). *Dependency road: Communications, capitalism, consciousness, and Canada.* Norwood, NJ: Ablex.

Snow, D., & Anderson, L. (1987). Identity work among the homeless: The verbal construction and avowal of personal identities. *American Journal of Sociology, 92*(6): 1336–1371.

Snow, D., & Anderson, L. (1993). *Down on their luck.* Berkeley, CA: University of California Press.

Snow, D.A., Rochford, E.B., Jr, Worden, S.K., & Benford, R.D. (1986). Frame alignment processes, micromobilization, and movement participation. *American Sociological Review, 51*, 464–481.

Soja, E. (1996). *Thirdspace: Journeys to Los Angeles and other real-and-imagined places.* Oxford, UK: Blackwell.

Spector, M., & Kitsuse, J.I. (1977). *Constructing social problems.* Menlo Park, CA: Cummings.

Spitzer, S. (1975). Toward a Marxian theory of deviance. *Social Problems, 22*, 638–651.

Spreitzer, G.M., & Sonenshein, S. (2004). Toward the construct definition of positive deviance. *American Behavioral Scientist, 47*(6), 828–847.

Spring, J. (2009). *Globalization of education: An introduction.* New York, NY: Routledge.

Stanworth, M. (1987). *Reproductive technologies: Gender, motherhood and medicine.* Cambridge, UK: Polity Press.

Stapleton, J., with Kay, J. (2015). *The working poor in the Toronto region.* Toronto, ON: Metcalf Foundation.

Stasiulis, D. (1980). The political structuring of ethnic community action. *Canadian Ethnic Studies, 12*(3), 19–44.

Statistics Canada. (1983a). *Historical statistics of Canada.* Catalogue no. 11-516-X. Ottawa, ON: Statistics Canada. Retrieved 6 January 2016 from http://www.statcan.gc.ca/pub/11-516-x/3000140-eng.htm

Statistics Canada. (1983b). Total expenditures on education, by direct source of funds and type of education, annual (dollars). CANSIM Table 478-0001, W301–306 and W519–532

Statistics Canada. (1993,1 June). 1991 Census of Canada highlights: Religion. *The Daily.*

Statistics Canada. (2000). *Canadian Social Trends.* Catalogue 11-008.

Statistics Canada. (2002). *Mortality, Summary List of Causes.* Catalogue 84F0209X.

Statistics Canada. (2004). "Update on Economic Analysis." Catalogue no. 11-623. XIE. Ottawa, ON: Statistics Canada. Retrieved from www.statcan.ca/english/freepub/11-623-XIE/2003001/trdescrip.htm

Statistics Canada. (2006). Median earnings, in 2005 constant dollars, of male and female recent immigrant earners and Canadian-born earners aged 25 to 54, with or without a university degree, Canada, 1980 to 2005. *Income and earnings, 2006 Census.* Catalogue 97-563-XWE2006002, Table 8. www.statcan.gc.ca/bsolc/olc-cel/olc-cel?catno=97-563-XWE2006002&lang=eng

Statistics Canada. (2008). Women in Canada: Paid work. Ottawa, ON: Statistics Canada. Retrieved from www.statcan.gc.ca/daily-quotidien/1012091/dq101209a_eng.htm

Statistics Canada. (2009a). Census of population, 1851 to 2006. Ottawa, ON: Statistics Canada. Retrieved from www.statcan.gc.ca/tables-tableaux/sum-som/l01/cst01/demo62a-eng.htm

Statistics Canada. (2009b). Total first marriage rates and age-specific first marriage rates per 1,000 females, all marriages, Canada, provinces and territories, annual (rates per 1,000 females). CANSIM Table 101-1012. http://www5.statcan.gc.ca/cansim/pick-choisir?lang=eng&p2=33&id=1011012

Statistics Canada. (2010a, 10 May). Canadian Internet use survey. *The Daily*. Retrieved from http://www.statcan.gc.ca/daily-quotidien/100510/dq100510a-eng.htm

Statistics Canada. (2010b, 10 May). Characteristics of individuals using the Internet. *The Daily*. Retrieved from www40.statcan.gc.ca/l01/cst01/comm35a-eng.htm

Statistics Canada. (2010c). Labour Force Survey estimates (LFS), employees by union status, North American Industry Classification System (NAICS) and sex, Canada, annual (persons unless otherwise noted). CANSIM Table 282-0223. Ottawa: Statistics Canada.

Statistics Canada. (2011a). Education indicators in Canada: Fact sheets. Retrieved 26 February 2014 from http://www.statcan.gc.ca/pub/81-599-x/81-599-x2011006-eng.htm

Statistics Canada. (2011b). Labour force survey 2011. Unpublished data.

Statistics Canada. (2011c). *National Household Survey: Religion, immigrant status, and periods of immigration.* Catalogue 99–010-X2011032. Ottawa: Statistics Canada.

Statistics Canada. (2012a, 26 November). Canadian Internet use survey, 2012. *The Daily*. Retrieved from http://www.statcan.gc.ca/daily-quotidien/131126/dq131126d-eng.htm

Statistics Canada. (2012b). *The Canadian population in 2011: Population counts and growth.* Catalogue no. 98-310-XWE2011001. Ottawa: Statistics Canada.

Statistics Canada. (2012c). Persistence of low income, by selected characteristics, every 3 years. CANSIM Table 202–0807. Retrieved from http://www4.hrsdc.gc.ca/.3ndic.1t.4r@-eng.jsp?iid=83

Statistics Canada. (2012d). Population and dwelling counts, for census metropolitan areas and census agglomerations, 2011 and 2006 censuses. Retrieved from http://www12.statcan.gc.ca/census-recensement/2011/dp-pd/hlt-fst/pd-pl/Table-Tableau.cfm?LANG=Eng&TABID=1&T=201&SR=1&RPP=150&S=3&O=D&CMA=0&PR=0#C2

Statistics Canada. (2012e). *Portrait of families and living arrangements in Canada.* Catalogue no. 98-312-X2011001. Ottawa, ON: Minister of Industry.

Statistics Canada. (2013a). *2011 National Household Survey.* Catalogue 99-014-X2011041.

Statistics Canada. (2013b). *2011 National Household Survey.* Catalogue 99-010-X2011032. http://www12.statcan.gc.ca/nhs-enm/2011/dp-pd/dt-td/Rp-eng.cfm?LANG=E&APATH=3&DETAIL=0&DIM=0&FL=A&FREE=0&GC=0&GID=0&GK=0&GRP=0&PID=105399&PRID=0&PTYPE=105277&S=0&SHOWALL=0&SUB=0&Temporal=2013&THEME=95&VID=0&VNAMEE=&VNAMEF=

Statistics Canada. (2013c, 9 May). 2011 National Household Survey: Immigration, place of birth, citizenship, ethnic origin, visible minorities, language and religion. *The Daily*. Retrieved from http://www.statcan.gc.ca/daily-quotidien/130508/dq130508b-eng.htm

Statistics Canada. (2013d, 26 June). 2011 National Household Survey: Portrait of Canada's labour force. *The Daily*.

Statistics Canada. (2013e). The educational attainment of Aboriginal peoples in Canada. *National Household Survey (NHS) 2011.* Catalogue 99-012-X2011003. Ottawa: Statistics Canada.

Statistics Canada. (2013f). Labour force survey estimates (LFS), by North American Industry Classification System (NAICS), sex and age group, annual (persons unless otherwise noted). CANSIM Table 282-0008

Statistics Canada. (2013g). National Household Survey: Data tables. Selected Demographic, Income and Sociocultural Characteristics (109), Income Statistics in 2010 (3) and Income Sources (16) for the Population Aged 15 Years and Over in Private Households of Canada, Provinces, Territories, Census Metropolitan Areas and Census Agglomerations. 2011 National Household Survey. Catalogue no. 99-014-X2011032. Retrieved from http://www12.statcan.gc.ca/nhs-enm/2011/dp-pd/dt-td/Rp-eng.cfm?LANG=E&APATH=3&DETAIL=0&DIM=0&FL=A&FREE=0&GC=0&GID=0&GK=0&GRP=0&PID=106736&PRID=0&PTYPE=105277&S=0&SHOWALL=Yes&SUB=0&Temporal=2013&THEME=98&VID=0&VNAMEE=&VNAMEF=

Statistics Canada. (2013h, November 27). Postsecondary enrolments by institution type, registration status, province and sex (Both sexes). Retrieved 26 February 2014 from http://www.statcan.gc.ca/tables-tableaux/sum-som/l01/cst01/educ71a-eng.htm

Statistics Canada. (2014a, December 10). Canadian Income Survey, 2012 (Table 3). *The Daily*. http://www.statcan.gc.ca/daily-quotidien/141210/t141210a003-eng.htm

Statistics Canada. (2014b). Federal government indirect support to provinces and territories for postsecondary education, by type of contributions, annual (dollars). CANSIM Table 478-0002 (accessed 11 December 2014).

Statistics Canada. (2014c). Homicide offences, number and rate, by province and territory. Retrieved from http://www.statcan.gc.ca/tables-tableaux/sum-som/l01/cst01/legal12a-eng.htm; http://www.statcan.gc.ca/tables-tableaux/sum-som/l01/cst01/legal12b-eng.htm

Statistics Canada. (2014d). Labour Force Survey estimates (LFS), average weekly earnings, average hourly wage rate and average usual weekly hours by union status and type of work, Canada and provinces, annual. CANSIM Table 282-0225. Ottawa, ON: Statistics Canada.

Statistics Canada. (2014e). Postsecondary non-university education (college) expenditure, by direct source of funds, type of college and type of expenditures, annual (dollars). CANSIM Table 478-0004 (accessed 11 December 2014).

Statistics Canada. (2014f). Public and private elementary and secondary education expenditures, annual (dollars). CANSIM Table 478-0014 (accessed 11 December 2014).

Statistics Canada. (2014g). Public and private elementary and secondary education expenditures, by direct source of funds, annual (dollars). CANSIM Table 478-0015 (accessed 11 December 2014).

Statistics Canada. (2014h). School board expenditures, annual (dollars). CANSIM Table 478-0012 (accessed 11 December 2014).

Statistics Canada. (2014i). School board revenues, by direct source of funds, annual (dollars). CANSIM Table 478-0010 (accessed 11 December 2014).

Statistics Canada. (2014j, 29 January). Survey of household spending, 2012. *The Daily*. Ottawa, ON: Statistics Canada. Retrieved from http://www.statcan.gc.ca/daily-quotidien/140129/dq140129a-eng.htm

Statistics Canada. (2014k). Total expenditures on education, by direct source of funds and type of education, annual (dollars). CANSIM 478-0001 (accessed 11 December 2014).

Statistics Canada. (2014l). Total expenditures on university education, by type of expenditure, annual (dollars). CANSIM Table 478-0008 (accessed 11 December 2014).

Statistics Canada. (2014m). University education expenditures, by direct source of funds and type of expenditures, annual (dollars). CANSIM Table 478-0007 (accessed 11 December 2014).

Statistics Canada. (2014n). Vocational training education expenditures, by type of program and direct source of funds, annual (dollars). CANSIM Table 478-0005 (accessed 11 December 2014).

Statistics Canada. (2015a). *Aboriginal statistics at a glance* (2nd edn). Catalogue no. 89-645-x2015001. Ottawa, ON: Statistics Canada.

Statistics Canada. (2015b). Annual demographic estimates: Canada, provinces and territories. Catalogue no. 91-215-X. Ottawa, ON: Statistics Canada. Retrieved 2 February 2016 from http://www.statcan.gc.ca/pub/91-215-x/91-215-x2014000-eng.htm

Statistics Canada. (2015c). Annual demographic estimates: Subprovincial areas, July 1, 2014. Catalogue no. 91-214-X. CANSIM Table 051-0056. Ottawa, ON: Statistics Canada. Accessed 2 February 2016.

Statistics Canada. (2015d, 8 July). Canadian income survey, 2013. *The Daily.*

Statistics Canada. (2015e). Canadian vital statistics, 1981 to 2011, Survey 3231(Births), 3233 (Deaths) and Demography Division, demographic estimates. Ottawa, ON: Statistics Canada. Retrieved 1 February 2016 from http://www.statcan.gc.ca/pub/91-209-x/

Statistics Canada. (2015f). Criminal victimization in Canada, 2014: Highlights. *Juristat, 35*(1). Catalogue no. 85-002-X.

Statistics Canada. (2015g, 3 November). High-income trends among Canadian taxfilers, 1982–2013. *The Daily.*

Statistics Canada. (2015h). Low income lines, 2013–2014: Update. Catalogue no. 75F0002M, No. 002. Ottawa, ON: Statistics Canada.

Statistics Canada. (2015i). Low income statistics by age, sex and economic family type. CANSIM Table 206-0041, accessed 24 March 2016. Ottawa, ON: Statistics Canada.

Statistics Canada. (2015j). Postsecondary enrolments by institution type, registration status, province and sex. CANSIM Table 477-0019. Retrieved 6 January 2016 from http://www.statcan.gc.ca/tables-tableaux/sum-som/l01/cst01/educ71a-eng.htm

Statistics Canada. (2015k, 24 June). Study: Employment patterns of families with children, 1976 to 2014. *The Daily.*

Statistics Canada. (2017). Life expectancy. Catalogue 89-645-x. Retrieved from http://www.statcan.gc.ca/pub/89-645-x/2010001/life-expectancy-esperance-vie-eng.htm

Statistics Canada. (n.d.a) Deaths, by selected grouped causes and sex, Canada, provinces and territories. CANSIM Table 102-0552.

Statistics Canada. (n.d.b). Estimates of population, by marital status or legal marital status, age and sex for July 1, Canada, provinces and territories, annual (persons). CANSIM Table 051-0042. Last modified 2 November 2015.

Statistics Canada. (n.d.c). Full-time and part-time employment by sex and age group. Retrieved from http://www.statcan.gc.ca/tables-tableaux/sum-som/l01/cst01/labor12-eng.htm

Statistics Canada. (n.d.d) Labour force survey estimates (LFS), by educational attainment, sex and age group, annual. CANSIM Table 282-0004 (accessed 23 August 2016).

Statistics Canada. (n.d.e) Postsecondary graduates, by Pan-Canadian Standard Classification of Education (PCSCE), Classification of Instructional Programs, Primary Grouping (CIP_PG), sex and immigration status, annual (number). CANSIM Table 477-0020 (accessed 6 January 2016).

Statistics Canada. (n.d.f). Suicides and suicide rate, by sex and by age group. CANSIM Table 102-0551. http://www.statcan.gc.ca/tables-tableaux/sum-som/l01/cst01/hlth66a-eng.htm

Stelter, G.A., & Artibise, A.F. (1984). *The Canadian city: Essays in urban and social history* (Rev. & enl. edn). Ottawa, ON: Carleton University Press.

Stevens, R., Gilliard-Matthews, S., Dunaev, J., Woods, M.K., & Brawner, B.M. (2016). The Digital Hood: Social Media Use among Youth in Disadvantaged Neighborhoods. *New Media and Society.* doi: 10. 1461444815625941

Stiglitz, J.E. (2002). *Globalization and its discontents.* New York, NY: W.W. Norton.

Stonechild, B. (2006). *The new buffalo: The struggle for Aboriginal post-secondary education in Canada.* Winnipeg, MB: University of Manitoba Press.

Strasburger, V.C., Wilson, B.J., & Jordan, A.B. (2009). *Children, adolescents and the media* (2nd edn). Thousand Oaks, CA: Sage.

Strauss, A. (1959). *Mirrors and masks: The search for identity.* Chicago, IL: Free Press of Glencoe.

Strauss, A.L. (1978). *Negotiations: Varieties, contexts, processes, and social order.* San Francisco, CA: Jossey-Bass.

Stuber, J., Galea, S., & Link, B.G. (2008). Smoking and the emergence of a stigmatized social status. *Social Science and Medicine, 67*(3), 420–430.

Sutherland, E. (1939). *Principles of criminology* (3rd edn). Chicago, IL: Lippincott.

Sutherland, E. (1940). *White collar crime.* New York, NY: Holt, Rinehart and Winston.

Swain, J. (2004). The right stuff: Fashioning an identity through clothing in a junior school. In M. Webber and K. Bezanson (Eds), *Rethinking Society in the 21st Century: Critical Readings in Sociology* (pp. 81–92). Toronto, ON: Canadian Scholars' Press.

Swanson, J. (2001). *Poor bashing: The politics of exclusion.* Toronto, ON: Between the Lines.

Swiss, L. (2009). Decoupling values from action: An event-history analysis of the election of women to parliament in the developing world, 1945–90. *International Journal of Comparative Sociology, 50*(1), 69–95.

Swiss, L. (2012). The adoption of women and gender as development assistance priorities: An event-history analysis of world polity effects. *International Sociology, 27*(1), 96–119.

Sykes, G.M., & Matza, D. (1957). Techniques of neutralization: A theory of delinquency. *American Sociological Review, 22*(6), 664–670.

Syndicat Northcrest v. Amselem, 2004 SCC 47, [2004] 2 SCR 551.

Tait, S. (2007). Television and the domestication of cosmetic surgery. *Feminist Media Studies, 7*(2), 119–135.

Tannenbaum, F. (1938). *Crime and the community.* Boston, MA: Ginn.

Tanner, J. (2015). *Teenage troubles: Youth and deviance in Canada* (4th edn). Toronto, ON: Nelson.

Tannock, S. (2001). *Youth at work: The unionized fast-food and grocery workplace.* Philadelphia, PA: Temple University Press.

Taras, D. (2001). *Power and betrayal in the Canadian media* (updated edn). Peterborough, ON: Broadview.

Tarrow, S. (1988). National politics and collective action: Recent theory and research in western Europe and the United States. *Annual Review of Sociology, 14,* 421–40.

Tarrow, S. (2005). *The new transnational activism.* New York, NY: Cambridge University Press.

Taylor, A. (2005). Finding the future that fits. *Gender and Education, 17*(2), 165–87.

Taylor, C., & Peter, T. (2011). "We are not aliens, we're people, and we have rights": Canadian human rights discourse and high school climate for LGBTQ students. *Canadian Review of Sociology, 48*(3), 275–312.

Teelucksingh, C. (2009). Social inequality and brownfields redevelopment in downtown Toronto. In L. Adkin (Ed.), *Environmental conflict and democracy in Canada* (pp. 262–278). Vancouver, BC: University of British Columbia Press,.

Teelucksingh, C., & Zeglin, L. (2016). Green prosperity series. Toronto, ON: Metcalf Foundation. Retrieved from http://metcalf foundation.com/wp-content/uploads/2016/05/Metcalf_Green-Prosperity-Papers_Building-Toronto.pdf

Tezli, A., & Gauthier, A. (2009). Balancing work and family in Canada: An empirical examination of conceptualizations and measurements. *Canadian Journal of Sociology, 34*(2), 433–462.

Thiessen, V. (2009). The pursuit of post-secondary education: A comparison of First Nations, African, Asian, and European Canadian youth. *Canadian Review of Sociology, 46*(1), 5–40.

Thomas, D.S., & Thomas, W.I. (1928). *The child in America: Behavior problems and programs.* New York, NY: Knopf.

Thomas, W.I., & Znaniecki, F. (1958). *The Polish peasant in Europe and America* (Vol. 1). New York, NY: Dover.

Thompson, W.S. (1929). Population. *American Journal of Sociology, 34*, 959–975.

Thomson, A. (2010). *The making of social theory: Order, reason, and desire* (2nd edn). Don Mills, ON: Oxford University Press.

Thomson, A. (2016). *Modern social thought: An introduction.* Don Mills, ON: Oxford University Press.

Thrasher, F.M. (1927). *The gang: A study of 1,313 gangs in Chicago.* Chicago, IL: University of Chicago Press.

Tiessen, K. (2015). *Making ends meet: Toronto's 2015 living wage.* Ottawa, ON: Canadian Centre for Policy Alternatives.

Tilleczek, K.C., & Hine, D.W. (2006). The meaning of smoking as health and social risk and adolescence. *Journal of Adolescence, 29*(2), 273–287.

Time Warner. (2010, December). Time Warner Inc's worldwide subsidiaries and affiliated companies list. Retrieved from http://www.timewarner.com/sites/timewarner.com/files/ckeditor/public/files/Time_Warner_Inc_Entity_List_v4_FINAL.pdf

Timson, J. (2011, 26 May). The genderless baby? Well-intentioned but wrong. *Globe and Mail.*

Tindall, D.B. (2013, 12 August). Twenty years after the protests, what we learned from Clayoquot Sound. *Globe and Mail.* Retrieved 5 February 2014 from http://www.the-globeandmail.com/globe-debate/twenty-years-after-the-protest-what-we-learned-from-clayoquot-sound/article13709014/#dashboard/follows/

Tönnies, F. (1957 [1887]). *Community and society (Gemeinschaft und gesellschaft).* New York, NY: Harper and Row.

Torjman, S. (2015a). *Disability supports: Missing on the policy radar.* Toronto, ON: Caledon Institute of Social Policy.

Torjman, S. (2015b, July). We are all disabled. *Caledon Commentary.* Ottawa, ON: Caledon Institute of Social Policy.

Touraine, A. (1981). *The voice and the eye: An analysis of social movements.* Cambridge, UK: Cambridge University Press.

Truth and Reconciliation Commission of Canada (TRC). (2015a). Truth and Reconciliation Commission of Canada: Calls to Action. TRC.ca. Retrieved 30 August 2016 from http://www.trc.ca/websites/trcinstitution/File/2015/Findings/Calls_to_Action_English2.pdf

Truth and Reconciliation Commission of Canada (TRC). (2015b). *What we have learned: Principles of truth and reconciliation. Final report of the Truth and Reconciliation Commission of Canada.* Ottawa, ON: Truth and Reconciliation Commission of Canada.

Turk, A.T. (1976). Law as a weapon in social conflict. *Social Problems, 23*, 276–292.

Turkle, S. (2011). *Alone together: Why we expect more from technology and less from each other.* New York, NY: Basic Books.

Turner, V. (1969). *The ritual process: Structure and anti-structure.* Ithaca, NY: Cornell University Press.

Tweedle, A., Battle, K., & Torjman, S. (2015). *Welfare in Canada, 2014.* Ottawa, ON: Caledon Institute.

Tylor, E.B. (1920) [1871]). *Primitive Culture: Vol. 1. Researches into the development of mythology, philosophy, religion, language, art and custom.* London, UK: John Murray.

Tyyskä, V. (2009). *Youth and Society: The Long and Winding Road.* 2nd edn. Toronto: Canadian Scholars' Press.

United Nations Department of Economic and Social Affairs, Population Division. (2009a). *World Population Prospects: The 2008 Revision, Highlights.*

SA/P/WP.210. New York, NY: United Nations.

United Nations Educational, Scientific and Cultural Organization (UNESCO). (2014). *UNESCO education strategy 2014-2021.* Paris, France: UNESCO.

United Nations Educational, Scientific and Cultural Organization (UNESCO). (2015a). *Education for All 2000-2015: Achievements and Challenges.* EFA Global Monitoring Report 2015. Paris, France: UNESCO.

United Nations Educational, Scientific and Cultural Organization (UNESCO). (2015b). *Education 2030: Framework for Action. Towards inclusive and equitable quality education and lifelong learning for all.* Paris, France: UNESCO.

United Nations High Commissioner for Refugees (n.d.) Syria regional refugee response. Retrieved from http://data.unhcr.org/syrianrefugees/regional.php

United Nations Women. (2010). *Beijing and its follow up.* New York, NY: United Nations Entity for Gender Equality and the Empowerment of Women. Retrieved from http://www.un.org/womenwatch/daw/beijing/

Uppal, S. (2015). Employment patterns of families with children, 1976 to 2014. *Insights on Canadian Society.* Catalogue no. 75-006-X. Ottawa, ON: Statistics Canada. Retrieved from http://www.statcan.gc.ca/pub/75-006-x/2015001/article/14202-eng.pdf

Urmetzer, P. (2005). *Globalization unplugged: Sovereignty and the Canadian state in the twenty-first century.* Toronto, ON: University of Toronto Press.

Ursel, J., Tutty, L., & LeMaistre, J. (2008). *What's law got to do with it? The law, specialized courts and domestic violence in Canada.* Toronto, ON: Cormorant Press.

Van Gennep, A. (1960) [1908]). *Rites of passage.* London, UK: Routledge.

Vanier Institute of the Family. (2016). Definition of family. Ottawa: Vanier Institute of the Family. Retrieved from http://vanierinstitute.ca/about-us/approach-family/definition-family/

Veblen, T. (1899). *The theory of the leisure class.* New York, NY: Penguin.

Veenstra, G. (2015). Class position and musical tastes: A sing-off between the cultural omnivorism and bourdieusian homology frameworks. *Canadian Review of Sociology, 52*(2), 134–159.

Venkatesh, S. (2009). *Gang leader for a day.* London, UK: Penguin.

Vézina, M. (2015). 2011 General Social Survey: Overview of families in Canada—Being a parent in a stepfamily:

A profile. Catalogue no. 89-650-X, No. 002. Ottawa, ON: Statistics Canada. Retrieved from http://www.statcan.gc.ca/pub/89-650-x/89-650-x2012002-eng.pdf

Vosko, L. (2000). *Temporary work: The gendered rise of a precarious employment relationship.* Toronto, ON: University of Toronto Press.

Vosko, L. (2003). Gender differentiation and the standard/non-standard employment distinction in Canada, 1945 to the present. In D. Juteau (Ed.), *Patterns and processes of social differentiation: The construction of gender, age, "race/ethnicity" and locality.* Toronto, ON: University of Toronto Press.

Vosko, L. (2006). *Precarious employment: Understanding labour market insecurity in Canada.* Montreal, QC: McGill-Queen's University Press.

Vosko, L. (2010). *Managing the margins: Gender, citizenship, and the international regulation of precarious employment.* Oxford, UK: Oxford University Press.

Wajcman, J. (2013). *Feminism confronts technology.* Hoboken, NJ: Wiley. Retrieved from http://gbv.eblib.com/patron/FullRecord.aspx?p=1215734

Waller, W. (1965 [1932]). *The sociology of teaching.* New York, NY: Wiley.

Wallerstein, I. (1976). *The modern world-system: Capitalist agriculture and the origins of the European world-economy in the sixteenth century.* New York, NY: Academic Press.

Wallerstein, I. (1979a). Dependence in an interdependent world: The limited possibilities of transformations within the capitalist world-economy. In I. Wallerstein (Ed.), *The capitalist world-economy: Essays* (pp. 66–94). New York, NY: Cambridge University Press.

Wallerstein, I. (1979b). The rise and future demise of the world capitalist system: Concepts for comparative analysis. In I. Wallerstein (Ed.), *The capitalist world-economy: Essays* (pp. 1–36). New York, NY: Cambridge University Press.

Warren, C.A.B., & Karner, T.X. (2009). *Discovering qualitative methods* (2nd edn). New York, NY: Oxford University Press.

Waters, M. (1995). *Globalization: Key ideas.* London, UK: Routledge.

Watson, J.L. (Ed.). (1997). *Golden arches east: McDonald's in East Asia.* Stanford, CA: Stanford University Press.

Weber, M. (1946 [1915]). Religious rejections of the world and their directions. In H.H. Gerth & C.W. Mills (Eds), *From Max Weber: Essays in sociology* (pp. 323–359). New York, NY: Oxford University Press.

Weber, M. (1958a [1904]). *The Protestant ethic and the spirit of capitalism.* T. Parsons (Trans.). New York, NY: Scribner.

Weber, M. (1958b [1921]). *The city.* New York, NY: Free Press.

Weber, M. (1958c [1922]). *Essays in sociology.* H.H. Gerth & C.W. Mills (Trans.). New York, NY: Oxford University Press.

Weber, M. (1978 [1908]). *Economy and Society.* E. Fischoff (Trans.), G. Roth & C. Wittich (Eds). Berkeley, CA: University of California Press.

Weeks, J. (1993). *Sexuality.* London, UK: Routledge.

Weiner, G. (1994). *Feminisms in education: An introduction.* Birmingham, UK: Open University Press.

Weissman, E. (2012). *Dignity in exile: Stories of struggle and hope from a modern American shantytown.* Mount Forest, ON: Exile.

Weissman, E. (2014). *Spaces, places and states of mind: A pragmatic ethnography of liminal critique.* PhD dissertation, Concordia University.

Weissman, Eric. (2017, forthcoming). *Tranquility on the razor's edge: changing narratives of inevitability.* Toronto, ON: Rock's Mills Press.

Weitz, R. (Ed.). (2002). *The politics of women's bodies: Sexuality, appearance and behaviour* (2nd edn). Oxford, UK: Oxford University Press.

Wellman, B. (2001). Physical place and cyber place: The rise of personalized networking. *International Journal of Urban and Regional Research, 25*(2), 227–252.

Wellman, B., Quan-Haase, A., Witte, J., & Hampton, K. (2001). Does the Internet increase, decrease, or supplement social capital? Social networks, participation, and community commitment. *American Behavioral Scientist, 45*(3), 437–56.

Welsh, S. (1999). Gender and sexual harassment. *Annual Review of Sociology, 25*(1), 169–190.

Western, D., & Wright, R.M. (Eds). (1994). *Natural connections: Perspectives in community-based conservation.* Washington, DC: Island Press.

Westhues, K. (1982). *First sociology.* New York, NY: McGraw-Hill.

Whitman, S. (2012). Sexual violence, coltan and the Democratic Republic of Congo. In M.A. Schnurr & L.A. Swatuk (Eds), *Natural resources and social conflict: Towards critical environmental security* (pp. 128–151). London, UK: Palgrave Macmillan.

Whorf, B. (1956). *Language, thought, and reality: Selected writings of Benjamin Lee Whorf.* J.B. Carroll (Ed.). Cambridge, MA: MIT Press.

Widman, L., Choukas-Bradley, S., Helms, S.W., & Prinstein, M.J. (2016). Adolescent susceptibility to peer influence in sexual situations. *Journal of Adolescent Health* doi: 10.1016/j.jadohealth.2015.10.253

Wiesner, M., & Rab, S. (2015). Self-control and lifestyles: Associations to juvenile offending, violent victimization, and witnessing violence. *Victims & Offenders, 10*(2), 214–237.

Wigginton, B., & Lee, C. (2013). A story of stigma: Australian women's accounts of smoking during pregnancy. *Critical Public Health, 23*(4), 466–481.

Wiley, S.A., & Esbensen, F.-A. (2013). The effect of police contact: Does official intervention result in deviance amplification? *Crime & Delinquency* doi: 0011128713492496

Wilkes, R. (2001). *Competition or colonialism? An analysis of two theories of ethnic collective action.* PhD dissertation, University of Toronto.

Wilkes, R., & Kehl, M. (2014). One image, multiple nationalisms: Face to face and the siege at Kanehsatà:ke. *Nations and Nationalisms.* doi: 10.1111/nana.12067

Williams, C. (2010). Economic well-being. In *Women in Canada: A gender-based statistical report* (6th edn). Ottawa, ON: Statistics Canada. Retrieved from http://www.statcan.gc.ca/pub/89-503-x/2010001/article/11388-eng.pdf

Williams, F.P., & McShane, M. (2013). *Criminological theory* (6th edn). Englewood Cliffs, NJ: Prentice Hall.

Williams, R. (1975). *Television: Technology and cultural form.* New York, NY: Schocken.

Wilson, D., & Macdonald, D. (2010). The income gap between Aboriginal peoples and the rest of Canada. Canadian Centre for Policy Alternatives Ottawa. Retrieved from http://mail.policyalternatives.org/sites/default/files/uploads/publications/reports/docs/Aboriginal%20Income%20Gap.pdf

Wilson, E.O. (1975). *Sociobiology: The new synthesis.* Cambridge, MA: Harvard University Press.

Wilson, J., & Anielski, M. (2005). *Ecological footprints of Canadian municipalities and regions.* Report prepared for the Canadian Federation of Canadian Municipalities. Edmonton, AB: Anielski Management.

Wilson, S.J. (1991). *Women, families, and work* (3rd edn). Toronto, ON: McGraw-Hill Ryerson.

Winter, E. (2014). Becoming Canadian: Making sense of recent changes to citizenship rules. *IRPP Study, 44* (January), 1–28.

Wirth, L. (1938). Urbanism as a way of life. *American Journal of Sociology, 44,* 1–24.

Witte, J.C., & Mannon, S.E. (2009). *The Internet and social inequalities.* New York, NY: Routledge.

Witterick, K. (2013). Dancing in the eye of the storm: The gift of gender diversity to our family. In F.J. Green & M. Friedman (Eds), *Chasing rainbows: Exploring gender fluid parenting practices.* Bradford, ON: Demeter Press.

Witz, A. (1992). *Professions and patriarchy.* London, UK: Routledge.

Wolfe, D.A., & Gertler, M.S. (2001). *The new economy: An overview.* Discussion paper produced for the Social Sciences and Humanities Research Council of Canada.

Wolfgang, M., & Ferracuti, F. (1967). *The subculture of violence: Towards an integrated theory in criminology.* Beverly Hills, CA: Sage.

Wollstonecraft, M. 1986 [1792]. *Vindication of the rights of women.* Middlesex, UK: Penguin.

Woodhead, L. (2007). *Religion as normative, spirituality as fuzzy: Questioning some deep assumptions in the sociology of religion.* Paper presented at SISR/ISSR, Zagreb.

Woods, P. (1979). *The divided school.* London, UK: Routledge and Kegan Paul.

World Bank (2015). *World Development Indicators.* Retrieved from http://data.worldbank.org/products/wdi

World Bank (2015). Migration and Remittances Factbook 2016. World Bank Group. http://go.worldbank.org/QGUCPJTOR0

World Health Organization (WHO). (2012). Understanding and addressing violence against women. Retrieved from http://apps.who.int/iris/bitstream/10665/77432/1/WHO_RHR_12.36_eng.pdf

World Wildlife Fund. (2010). *Living planet report 2010.* Gland, Switzerland: World Wildlife Fund.

Wortley, S. (1999). A northern taboo: Research on race, crime and criminal justice in Canada. *Canadian Journal of Criminology, 41,* 261–274.

Wotherspoon, T. (1995). The incorporation of public school teachers into the industrial order: British Columbia in the first half of the twentieth century. *Studies in Political Economy, 46,* 119–51.

Wotherspoon, T. (2000). Transforming Canada's education system: The impact on educational inequalities, opportunities, and benefits. In B.S. Bolaria (Ed.), *Social issues and contradictions in Canadian society* (pp. 250–72). Toronto: Harcourt Brace.

Wotipka, C.M., & Ramirez, F.O. (2008). World society and human rights: An event history analysis of the Convention on the Elimination of All Forms of Discrimination against Women. In B.A. Simmons, F. Dobbin, & G. Garrett (Eds), *The global diffusion of markets and democracy* (pp. 303–343). Cambridge, UK: Cambridge University Press.

Wright, T. (1997). *Out of place: Homeless mobilizations, subcities, and contested landscapes.* Albany, NY: State University of New York Press.

Wrong, D. (1961). The oversocialized concept of man in modern sociology. *American Sociological Review, 26,* 183–193.

Yang, S., Quan-Haase, A., & Rannenberg, K. (2016). The changing public sphere on Twitter: Network structure, elites, and topics of the #righttobeforgotten. *New Media & Society.* doi: 1461444816651409

Yates, C. (2008). Organized labour in Canadian politics: Hugging the middle or pushing the margins? In M. Smith (Ed.), *Group politics and social movements in Canada.* Toronto, ON: University of Toronto Press.

Yoder, J.B., & Mattheis, A. (2016). Queer in STEM: Workplace experiences reported in a national survey of LGBTQA Individuals in science, technology, engineering, and mathematics careers. *Journal of Homosexuality, 63*(1), 1–27.

Yoo, E. (2011). International human rights regime, neoliberalism, and women's social rights, 1984–2004. *International Journal of Comparative Sociology, 52*(6), 503–528.

Young, D. (2006). Ethno-racial minorities and the Juno Awards. *Canadian Journal of Sociology, 31*(2), 183–210.

Young, D. (2013). Why Canadian content regulations are needed to support Canadian music. In J. Greenberg & C.D. Elliott (Eds), *Communication in question: Competing perspectives on controversial issues in communication studies* (2nd edn, pp. 210–216). Toronto, ON: Thomson Nelson.

Young, D., & Keil, R. (2007). Re-regulating the urban water regime in neoliberal Toronto. In N. Heynen, J. McCarthy, S. Prudham, & P. Robbins (Eds), *Neoliberal environments: False promises and unnatural consequences* (pp. 139–152). New York, NY & London, UK: Routledge.

Young, M. (2015). Work–family conflict in context: The impact of structural and perceived neighborhood disadvantage on work–family conflict. *Social Science Research, 50,* 311–327.

Zephoria. (2015). The top 20 valuable Facebook statistics—updated October 2015. Retrieved 9 November 2015 from https://zephoria.com/top-15-valuable-facebook-statistics/

Zola, I.K. (1972). Medicine as an institution of social control. *Sociological Review, 20:* 487–504.

Zukin, S. (1980). A decade of the new urban sociology. *Theory and Society, 9*(4), 575–601.

INDEX

Milestones in Canadian Sociology

Talcott Parsons
1902–1979
American sociologist promoted a conception of society as a social system with subsystems of human action, in which individuals fulfill the systems needs of the societies of which they are members.

Herbert Blumer
1900–1987
American student of Mead, who coined the term "symbolic interactionism."

Everett C. Hughes
1897–1983
American sociologist studied economic organization, work and occupations, and ethnic relations, including a key study of the "ethnic division of labour" in Quebec.

Samuel Delbert Clark
1910–2003
Canadian historical sociologist and educator founded the University of Toronto's Department of Sociology (1963).

Theodor Adorno
1903–1969
German Frankfurt School philosopher argued that philosophical authoritarianism is inevitably oppressive.

Oswald Hall
1908–2007
Canadian educator researched the sociology of work and medicine and served on the Royal Commission on Health Services and the Royal Commission on Bilingualism and Biculturalism.

Robert K. Merton
1910–2003
American sociologist and educator developed middle-range theory, which sought to bridge the gap between high-level theories and low-level observations.

Erving Goffman
1922–1982
Canadian-born sociologist advanced microsociology and studied social roles, deviance, stigma, and "total institutions."

John Porter
1921–1979
Canadian sociologist examined connections between ethnicity and barriers of opportunity in Canadian society, which he characterized as a "vertical mosaic."

C. Wright Mills
1916–1962
American critical sociologist studied power structure in the US and coined the term "sociological imagination."

Guy Rocher
b. 1924
Canadian educator and pioneer in the sociology of education, law, and medical ethics has sat on several commissions and boards of inquiry at the provincial and federal levels and wrote a lucid and highly regarded introduction to the discipline, *Introduction à la sociologie* (1968).

Michel Foucault
1926–1984
French thinker, famous for historical studies of madness and civilization, imprisonment, and sexuality, portrayed science as an arbitrary instrument for control and power and constructed a theory of power as actions and relations.

Dorothy Smith
b. 1926
English-born Canadian sociologist developed standpoint theory, which sought to frame and understand everyday life from a feminist point of view.

Arlie Russell Hochschild
b. 1940
American sociologist has studied the alienating effects of emotional labour, which requires workers to manage their feelings in accordance with workplace rules.

Jean Baudrillard
1929–2007
French cultural theorist influenced postmodernism and showed how capitalist consumer society erases distinctions between reality and reference, leading to a loss of meaning.

Saskia Sassen
b. 1949
Dutch-born critical sociologist coined the term *global cities* in her work on globalization, immigration, and the disparity between wealthy neoliberal states and developing countries.

Michael Burawoy
b. 1947
British-born public sociologist is known for ethnographic studies of industrial workplaces under monopoly capitalism.

Margrit Eichler
b. 1942
Canadian sociologist has studied family sociology, feminist research methods, and gender inequality.

Manuel Castells
b. 1942
Spanish sociologist is a leading theorist on urban planning and communication technology, including urban social movements and social changes in the information society.

1900 — 1950 — 2000

1969
Doctors and Doctrines: The Ideology of Medical Care in Canada, an examination of Canada's healthcare system in terms of role strains, conflict in values, and relations to the public, by Bernard Blishen (b.1919)

1968
Introduction to the Mathematics of Population, a landmark contribution to the field of population studies, by Canadian demographer Nathan Keyfitz (1913–2010)

1965
Lament for a Nation: The Defeat of Canadian Nationalism, an examination of the dangers of Canadian cultural absorption by the US, by Canadian social philosopher George Grant (1918–1988)

The Vertical Mosaic: An Analysis of Social Class and Power in Canada, a ground-breaking and influential study of Canada's class structure, depicting a complex system of groups organized in hierarchy across lines of ethnicity and class, by John Porter

1978
The Double Ghetto: Canadian Women and Their Segregated Work, a study of gender inequality in the labour force and the home, by Pat Armstrong (b. 1945) and Hugh Armstrong (b. 1943)

1975
The Rise of a Third Party: A Study in Crisis Politics, a sociological analysis of the growth of nationalist politics in Quebec, by Maurice Pinard (b. 1929)

The Canadian Corporate Elite: An Analysis of Economic Power, a response to *The Vertical Mosaic* examining corporate elites and their impact on class and social stratification, by Wallace Clement

1983
Green Gold: The Forest Industry in British Columbia (1983), an early study in the social, political, and economic aspects of a particular staples industry, the BC forest industry, by Patricia Marchak (1936–2010)

Families in Canada Today: Recent Changes and Their Policy Consequences, a study of how the way we think and talk about gender roles pre-empts useful changes in family policy, by Margrit Eichler

1986
"The 'Wets' and the 'Drys': Binary Images of Women and Alcohol in Popular Culture," a study of gender inequalities and mass media, by Thelma McCormack (b. 1921)

1987
The Everyday World as Problematic: A Feminist Sociology, an argument that sociology has developed without proper insight into women's experiences, by Dorothy Smith

1988
Quebec Society: Tradition, Modernity, and Nationhood, a study of Quebec's rising middle class and the separatist movement, by Hubert Guindon (1929–2002)

1989
The Social Significance of Sport, a study of how individuals take control of and participate in society through voluntary association, by Barry D. MacPherson, James Curtis (1943–2005), and John W. Loy

1996
The Barbershop Singer: Inside the Social World of a Musical Hobby, a study of leisure and hobbies in society, by Robert Stebbins (b. 1938)

2002
"The Impact of Feminism on Canadian Sociology," a study of the rise of sociology as a feminist discipline, by Margrit Eichler

2004
Perspectives de Recherche en Santé des Populations au Moyen de Données Complexes, an analysis of the Quebec healthcare system, by Paul Bernard (1945–2011) and colleagues

2006
Do Men Mother? Fathering, Care, and Domestic Responsibility, an examination of the changing role of fathers, by Andrea Doucet

2008
Canada's Rights Revolution: Social Movements and Social Change, 1937–82, a study of post-war Canadian social movements, by Dominique Clément

2010
Measuring the Mosaic: An Intellectual Biography of John Porter, the first intellectual biography of pre-eminent Canadian sociologist John Porter, by Rick Helmes-Hayes

2012
Direct Action, Deliberation, and Diffusion: Collective Action after the WTO Protests in Seattle, a study of strategies that underlie the tactics used by activists, by Lesley Wood